ships
FOR A
NATION

JOHN BROWN & COMPANY
CLYDEBANK

West Dunbartonshire
Libraries & Museums

2000

ships
FOR A
NATION

JOHN BROWN & COMPANY
CLYDEBANK

Ian Johnston

West Dunbartonshire Libraries & Museums

2000

Frontispiece
The Canadian Pacific liner Empress of Britain *on her building slip photographed on 10 June 1930 the day before her launch.*

Copyright @ Ian Johnston 2000
First published in Great Britain in 2000 by West Dunbartonshire Libraries & Museums

ISBN 0-953 7736-0-4 (Hbk)
       0-953 7736-1-2 (Pbk)

Maps, illustrations and book design by
Ian Johnston.

Printed by Mackay & Inglis Limited, Glasgow

CONTENTS

ACKNOWLEDGEMENTS

Many people assisted in writing this story. In recording my sincere thanks, I have attempted to list them as individuals and in the organisations with whom they are or were involved. It is worth noting that Clydebank District Council commissioned this book in 1994. In 1996, this Council became part of the newly created West Dunbartonshire Council. I therefore owe both authorities a debt of gratitude in making it possible for me to tell what is arguably one of the greatest of all stories in British industrial history. In particular, I would like to thank John Hood, who started the process off and his successor Susan Carragher who brought it to a conclusion. I would also like to thank those who read the final manuscript: Sir John Brown, Brian Newman, Dr Lewis Johnman, Dr Ian Buxton and David K Brown. To Graeme Smith, a special thanks for making sense of the financial papers of J&G Thomson and John Brown & Co. In acknowledging the assistance of the above, I immediately absolve them from any errors of fact or judgement which remain mine alone.

Babtie Shaw & Morton, Glasgow:
Bill Paterson
The Ballast Trust, Johnstone:
Delaine Colquhoun, Dr William Lind and Duncan Winning MBE
The Bank of Scotland Archives, Glasgow:
Alan Cameron and Derek Burns
Former employees of John Brown & Co Ltd:
Lord Aberconway (Chairman of John Brown & Co. Ltd), Joe Brown (plumber and shop steward's convenor), Sir John Brown, (Managing Director 1959-63), Willie Clydesdale (welder), Bob Dickie (joiner), Isabel Dickie (wages clerkess), Isabel Dickie nee Downie (dilutee electrician), Bob Gourlay (patternmaker), Charlie MacIntyre (foreman rigger), Tom McKendrick, Roddy McKenzie (welder), Andrew McLaughlin (outfit manager), Willie McLaughlin (engine designer) (loftsman), Willie Miller (timekeeper), Johnny Moore (apprentice fitter), Jimmy Reid (fitter and shop steward), John Starks (Technical Director), Robin Williamson (Company Secretary).

Kvaerner Power, John Brown Engineering:
Tony Bird, John Innes, Tom and Marion Love, Bill Connell, Jim Turner, Stephen Rodgers
Clydebank Library & Clydebank Museum:
Pat Malcolm and Mary Land
Clydeport Authority:
James Young, David Sommerville, Barclay Braithwaite, Bill Girvan and Harry Osborne
Glasgow City Archives:
Dr Irene O'Brian and Alison Gordon
Glasgow University Archives & Business Record Centre: George Gardner, Kate Hutcheson, Michael Moss, Jim Nixon, Moira Rankin, Frank Rankin, Leslie Richmond, Vanora Skelly and Alma Topin
The Huntington Library, San Marino, California:
Karen Kearns, Jennifer Watts
The Institute of Engineers and Shipbuilders in Scotland, Glasgow:
Doris Callaghan
The Mitchell Library, Glasgow:
Elizabeth Carmichael, Ann Escott, Ian Gordon and Murdoch Nicolson
McGrigor Donald & Co., Solicitors, Glasgow:
Malcolm Livingston
National Archives of Scotland, Edinburgh;
Hazel Anderson, Dr Peter Anderson and Hugh Hagan
Sheffield City Archives:
Ann Heath and Rachel Moffat
UiE Scotland Ltd:
Brian Divers, Tom Allison, Jim Allan, Leslie Sillars and Dawn McKellor
University of Liverpool Archives:
Adrian Allan and Andrea Owens

Individuals:
Michael Bell (nephew of Sir Thomas Bell), Dugald Cameron, Ken Colville, Norman Gilchrist (chief draughtsman, Swan Hunter), Ian Gorrie, Barbara Graham, Meg Henderson, Tom Kameen (superintendent engineer, Cunard), Vivian Kitt (grand daughter of George Paul Thomson), Neil McCart, Frank McCrae (Sir William Arrol & Co), Ronald

Opposite.
The starboard anchor recess on Empress of Britain. *The horizontal line is the dark blue painted line of her livery.*

McNeill (Sir James McNeill's son), Rodderick
McConnell (grandson of James Roger Thomson),
Steve McLaughlin, Carol Marshall, Alex Morrison,
Marion Mowat (Dr John Rannie's daughter), George
Moore, Linden Moore, Hugh Murphy, Ian Ramsay
(Sir JH Biles & Co.), Fred Reid (Asst. Chief Ship
Surveyor, Lloyds), Johnston Robb (Scott Lithgow),
Donald Robertson, Jan Rudzinski (ORP Piorun),
Christine Schmitt-Mackinnon (niece of Sir John
Brown), Eleanor Shipp (Sir Stephen Pigott's
daughter), Professor Tony Slaven, Sir Robert Smith,
Jim Sorbi, Sue Stephen (great grand daughter of
James Thomson), Sandy Stephen (Alexander
Stephen & Co. Ltd), Elsie Tannoch (grand daughter
of James Thomson). PN Thomas, Roy Turner (naval
architect, Vickers Armstrong at Barrow in Furness),
Fred Walker.

Thanks are also due to my good friend David Wilson
for assisting in the design and layout of this book.
Lastly, as ever, thanks to my wife Linda for unfailing
support and endless proof reading and to my
children Andrew and Laura for permitting me to be
an absentee member of their family.

The stern of the Cunard liner
Carmania *before launching on*
21 February 1905

FOREWORD

After half a century of service to the Clydebank firm which is the subject of this history, I feel uniquely qualified to contribute a foreword to this book and to compliment the author on his comprehensive and meticulous record of its endeavours and achievements.

It is fitting that the record should be preserved not least as a memorial to the work of countless skilled tradesmen over the years which made possible the unique place the firm occupied in shipbuilding history.

In 1919, after commencing a course in naval architecture at Glasgow University on the assumption that I could obtain employment under the so called sandwich system with a Clydeside shipyard, I found that none of the yards would honour that arrangement so that I had to accept a five-year apprenticeship. The slump in shipbuilding in 1921 made it possible to obtain release to pursue the sandwich course and I then obtained my degree of BSc in 1923. Continuing my apprenticeship with the shipyard I worked under Sir James McNeil to whom I owed every encouragement then and later. After two years of secondment to an associated Spanish shipyard, I was appointed Assistant Naval Architect at Clydebank and so started my involvement with the design of some of the most outstanding liners in British shipbuilding history. For me, pride of place is taken by the *Queen Mary* although many other examples of ship design contributed to my enjoyment of this work. This led eventually to my appointment as Managing Director at Clydebank and satisfaction in the fulfilment of a worthwhile working life. My pride in the term 'Clydebank Built' must be shared by literally thousands who participated in establishing that phrase. Alas, the shipyard is no longer building ships but will, however, stay forever in the memory of all those in any way linked with it. I feel certain that this excellent history will ensure that this memory will not fade.

Sir John Brown
29 February 2000

The elegant bow of the Inman liner City of New York *in the fitting-out basin at Clydebank in 1888*

INTRODUCTION

On 26 September 1934, during rain which poured down with arresting determination, the largest assembly of steel in history was launched into the River Clyde at Clydebank near Glasgow. From behind a protective glass canopy, the words of Her Majesty, Queen Mary, were carried across the shipyard and by radio to the world beyond. The ship was the Cunard liner which bore her name, *Queen Mary*, afloat at last after her construction had been halted during the Depression. Sixteen years earlier another vessel, sleeker in form and built for an altogether different purpose, was launched from the same yard. This was the battlecruiser *Hood*. Both ships were destined to occupy a special place in the minds of British people, representing tangible objects of national achievement.

The events between 1847 and 1972 which form the chronological book-ends of this history witnessed the expansion of the British shipbuilding industry to a position of world leadership. This was sustained for one hundred years and followed by a remarkably sudden decline into statistical irrelevance. As that period in British industrial history recedes, there is perhaps no better example of the excellence and achievement with which it was associated than with the products of this shipyard, known for the greater part of its life as John Brown & Co.

Although much of the skill and reputation associated with Clydeside's heavy industries has been retrospectively focused on John Brown's, that yard was not an isolated enterprise but part of a remarkable and complex industrial dynamic which overtook the River Clyde, Glasgow and Britain in the 19th Century. In 1847, shipbuilding in wood was long established in ports around the British Isles. Although Greenock was such a port, the Clyde was not particularly noted for endeavour in this field. That changed with the adaptation of the steam engine to marine propulsion. The revolution in marine transportation which followed had its origins on Clydeside and created a momentum which placed the Clyde and Glasgow at the epicentre of marine engineering and iron shipbuilding.

Two brothers, James and George Thomson, founded the business, known in the 20th Century as John Brown & Company, in 1847. As former employees of the pioneering engineer, shipbuilder and entrepreneur Robert Napier, the Thomson brothers were well equipped to enter into the new and advanced technology of designing and building marine steam engines. Recognising that iron and not wood was the future material of ships, the Thomsons expanded their business in 1851 by establishing the Clyde Bank Iron Shipyard at Govan on the south bank of the Clyde. A third brother, Robert, became Samuel Cunard's first superintendent engineer in the shipping line which Cunard had established in 1839. Thus a link was established between the new firm of engineers and shipbuilders and Cunard that would endure for over one hundred years. The business of James and George Thomson was to have its share of peaks and troughs. Initially, the business thrived, building ocean going ships and river steamers alike. In 1863, James and George, now wealthy men, quarrelled, and James resolved to leave the business to establish a rival marine engineering business with his two sons. George continued on his own until 1866 when he died suddenly at the age of 55. The business was plunged into deep crisis and had to be operated by a Trust formed of Glasgow businessmen until George's young sons, confusingly named James and George, became of age.

By now, the remarkable success of Glasgow as a port as well as a shipbuilding, marine engineering and manufacturing centre was well established. The port needed new wharves, sheds and facilities, forcing the relocation of Thomson's Govan shipyard. This was to prove an acrimonious and protracted procedure which resulted in a poor financial settlement. Nevertheless, the ambition of young James Roger Thomson, who assumed control of the business with his brother, George Paul Thomson, in 1874 at the age of 30, ensured that the Clyde Bank Iron Shipyard was moved to a large site on farmland seven miles down river. With no amenities whatsoever, the new yard had enormous hurdles to overcome before an adequate infrastructure, including homes for working people, could be provided. Over the course of the 1870s and 1880s, the town of Clydebank, which took its name from the shipyard, was established, recording in the process the highest growth rate for any town in Scotland at that time. Throughout this period, the new works struggled financially, partly as a result of the need to organise 2,000 working people daily to carry on the business of building ships at a yard in the middle of a field. The Union Bank of Scotland became increasingly involved in supporting the Company over a long period of time. The Thomson brothers tested the Bank's patience by proving to be profligate in their pursuit of lifestyle. Nevertheless, J& G Thomson & Co. succeeded in establishing itself as second in importance to that of its great Clydeside rival, John Elder & Co. at the Fairfield Works. For a time, the battle to take the coveted Blue Riband for the fastest Atlantic crossing was purely a Clydeside affair between Thomson's and Elder's as numerous record-breaking liners left their Clydeside yards. From the mid 1880s onward, warships became the other prestigious and lucrative market for which Clydebank became renowned. In 1890, the Union Bank of Scotland converted the business to a public company with the ultimate aim of returning it to private ownership. Now, highly profitable and with prestigious naval and mercantile contracts, the business attracted the attention of John Brown & Company of Sheffield, a leading manufacturer of armour plate and other steel products. In 1899, John Brown & Company acquired the Clydebank works. Under the innocuous name of John Brown, Clydebank shipyard would become world famous. The Thomson brothers were obliged to leave the company they had managed in ignominious circumstances.

John Brown's timing in acquiring the Clydebank works was to prove more apposite than even the most optimistic could have imagined. The backdrop was the growing international competition and tension between the Germany of Kaiser Wilhelm II and Great Britain. By the end of the 1890s, the Blue Riband for speed on the prestigious North Atlantic sea route was firmly in German hands while a naval race between Britain and Germany was in the making. British response was in the form of several remarkable ships, the Cunard liners *Lusitania* and *Mauretania* which reasserted dominance of the North Atlantic and the revolutionary battleship *Dreadnought*. John Brown's won the order for *Lusitania* and the dreadnought battlecruiser *Inflexible*. In the years before World War One, the Brown-Curtis steam turbine, particularly suited to warship propulsion, was developed at Clydebank. This advanced technology proved to be of great interest to the Admiralty, resulting in significant machinery contracts and licence agreements with other British shipbuilders. Completion of the Cunard liner *Aquitania* coincided with the outbreak of war during which time John Brown's turned out a host of ships including the dreadnoughts *Tiger, Barham, Repulse* and, after the end of the war, the battlecruiser *Hood*. The post-war desire to cut defence spending caused the progressive collapse of the armaments industries. This, coupled with the onset of a severe trade depression, resulted in fewer contracts and reduced employment at Clydebank. By the end of the 1920s, the situation had temporarily improved and a succession of elegant liners for Canadian Pacific, including *Empress of Britain*, was built.

The growth which the shipbuilding and marine engineering industries had known since inception, and which peaked in 1913, had been halted during the 1920s and turned into decline during the early 1930s. The difficulties in which the West of Scotland found itself highlighted an acute overdependence on the heavy industries which had been its making. Efforts were made by shipbuilders to reduce the industry by eliminating redundant yards. In 1930 the adjoining shipyard of William Beardmore at Dalmuir was closed as part of this effort.

The future of John Brown & Co. was in the balance. The signing of the high profile contract in December 1930 for the Cunard liner *Queen Mary* kept the yard open. However, within a year, elation at winning the contract gave way to abject misery as the ship was suspended as a result of deepening financial chaos internationally and the onset of the Great Depression. Her incomplete hull towering above the yard, visible for miles around, signalled the deepest crisis of the depression. John Brown's, and its employees were brought to their knees. Dole queues lengthened while the Government moved slowly towards a settlement which would allow the ship to continue. The resumption of work in April 1934 was interpreted nationally as an end to the worst effects of depression. The beginning of rearmament in the mid 1930s pulled John Brown's and the heavy industries out of recession although many yards had closed permanently with the loss of what would prove to be irreplaceable skilled jobs. By the end of the decade, the order for a second Cunarder ensured full employment. The launch of this ship, *Queen Elizabeth*, coincided with the Munich crisis of September 1938 and the start of a short timetable to world war. During this conflict, Clydebank paid a cruel price for its association with shipbuilding. The Luftwaffe offensive of March 1941 failed to inflict significant damage on the shipyard, but succeeded in severely damaging the town and claiming 448 lives. Despite that, the yard produced a vitally important fleet of warships from battleships to landing craft.

The end of the war brought many orders to replenish the world's merchant fleets and a period of sustained building which lasted well into the 1950s began. John Brown's was in a position to pick and choose its orders. The apparent domination of the market by British shipbuilders nevertheless masked the rise of new shipbuilding nations whose yards were established on a more productive basis in terms of plant, practice and labour. By the end of the 1950s, Britain had been overtaken by Japan and Germany as the world's leading shipbuilder. By the early1960s, the British shipbuilding industry was moving into deep crisis forcing many yards to close, unable to win orders at remunerative prices. Despite the excellence of John Brown's product, the company became uncompetitive. Lucrative warship orders dwindled as

the Royal Navy adjusted to a greatly reduced strategic role. The yard's other niche market, passenger liners, declined against steep competition from the passenger airliners of the jet age. The long-standing relationship with Cunard stalled as the shipping line deliberated over a replacement for *Queen Mary*. To hold its skilled workforce together, in anticipation of the latter, a ruinous contract was entered into with the Swedish America Line for *Kungsholm*. Massive losses on this contract were obscured by jubilation after winning the *QE2* contract. Concern expressed over the difficulties faced by the shipbuilding industry spurred the Government into an interventionist role. The Geddes Committee of Enquiry was established to recommend ways in which the industry could once more be put on a sound footing. In 1966, this Committee recommended the formation of shipbuilding groups. Thus Upper Clyde Shipbuilders was formed on the upper reaches of the Clyde. John Brown's became the Clydebank Division thus relieving the parent John Brown company of a financially burdensome yard. The brief and troubled history of Upper Clyde Shipbuilders finally tore the heart out of shipbuilding at Clydebank. In its final moments, Upper Clyde Shipbuilders put Clydebank in the headlines one more time although this had little to do with ships and everything to do with the fight to retain shipbuilding jobs.

After 120 years ranging between the lows of economic depression, the carnage of 1941 and the production of some of the world's most spectacular ships, the unthinkable had happened – shipbuilding at Clydebank ended.

Although hardship often attended shipbuilding, either through grim working conditions or periods of chronic economic depression, many thousands of people, acquired, and were able to apply, great skill in building ships. In this respect, society is poorer at the end of the 20th century than it was at the start. For shipyard workers, there was a clear sense of purpose in constructing products of such obvious utility. To this sense of purpose was added the overawing scale of both the ships and the shipyard environment. Ships were punched, bent and forced into existence out of a reluctant material. The shipyard was the scene of an all-weather elemental confrontation between man and steel. This gave rise to camaraderie in and out of the yard and to the emergence of 'characters' who became embedded in the folklore of shipbuilding communities. Although not always admitted, building ships generated tremendous pride. Perhaps overly focused on the product, shipbuilding has often been portrayed as a romantic activity. Although the reality was very different, there was an undefinable moment at a launch or when a ship sailed away in which the day to day issues, disagreements or the fears over job security which beset the company were suspended. As one Clydebank manager succinctly put it - 'shipbuilding was a hell of an industry for emotion.'[1]

Despite the demise of John Brown & Co. and shipbuilding at Clydebank, its story remains a remarkable one of achievement comparable with the best that any industrialised society could hope to recount.

Ian Johnston
July 2000

A NOTE ON PHOTOGRAPHS

The John Brown photographic archive is exceptional in its scale and quality. Photography did not become a feature of shipyard activity at Clydebank until the 1880s. Its function was to record progress on a contract and demonstrate to owners that construction had been achieved in line with stage payments. The period before the 1880s suffers from a paucity of directly relevant images. There would appear to be no photographs of J&G Thomson's Govan shipyard whatsoever although if there are any, they will no doubt appear soon after publication of this book. Many ships built at Clydebank have been exceeded only by the number of books written about them many of which are well illustrated. In selecting images for this book, priority was given to showing ships under construction as well as the yard itself. Although employed to make a factual record, staff photographers at Clydebank often transcended mere record photography. The sheer scale of shipbuilding and the majesty of the product has often been poignantly captured.

It is this record of often haunting images perhaps more than any other which underlines the inherent sadness in the end of shipbuilding at Clydebank. While the majority of images are by courtesy of the National Archives of Scotland, I would also like to thank the Scottish Media Group, John Hume, John Innes, Neil McCart, the Imperial War Museum and Glasgow City Council Cultural and Leisure Services Libraries for permission to reproduce images from their collections.

One of the unsung heroes of this book, the shipyard photographer, here unusualy caught in frame at the launch of the cruiser Europa *on 23 March 1897*

1847 - 1871   SET IN MOTION

The events which placed Clydeside in a position world prominence in marine engineering and shipbuilding were underpinned by inter-related developments. The emergence of the iron industry in the mid-eighteenth century using locally mined ore served as a starting point. The Carron Iron Works near Larbert, established in 1760, is generally regarded as the beginning of the modern Scottish iron industry. In 1782, the Clyde Iron Works began production to the north east of Glasgow. These developments encouraged exploitation of the Lanarkshire coalfields leading to a significant mining industry. In addition, Glasgow already had an important textile industry first established with flax spinning and then, by the end of the 18th century, further consolidated with cotton. By 1840 the population of Glasgow numbered 255,000 and the city rivalled Manchester as a cotton spinning and weaving centre. These industries, of recent introduction in themselves, were soon to be eclipsed by the engineering products of the new iron industries which they had indirectly spawned. The machinery employed in the textile industry was generally not of local manufacture and this encouraged a number of millwrights and iron founders, working in and around Glasgow, to specialise in the repair and manufacture of spares for these machines. From these modest beginnings, the design and manufacture of textile machinery was undertaken. This had the twin effect of stimulating the growth of iron foundries in the Glasgow area and, at the same time, creating a pool of skilled metal workers.

However, it was the commercial development of steam navigation that provided the impetus for the next series of developments in the growth of engineering.

In August 1812, when Henry Bell made his historic voyage down the Clyde in the Port Glasgow built *Comet*, it was with a steam engine designed and manufactured by John Robertson in Glasgow and a boiler made by David Napier in Glasgow[2]. While others had built steam engines for marine purposes,

most notably William Symington with the successful Charlotte Dundas of 1803, it was the *Comet* and its 3.5 hour pioneering voyage covering only twenty or so miles from Glasgow to Greenock, which beckoned new horizons in marine transportation. Steam powered machinery had made a small but significant impact on the vagaries of sail, wind and tide. While there was little new about the nature and function of ships, driving them through the seas by mechanical propulsion was novel. By 1816, no fewer than twenty steamboats were plying the Clyde, with machinery ranging from 6 to 30 horsepower.[3] Of these twenty vessels, five were built at Dumbarton, twelve at Port Glasgow and three at Greenock; all were of wooden construction. The engines for all but two of these vessels were made in Glasgow and the remaining two were both the product of James Watt's firm in Birmingham. Although Glasgow had as yet played little part in the construction of vessels, it was through steam propulsion and engine building that the city's association with shipbuilding was established.

David Napier and his cousin Robert are widely recognised as having laid the foundations of marine engineering and shipbuilding on Clydeside. David Napier, two years older than his cousin, established his first engine works in 1816 at Camlachie in Glasgow. An engineer of considerable talent and ingenuity, he perfected the steeple engine employed in many early steamers. Napier moved from Camlachie and set up new engine works at Lancefield Street, west of the city centre in 1821, leaving the old works to the equally talented Robert[4]. At this time, David Napier employed John Wood and other shipbuilders in Port Glasgow to build hulls for his engines.

By 1835, David had abandoned Clydeside and a successful business for London, and Robert had taken over the Lancefield engine works. The success of the marine steam engine in propelling ships soon encouraged others to establish themselves as engineers and engine builders. The role of both David and Robert Napier in training a cadre of talented engineers and shipbuilders in their works at Lancefield and, later Govan cannot be underestimated. Distinguished shipbuilders such as David Tod, John McGregor, William Denny, John Elder, and of course, the subjects of much of this book, James and George Thomson, were under the tutelage of Robert Napier at the outset of their careers.

A NAVIGABLE CHANNEL

The development of shipbuilding in Glasgow and the upper Clyde was inextricably linked with the development of Glasgow harbour and the River Clyde. In 1800, the upper part of the river was barely navigable by vessels drawing more than 3 feet, which effectively prevented ships of any reasonable size sailing to Glasgow. To some, the solution lay in bypassing the Clyde altogether. In 1806 work started on the construction of a canal linking Glasgow to the Ayrshire coast at Ardrossan. By 1810 the money ran out, leaving only an eleven-mile section of canal from Glasgow to Johnstone.[5] It was largely down to the far sighted efforts of the River Improvement Trust, constituted in 1809 by Act of Parliament, that both widening and deepening operations were carried out over a long period of time with the aim of making Glasgow accessible to ocean going vessels.[6] This process made it equally possible for ships of similar size to be built there. The first builder of vessels of a reasonable size in Glasgow was John Barclay, later to become associated with Robert Curle, who established a small slip and yard for building and repairing wooden vessels at Stobcross Pool in 1818. It was the advent of iron, rolled into flat plates, as a shipbuilding material, which distinguished the rise of shipbuilding on the upper part of the Clyde. The realisation that iron would enable ships of much larger dimensions to be constructed in addition to providing a more rigid structure for steam engines provided the stimulus for development. Heavy cast iron engines fitted into wooden hulls, no matter how well built, were a marriage of limited future. It was the combination of iron hull, steam engine and commercial incentive that enabled the Clyde to rise to a position of prominence in marine engineering and shipbuilding.

There were many shipyards throughout the UK building wooden ships although few had experimented with iron. The first builders of iron ships on a regular basis were not far-seeing builders of wooden vessels but the engine builders who saw hulls constructed of iron as a natural extension of their existing metal working skills. Among the first to exploit this new development in Glasgow were Tod and McGregor, later described as the 'originators of iron architecture as applied to the construction of vessels'. In 1839, they set up an iron shipyard at Greenlaw on the south bank of the River Clyde having previously built a number of small iron vessels at their Clyde Foundry on the north side of the river.[7] Robert Napier entered iron shipbuilding at an early stage taking over McArthur and Alexander's shipyard at Govan in 1842. Within a very short space of time Napier became the most important of the early Clyde shipbuilders.

Thus, the second phase in the development of shipbuilding on the upper Clyde began with the evolution of marine engineers into iron shipbuilders. This phase is described by the following comment, which appeared in a newspaper:

'Out of a hundred or more vessels now being constructed on the Clyde there are only seven of wood: and of all the rest 94 are steamers. There can be little doubt that the time is hastening fast when timber ships will be obsolete, and that the world's traffic will be conducted mainly by steam as an auxiliary power to the uncertain and precarious winds.

It is a curious phase in the art and mastery of shipbuilding, that hitherto nine tenths of these vessels made of iron have been built by engineers who never studied naval architecture, and all at once took a lead in the art, leaving the professional shipbuilders to jog on at heckmatock and oak, until they were distanced in the race of

Henry Bell (1767 - 1830) Bell placed the contract for the steamer Comet *with the Port Glasgow shipbuilder John Wood & Co. Bell was a millwright to trade who later studied under the Scottish engineer John Rennie*

The first commercial staemboat in Europe, Comet *was launched in 1812 and sailed successfully until wrecked in 1820. Her engine was constructed by John Robertson and her boiler by David Napier.*

competition and had to convert their adzes into huge iron shears, and their augers into punching machines, in self defence. And yet it is a study to see how soon carpenters became cunning in bending plates, and shipwrights in fashioning angle-iron.'[8]

The first steam ship to cross the Atlantic was the wooden-hulled *Sirius* which had side lever paddle

An early image of industrialisation on the Clyde around 1840. The painting shows Tod & McGregor's works on the south bank of the river at Windmillcroft

Another illustration painted in 1840 by the same artist this time showing the wood shipyard of John Barclay to the west of Finnieston Quay

engines constructed by Thomas Wingate of Glasgow. As the Clyde emerged as an iron shipbuilding centre it was by no means the only one of importance. Much of the shipbuilding industry was concentrated on the Thames and for a time, thanks largely to the exertions of Isambard Kingdom Brunel, and ships like *Great Britain* and *Great Western*, it seemed as if Bristol might

also develop into a major shipbuilding centre. There can be little doubt that great excitement must have been generated by the promise of this new industry, the products of which brought far off places a little closer through reliable, swifter, mechanical propulsion. The creation of engine works, boiler shops, forges, foundries, yards and a host of related industries in its midst set Glasgow on the path to becoming the major centre of heavy industry which it would remain for over one hundred years. Of the men who developed this industry the Mechanics Magazine said in April 1853:

> ' . . . the employers in nearly all the establishments were working men themselves within the last thirty years. Most of them had attained the period of middle life before they turned their attention to iron boat-building at all. The men are not only the architects of their own fortunes but the creators of a new branch of industry'[9]

Even before it was certain that Clydeside would play a major part in the development of marine engineering and shipbuilding, a Partick grocer named John Thomson sent three of his sons into apprenticeship with a firm of millwrights and engineers in Glasgow.

THE THOMSON FAMILY

Details of the Thomson family before 1800 are scant. John Thomson was born on 1 December 1768 at Holm of Cathcart on the south side of Glasgow. His wife to be, Jean Paul, was born on 9 April 1777 in the Gorbals, then a rather affluent suburb on the south bank of the river. On 17 October 1800, John married Jean Paul in the Parish of Govan and the first of nine children, three girls and six boys, was born on 9 October 1801. When John Thomson died on 21 January 1837, he was recorded as being a grocer working in Partick, 'leaving a piece of ground with house thereon in the village of Partick, Glasgow, Lanarkshire.'[10] However, other accounts attribute John with involvement in 'smith-work'. Three sons, James born 19 December 1803, Robert, born 5 February 1811 and George born 25 March 1815,[11] were to become involved in the new business of marine engineering. Whatever plans John had for his sons were probably influenced by the excitement surrounding the development of steam navigation, events which were happening on their own doorstep. All three brothers were apprenticed to the Partick firm of Graham Wellington & Company, millwrights and engineers. The apprenticeships were as joiners.

Engineering in the modern sense was of recent origin and many of the skills and methods associated with metalworking were carried over from woodworking. Certain wood-working trades had a considerable bearing on engineering, especially pattern making, a highly skilled trade where an understanding of the characteristics of molten iron and of metal in general were a prerequisite for the manufacture of accurate metal castings. It was as pattern makers that both James and George Thomson were later to find employment as journeymen.

JAMES THOMSON

On completion of his apprenticeship, James left Glasgow to take employment in Manchester. In 1828, he returned to Glasgow to work for Robert Napier as his leading smith, finisher and turner, at the Vulcan Foundry in Washington Street. Napier's move from Camlachie to Lancefield was completed in the same year. James Thomson's return to Glasgow was facilitated by Napier who paid him the sum of £10 to defray the expense of conveying him from Manchester and a wage of 36 shillings per week to be paid fortnightly. Thomson was to work for Napier for almost twenty years during which time Napier's' reputation as a marine engine builder was firmly established

In 1838, a new agreement was signed between Robert Napier and James Thomson, who was now an assistant foreman engineer:

> 'It is hereby agreed between James Thomson and Robert Napier that the said James Thomson shall give the whole of his personal services for the term of Five Years from and after this date. On the other hand Robert Napier to pay the said James Thomson a yearly salary of One Hundred and Twenty Pounds Sterling with a bonus of Five Pounds for every pair of engines that are finished and set agoing from the two works of Vulcan & Lancefield Foundries commencing with the following engines - the Victoria's, the Fire King's, Glow Worm's, Aberdeen Company and Arran Companies engines. These bonuses to be paid at the end of each year for all Engines set agoing and finished during the preceding year and we agree to put this on stamp paper.'[12]

On 22 November 1842, the agreement with James was renewed for a further five years with salary fixed at £175 with a bonus of £10 for every pair of engines (meaning an engine with two cylinders) completed at Napier's works.

On 24 August 1834, James married Grace McIntyre in Govan Parish Church. Grace was the daughter of John McIntyre, who had prospered as cashier at Robert Napier's Vulcan Foundry, living at Greenlaw on the south bank of the Clyde. Between 1835 and 1848, James and Grace had six girls and two boys. In 1851 they were living at 13 Kelvin Grove Place, an affluent address in Glasgow[13].

ROBERT THOMSON

On completion of his apprenticeship, Robert went to sea. He served as an engineer with the small steamship company, G&J Burns, sailing from Glasgow to Liverpool on the steamer *Commodore*. When, in 1839, George Burns and David McIver decided to put up the capital for Samuel Cunard to realise his ambition of establishing a North Atlantic shipping company, Robert joined the company in Liverpool and became their first superintendent engineer with responsibility for all machinery in the company's growing fleet. Robert's close association with the Cunard's company was fortuitous in light of his brother's future aspirations as marine engineers and shipbuilders.

GEORGE THOMSON

On completion of his apprenticeship, George also went to sea for a brief period before following his brother James into employment with Robert Napier at the Lancefield works in 1835. Robert was evidently impressed by young George and in 1841 entered into a five-year agreement in which George was employed in the capacity of foreman at the 'Lancefield Foundry and Engineer Works'. George's salary, to be paid quarterly, was £160 for the first year, £170 for the second, £180 for the third and £200 for the last two years.

On 8 August 1841, George married Elizabeth Rodgers at Gorbals Parish Church. Between 1842 and 1860, George and Elizabeth had nine children (six girls and three boys) In 1851, the family were living at 8 Royal Terrace, Glasgow, an equally affluent part of the city.

ROBERT NAPIER AND SAMUEL CUNARD

In 1839 an agreement was struck which did much to consolidate Clydeside's emerging position in shipbuilding as well as creating an alliance of interests which lasted until the completion of the QE2 in 1968. Samuel Cunard arrived in Britain from Nova Scotia early in February 1839 to try and secure the Admiralty contract for the first Atlantic Mail Steamer Service. This had been advertised in The Times in November of the previous year. Cunard was not a

Top
James Thomson, the older of the two brothers who started the business of James & George Thomson.

Middle
George Thomson, who, with his brother, worked for leading engineer and shipbuilder Robert Napier

Bottom
Grace MacIntyre, whom James Thomson married in 1834. Her father, was cashier at Robert Napier's Vulcan Foundry in Glasgow

Above
David Napier, built the boilers for
Comet *while working in his*
father's engineering business. He
founded the Camlachie Foundry
in 1814 and the Lancefield
Foundry in 1824.

Right
John Robertson, a Glasgow
engineer, posing in front of part
of the engine that powered Henry
Bell's steamship Comet.

The wooden paddle steam ship
Acadia *one of four designed and*
engined by Robert Napier for
Samuel Cunard in 1840. All four
ships were built by John Wood at
Port Glasgow as Napier had yet
to start shipbuilding activities

newcomer to shipping and already owned, through his company Samuel Cunard & Co., over forty sailing vessels. Cunard's tender, delivered by 11 February 1839, promised three steam boats each of 300 horse power and 800 tons, able to carry the mail by May 1840. Cunard was faced with the problem of making the terms of his tender a reality. Through his friend, James Melville, Secretary of the East India Company, Cunard was directed to Robert Napier and John

Wood in the belief that they would be capable of building the ships promised for the Atlantic route. Cunard made the journey north to Glasgow and met Napier at his home, Lancefield House, adjacent to his engine works at Lancefield Quay. The meeting went well and on 18 March, Napier signed the contract to build Cunard's three Atlantic wooden paddle steamers. The Admiralty contract, worth £55,000 per annum, was signed on 4 May 1839.

When Napier advised the construction of larger, stronger vessels, better able to keep to a Trans-Atlantic schedule in the face of steep penalties, Cunard was forced to seek additional capital for these costlier vessels. James Melville suggested that Cunard discuss this in another meeting with the Scottish engineer. Napier introduced him to David and Charles McIver and George and James Burns, successful Glasgow ship owners who operated in competition with one another. After some deliberation, David McIver and George Burns agreed to become partners in Cunard's contract. Thus The British and North American Royal Mail Steam Packet Company was brought into existence. With such a long designation it is little wonder that the new company was soon referred to as Cunard's Company long before being officially titled the Cunard Steam-Ship Company in 1878. While George Burns remained in Glasgow to supervise construction of the ships, David McIver went to Liverpool from where the new ships would operate. By 1840, the first of four 'Cunarders', *Britannia*, had made a successful crossing of the Atlantic from Liverpool to Halifax. Napier constructed the engines for all four vessels, the hulls by Robert Duncan at his Greenock shipyard. However, Napier clearly saw financial as well as technical advantage in building his own hulls and, in the year 1841, he purchased a shipyard in Govan.[14] The first iron ship built by Napier was the 700 ton *Vanguard* in 1843. After launching, ships were taken from Govan up-river to a small basin which had been cut into the bank near the engine works at Lancefield where vessels were completed after having their engines fitted.

EARLY STEAM ENGINES

Above all, it was the development of the marine engine which acted as the stimulus for the growth of engineering on Clydeside. The necessity to produce engines of greater power coupled with greater economy and yet of minimum size, challenged the skill and inventiveness of the most able engineers. For those used to horse and wind as the motive

power of the day, the sight of towering steam driven engines must have been awe inspiring. Cast in iron, with cranks and beams in rapid motion these engines filled the inside of cramped machinery spaces lit only by oil lamps and candles.

In many respects, the first commercially successful marine steam engines were adapted directly from James Watt's beam engine, which, in turn, stemmed from Newcomen's engine of the 18th century. The 4 horse power engine built by John Robertson in 1812 for Henry Bell's *Comet* was an early version of the side-lever engine which, in essence, provided the pattern for the multiplicity of engine types which followed over the next few decades.

As paddle wheels were then the only method of converting the power of the engine into motion, developments of the side lever engine were concerned with maximising the relationship between engine and paddle wheel. Largely down to the efforts of David Napier, a series of derivatives based on the side-lever engine were successfully introduced and his steeple engine, in which the piston operated more directly with fewer parts than the side lever, was widely adopted. This engine also had the added commercial advantage of occupying less horizontal space thereby enabling more cargo to be carried. The oscillating trunk engine developed by Maudslay on the Thames and improved by Penn during the 1830s also found favour as did twin cylinder and direct acting engines. With the advent of the screw propeller during the 1850s, paddle engines were geared to make the faster revolutions required for efficient operation of the propeller. This arrangement was soon replaced by the direct acting engine where horizontal cylinders drove the propeller shaft directly at a higher speed[15] As the end of their working relationship with Robert Napier drew closer, the Thomson brothers, both senior employees at his Lancefield Foundry, had received first class experience in the design and building of some of the most notable marine engines of the day.

J&G THOMSON & COMPANY

On 1 April 1847, James and George took the plunge and went into business under the title J&G Thomson & Company, Engineers. Capital for the new company was provided by James' wife Grace, who contributed the substantial sum of £4,000. The source of this loan was almost certainly Grace Thomson's father, John McIntyre.[16]

James Lumsden, a former Lord Provost of Glasgow and founder of the Clydesdale Bank, granted the brothers ground to the value of £4,500 and James Ewing Mathieson gave land to the value of £4,977 on which to erect the works. [17] Although the brothers had contributed considerable sums of money to the business Lumsden and Mathieson's support was invaluable.

Whether Robert Napier's benevolence in sharing his pioneering expertise extended to encouraging competitors is unknown. His failure to attend either George or James' farewell supper, held in the Crow Hotel, George Square, Glasgow, may provide an indication.

The Thomson brothers built their new engine and boiler shops, which covered an area of 2.5 acres, in Finnieston Street a newly industrialised part of Glasgow and a short distance from their former employer's works. The new works were later described as slavish copies of Napier's Lancefield Works 'low in height and dimly lighted, with superimposed shops for finishing and pattern work; the hoisting and handling of the pieces of machinery being performed almost entirely by manual labour, and the haulage of machinery in yard or to the crane by the employment of a large gang of men and boys'[18] In December 1847, the brothers engaged John Grant as company secretary at a salary of £178, a position he would keep for nearly fifty years. The following year, Andrew Burns was employed as manager at an approximate salary of £150.

The new works were given the name Clyde Bank Foundry, thus bringing into being the name that would subsequently be applied to the town some fifty years later.[19] The first marine engine constructed by the new company was a single steeple engine of 50 hp for the iron paddle ship *Ben Nevis*, later renamed *Cygnet*. This vessel was built by John Reid at Port Glasgow for the Glasgow shipowners G&J Burns and intended for the Glasgow and Inverness trade through the Crinan and Caledonian canals. The engine had a single cylinder of 41 inches diameter with a stroke of 42 inches.[20] The Thomsons had learnt their business well and plaudits were not long in coming. In October 1850, with the launch of the Bibby Line paddle ship *Arno* at Wood and Reid's Port Glasgow yard, it was reported that 'Her engines, which are constructed on the direct acting principle, have been made by Messrs. James and George Thomson of Glasgow, whose celebrity as marine engineers is now rapidly extending.'[21] The Thomsons quickly established themselves as builders of land and marine engines as well as cranes and derricks for use on board ships. Some of the orders which the

Robert Napier, followed his cousin David into engineering and later started iron shipbuilding. Napier did more than anyone to start the momentum behind marine engineering and shipbuilding on Clydeside.

Below
Sam Cunard, who met Robert Napier in Glasgow to discuss details and construction of the first ships of the Cunard Line

Bottom
James Burns who with his brother entered into a financial arrangement with Cunard to bring the latters shipping line into existence

A view of the Clyde at Govan painted by James Adderson in 1839 where soon after an iron shipbuilding yard would be established by McArthur & Alexander. This would be taken over by Robert Napier in 1842

young firm took included the hull of the ship as well as the engines. Initially, the hulls were sub-contracted out to shipbuilders, principally Wood & Co. in Port Glasgow. However, James and George were not slow to recognise the commercial advantages in building their own hulls.

IRON SHIPBUILDING

In 1851, James and George made the decision to extend the business into iron shipbuilding following the lead which other marine engineers had successfully taken before them. The site chosen was on the south bank of the Clyde at Govan about half a mile from their engine works. An article in the Glasgow Herald noted that:

> 'As another evidence of the increase of the trade on the River Clyde we may notice that the

Messrs. Thomson of the Clyde Bank Foundry Finnieston have purchased the property of Cessnock Bank with a view to converting it into a shipbuilding yard. Already a long range of workshops has been built and roofed in, and we are informed that the fine house of Cessnock Bank is doomed to demolition to make way for the keels of iron ships. The widening of the river at this point will enable the builders to launch their vessels from the yard with the utmost facility.

As a matter of course the owners of the five little villas in the neighbourhood will not be very well pleased with their new neighbours, for the riveting of bolts do not produce any very pleasing sounds. The increase in the value of property of late on the margin of our river is really astonishing. We have been informed that not long since the proprietor of Cessnock Bank bought the house and ground attached for less than £3,000. The Trustees requiring a strip of it to enable them to widen the river, paid him £1,000 for so much as they needed and now the remainder, purchased as before stated by Messrs. Thomson, has brought £7,500'[22]

What actually happened was rather different. Two adjoining plots of ground were acquired, Cessnock Bank and Hornbank. As with their engine works, the ground was effectively given free of charge for a period of time.[23] The total area of both plots was about five acres.[24] A public right of way maintained along the river's edge was removed for launches and reinstated immediately after.[25] At least part of the villa standing at Cessnock Bank was retained and incorporated into the new shipyard office buildings.

An 1860s map of the Clyde showing the location of Thomson's Clyde Bank works at Finnieston and Clyde Bank iron shipyard at Govan. At this time the Clyde opposite Thomson's yard had not been widened

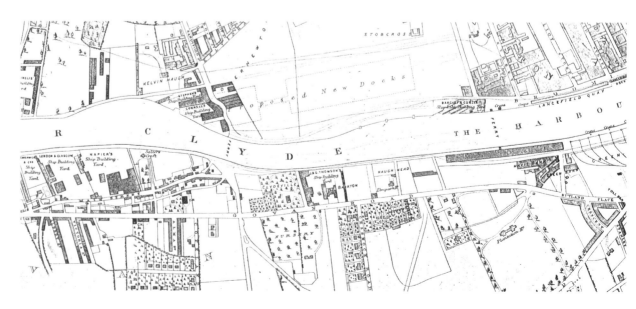

After a few years, together with the new Govan yard, the Clyde Bank Foundry at Finnieston had a workforce of around 1,500.

The first vessel to be built by J&G Thomson, and thus inaugurate a remarkable series of over 750 ships, was an inauspicious, small, double-ended paddle tender named *Jackal*, built to the order of Charles McIver.[26] This 165-ton vessel was intended to operate between Cunard's passenger ships on the Mersey and the quays at Liverpool. The new shipyard was sufficiently complete to permit the keel laying of this vessel on 22 December 1851.

> 'Both ends of the vessel are alike; and in what may be called the deadwood at each end is a rudder. The object of this arrangement is that the vessel may be steered either way without the necessity of turning, each end in turn becoming the stern. The rudders fill the opening in the deadwood in which they work, and the one at the advancing end of the boat is fixed firmly, while the after one is in action to steer by. The paddle boxes are flat on the top, and are on the level of the gunwale, so as to afford facilities for shipping passengers luggage etc. This arrangement will necessitate very small paddles which must be made to rotate more rapidly in consequence. Altogether the tender is worth a visit as exhibiting a judicious adaptation of means to an end irrespective of the conventional rules of marine architecture'[27]

Other marine engineers were set to follow the Thomsons into shipbuilding in a period of great activity. In June 1852, the North British Daily Mail, took up this point:

> 'The notion that most of our iron steamboat building firms are acquiring rapid fortunes, is likely, we hear, to cause a considerable rush into the trade. We are informed that sites for no fewer than four additional building yards have just been secured by different parties on the banks of the river - all within a few miles of the city - with a view to a roaring competition! When the projected establishments are in operation, the Clyde will, if we mistake not, be able to put forth a greater amount of work in this important department of naval architecture than all the rest of the Kingdom put together'[28]

Two similar sized vessels followed *Jackal*, *Venus* for the Largs Steamboat Co. and *Mountaineer*, for Glasgow owners David Hutcheson & Co. The fourth vessel *Corriere Siciliano* for Samuel Howes & Co. of Liverpool, was larger and indicative of the type of ship for which the Thomsons would become famous. Of nearly 500 tons, *Corriere Siciliano* had internal arrangements described as most complete, 'the saloon is wainscoted with bird's-eye maple and provided with sleeping berths for 38 first-class passengers. The accommodation in the second cabin is very commodious, 40 berths being fitted up.'[29]

As the engines and boilers intended for these ships were built on the other side of the river and there was, in any case, no crane at the shipyard capable of lifting them, *Jackal*, and all the other ships to follow from this yard, was taken up river to have her engines and boilers installed. There were only two cranes in Glasgow capable of doing this work, one at Windmillcroft Quay on the south bank and the other at Lancefield Quay on the north bank.[30]

The separation of the Thomsons' principal business assets - engine works at Finnieston and shipyard at Govan - was entirely typical of the early development of this industry on Clydeside. Transporting engines and boilers from the works at Finnieston to the crane at Windmillcroft, as happened frequently during the 1850s, was often a dangerous business as the following contemporary account illustrates:

> 'Steamboat building was never so brisk on the banks of the Clyde as at present: and never were

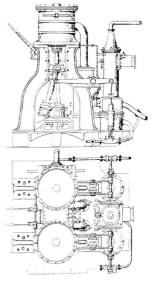

Above
The direct acting compound engines for Frankfort *constructed in 1851.*

Left
The diagonally opposed geared screw engines for Bordeaux.

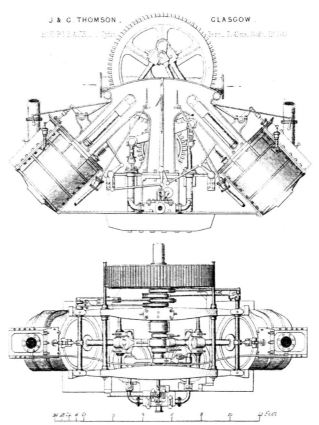

A ticket to the 'soiree' held in 1852 for the men and women of the Clyde Bank Foundry and Shipyard.

The Australasian built for Cunard in 1857 and the largest ship so far built by the Thomsons.

so many large steamers and engines being built. Steam boilers of 20 to 35 tons are put on board ship at the rate of probably one a week. All the large engineering shops where such structures are built are situated on the north side of the river, but the only crane powerful enough to put them on board is situated half a mile down on the south side of the harbour, it having been so placed, as we once heard a waggish official say "Because it would be there most out of the way" All these boilers and other heavy machinery must be therefore conveyed on strong four-wheeled trucks a distance of from one to nearly two miles along our most crowded quays and across our principal bridge, interrupting traffic, endangering life, and injuring the causeway. The two boilers dragged to the large crane on Tuesday were from Messrs. J&G Thomson's engine works and are to be put on board the Telegraph iron steamer launched a few days ago from their building yard. There were about 600 men employed in dragging each boiler, and it took nearly two hours to accomplish the distance. The question of erecting a large crane on the north side of the river was lately discussed by the River Trustees but we have not heard of any further steps having been taken to obviate the present inconvenient and annoying arrangement'[31]

The image of massive, riveted, wrought-iron boilers and cast iron steam engines inert on wooden bogies being dragged through the narrow cobbled streets of Glasgow seems wholly contradictory to their use as sophisticated prime movers in the new age of steam navigation. The reliance on manpower brought with it risks to life and limb:

'Yesterday afternoon, as a great many of Messrs. Thomson's workmen were engaged in conveying a truck on which was a large steamboat funnel southward across Jamaica Street Bridge, one of their number named Soper was accidentally forced in upon one of the wheels, the edge of which passed over the fore part of his left foot, bruising it very severely. The poor fellow was carried to the shop of a surgeon, and thence taken home in a cab'[32]

The integration of shipbuilding and marine engineering facilities was first achieved when John Elder's new shipyard and engine works opened at Fairfield in 1871. The Thomsons were not to achieve such integration until 1884 on another site at Clydebank. In the short term, the solution to the early difficulties of lifting heavy engines and boilers onto ships in Glasgow Harbour was rectified by building a sixty-ton crane at Finnieston.

In a diversification of their activities, the Thomsons built this crane for the Clyde Trust in 1855 at a cost of £2,450[33] From this time onwards, ships launched at Govan were taken to Finnieston to be fitted-out by

this crane which was the largest on the Clyde for twenty years.

An early employee of the Thomsons was Edward J Harland, who, on completion of an apprenticeship on the River Tyne in 1851, accepted employment at the Clydebank Foundry for £1 a week. Harland later moved to the new Govan shipyard as chief draughtsman at the same rate of £1 per week! Despite being offered a rise in wages and a long-term contract, Harland declined and left the Clyde to return to Tyneside. Of his time with the Thomsons, Harland later said 'I found the banks of the Clyde splendid ground for gaining further mechanical knowledge'[34] Ten years later Harland established his own shipyard at Belfast later taking Gustav Wolff into partnership.

After shipbuilding was successfully begun at Cessnock Bank, the Thomsons continued to use spare capacity at their engine works to build machinery for ships other than their own, an activity which would continue throughout the life of the Company. Several engines attracted favourable comment such as the geared screw engines built for *Bordeaux* in 1851: ' . . . the general arrangement of the engines, and the adjustment of the details manifest much judgement and aptitude in the art of mechanical combination'. The engines of *Frankfort*, also built in 1851, were described as 'among the best examples of direct acting screw engines that we yet possess.'[35] The *Frankfort's* engines were the first to adopt the form of direct acting engine in which the cylinders were inverted vertically.[36] One authority in marine engineering[37] describes Thomsons inverted or 'steamhammer' engine as 'the most successful of all direct-acting screw engines . . . (which) . . . eventually became to be acknowledged as the only form of engine for screw propulsion and has survived a century of experimentation with many engines working on widely different principles.'[38] Although they were perhaps not as inventive as Napier or Elder, Thomson's development of the latter engine was highly significant. In 1855, George Thomson took out a patent for the invention of 'Improvements in Steam Engines' This patent covered a variety of modifications to the valves of steam engines to improve economy by shutting off steam as well as balancing the action of direct-acting engines.

On 8 January 1857, George Thomson wrote the following letter concerning his patent.

'Dear Sir,
I am duly in receipt of yours of 6th instant and have sent you by this post one of the printed Specifications and Drawings (by the Patent Office) of my expansion gear, which will explain the whole making of it; we have applied it very successfully to the Governor Higginson lately fitted out by us. . . should you . . . think of adopting this Expansion Gear I could give you all particulars as to how it should be fitted up, the patent right is one pound per Horse Power.'[39]

In April 1854, sensitivity over engine design was revealed when the Company set the police after their

Part of the programme for the 1852 social event.

A busy scene in Glasgow Harbour during the 1860s. The increase in seaborne trade made demands on river frontage forcing several shipbuilders to relocate

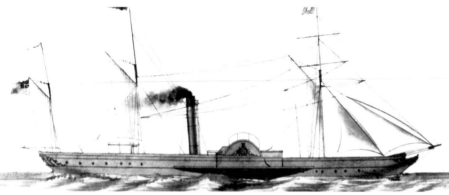

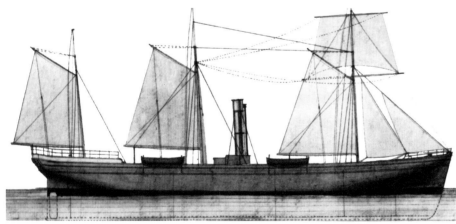

Contemporary drawings of early Thomson built ships from top to bottom:
  Chevalier *1853*
  Jura *1854*
  Clansman *1855*
  Ossian *1855*

chief draughtsman, David Rollo, who had recently been in their employ. Rollo's job had been to prepare drawings of finished engines which the Thomsons had designed and constructed. Initial sketches were made in sketchbooks by Rollo and other draughtsmen at the engine works in preparation for

the final drawings. When he left Thomson's employment, Rollo took eight of these sketchbooks with him and the Thomsons took action to recover them. Although Rollo contested ownership of the sketchbooks he was ordered to return them[40]

By March 1852, the new yard had orders for four ships and engines to build for a fifth. Of these, two were screw steamers the remainder being paddle steamers. In March the following year, a total of eight vessels were on order, all but two of which were screw ships. In addition, the Company had orders for the machinery for three ships being built by Denny at Dumbarton. It also seems likely that between the years 1855 and 1856, 19 sets of engines of 70nhp[41] each were constructed for wooden screw gunboats building at various yards in St Petersburg for service in the Crimea.[42]

Many of the vessels built during the 1850s became well known. In 1854, the Cunard Atlantic liner *Jura* was completed at 313 feet and 2,240 gross tons, the largest ship so far built by the Thomsons. In the space of ten years, the yard built three vessels called *Iona*. The first *Iona* was built for David Hutcheson and completed with two oscillating engines of 180 horsepower in 1855. This paddle steamer generated considerable interest in the local press ' (*Iona*). . . promises to outrun any steamer in Europe . . . this speed is beyond what the ordinary railway trains accomplish between Glasgow and Greenock, and quite up to anything yet attained in the United States'[43] *Iona* was built for the Glasgow to Ardrishaig run and on her trial trip in June made the 15 .75 miles from Cloch Point to Cumbrae light house in nearly 48 minutes, a speed of almost twenty miles per hour '. . . a rate of speed unparalleled in this quarter'

By the early 1860s, J&G Thomson had built over fifty vessels and engined many more on a profitable basis. In the first eight years of trading, annual profits averaged £1,890. In the three years from 1856 to 1858 profits jumped to an average of £12,667 before a one-off loss in 1859 of £3956, the only loss made in nineteen years. The principal sources of orders were Burns, McIver and Cunard although others like David Hutcheson and the Papayani Brothers also placed orders regularly. Other major customers were sought including the Admiralty and P&O. While Robert Napier had built many of the first vessels for the Cunard Company, the Thomsons were steadily encroaching on Napier's market, first with relatively small vessels, but increasingly with larger and better appointed ships. While Robert Thomson's position as Superintendent Engineer with Cunard could only

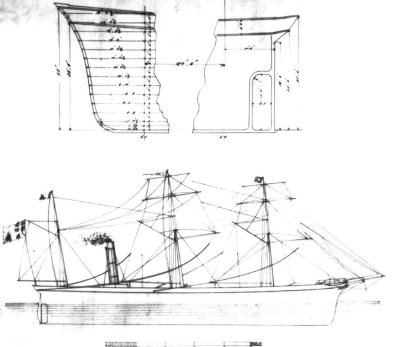

Dimensions of Masts, Spars &c.
of the

"Elizabeth Jane."

Fore Mast. Length over all 68', Head 9'

Main Mast.   Do   70'6", Do 9'

Mizen Mast.   Do   55' , Do 6'

Bowsprit. Length over all 33', Length outboard 18'

Jibcom .   Do 26' ,   Do   14'

Fore - Main Top Masts. Length 22' for. 24' main .

Mizen Top Mast.   Do   38 feet -
Fore - Main Top Gall. Masts. Length 12'
Fore - Main Poles Length 4' Mizen pole 3'
Fore + Main Gaffs   Do - 29 feet .
Mizen Gaff   Do - 20 -
Fore Boom   Do - 78'6"-
Main Boom   Do - 40'6'-
Mizen Boom   Do - 32' 0'-
Fore + Main Lower Yards _ Do over all 59', arms 3',
     Do Topsail Do . Do - - 40'6', Do 2',
     Do Top Gall. Do - / Do   30' 0', Do 1'5',

Glasgow, July 15th 1858

Elisabeth Jane, *31st ship built by Thomson, completed in 1857*

have been beneficial in this respect, there is little doubt that the engines and ships turned out by his brothers were of the highest quality. The *Australasian* of 1857, built for the European & Australian Royal Mail Company, was evidence of the Company's ability to attract orders for the most significant ships of the day. The contract for *Australasian* stipulated severe penalties for failure to meet the required speed. On trials at the Stokes Bay measured mile off Portsmouth, the ship made a maximum of 14.575 knots, which was considered highly satisfactory. A contemporary report describes the ship:

> '. . . She has three decks: on the spar deck is a spacious poop, fitted entirely for first class passengers; also topgallant forecastle for crew, and the usual deck houses, sculleries, butcher's and baker's shops, cowhouse etc. On the main-deck is a magnificent saloon, capable of dining upwards of 200 passengers; alongside the saloon, and the entire length of the vessel, accommodation for passengers is fitted; the lower-deck is appropriated to mail-rooms, bullion-rooms, store-rooms, wine-cellars etc. . . .'[44]

When the European & Australian Royal Mail Company went bankrupt in 1860, the *Australasian* was purchased by Cunard to become their first screw driven mail ship.

Until March 1855, the Company had shown no requirement for finance to support business. In that month, however, credit of £20,000 was arranged with the Union Bank of Scotland to support the continued growth of the business. In September 1858, at the onset of a trade depression, the Company asked if this could be increased to £35,000. The Bank agreed on the basis that this should be reduced to the original limit of £20,000 over the next two years. This straightforward transaction established a relationship with the Union Bank of Scotland, and their successors, the Bank of Scotland, which would last through good times and bad for the next one hundred years.

Relations between James and George and their brother Robert were cordial and businesslike and the following letter dated 16 April 1861 indicates that no privileges or special treatment was expected. It describes also the very loose way in which prices were quoted on the basis of minimal information, principally - dimensions, cargo capacity, speed and accommodation. It seems likely that the vessel described was not ordered.

> 'Dear Brother,
> We are in receipt of yours of 9th inst. enclosing letter from Mr Cunard of New York, relative to screw steamer required for Panama Rail Co. From the dimensions and requirements stated we think such a vessel would require about 130 hp to propel 9 to 10 knots in moderate weather, with a consumption of fuel (best Welsh coal) of from 12 to 14 tons per day. Not knowing anything of the qualities of the hard coal Mr Cunard mentions

we cannot say as to the consumption . . . but in all likelihood, Mr Cunard will be in a position as to the relative steaming qualities of the two kinds of coal from seeing them used probably in the same vessels, and will thus be able to form an idea of the quantity of hard coals that would be burned. Our price for the vessel we give as exactly as possible, not having specification or fuller details to guide us, one estimate for a vessel as stated 215 x 30 x 21 feet, with engines of 130 ihp[45] and tubular boilers (iron tubes) with storage for 800 tons cargo and accommodation in deck houses for 50 cabin passengers all fittings plain but substantial and the whole make first class materials and workmanship equal to anything we have turned out in these respects, finished complete for sea and delivery here, with exception of stewards furnishings, say the sum of £21,500 this estimate we give to the best of our knowledge from the idea conveyed to us by Mr Cunard's letter. The amount of course subject to modification more or less according to extent of specification and the price we may mention is at current rates of material and wages.

We trust you will find the foregoing sufficiently satisfactory to transmit to Mr. Cunard. We would have great pleasure in building this or any other vessel to his order, and would do our utmost to make it as moderate as possible in cost, and thoroughly substantial and workman like in execution as we could turn out.

We remain, Dear Brother, Yours very truly, James and George Thomson'[46]

Later the same year, the brothers sprang to the defence of their reputation after the Glasgow shipping agents Robinsons & Marjoribanks referred to the business in dismissive terms.

'Dear Sirs,

We were not a little surprised at what you mentioned to us yesterday regarding the opinion entertained of us by some of your friends in Paris as being only 'young constructors' of marine engines, more especially referring to those of the 'balanced liner construction' we think we can give the most unqualified proofs of having had unusually large experience and success in making such engines.

Firstly, we beg to state that all the Clyde paddle steamers (we mean those sailing from the Clyde to Liverpool, Belfast, Dublin etc.) having balanced liner engines (and nearly all have such engines) received them from us. Moreover, we

have to say, that when the *Scotia*, the new paddle steamer now fitting out for the Cunard Company, 4,000tons and 1,000 horse power was contracted for, we, along with Messrs Napier were the only parties applied to by the owners to tender for the construction, as being the only builders they would entrust with such work. The *Scotia's* engines are of the balanced liner description and are probably the largest of the kind made. We may mention further that the first six vessels built for the Cunard Company were fitted up under our superintendence while we were managers with Mr Napier, also that the swiftest despatch boat in the Black Sea during the Crimean War, the Telegraph, (the favourite steamer of Lord Lyons) was both built and had balanced liner engines of our construction – so much for our experience in making balanced liner engines.

As regards our experience and success in building steamers, whether paddle or screw, with engines either oscillating, direct acting, or of other kinds, we can refer with confidence to the vessels we have built for the Cunard and other large companies many of which are celebrated for their speed and efficiency among others we may mention the trans-Atlantic mail screw steamer *Australasian* belonging to Cunard Company, which has made some of the quickest runs on record, also the *Jura, Olympus, Atlas*, all of large size belonging to the Cunard Company and a whole fleet of vessels in the Mediterranean and other trades. We have also built the swiftest steamer (the Iona) on the Clyde.

As a proof of our standing and estimation by Government, we have repeatedly received schedules for tendering for marine work. We trust that the above remarks will fully disabuse the minds of your friends of the erroneous impressions entertained as to our ability in engine making . . .'[47]

ENGAGING THE ADMIRALTY

The above letter makes reference to Government contracts. The fact was that despite enquiries, no order had been placed for either machinery or hulls. During the 1860s, repeated attempts were made to win Admiralty work. This is hardly surprising considering the size of the Royal Navy, then by far the largest in the world. Moreover, the Thomsons would have been aware that Robert Napier, had for some time been building warships and engines for the Admiralty, culminating in the order for the *Black Prince* of 1859 which, with her sister *Warrior*,[48] was the first of the British ironclad battleships. Commercially, a great deal of prestige was associated with building these large, complex and technically advanced vessels.

Robert Napier had first attracted the Admiralty to the Clyde. His inventiveness and success in constructing engines for commercial interests, persuaded the Admiralty, despite their initial reluctance and tendency to support firms on the Thames, to place orders with him. In 1838, Napier was awarded the contract to supply the engines for *Stromboli* and *Vesuvius*. This decision was to be amply rewarded. In a return made by the Admiralty in 1843 assessing the time and cost of warships spent out of commission due to engine breakdowns and repairs over a three year period, Napier's engines were proved to be the most reliable in comparison with Thames builders Maudslay Son & Field and Seaward & Capel.[49] It is more than likely that the Thomson brothers worked on these engines while in Napier's employ. With confidence in Napier established, further orders for engines and, later, hulls followed. Nevertheless, the majority of new warships continued to be constructed in the Royal Dockyards with only a few orders going to the private yards on the Thames. Subject to a site examination of facilities and plant, together with confirmation of appropriate building experience, the Admiralty might agree to place the firm on their list of contractors.

In June 1858 an Inquiry into the 'present condition and care of the steam machinery in Her Majesty's ships of war' was appointed[50] under the direction of Mr James Nasmyth. In the course of this inquiry, the Committee visited several shipbuilders and engineers on the Clyde including Tod & McGregor, Robert Napier, Inglis Brothers, Tulloch & Denny, Scott & Sinclair and Caird & Co. In August 1858 J&G Thomson was selected for a visit.

The ensuing report of the Committee offered the following description of the engine works and shipyard:

> 'The works of Messrs Thomson are extensive and well adapted for the construction of marine engines.
> The boiler shed is lighted with a coarse kind of naptha placed in iron basins in the upper part of the pillars that support the roof. A jet of flame from the forges proceeds up a tube and keeps the naptha burning. The expense was stated at 3d per hour, and lighted the place completely.'[51] In reply

to questions placed by the Committee, Thomson stated that they had employed 1,800 men in their works and had built the Australasian of 2,800 tons and 700 horsepower in 11 months. George stated that he had been to sea in charge of engines and had found it very useful in his business as a maker as well as a repairer of engines.[52] Generally, the Committee found the works ' . . . admirably arranged and capable of executing work of the largest class, their tools being of the most approved modern construction. The iron ship-building yard of this firm is on the most extensive scale, and admirably arranged and equipped with the most powerful and improved machinery for the work in question'[53]

The first record of any correspondence between the firm and the Admiralty concerning contracts was in July 1860 when they were invited to tender for the machinery for three small gunboats. The tender was unsuccessful. The Thomsons did not give up, however, and in June 1862 the following letter was sent to Admiral Robinson, Third Sea Lord and Controller of the Navy with responsibility for placing contracts.

> 'We beg to make application that our firm may be placed on the Government list, as engineers and shipbuilders for tendering for work in connection with these branches of trade.
> Surveyors from the Admiralty have already inspected our premises and we have merely to state that in our Shipbuilding Yard we can construct vessels up to 6,000 tons and in our engineering establishment we have facilities for constructing, with despatch, engines up to 1,500 HP'.[54]

J&G Thomson was given the opportunity to tender for the engines of the ironclad sloop *Research* building at Pembroke Dockyard and on submitting their tender, included the following comment -

> 'We trust their Lordships will give our tender, which we have made as low as possible, their favourable consideration. We have repeatedly had the honour of tendering for their Lordships' requirements, but we regret to say without success. We trust that on this occasion we may be so fortunate as to receive their Lordships' orders'.[55]

As with the previous tenders, this one was also unsuccessful. However, at the start of the 1860s, a remarkable series of events caused the role of the Royal Dockyards in building warships to be challenged. This was triggered by Admiral Robinson, who, in a rather outspoken attack, criticised the private shipbuilding yards as being 'untrustworthy, unreliable and producers of poor workmanship'. In making this case, Admiral Robinson so infuriated a member of the London press, Patrick Barry, that the latter delivered a stinging rebuke to the Admiralty in general and Admiral Robinson in particular. In a pamphlet published in 1863, Barry argued that the private shipyards were scientifically organised, more economic in production, in direct competition with one another and therefore offered better value to the nation. Further, the private yards, unlike the Royal Dockyards, had made advances in developing steam engines and introducing iron as the new building material. The large private yards and engine builders of the day were concentrated on the Thames such as Penn, Maudslay, Mare (later the Thames Iron Works) etc. As part of a survey carried out in support of his argument, Barry visited these yards in addition to the Dockyards. He also visited Laird's yard at Birkenhead and wrote to Robert Napier. However, although the private yards had found a champion in Barry, there was no immediate change in Admiralty building policy.

The Admiralty was not the only source of warship orders and in 1862, an attempt was made to obtain contracts from the Turkish Navy, following their decision to build a small fleet of ironclads. In the eyes of the Turkish Government, however, acceptability lay in being a named contractor on the British Admiralty list. As there seemed no way round this impasse Thomson wrote another letter to Admiral Robinson in June 1862 anxious to ensure, that in this at least, the Admiralty would oblige.

> ' . . . meanwhile, we trust . . . this may not prevent our name being placed, with your kind instructions, on the Admiralty list, so as to enable us to tender for requirements of the Turkish Government (for iron cased ships and engines)'[56]

Although the Admiralty agreed, the outcome was yet more disappointment for the Company in a rejected Turkish tender and a reminder that they were not yet in the same category for warship building as their former employer, who received an order for three Turkish ironclads in 1863.

Despite attempts to win favour at the Admiralty, the company was not successful in obtaining contracts for either machinery or hulls and it was not until 1868, ten years after the first attempt, that an order for the Royal Navy was received for *Hart*, a gunboat of 600 tons. Ironically, Thomson's first warship contract was not for the Royal Navy, but for the Confederate States Navy.

THE AMERICAN CIVIL WAR

The outbreak of the American Civil War on 14 April 1861, provided an unexpected opportunity for British and French shipbuilders to supply the Confederate States with warships, commerce raiders and fast vessels able to outrun the blockade which had been imposed by the Union Government. From the outset, the building of such ships in Britain was undertaken clandestinely because of the British Government's policy of neutrality, which was declared on 13 May 1861. The Foreign Enlistment Act of 1819, stipulated that no ship could be fitted-out in a British yard for a war in which Britain remained neutral. Nevertheless, there were many in Britain who sympathised with the Southern States not least those who depended, for the success of the British cotton industry, on plentiful supplies of cotton from the South. Equally, the opportunity to stimulate trade in providing materials to both the North and South led to a flexible interpretation of the 1819 Act. While completing a ship equipped for war was forbidden, building of the hull for subsequent completion as a warship outside British waters was not. In this muddied arena, Confederate agents took steps to obscure contract details of ships under construction on their behalf while Union agents kept suspected Confederate ships and agents under close scrutiny.

With limited shipbuilding capacity and almost no capacity to roll iron armour plates or to construct marine engines, the predicament of the Confederate States was real enough. Urgently, Confederate vessels were contracted from British firms including, on Clydeside, John Elder, Alexander Stephen, Tod & McGregor, William Denny and J&G Thomson. Between the years 1862 and 1864, no fewer than 111 blockade-running vessels were built on the Clyde.[57] Initially, Britain proved the most plentiful source of war materials and ships and it was there that the Confederates set up a network of agents to procure equipment for shipment to the South. In May 1861, Stephen R Mallory, Secretary of the Confederate Navy, appointed James Dunwoody Bulloch, a Georgian with fourteen years of service in the US Navy, to organise a shipbuilding programme in Britain. Bulloch immediately set about the task and established a base in Liverpool on his arrival there in June[58] Fraser Trenholm & Company of Liverpool were appointed to act as bankers for the Confederacy. One of Bulloch's early successes in the war against the North concerned the purchase of the J&G Thomson built steamer *Fingal*, which, with Bulloch in command, delivered a vast amount of military equipment to Savannah, Georgia, in the autumn of 1861. *Fingal* was stripped down to the main deck and rebuilt as the Confederate ironclad steamer *Atlanta* during 1862/3. In June 1863 she ran aground while engaging the Union monitors *Weehawken* and *Nahant* and was captured.[59]

SANTA MARIA

Mallory appointed other agents to work with Bulloch as part of his network in Britain. One of them was Lieutenant James H North of the Confederate Steam Navy who was despatched to Britain in November 1861 to arrange for the construction of ironclads.[60] By May 1862, North had taken up residency in London had been put in touch with George Thomson through a third party. At North's behest, a meeting was arranged with George Thomson in London to discuss the building of a large and powerful armour-clad warship. On his return to Glasgow, George quickly put preparations in hand and wrote to North on 9 May stating that the ship 'was draughted and a model made' and also that the plans for the arrangement of armour plates, engines, boilers, coals etc., were in production. George made it clear that he understood and acknowledged that Lieutenant North had to wait for instructions from his superiors before proceeding.[61] The contract for this ship was signed on 21 May at a price of £182,000 with a delivery date of 1 June 1863.[62] However, within a month of signing the contract, it seemed as if Thomson's ironclad would be cancelled. On 18 June, North wrote to Thomson with the news that he would be leaving the country and would have to transfer the contract to another builder. George Thomson wrote back on 20 June saying that the contract had been entered into on the basis that North would be in Glasgow and that transferring the contract to another party was 'not in accordance with the spirit or the letter of our agreement with you.'[63] In the event North was not recalled and the contract went ahead.

As the principal ship of war, the ironclad was of recent origin, the first British examples being the sister ships *Warrior* and *Black Prince*; the latter built by Robert Napier. Although not as big as *Warrior*, Thomson's ironclad was a formidable warship and easily the equal to anything in service with the Union Navy. Designed to carry ten 68 pounder guns down each broadside,[64] the ship was equipped with a ram bow to enable her to run down enemy vessels unfortunate enough to get within striking distance. The return of the ancient concept of the ram came from the belief that sinking an ironclad by gunfire

alone might prove difficult because of the resistance of the armoured sides. The ability to hole the ship beneath the waterline by striking it with a ram bow was therefore perceived as an important element in the offensive power of this warship.

Although complete secrecy was not possible in the construction of such a large warship, she was entered into the books of J & G Thomson as *Santa Maria*. Her

The armourclad warship given the cover name Santa Maria *in a vain attempt at disguising Confederate owners. This illustration shows the ship fitting-out beside the crane that the Thmsons built on the north bank at Finnieston.*

intended name in the Confederate navy is unknown. On 17 July, George Thomson wrote another letter to North, now living in Liverpool, in which various details of the ship's design were discussed, including

The Confederate raider Canton *lying adjacent to the big crane at Finnieston. This ship was confiscated in 1864 to prevent her serving in the Confederate Navy.*

31

the ram bow. In this letter, George displayed great commercial instinct in his partisan attitude towards the Civil War.

> 'I do honestly assure you that my intentions are to complete the whole ship and more especially the stem and prow of such strength that it will be almost impossible to crush it when running down any other vessel of the same class even. I really think the plan I am carrying out is superior to any other that I have yet seen or heard of . . . I sincerely trust that the recent success of the South may be followed up, and that Richmond may be placed beyond danger. The fortunes of war are too varying to speak confidently, but surely such men as Beauregard and Stonewall Jackson commanding will be able to keep the Yankees at bay.'[65]

By August 1862, George Thomson had to apologise to North for the delay in sending him drawings:

> 'the truth is the matter in hand is one of such magnitude and involving so much time and thought in planning the arrangements to suit all requirements that I have not been able to get the detailed drawings forward so early as I expected . . . the machinery is going ahead we have the cylinders boring and a large quantity of castings in from the foundry'[66]

When the drawings were sent two weeks later, George was careful to ensure that they were not marked with any names or flags.[67] While North was responsible for the construction of the ship, it was Bulloch who arranged for the stage payments. By January 1863, £98,000 had been paid into the company.

The activities of the Confederate agents and Clyde shipbuilders came under the close scrutiny of the US Consul in Glasgow, Warner Underwood, who kept the US Ambassador in London, Charles Francis Adams, fully informed. Adams was determined to ensure that British recognition of the Confederate States was not forthcoming. Repeated attempts to get the British Government to seize the Confederate ship contracts were at first unsuccessful, however, the fate of two Confederate warships under construction at Laird's Birkenhead shipyard, builders of the most famous of all Confederate cruisers *Alabama*, forced the issue. With the likelihood of the Northern States winning the war, the British Foreign Secretary, Lord John Russell, told James Bulloch, in January 1863, that the vessels building at Laird's would not be permitted to leave the UK as the property of a belligerent. In September 1863, the Government took

action and in the following month, the ships were seized on the Mersey and eventually purchased by the Admiralty for service in the Royal Navy.[68] When it became evident that the same fate was likely to befall *Santa Maria*, North consulted Mason & Slidell, Confederate Commissioners on the course of action to take. On their advice, North terminated Thomson's contract on 21 December 1863 by which time the ship was well advanced on the stocks. North was also requested to hand the proceeds of the sale to Bulloch.[69] The as yet officially unnamed ironclad became the property of J & G Thomson for a brief period while a purchaser was sought. In a remarkably short space of time, the Danish Government, embroiled in a dispute with the German Confederation over Schleswig Holstein, paid Thomson £240,000 for the ship at the end of December 1863.[70] The following article appeared in a local paper:

> 'We learn that the formidable steam ram which is now approaching completion at the yard of Messrs. J & G Thomson has been purchased for the Danish Government by a naval officer empowered to make such a bargain. One consequence of this sale will be to relieve the Messrs Thomson and their workmen from the pressing attentions of a host of scouts and spies, who, acting it is presumed in the interests of the Northern States of America, if not actually hired for that purpose, have been most assiduous in watching progress and trying to catch up information . . . Her burden is 3,500 tons; her engines are of 500 horsepower; and she has a prow which it would be a very awkward thing for another vessel to come into collision with'[71]

The ironclad joined the Danish Navy on completion in August 1864 and was named *Danmark*.[72]

CANTON

The other Confederate warship ordered from Thomson was the commerce raider *Texas*, built, confusingly, under the cover names *Canton* and *Pampero*. The first reference to this vessel appears in September 1862 when the Company wrote to Captain George T Sinclair, another Mallory appointed agent and a serving officer in the CSN, quoting a price of £43,340 for a 'steamer'.[73] Efforts to conceal the true identity of this ship resulted in various owners being named including Glasgow shipping agent James Galbraith and Liverpool agents Edward Pembroke and Smith Fleming & Co.

The following quotation for the *Canton* was sent to Galbraith on 10 October 1862:

Hull 1150tons	£23,000
Engines 350hp	£13,000
Extra cost of teak planking less plating under teak	£2,900
Coppering vessel material and labour	£1220
Covering stern frame with brass, welding all brass work at stern material and labour	£1420
Extra cost of brass propeller and lifting frame, material and labour	£1800
Total	**£43,340**

In a letter to Edward Pembroke written in October, the price had risen to £46,600[74]

Ordered in the late autumn of 1862 by Lt. George T Sinclair, Canton was subject to intense Northern surveillance. When *Canton* was almost complete, Charles Adams urged Lord Russell to detain the ship. For this, however, evidence of *Canton's* true ownership and function was needed. In attempts to provide this, Northern agents approached a number of J&G Thomson's workmen to solicit details of her construction. On 22 September 1863, two men asked James Goldie, a draughtsman, to accompany them to a hotel in Glasgow where they asked if war fittings had been or were being fitted to the ship. He was urgently requested to provide a tracing of the ship without his employer's knowledge. Thomson's foreman joiner, John Gilchrist, was approached at his home by a man on 23 October

> 'who informed him that he was commissioned to offer him a handsome sum, and also to pay his passage to North America, and guarantee him an excellent situation there, if he would give certain information respecting the *Pampero*'

Intrigued by this offer, a further meeting was arranged at which the following was proposed:

> 'If he objected to emigrate, a sufficient sum to render him independent of work ever afterwards would be paid him at once; also, that he would leave his employers immediately and enter the services of the parties who were treating him, at a larger salary than he was receiving.'

In return for this, Gilchrist would have to watch and report on the *Pampero*.[75] It is not clear whether these offers were accepted.

With *Pampero* almost complete, application for a certificate of registry and declaration of nationality in compliance with the Merchant Shipping Act had to be made, When no one stepped forward to do this Russell authorised the seizure of the ship having first placed the gunboat *Goldfinch* alongside.[76] *Pampero* was seized by William Trevor, HM Collector of Customs, on 10 December 1863. Thomsons and the agents for the ship were both charged with breaching the Foreign Enlistment Act on 98 points, principally, that they constructed a ship which was intended to commit hostilities against a nation with whom the Government was not at war. On 21 January, Thomson lodged a claim that they had the right of retention as they were still owed £16,000 for the vessel. The following day, Smith Fleming & Co. claimed to be the owners of the vessel. With sufficient evidence at their disposal, the Government responded by impounding the ship in Glasgow Harbour on 10 January 1864 from where she was not released until September 1865 well after the war was over.[77]

In February 1863, North, now living in Bridge of Allan,[78] ordered 12 sets of machinery from Thomson to be fitted into small craft building in the Southern States and elsewhere. These engines left the Clyde loaded on three blockade-runners in September 1864.[79]

Henry Lafone was a Liverpool shipping agent working for the Confederacy through the Choicer Importing & Exporting Company of South Carolina. He had dealings with seventeen blockade-runners during the war and ordered no less than five vessels *Lilian, Little Hattie, Wild Rover, Emma Henry* and *Corcovado* from Thomson at the end of 1863. All of these vessels saw service with the Confederacy with varying degrees of success.

The other strategy employed by Confederate agents was to buy existing ships and sail them across the Atlantic for conversion to blockade-runners. In 1862 the Thomson built *Iona* was bought by Henry Lafone to serve as a blockade-runner, the attraction being her high speed. The vessel was stripped of many fittings, painted drab grey and loaded with coal for the Atlantic crossing. After adjusting her compass in Loch Long, the *Iona* returned to the Gourock side of the channel and set course for the open sea with no lights in the event that attentive Federal agents might be on the look out. While off Kempock Point, the *Iona*, rather too effectively concealed by her grey paint, was hit by the new steamer *Chanticleer* and sunk.[80] The second *Iona*, completed in June 1863 for David Hutcheson before acquisition by Lafone, was equally unsuccessful, foundering in a storm off Lundy Island en route to Nassau at the start of her blockade running career. By the end of the war, Confederate agents had placed contracts to build two warships and five blockade-runners. A further seven vessels built at the Govan yard for other owners were later acquired by Confederate agents. The Confederates paid large sums into the Company during the years 1862 to 1865. It is not entirely clear what happened to these funds following the British Government's seizure of *Santa Maria* and *Canton*. There is no evidence to show that this money was returned to the defeated Southerners following the sale of their vessels to other interests. It is a distinct possibility that the *Santa Maria* was paid for twice, resulting in a fabulous windfall for the Company[81]. With the benefit of this money, profits for the years 1865 and 1866 rocketed from an annual average of £8,020 over the past five years to £90,273 and £40,711 respectively.[82]

END OF THE PARTNERSHIP

In 1863 the business was dealt a severe blow when James Thomson indicated his intention to withdraw from the partnership. The events leading up to this

decision are unknown but it is certain that the split was acrimonious. James was now 61 years of age with two sons in their early twenties hopeful of following their father in business. Well aware that large sums of Confederate money were flowing into the Company, James decided that there was a unique opportunity to leave with a considerable fortune and set up business for himself and his sons. Moreover, once James had extracted his share of the partnership, it was evident that the original business would not be damaged financially so large were the profits in prospect.

James's departure required termination of the original partnership and two arbiters, Peter Denny, the Dumbarton shipbuilder and James McNaught, a consultant engineer, were appointed to make a valuation of the Company. The arbiters appointed William Anderson CA to report on the balance sheet and establish the partners' interests at June 1863. The Partnership was dissolved on 6 August 1863 although trading continued as normal.[83] Anderson's report was

Part of an atmospheric engraving from the London Illustrated News of 1860 showing the Clyde and the growth of industrialisation particularly on the north bank. This area behind and to either side of Napier's Dock (inshot on north bank at left with large crane) had a heavy concentration of engine works and foundries

completed in March 1864, leaving only the value of unfinished contracts to be calculated. In June 1864, James received an initial £22,603, which included his half of the profits for the year 1863, which amounted to £6,887. On 4 May 1865, the arbiters, having fully investigated the value of work in hand including the lucrative Confederate contracts, reported that James was entitled to a further sum of £38,938 13s 7d. This was paid in May 1865.[84] He was also awarded 'half of the Confederate Bonds'. At the foot of their report the arbiters felt moved to add the following:

> 'The arbiters have hitherto refrained from making any allusion to the painful state of feeling which obviously exists between the parties but they cannot close the submission without expressing a hope that this state of feeling will now be changed and the arbiters deem it right to add that in so far as the proceedings in this submission are concerned there is no fair ground for recrimination on the one side or the other'[85]

In total, James received a staggering £61,542 from the business. Evidence from relatives suggests that he and his brother George were unable to reach the accommodation desired by the arbiters and had nothing further to do with one another.

J&J THOMSON & COMPANY 1868 - 1893

Contemporary accounts refer to James Thomson's 'retiral' from business, a euphemism which masked the reality of the bitter split. Retiral was the last thing in James' mind and, in 1865 and 1866, he spent £9,000 acquiring ground on which to set up rival engine and boiler works. He was unable to find a plot large enough to build a single works and thus two separate plots were purchased. The engine works were established at 36 Finnieston Street only a few doors away from his former business, and the boiler works a mile westwards at Kelvinhaugh Street. Trading commenced in 1868 at which time James introduced his sons John and James into the business. On 14 March 1870, James died in his home at Linnburn, Shandon after an illness of one year. He was 67 and left his sons James and John, then only 20 and 17, to continue with the business. One newspaper described James Thomson as:

> 'an excellent specimen of an honest Scotchman, and shrewd man of business. He was noted for downright integrity, striaghtforwardness and frankness of manner in all his dealings; and was highly respected, not only by the large body of men whom he employed, but by all with whom he came in contact, either in a social or business capacity.'[86]

For the next twenty years, J&J Thomson manufactured propelling machinery successfully for various shipbuilders on the Clyde and elsewhere. By the early 1890s, being men of some means, both John and James elected to pursue the life of gentlemen and dispose of the business. In 1893, Barclay Curle & Company, finding their engine works restricted by the new Glasgow Harbour tunnel, were forced to

look for alternative works. In August, they signed an agreement with J&J Thomson for a ten-year lease on their premises at an annual rent of £1,900. On expiry of this lease in 1903, a new lease for twenty years was taken out at £2,100 per annum in addition to which Barclay Curle agreed to buy all tools in the works for £8,000.[87]

With the departure of John and James, the association with marine engineering on this side of the Thomson family was effectively at an end.

LOCKOUT

In the 1860s, a number of features which would dominate the trading and general environment in which the Company and the shipbuilding industry operated, were set in place - trade depressions and labour strife. With the exception of the depression of 1859 when only a few vessels were launched, the shipyard had maintained a steady output of 6 or 7 ships per year. Over the first few years of the 1860s, demand for new tonnage increased, spurred by the need to replace the river and coastal vessels withdrawn from home service to run the American blockade. In 1851, when the Thomsons first started iron shipbuilding, 41 iron ships with an aggregate tonnage of 25,322 were built on the Clyde. By 1863 this figure had grown to 140 vessels of 130,000 tons.[88] To keep pace with production, James and George were evidently unconcerned about employing

James MacIntyre Thomson, son of James Thomson, joined his father following the acrimonious split between the brothers James and George Thomson.

Left
Glentower, the house built by James MacIntyre Thomson on Great Western Road, Glasgow and now part of Glasgow Homeopathic Hospital.

unionised labour. In April 1863, an incident occurred in the yard as a result of hiring non-union riveters which demonstrated their thoughts on the subject. When riveters already in Company employment complained that 'it was not legal that men not belonging to the union should be employed' they were told that they could pick up their wages and leave. Although some journeymen did just that, several apprentice riveters pounced on one of the unaffiliated riveters at the yard gate and threatened to throw him into the Clyde. The three apprentices were charged with assault and fined £5 each.[89]

The end of the American Civil War in 1865 signalled a reduction in demand for new tonnage and a depression in the shipbuilding industry followed. In 1866 a dispute of major proportions affected much of the shipbuilding and engineering industry on Clydeside. The issue revolved around the length of the working week and was precipitated by the men of the iron trades. In essence, the men wanted a reduction in the working week from 60 to 57 hours with no reduction in wages while the employers were prepared to concede 57 hours but wanted to reduce wages accordingly. The dispute had wide reaching consequences one of which was the organisation of employers into a single body named the Clyde Shipbuilders and Engineers Association (later known as the Employers Association) and the deployment, for the first time, of the lockout as a tactic against organised labour. The unions involved in the dispute were the Amalgamated Society of Engineers, the Boilermakers and Iron Shipbuilders' Society, the Operative Blacksmiths' Society, the Shipwrights' Society and the Shipjoiners' Society.

The general trade depression in which this dispute flared gave some advantage to the employers and they resolved that if the men continued with their demand, a lockout of three months duration would be imposed across the industry. The Glasgow Morning Journal declared:

> 'A three months' lockout is tremendous - a ukase, indeed. Imperial in its hauteur and Russian in its rigour. It can not but inflict great loss on the firms themselves, but it amounts to the utter banishment and ruin of the operatives if they should be so foolhardy, or so spirited as doubtless some of them will think, as to risk it.'[90]

On 28 May 1866 the lockout was imposed and an estimated 20,000 men in the shipbuilding and engineering establishments in Glasgow were on the street. At the Govan shipyard, George Thomson locked out between 1,800 and 2,000 men leaving only

100 foremen and apprentices in employment. At their engine works, 600 men were set to be locked out following the expiry of the two weeks warning period which their employers had given them.[91] In imposing the lockout, the employers determined to break the unions by demanding that the men leave the union as a condition of return to work. After a lockout of thirteen weeks, the employers gave in and the 57-hour week was adopted.

GEORGE CONTINUES

After James left the company in 1863, George continued the original business retaining the name James & George Thomson. For George, however, time was running out. On 29 June 1866, in the middle of the lockout, he died at his home in 2 Newton Place, Glasgow, after a short illness. George was only 55 years old and his passing plunged the business and his family into crisis.

One year before his death, George had drawn up a Trust Disposition and Settlement, which detailed the manner in which his estate and its future management would be maintained. The Settlement, which came into effect on 7 July 1866, established a Trust responsible for administering his entire estate. Trusts were regularly used before the growth and acceptance of Limited Liability Companies. This Trust was necessary, as George's sons were too young to take over the business, although the terms of the Settlement allowed for that event when they came of age. This complex arrangement was set in place and meant that both business and family affairs were inextricably bound together. Consequently, the events of the next thirty years cannot be recounted without frequent reference to the Trust, Trust members and the affairs of the Thomson family.

In accordance with George's wishes, the following persons were named as Trustees - Elizabeth Rodger Thomson, his wife; Robert Thomson, his brother and Cunard's Resident Engineer at Liverpool; George Gibson, merchant in Glasgow; George Webster

George Thomson who died in 1866 plunging the business into difficulty as his sons were too young to take over.

Right
Dhalling Mhor, the house which George Thomson was building in Dunoon at the time of his death. His widow Elizabeth was determined to retain the house despite the Trust's desire to sell it. The house survived in a number of guises including that of a hotel and was demolished in 1999 after a fire

Snodgrass, Manager of the North British and Mercantile Insurance Company in Glasgow; William Johnston, Engineer to the Glasgow and South Western Railway Company; James Stevenson, writer in Glasgow at Messrs. McGrigor Stevenson & Fleming; John Grant, the company secretary; James Roger Thomson, George Paul Thomson and Robert Thomson, his three sons. Although George's sons were nominated as trustees, under the terms of the settlement, they were unable to assume this role until the age of 24. Such was the rift between James and George that even in this crisis and despite his obvious knowledge of the business, James was not named as a trustee.

George's eldest son, James Roger Thomson, would eventually become managing director of the business, the first Provost of the new burgh of Clydebank and later still see the company become part of John Brown & Co. Ltd. He was, however, only twenty-two at the time of his father's death. His brother George Paul, who would also play a significant role in the business, was twenty. George Thomson's contribution to the development of industry in Glasgow was later acknowledged in a tribute published in 1886[92]

'. . . . While claiming for George Thomson no speciality as an inventor or an 'epochal' man in his profession it may be said that he was one of those who carried forward the lamp, ever ready to make any needed invention, to perfect any design to meet, in a word, all the constantly recurring calls and exigencies of a laborious and exacting profession, with workmanlike ability and suggestiveness, as to the success of his work there can be no question. Mr. Thomson devoted himself thoroughly to his business and was little seen or known in public. To those who knew him his untimely death came as a painful shock. He was handsome and manly of presence, kindly and modest in manners, with an abounding cheeriness, and, we may add, with a touch of the Anderston 'Doric' in his speech, which in him was an added charm.'

NINE CHILDREN, AN ENGINE WORKS AND A SHIPYARD

The creation of the Trust brought the business under the attention of McGrigor Stevenson & Fleming, a major Glasgow legal practice. Minutes of the Trust were kept meticulously and provide an insight into some of the decisions taken. Through this narrative, James Roger Thomson rapidly assumes a prominent position over a few short years in the running of the firm. Equally, the narrative reveals some of the character traits which later contributed to his downfall.

At the first meeting of the Trustees on 14 September 1866, one of the initial tasks undertaken was to initiate a complete valuation and inventory of the business and establish the financial position of the Company in order that the family's position might be

At the time of his death, George's Glasgow home was in Newton Terrace to the west of Charing Cross in Glasgow.

determined. William McNaught, a consulting engineer from Manchester, and Peter Denny, the Dumbarton shipbuilder, were asked to prepare a carefully detailed valuation of the works, machinery and tools. Robert McTear, a licensed valuator in Glasgow, made the valuation of the family house. William Anderson CA was appointed to prepare a financial statement of the business and to act as Reporter. The Trustees decided to meet on the first Wednesday of every month at the offices of McGrigor Stevenson & Fleming, 136 St Vincent Street Glasgow. In addition to the family home at Newton Place, George Thomson was, at the time of his death, completing a magnificent villa named Dalling Mhor in Dunoon on the Cowal Peninsula. The total valuation of his estate including both houses and Works, was provisionally estimated at £81,294[93] The contents of the house at Newton Place alone were valued at £2,073 15s 6d while that of Dalling Mhor was £1,700.[94] Full valuation showed the estate and Works to be worth £141,526.[95] In light of several outstanding and unfinished contracts, the Trust decided to limit the sum to £120,000.

At the meeting of the Trustees in November 1866 a number of business and family matters were raised.

John Grant, the Company Secretary, was requested to ensure that all family and household accounts no longer passed through the firm and that henceforth they were to be paid by Mrs Thomson out of the annuity she received under the terms of the Trust. Eight children received annual allowances of from £150 for the oldest to £50 for the youngest. James Roger received £500 for 'attending to the business

The screw steamship Russia *completed for Cunard in 1867.*

which James Stevenson, solicitor and Trustee, had submitted. One of these loans, for £4,000, was granted to Thomas Corbett who was to become a significant property owner in Glasgow and London.[96] While these events were in train, the Trust's principal concern was the continuation of marine engineering and shipbuilding. During this period, no fewer than nine vessels were under construction: *Tornado, Linnet,*

generally' while his mother Elizabeth received £800. The Trust felt obliged to honour the late George's desire to give his eldest daughter, Jane Paul Thomson, on her forthcoming marriage to James Neilson of Mossend, 'a handsome trousseau or outfit. . . . and to furnish the drawing room of her and her intended husband'. In consequence of this, John Grant was authorised to give Miss Thomson £1,000. James Neilson, who would later become a Trustee and a spokesman for the rest of the family, was the son of James 'Hot Blast' Neilson whose blast furnace of 1828 had been instrumental in the development of the Scottish iron industry.

Exercising its right to invest surplus funds, the Trust used the proceeds of George Thomson's insurance policies, £11,160, to invest in three separate loans

Weasel, Malvina, Russia, Salto Iona, Gondolier, Chevalier and *Snipe.* Of these, *Russia* built for Cunard, was probably the most significant. At almost 3,000 gross tons she was the largest vessel turned out so far and also the most powerful with engines of 3,000 horse power and a service speed of 13.5 knots.

Russia demonstrated the rapid advances made in marine engineering, particularly in reducing fuel consumption, since the paddle steamer *Scotia* of 1862. This ship used 159 tons per day for a speed of 13 knots in comparison to the screw driven *Russia,* which burned only 90 tons for the same speed. *Russia* became the first screw driven ship to hold the Blue Riband after a record eastbound Atlantic crossing of 8 days and 28 minutes in November 1867. Her record was almost immediately challenged by the Inman

Line's *City of Paris* built by Tod & McGregor.[97] Engines for *Asia* and *Scotia* were also under construction for Henry Lafone the former Confederate agent who had defaulted on the bills granted him. His affairs 'had become embarrassed' and Grant was asked to determine the exact amount outstanding and present the debt to Stevenson that legal proceedings might be initiated.

JAMES ROGER THOMSON

James Roger Thomson was born on 9 May 1844 at 2 Newton Place, Glasgow. In 1861, he matriculated into the Faculty of Arts at Glasgow University, taking classes in Natural Philosophy (physics) under William Thomson, later Lord Kelvin. He also took classes in technical drawing at the Government School of Design, later known as Glasgow School of Art. He was present at the very first meeting of his late father's Trust in September 1866 at which time he stated his intention, under the terms of the Trust, to join the business as a partner when he was 25 years old. He attended all Trust meetings taking an active part in the business in preparation for his eventual role.[98] A lifelong interest in the army began in 1860 when he was made a sergeant in the 69th Lanarkshire Volunteer Rifles. By 1868, he was Captain of the 105th Lanarkshire Volunteer Rifles, otherwise known as the Glasgow Highlanders.

James Roger was given a significant responsibility in the running of the business. One of his first tasks, at the age of 22, was authorisation to engage James Pattison 'foreman of the engineer work' for three years at an annual salary of £300 and to engage a fitter at the engine works in place of John Dow, who was 'leaving on the best terms that he can'.[99] Young James was told that no work was to be taken on, or estimates given out, without the prior approval of the Trust. In June it was agreed that his allowance be increased from £500 to £750.[100] Within six months the Trust, evidently satisfied with his progress, authorised a further increase to £1,000.[101]

PART EXCHANGE

In December 1866, The British and North American Royal Steam Packet Company (the Cunard Company) in conjunction with the British and Foreign Steam Navigation Company, agreed to purchase the *Malta*,[102] which had been laid down on a speculative basis. The nature of the contract entered into with Cunard illustrates the ability of the ship owner to extract favourable deals at the expense of the shipbuilder. In order to sell the ship, Thomson agreed to receive three worn out steamers for resale or scrap in part exchange. £58,000 changed hands between companies together with the three vessels *Europa*, *Niagara* and *America* each valued in the contract at £5,000. Any profit or loss made on the sale of the ship would be split between both Companies. In the event, a small profit was recorded on the resale of the vessels and the *Siberia* consequently returned a profit of £6,000.[103]

Looking westward along the Clyde about 1880. Napier's yard is to the immediate left while the Inglis and Henderson yards are visible to the right. The public right of way along the south bank is clearly visible. This walkway had to be dismantled for launches and re-erected afterwards. Thomson's shipyard was a few hundred yards to the east of this photograph

The method by which the £58,000 was to be paid was typical throughout the shipbuilding industry. Payments were made in five instalments each one equivalent to the completion of a part of the contract such as keel laying, hull in frame, launching etc. The first and second payments were made in cash, the remaining three either in cash or in 12-month bills at the owner's discretion. Bills i.e. a promise to pay in twelve months (in this instance) attracted interest of 2.5% while cash qualified for a 2.5% discount. While cash was the preferred option by all builders, it was not always possible to take contracts on that basis. The purchase of ships was generally a buyer's market and shipowners, particularly in slack periods for shipbuilders, could often command favourable terms of payment such as the one above.[104]

As a bad debt of £1,500 against engines originally built for *Scotia* and *Asia* looked increasingly difficult to recover, it was agreed, in June 1867, to act on James Roger's suggestion of building a new vessel in which

James Rodger Thomson was George Thomson's eldest son. When George died in 1866, James Rodger was only 22 years old and had to wait until 1874 before he could take control of the business.

to fit the engines 'under the advice and assistance of Robert Thomson', James's uncle.[105]

Having concentrated on the shipbuilding aspect of their remit, the Trustees turned their attention to a letter from Mrs Thomson, James Roger's mother, asking for an increase in her children's allowance from £850 to £1,200 ' . . . I find from the experience of the last six months, that with the present expensive

The liner Abyssinia *completed in 1870. Although* Abyssinia *and her sister* Algeria *were built to the order of George and James Burns, the vessel was for service in Cunard's shiping line. At 3,253 gross tons, she was the largest ship built at the Govan yard.*

George Paul Thomson, George's second son.

living, and the children being at a time of life when clothes are especially worn quickly out, together with their education, I find I have just too much to do. . . .'[106] At the same time, the Trustees were anxious to sell Dalling Mhor in Dunoon as they considered that Mrs. Thomson's circumstances made it difficult for her to maintain the house. She took the opposite view and agreed to pay a rent of £300 for the coming year in order to retain its use.

In April 1867, tenders were prepared and sent out for the following - six collier screw steamers; seven screw steamers for interests in Monte Video; two sailing vessels and two gunboats for the Navy. Of these vessels, the Company was successful in getting the order for one iron sailing ship, *Clanrannald* and for the gunboat, *Hart,* for the Navy. This was the third warship built at the Govan yard and the first for the Royal Navy.

In April 1868, James Roger made first reference to the inadequacies of the present shipyard thereby precipitating a series of events that would lead to the move down river. He considered that the firm was ' . . . very much hampered for space in the building yard the consequence of which was that they carried on the shipbuilding operations at a great disadvantage

and not so economically as could be done if they had a larger extent of ground.'[107] His proposal, for which he had drawn plans to show the Trustees, was that the adjoining land known as Clyde Villa be leased from the Clyde Navigation Trust for a period of ten or twelve years. The Trustees received this favourably and instructed him to contact the Clyde Trust to ascertain their preparedness to lease Clyde Villa.[108] Meanwhile, in July 1868, the Trustees had to contend with several loss making contracts. The first was for the gunboat *Hart*, which, according to John Grant, was 'caused by the Government inspectors starting one difficulty after another and then constantly reforming to headquarters for instructions'[109] As a direct result of this indecision and the consequent delay in completion, *Hart* lost nearly £4,000. The second contract, for the sailing ship *Clanrannald*, was more troublesome. John Grant told the Trust it had made a loss of about £3,261 and that secondly, it was part owned by Andrew Burns the shipyard manager. Needless to say, the Trustees strongly disapproved of this and instructed Mr Stevenson to express their great disappointment to Burns, Grant and James Roger Thomson.[110] The Trustees agreed that both contracts represented areas of shipbuilding in which they had little experience.

During 1868, orders were becoming difficult to win and a loss of £13,014 was recorded. Early in the following year, James Roger put forward a proposal to build an iron sailing ship speculatively which 'would keep the building yard more fully occupied and at the same time enable him to retain the best of the workmen'. The Trustees concurred, with the caveat that while he must 'produce a first class job it must be at such a rate as will be remunerative.'[111] By May the position had improved and two vessels for the Cunard Company through G&J Burns, *Algeria* and *Abyssinia* were booked, together with a smaller vessel for William Cunard, *Bear*. The first two named vessels were the largest so far built by the Thomsons with a length of 360 feet and a gross tonnage of nearly 3,300. They represented the next step in development of the Atlantic liner, being larger and faster than *Russia*. The price for *Algeria* was £95,400 and, as was now frequent practice in accepting orders from G&J Burns, the Thomsons had to accept the steamer *Palestine* for the sum of £8,000.[112]

The same month, James Roger Thomson was 25 years old and, under the terms of his father's settlement, was assumed as a partner. This entitled him to a three fifteenth interest in the business and a corresponding share in the profits. This was in addition to his salary, which remained at £1,000. As James Roger had announced his intention to marry Marion Neilson, daughter of James Neilson, the Trustees also agreed to provide him with an advance to enable him to furnish his new house.[113]

'NOT PRUDENT'

At the meeting of the Trust held in May 1869, James Roger again referred to the small size of the building yard and indicated the possibility that the Clyde Navigation Trust might want the ground the yard was built on for port developments. He cited locations further down the Clyde at Shieldhall belonging to the Johnston's Trustees, and at Shiels, belonging to a Mr McLean, as being suitable. Having discussed the matter, the Trustees considered his proposal 'not prudent' and rejected it.[114]

At the beginning of 1869, the shipyard was almost without work. James Roger stated the need to lay down a sailing ship on their own account (*Orissa*) with the object of retaining the best of the workforce. He added that he had written to his Uncle in Liverpool and obtained his approval for this.[115] By the middle of 1869 the trading position of the Company was deteriorating. It transpired that the late shipyard cashier had misappropriated £251[116] of wages, and that a loss of £5,034 had been recorded for the year attributable largely to taking the old vessels *Racoon*, *Raven* and *Weasel*, in exchange for a ship order.[117] *Weasel* had been acquired by the Trust for £13,000 but 'had been taken into stock at only £8,000'. She was finally sold to Handyside & Henderson for only £7,500 because of her poor internal arrangements and old engines, resulting in a loss of £5,500. The Trustees' reaction to the news was predictable. James Roger and John Grant were told to be as 'economical as possible in regard to carrying on the expenses of the works and especially to take care and see that the workmen and overseers of the various departments attend properly to their duties so that no loss arises from the want of arrangement in regard to their time being fully occupied.'[118] Moreover, the Trustees told Thomson and Grant, that under no circumstances must contracts for ships or engines be contracted for without their approval. Having delivered this caution, the Trustees turned to the matter of financing Mrs Thomson's daughters, two of whom were at boarding school, one in Edinburgh, the other in London. It was noted also that George Paul, James Roger's younger brother, who was 'now in the works', should receive the sum of £100 annually in addition to his family allowance.[119]

At the end of 1869, the speculatively built screw steamer *Stamboul*, constructed to accommodate unwanted engines, was sold to the Ottoman Government at a considerable loss. The loss was attributed to the 'extreme depreciation 'on the old fashioned engines which were not of the compound type so much in use at present'[120]

The sailing ship *Orissa* was sold at cost to John Kerr,

Managers and foremen from J&G Thomson's Govan works in the year 1868

Greenock while the Cunard ships *Australasian* and *Calabria*, were refitted and re-engined at a profit. The Cunard vessels *Algeria* and *Abyssinia* were still on the stocks and only one new contract had been taken, *Clansman*, a relatively small vessel of 600 gross tons and 150 horsepower for David Hutcheson of Glasgow. A pair of paddle engines and two boilers were under erection at Finnieston in addition to the machinery for the above ships.

Significantly, as subsequent events were to prove, a report at the end of the minutes for December 1869 records that James Roger Thomson had drawn cash of £4,684 to 30 December, bringing his total debt to the Company to £5,171.[121]

FAIRFIELD

By 1869, John Elder's new shipyard and engine works on the site of Fairfield Farm at Govan were nearing completion. This yard was unlike any other on Clydeside, reflecting in its size and organisation, the next generation in the evolution of shipbuilding facilities. The Fairfield works were, by the standards of the day, large and well equipped, embodying all

John Elder set the standard both in the ships he built and in shipyard facilities.

The Fairfield works, shown below at the close of the 19th Century, had a reputation second to none.

the knowledge and expertise which had been accumulated by iron shipbuilders over the past three decades. In addition to providing for ships of the largest proportions, the Fairfield works incorporated a complete engine and boiler works on the same site. Further, Elder applied for and received, with difficulty, permission from the Clyde Trustees to construct a large fitting-out basin where ships could be completed away from the river channel.[122]

A brief description of the origin of the Fairfield works is useful in understanding the nature of the technical and commercial rivalry that ensued between Fairfield and Clydebank as well as recognising the spur it provided to young James Roger Thomson.

Like many other Clydeside shipbuilding firms, Fairfield began as engineers and engine builders opening works in Tradeston, Glasgow in 1834. Charles Randolph and Richard Cunliff were the original partners and output from the works largely consisted of machinery for mills and factories.[123] The company traded successfully if unspectacularly until 1852 when John Elder joined the firm bringing with him originality, skill and a great aptitude for designing marine engines. John's interest and ability undoubtedly owed much to his father David who served as Robert Napier's manager at the Lancefield Engine Works. John Elder's contribution to marine

engineering soon emerged in his compound engine of 1854, which was successfully demonstrated in the steamer *Brandon*, resulting in a 30 to 40% reduction in coal consumption. Ship owners were not slow to recognise the commercial advantage promised by this new engine and orders flowed. In 1860, the business, now named Randolph, Elder & Company, added shipbuilding to its activities acquiring Robert Napier's original Govan yard. After only four years at this location, the company was in a position to finance major new works on Clydeside. Sixty-eight acres of ground were acquired at Fairfield farm for the sum of £60,000. On this site, a shipyard, engine works and fitting out basin were constructed and completed by 1870 at a cost of £80,000, £100,000 and £20,000 respectively.[124] This enormous investment speaks loudly of Elder's confidence and of the profits made by his compound engine. By 1874, the old engine and boiler works at Tradeston were closed, allowing the firm to concentrate all of their activities at Fairfield. Not surprisingly, given the massive investment, the new works were unquestionably the finest private shipyard and engine works in Britain and well beyond the means of the Thomson Trust. The reputation for engineering excellence, innovation and reliability established by Elder, was maintained for decades after his early death at the age of 45 in

1869.[125] Seven Blue Riband holders were built at Fairfield during the 1880s and 90s.

The significance of the new Fairfield works was not lost on James Roger Thomson. From a starting point in 1853, Elder's firm had pioneered the compound marine engine, enabling the creation of vast new works eleven years later. In this, they had eclipsed all other Clyde engineers and shipbuilders. Thomson's comment to the Trustees made in April 1868 about the inefficiencies of the cramped yard at Govan had been stifled. Now, when the Company was forced to relocate through port expansion, the opportunity existed to challenge Fairfield and build another major yard on Clydeside.

PORT EXPANSION

The commercial success of Glasgow as a shipping port was proving difficult to sustain partly because growth placed an increased pressure on existing wharfs and warehousing. As a consequence, the Clyde Navigation Trust was compelled to embark on the westward expansion of port facilities. This required another Act of Parliament to empower the Clyde Trust with a compulsory purchase mandate and this was duly provided for in the Act of 1869. As with earlier harbour expansions, shipbuilders were forced to make way for new wharfs and relocate elsewhere on the river.[126] Despite the difficulties involved, relocation was not necessarily a harmful experience as it enabled the creation of larger yards better able to deal with the growing size of steamships. In the case of Thomsons, it was both timely and fortuitous. The increasing size of ships was outstripping the capacity of the small Govan yard to build them.

The Clyde Trust required Thomson's shipyard for the construction of Plantation Quay.[127]

Negotiations between the Thomson Trust and the Clyde Navigation Trust, referred to as the Clyde Trust hereafter, were difficult from the start. The first recorded intimation from the Clyde Trust was on 4 December 1869, when George Reith[128], General Manager of the Clyde Trust wrote:

> 'I think it right to inform you this early that the Trustees of the Clyde Navigation, will not be able to allow you to retain possession of the ground belonging to them at Bankton. . . after Whitsunday next, and you will therefore be so good as to make arrangements for giving up the ground at that term'[129]

This letter, which seems unnecessarily terse, outlined a hopelessly unrealistic time scale of five months in which the shipbuilder was expected to find and equip new premises, whilst maintaining commercial and manufacturing continuity. In reply for the Thomson Trust, John Stevenson, a trustee and lawyer with the Glasgow firm of McGrigor Stevenson & Fleming, asked for an extension to this period on the basis that they had entered into contracts which, apart from being legally binding, would not be completed until after this date. In a letter dated 13 January 1870, Reith refused this request:

> '. . I really cannot hold out the least hope that the Clyde Trustees will be able to permit the Messrs. Thomson to remain in possession of the ground at Bankton, for any time, however short, after the term of Whitsunday. The ground will certainly be required for purposes of the Trust by that time and your clients must not rely on getting any extensions of their occupancy'[130]

Only after McGrigor Stevenson and Fleming placed a Petition against the Clyde Navigation Bill did the Clyde Trust agree to extend the time until 2 August 1870. Stevenson's firm prepared a claim against the Clyde Trust while James Roger was asked to look for suitable ground on the banks of the river for a new yard.[131] In July, James Roger proposed ground at Lady Burn, Port Glasgow as being suitable and the Trustees requested that James Stevenson look into this.

On 4 August 1870, Reith wrote that:

> 'Your clients, Messrs Thomson have not given up possession of the ground at Bankton belonging to the Clyde Trustees . . . we are bound now to give possession to our contractors and must do so'

The eastern portion of the yard was made available to the Clyde Trust to allow completion of the first phase of Plantation Quay. The Thomsons were obliged to purchase a small strip of land at Belize Villa adjacent to the shipyard in which to store the materials vacated from the portion of the yard given over to the Clyde Trust. This sale was completed in August 1870 for the price of £4,000.[132] Although building space at Govan had now been reduced, the question of an alternative site was still to be settled.

New orders were booked in the first three months of 1870 - three steamers for Currie & Co. and one for the London & Edinburgh Shipping Co. With no space in the yard to lay down all four, one was subcontracted to JG Lawrie's shipyard at Port Glasgow. The new Cunard steamer *Abyssinia* was completed and ran successful trials in May. Of this vessel, a contemporary account stated

> '. . . She has accommodation on the spar-deck for about 120 first-class passengers, the dining

saloons and sleeping apartments for whom are very well lighted, heated and ventilated, and for whose comfort and security neither trouble nor expense has been spared. On the main and lower decks is accommodation for 1,000 third-class passengers or if need were, a regiment of two battalions of soldiers.'[133]

When James Roger informed the Trustees that he was negotiating with John Burns for the construction of a vessel similar to *Bear*, the Trustees instructed him not to proceed as this contract would be conditional, once again, on accepting an old vessel for £12/13,000.[134] James Roger did not heed this instruction and made a contract with John Burns for a screw steamer at the price of £24,500 in addition to the steamer *Wolf* at the reduced price of £9,000. The Trustees reluctantly agreed to this after James Roger assured them that the contract would be profitable.

The Trustees were also informed of the death of James Pattison, the engine works manager, and agreed to fill this 'important position' with John Parker, the chief engineer on the Cunard steamer *Java*, at an annual salary of £360. The minutes recall that James Pattison, an 'excellent manager', had worked for the Thomsons for fifteen years and that 'his illness had to some extent at least been caused by his long and constant attention to his duties'. James Roger recommended that as Mr Pattison had left a family of ten or eleven children unprovided for, an allowance of £25 per annum for four years be given to his widow to assist with the education and upbringing of the family.[135]

By November 1870, the Cunard steamer *Algeria* was completed together with *Bear* for G&J Burns, leaving four vessels on the stocks, three for Currie & Co., *Westmoreland*, *Gothland*, *Iceland* and one, *Bison*, for G&J Burns. In a joint report to the Trustees, the Secretary, John Grant, and James Roger Thomson presented information at the November meeting designed to galvanise minds over the question of a new yard.

> 'We have the early prospect of being called upon for several vessels mostly mail steamers of a large size, larger than any we have hitherto built: (we need hardly remind the Trustees that all the recently contracted for mail steamers are of a much greater length than formerly) we are not however, while in our present yard, in a position to tender for such vessels, the increased dimensions place it out of our power to build them . . . The Trustees will find by reference to our balance sheet for years past that the only

vessels that have been at all remunerative are the larger class of screw steamers and especially those for the mail service . . . '[136]

This is the first recorded statement from the Company which defines a clear, commercial reason for expansion and which also identifies the large, fast mail steamer as the class of ship likely to be the most profitable. In response, the Trust asked James Roger Thomson and Andrew Burns, the shipyard manager, to investigate potential sites and report to the Trustees at the next meeting.

In his review of the financial year to June 1870, William Anderson CA, stated that the net profit for the year was £14,845. The Trustees instructed William Anderson to credit the account of James Roger with £24,000, that being the amount of his share of the estate and held as capital in the firm. This was in recognition of his status as a partner from 1869 onwards.[137]

Concern over James Roger's personal finances, which would become a persistent feature throughout his life, again merited a minuted comment when, after agreeing to confirm his salary at £1,000, the Trustees 'would impress upon Mr Thomson the necessity of restricting his drawings for personal expenditure as they have hitherto been much too large, more than the state of the business during the last two years justifies.'[138] The Trustees were always conscious of their duty to the remainder of the family who would eventually demand their share of the capital.

James Roger Thomson's desire to explore and develop new ventures emerged when, at a special meeting of the Trust, he outlined a proposal for joint ownership of one or two vessels in account with Donald Currie the shipowner. This arrangement, in which Thomson would own 30/64ths of the vessels, was an attempt at establishing the nucleus of a shipping line rather than a method of finding orders for new vessels. The Trust, however, wanted none of this, stating that 'under no circumstances recommend them (the Trustees) to be parties to an agreement for sailing and trading with vessels'. They did, however, ask James Roger to meet with Currie and get better terms for the building of ships.[139] While the Trustees might well have been concerned about James Roger's ambitions, involvement in shipping lines was commonplace and often much in the commercial interests of shipbuilders. Donald Currie and his elder brother James were important Scottish shipowners. Donald (later Sir Donald Currie) established the Castle Line in 1876 and later was the driving force behind the Union-Castle Line of which he was

Chairman. Had James been allowed to proceed with this venture, there might have been significant benefits for the developments of the business.[140]

'THE GROUND ADJOINING THE CANAL A SHORT DISTANCE TO THE WEST OF RENFREW FERRY'

In December 1870, James Roger Thomson and Andrew Burns reported on their attempts to identify a suitable tract of land for a new yard:

> [James Roger Thomson] ' . . . recommended as the best and most suitable the ground on the north side of the river at the point where the canal joins it and immediately opposite the mouth of the Cart a short distance west of Renfrew ferry. This ground, he thinks, may be got at a reasonable price while considerable advantages may be obtained from its connection with the canal for the carriage of coal, machinery and other materials'.[141]

As with the ground at Lady Burn, James Stevenson was asked to investigate the terms on which 30 acres of ground could be obtained. The Trustees considered that the £650 per acre asked for was too high a price and instructed Stevenson to find the lowest price that would be acceptable for 'the ground adjoining the canal and a short distance to the west of Renfrew Ferry'.

Agreement from all Trustees was necessary before this transaction could be completed and, while Elizabeth Thomson readily concurred, Robert, her brother-in-law, writing from Liverpool, said in a letter of 18 February

> ' . . . Mr James is inclined to be very extravagant and if the Trustees do not keep a tight hand on him (especially when he has got thirty acres to cut and carve at) we may find some day that more money has been spent than will ever pay. You know he has not got the best advisor, they are rather selfish to my taste. The money on the ground is not so much, if care is not taken in laying out the yard and carving in buildings and tools the whole may turn out a bad speculation . . . '[142]

The 'advisor' is unknown but may be John Grant or Andrew Burns. The trustees did consider an alternative to building a new yard – that of winding up the business. However, that would have resulted in a serious loss[143] and, as the Trustees were acting as much in the interest of the Thomson family as for the business, it was agreed that the purchase should proceed on the basis that James Rodger and his brother George Paul would eventually take over the business and pay out the money which the Trust had invested.

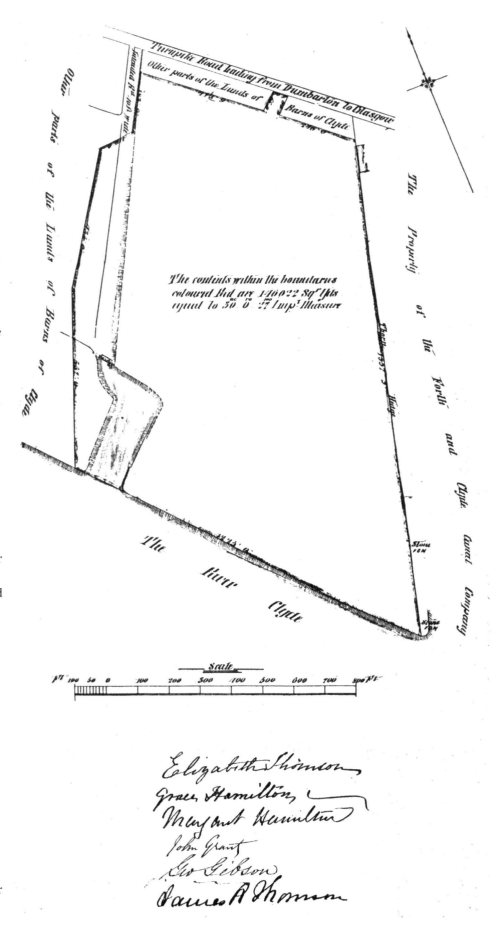

Authority to purchase was enshrined in the Trust minutes of the meeting of 1 March 1871:

> 'The Trustees therefore resolve on acquiring the ground necessary for a new shipbuilding yard and instruct Mr Stevenson to arrange for the purchase or feu from Miss Hamilton of Barnes as part of her lands of the Barns of Clyde lying immediately to the west of the canal where it enters the river and that on the best terms that he can procure.'[144]

The 30 acres and 27 roods of land purchased for £600 per acre on Whitsunday 1871 represented a six-fold increase in area over the Govan yard. The ground was part of the 'Barns of Clyde' Estate in the Parish of Old Kilpatrick owned by Grace Hamilton of Cochno. The site was bounded to the east by the canal, to the north by the Dumbarton to Glasgow turnpike road and to the west by a small stream which ran down to the Clyde in a line roughly parallel with the canal. The long axis of this plot was roughly in line with the River Cart, which joined the Clyde opposite the southeast corner of the ground. The ground was a green field site with virtually no buildings in the general area with the exception of the West Barns of Clyde farmhouse, which lay on the east side of the canal. The location had much to commend it. Although bound on two sides by the canal and the road, westward expansion was possible across green fields. The nearest development in that direction was the Clyde Trust's marine repair workshops at Dalmuir Shore which had been erected in 1860 to repair harbour and river craft. Communication links were reasonable, with access by canal, road and, of course, the river. Railway links, very much the transport system of the day, and by far the most important for the delivery of materials were less convenient. The Helensburgh to Glasgow line lay about a mile to the north. The principal disadvantage was the remoteness of the new location from the supply of labour and materials. The latter would not be properly rectified until the works were connected by a spur from the main line in 1882. Initially, materials were carted in by road or brought from Glasgow by

Map showing the distance in miles from Thomson's engine works at Finnieston and the new shipyard at Dalmuir. Until a fitting-out basin was cut into the land, it was not possible to work on a ship once launched. Fitting-out had to be completed at Finnieston where a number of large cranes were available to place the ship's machinery on board

boat. Glasgow lay some seven miles to the east while the nearest town was across the river at Renfrew. The greatest problem confronting the new works was the total absence of housing and utilities like water supply and sewerage. It was clear from the outset, that providing accommodation for workers would be an essential element of the shipyard.

Detailed plans for the new works went ahead with the appointment of an architect to prepare drawings. At a meeting held on 4 May, the following building contracts were authorised:

Bell Hornstey & Co.	Brickwork	£3,413
John Bayne	Masonwork	£1,226
G&J Findlay	Joinerwork	£7,999
Thomas Leadbetter & Co.	Plumberwork	£1,212
John Morison	Slaterwork	£1,484
McElroy & Son	Ironfounders	£3,349
C&J Malloch	Glazierwork	£585[145]

James Roger was authorised to proceed with the ordering of tools, machines and equipment to a combined value of over £13,000 which together with the building work itemised above, came to a total of over £32,000.[146] By June, this figure stood at £64,355 principally because of the need to build tenement houses, a gasometer, foundations, cranes, a steam lighter and numerous smaller items. Additionally, a strip of land parallel to the turnpike road was purchased from Miss Hamilton for building tenements earmarked for 'foremen and other superior servants'[147]

Expenditure of this order was not likely to be forthcoming from the business or the Trustees, and a meeting with the manager of the Union Bank of Scotland, Charles Gairdner, was sought. James Stevenson had died suddenly, a few days before the June meeting of the Trust, and his partner James Fleming was appointed as the Trust's law agent. He and William Anderson were requested to call on Gairdner by the Trustees. Following meetings with Gairdner in which a figure of £90,000 was proposed as the new cash credit limit, the Trust was told that while under normal circumstances the Bank would

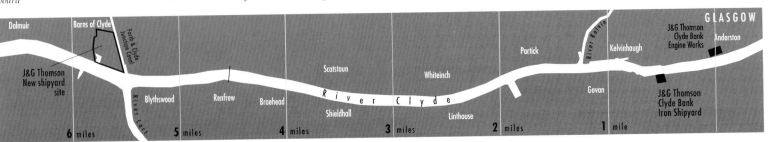

not entertain such a request, it was, in view of the time in which the account had been kept, anxious to meet the wishes of the Trustees as far as possible. In this manner, Gairdner made clear his desire to support the expansion of the business. The numerous difficulties of the following two decades would provide ample time for Gairdner to reflect on his magnanimity. However, at this point, his only conditions were that the Govan works be properly valued. It was also made clear that the Trustees would personally be liable for any debt incurred. When Robert Thomson heard of this proposal he wrote a letter from Liverpool on 10 June admonishing his nephew James Roger:

> ' . . . I see that James does not seem to study economy . . . he wants to borrow about £100,000 and give his brothers and sisters money as security . . . and I think that putting up such large works is going to reduce the value of the old. I wonder if James Thomson and his advisors think that if the large yard is finished that they will get ships to fill it, they may, but the chances are against them, it is not long since they could not get ships to build to fill their old yard, and if a slack time should come this new yard will ruin them. It appears to me that Clyde shipbuilders are vying with each other who will have the finest yard. I cannot agree with the amount James and Grant has down for buildings etc., instead of reducing as he promised me he has been adding and keeping me in the dark. I should like to write you a longer letter but feel I cannot do it as I am quite exhausted. This affair worries me more than my own business.'[148]

Robert was not the only one to take a poor view of the proposed new yard. William Johnston, a Trustee, declared at the meeting of 19 June 1871, that he too had 'all along been averse to the acquisition of ground for the new shipbuilding yard' but had acquiesced as the likely outcome of not proceeding was the winding up of the business. He was also very unhappy that tenders for the construction of the new yard were accepted despite the lack of financial arrangements being in place.[149] Following discussion, the Trustees recommended that:

> 'one or more new partners with capital should be taken into the business with a view to a transference thereof to Mr James Thomson and his brother George Thomson and to the liberation of the Trust from the Co-partnery. The Trustees recommend this course to the favourable consideration of Mr James R Thomson looking at the heavy prospective outlay in connection with the Dalmuir works'[150]

Clearly concerned about the large borrowings necessary to equip the new yard, the Trustees sought to divest themselves of the business to James and George whose position, as co-partners, would be bolstered by new partners able to make fresh investment in the concern.

Meanwhile the Trustees agreed that no further contract of any kind concerning the new yard would be entered into without proper financial arrangements being in place. Mrs Elizabeth Thomson's request that James Neilson, her son-in-law, should be admitted as a Trustee, was acted upon. William Anderson moved to "bring the financial arrangements of the shipbuilding yard under the direct control of the Trustees' by establishing a finance committee to oversee all transactions on a monthly basis.[151] A new and reduced estimate of expenditure to be incurred at the new yard was requested. It seems probable that the sheer scale of the venture was causing anxiety in the Trustees particularly as the young James Roger, aided by John Grant, was proving difficult to restrain.

In light of the Trust's growing concern, reduction of the borrowing requirement assumed a new importance and it was further agreed that Trust Funds amounting to £12,000 from life policies which had matured on the death of George in 1866, be used to finance the cost of building tenements at the new works. To this, it was hoped, would be added the proceeds of the sale of the large house Dalling Mhor in Dunoon, which was to be offered on the market at the much reduced price of £5,000. Borrowing was now estimated to be in the region of £60,000, a significant reduction from the earlier contemplated £90,000.[152] On 23 August 1871, Charles Gairdner granted a credit account of £60,000 on security of the works at Finnieston, which were valued at £108,352.[153] Work on forming the building berths began on 1 May 1871 while shipyard buildings were started on 14 May with the laying of the first brick.[154] Whatever present or future difficulties, James Roger Thomson had nevertheless succeeded in creating the second largest shipyard on Clydeside after John Elder's Fairfield Works.[155] The site was large enough to accommodate the engine works and thus create a fully integrated development on the Fairfield model although it would be many years before the company was able to finance this move.

Throughout this period, a succession of ships left the Govan yard. The loss of the ground to the Clyde Trust had limited the number of ships capable of being laid down, resulting in several orders being declined. On hand in May 1871 were the following vessels and contracts: *Bison*, for G&J Burns recently launched; *Iceland*, completing for D Currie & Co. together with new engines for *Verona*; *Marmion*, completed for the Leith Company; *Drummond Castle* and *Gordon Castle* both on the building berths for Thomas Skinner and *Trinidad* and *Demerara*, for G&J Burns' West India trade. Two additional orders were booked - a small steamer for G&J Burns' Belfast trade and a pair of engines for shipbuilders JG Lawrie. In July, a contract to lengthen and re-engine the Cunarder *Hecla* was in progress, the lengthening having been sub-contracted to Harland & Wolff at Belfast. Sister ships *Olympus* and *Marathon* were about to receive similar treatment.

The Company continued to receive invitations to tender from the Admiralty and in April 1870, tenders were prepared for building the engines of the *Vigilant* and *Lively* while, over a year later, in August 1871, a tender to build gunboats of the Snake Class at the price of £10,500 for the hull and £2,500 for the engines was submitted.[156] Neither tender was accepted. Negotiations with Cunard to build the largest and fastest ships yet built,[157] *Bothnia* and *Scythia*, were in progress. Whether it was purely a commercial decision or a question of pride, the Company was anxious to enter the field of warship construction and on 7 December 1871, wrote to the Turkish Minister of Marine offering to build an ironclad 'similar to *Hercules*, designed by Mr Reid chief constructor of the English navy.'[158] Two days later, another letter was written to a London firm of agents, Mirabita Brothers, offering to build gunboats similar to *HMS Staunch* for an unknown power. Again, these offers bore no fruit.

A BATTLE OF TRUSTS

From the outset it was clear that the award of appropriate compensation for the removal from the Govan yard would be a matter of some difficulty. As early as March 1870, George Reith wrote to the Thomson's lawyers, McGrigor Stevenson & Fleming, following a verbal indication of the amount Thomson hoped to receive, saying that Thomson's terms were 'so far beyond any estimate of the value of the property ever formed by the Trustees as to preclude all hope of an arrangement by negotiation.'[159] Equally, the £45,000 offered by the Clyde Trust was clearly nowhere near the Thomson's expectations.[160] The foregoing was compounded by Thomson's difficulty in clearing the Govan site. On 2 March notice was served on J&G Thomson for the immediate and compulsory removal of its works. The

Clyde Trust agreed however that three ships under construction in the yard could be completed but that four other contracts recently taken could not be started even although the material for one had been delivered and many of the frames set. In reply, Thomson stated that the new works and accommodation for workmen were under construction but that a water supply would not be available until the end of the year and that shipbuilding work could not commence until then. On 23 March 1872, the Thomson Trust made its claim for compensation:

> '. . . for the said lands . . . with the buildings and erections thereon and for all loss injury and damage sustained or to be sustained by them in consequence of the acquisition of the same by the Trustees of the Clyde Navigation Trust, the sum of £200,000 besides all costs, charges and expenses incurred or to be incurred by them . . .'[161]

It was agreed that the question of compensation would be subject to arbitration although the appointment of an arbiter was the source of disagreement. This was only solved when both parties appointed their own arbiter. For Thomson, this was James Morton of Greenock. In support of their case, the Thomsons listed the disadvantages of the new site in addition to fixing the costs of the buildings, plant and ground at Govan, the latter based on a valuation of Clyde Bank Shipyard, Govan on 1 February 1870 by James McNaught.[162]

1. Ground in yard	45,767
Footpath at yard	1,213
2. Buildings	12,345
3. Machinery and tools	15,083
4. Compensation claim –	
a) extra expense entailed by increased distance from Glasgow for wages say, overhead 1,000 men at one shilling per week equal to per annum	2,600
b) extra expense for increased distance betwixt engine shop and new shipyard for men working in vessels at harbour, engineers at harbour, managers clerks etc. per annum	2,500
c) Extra expense for carriage of material cartage tolls etc.	500
Seven years purchase (7 x £5,680)	39,200
Total	**£119,208**

The above provided the basis for the original claim of £110,000 to the Clyde Trust. Even this was considered inadequate in light of additional expense likely to be incurred, namely, loss through delay in completion of certain contracts and loss on house accommodation which had to be provided in order to alleviate the necessity of permanently maintaining a steamboat service to bring men to and from work. These additional costs together with an assumed safety margin took the figure to £200,000.

LAST SHIP AT GOVAN

While the above events were in train, vacating the Govan yard became a major problem for both the Thomson and Clyde Navigation Trusts. In exasperation, George Reith wrote, on 17 August 1872, '. . . the delay in launching the vessel still on the stocks is putting the Clyde Trustees to great inconvenience and loss, and it is now long past the time you said the ground would be clear of the last vessel . . .' Until December 1872, the Thomsons were subjected to a barrage of similar letters requesting their immediate removal.

With the transfer of the works underway and keels laid at Dalmuir, the majority of workers were travelling daily to the new yard in the lighter *Vulcan*. It was expected that the new yard would employ around 2,000 men when completed. Prior to the transfer, 1,500 men were employed at Govan.[163] The completion of contracts at Govan became a severe problem as John Grant explained in a letter to solicitors McGrigor Donald & Co. on 21 August 1872:

> ' . . . with regard to Mr Reith's enquiry as to the probable date of evacuation of the Govan yard, we expect to launch the vessel therein in the first week of September. In order to accomplish an early clearance we have been doing everything in our power to get a sufficient number of hands to finish the work - a very difficult matter at present - and among other sacrifices for this end have nearly denuded our new yard of the squads of riveters working there, to get the vessel off our hands . . .'[164]

The vessel in question was *Demerara* which was launched on 6 September and completed on 23 November 1872. This was the last ship to be constructed by J&G Thomson at Govan. Originally, it had been the intention to build *Cawdor Castle* and *Braemar Castle* for Thomas Skinner at Govan. Much of the material had been gathered there and many frames bent. The pressure to evacuate the yard required the removal of 1,312 tons of this

material to Dalmuir at great expense and both vessels were not laid down until the early months of 1872.[165] The delay in constructing both Castle ships meant that no stage payments were made to the Company despite heavy outlay in materials and wages. Six months were lost in their construction and Charles Gairdner was asked to provide additional credit of £25,000 to cover the period.

On acquiring the shipyard site, the Clyde Trust immediately set about the construction of Plantation Quay which was not fully opened until 1875.[166] Most of the shipyard buildings were retained and converted into grain stores. In the 1880s, the entire site was cleared to make way for Cessnock Dock, which was opened in 1897 under the name of Princes Dock.[167]

In twenty years at Govan the Company had built 126 ships ranging in size from the *Jackal* of 125 feet and 165 tons to the *Abyssinia* of 360 feet and 3,253 gross tons, the latter amongst the largest built anywhere at that time. The fast mail steamer was established as the type of ship to which the yard was most suited. With few exceptions the business at Govan had been consistently profitable and both James and George, the founders of the firm, had become very wealthy, although neither lived long to enjoy it. Important customers had been won and maintained, particularly the Cunard Company.

Tentative experiments with steam engines and iron hulls described at the beginning of this book had, by the 1870s, blossomed into a national industry during which time Clydeside had replaced the Thames as the leading shipbuilding and marine engineering district in Britain. Employment in these industries on Clydeside alone had grown from 3% of the UK total in 1831 to 21% in 1871, equivalent to a total of 60,000 men.[168] Although sailing ships continued to be built in sizeable numbers, the steamship had become the predominant means by which goods and people were transported on the world's seaways. With the development of the compound engine, the 'Scotch' boiler and screw propulsion, the steamship had become reliable and economic.

THE GOVAN SHIPYARD OF J&G THOMSON

No published description or plan of the Govan shipyard has been located. Maps of the period show the basic layout but not the disposition of specific shops. It seems likely that the ironworking sheds were arranged down the western boundary of the yard and the joiner shops closer to the eastern side near the old mansion, which served as offices. There was a public right of way between the shipyard and the River Clyde which had to be maintained at all times with the exception of launches. The following is a list of principal buildings taken from the inventory of Clyde Bank Iron Shipyard made in 1866.[169]

- Sawmill, Joiners Shop and Loft with store for moulding and turning shop machine room including engine house chimney.
- Carpenters Shop, Moulding Loft Riggers Loft and Sawpit.

- Upper Smiths Shop turning and erecting shop and Engineers Loft with wooden stair. Pattern Shop, Shipsmiths Store and Painters Shop.
- Lower Smiths Shop Engine Room, store etc.
- New Frame Shed with zinc roof, new shed over punching machine and donkey engine.New Water Closet with McFarlane's Patent Apparatus, Cistern etc.
- New shed over beam bending and punching machines
- Furnaces for heating plates and angle iron. 3

A plan showing the main shipyards and engine works in the upper reaches of the Clyde at Govan and Glasgow. It was this remarkable concentration that put Clydeside at the centre of the marine engineering and shipbuilding industries.

Shipyards and Engine Works in Govan and Glasgow Harbour about 1870

The main concentration of shipyards, engine works and cranes in Glasgow Harbour and Govan at 1870.
Previous and subsequent owners of sites are listed under 1870 occupant

Based on a map by J Deas published in the Transactions of the Institute of Civil Engineers 1872/73

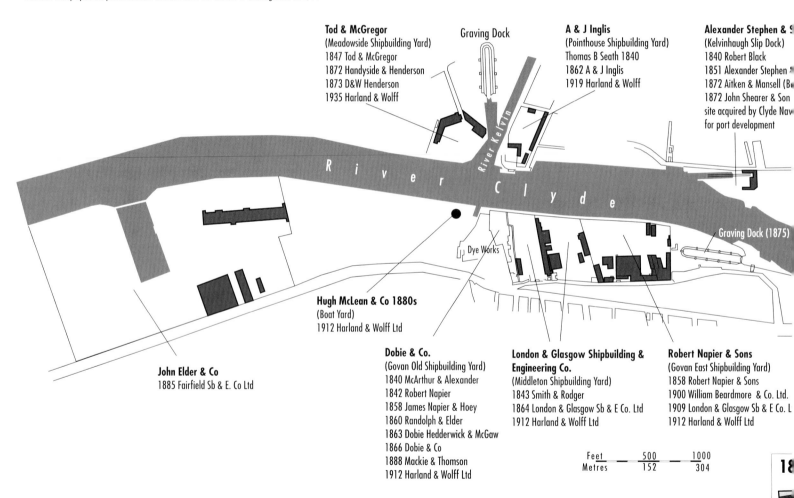

Tod & McGregor
(Meadowside Shipbuilding Yard)
1847 Tod & McGregor
1872 Handyside & Henderson
1873 D&W Henderson
1935 Harland & Wolff

Graving Dock

A & J Inglis
(Pointhouse Shipbuilding Yard)
Thomas B Seath 1840
1862 A & J Inglis
1919 Harland & Wolff

Alexander Stephen & S
(Kelvinhaugh Slip Dock)
1840 Robert Black
1851 Alexander Stephen
1872 Aitken & Mansell (B
1872 John Shearer & Son
site acquired by Clyde Nav
for port development

River Kelvin

River Clyde

Graving Dock (1875)

Dye Works

Hugh McLean & Co 1880s
(Boat Yard)
1912 Harland & Wolff Ltd

John Elder & Co
1885 Fairfield Sb & E. Co Ltd

Dobie & Co.
(Govan Old Shipbuilding Yard)
1840 McArthur & Alexander
1842 Robert Napier
1858 James Napier & Hoey
1860 Randolph & Elder
1863 Dobie Hedderwick & McGaw
1866 Dobie & Co
1888 Mackie & Thomson
1912 Harland & Wolff Ltd

London & Glasgow Shipbuilding & Engineering Co.
(Middleton Shipbuilding Yard)
1843 Smith & Rodger
1864 London & Glasgow Sb & E Co. Ltd
1912 Harland & Wolff Ltd

Robert Napier & Sons
(Govan East Shipbuilding Yard)
1858 Robert Napier & Sons
1900 William Beardmore & Co. Ltd.
1909 London & Glasgow Sb & E Co. L
1912 Harland & Wolff Ltd

	500	1000
Feet		
Metres	152	304

brick chimneys for furnaces and engine furnace.
• Smiths fires in Smith Shop with hearths and hearth covers.
• Smiths fires in Upper and Lower Smith Shop with hearths and hearth covers.
• Large fires in Lower Shed with hearths and hearth covers.

The following lists the various shops and rooms with a brief indication of what they contained.
Painter's Shop - paint brushes, camel hair pencils, quill tools, iron paint pots;
Bellows Mender's House - sewing awls, drills, chisels, riveter's fires;
Pitch House - iron pails, pitch ladles, ships scrapers;
Naptha House - naptha lamps, torches;
Shipsmith's Shop - hammers, cresses, flatteners;
Upper Smithy - anvils, tongs, punches and chisels;
Lower Smithy - cast metal blocks, hammers, anvils, flatteners;

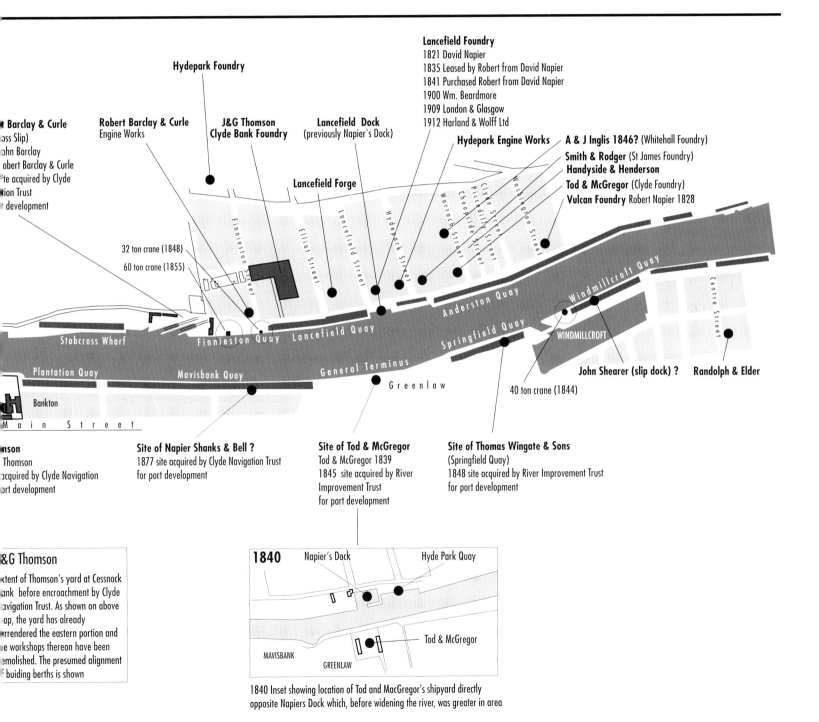

1840 Inset showing location of Tod and MacGregor's shipyard directly opposite Napiers Dock which, before widening the river, was greater in area

Lower Store - riveter's boxes, caulker's boxes, riveter's and caulker's hammers, caulker's chisels;

Bolt Store - vice;

On Hill - iron tresses

Finishing Shop - vices, nibbling tools, vices, chisels

Engineers Shop - vices, oil lamps, pots for melting lead, tackle with iron blocks

Joiners Shop - benches, cramps, glue pots and boilers, augers, moulding planes, chisels, gouge, slog frame saws, jack planes, grooving planes

Upper Joiners Shop - benches, yellow pine tresses

Machine Shop - augers

Carpenters Shed - launching ways, launch shores, bilge wedges, shovels, picks, barrows, stage planks, stage uprights, frame ribbands, keel blocks

Rigging Loft - lufftackles, purchase blocks, marlinespikes, lignum vitae dead eyes

Launching Gear - hawsers, mooring ropes and chains, notch blocks

Masting Falls - tarred ropes

Counting House - desks, copying press

Time Office; Consulting Rooms

Drawing Room - table, presses, drawing boards, drawing tools

Model Room - moulding bench, gouges and chisels etc.

Managers Rooms

Machine Shed - punching machines, keel plate bender, plate bender, plate rolls, lathes, angle iron cutting machine, grindstones, vertical drilling machines, plate planing machines, Rigby steam hammer

Stables - 5 horses, harnesses, belly bands etc.

The skills and machine tools required in iron shipbuilding came from established iron-working industries such as boiler, tank and girder making.[170] The engineers who applied them to shipbuilding adapted the machines. By the time the Thomsons established their iron shipyard at Govan, riveted iron construction methods were well established and were fundamentally to remain the same until the advent of welded construction after the Second World War. In the period 1850/60, the basic components of the iron ship - angle iron, frames, deck beams and shell plates, were heated in furnaces, bent on iron beds, punched and cut by machines, handled by men and fixed together by squads of riveters using nothing more than rivets and rivet hammers.

In comparison with later developments, building a ship in the early days of iron shipbuilding was very much a craft. Unlike woodworking trades where highly developed skills and practices existed, iron working had to evolve from a rudimentary craft into an industrial process. Plates weighing several tons were manhandled from furnace to machine or to a plate-former in sheds dimly lit by paraffin or naptha lamps. Machines of a new type such as punching and shearing machines, keel plate benders and plate rolls were in their infancy as were the skills associated with their use. These machines were steam driven, crude and awkward to operate. Once prepared in the shed or in the open, plates and angles were taken by cart to the berth for erection. Simple wooden derricks, slings and tackle held the plate in position ready for riveting where it would first be fixed temporarily using bolts.

A rivet squad usually comprised four men; a heater boy to heat the rivets to red heat; a holder-on to keep the rivet in place at the back of the plates and two riveters, one left handed the other right handed. Standing either side of the rivet, the riveters would alternately strike the red-hot rivet until the shaft was forced into a mushroom-like shape over the plate. As a rivet might require up to ten blows from each riveter, this was heavy, tough, noisy work, which demanded accuracy as well as strength. Working in confined spaces, often the case in certain compartments where the hull narrowed at the stern or stem, could only have made this task more unpleasant. A fifth person called a catch-boy might also be part of a squad where access to the work was difficult. His task was to receive the rivet thrown to him by the heater-boy and insert it into the rivet hole. Working in this fashion, a squad might close up to 1,000 rivets per shift. The demonstrably physical aspect of their contribution to the construction process earned the riveters great respect and, for their part, they considered themselves to be the elite of the shipyard trades. The introduction of piecework, where payment was made by the number of rivets driven, added the element of urgency to their work. The traditional builders of ships - shipwrights - had little part in the direct process of iron construction the transition from wood to iron having reduced their role largely to the timberwork associated with launching, decks etc. The core of the new ironworkers, riveters, caulkers and platers, came from other branches of industry most notably boilermaking. The organisation of trades into societies and unions took place after the repeal of the Anti-Combination law of 1824/5. The United Society of Boilermakers and Iron Shipbuilders was formed in 1832 and the Amalgamated Society of Engineers in 1850.

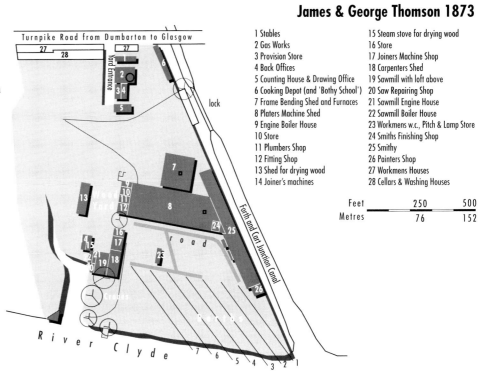

James & George Thomson 1873

1 Stables
2 Gas Works
3 Provision Store
4 Back Offices
5 Counting House & Drawing Office
6 Cooking Depot (and 'Bothy School')
7 Frame Bending Shed and Furnaces
8 Platers Machine Shed
9 Engine Boiler House
10 Store
11 Plumbers Shop
12 Fitting Shop
13 Shed for drying wood
14 Joiner's machines

15 Steam stove for drying wood
16 Store
17 Joiners Machine Shop
18 Carpenters Shed
19 Sawmill with loft above
20 Saw Repairing Shop
21 Sawmill Engine House
22 Sawmill Boiler House
23 Workmens w.c., Pitch & Lamp Store
24 Smiths Finishing Shop
25 Smithy
26 Painters Shop
27 Workmens Houses
28 Cellars & Washing Houses

	Feet	250	500
	Metres	76	152

A plan of Clydebank shipyard as completed in 1873 showing the layout of the berths and principal shops. The small inlet at the bottom left had been cut some years before by the Clyde Navigation Trust.

1872-1899 RELOCATION & EXPANSION

Establishing new works at Dalmuir had not been unanimously supported by the Trustees. Both Robert Thomson and William Johnston had been wary of the scheme. Now, against a background of spiralling costs, they were concerned that their ability to influence events was limited. On the other hand, James Roger Thomson and John Grant were pushing hard to create the best possible facility out of the demise of the Govan yard. The other members of the Trust became increasingly cautious.

The new works were much larger than the old, and the relatively modest financial arrangements previously enjoyed with the Union Bank of Scotland had to give way to greater dependence. The ensuing pressures caused the Trust to polarise with James Roger Thomson and George Gibson taking opposing views, making any form of collective decision-making all but impossible. The first evidence of division in the Trust emerged in July 1871 when Robert Thomson indicated that ill health might soon force him to give up his position as a Trustee. While Robert was merely pointing out a simple fact, George Gibson saw an opportunity to leave the Trust declaring that his membership of the Trust was conditional on that of Robert's. He also wished to see William Neilson, an ally, assumed as a Trustee. In

September, James Neilson wanted to withdraw £8,000 of his wife Jane Paul Thomson's money. James Fleming told him that this would not be possible and 'if insisted upon would force winding up of the business' [171]

Robert Thomson's position was decided in October when he died at his home in Bootle, Liverpool, at the age of sixty. With his death, all three grocer's sons from Partick had passed into history.

In December, William Neilson was assumed into the Trust in place of William Johnston, who resigned. Although Trust minutes offer no reason for this, it is likely that his disagreement over the decision to move to Dalmuir precipitated this action.

In the same month, Andrew Burns', shipyard manager, contract was due for renewal and the proposal was put forward by the Trust that he should be retained for five years at £600 per annum plus 5% of all profits made by the Company.[172] This amounted to a large cut in his salary as determined by his previous contract in which he had been guaranteed a minimum of £1,000 annually, £600 of which was salary, the rest made up as a percentage of shipyard profits.[173] The trust eventually agreed to reinstate the £1,000 guaranteed minimum and also agreed to build a house near the yard for him, Clydebank Cottage, provided that it cost no more than £1,000.[174]

COMPETITION ACROSS THE IRISH SEA

On 31 December 1871, construction of the first ship at the new yard, the Cunard liner *Bothnia*, was begun. The contract for this highly prestigious ship, and her sister *Scythia*, had been won in the previous August and represented the most important so far received from Cunard. Of 4,535grt, *Bothnia* and *Scythia* continued the upward trend in size, speed and standard of accommodation. However, unlike previous Cunarders, these vessels were not destined to be leaders on the North Atlantic.

In the late 1860s, a new shipping line emerged to challenge the Cunard and Inman lines. This line chose to place all its contracts with one shipbuilder. The shipping line was White Star and the shipbuilder

Although Bothnia *was the first ship to be laid down at the new yard, her protracted building time allowed the third ship to be laid down,* Braemar Castle, *shown here, to be launched first.*

was Harland & Wolff. Both Cunard and J&G Thomson now had serious competition.

The Oceanic Steam Navigation Co., was formed by Thomas Ismay in 1869 to take over the bankrupt White Star Line. Both Edward Harland and Gustav Wolff, partners in Harland & Wolff, had taken a significant interest in the new company in exchange for which, it was agreed that all White Star ships would be built by them.[175] Thomas Ismay resolved to out-build Cunard and thus he gave the Belfast yard the opportunity to rise to the first rank in passenger ship construction. The first White Star ship, *Oceanic*, was delivered in February 1871 followed by four similar ships over the next two years. The spacious and luxurious White Star ships, designed from the outset to be the best, immediately established supremacy over their competitors on the North Atlantic. *Bothnia* and *Scythia*[176] despite being large, swift and well appointed, were not the ships to redress this situation and almost ten years passed before Cunard was able to challenge White Star. The Belfast yard had been building small vessels since the early 1850s and, under the direction of Edward Harland, had, from 1858, built many ships for J Bibby Sons & Co. Harland's yard relied on Clydeside for the supply of materials and components and engines for the first ships were supplied by McNab & Co. of Greenock. Small cargo handling cranes were supplied by none other than J&G Thomson.[177]

The relationship established between Harland & Wolff and White Star enabled ships to be built very competitively. Ships were built for White Star at cost plus 4% commission and no establishment charges (overheads). Other shipbuilders, including J&G Thomson, priced ships by adding establishment charges to the cost of materials and wages to give the basic cost. The price was finally determined by applying profit, usually about 10%, to the cost. In times when contracts were difficult to secure, shipbuilders might build for no profit or even waive charges. Harland & Wolff were able to sustain such low margins because of the volume of work they were able to attract. This arrangement gave them a major advantage in tendering for new tonnage and posed a serious problem for other shipbuilders, who were quite unaware of the commission arrangement. As a result of pressure of work on the engine shops at Finnieston in January 1872, plans to build an additional engine erecting shop there were brought forward at a cost of £2,300.[178] This was evidence of the increased capacity of the shipyard. Unable to take

any orders while the new yard was under construction, an order was accepted in March 1872 from G&J Burns for the West India steamer *Saragossa* at the contract price of £49,600.[179] In May 1872, G&J Burns asked the company to build two or three vessels of 1,200 tons for their Le Havre service. Because of its difficulties with the new yard, Thomson was set to decline when Thomas Skinner's Australian Line collapsed, freeing the yard of a commitment to about 8,000 tons of shipping. One of the Burns ships, *Cherbourg*, was taken on and another, reluctantly, allowed to go elsewhere.[180]

The workforce at Dalmuir was steadily increasing, reaching between 700 and 800 men in September 1871 and 1,300 by December. As most workers travelled from Govan or Glasgow, the paddle steamer *Vulcan*[181] was bought for £1,525 to take men to and from Dalmuir, a task shared with *Maggie*, a lighter built by the Company. Writing in 1923, one author said of *Vulcan*, having seen her arriving in Glasgow loaded with Clydebank workmen:

> 'I can well remember seeing her come alongside the quay on her upward journey one evening. No gangway was required to accommodate her passengers; all along her length they climbed on the bulwarks and scrambled up the quay-wall, and before she was even moored the boat was emptied.'[182]

Throughout 1872, only three ships were laid down, *Cawdor Castle*, *Braemar Castle* and *Saragossa*, underlining the continuing difficulties experienced at the new yard. Greater difficulties were soon to engulf the Trust.

HARD FACTS

The optimism generated by the new yard was dashed by the onset of serious financial difficulties. Fear of collapse prompted a struggle within the Trust and placed members under great pressure. George Gibson in particular became outspoken in his desire to minimise losses and therefore his personal liability. The Thomson Trust owned the business and each Trustee was personally liable for any debt the business was unable to honour. Had the Company failed, each member would have suffered serious financial loss. Although Limited Liability had come into existence under the Companies Act of 1861, this was regarded as an innovation of questionable morality.

In December 1872, indebtedness to the Bank had soared to £108,000,[183] and climbed even higher to £123,391 in the following January. This was partly attributable to the slow progress on contracts at the new and incomplete shipyard, compounded by difficulties in attracting tradesmen. The consequent delay in progressing contracts meant that stage payments were late, increasing indebtedness to the Bank.

On 8 January 1873, the Trust requested that John Grant, Company Secretary, provide a statement showing the amount and value of unfinished work, together with the stock of materials in the Company, with the object of finding to what extent the money owed to the Bank could be accounted for by these assets.[184] John Grant's statement to the Trust on 13 January showed a deficit of £26,000 in the trading account. It also showed that the outlay at Dalmuir to date was a massive £88,000. Trust members, by now suitably concerned, had to wait until William Anderson, reporter to the Trust, could complete the audit for the year to June 1872.[185] This was completed by March 1873 and showed a loss of £22,079 for the year before interest, the third loss in the 25-year history of the Company.[186] The loss was largely attributed to the contracts for *Braemar* and *Cawdor Castle*, which had been relocated from Govan to Dalmuir. The Trust's response was to insist that no new contracts were taken, as the initial burden of financing them was unacceptable given the present straitened circumstances.[187]

Attempts to sell Dalling Mhor for a much-needed £5,000 were frustrated when Mrs Thomson stated her intention to use the house over summer for a rent of £120. Although she also agreed to pay the gardeners' wages, the Trust had to insist that she pay the appropriate rent of £245, the Trust maintaining the property as before. Dalling Mhor was finally sold in November 1873 for £5,000 to John Ewing Walker, Postmaster at Glasgow.[188]

The results for the year 1872 revealed a sharp plunge into deficit with the loss of £22,079 compared to a profit of £14,239 in 1871. The Bank became concerned. Events reached a head on 9 May 1873 when Charles Gairdner, manager of the Union Bank, having received William Anderson's audited accounts for the year, wrote to Colin Dunlop Donald, a Thomson Trustee and partner in Glasgow solicitors McGrigor Donald & Co.:

> 'I find from Mr. Anderson's report on the balance sheet of Messrs. J&G Thomson's books of 30 June last that the capital of the firm was then £123,000. This is brought out on the basis of valuations which it is stated were very inadequately checked. I find further that at the same date there was sunk

in fixed property £190,000 so that the whole capital and £67,000 besides was sunk and there were no funds therewith to carry on the large business they have in hand. No doubt you expect to get in £90,000 from the River Trust in a few days which will so far improve matters but on the other hand there must have been further outlay at Dalmuir since June last and probably a loss on contracts besides. The account at the bank has increased from £87,000 in June to £154,000 where it stands today and as the position of the finances of the firm is evidently not satisfactory and we cannot agree to increase this amount or let it remain as it is, I must ask you to bring the matter under the consideration of the Trustees as requiring their urgent and immediate attention.'[189]

The Trust immediately set about the task of controlling costs while a long-term strategy to deal with the structural weakness of the business was developed. It resolved that James Roger's drawings were not to exceed £1,000 per annum, that Mrs Thomson's allowance for the younger children would be reduced from £1,050 to £750, that George Thomson's allowance would be reduced from £400 to £250 and lastly, that John Grant's salary would be restricted to £750.[190]

The above points were of a relatively minor nature and much depended on the size of the award made in the claim against the Clyde Navigation Trust as a consequence of the compulsory removal of the shipyard to Dalmuir.

It will be recalled that the Thomson Trust had made a claim of £200,000 in March 1872.

At the hearing of May 1873, the Lord Advocate in summing up was dismissive of this claim.

> '. . . Good Heavens! these people come here claiming £200,000. I am not sure if they do not claim more. They might as well have claimed the expense of the National Debt; it would only have been a shade more extravagant and ridiculous – scarcely more ridiculous, because, when you get a certain length, it does not matter how you multiply'[191]

The sum found in favour of Thomsons was only £85,270 plus interest and expenses. The Trustees were very dissatisfied with the 'smallness of the sum awarded' particularly as it had ignored their claim for future losses as a consequence of the move.[192] The repercussions following this low award were to add greatly to the problems in financing the new works. From the outset, taking into consideration the real costs associated with the move and the inadequacy of

Top
Colin Dunlop Donald the Thomson Trust's law agent and a partner in Glasgow solicitors McGrigor Donald & Co.

Bottom
Charles Gairdner, Manager of the Union Bank of Scotland, took a firm but supportive role in the financial difficulties of the Thomson Trust.

the compensation, the business was in a financial pit from which it would take almost two decades to escape.

The Trust revisited the idea of bringing a 'monied partner' into the business and initially proposed to advertise for such. Instead, Colin Donald wrote to George and John Burns, very wealthy partners in the Cunard Company, and, moreover, Thomsons' most important customer, asking if they 'would assist the Trustees in their efforts to effect this object' i.e. bringing a monied partner into the business.[193] At a meeting of the Trust in August, it was Donald's unfortunate duty to tell the Trustees that while John Burns expressed 'warm interest in the prosperity of the firm and an anxious desire to assist . . . he had at last confessed himself utterly unable to suggest anyone who would answer the purpose in view.'[194] John Burns had, one assumes, neatly evaded the thinly disguised attempt to co-opt him and his money onto the Trust.

Disappointing as it was, the Clyde Trust award nevertheless reduced borrowing from the bank to £72,000 - still an unacceptably high figure. As work on contracts progressed, money flowed into the business and, with a freeze on new contracts causing spending to be reduced, the debt to the bank was slowly reduced. The Trust reaffirmed that, at the earliest time, the business should be separated from the Trust and be converted into a Joint Stock Limited Company.[195]

However, the fundamental problems which beset the business remained and pressure on the Trustees grew resulting in disagreement. At a meeting on 20 October 1873, James Roger reported that he had offered to build a large steamer for Thomas Skinner's China trade at what he considered were remunerative prices, adding that, unless new contracts were to be taken on, they would eventually be out of work and out of business. In this he had more than a point. The last contract booked by the Company had been taken in April 1872, almost sixteen months before. Workmen would soon have to be paid off and the business would loose momentum. At a time when reliable skilled labour was at a premium, continuity of employment was a crucial consideration.

George Gibson immediately declared his intention to retire from the Trust and said that under no circumstances would he permit any new contracts to be taken until he had gone. Following this, William Neilson stated that he had only joined the Trust on the express condition that George Gibson remained and that under the circumstances, he too, had no

option but to resign. The minutes of this meeting record that a 'long and anxious conversation ensued' during which time the likely effect of these resignations on the credibility and confidence of the business was considered. The only agreement reached when the meeting broke up was that they would meet again nine days later.[196]

At this meeting, William Anderson submitted his

report on the current financial position of the business and also reported a meeting with Charles Gairdner, manager of the Union Bank, at which he had appraised him of events at the troubled meeting. Gairdner's response was to request information about the profitability of current contracts and to determine the amount required by the business to continue after these contracts were completed. As the answers to this required knowledge of the practical workings of the business, it was agreed that James Roger Thomson should personally see Gairdner and provide the details.[197]

At the next meeting of the Trust on 26 November, James outlined the conditions which Gairdner had laid down at their meeting – the Trust should bring its debt to the bank down to a figure of £35,000 by the following February, in return for which Gairdner would recommend new credit of £50,000 to his directors. The retiring Trustees could then be relieved of their liability.[198]

Having described Gairdner's proposal, James optimistically said that he hoped the Trustees would now be able to let him book one or two new contracts to maintain the business. To this Gibson delivered an emphatic no, unless both he and Neilson could be discharged from the Trust forthwith. To add to the drama, Anderson was instructed to see Gairdner at his Glasgow head office immediately and put to him

The liner Bothnia, *completed in June 1874 for Cunard, was followed by her sister* Scythia *in the following year. Although both were intended to win the honours on the North Atlantic, they were trumped by the newly formed White Star Line's* Oceanic *built by Harland & Wolff at Belfast.*

the possibility of the instant discharge of two Trustees. The Trust meeting was meanwhile adjourned until 3pm later that day when Anderson returned with Gairdner's decision.[199] Anderson described how Gairdner would have none of this proposal stating that in his opinion, the retiring Trustees' object in being relieved of their obligation to the bank would be equally served by reducing the debt as his proposal suggested. The meeting broke up with Gibson agreeing to give the matter some thought. On 5 December the Trust met again. Even though he was present at the meeting, Gibson felt the need to formally state his position in writing:

> 'I have been considering very anxiously the proposal made by the bank as explained at the last meeting of George Thomson's Trustees but the more I think of it, I am satisfied that it would be folly on my part to accede to it.
>
> As I therefore do not see my way at present to retire from the Trust believing that might prove injurious to the Estate, the only alternative left me, is to adhere to my former resolution that no further contracts be taken for work. It seems to me that the business can only be brought to a workable focus by having existing contracts completed and a new start made upon such terms as may then seem the best.
>
> I am quite sensible that in following this course which I propose there may be loss sustained, but I think you must look at it as the least of two evils. I must ask therefore that this intimation be respected with reference to new contracts and hope that any further action on my part will be quite unnecessary to compel that'

This letter, a return to Gibson's original position, was unacceptable not just because Gairdner's solution had largely circumvented Gibson's fears but also because it did not permit the Company to trade. James Roger's response to Gibson's letter was predictable and appropriate. He explained that it would 'be wholly impossible for him to keep the workmen together, and to carry on the business successfully after a certain period unless a limited number of new contracts are taken.' He added the inducement that such contracts would, of course, require the approval of the Trustees. Gibson relented and wisely agreed to reconsider his position.[200] The following day, he wrote a letter to the Trust agreeing to the contract for one ship.[201] The immediate crisis was over although the rumblings were to continue. James Roger duly asked the Trust to give him permission to finalise an order with Gay & Thomson

William Anderson CA, had the task of dealing with the Thomson Trust's difficult financial position.

to build a sailing ship of 1,250 tons. Before agreeing to this, Gibson asked the shipyard manager, Andrew Burns, whom he had asked to attend the meeting, to confirm Thomson's description of the contract. Burns corroborated Thomson's statement in every respect'[202] Evidently, James Roger Thomson was as much a part of George Gibson's concern as were the finances.

In April, another order was in prospect, this time a steam ship for clients of William McNaught of Manchester at a price of £51,400. James Roger asked for permission to proceed whereupon George Gibson expressed himself '. . . decidedly opposed to any new contract . . .' Although permission was granted, it was against his express wishes and he wanted it minuted that should any loss be made on this contract, he would hold James Roger and John Grant personally liable. James Neilson supported Gibson's position. The Trust had become unworkable.

In November 1874, James Roger submitted the proposal that he and his brother George Paul take over the business for the sum of £45,000 secured by the Dalmuir works. They agreed that a further sum of £15,000 would be paid when circumstances made this possible and that the £12,000 used to finance the tenements at Dalmuir would similarly be repaid. The Trust concurred with this proposal, and specified that the whole sum of £60,000 be paid off in twelve yearly instalments of £5,000.[203] The recorded loss for 1873 was £13,736, and George Gibson would undoubtedly have been relieved to be free of the leaden weight that Dalmuir shipyard had become. From 29 December 1874, the business was now a co-partnery in the hands of James Roger and George Paul Thomson.[204]

The first ship to be launched from the Dalmuir yard was *Braemar Castle*, ship number 125, for Thomas Skinner & Co., on 13 February 1873. This ship was launched by Marion Thomson[205] James Roger's wife. *Braemar Castle* left the Clyde on 17 May, two days after her sister ship *Cawdor Castle* was launched by Maggie Thomson, James Roger's sister.

In June 1873, the Company wrote to the Turkish Minister of Marine, Riza Pacha, offering to build an armour-clad steam frigate 'similar to the one building for them by the Thames Company'[206] adding 'We have the second largest shipbuilding premises on the Clyde and we may mention, among other series of contracts, have built nearly all the Cunard mail steamers for the last 10 or 12 years.'[207] The price quoted for the vessel was £438,850. The Thomsons had every reason to be circumspect in soliciting work from the Turkish Government. Payments for the speculatively built steamer *Stamboul*, which they had sold to them a few years previously, were still outstanding in April 1872.[208] Nothing came of this offer.

The launch of *Bothnia* on 4 March 1874 was a demonstration of what the new yard could produce. As well as being the largest Cunarder, this ship was also the largest yet built on the Clyde. The launch attracted many dignitaries and assured coverage in the national and international press. The shipyard diary records the following entry:

> 'Bothnia launched at 1.30pm by Miss Hamilton of Cochno. Vessel named by Miss Arbuthnot. A grand stand erected and a large number of visitors present. Johns Burns Esq., Sir James Watson, Lord Provost of Glasgow, the magistrates and Council of Paisley, Mr Sankey and the American evangelists etc. A magnificent launch. Company afterwards entertained to lunch in the dinning hall which was tastefully decorated for the occasion. Misses Hamilton and Arbuthnot were presented each with a silver mallet.'[209]

Throughout 1874, trade was disappointing causing the engineers at the Finnieston Street works to be notified of a 15% cut in wages.[210] On 26 April 1875, the first recorded strike at the new works occurred when joiners walked out over the issue of wages. On 1 June they returned to work having achieved an increase.

As the new partnership was being formed, five ships were in various stages of construction - *Scythia, Cherbourg, Dunnottar Castle, Fleurs Castle* on the slips, *Klopstock* newly launched and *Bothnia* and *Saragossa* just completed.

A NEW COMMUNITY

The absence of any accommodation for workers at Barns o' Clyde required the building of houses at the same time as the shipyard. Within a radius of a few miles, there were a number of small villages, the nearest of which was Dalmuir. However, none of these was capable of supporting the influx of workers taking employment in the yard. The first tenements to be constructed were on the northern boundary of the yard fronting the turnpike road and were known locally as 'Tamson's Buildings'. They were plain fronted, four storey, stone-built tenements comprising a total of 136 dwellings. The houses were either of two or three apartments with water closets located on every floor i.e. one water closet shared by two houses.[211] The main shipyard workshops and sheds were completed at the end of February 1872 with the

first of the tenements ready for occupation in March. Nevertheless, James Roger recognised the inadequacy of these arrangements 'As we approach completion of the new yard, we see every day more clearly the total inadequacy of the house accommodation as yet provided for, to meet even the first few months requirements . . . ' The Trust agreed that 100 houses in Duntocher be rented for two years. This was duly

arranged at an annual rental of £337 16s.[212] Meanwhile, the lack of a connection to the public water supply was creating another problem, which was addressed by asking the Glasgow Water Commissioners to extend their pipes to the new yard from Yoker and by having the area declared a special water district by the local authority.[213]

The area was without amenity of any kind placing great hardship on the first tenants. Shipyard buildings had to assume a dual role, one during working hours and another outside hours, to support the new community. The canteen was used as a makeshift hall for a variety of activities including that of a church on Sundays, earning the shed the name of the 'Tarry Kirk'. The Tarry Kirk was fully committed to spiritual matters on Sundays until the first church was built in 1876. A Penny Bank was established in 1872 under the guidance of Robert Carswell, the shipyard cashier.

The first school was set up in a room in one of the tenements in Thomsons' Buildings. Mrs Pitblado, wife of a shipyard engineer, provided simple schooling for forty children. This school known as

The 'Bothy School' was built initially to offer men accommodation while tenements were under construction. It was used as a school building between 1873 and 1876 when a purpose built school was opened. It is shown here at the end of its life.

Pitblado's Clydebank Adventure School, lasted for only one year. When the first Old Kilpatrick School Board was elected in 1873 under the chairmanship of James White of Overtoun, Mrs Pitblado's Adventure School was closed down, as she was not qualified. Alternative school accommodation was found in a long low 'bothy' which had been built as a place where workmen could eat and sleep. Classes in what was known as the 'Bothy School' began on 11 August 1873 and continued until 1876 when a purpose built school was opened by the School Board in Kilbowie Road.[214] James Roger Thomson took a keen interest in the School Board and acted as Chairman in the years 1875 and 1876.

The only way in which men and material could be transported to the shipyard was by river or by road. There is no evidence that the Forth and Clyde Junction Canal was used for this purpose despite its proximity to the yard. The railway was the obvious means of transportation and this was provided in August 1873 when a spur from the main Glasgow to Dumbarton railway line was opened at Kilbowie although the first train for shipyard workers did not run until 15 December 1873.[215] An omnibus service operating between the shipyard and Partick was inaugurated on 6 March 1876.[216] By the end of 1881 a new railway line was in operation between Glasgow and the Works[217] the result of persistent applications to the North British Railway Company by the firm,

The basic elements of a township were slowly added, although in the early days a sense of rural isolation was present. This is perhaps illustrated by a comment in the shipyard diary for 23 October 1874 – 'Terrific storm last night. *Vulcan* not down from Glasgow and no communication with Renfrew' In 1881, the arrival of American manufacturer I M Singer & Co.,[218] placed even greater strains on an already inadequate infrastructure. Singer purchased 46 acres of ground at Kilbowie, a short distance from the shipyard, and in the next four years, erected a manufacturing plant for the production of sewing machines. By the end of 1885, 5,000 people were employed. The budding town became the fastest growing in the United Kingdom and by 1900, had a population of almost 20,000. In 1886, James Roger Thomson instigated the successful move to establish a Burgh which included Dalmuir, Yoker and Clydebank. On 18 November 1886 the Burgh of Clydebank came into existence. At the election of commissioners in December, James Roger Thomson was voted in as Provost.

A study of John Grant from shipyard records. Grant served with the company as secretary from 1847 until his accidental death in 1897 when he fell into the Forth and Clyde Canal and drowned.

SLUMP

The shipbuilding industry suffered from periodic slumps in demand which could be triggered for a number of reasons. The high cost of coal in the mid 1870s resulted in falling demand for new steam tonnage. Ten years earlier, the American Civil War initially induced ship owners to be cautious in placing new orders.

The slump of 1874/78 prompted John Grant to write to Charles Gairdner in November 1875 asking for an extension to the overdraft of £15,000.

> 'to enable us to keep our workmen (especially those in our houses) employed on short time, until fresh contracts come in . . . it is only the extreme scarcity of orders that has obliged us to ask this concession in the meantime.'[219]

To obviate the high cost of coal, ship owners returned to using sailing vessels and during 1875 to 1878, fifteen sailing ships were booked. This must have been a last resort, as they provided no work whatsoever for the engine works. In 1876 the only steam ship contracts were two gunboats for the Admiralty. These vessels *Firebrand* and *Firefly* of the Forester Class were only 125 feet in length and of 455 displacement tons. In December 1875, Grant wrote to

John Burns declining the offer to build yet another sailing ship:

> 'We have yours of today with enclosures (specification of sailing ship): this will be given to James Roger immediately on return, but I would beg meanwhile to say that I fear . . . that we must deny ourselves the honour of tendering for these ships. We have contracted within the last few days for 5 sailing ships of large size which is quite beyond our requirements in that way in the meantime: we want steamers, not ships, as our engine shops are in a starving condition.'[220]

Inevitably, the dearth of suitable contracts led to a further deterioration in the financial position of the business with losses of £53,012 recorded over four years since 1872.[221] Nevertheless, the yard was busy during 1876. No fewer than thirteen vessels were laid down nine of which were sailing ships. The most impressive ship of this period was the 2,472 ton *Loudoun Castle* launched for Thomas Skinner's China and East Indies service on 19 October. The largest vessel in Skinner's fleet, *Loudoun Castle* had compound engines of 2,740 ihp giving her a service speed of 13 knots to enable her to make the voyage to China in under 35 days.

In August, management succeeded in introducing the piecework system of payment to the joiners despite union advice to the contrary. This was achieved by sub-contracting joiner work to outside firms who quoted for the work and employed joiners as necessary.[222]

In the summer of 1876, the shipyard diary recorded an event which was to become a Clydebank ritual for decades to come. The unpaid summer holiday lasted for ten days, after which work was due to resume at 6.30am on the morning of Monday 24 July. By 10am, the machinery in the yard had been switched off because many men had not returned and most of those who did had left again. A notice was posted at the main gate stating that the works would remain closed until 9.45am on the 27th.[223] This dilatory return to work occurred regularly at the summer or 'Fair' holiday and at the 'New Year' holiday.

By the end of 1876 the yard was again on short time working with a 7.30 am start and 4.45pm finish. Normal winter working hours were 7am until 5.15pm with half-hour meal breaks at 9.30am and 2pm. Saturday was a normal working day. To maximise daylight, summer working hours were different. Work started at 6.30am and ended at 5.30pm with two three quarter hour breaks at 9am and 2pm.[224]

Early in 1877, the shipwrights asked for an increase of

10%. The carpenters followed, demanding 15%. On 5 April 1877, the carpenters went on strike. The employers replied with a lockout affecting all trades which took effect from 19 May. All shipyard workers except pieceworkers, apprentices and foremen were paid off. At Clydebank, the lockout did not end until 24 September when a resumption was made on the old terms in the understanding that the question of

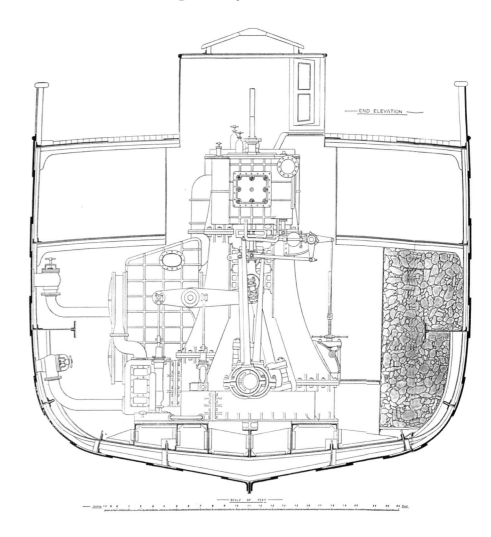

wages would be re-examined in six months time. This damaging dispute further compromised operation of the yard and the gunboats *Firefly* and *Firebrand* had to be taken to Bowling harbour for completion by joiners.[225] In August 1877, in the midst of this difficult labour period and a trade depression, the order for what would become one of the best loved of all Clyde paddle steamers was announced. This was *Columba* built for a cost of £28,500 and capable of a speed of 19.5 knots. Completed less than a year later, *Columba* operated on the Glasgow to Ardrishaig route carrying professional classes to their country houses and shooting lodges.

A section through the single screw steamer Loudoun Castle *completed in 1877 for Thomas Skinner. The size of her compound engines relative to the hull is clearly shown as are the coal-bunkers at right. The engine developed 2,790ihp for a speed of 13.5 knots.*

By June 1878, with trade still in a very depressed state, the employers had decided to take the opportunity to increase the working week and drive wages down. The working week stood at 51 hours as a consequence of events in 1871 when action across the country resulted in the adoption of the 54-hour week with no reduction in wage rates. These conditions had been won relatively easily and in the

The paddle steamer Columba, *completed in 1878, one of the fastest and considered by many to be one of the finest of the Clyde steamers.*

following year, 1872, when unemployment was all but non-existent, Clyde employers went further and acceded to the 51-hour week. When the issue of wages came to be considered in 1878, far from offering an increase, the employers demanded a cut of 7.5% and a return to the 54-hour week. With unemployment running at 9%, all trades with the exception of the boilermakers gave in to the employers' demands. The boilermakers struck, and continued alone until February 1879 when they too returned on the employers' terms.

In July 1877, Andrew Burns employment with the Company ended. Burns had been an employee from 1847 and the shipyard manager since 1851. On his last day, he walked round the works to say farewell to those in the yard. His replacement was Samuel Crawford.

Despite the depression, Clydebank managed to lay down ten hulls in 1878 and five in the following year. These included important orders from Cunard for *Gallia* and *Trojan* for the Union Steam Ship Co. At 4,809 gross tons and a length of 450 feet overall, *Gallia* she was designed principally for comfort and not speed. *Gallia* had richly decorated first class accommodation with Japanese panelling, oak

parquetry flooring and the copious use of onyx. Her compound engines developed 5,300 ihp to give her a service speed of 15 knots for which 98 tons of coal was consumed each day.

On 3 November 1879, John Burns, Chairman of Cunard, wrote to The Times in response to speculation that Cunard were contemplating construction of a steamship of greater size and power.

'it may interest the public to know that my partners and I have just concluded a contract with Messrs James & George Thomson, by which that firm is to build on the Clyde, for our fleet, a screw steamship, the size of which will be exceeded only by that of the Great Eastern, whilst the speed will be greater than that of any ocean steamship afloat.'[226]

The ship was *Servia* of 7,500 tons, set to be the flagship of the Cunard fleet.

Despite this activity, the Company remained unprofitable. The removal to Dalmuir, the depressed market and lack of employment for the Finnieston Works ensured that the run of losses continued. The Company wrote to the Union Bank in December 1874, November 1875 and March 1876 to ask for an increase in borrowing limit which, by January 1876, had reached £90,000 from the previous years limit of £50,000.[227] The lockout of 1877 provoked more difficulties forcing the request for a further £20,000. In a letter to James Roger in August 1877, Charles Gairdner wrote testily - 'The bank will let you have the extension of £20,000 on your account temporarily and I hope that it will be not long needed'[228] By October 1879 the overdraft had risen to £134,000. The dislocation caused to the business in moving the shipyard interrupted the flow of work and results as measured in output tons were disappointing. Over the years 1871 to 1881, J & G Thomson, with 126,465 tons managed only sixth place behind Elder & Co. (245,791 tons) Denny & Brothers (181,392 tons), Alexander Stephen (159,484 tons), Cairds (159,278 tons) and Barclay Curle (128,700 tons). Nevertheless, some significant and sophisticated ships were built. *Servia* was launched on 1 March 1881 amidst scenes that would be repeated over and over again at Clydebank for the next 80 years. The shipyard was packed to capacity with spectators, as were the fields to either side of and opposite the Works. At 1.15pm, Mrs John Burns, wife of Cunard's Chairman, cut the rope which freed the last of the dogshores, sending *Servia* into the Clyde. At the luncheon held afterwards, James Roger Thomson toasted *Servia* '. . .

In asking you to drink this toast I would express

the hope that *Servia*, the first of a new type of vessel for the Cunard Company , and the others to follow, may prove as successful and as much a credit to all concerned as the many ships we have already built for them.'

In recognition of the importance of *Servia*, the Glasgow society paper 'The Baillie' ran a feature on James Roger Thomson guaranteed to discourage

Steam Ship Co.; *Thames* for P&O and Claymore for MacBrayne. *Servia* was safely berthed in Glasgow Harbour having her engines and boilers fitted. Shortly after 9pm on 18 April, residents in the township were alarmed when the Works steam horn blew, signalling the discovery of a fire in the sawmill. The watchman immediately telegraphed the central office of the Glasgow Fire Brigade for assistance:

recruitment into the industry.

'Few positions in active life can be more harassing than the management of a large shipbuilding and engineering concern, and if some of our (readers) could have some glimpses of the arcana of such a business as that of the Thomsons, the sight would simply cause them to stand aghast. Fierce competition in trade, never-ending troubles and difficulties with workmen, increasingly exacting requirements in every department, contingencies of weather, rises and falls in prices, casualties of all kinds, these are the trials the shipbuilder has to meet and combat, and that incessantly.[229]

FIRE!

By April 1881 Clydebank shipyard was busy with seven vessels on the stocks *Aurania, Pavonia* and *Catalonia* for Cunard; *Spartan* and *Moor* for the Union

'From J & G Thomson Clyde Bank, to Glasgow Central Fire Brigade.

"Terrible fire in yard; send steam fire-engines at once; as many as possible. Wire reply when you will be at once"

The reply was, to the presumed astonishment of the sender:

'From Bryson, Glasgow to Thomson, Clyde Bank'
"Cannot attend fire. Try and get Partick Brigade engine"

'From Thomson, Clyde Bank to Bryson Glasgow
"For anysake try and send some steam fire-engines; it is a fearful fire and may extend over yard. Expenses will be paid"[230]

The Glasgow Fire Brigade would not turn out as Dalmuir was outwith its operational area.

As the blaze spread to the adjoining four storey high Joiner Shop, a messenger was sent on horseback to Partick Police Station from where he telegraphed the

The Cunard liner Servia *which at 505 feet (153 metres) in length and 7,392gt, represented another leap in the size of Atlantic liners. Her completion was delayed when a fire in the joiner shop on 18 April 1881 destroyed many of her fittings.*

fire brigades at Elder's Fairfield Works and Lobnitz's works at Renfrew. Meanwhile Thomson's own fire tender had turned out assisted later by the arrival of tenders from Partick and Renfrew. By midnight, the Joiners Shop was engulfed in flames fierce enough to be visible from the east end of Glasgow nine miles away. A crowd of 6,000 gathered to watch as the fire was fought and eventually quenched at 3am. The

The Works firebrigade comprising men from shipyard departments stand by their fire tender in this photograph taken in 1884.

Joiners Shop was gutted and with it went most of the fittings for *Servia*, *Catalonia* and other vessels being built in the yard. James Roger Thomson was summoned from his house at Dowanhill and estimated that losses of materials, machinery, fittings and buildings amounted to £35,000. Although the Company was insured, the blow was a serious one and set back the building programme for all vessels in the yard. With the Company under great pressure to manufacture fittings lost in the fire, the joiners, with an acute sense of timing, struck on 27 April for a rise of 7.5%. The Company had little alternative but to comply and the joiners returned to work on 4 May having achieved their objective.[231]

More bad luck overtook the Company when the South Eastern Railway Company refused to accept the *Duchess of Edinburgh*, as she did not fulfil contract conditions. Completed in October 1880 for the Folkestone - Boulogne service, *Duchess of Edinburgh* was of 812 gross tons with compound engines of 2,750 ihp. James Roger wrote to the owners with the

following proposal. 'We will take the ship to Deptford and have everything made perfect and strong and as soon as completed we will run her as often across the channel on our own responsibility as you may require and test her in every way to your entire satisfaction.' Unfortunately, the letter does not explain in what respect the ship was deficient, although it seems reasonable to assume that it was in speed. The railway company accepted this offer without waiving their right to reject the ship and have the purchase price returned with interest 'if the steamer should again fail within a period of 6 months'[232] A loss of £5,000 was made against this contract.[233] After one year of service, the railway company sold the ship to Manx Line who renamed her *Manx Queen*.

REORGANISATION

In comparison with the fully integrated works of Fairfield and Harland & Wolff, Thomson's separate engine works and shipyard seven miles apart was proving to be highly inefficient. Endemic loss making throughout the 1870s must be partially attributed to the high overheads that resulted. The sums required to merge production on one site were large, and initially, the Thomsons wanted to raise the capital by converting the firm into a Joint Stock Company. A report which considered flotation was prepared by two leading Glasgow firms of accountants in 1882.[234] The report looked at three main elements:

1. Capital of the Proposed Company

This was estimated at £300,000, based on the valuations of the existing works by Peter Denny, the Dumbarton shipbuilder. He valued the shipyard and engine works at £235,000 to which was added the cost of £39,000 for the removal of the Finnieston Works to Dalmuir and working capital at £36,000.

2. Capability of the Works over other Works

Peter Denny was asked by the accountants to compare the cost sheets of two identical ships, *Thames* and *Clyde*, which were built by Thomson at Dalmuir and Denny at Dumbarton. Denny found the costs in carpenter's timber at Dalmuir to be 'out of all idea of right' and in the total for wages 'considerable differences in excess of ours.' He conceded, however, that his yard had excellent building weather and that they were able to press ahead with the work before the cost of wages had risen. He also found that charges in the engine department at Dumbarton were heavier than those at Finnieston. However, this was hardly a conclusive comparison as any number of variables over such a narrow sample, could affect an individual contract.

3. Reduction in Costs through concentration of Works at one Site

James Roger Thomson estimated that savings through the removal of the engine works and introduction of the railway into the Works to be about £15,000 per annum. This figure was based on an output of 20,000 tons of shipping which he thought the works would be fully capable of turning out annually when concentrated at Dalmuir. These costs amounted to over £14,500 per annum added to which was an expected saving of £3,000 through combining management at one site.

The manager of the Finnieston engine works, John Parker, was asked to submit a report on 'Saving Fitting and Finishing Engines & Boilers when all Combined at Shipyard' His report made a forceful argument for integration of the two works.

> '. . . I am convinced they (the savings) are so many and so important that I could not exaggerate either but very much the reverse. It is undoubtedly principally to their being so fortunately placed that Messrs Elder & Co. are able to show yearly so large an output and no doubt both them and Stephen must manage to complete their ships much more economically from the same cause.
>
> I ought to be at the works in Finnieston Street the most part of every day, and at the same time I am almost as much wanted at the shipyard but as this is impossible of performance, it is clear my duties must be imperfectly performed and this also applies to the outside foremen to some extent and likewise a number of the men such as brass finishers etc. . . Of course before the engine works should be removed to Clydebank and even before either them or the boilermaking could be managed properly a sufficient number of workmen's houses must be erected and indeed even at present we are labouring under great difficulties at the early hour at which the steamer leaves Glasgow in the morning is the cause of a great many absentees in fact about 30% are on an average absent and this makes us only too glad to employ indifferent hands as the best men not even for better pay will join the squad at the shipyard and as the absentees are mostly tradesmen, the labourers are not kept so well employed as they otherwise would. I mention these matters to show that there are losses going on at present which cannot be reckoned up with precision but for going to the shipyard, men receive one penny per hour extra and as there are about 160 men on an average this gives £36 per week then I reckon we could do as much with one fourth less men this gives £54 per week and the cost of carriage amounts to about £6 per week. So in all a ship like the *Savonia* has her cost increased by about £500 and as her indicated horsepower is about 4,000 being about a sixth part of our whole output we get a total loss of about £3,000 per annum. . . Of

One of the very few photographs showing Thomson's Finnieston Engine Works. The paddle steamer on the left is Bonnie Princess *built at Rutherglen by TB Seath. She is seen here having her engines, constructed by A Campbell & Co., and fitted by the crane which the Thomsons built for the Clyde Navigation Trust in 1855. Thomson's works are immediately in front of the bowsprit of the ship on the right.*

course but for the fortunate circumstances that are occurring at this time such as the completion of Clyde Bank railway and the establishment of Singers factory I could not have seen my way to hope for men settling in such numbers as we require, but being as I have stated, I consider your proposal a very proper one.'

The case for concentrating activities at Clydebank was overwhelming. Preparations for conversion of the business to limited liability did not proceed because of poor financial performance. The accumulation of trading losses since 1872 had effectively exhausted the capital of the business. Nevertheless, and quite surprisingly given the circumstances, work started as early as May 1878 on the construction of a fitting-out basin, the first step towards the realisation of the single integrated site. By December, a dredger and two hoppers were excavating the new basin which was about 600 feet long but limited to a width of 100 feet by lack of ground to the west.

The first vessel to use the fitting-out basin was the *Lake Winnipeg* for the Canada Steam Ship Co. on 26 May 1879. This development was sound enough but by itself inadequate as ships still had to go to Glasgow to have their machinery fitted.

The re-siting of the entire Finnieston Street Works at Clydebank formed the next part of the capital programme, followed by the purchase of an additional sixteen acres of ground from the Barns of Clyde Estate. Transfer of the boiler shop from Finnieston to Clydebank began in April 1880. This shop covered 6,000 square yards and was situated at the north end of the Works butting on to the back of Clydebank Terrace otherwise known as 'Tamson's Tenements', spoiling the uninterrupted view of the yard and the Clyde which the tenants had previously enjoyed. In July 1883, negotiations commenced for the purchase of an additional sixteen acres of ground from the Grace Hamilton Estate to enable westward expansion of the works. These negotiations were completed in the following year and the ground was immediately used to accommodate part of the new engine shops on which work had been started in 1883. This phase of the programme, which had begun with the new boiler shop, was completed in February 1884 with the inauguration of the new engine works. These Works were described as the largest of their kind in existence, designed for an annual output of 40,000 ihp of steam machinery.

The Union Bank had little alternative but to finance this programme. In September 1882 the Thomsons received an advance of £115,000 secured against the Finnieston Street property, tenements, shares in ships and a partners' guarantee. In the following year they received a further advance of £50,000 secured by an additional partners' guarantee. The total indebtedness to the Union Bank now stood at £300,000. In addition, the partners owed the George Thomson Trust, i.e., their mother, brother and sisters, a further £72,000.[235] In effect, the Bank had control of the business assets as security for borrowings and insisted that William McKinnon be appointed to manage the accounts and supervise improvements in the management of the Works.[236] In May 1883, McKinnon reported on the 'Affairs of J & G Thomson with suggestions for a re-arrangement of the finances of the firm and for the better management and conduct of the business generally'. The report attributes a serious loss of £42,732 for 1882 to the reasons already stated in the 1882 report and reiterates that losses were also due 'in great measure to the want of really capable and efficient management.'[237] By July, news of endemic loss making gained currency and the London office manager of the Union Bank wrote to Gairdner to say

that he had been overwhelmed with enquiries about repeated rumours of the failure of the business of J & G Thomson.[238]

William McKinnon's dissatisfaction with the commercial operation of the Works led to Robert Carswell, cashier at Clydebank, being sent to the shipyard at Barrow to study their commercial system. Carswell reported back on 26 June with details of the methods employed at Barrow finding:

> '. . . it is in many ways admirable, but it is much too costly and somewhat complicated in the process of obtaining results - I think the groundwork of our system is preferable if it was as well organised and this could be done in the manner I have sketched and with a comparatively small addition to the present staff'.

One of McKinnon's first acts was to place an advert in the journal 'Engineering':

> 'Wanted. A thoroughly qualified manager for a large shipbuilding yard'

McKinnon's plan was to appoint a General Manager who would be senior to the shipyard and engine works managers but under the Managing Director, James Roger Thomson. In his search for such a manager, McKinnon was assisted by James Currie of the shipping line James Currie & Co., who wrote to Charles Gairdner recommending the appointment of John Paul Wilson as the General Manager at Clydebank. Wilson was a man of considerable experience. He had received his training at Denny & Rankin's in Dumbarton before holding senior positions at Palmers, Napiers and the Barrow works. Wilson was appointed General Manager in 1883 for a period of five years at a salary of £1,250 increasing by £100 per annum.[239]

The Bank had resolved in the long term to prepare the business for flotation. This would provide the best chance of recovering the capital sunk in both the business and the Thomson brothers personally whilst securing the future of the Works.

By 1882, transport links with the Works had been greatly improved. In March the tramway was extended from Partick, to the west of Glasgow, to Clydebank replacing the horse-drawn bus which the Company had been running since August 1875.[240] The river continued to be used as a means of transporting people to work and steamers were chartered from several owners for this purpose. A new train service from Queen Street Station in Glasgow began in December 1881 which left at 5.30am. However, by June of the following year this train was discontinued owing to insufficient use. On

14 September 1882, direct connection to the main line was made and the first train carrying materials entered the yard.[241] The Clydebank & Yoker Railway, of which James Roger Thomson was a director, was formally opened in December 1882.

In November 1883, the Employers Association acted to reduce wages in view of the general lack of orders and in the following month the ironworkers had to accept a 10% reduction. A few weeks later on 1 January 1884, the 10% reduction was applied to all classes of workmen. At this time the Clydebank yard employed 1,500 men.[242]

The cost of building and equipping the new engine works was £20,865.[243] With a full order book, the Clydebank Works could now employ up to 4,500 men, 3,000 in the shipyard and 1,500 in the engine works.[244] Completed engines and boilers could now be taken the short distance to the fitting-out basin

where a set of sheerlegs had been installed in December 1883. The sheerlegs, made by Taylor of Birkenhead, were capable of lifting 100 tons to an outreach of 57 feet.

In July 1886, the fitting-out basin was broadened to 300 feet utilising the new ground to the west. The Works now occupied an area of 46 acres making it the second largest in area on the Clyde after Fairfield. These developments transformed the business into an efficient, well organised shipbuilding and marine engineering establishment and finally removed the burden of heavy overheads.

Shipbuilding was a hazardous and often lethal activity. Working conditions in the shops or at the berths were often appalling. Simple safety measures like handrails were not considered. Thus, negotiating staging high on the side of a hull or openings in a deck could result in injury or death. For survival, it

An interesting perspective engraving of Clydebank shipyard from the March 1885 edition of Iron magazine showing the new engine and boiler works at the head of the fitting-out basin.

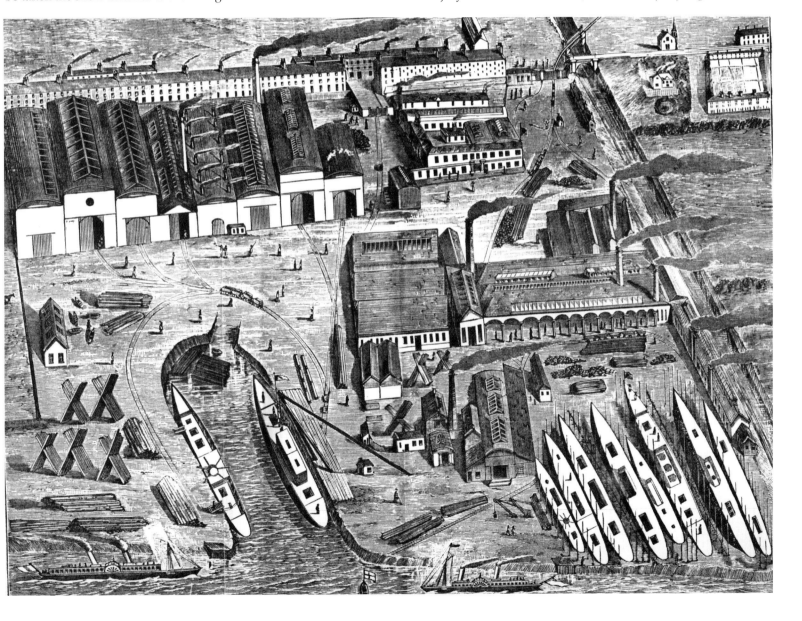

was necessary to have a well developed sense of activities in the immediate working area. Work proceeded often in poorly ventilated, confined compartments, lit only by candle light or paraffin lamps. In the shipyard and engine shops, machines driven by exposed drive belts from line shafting operated without guards. Accidents happened with great regularity. The following entries from the Shipyard Diary and the Dumbarton Herald illustrate several from the 1880s and 90s.

Archie Nisbet
Archie Nisbet killed today in Boiler Shop caught in shafting.[245] 'Nisbet lived in Cavendish Street, Glasgow. His head was much mutilated before he could be released.'[246]

Charles McKechnie
'Last Wednesday night a man named Charles McKechnie, employed at the sawmill in Clydebank shipyard, accidentally came into contact with a circular saw, and had his hand severely damaged, two of his fingers being taken off.'[247]

McFarlane
'Last Wednesday an apprentice engineer named McFarlane, belonging to Glasgow and employed in Messrs. J & G Thomson's shipbuilding yard, fell from a scaffolding to the ground, a distance of 25 feet. Several of McFarlane's ribs were broken and

he was otherwise internally injured.'[248]

John Meek
'John Meek, boilermaker, while coming ashore from No 222 at stopping time jumped from one of the steel doors instead of going out by the gangway. While jumping his head came into contact with the top of the door and he fell into the dock. He was taken out dead supposed.'[249]

Philip Derby
'The other day while a craneman, Philip Derby, in the employment of Messrs. J & G Thomson, shipbuilders, was attending to a travelling crane in the engine shop, his arm got entangled in the machinery, with the result that the sleeve of his shirt and semmit was torn off, as also a large piece of flesh from the shoulder to the elbow. He was attended to by Dr Stevenson[250] who ordered his removal to the Infirmary.'[251]

James Faulds
'A man named James Faulds was engaged letting off foul air from one of the compartments (on *Reine Regente*) situated at the stern of the vessel, and in doing so had unscrewed the nuts in a manhole plate, and had accidentally brought the light which he carried into contact with the foul air. An explosion followed, the manhole plate was blown in, and the stern pin plate near the propeller burst. The water rushed in, and before any measures could be taken had caused the cruiser to sink several feet.'[252]

John Woods
'A man named John Woods, a borer employed on tank edge of No 240 was killed today at 12.45 by a wooden roller used by fitters falling from lower deck and striking him on head.[253]
'It appears the unfortunate man was engaged in the hold of the vessel, while on the upper deck a number of platers were pulling across the deck one of the ship's iron plates on a wooden roller. A nut, it is stated, caused the roller to spring out under the plate. It fell into the hold, and striking the lower deck, it fell onto the right side of the unfortunate man's head, rendering him insensible. He was conveyed to the general store of the works, and Dr Jas. Stevenson, who was immediately in attendance, found that he had expired from a fracture of the skull. The deceased was only 26 years of age, and leaves a widow and two young children to mourn his loss.'[254]

Robert Anderson
'While a squad of riveters were engaged on the hull of one of the large Transatlantic steamers

A plan of the works in 1884 showing the new engine and boiler shops. The fitting-out basin has been constructed but severely restricted in width by the western boundary of the site. The purchase of an additional 16 acres of ground in 1883 made it possible to rebuild the basin to a width of 300 feet (91.5 metres).

James & George Thomson 1884

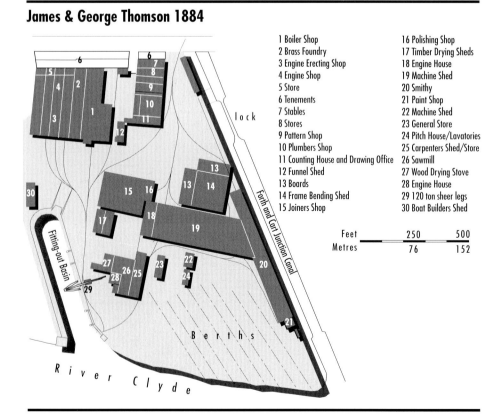

1 Boiler Shop
2 Brass Foundry
3 Engine Erecting Shop
4 Engine Shop
5 Store
6 Tenements
7 Stables
8 Stores
9 Pattern Shop
10 Plumbers Shop
11 Counting House and Drawing Office
12 Funnel Shed
13 Boards
14 Frame Bending Shed
15 Joiners Shop
16 Polishing Shop
17 Timber Drying Sheds
18 Engine House
19 Machine Shed
20 Smithy
21 Paint Shop
22 Machine Shed
23 General Store
24 Pitch House/Lavatories
25 Carpenters Shed/Store
26 Sawmill
27 Wood Drying Stove
28 Engine House
29 120 ton sheer legs
30 Boat Builders Shed

Feet	250	500
Metres	76	152

presently being built for the Inman Line, a plank slipped from the crossbeams, precipitating one of their number, Robert Anderson, to the ground, a distance of 20 feet. He fell on his head, sustaining severe injuries. Dr Stevenson was at once in attendance, and ordered his removal home. Small hope is entertained for his recovery. Anderson is a married man residing at Belmont Street, Clydebank, and has a large family of young children.'[255]

'A man named Robert Anderson, a riveter employed on the shell of No 240 fell from staging at bow to ground a distance of from 18 to 25 feet today at 12 o'clock and broke his neck. He died at 5pm.'[256]

William Kerr

'On Monday morning a very sad accident befell a young man named William Kerr, helper, Clyde Street, while working with an iron plate in the shipyard of J & G Thomson. Kerr was handling a plate when it accidentally came to the ground and knocked his thumb off. Dr Stevenson, who was called in, ordered his removal to the Western Infirmary.'[257]

David White

'While a man named David White, a driller, residing in Belmont Street Clydebank, was engaged working on a recent evening, on board H M gunboat 'Phoenix' - at present undergoing repairs at Messrs Thomsons' yard - the flame of his lamp caught some naptha which had been spilt, and his clothes were immediately ignited. Before the flames could be subdued his clothes were literally burned off his body, and the poor fellow was found to be very seriously burned. He was removed at once to the Glasgow Western Infirmary where he lingered in agony till Wednesday when he succumbed. The deceased, who was about 28 years of age, was married.'[258]

'An accident happily not attended with serious results occurred today at about 1.40pm during an experimental forced-draught trial in *Shark* while at moorings in the dock. Several men in one of the stokeholds were slightly burned on the hands and arms in consequence of the flames rushing out through the furnace doors. The operations were temporarily suspended.'[259]

NEW MEN AND NEW IDEAS

Criticisms of the management must to a large extent be borne by the two partners, James Roger Thomson

and George Thomson. James had overall responsibility for the firm. George's role is less clear. New and recent appointments had, however, laid the foundation for a core of talented managers. As General Manager, J P Wilson had seniority over Samuel Crawford, Shipyard Manager and John Parker, Engine Works Manager. In July 1880, John Harvard Biles became the first naval architect to be employed at Clydebank. This was a reflection of the growing influence of scientific ship design.[260] Ship design had hitherto been a rather rule-of-thumb activity taking the most recently completed ship as the model for the succeeding one. The latter half of the nineteenth century witnessed major advances in the application of scientific principles to the practical problems of ship design. The work of William Froude in exploring resistance and stability established naval architecture as a science. At Clydebank, Biles set about applying these new ideas.

Two key appointments were made in the engine works during 1888. The first was John Gibb Dunlop as Engine Works Manager following a period of nine years as superintendent engineer for the Orient Line. Dunlop trained as an engineer with Randolph & Elder becoming Engineering Manager at Fairfield in 1872. He would later become Managing Director at Clydebank from 1897 to 1909.[261] The other was Thomas Bell, a young graduate of the Royal Naval Engineering College at Plymouth who joined the engineering staff. Poor eyesight had prevented Bell from pursuing a career in the navy but this did not mask his obvious abilities and he too was destined to play a major role in the management of Clydebank.[262] The pursuit of more efficient marine engines was a ceaseless activity. The triple expansion engine attributed to Dr. Alexander Kirk of Fairfield, was destined to be the successor to the compound engine. These engines extracted more energy from steam by expanding it not twice as in the compound engine, but in three stages. To work successfully, the triple expansion engine required steam of a higher working pressure than generally available. Kirk's first triple expansion engine was fitted in the steamer *Propontis* of 1874 although an unreliable boiler limited the overall success of the machinery. It was not until the advent of *Aberdeen* of 1881 that the triple expansion engine allied to a reliable 'Scotch' type boiler delivering steam at 125Psi, demonstrated a significant improvement over compounding. The quadruple expansion engine was the logical development of the triple and by the end of the 19th Century, quadruple expansion was the rule for large ships

John Harvard Biles joined the company in 1880 as their first naval architect. He resigned in 1890 but acted as agent to the company, particularly in Japan for many years thereafter. He was appointed to the John Elder Chair of Naval Architecture at the University of Glasgow in 1891.

In the early 1880s, iron gave way to steel as the principal material used in shipbuilding. Steel was not a new material but the Siemens Martin open-hearth process made it economic to produce in large quantities. Steel had ductile qualities which made it superior to wrought iron. The one major disadvantage was the rapidity with which it corroded. To deal with this, an industry based on protective paints and finishes developed. Steel enabled plates of greater dimensions to be prepared and worked which led to the introduction of more powerful and larger plate working machinery.

FIRE AND FORCE

In competition for honours on the North Atlantic, Thomson's main competitors were Fairfield on the Clyde, Harland & Wolff at Belfast and the Barrow Engineering & Shipbuilding Co. at Barrow-in-Furness. During the 1880s, the battle for supremacy on this prestigious route became a purely Clydeside affair between Thomson's and Fairfield. Increasingly, the issue of which was the better ship turned on speed and the ability of engine builders to design machinery capable of generating the maximum horsepower for every ton of coal burned. The express mail steamers built by John Elder at Fairfield were proving almost unassailable. The pace was set by the Guion liner *Arizona*, which captured the Blue Riband in 1879, with a crossing of 7 days 10 hours and 53 minutes. However, great speed was achieved at considerable cost in fuel and, in making one extra knot of speed over *Gallia*, *Arizona* burned an additional 125 tons of coal per day. The next Cunard ship, Thomson's *Servia*, was different. Launched on 1 March 1881, she was designed from the outset to be one step ahead of the competition and in particular of the Fairfield ships built for Guion. The biggest ship afloat excepting *Great Eastern*, *Servia* measured 530 feet (161.6 metres) overall. On trials with engines developing 10,350 ihp she made a speed of 17.85 knots. *Servia* was also the first Cunard vessel to be built of steel, have electric lighting and remotely controlled watertight doors. She did not, however, take the Blue Riband.

At Fairfield the aim of increased speed was met by the construction of ever bigger and more powerful engines. At Clydebank, a slightly different approach was taken. John Biles, influenced by Froude's ideas, became increasingly concerned with the application of more scientific methods in developing the form of a ships hull. In simple terms, this resulted in what was termed the 'fine ended model' where increased

beam amidships tapered to fine lines at either end and helped to reduce the resistance of the hull through the water.[263] *Aurania*, built for Cunard in 1883, developed this principle and, although designed to be half a knot slower than *Servia*, *Aurania* took two hours off *Servia's* best Atlantic crossing of 6 days 23 hours and 57 minutes. At sea, *Aurania* was met by *Oregon*, Guion Line's latest flyer from Fairfield. The Fairfield ship won the contest, taking the Blue Riband at an average speed of 18.05 knots. In 1883, the National Line ordered *America* from Clydebank, and she too was designed with the new hull form. Thomson claimed she was capable of steaming at the same speed as her competitors with little more than half the power and with much the same passenger accommodation.[264]

Record passages across the Atlantic were watched with great interest and, at the height of the *Servia/Arizona* confrontation, both Clydeside shipbuilders felt obliged to write to the Glasgow Herald to correct 'errors' in crossing times accredited to their ships. The actual differences in the time taken to cross the Atlantic were slight and at all times subject to the vagaries of sea and weather. The eventual consensus was that while Fairfield ships were quicker, the Clydebank ships were more fuel-efficient. This leader from the Glasgow Herald makes the point:

'Considerable excitement was caused recently by what substantially amounted to a race across the Atlantic between the Oregon built by John Elder & Co., and the Aurania built by J&G Thomson & Co. The palm of victory was won by the Oregon, which bounded across the Atlantic in the short space of six days, ten hours and ten minutes, making the fastest trip on record, and beating the Aurania by twenty hours. . . The public will not enquire into the conditions of the race, nor will passengers enquire how many tons of coal were burned by these rival 'greyhounds' of the Atlantic. . . Meanwhile the scientific world, and especially that section of it connected with shipbuilding, insists upon discussing the merits of the contest. Each steamer has the same displacement, or a draught of water of 26 feet; but the Aurania has 3 feet more beam, 30 feet less length, and indicates only two-thirds the power. Moreover, she burns less coal per day by one-third than does her successful rival, the Oregon, and yet, in spite of these differences, and especially the economy of fuel, she is not much inferior to the Oregon in speed. . . The expenditure of fire and force seems to us out of proportion with the advantage gained'

DEFECTION

Nevertheless, when it came to ordering succeeding ships for their express Atlantic service in 1883, Cunard turned their back on J&G Thomson and placed the order with Fairfield. This left Clydebank with only one small vessel, the tender *Skirmisher*, to be completed for Cunard. The loss of such an important customer must have been the cause of

The liner America *was built with a new hull form developed by Biles called 'the fine ended model'. Thomson claimed this enabled her to steam at the same speed as her competitors on greatly reduced horsepower. The ship was completed in 1884. On her first eastward crossing of the Atlantic,* America *broke all records completing the voyage in 6 days 14 hours and 18 minutes.*

great dismay to the Clydebank management. Cunard was more than a customer. Their ships were both prestigious and technically advanced.

Both Thomson and Fairfield were at the forefront of shipbuilding and marine engineering in the UK. Cunard's decision to switch to Fairfield might have been taken as verification of Fairfield's better record in building fast ships for the all-important North Atlantic market where the fastest ship attracted both plaudits and passengers. Equally, it may have been rumours of the dire financial straits in which the Company was floundering, or, simply a matter of exercising choice after a long period with one contractor. Whatever the reasons, Cunard's decision to switch must have contributed to the 'rumours of failure' already described and to a loss of confidence in Thomsons generally.

Although Directors' minute books for this period are not available, there is reason to believe that relations between Thomson and Cunard had deteriorated. Between the construction of *Servia* and *Aurania*, two intermediate ships, *Catalonia* and *Pavonia*, were also built for Cunard. All four vessels appear to have been delivered late as the following letters from the Cunard's Secretary indicate:[265]

10 September 1881
'I have received your communication of yesterday's date and feel sure that my directors will regard it as a very unsatisfactory reply to my letter of 7th inst. as it contains no assurance whatever that the Aurania and Pavonia will be delivered within the time specified within their respective contracts. The reference which you make to Servia and Catalonia appears to me singularly unfortunate. According to my instructions the former named vessel is not yet completed or anything like it.'

14 September 1881
' . . . The directors are entirely unable to admit that since you entered into the contracts to build the Aurania and Pavonia the circumstances you narrate have been such as to adequately account for the slowness in the progress of construction of these vessels, and the same remarks apply with equal force to what you urge in respect of the detention of the Catalonia and Servia.

With regard to the Aurania and Pavonia which my letter of the 7th Inst. more particularly alluded, I am to impress upon you that if they are not delivered within the time stipulated for their respective contracts, it will most gravely affect the Company's business, and I am to request that you will favour my directors with such assurances as will relieve their anxiety in this matter.

With regard to the Servia the board are advised that she is by no means completed and furthermore that the work remaining to be done is not being carried out as expeditiously as it might be. I therefore have to request that you will be good enough that you will at once take steps to finish all that remains to be done without further loss of time.'[266]

In the assumption that Thomson was pleading delay caused by the Joiner's Shop fire, Cunard were unimpressed and under the terms of the contract the penalty of £5,000 was deducted for the late delivery of *Servia* in December 1881.[267] An identical sum was

A model of the torpedo cruiser Scout. *The order for this small warship in 1883 marked a turning point in the company's efforts to secure profitable warship work.*

deducted for the late delivery of *Pavonia* in April 1883. Altogether a loss of £13,000 was made on this ship.[268]

During this period of strained relations, an unfortunate event at sea further exacerbated the situation. On her maiden voyage, one of *Aurania's* cylinders collapsed jamming the engine while a short distance from New York and required six tugs to assist her into port. Following a temporary patch-up, the ship sailed back to the Clyde for permanent repairs, where it became clear that the high-pressure cylinder connecting rod had broken. Free from any restraint, the piston and piston rod had been driven through the top of the cast iron cylinder which shattered into pieces. The other end of the connecting rod was driven round by the engine, which was still running at high speed. The rod came crashing down on the iron column which held it in place, tearing a hole seven feet by two feet. Seconds later, with the last of its energy, the rod smashed the cast iron bedplate which supported the engine. The consequences of this might well have been yet further financial difficulties for the Company as the ship was within her guarantee period. The outcome of the independent report into the accident by AD Bryce Douglas, formerly Engineering Director at Fairfield and now Managing Director at Barrow shipyard, was awaited with some apprehension by the Thomsons. Inspection of the broken connecting rod showed that

a faulty weld was to blame. The manufacturer of the connecting rod, the Mersey Steel & Iron Co. was liable and no discredit attached to Clydebank. In September, J P Wilson, firmly in charge at Clydebank, wrote to William McKinnon about this incident and his meeting with John Burns, the Chairman of the Cunard Company:

'I met Mr. Burns today at his office in Jamaica Street concerning the report by Messrs. Bryce and Wallace and on the whole it is what we expected. The condensers about which we were afraid there might be some contention are all right. I find that owing to the arrangement of the machinery it will be necessary to take out the whole of the cylinder and columns but in order to get the work fitted and save time it is better to take the whole thing to the engine shops as it can be much better done there than on the ship. I am glad we have arranged the matter in an amicable spirit. I think we are likely to get an order from Mr. Burns for an iron screw so we may as well keep friendly. I was at Liverpool on Friday awhile and there learned that the present forge company took possession on 18 January 1882 at midnight in that case it is the present company and not the old company who have done the work. I think we ought to lay a claim for £10,000 against them. There will be no difficulty in bringing the thing home to them as there is ample testimony.'[269]

SEND A GUNBOAT

The boom years of the early 1880s were the most productive for Clyde yards. In 1883 an all time record output of 419,664 tons was achieved, a record which was to stand until 1896. The slump which followed, saw that figure plummet to 169,710 tons in 1887. The onset of what was to be the worst recession in shipbuilding until the 1930s coincided with Cunard's departure to Fairfield. Once again, and despite the greatly improved organisation of the works, the future of the yard seemed uncertain. On 1 October 1884, short time working was introduced.[270] The change from boom to slump was mirrored in the results for 1884 and 1885 in which a profit of £20,749 was turned to a loss of £13,572. For the rest of the decade, the Company was only able to break-even or record a small loss.

The situation might have been worse had it not been for the timely arrival of the Admiralty. Despite their almost complete lack of success in previous years, Thomson had continued to tender for Admiralty work. At the end of 1883, the contract for the torpedo cruiser *Scout* of 1,580 tons was won which would prove to be a turning point in the fortunes of the Company. Winning this contract was not so much a question of perseverance as of quoting a low price to get the work. This was followed the year after with contracts for six additional torpedo cruisers to an improved Scout design known as the Archer Class. The general scarcity of work compelled many yards to tender at very low prices and few had more cause than J&G Thomson. Before the Admiralty announced the successful builder for the Archer Class, James Roger wrote to William McKinnon of the Union Bank: 'I have just seen Dunn (of the Admiralty) he tells me our tender is the lowest - we are to get the six but it is not to be decided upon until tomorrow . . . it must not leak out. The next tenders to ours were Laird at £3,000 over ours or £500 a boat"[271] Taking contracts at a loss was not new. At best, the six warships provided

continuity of employment.

In April 1885 with a Russian war scare about to break, James Currie, a director of the Union Bank wrote to Gairdner expressing his concern about the effect this war might have on J&G Thomson:

'The Russian difficulty seems no nearer a solution and I think war can hardly be averted. In that event there will be increased activity on the part of the Admiralty and probably more war vessels will be ordered perhaps of a smaller class. I mention this in as much that I think Thomson should be cautious about taking new work at enhanced prices; and if pressed by the Government to hasten the completion of the Scout cruisers, they must take care that they are reimbursed for the extra cash. It is a matter of comment among shipbuilders that the six scouts have been taken at too low a price and this may be true if the sudden

A detail of the Royal Sovereign Class battleship Ramillies *in 1893, Clydebank's first battleship. The Naval Defence Act of 1889 called for a large fleet expansion programme from which Thomson and a number of other private shipbuilders benefited.*

A view of the fitting-out basin in 1890 showing from left, the Channel steamer Frederica, *the Australian 3rd Class cruisers* Tauranga *and* Ringarooma *and the Japanese cruiser* Chiyoda.

demand of the Government should raise the wages of the workmen. In that case Thomson's must protect themselves by enhanced prices whether for new work or for modifications of the existing contracts'[272]

During the early 1880s, public dissatisfaction at the state of the Navy prompted the Admiralty to embark on additional warship construction in what became

significant effect on the growth of the warship building and armaments industries in the United Kingdom and later set the scene for the formation of large armaments combines. In the interim, however, the market for warships had been transformed. The only immediate benefit to Thomson from the Northbrook Programme was the machinery contract for the cruiser *Aurora* under construction at Pembroke

known as the Northbrook Programme. Although this programme was limited, events abroad, particularly in Russia, and a realisation that the British fleet was not capable of fulfilling colonial commitments, led to the Naval Defence Act of 1889. This Act provided for a greatly increased building programme of 70 ships at a cost of £21.5 million and identified cruisers as the class of warship most urgently required.[273] More importantly, the Act reaffirmed the Two Power Standard, which ensured that the Royal Navy would be maintained at a strength equivalent to the combined strengths of the two next largest fleets - the French and Russian. This commitment had a

Dockyard, tenders for ironclad battleships and belted cruisers having been rejected.

International tensions had the side effect of reviving the possibility of foreign warship orders. Several British shipbuilders already had made significant progress in this market, among them Armstrong's on the Tyne and the Thames Iron Works. Increasingly, James Roger Thomson's time became taken up with sales trips abroad. October 1885 found him in Madrid pursuing work from the Spanish Navy.[274] This resulted in two contracts being placed, the first for a small torpedo boat, *Destructor*, the second for the protected cruiser, *Reina Regente*. The order for the latter was taken in competition with fourteen other yards in Britain, France, Germany and Italy. The ability to guarantee the high speed of 20.5 knots was one of the features of Thomson's design which helped win the contract. In the same year, a trip to St Petersburg secured the contract for the small torpedo boat *Wiborg* for the Imperial Russian Navy. Following an introduction to the Austrian Consulate in Glasgow arranged by William McKinnon,[275] in July 1886, James Roger was in Vienna delivering a tender for a cruiser for the Austro-Hungarian Navy. On this occasion, Thomson was unsuccessful but nevertheless, orders for other warships came flowing in. In 1888 the Admiralty placed an order under the auspices of the Australian Navy for two cruisers, *Ringarooma* and *Tauranga*. One year later, the Imperial Japanese Navy placed the order for the cruiser *Chiyoda*. The contract for the first class cruiser *Blenheim* of the 1887/88 Programme was pursued but not won. The price of £339,000 was not sufficiently competitive to prevent the ship going to the Thames Iron Works.[276] The second class cruisers of the Apollo class, *Terpsichore, Thetis* and *Tribune*, a direct outcome of the 1889 Act, were won at a hull and machinery price of £444,000 for the three. In 1890, the contract for the 14,000ton Royal Sovereign Class battleship *Ramillies* was taken, demonstrating that Clydebank had finally achieved Admiralty recognition as builders of the highest class of naval work. Typically, the percentage of failed tenders was high. In 1889, the Company prepared thirty four tenders of which only three (comprising a total of seven vessels) were successful - *Brazil* for the Brazilian Steam Navigation Co., the Apollo Class cruisers and the steamers *Frederica, Lydia* and *Stella* for the London & South Western Railway. Efforts to win a contract from Canadian Pacific through the submission of seven separate tenders in 1889 failed.[277]

The seven torpedo boat cruisers of the Scout and Archer Class completed by the end of 1886 were of interest mechanically as they employed the Forced Draught System invented by Glasgow based engineer James Howden. This system permitted more efficient combustion of coal in the boilers which, in turn, delivered steam of greater pressure and higher temperature to the pistons. The result was a substantial increase in power which was illustrated in the trials of *Cossack* in October 1886. The use of this system increased ihp from 3,500 to 4,200.[278] During this period, the manager of the Union Bank of Scotland, Charles Gairdner, and his appointee at Clydebank, William McKinnon, took an extraordinary interest in the progress of individual ship contracts. McKinnon wrote Gairdner a series of letters throughout the 1880s keeping him abreast of developments at the yard. Increasingly, the letters introduced a technical element. In one letter to Gairdner, McKinnon passed on technical gossip concerning the installation of engines of the cruiser *Aurora* at Pembroke Dockyard. This was to the effect that Harland & Wolff's engines for the torpedo cruisers *Serpent* and *Racoon* had been a complete failure, making only 3,700 ihp instead of 4,500 despite forced draught. McKinnon added 'We had trouble enough with the Archer Class of cruiser with boiler leakage but the engines were perfect and in this department the Thomson's have always stood highest'[279]

RETURN TO THE NORTH ATLANTIC

Throughout this period of naval work, merchant vessels were not ignored and a number of contracts were booked for British and foreign owners. In April 1887, the contract to make alterations and additions to the International Line steamer *Ohio* was secured and the work carried out in the fitting-out basin.[280] If James Roger Thomson was smarting at the departure of Cunard to Fairfield, he was admirably recompensed in 1887 when he won the contract from the Inman International Steam Ship Co., for the *City of New York* and *City of Paris*. Both ships enabled the Company to return to the highest class of merchant work and placed them once again at the forefront of marine engineering technology. The Inman Line gave the yard a free hand in their design and the result was handsome, magnificently appointed and technically advanced ships. The first vessels to exceed 10,000 tons since *Great Eastern*, they set new standards in subdivision, incorporated anti-rolling tanks, employed electric lighting and had a twin screw machinery arrangement which employed triple expansion engines. The building of these ships presented unforeseen difficulties. When *City of New York* was launched on 15 March 1888 by Lady Randolph Churchill, the ship grounded at the mouth of the River Cart and could not be refloated for some time. Prior to the launch of these vessels, the fitting-out basin was increased in length to 700 feet. In May, when *City of New York* was being manoeuvred in the basin at four o'clock in the morning, control of the vessel was lost and she started to drift into the river. Her bowsprit became enmeshed with the sheerlegs on the dockside and pulled this huge crane into the basin. Damage was confined to the ships wooden bowsprit and figurehead. The sheerlegs were destroyed and a new set of 120 tons capacity was built and installed by Thomson in the following year. Despite these difficulties, *City of New York* was built in the remarkably short time of only one year and ran trials in July 1889. The complexity of the machinery caused numerous mechanical breakdowns, particularly to the circulating pumps, and it was

'virtually unsinkable' because of the subdivision of the hull into eleven watertight compartments. Another development, the adoption of twin screws, not only allowed for the delivery of more thrust and therefore more speed, it theoretically enabled the ship to maintain passage should one of the engines break down. Much was made of the latter point which was immediately challenged on the high seas. On 19

Right
One of the earliest photographs taken at Clydebank, showing the keel and bottom of the Inman liner City of New York *on 19 July 1887 over five weeks after keel laying.*

Opposite page
Work proceeding on the inner bottom of the City of New York *showing plates being 'screwed up' by hand prior to riveting. A hydraulic riveter suspended from a counterbalanced trolley is in use in the background.*

some time before she was able to demonstrate her true capabilities at sea.

The mechanical difficulties encountered by *City of New York* during her guarantee period extinguished any prospect of making money on the contract. The scale of these losses exceeded even the Bank's most pessimistic expectations.

> 'The long voyage of the 'City' was caused by sundry small mishaps in connection with the machinery and those dreadful pumps. A good deal will have to be done on her return to Liverpool and I fear one must make up one's minds to see all the profits disappear . . .'[281]

Contemporary descriptions refer to these ships being

March 1890, *City of Paris* left New York complete with 687 passengers, a crew of 373, and a full cargo including 2,000 bales of cotton, leather, bacon and cheese. On 23 March, while steaming at high speed, she suffered a fracture of the starboard propeller shaft. The engine began to race 'and they heard a terrible crash in the starboard engine room'.[282] The sudden and complete disintegration of the starboard engine followed, sending large pieces of metal flying in all directions. These fragments punctured the bulkhead of the port engine room flooding the space and causing the port engine to be stopped. *City of Paris* lay completely dead in the water and required several tugs to tow her into Queenstown (now Cobh).

The City of New York's *stern and shaft bracket castings bolted together and awaiting transportation to the building berth on 15 September 1887.*

City of New York's *magnificent dining saloon. The arch rose 22 feet (6.7 metres) high from deck level, was 45 feet (16.4 metres) wide and 70 feet (21.3 metres) long.*

The accident was important enough to warrant a Board of Trade enquiry, which was held on 24 June 1890 at St George's Hall, Liverpool. The enquiry found that the fracture was caused by premature wear of the lignum vitae bushes in the shaft bracket. The report nevertheless found that 'she has proved herself to be one of the finest and safest vessels in the Mercantile Marine.'[283]

Once repaired, *City of Paris* performed magnificently and took the Blue Riband at an average speed of 19.95 knots westward and 20.02 eastward.[284] Both ships were a triumph for their builders and particularly for J H Biles, John Dunlop and Samuel Crawford. In winning the Blue Riband they gave the Company the satisfaction of beating the Cunard liners *Umbria* and *Etruria* which

had been built at Fairfield a few years earlier.

RICH & FAMOUS

The growing reputation of the firm resulted in visits to the Works by the rich and famous. In August 1888 Prince Henry of Battenberg sailed up the Clyde on the Royal Yacht *Victoria and Albert* and into the basin at Clydebank on the 20th, leaving three days later for Fairfield where Princess Beatrice launched the cruiser *Marathon*. On 18 July 1889, it was the turn of the Shah of Persia to visit the Works. The Shah arrived at Kilbowie Station about 5.30 in the evening to be greeted by a guard of honour consisting of 100 men of the 1st Dumbarton Rifles Volunteers - James Roger Thomson's regiment. At the Works, the Shah was

Looking forward on City of New York's *promenade deck during trials on the Firth of Clyde.*

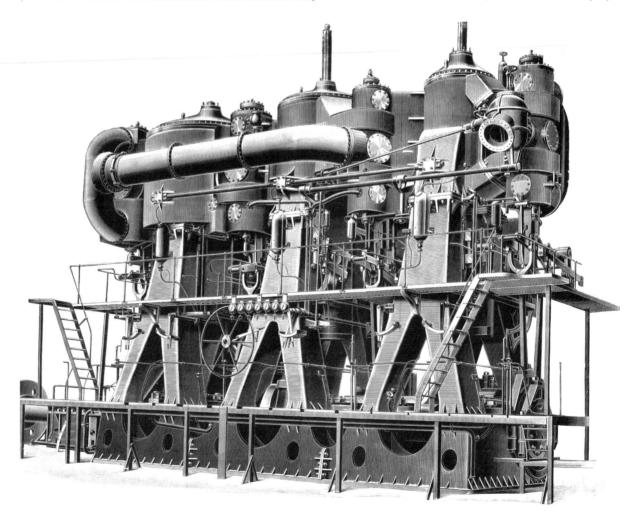

Right
A page from George Paul Thomson's diary recording the westward and eastward Atlantic passage of the City of Paris.

Second Right
An invitation made out to Mrs George Paul Thomson to attend the launch of City of Paris.

An engraving of the massive twin-screw triple expansion engines fitted in both Inman liners. They developed 20,600 ihp for a speed in excess of 21 knots. City of New York *made the fastest westward crossing in 5 days 14 hours and 24 minutes while* City of Paris *made the eastward crossing in 5 days 19 hours and 57 minutes.*

Messrs James and George Thomson request the honour of the Company of
at the LAUNCH of the Inman & International Co's Twin Screw Steamer
"CITY OF PARIS"
on Tuesday, 23rd October, 1888, at 1·30 p.m.

The ceremony will be performed by The Hon. Lady Campbell of Blythswood.

NOT TRANSFERABLE.

Clydebank, October, 1888.　　　Please Answer

received by George Thomson and Sir James King, Lord Provost of Glasgow. A forty-minute tour included the Model Room, engine works and shipyard where he was shown round *Friesland*. In June 1890, the Lord Provost of Glasgow again performed the honours escorting HM Stanley, the African explorer, round the Works accompanied by both Thomson brothers.

Four disputes were recorded in the latter half of the 1880s. The first in 1887 involved riveters who struck because of concern over the 'patent' furnaces employed on the shell of ship number 240. This dispute lasted nearly one month. In 1889, riveters struck for nine days over dissatisfaction with the 'Price List' the document in which piece rates of payment for riveting were printed. In October the fitters' helpers struck for more pay, returning after five days with no advance having been won. In September 1890, shipyard engineers struck because plumbers were jointing pipes and valves as well as fitting storm valves to ships, work the engineers considered to be theirs. After five days, the engineers returned on the basis that plumbers would do this work on fittings of up to 3" in diameter and engineers everything over.[285]

Wages fluctuated in accordance with the state of trade. Employers reluctantly permitted increases in good times and men reluctantly accepted reductions in bad times. Although this was the source of many disputes, it appears to have been accepted as a crude method of regulating wages. The relative scarcity of orders during 1890 and 1891 caused employers to announce reductions in wages.[286] After the Fair Holiday in July 1891, fitters, riveters, angle iron smiths, angle iron hammermen and caulkers, decided to join a strike against their own executive who had agreed to a reduction of 5% with employers. After a month, the men were forced to return on the employers' terms, with the exception of the angle iron hammermen who stayed out for a further four weeks. They returned at the old rate with angle iron smiths having to absorb their 5% reduction.[287]

In October 1892, notices were posted in the yard announcing a general reduction in wages across the industry. Two days later, a circular stated that on 10 October all piecework rates in the shipyards and engineering shops be reduced by 5% and that the following time workers' wages would be reduced by one farthing per hour – carpenters, joiners, cabinetmakers, engine fitters, ship smiths, smiths finishers, boilermakers, machinemen, caulkers, riveters, smiths, patternmakers, brassfinishers, shipyard fitters. Hammermen, redleaders, helpers, labourers and boys were to be dealt with by their own employers. On 9 December 1893, the shipyard, but not the engine works, was closed because of 'the action of a section of tradesmen and the difficulty of obtaining fuel' The shipyard workers were not permitted to return to work until 15 February, having received no wages for nine weeks. The section of tradesmen referred to were the joiners who were in dispute for eighteen weeks over working hours.

LIMITED LIABILITY

By the end of the 1880s, it was clear that Thomsons had finally succeeded in making significant inroads into the lucrative warship market. From a modest start in 1884, the Admiralty increasingly entrusted the yard with orders for larger warships, which culminated in the contract for the battleship *Ramillies* in 1890. Moreover, important naval contracts from foreign governments,

The 2,000gt passenger ship Brazil *built for the Brazilian Steam Navigation Co. in 1890. The ship is under the sheerlegs which Thomson built themselves after the previous pair had been brought down by the bowsprit of* City of New York *in 1888.*

Spanish, Russian, Australian and Japanese, had been booked. The vacuum created by the departure of Cunard was filled to some extent by the Inman Line and the contracts for the *City of New York* and the *City of Paris*, were highly prestigious. While the Thomsons had demonstrated yet again that the technical excellence of the product was beyond question, profits remained elusive.

Throughout 1889 the Union Bank worked towards the conversion of the business into a Limited Liability Company.[288] Even in this, there was rivalry with

The paddle steamer Glen Sannox *and, below, her 2 cylinder compound diagonal paddle engines which drove her in excess of 19 knots.*

Fairfield which was known to be pursuing a similar objective.[289] By 31 March 1890, the Partnership owed the Union Bank a staggering £425,957. In addition, the sum of £62,000 was also owed to the Family Trust. The basis for conversion was an asset valuation of the Partnership made in August 1889 by A D Bryce Douglas, managing director of the Barrow shipyard, which valued the business at £400,000. The new Limited Company would pay for this by issuing 25,000 £10 shares and raising a £150,000 mortgage debenture. To secure the money owed them by the Thomson brothers, the Bank bound them very tightly into the restructuring by advancing £250,000, through a Trust Deed dated 19 April 1890, which enabled the brothers to buy the bulk of the new shares. This was an important element of continuity for the business and reassurance to customers, suppliers and the public that the Company was safe. The Thomsons indebtedness to the Bank was e repaid either out of the subsequent sale of their shares or by dividends which the shares might earn. In the event of their insolvency, the Bank had the right to take over all their remaining shares and under the terms of the Trust Deed, the Trustee (for the Bank) was empowered to acquire all assets, contracts, properties and securities they may have except household furniture, chattels, horses and carriages. Further, the Trustee was empowered to 'take out of our yearly salary or salaries to an extent not exceeding the sum of £3,000 a year (JRT) and £2,000 a year (GPT)' Both brothers were in a straitjacket from which the only hope of liberation was large profits.[290]

The Partnership of James & George Thomson was dissolved and the new firm James & George Thomson & Co. Limited, began trading on 1 April 1890. The shareholders in the new Company were:

William A Donaldson	50	Ironfounder
John Grant	1	Company secretary
George P Thomson	11,924	
James R Thomson	11,924	
Colin Donald	50	For the Union Bank
Mrs E Thomson	1,000	Mother
J Parker Smith MP	50	MP for Partick and Director of Union Bank
John Wilkes	180	Brother-in-law of J.R.T

The continued pursuit of the grand lifestyle by both Thomson brothers, reflected in growing indebtedness to the Bank, led them to ask the Bank for an advance on their salaries, in contravention of the agreement described above. Making this request was at best insensitive on the part of the Thomsons, as Gairdner, in securing the Bank's interest, had always been considerate of their position. On learning that the Thomsons were yet again adding to their financial difficulties, Gairdner reached the end of his patience. On 19 June 1891, he wrote to the Company's lawyer and shareholder, C D Donald, with the following stinging rebuke:

'I have consulted my directors regarding the position Mr. James R Thomson has again brought himself to in his personal finances. I have also reported that I am given to understand that Mr. George P Thomson is likewise heavily in arrears with his personal and household debts. These facts my directors regard as the result of extravagance which in the circumstances is wholly unjustifiable and which, coming after so many promises made and broken is calculated to destroy all confidence in the prudence of Messrs. Thomson in the conduct of their personal affairs. The bonus on their salaries for last year which they now ask permission to draw for the purpose of meeting these debts, it was expressly agreed, should be applied in reduction of their indebtedness to the bank. It is with the greatest reluctance that the directors have brought themselves to concede to the Thomsons' request. In so doing they have given instructions that the ordinary shares of the limited company standing in Messrs. Thomson's names be now transferred in the Company's books to the nominees of the bank reserving only the necessary qualification for the board of directors. I have already stated to you the mode in which this had better be done and will thank you to see Messrs. Thomson and communicate the purpose of this letter.'[291]

At a stroke, the Thomson's shareholding was reduced to 50 shares each and any prospect of participating in improved Company performance had gone. The brothers were now little more than salaried executives in a public company. As the trading position of the Company went from strength to strength over the course of the 1890s, James and George had much to regret.

The composition of the Board of the new Company comprised James Roger Thomson, Managing Director, George Paul Thomson, director and a manager of the Works, John Parker Smith MP, Colin Donald, a partner in the firm of solicitors McGrigor Donald & Co., and William Anderson Donaldson of Cochno, a Glasgow iron merchant who was voted as Chairman. John Grant remained as Secretary.

Departmental management remained the same with John Gibb Dunlop as Engine Works Manager and Samuel Crawford as Shipyard Manager.

With the Thomson's shares now available, the Union Bank of Scotland sold them at an average of £10 per share to other members of the Glasgow business community and by 1897, the shareholders were:

William A Donaldson	5,500	Chair. of J&G Thomson
John Grant	1,000	Company Secretary
Paul & Fritz Rottenburg	1,500	Chemical merchants
John G Dunlop	2,000	Engine Works Manager
George P Thomson	50	
James R Thomson	50	
Robert M Paterson	1,000	Chemical manufacturer
Creswell D Haynes	700	Company agent
Alex Grigor & A H Donald	8,670	For the Union Bank
Lord Overtoun	1,000	Chemical manufacturer
Robert & William Chrystal	800	Chemical manufacturer
D Scott Ferguson & George Willock	1,000	Gentlemen
Mrs E Thomson	1,000	Mother
J Parker Smith MP	200	MP (Director of Union Bank)
A S McClelland CA	50	
John Wilkes	180	Brother-in-law of J.R.T
William Houldsworth	200	Coltness Iron Co.[292]

William A Donaldson's position as Chairman of the Company was appropriate. He had served an apprenticeship with the original James & George

William Donaldson, the Glasgow ironfounder who became Chairman of James & George Thomson & Co. Ltd in 1891.

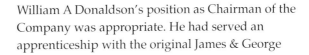

The large Red Star liner Friesland on trials in November 1889. Carrying 4,000 tons of cargo in addition to a large number of passengers at an economical 14.5 knots, Thomson built many examples of this type of Atlantic liner as well as ocean racers.

Thomson in the early 1860s before joining Glasgow stockbrokers and accountants James Watson & Co. He had become a partner of that Company in 1866 and later became Chairman of James Dunlop & Co., the Lanarkshire steel company. He was also a director of the Barrow Steel Company.[293]

In 1890, George Paul Thomson asked the shipyard manager, Sam Crawford, and the chief cashier Don Bremner, to visit Harland & Wolff's yard at Belfast and compare that establishment with his own. The ability of Harland & Wolff to win orders for large passenger steamers at very low prices was a source of frustration at Clydebank where they would be quite unaware of the low commission basis on which Harland & Wolff operated. Crawford and Bremner's report, dated 11 October 1890, finds that in only one department, the ironworkers, does Harland & Wolff have superior facilities to Thomson. The importance of joinery work in passenger ships ensured that this department was given close scrutiny. When provided with joinery costs on the *Teutonic*, and comparing them with *City of Paris*, the reporters found that the cost

'. . . shows that they cannot do this work nearly as favourably as we can and especially when it is borne in mind that the accommodation on board the Teutonic is very far short of that on City of Paris. . . . From the general information obtained, and considering the somewhat extravagant expenditure in many of the departments (at Harland & Wolff) compared with what it is here, it does appear somewhat curious how they can work so cheaply or to procure such an enormous amount of freight carrying tonnage as with the exception of their iron department, we consider that your establishment is all over as well equipped as theirs and in many respects superior'[294]

In summary, the reporters could find no obvious way in which Harland & Wolff could be building ships cheaper than Clydebank. At the time of their visit, Harland & Wolff had 25 ships under construction none of which were less than 400 feet in length. 5,000 men were employed in the shipyard and 1,600 in the engine works. What George Thomson made of the report is not known. In any case, warship work was

Right
A plate for the protected cruiser Terrible *being manipulated into a punching and sheering machine made by Craig &Donald at Johnstone.*

Opposite page
Top right
A bogey track laid between the decks of the cruiser Terrible *is used to run material and a hydraulic riveter through the ship.*

Bottom left
A view of the engine erecting shop showing the triple expansion engines for Terrible *on the right and the diagonal compound machinery for a paddle steamer on the left.*

Bottom right
Terrible *nears completion in the summer of 1896.*

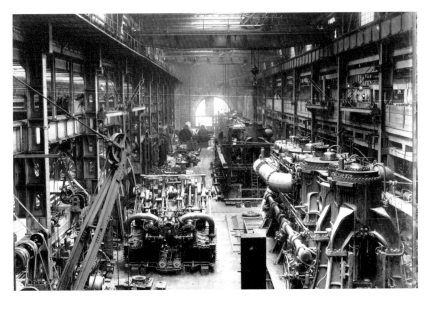

highly profitable, a category of work in which Harland & Wolff were not involved.

With the fundamental elements of manufacturing site, plant, able managers and finance now in relatively good order, the new Company was almost immediately successful and in its first year recorded a trading profit of £38,313. The yard delivered three cruisers of 7,800 displacement tons and 23,500 ihp

A group of riveters who worked on Terrible. *Riveters regarded themselves among the elite of shipyard trades.*

and four passenger steamers of 5,300 tons and 20,300 ihp. Three cruisers, a battleship and four merchant steamers were in progress and £13,231 had been spent on new machinery and plant.[295]

In the conversion of the Company there was one notable staff change. JH Biles, the Company's eminent naval architect, had hoped for a position on the new Board. At the same time he was offered the job of General Manager of the Southampton Naval Works at Woolston at a salary of £2,000 plus a £10,000 share of the business after five years. Biles' position at Clydebank attracted a salary of only £550, the same as that paid to the Shipyard and Engine Works Managers. When Biles suggested that his position at Clydebank could be placed on a similar footing to the job offered him at Southampton, the Company declined. Negotiations deteriorated suddenly and the Company wrote to Biles asking him to resign at once. Biles resigned his position by letter on 23 January 1890 saying 'I take this opportunity of saying with how much regret I take this step.' In a letter written a

few months later in March, Biles said the Southampton job was offered him by the 'wealthy people in London' and that in the restructuring of Clydebank 'no reference has been made to me . . . you were not prepared to offer terms.'[296] On Biles' departure, William David Archer was appointed as Naval Architect.

It was not to be the last contact Biles had with the firm. Following a brief period at Southampton as General Manager, Biles returned to Glasgow in 1891 after being appointed to the John Elder Chair of Naval Architecture at Glasgow University. He also established a marine consultancy in Glasgow.[297] Within a few years Biles was contracted as the Company's agent to Japan in pursuit of warship orders. In February 1896, he was behind a proposal to take over the Southampton Naval Works for repair work. Both James Roger Thomson and John Dunlop visited Southampton to consider this proposal but decided against it.

The Company continued to be profitable throughout the early 1890s, with the exception of 1894 during which a loss of £31,882 was made, attributed to 'several serious hindrances to continuous work'[298]

AGENTS AND AVIATORS

Minute Books for the late 1890s give insight into the network of agents employed to win foreign contracts. These agents were paid an annual fee plus commission for any orders booked.[299] For example, Professor Biles' two year contract signed in December 1895, paid him a fee of £600 per annum for 'services he may render in connection with securing orders in Japan' together with 1% commission on the price of a cruiser and 0.5% on the price of a battleship.[300] The importance of the Spanish Government to the Company ensured that Creswell Haynes was re-appointed Spanish agent for three years at £1,500 per annum.[301] Both Spain and Japan were pursuing naval building programmes and looked to the United Kingdom as the source of the most technically advanced ships. British share of the world market in warships was high, although France, Germany, USA and Italy were in competition.

The pioneer aviator, Percy Sinclair Pilcher, had a short period of employment at Clydebank in the wake of John Biles' departure. Having served an engineering apprenticeship at Fairfield, Pilcher met Biles at Southampton and when the latter moved to Glasgow University, Pilcher followed as an assistant lecturer in naval architecture, managing to combine this with work in the drawing office at J & G Thomson's. In

1896, Pilcher left Glasgow to work with the inventor Sir Hiram Maxim. Pilcher's investigations into manned flight, which were leading directly to powered flight, were brought to an abrupt end when he died following a crash in the glider Hawk near Rugby in September 1899[302].

As early as 1891 the purchase of additional ground to the west of the yard was under consideration but rejected as the terms were thought to be exorbitant.[303] Further enquiries were made in 1896 for the purchase of ground owned by the Caledonian Railway Co. to the east of the yard and a tentative agreement reached at £800 per acre. This proposal foundered when the railway company insisted that the sale would be contingent on acquiring the shipyard's traffic for a period of 25 years.[304] Attention again focused on expansion to the west and £500 per acre was offered for 22 acres in June 1896. In November, a price of £650 was agreed and the ground purchased.[305] The total area of the Works was now over 71 acres and no further substantial additions were to be made. The following February, proposals were submitted for erecting a new sawmill on this ground at an initial cost of £10,000. At the same time, £29,000 was also spent building a new brass foundry and copper shop.

With trading continuing successfully, the question of changing the name of the Company was raised at a Board meeting in July 1896. In December 1895 a company called Clydebank Engineering & Shipbuilding Co. Ltd. had been registered partly to stop a potential competitor using it and partly to enable the existing company name to be changed to that title 'as and when desirable.'[306] However, the absence of James Roger Thomson from the Board meeting deferred the matter until his return. At a meeting on 11 August 1896 at which James Roger was present, the decision to change the name was passed, and from 1 April 1897 the business was known as the Clydebank Engineering & Shipbuilding Co. Ltd. The reason for making this change is not clear but it is certain that the Union Bank of Scotland had eventual sale of the Company in mind. Investment in both facilities and personnel over many years had enabled the full realisation of the Company's potential through many magnificent vessels and large profits. The name J&G Thomson was synonymous with the best in shipbuilding and the business had few peers. The financial crisis of past years together with the profligacy of the Thomsons would not have been widely known. Nevertheless, in selecting a new name, the Bank was consciously repositioning the

Company with a fresh identity.

Set against the world role which the Royal Navy performed, the continued demand for warships caused a number of armaments firms to acquire shipbuilding capacity. In 1897, Vickers Son & Maxim took over the Barrow Naval Construction & Armaments Company and Armstrong Mitchell joined with Whitworth to form Armstrong Whitworth. Both companies, with capacity in shipbuilding, amour and armament manufacture, were concentrating efforts to win a greater share of lucrative defence contracts. These events must have caused some concern at Clydebank whose recent success was due in no small part to naval contracts. Tentative interest in broadening armaments capacity first presented itself in January 1896 when a letter was received from Société Nordenfeldt with a proposal for the joint manufacture of guns. In March of that year the possibility of setting-up a gun factory was explored but later abandoned.[307] In 1898, to strengthen links with the Admiralty, the company employed William Joseph Luke, a former naval constructor, to replace William Archer in running the ship designing department. Luke's salary was £800 per annum rising to £1200 after five years. [308]

Output during the 1890s illustrates the yard's versatility in producing a remarkable range of ship types including warships, paddle steamers, channel ferries, yachts and merchant ships.

Six cruisers, one Japanese, two Australian and three

The battleship Jupiter *being prepared for launch in November 1895.*

The torpedo boat destroyer Rocket *is prepared for her launch on 14 August 1894. The early destroyers were small vessels as this photograph demonstrates.*

British, were completed by 1892. On 1 March the first battleship to be built at Clydebank for the Royal Navy, *Ramillies*, was launched. A distinguished list of guests including the Director of Naval Construction, Sir William White, watched as the Duchess of Abercorn performed the ceremony. This battleship proved reluctant to enter the water and her progress down the ways was so slow it was barely perceptible. As the tide was falling, efforts were made to block the ship up on the ways without success and the prospect of her entering the mud rather than the water became a worrying possibility. After one and a half hours had passed, *Ramillies* entered the Clyde with only just sufficient water for the launch to be

declared a success.

Further Admiralty contracts included engines for *Hermione* at Devonport and the rebuilt ironclad *Sultan*, three torpedo boat destroyers, *Rocket*, *Shark* and *Surly*, the first class protected cruiser *Terrible* and the battleship *Jupiter*, all of which were laid down in 1894. *Terrible*, although a cruiser, was longer than contemporary battleships. She was also fitted with 48 Belleville water-tube boilers, a French design, which permitted higher steam pressures without an increase in weight. At any one time, a water-tube boiler contained much less water than the cylindrical or 'Scotch' boiler. This was an obvious advantage in many ship types including warships where great efforts were made to minimise weight. As the Admiralty decided to make a major commitment to Belleville boilers, in May 1891, a new boiler shop was built at Clydebank for their manufacture. By the end of the Century, Belleville boilers were the subject of debate in what became known as the 'Battle of the Boilers.' In 1901, an Admiralty report recommended the abandonment of the Belleville boiler in favour of the Yarrow and Babcock type, each of which were later manufactured at Clydebank.[309]

In addition to the ships of war, four magnificent steam yachts were built in the last half of the 1890s, *Urania, Mayflower, Nahma* and *Sheelah*. Largest of the four were the *Mayflower* and *Nahma* built for Ogden Goelet and his brother Robert. *Nahma* was later sold to Sir Thomas Lipton for £80,000.[310] Both yachts, designed by the eminent Glasgow firm G L Watson & Co., were large and sumptuously appointed. *Mayflower* was acquired in 1902 by the American Government and served as the presidential yacht for three decades. Perhaps the most historically significant event in her career was the signing of the peace treaty between the Russian and Japanese Governments following the war of 1905. The smaller yacht *Sheelah*, was built for William Donaldson, Chairman of the Company.

The 1890s also reaffirmed Clydebank's position as a leading builder of channel and river steamers with no fewer than seventeen examples built. Among these, five channel steamers were built for the London & South Western Railway Co., *Frederica, Lydia* and *Stella* for the Southampton - Channel Islands service and *Columbia and Alma* for the Southampton - Le Havre service. The Glasgow & South Western Railway Co. ordered five paddle steamers for Clyde services *Glen Sannox, Minerva, Glen Rosa, Jupiter* and *Juno*. Built following model experiments in the Forth & Clyde Canal, *Glen Sannox* won the day against rival steamers of the Caledonian Steam Packet Co., upholding J&G Thomson's tradition for speed. *Glen Sannox* proved to be the fastest steamer on the Clyde.

TORPEDOED

The following contract is described in detail because it illustrates one of the less obvious vagaries which shipbuilders faced. By the end of the century, warship design was evolving rapidly in response to new weapon systems. The introduction of the self-propelled torpedo as a credible weapon prompted the design of small, fast vessels to carry them, known as torpedo boats. Inevitably, larger faster vessels were designed to pursue the torpedo boats. These ships

were known as torpedo boat destroyers (TBD's, later simply as destroyers) the first examples of which were ordered by the Navy in 1892. Between 1892 and 1894, the Admiralty ordered no fewer than forty-two torpedo boat destroyers from private yards. Unlike Yarrow and Thornycroft, J&G Thomson had not specialised in the development of high speed vessels of this type but nevertheless their proven reputation

as designers and makers of high performance steam reciprocating machinery made them an obvious choice. The first torpedo boat destroyers built by the Company, *Rocket, Shark* and *Sturdy*, designed for a speed of 27 knots, were ordered in 1894. Although a TBD of this period required about six to seven months of construction before launch, and about

Top
One of the gunboats built at great speed for the Spanish Navy running trials in 1895.

Above
A torpedo boat destroyer sails back up the Clyde to the shipyard after trials.

89

another three to physically fit-out and complete the contract, all three 'Rockets' required seventeen months to achieve contract speed. *Rocket*, for example, required seventeen separate trials over a six month period to make a mean speed of 27.4 knots. Adjustments to her machinery and propellers were carried out and although improvements were made, they were not sufficient to enable a speed of 27 knots

The fitting-out basin about April or May 1897 with eight vessels present not all of which are identifiable. From left is one of the Spanish TBD's, the steam yacht Mayflower, *one Spanish TBD, one British TBD, one other, the steam yacht* Nahma *a further TBD and unidentified craft to the rear.*

to be achieved. As a last resort, partial rebuilding of the after section of the lower hull was necessary. Although time consuming and expensive, these changes worked and the last of the three, *Surly*, proved to be the fastest, with a mean speed of 28.05 knots.

Evidently satisfied with these vessels and their performance, the Admiralty included Thomson in the next round of TBD orders. The main difference between this and preceding classes was speed, which was increased to 30 knots. Thus, in November 1895, *Brazen, Electra, Vulture* and *Recruit* were laid down. The last three were tendered for at a price of £152,688, which included a profit of £30,000.

Earlier in 1895, the relationship between the Spanish Navy and Thomson was strengthened when seven small gunboats ranging between 100 feet to 150 feet in length overall and 100 to 300 tons displacement, were built. These vessels in which high speed was not a feature, were destined for service in Cuba. These

contracts were executed with great speed and all vessels were built within the space of only two months. At the end of 1895, the Spanish Navy issued specifications for two 27 knot TBDs similar to the Rocket type built by Thomson. J&G Thomson was awarded the contract and both vessels, *Terror* and *Furor,* were laid down in February 1896. With the experience of *Rocket* behind them, both TBDs were completed to contract in nine months. As *Terror* and *Furor* were under construction at Clydebank, deteriorating political events in the Caribbean forced the Spaniards to consider placing orders for additional and even faster TBDs.

Spain was steadily becoming embroiled in insurrection in Cuba, then a Spanish colonial possession. Much to the irritation of the Spanish government, Cuban rebels were supplied with men and munitions by sea from agents in the United States. Spanish naval forces deployed there were light and inefficient, consisting of gunboats and small steam launches unable to impose an effective blockade.

The solution lay in the construction of fast warships able to overtake and overwhelm the blockade-running vessels. Thus, an outline specification for fast torpedo boats to be delivered in eight months was formulated in 1896 and tenders requested from several British and one French shipbuilder. This specification included the following sentence:

'The time for delivery to be considered a very essential point and consistent with the price – that is to say, without increasing the cost of the vessels by the quick delivery demanded as an important condition, builders are requested to state the shortest time for building the ships and delivering same ready for sea; and also stipulate clearly what penalties are they willing to pay for non-fulfilment of speed and for every week's delay beyond the date that may be agreed upon for the delivery'

Technically, the key element of the specification was speed, which was to be a minimum of 30 knots. No vessel of this, or indeed, any type, had so far made a speed of 30 knots and in that respect the Spanish TBDs would require careful consideration given the difficulty in getting 27 knots from the earlier vessels. Despite the specified requirement of eight months for completion, James Roger Thomson nevertheless drew his company into an even tighter position writing on 2 May 1896:

'We could give delivery of the first vessel in six and three-quarter months and of the second in seven and three-quarter months from date of signing of contract and final approval of plans'. The penalty for deficiency in speed was set at £150 per tenth knot under the contract speed and the penalty for delay in delivery at £500 for each week beyond the contract time. The last mentioned figure of £500 was stipulated by Clydebank management presumably influenced by a bullish James Roger

Thomson's price allowed for a profit of £8,000 on each ship.[311]

On 26 May 1896, Admiral Manuel De La Camara, chief of the Spanish Naval Commission, wrote to the shipyard saying that he had been authorised by his Excellency the Minister of Marine to sign the contract, but referred to a further and absolute condition which must be observed as part of the contract:

Thomson. Clearly, he felt confident about the ability of the Company to deliver these ships within contract.

Five firms tendered with prices and delivery times for two ships as follows:

Company	Price each	Delivery time
Thornycroft and Co.	£55,000	15 and 16 months
Thames Iron Works	£60,000	10 months
Palmers Shipbuilding Co.	£59,500	12 months
Laird Brothers	£65,000	13 and 14 months
J & G Thomson	£67,180	6.75 months the first and 7.75 the second

As the Clydebank tender was chosen, it was clear that quick delivery was of paramount importance.

'The speed of the vessels must not be less than 30 knots an hour, to be demonstrated by trials under conditions given in the contract, and should the vessels not reach the said speed of thirty knots, the Spanish Government will not admit any penalty for deficiencies from the contractors, but reject the acceptance of the ships, contractors being bound to reimburse all moneys already paid in way of instalments.'

Thomson replied on 27 May saying that 'The condition laid down by you is one that is quite unprecedented in our experience, and certainly is not customary in our trade . . .' (i.e. the outright rejection of ships should they fail to make contract speed) On 1 June Thomson wrote again '. . . we are prepared to meet you in this matter and will insert a clause in the contract in accordance with the same'. The contract

The protected cruiser Europa *leaving Clydebank in April 1898. The west part of the yard is relatively undeveloped being used largely for storing timber and the construction of one small unknown vessel. To the left, the funnels for the cruiser* Ariadne *lie on their side awaiting the launch of the ship.*

for two ships *Audaz* and *Osado* followed almost immediately and was signed on 4 June 1896. On 24 November 1896 an identical contract for two further ships, *Proserpino* and *Pluton* was signed although the price had dropped to £65,650 each.[312]

The first two ships were laid down in August and September 1896 and almost immediately ran into problems. The shipyard found great difficulty obtaining the type of steel (later known as high tensile steel) required which, having a greater unit strength, could be employed in lighter sections therefore enabling a lighter hull to be built. This steel was of recent introduction and in view of the large number of torpedo boat destroyers being built in Britain, was in great demand and consequently in short supply.

The Steel Company of Scotland Ltd., with works at Newton and Blochairn outside Glasgow, were makers and suppliers of this steel.[313] Contracts that would normally have taken no more than four weeks to fulfil, stretched, in some cases, to twenty weeks. Despite repeated letters and visits to the steel works by Clydebank personnel, delivery of material remained highly unsatisfactory throughout the duration of the contracts. According to David McGee, Shipyard Manager at Clydebank, this added at least two and a half months to the building time of the ships.

While progress on the hulls continued, there was a further setback which delayed construction of the main propelling machinery. As a consequence of strikes in London over the reduction in working hours, the Employers' Federation, through a resolution made on 1 July 1897, imposed a lockout of engineers to commence in July. When notice of the lockout was given, the engineers pre-empted the employer's action and struck en masse on 13 July. This dispute, one of the longest in which the engineers were involved did not end until January of the following year. Work on the engines and boilers which had been fairly well advanced, slowed as the Company could only rely on a handful of foremen and between 130 to 140 apprentices who, traditionally, did not take part in strike action. According to Thomas Bell, the assistant manager of the engine works:

> 'Only those apprentices nearing the completion of their time could be trusted with work of such importance as this. The staff was not sufficient to enable us to carry on, and the whole work of the engine works was stopped. As a matter of fact, what staff we had was devoted solely to the work

on these Spanish destroyers.'[314]

On 13 March 1897, just five weeks after launching, *Audaz* was sufficiently complete to make her first trip down river to conduct trials on the Firth of Clyde. Although possibly lacking in some items of equipment, *Audaz* had indeed been built in six and three-quarter months. However, Thomson's problems were only beginning.

The first of the four Admiralty 30 knot destroyers, *Brazen*, had been launched much earlier than her Spanish 30 knot counterpart and had run her first trial on 5 September 1896 - a period of eleven months from keel laying. By the time *Audaz* ran her trials, *Brazen* had been attempting to reach 30 knots for six months without success. Inevitably, *Audaz* could not make 30 knots either.

Rectification of this was to prove a protracted business of trial and error. At first, different propellers were fitted and after many weeks spent unsuccessfully trying to achieve the speed, it was decided to pursue the only alternative - altering the shape of the hull. This necessitated hauling the vessel out of the water at the patent slip at Dalmuir, adjacent to the yard or taking it upriver to a dry dock. This was followed by the partial dismantling and rebuilding of the stern section of the ship. Finally, after several major modifications, *Audaz* made her contract speed leaving for Spain in company with *Osado* on 9 March 1898.

After *Audaz's* and *Osado's* trials had been successfully completed, the other two TBDs *Pluton* and *Proserpina* were modified along similar lines. Work on these vessels was suspended on the stocks in order that they could be built with the new form of hull from the outset. As a result, despite being ordered almost six months after the first pair, *Pluton* and *Proserpino*, were able to make contract speed almost immediately. *Pluton* was the first to complete successful trials with a speed of 30.15 knots on 4 November 1897. The other three left the Clyde for Spain in March 1898. The Spanish American War broke out on 22 April. *Pluton*, the only one of the four fit to be despatched to Cuba in anything like warlike manner was sunk at the battle of Santiago Bay on 3 July 1898.

Following delivery of the four vessels, Clydebank management did not expect the penalty clause to be applied, although some form of compensation was anticipated. They considered the unfortunate events surrounding the contracts to be outwith their control claiming force majeure. On 16 July 1897, a letter from the Spanish Government to the Spanish Commission in London hinted at what was to come:

'. . . the Government has decided to make them (the builders) responsible as per contract of their default in the fulfilment of their agreement'

On 30 July, George Paul Thomson, James Roger Thomson's younger brother and a manager at Clydebank, wrote to the Spanish Commission with a very full explanation of the delays in building and testing the ships. Throughout this time, other Spanish contracts were in the offing forming part of their awaited fleet expansion programme. In September 1896, Thomson quoted for a battleship at the price of £727,650 and a cruiser at £521,220.[315] In April 1897, they tendered for a Spanish Royal Yacht at a price of £166,000,[316] while in September, Thomson considered acquiring the shipyard at Bilbao to assist in securing Spanish orders.[317] At the Board meeting of 27 July 1897 held at Clydebank, Creswell Haynes, Thomson's agent in Spain suggested that:

'. . . it might be a good idea in view of possible further contracts to present the King of Spain with a sailing yacht or small gunboat if they waive their claim for penalties for late delivery of destroyers' and that 'no mention of this was to be made'.[318]

The Board decided to consult with Admiral Camara, the Spanish Minister of Marine, on the matter and meanwhile authorised spending up to £6,000 on a yacht. In September, the Board met again to consider the situation. Admiral Camara had written to them on 10 September stating that penalties were to be 'inflicted in full'. The company response was to propose a yacht of 60 metres length and of 13 to 14 knots speed if the penalties were not pressed. At the same meeting a full discussion took place regarding the inability of *Brazen, Electra, Recruit* and *Vulture* to reach 30 knots[319]. It was agreed that they should alter the lines of these vessels with the utmost despatch.[320] One month later, the Spanish yacht had grown in cost to £15,000 on condition of waived penalties.[321] With Spanish authorities showing no willingness to accept this compromise, the yacht proposal was dropped.[322] On 27 October 1898 the Spanish Commission wrote to Clydebank claiming that the *Audaz* was 50 weeks late, the *Osado* 46 weeks late, the *Pluton* 25 weeks late and the *Proserpino* 30 weeks late and stated its intention to pursue the Company for penalties of £75,000, and asking for their attendance at an Administrative Inquiry. On 3 November 1898, John Gibb Dunlop, engine works manager, replied:

'we would remind you that these contracts have been completed for some considerable time to

your Government's satisfaction, and we cannot now recognise any claim for penalties alluded to '

The Company stuck to this line replying to a letter from the Spanish Commission on 9 January 1900 in which they repudiated liability.[323] The Spanish Commission were not inclined to this view and issued a Royal Decree on 27 March 1900 ordering legal proceedings to recover penalties. The case was not brought to the Court of Session in Edinburgh until 1902 during which time evidence was heard from a variety of persons including a shipyard plater, a carpenter, a meteorologist, consulting engineers, naval architects, the shipyard and engineering managers including Thomas Bell and, of course, James Rodger Thomson. When asked if a destroyer had been built before with a speed of 30 knots Thomson gave an answer which probably comes closest to illustrating the climate in which TBDs were built:

'It was purely an experiment, and that was thoroughly well known by everyone. We had contracts at the time for a number of ships of the same description for the British Government, some of a high rate of speed. It [speed] is not susceptible by precise scientific ascertainment, and it depends largely on experiment. It may be got at once by accident or luck, or it may take a great number of trials.

No government ever did exact penalties from our firm, although we were late. In this instance it was we who fixed the penalty. The clause in the contract giving the Spanish Government the right to reject the ships if they did not attain the contract speed was unusual. Our directors carefully considered it before they agreed to it, and we did agree to it, influenced by the fact that, if they were rejected they were boats that were very saleable. We would have no difficulty whatever in disposing of them.

We considered that the delay in delivering all of these boats was caused by the discovery that the contract speed could not be obtained on the model we originally worked upon'[324]

In summing up on 18 February 1903, Lord Kyllachy found in favour of the pursuers placing the total number of weeks in penalty at 135. His long statement included the following remarks:

'. . . I think it quite probable, and perhaps more than probable, that if the Spanish Government had even in the spring of 1897, been in a position to establish around the coast of Cuba, or even certain parts of that coast, a really effective

James Rodger Thomson in regimental uniform

blockade – I mean effective as against the landing of munitions of war – the Cuban insurrection might have been crushed, and American intervention avoided'.

It was one thing to be late with a ship but to be blamed for contributing to if not causing the Spanish American war added a new aspect to the trials and tribulations of shipbuilders. The Spanish Commission was awarded £67,500 with interest plus expenses which in total, amounted to over £80,000. An appeal heard in June 1903 was dismissed although the following statement summarises the position advanced on behalf of the builders:

> 'The proof discloses no lack of diligence on the part of the Appellants but on the contrary shows, that under difficult circumstances, which could not have been foreseen, they used the utmost exertions to perform an unprecedented task, and also that the cause of most of the delay was the experimenting necessary to attain an unprecedented speed.'[325]

To the sum awarded the Spanish Commission, must be added the real cost in labour and material of working on these vessels for a considerably greater time than originally estimated.

In the interval between delivering the ships and the court case, major changes had occurred at Clydebank. In 1897, J&G Thomson Ltd became the Clydebank Engineering & Shipbuilding Co. Ltd. Although this was largely a change of name only it marked the continued resolve of the Union Bank of Scotland, the largest shareholder in the Company, to free itself of the Clydebank Works.

The four TBDs of the Brazen type, which had been laid down almost a year before the four Spanish boats, were not able to reach contract speed until the end of 1899. *Brazen* took a total of fifty months from keel-laying to acceptance. Although penalties of £32,900 were discussed by the Board at Clydebank,[326] there is no evidence of these penalties being applied.[327]

Thomsons had been unfortunate in their Spanish contract perhaps believing that Spanish naval authorities would take the same understanding if not benevolent view towards them as the Admiralty. The latter, more anxious to nurture than penalise shipyards particularly where new types of ship were involved, tended not to press for contract penalties in the recognition that builders were making great efforts in technically demanding circumstances. The Spanish Government, with no inherent interest in a British yard, had little

compunction about pressing penalties, particularly after their defeat at the hands of the Americans. The Admiralty took a generally sympathetic view of the other private shipbuilders who had also experienced similar difficulties in achieving contract speed.[328] The only outright casualty of the early torpedo boat destroyer contracts was the small firm of Paisley shipbuilders, Hannah Donald & Wilson, who did not have the financial resources to endlessly modify *Fervent* and *Zephyr*. This contract forced the Paisley firm out of business in 1900.

Nevertheless, the experience of building the battleships *Ramillies* and *Jupiter* placed the Company in a strong position to tender for foreign battleship contracts. Many were pursued and one, *Asahi*, for the Imperial Japanese Navy, was successful. Winning contracts was often a protracted business as the following chronology for *Asahi* shows:

---

26 March 1896
Professor Biles 'to be sent to Japan immediately'
28 April
Captain Takayama and 2 other Japanese officials visit Clydebank.
20 July
James Roger Thomson visits the Japanese legation and is told that he would get details of battleship in a few days. It is stressed that design is to be the chief element in securing order.
11 August
Board agree to tender for Japanese battleship.
4 September
Estimates – A Design £792,000 and B Design £814,000, commission and profit not added
8 September
Profit of £50,000 to £60,000 to be added to Japanese battleships at James Roger Thomson's discretion
22 September
Tender prices. Design A £864800, Design B £888,800 (Design B – Hull £360,000, Armour £302,000, Machinery £143,000, Aux. machinery £9,000)
16 November
Letter from Bolling & Lowe (Company agents in Japan) recommending that we offer to build battleship in 27 months rather than 30. Done.
26 January 1897
Letter from Bolling & Lowe detailing differences between our tender and Thames Iron Works.
20 April
Revised prices given to Professor Biles for forwarding to Mr Sassoio in Japan.
5 May
Revised prices are – Cost £836,042, profit £27,000, commission £16,500 Price £879,542.
1 June

Letter from Japanese delegation offering battleship contract to Clydebank for £873,000. Accepted.

12 July

Contract signed on 5th and first payment of £87,300 made.[329]

One advantage which naval contracts offered over their merchant counterparts was payment of the first instalment in advance. The *Asahi* tender included armour and armament. Tenders for Admiralty ships were usually exclusive of these items.[330] The armour for *Asahi* was supplied by Sheffield steel makers John Brown & Co., as their price was the lowest by 2.5%.[331] The last years of the 1890s were dominated by warship orders. These included the Diadem Class cruisers *Europa* and *Ariadne*; destroyers *Brazen*, *Electra*, *Recruit*, *Vulture*, *Thorn*, *Tiger* and *Vigilant*, Cressy Class cruisers *Sutlej* and *Bacchante*. Efforts to win orders in Russia resulted in the troopships *Kiev* and *Moskva* for the Russian Volunteer Fleet. A number of large merchant ships were built including the refrigerated ships *Fifeshire* and *Nairnshire*, the Red Star liner *Vaderland* and *Zeeland* and *Haverford* for the International Navigation Co. 1898 was of particular significance as it marked the return of Cunard to Clydebank after an absence of 14 years with the order for the intermediate 14,000ton liner *Saxonia*. Cunard's relationship with Fairfield had produced four record breaking, Blue Riband express steamers. Although the last pair, *Campania* and *Lucania*, were outstanding ships, they were the source of a bitter dispute between Fairfield and Cunard over contract details.[332]

News of Cunard's order was tempered by the death of John Grant in October 1897, secretary to the Company from its inception in 1847. While walking home to Dalmuir House along the banks of the Forth & Clyde canal, Grant stumbled, fell in and drowned. Grant had worked for the first James and George Thomson before supporting young James Roger Thomson against strong Trust opposition in the move to Clydebank. On the inauguration of the engine works in February 1884, it was Grant who foresaw the day that great passenger liners of the future would be launched into the mouth of the River Cart. The report for the year 1898 said of him: 'for over 50 years (he) made the welfare and success of this business his one object and desire'[333]

By the end of the 19th Century, the Clydebank Company was almost 53 years old with an excellent order book and an impressive balance sheet. In nine years as a public limited company, profits of over

Sir John Brown started selling cutlery for a local Sheffield firm in the 1830s but soon successfully established his own firm which grew rapidly. After disagreeing with his Board, he left the company which he had built up in 1871. It is likely that he never visited the shipyard that later bore his name.

The Atlas Works at Sheffield in 1903.

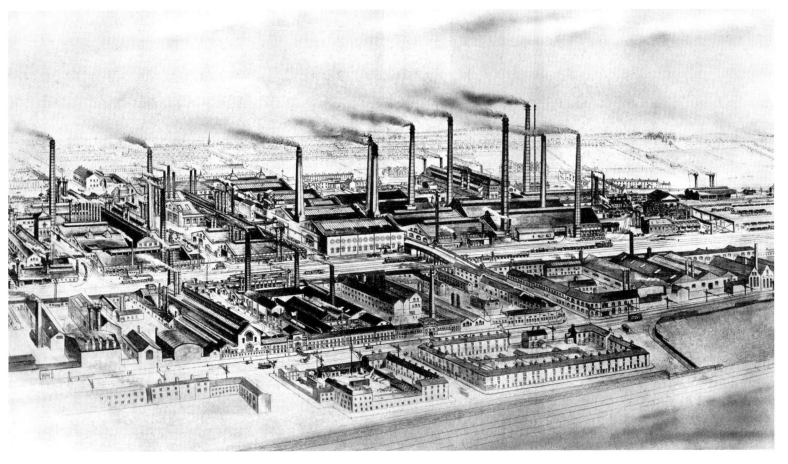

£503,000 were made from which £150,000 was paid in dividends to shareholders and a reserve fund of £150,000 created. In a British dominated industry, Clydebank stood in the forefront of world shipbuilding. However, the emergence of powerful armaments companies with shipbuilding capacity brought with it concern over Clydebank's ability to continue on its own as a major warship builder. In

with the intractable financial problems that had plagued the Thomsons.

John Brown was born at Fargate, Sheffield on 6 December 1816, the second son of Samuel Brown, a slater. At the age of 14, despite his father's wish that he should be a draper, he was apprenticed to Earl Horton & Co., a Sheffield firm of merchants who traded in locally made steel products. For the first

Looking eastwards over the head of the building berths in 1900 to the plater's sheds which are conspicuous by the number of outlets venting steam.

1899 this concern was met when the success of the Clydebank yard attracted one of the largest and most successful steel and armour making companies in the United Kingdom. This, of course, was John Brown.

JOHN BROWN: 1816 TO 1899

The patterns traced by J&G Thomson and John Brown & Co. from inception to conjunction share the common background of economic and industrial expansion. John Brown was a contemporary of the original James and George Thomson and equally successful in exploiting the opportunities offered by the new iron and steel technologies. Like James and George, John came from a modest background succeeding through his own efforts and abilities. The transition of Brown's company to the industrial first rank was a much smoother process by comparison

two years of his apprenticeship, John received no wages at all. In 1836, Earl Horton became a manufacturer of steel products such as cutlery and files for which Sheffield became world-renowned. In the following year, John Brown was offered the job of factoring for Earl Horton, which involved travelling the country in a horse and gig, selling the company's wares. Brown's success led him to leave the company in 1838, and establish his own business. He now set about making cutlery, pocketknives, scissors and files for which he made his own crucible steel. This business expanded rapidly and soon Brown moved to larger premises in Furnival Street, Sheffield. He called the new works the Atlas Steel Works. In 1848, Brown invented a conical spring buffer, which found a ready market in the rapidly growing railway network. The success of his business was assured and by 1856, the

Atlas Works were moved to premises of three acres in extent at Savile Street. In 1857, he started wrought iron making and, finding a ready outlet for his products, expanded production to 100 tons per week. In 1859, Brown began the manufacture of steel by the Bessemer process, then a largely untried method. This gamble paid off but required numerous additions to plant in order to keep pace with orders, many of which were for railway products including axles, tyres and rails. [334]

ARMOUR

By the end of the 1850s, John Devonshire Ellis, a brass founder, and William Bragge, an engineer, both from Birmingham had joined John Brown as partners and together they set about establishing the manufacture of rolled armour plate in Britain. They had been encouraged in this direction by the technical revolution which had taken place in the 'line of battle' ship following the appearance of the first ironclad, the French *Gloire* in 1858. It was recognised more or less immediately that the 'wooden walls' of the Royal Navy were no longer adequate and a programme of ironclad building was initiated to preserve British naval ascendancy over the French. [335] Thus a new industry, armour plate making, was brought into being. At first, armour was simply wrought iron rolled to the required thickness and did not differ in composition from the rolled or wrought iron used widely. The function of the armour was to keep out 'shot', a solid mass of iron, fired from an opposing ship. However, the development of ballistically superior explosive shells of greater penetrating and destructive power forced the metallurgical development of armour plate, using special steels, to resist these projectiles.

By 1867, the majority of ironclads in the Royal Navy were protected by simple wrought iron armour plate rolled in the Atlas Works. The effect of this was to transform the business from 200 employees and three acres in 1857 to 4,000 employees and 21 acres in 1867. Armour plate accounted for half of the output.

To permit adequate financing of what was now a large manufacturing concern, the business was converted in 1864 into a limited liability company, taking advantage of the first Companies Act which had been passed in 1861. The flotation of the company attracted the attention of several wealthy Manchester businessmen who had previously invested in a number of iron and coal companies. They now made a significant investment in John Brown & Company and occupied four out of ten seats on the new board. John Brown was elected chairman and John D Ellis and William Bragge were appointed joint managing directors.

The expansion of the business had brought problems for John Brown. When the Board considered their chairman more extravagant with capital for new foundry plant than they thought wise, relations between the two grew steadily worse. John Brown departed from the business in 1871 about the same time that James Roger Thomson was contemplating the move from Govan to Dalmuir. [336] John Brown, who was knighted in 1867 for his part in establishing the steel industries of Sheffield, moved on to other business ventures. Although his name would live on in the company he had founded, he ceased to have any further connection with it.

One of the ventures he pursued was a directorship in Earle's Shipbuilding & Engineering Co. Ltd. of Hull, taken up in 1871. Among his co-directors were Edward J Reed, a former Chief Naval Constructor with the Royal Navy, and Admiral Robinson, formerly Third Sea Lord. Sir John Brown became Chairman of Earle's in 1874, a position he held until resignation in 1892. [337] Few of Sir John's business activities were financially rewarding and he died on 27 December 1896 at Bromley, Kent. [338]

Under the chairmanship of JD Ellis, John Brown & Co. Ltd., Sir John's former company, continued to grow, acquiring collieries at Rotherham and ore mines in Northern Spain. In 1878, the Company shifted the emphasis of production from railway products to the manufacture of ships' plates and boiler end plates. In 1879, Siemens Martin open-hearth steel making was adopted in addition to the Bessemer and crucible steel processes.

The 1880s and 90s saw the introduction of new plant and processes most of which were in response to rapidly evolving technical advances in the manufacture of armour plate and naval ordnance. Firstly, the company began making compound armour by the cementation process in which a hardened steel plate was welded to a backing plate of wrought iron. In 1886, a 4,000ton forging press for use in the manufacture of marine forgings and guns was installed. In 1892, Captain Tressider, an expert in ballistics and a manager in Company employment, patented his quenching process for face hardening steel armour plate, a method similar to the 'Harvey' process which was introduced around 1891. 1895 saw the introduction of Krupp Cemented armour which, through the use of nickel chrome alloy steel, was superior to all other armour and remained unchallenged throughout the life of the armoured warship.

By the end of the 19th Century, John Brown & Company was at the centre of armour and armaments manufacture in the United Kingdom together with the Armstrong Whitworth and Vickers Maxim companies. Two others, Cammell Laird and William Beardmore were keen to break into this exclusive club. The escalation in naval rivalry between Britain and Germany created an unprecedented period of expansion in naval shipbuilding which lasted until the end of the First World War. The acquisition of shipbuilding capacity was the logical expansion of business. The first of the armaments companies to be vertically integrated with shipbuilding was Armstrong, who had established a yard with Charles Mitchell on the Tyne at Elswick as early as 1883. Its merger with the Manchester firm of Whitworth in 1897 had added additional armour plate and forging capacity. In 1897, Vickers Maxim & Nordenfeldt, having broadly achieved a similar manufacturing profile to John Brown's, acquired the Naval Construction and Armaments Company at Barrow-in-Furness. With much of the market thus controlled, the John Brown board made the decision to secure and expand output from their works by acquiring shipbuilding capacity.

But which shipyard? By the turn of the century, the British shipbuilding industry was by far the largest in the world with over 140 yards distributed across the principal shipbuilding rivers. Brown's criteria for deciding which yard to acquire were based on product compatibility with the Sheffield Works. This could only mean large warships, particularly the battleship, as they required more armour, more heavy forgings and more armament than any other type of

George Paul Thomson and his family

warship. Yards capable of building such warships would necessarily be large establishments, thereby eliminating the majority of potential firms. The only available yards were Thames Iron Works at Blackwall, Lairds at Birkenhead, Palmers on the Tyne and both Fairfield and the Clydebank Engineering & Shipbuilding Co. on the Clyde. Surprisingly, the Board initially approached none of these and instead considered the purchase of Earle's shipyard at Hull.[339] This medium-sized firm had achieved a good record of naval construction but was verging on financial collapse.[340] With no way out of its financial difficulties, Earles finally went into voluntary liquidation in June 1900. A new company was formed under the same name at a purchase price of £170,000, less than half its value.[341]

Clydebank shipyard was thus eminently more attractive for several reasons. It had already built some of the largest and fastest ships in the world and possessed the space for even bigger vessels if required; profits over the last decade had been impressive and the business was now in very good shape. It had an excellent record in naval shipbuilding including battleships, and, in the form of the Union Bank of Scotland, which was its largest shareholder, it had a willing vendor.

Business relationships with the Clydebank firm were long established and castings, armour and other steel products had been supplied over the past twenty years.[342] Whether Sir John Brown ever visited the Clydebank firm, which later took his name with such distinction is unknown.

SOLD

Over the course of the 1890s, J&G Thomson had been consistently profitable with the exception of 1894. From 1897 to 1899, average annual profits had soared to £108,444. Negotiations for the purchase of the Works by John Brown's started early in 1899 and by 31 March the basis of the sale had been agreed. Negotiations at Clydebank were conducted by John Dunlop an indication that James Roger Thomson's future was uncertain.

On 5 June 1899, Charles Ellis, John D Ellis's son and a Board member, wrote to the Company's London solicitors with the form of words to be put to the John Brown shareholders.

'A favourable opportunity has arisen for strengthening the position of the Company by the acquisition of one of the best equipped and most successful shipyards and engine works in the United Kingdom. A provisional contract has been made with the Clydebank Engineering & Shipbuilding Co. Ltd. for the purchase of their property and business as a going concern on terms which the Directors believe are favourable to the shareholders'[343]

Discussion between members of the John Brown Board about the management of the Clydebank Works followed, with debate over the position John Dunlop would occupy. On 6 July, Ellis wrote to Dunlop offering him the position of manager of the shipyard and engine works and a directorship on the main John Brown Board adding that 'the general and financial control of the company would remain as at present.' Ellis explained that he wanted to operate separate Committees of the Board and that Clydebank would have such a Committee as would the Atlas Works and the Collieries.[344]

At a Board meeting held in Sheffield on 17 July 1899, the contract between the two Companies was sealed.[345] and the business, which had started on 2 April 1847 with £4,000 from Mrs James Thomson lodged in the Union Bank of Scotland, was sold to John Brown & Co. Ltd., for the sum of £923,255 3s 3d. At 31 March 1899 the business had a bank balance in its favour of £61,036, to which was added the sale proceeds making a total of £984,291. After deducting net liabilities of £195,950 repaying £133,157 to the remaining debenture holders and lodging £80,184 on deposit for the Spanish Government, the remaining £575,000 was distributed to shareholders, a sum equivalent to £23 per share. After a wait of nearly thirty years, the patience of the Union Bank of Scotland had been handsomely rewarded.

DISMISSED

The events of the last decade had witnessed the final elimination of the controlling interest in the Company which James and George had previously held. From 1874, partnership debts had grown and by 1884 onwards had reached a staggering £400,000. In the all embracing Trust Deed which they were obliged to sign on 19 April 1890, their shares in Messrs Caw's steamers held under Trust Deed of 1886 in favour of the Bank and their remaining property interests in Finnieston and Argyll Street and railway and shipping shares were put under the Trusteeship of William McKinnon CA acting for the Union Bank of Scotland. At that date they owed the bank £420,173-10s. Approximately three quarters of this was attributable to loans for capital investment in the yard, machinery and equipment and for the fluctuating levels of working capital required to fund

contracts. The remaining quarter represented 'the losses and overdrawings of the partners'.[346] The events surrounding the take-over by John Brown in 1899 prompted the last phase in their downfall. Although Directors, the positions they held in the management of the yard were, to some extent, supernumerary reflecting their past contribution and status. James Rodger was styled Managing Director

James Roger Thomson together with his brother George Paul had long since lost control of the business. When it was sold to John Brown & Co. in 1899, they were both dismissed ignominiously.

despite which, a considerable amount of his time was spent on sales trips abroad. Although a vital function, this barely concealed the fact that Clydebank was actually managed by John Gibb Dunlop. George Paul was Works Manager, a curious title which, in the line management structure of the Company, filled the position between Department Managers (Shipyard and engine works) and the Managing Director. On George's departure, this post was dispensed with. James Rodger and George Paul received salaries of £3,000 and £2,500 respectively together with director's bonuses, which for 1899 came to an additional £2,000 each. Their shareholding in the Company had all but been eliminated to reduce their debts to the bank and the income derived from the fifty shares they held was inconsequential. Given the lifestyle which they inherited from their father and so robustly developed, this income could barely have been adequate.

When the Clydebank Shipbuilding & Engineering Co. Ltd was in the process of being taken over by John Brown, a new Board was formed. On 2 May, James Rodger was informed that he would not be a member of this Board and that his position as Managing Director of the company would come to an end when the latter was wound up. Nevertheless, hopeful of being retained in some capacity, James Rodger indicated to the Chairman, William Donaldson, that he was content to leave the matter in his hands. The blow fell when Donaldson informed him that his services were no longer required in any capacity.[347]

For James, whose personal finances were in a critical condition, this course of events was disastrous. In June 1899 his solicitors, Watt Son & Co. wrote to the Company requesting compensation for his dismissal adding, in terms which understated the true position, 'He is very anxious to get a settlement at this time as he has some obligations to meet.' The Company refused to entertain this request maintaining that James had been paid in full for the year during which his employment was terminated. With his back against the wall, James Rodger had to fight the Company for what he could get. In October he took out a summons against the firm for £6,000 in respect of damages for dismissal and a claim for bonus. Meanwhile, with no income, his financial position collapsed and his estate was sequestrated on 28 July 1899. At a first creditors meeting held in the Elephant Hotel at Dumbarton in August 1899 it transpired that James's liabilities of £3,576, increased later to £4,718, were set against assets of only £1,270 the value of the contents of his home. At the time of sequestration, he was living in Richmond House, Dullatur, which, although rented, carried a staff of five.[348]

In the event, the Clydebank Engineering & Shipbuilding Co. (in liquidation) did agree to pay James £3,000 in full settlement of his claims against them in order to pay his creditors. In October, auctioneers Robert McTear & Co. realised £1,698 from the sale of Thomson's furniture, books, plate and pictures. James Neilson, his brother-in-law paid £20 for the family portraits. Together with the £3,000 from his old Company, Robert Reid, the Trustee, was able to pay his debts in full to 90 creditors totalling £4,718 in May 1900.

For James these events must have been a bitter conclusion to his life at Clydebank. His achievements are nevertheless worth recalling. He had been the prime mover in the decision to create the new shipyard at Clydebank in the first place with everything which that subsequently entailed. In addition to his position as head of the Company he had been the first Provost of Clydebank, Chairman of Old Kilpatrick School Board, Lieutenant Colonel in the First Dumbartonshire Rifle Volunteers (9th battalion Argyll and Southern Highlanders), Deputy Chairman of the Clydebank, Yoker & Partick Railway and a member of the Council of the Institution of Naval Architects.

His last years can only be described as miserable. He found work with the Clyde Shipbuilding & Engineering Co. Ltd of Port Glasgow and moved to London as their agent, living first in Gloucester Crescent then Regents Park and later still at St. Augustines Road, Camden. In March 1901, his eldest son, William Neilson Thomson, died in the Transvaal during, although not as a result of, the Boer War. The following year he was called to testify in the case brought by the Spanish Government against his company, a matter for which he undoubtedly felt responsible. On 12 March 1903 at the age of 58, he died suddenly of pyaemia, a form of blood poisoning while living at Morgan Mansions, Highbury. He was buried in Highgate Cemetery.

There was a sad corollary to James's death. On 18 December 1903, a letter from his widow, Emily Sarah Thomson requesting financial support was read at the monthly Clydebank Board meeting. The Board agreed that:

> 'in view of her destitute circumstances, and without in any way recognising a right to claim on the Company, a sum of 25 shillings per week should be allowed for a period of eight weeks, so that during that time, she might have an opportunity of getting employment'[349]

George fared little better. After the dismissal of his brother, George was assured that his services with the new firm would continue. On 23 September 1899, and quite unexpectedly, George received a letter from John Brown & Co. dispensing with his services from 31 March 1900 and stating that they were willing for him to go at once. George was paid his salary for the year, £2,500, together with a bonus of £1,250. George considered the bonus inadequate and asked the Company, through Watt Son & Co., to reconsider this. On 7 October 1899 his solicitors wrote:

> '. . . Our client has suffered very seriously through his loss of office and he has no immediate

prospect of employment. It will be difficult if not impossible for him to get a position as good in point of importance and involvement as that of which he is now being deprived so suddenly and without any fault or even dissatisfaction being expressed. . . . '[350]

The reply from Charles Ellis and John Dunlop stated that if he (George Paul Thomson) did not accept the offer made to him at an early date it would be withdrawn altogether.[351] George accepted. His period of unemployment was short. He died on 18 January 1902 at his home, Rosenlaui, Bearsden, Glasgow at the age of 56. George's wife also approached John Brown's for financial assistance. In May 1905, John Dunlop was authorised to give her 'a further sum of £50'[352]

It is understandable that in the circumstances of a take-over, the new board would wish to assert a fresh identity. The Thomsons' association with the Company over the last two decades had been unhappy. The poor financial performance of the Company, the inadequacies of management and the disastrous Spanish contract could all, to some extent, be laid at their door. Their personal financial excesses, so pointedly identified by Charles Gairdner of the Union Bank, did little for their credibility.

Nevertheless, it remains true that since the move to Clydebank, so enthusiastically pursued by James, the shipyard had grown into one of the most important in the world. At a time when British marine engineering skills were unsurpassed, only their Clydeside rivals Fairfield equalled the list of ships they constructed.

UNDER NEW MANAGEMENT

Clydebank shipyard and engineering works was no longer a family or even a local business. There was no single owner although there would be a dynasty of sorts through a succession of McLarens, who would remain at the head of John Brown at Sheffield and Clydebank for the next seventy years.

The events which led to the McLaren connection were first set in motion when Henry Davis Pochin took a seat on the John Brown board in Sheffield in 1861. Pochin, a manufacturing chemist, had invented a process of decomposing china clay in 1855. This process was later to become widely employed in the making of paper. His company, H D Pochin & Co., was very successful, making him a wealthy man. In addition to his membership of the John Brown board, Pochin counted many other directorships and shareholdings.[353] However, it was Pochin's son-in-

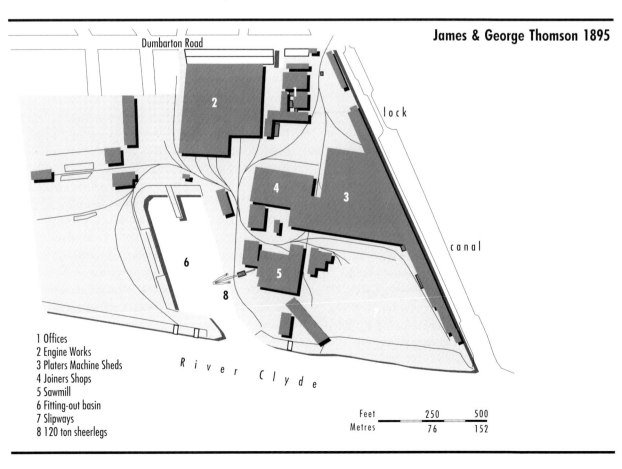

James & George Thomson 1895

1 Offices
2 Engine Works
3 Platers Machine Sheds
4 Joiners Shops
5 Sawmill
6 Fitting-out basin
7 Slipways
8 120 ton sheerlegs

Dumbarton Road

lock

canal

River Clyde

Feet	250	500
Metres	76	152

Clydebank shipyard in 1895. The purchase of additional ground to the west made the widening of the fitting-out basin possible.

law, Charles Benjamin McLaren, who was destined to carry his business forward and have a significant influence on the future of the John Brown Company. Charles McLaren was the third son of Duncan McLaren a farm servant who left his native Dalmally for Edinburgh in his early teens, later becoming Lord Provost of Edinburgh and a Liberal MP. His son Charles, later to become the first Baron Aberconway,

river, there was a small landing stage to allow the unloading of boilers and materials brought down from Glasgow as well as for the disembarkation of workmen. From the outset it was intended that the engine and boiler shops at Finnieston Street in Glasgow would be relocated at the new yard.[354] Lack of finance prevented this and consequently the operation of the new yard suffered from the same

Launch of the Japanese battleship Asahi on 13 March 1899.

married Henry Pochin's daughter. In 1883, Charles McLaren joined his father-in-law on the John Brown board followed, a year later, by Charles Ellis, the son of John Devonshire Ellis. Both newcomers to the Board were barristers. In 1895 when Henry Pochin died, Charles McLaren took over his father-in-law's business interests. When the Clydebank Engineering & Shipbuilding Company Ltd. was acquired in 1899, Charles McLaren was Deputy Chairman of John Brown.

CLYDEBANK SHIPYARD 1872/1900

On completion in 1873, the shipyard had eight building slips angled up river, large iron working machine shops, a sawmill and a joiner's shop. At the

inconvenience which afflicted the old yard principally, that after launching, ships had to be taken up river to Finnieston for the installation of engines and fitting-out. Berth dues and crane rental at Finnieston were a burdensome expense. Attempts were made to widen the small inlet at the river's edge at Dalmuir, possibly with the intention that small vessels could be completed there. The Clyde Navigation Trust was not slow to spot excavation work and stopped this in August 1872.[355] To minimise the difficulty and expense of having to send ships up to Glasgow for completion, it was decided to do as much to ships externally and internally as possible while they were still on the stocks. Boilers were brought by barge from the

Finnieston works to the yard. This required considerable manhandling and lifts of up to 30 and 40 tons, firstly to get the boilers off the barge and then to lift them into the ship. By this means, ships were virtually complete on launching and only had to be taken to Glasgow to have their engines installed. Fitting the latter took only a few days.

James Roger Thomson wrote to Cunard in August 1873 to inform them of the new procedure.

> 'We think it proper to acquaint you that we have decided in the matter of completion of your ships in our yard, to keep them on the stocks for a considerably longer time than usual, in fact until all the internal work is done that can be got done before taking on the engines. (the boilers too being put onboard before launching) This we do in the interests of the owners as much as our own and although, in the case of the *Bothnia* and *Scythia* it will entail our having to wait for the launching instalments for at least two months beyond the usual time, we shall be only too glad to accelerate the work by this arrangement . . . .'[356]

The *Espirito Santo* built for the Brazilian Steam Navigation Co., took this policy one step further. When she was launched in April 1875, it was with all machinery, boilers and engines, on board and steam up.[357] The perils of launching ships in this condition were signalled when the *Saragossa*, a large steamer of 315 feet length and over 2,260 tons, was launched on 5 May 1874. Complete with engines, boilers, masts, yards and sails, the *Saragossa* made two sudden lurches on leaving the ways and had to be drawn into the riverbank immediately to prevent capsizing.[358] The profitability of the Works from the early 1890s onwards, enabled major investment in plant and facilities to proceed and in 1896 various extensions and alterations were proposed. The engine and boiler works, now over twelve years old, required the addition of a brass foundry, copper shop and a new boiler shop for the manufacture of Belleville boilers. A total of £36,892 was voted for this purpose in February 1897. In the same year the purchase of 22 acres of land to the west of the yard for £14,300, permitted a major reorganisation and extension of capacity.[359] An additional three building berths for the construction of torpedo boat destroyers, were planned in 1897 to supplement the existing six in the main yard, at a cost of £14,953.[360] This development was postponed. £19,550 was spent on a new timber department at the extreme west of the yard. The existing sawmill was awkwardly located between the building berths and the fitting-out basin. The increasing size of ships required longer slipways and the sawmill and timber storage areas prevented the lengthening of the building berths. The foreman sawmiller and an engineer were sent on a comprehensive tour of all the leading sawmills in Great Britain and Ireland. The original estimate of £10,000 for this work eventually grew to a final total of £19,550.[361] Given the class of work undertaken at Clydebank this expenditure was fully justified and the new facility was estimated to be one of the foremost timber and woodworking departments in the country.

Between 1897 and 1900, an additional £53,1183 was spent on the shipyard, including the new timber department, and £12,243 on the engine works. Apart from a few minor additions to the ground made in the following century, the Clydebank Works had now reached their maximum extent.

Part of the above expenditure was spent equipping the Works with a new telephone system as the previous system, installed by Laurie of Falkirk in 1885 with 22 extensions, was subject to frequent breakdowns. The new Ericsson system installed in 1898 had 43 extensions to various departments throughout the yard. The Board also considered building a large four-sided steel clock tower with a 15-foot diameter clock on each side.

> 'The proposed steel tower clock should be electrically controlled and further, it should in turn, electrically control clocks in departments out west as well as alarm gongs when steam whistle cannot be heard. Whatever system is adopted it should be a thoroughly comprehensive and automatic one. The necessity can be more readily appreciated when it is recognised that every minute of our labour bill costs £3.'[362]

Although the tower was priced, it was never built. At the time of the sale to John Brown, the estate of the Company was as follows:

> Shipyard and engineering works covering an area of slightly over 70 acres; fifteen tenements, some with shops, at Dumbarton Road adjacent to the Works; Clydebank Cottage; four tenements at Union Place; feuing land at Dumbarton Road, Kilbowie Road, Roseberry Place and Union Place.[363]

1900-1913 FORGING AHEAD

John Devonshire Ellis, Chairman of John Brown & Company, presided over the first meeting of the Board at Clydebank on 22 September 1900.

A depiction of the yard about 1900.

The difficult removal of the Thomson brothers and the departure of William Donaldson simplified the creation of new management at Clydebank. The dramas of the Thomson Trust and the Thomson brothers, together with the constant financial difficulties which characterised the early years at Clydebank, were at an end. The management structure put in place during the 1890s, now shorn of the Thomsons, was augmented by the experience of a large, well established company, better able to advance its interests in home and foreign markets. William Donaldson, the outgoing Chairman, later demonstrated his satisfaction with events by placing an order for a second steam yacht, also called *Sheelah*. [364] John Gibb Dunlop's appointment as Works Manager in 1899 maintained the continued rise of Thomas Bell who became manager of the engine works. David McGee remained as manager of the Shipyard.

On 22 September 1899 the first minuted meeting of the new management took place at Clydebank. It was principally composed of members from the John Brown Sheffield board namely, Colonel Davies, Charles McLaren MP, Captain Tresidder, Charles Ellis and J E Townsend the company secretary. John Dunlop and Archibald McMillan, the assistant shipyard secretary, were the only members of Clydebank staff present. John Devonshire Ellis, the John Brown Chairman, was in the Chair. The business of this meeting was to form a Committee of the Board to oversee the operation of the Clydebank Works and to determine the manner in which Company finances would be conducted. The new management was evidently satisfied with existing financial arrangements and the Union Bank of Scotland continued to be the principal bankers. The new committee was appointed, comprising J D Ellis (Chair), CE Ellis, Colonel Davies and John Dunlop. It

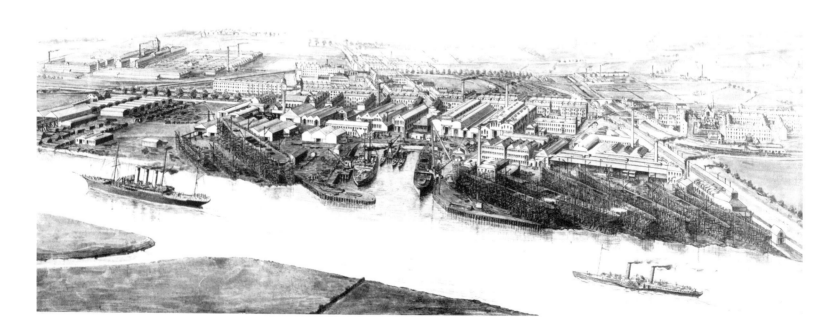

The Japanese battleship Asahi *was completed at the beginning of 1900 with the exception of her armament which was fitted elsewhere.*

The Devonshire Class cruiser Antrim *running trials in April 1905*

Opposite page
Top
Cunard decided to fit the liner Carmania, *here running trials at the end of 1905, with steam turbines to gain experience before fitting them in the much larger* Lusitania.

Bottom
A diver prepares to make a hull inspection of the Carmania *assisted by his crew.*

was agreed that this committee would meet once a month, at which time it would receive progress reports which would then be sent to the succeeding monthly meeting of the Sheffield board. The committee then established a pattern of business that would run for decades. Current enquiries and tenders were reviewed together with proposed expenditure on the Works. Some items from the first meeting follow to give an indication of details routinely discussed:

Tenders submitted:

- Lloyd Braziliero; 2 new boilers for *Porto Alegre*. Cost £2,400, profit £1,000, price £3,400
- Russian Government. Training ship. Cost £215,300, profit £15,000, Commission £5,900, price £236,200
- Admiralty; machinery for sloop *Espiegle*, cost £24,930, profit £5,000, price £29,930
- Admiralty; machinery of 22,000 ihp for first class cruisers *Essex* and *Kent*. The cost of the former was £193,735 and the latter £191,735. A profit of £18,690 was added to both figures.
- Admiralty; machinery for 2 first class battleships cost £172,180; profit £14,000, price £186,180 each
- Chinese Eastern Railway Co.; four 275' steamers. Cost £60,926, profit £6,092, commission £671, price £67,898, tendered at £67,500 for the first and £66,000 for each of the others, reserving the right of subcontract.

Enquiries received:

- G&J Burns for a 20 knot 320' paddle steamer and a 250' screw steamer of 13.75 knots.

106

Correspondence:

- Proposal from Schultz (agents) that Chinese orders should be taken on the basis of 7 to 10 years deferred payments was considered and declined.

Works expenditure:

- Piling of new slipways at west yard and forming wharf. Cost £1,400
- Piling and concreting under sheerlegs. Cost £1,200
- Mr Dunlop reported that a pension of £18 per annum had been paid for some years to Euphemia Neil, an old servant of the Clydebank Co., and it was agreed to continue this.[365]

The only successful tender from the above was the machinery for the twin screw cruiser *Essex*. As before,

The TBD Arab *running trials in October 1902. Difficulties in getting earlier destroyers to reach their designed speed had been overcome by the time* Arab *and her sister* Kestrel *were laid down.* Arab *made 31.78 knots on speed trials.*

the conversion of tenders into orders was low. In 1899, a total of 37 tenders was prepared from which the construction of five ships and one set of machinery resulted. This approximated to a one in six chance of winning an order.

While bidding for battleships and liners in the region of £1 million each, the Company was also tendering for thirteen foot long dinghies for the Admiralty at a price of £32 each. As John Brown built all of the lifeboats fitted in its ships, this was clearly intended to maintain employment in the boat shed.[366]

In October 1899, the Board became aware that other parties were bidding for the ground to the immediate west of the yard. As this was the only ground adjacent to the yard available for future expansion it was left to John Dunlop to decide on a counter bid. He decided not to proceed.[367] This ground was eventually acquired by William Beardmore & Co., Ltd. who, between the years 1900 and 1906, constructed a 100-acre shipyard and engine works on the site. Beardmore's intention to build the highest class of naval and merchant tonnage placed his new works in direct competition with Clydebank. The two miles of river from Clydebank to Dalmuir became arguably the most heavily concentrated shipbuilding and marine engineering site for the construction of warships and passenger vessels in the United Kingdom.

In the first few years of the century, ships of all types and sizes were under construction at Clydebank. Among these vessels were the paddle steamers *Mars* and *Duchess of Montrose*, the ferry *Duke of Connaught*, the Cunard liner *Pannonia*, the merchantmen *Suffolk* and *Essex*, the cruiser *Antrim* and the battleship *Hindustan*. On a much smaller scale was the paddle tug *Energetic* and William Donaldson's magnificent yacht *Sheelah*. The contract for the 19,500 ton Cunard liner *Caronia* was won in 1903, followed by a sister, *Carmania*, less than a year later.

Interest shown in the products of the various works within the John Brown group was satisfied by arranging visits. In June 1903, 500 workers from the Sheffield works travelled to Clydebank to see round the yard and view the launch of the New Zealand Steamship Co's *Kaikoura*, the first of two built for that company.[368]

The years leading up to the First World War were characterised by the rapid succession of events which were to change the political, commercial and technical environment in which the Company operated. Threats to British dominance of the North Atlantic, new systems of propulsion, the advent of the revolutionary battleship *Dreadnought* and the acceleration of Anglo-German naval rivalry, drove the Company forward to new levels of achievement and prosperity.[369]

INTERNATIONAL MERCANTILE MARINE

In 1900, J Pierpoint Morgan, the American financier and industrialist, set about creating a shipping

combine to secure a significant share of North Atlantic trade for American interests.

By February 1902, an agreement had been reached in which major shipping lines were incorporated into Morgan's syndicate – White Star Line, Ismay Imrie & Co., Dominion Line, American Line, Red Star Line, Atlantic Transport Co., and the Leyland Line. British maritime sensibilities were further shaken when two leading German lines, Norddeutscher Lloyd and Hamburg Amerika, pooled their ships with those of the syndicate. William Pirrie, Chairman of Harland & Wolff, had a particular interest in the formation of the syndicate through the White Star line and an agreement was reached whereby Harland & Wolff would receive 'all orders for new vessels and for heavy repairs requiring to be done in the United Kingdom'.[370] This was a major prize for Harland & Wolff, and of direct concern to British yards specialising in this class of work. In September 1902 the syndicate was given the name International Mercantile Marine with capital of $120 million at its disposal (then equivalent to £24 million). IMM made several offers for Cunard, which was particularly vulnerable. Cunard considered these offers inadequate. It was clear, however, that an improved offer might succeed.[371] The above events were rightly construed as an open attempt to wrest control of the Atlantic shipping trade from British hands. To ensure that Cunard remained British, an amalgamation with another British company was briefly considered. In March 1902, Vickers Son & Maxim courted the possibility of acquiring a major interest in Cunard.[372] In October 1902, John Brown's shipyard became the subject of a potential take-over bid by IMM. The London ship owners and agents, Little & Johnston, were authorised by 'New York gentlemen of very high social and financial standing' to make an offer for the Clydebank Works which would have included the yard as part of an American Shipbuilding Trust. In reply, John Dunlop informed Little & Johnston that his company had no intention of parting with the shipyard[373] The indirect outcome of Morgan's intervention on the North Atlantic was twofold; Government recognition of Cunard's position as the national shipping line and the contracts for *Lusitania* and *Mauretania*.

LUSITANIA

The concern and indignation created by the International Mercantile Marine's threat to British interests was compounded by German conquest of the North Atlantic. A succession of large German

liners, culminating in the *Kaiser Wilhelm II*, had eclipsed the pride of the British merchant marine - the ships of the Cunard and White Star Lines. This prompted a sustained public outcry, supported by the press, vociferously advocating a British reply. The climate created enabled Cunard to make an approach to the Government for financial support in the construction of two giant liners to

reassert British maritime supremacy. The Government was a willing partner and the ships which resulted were the legendary *Lusitania* and *Mauretania*. Two principal conditions were that Cunard should remain a British company and that the ships should be capable of operating as armed merchant cruisers in time of war.

As early as May 1901, Cunard had considered new, fast steamers for the New York trade and by August outline plans for a 700' steamer capable of 23.5 to 24 knots had been prepared by James Bain, Cunard's General Superintendent and Leonard Peskett, their naval architect.[374]

In February 1902, Cunard, intent on building two ships, prepared specifications which were sent to three leading shipbuilders, Fairfield, Vickers and John Brown, with the request that an indication of cost and delivery dates be given, adding that the enquiry was to be treated as private and confidential.[375] In March, Cunard raised the issue of a loan to build the ships

The Admiralty paddle tug Energetic.

Opposite page below
The paddle steamer Mars *built for the Glasgow & South Western Railway Co.*

with the Government and in September, the Prime Minister, Arthur Balfour, announced agreement subject to certain conditions.[376] In October, C S Swan & Hunter[377] wrote to Cunard stating their intention to tender for the new ships. In the following month, Albert Vickers wrote to Lord Inverclyde stating that if Vickers were appointed sole builders they would ' . . . enter into a permanent arrangement to be the builders of your company's ships . . .'[378] In December 1902, John Brown sent Cunard three different designs offering to build the ship on commission for an approximate price of £1,350,000. Interest in such prestigious contracts crossed national boundaries resulting in probably the most unwelcome request to tender given the reason for building the ships in the first place. This was from the German Vulcan Shipbuilding Company of Stettin who asked if they could tender for the ships on the basis of using British materials only. Cunard replied that 'their offer cannot be entertained even under the conditions proposed by them.'[379]

Government terms, announced in July 1903, allowed for a loan of £2.6 million to be repaid over 20 years, at a rate of 2.75% per annum. It was agreed that a further sum of £150,000 would be paid to Cunard annually, on the basis that the ships could be armed and called to national service in times of emergency. This condition attached to the loan was not a precedent. In 1887, by arrangement with the Admiralty, *Etruria, Umbria, Aurania, Servia*, and *Gallia* were to be taken into service as armed merchant cruisers in time of war.[380] Many ships of the White Star Line were similarly committed for possible employment as cruisers.

By 1903, Fairfield had dropped out of the running.[381] A series of model experiments to determine the principal dimensions of the proposed ships was conducted at the Admiralty Experiment tank at Haslar and the results passed to the potential builders to assist them in the design and estimating process. On 8 May 1903, the Cunard Board at Liverpool interviewed builders' representatives, including Charles Ellis and John Dunlop for John Brown. After this meeting John Brown and Swan Hunter were told that Cunard directors:

'were inclined to favourably consider the placing of an order with each of them for one of the proposed fast steamers, provided they would meet and collaborate with the view to producing duplicate ships . . . and submit for the consideration of the Directors the result of their deliberations and show the steamer which they would recommend.'

However, as the precise details of the ships had still to be determined, the contracts for *Lusitania* and *Mauretania* were not signed until 18 May 1905 at a meeting between both builders and Cunard in London. Charles Ker of the Glasgow firm of accountants McClelland Ker & Co. was appointed as auditor to the contracts and Mr C G Hall, an assistant naval constructor, was appointed Admiralty

Inspector. The ships were to be ready for trials in 30 months which indicated November 1907.

Speed was of critical importance as the following conditions specify:

Condition 1 required a mean speed of 25.25 knots on six runs between Ailsa Craig and Holy Island.
Condition 2 required a mean of 25.25 knots between Corsewall Light (Loch Ryan) and Chicken Light (Isle of Man)
Condition 3 required an average speed of 24.75 knots over 1,200 miles.
The penalty to be exacted if the average ocean speed fell below 24.5 knots over the first year of operation was £10,000 per 0.1 knot.

The cost of each ship to Cunard was calculated in four parts:

1. Materials, parts and wages
2. Establishment Charges of 15% on above
3. Cost of delivery to Liverpool, dry-docking, coal for trials and building insurance
4. 5% profit on all of above.

The hydraulic riveter suspended from the counter-balanced beam on the trolley, was made by the Glasgow structural steel company Sir William Arrol. It is seen here working on the shell of Lusitania. Note the complete lack of handrails or other supports for the platers.

Opposite page
The 150 ton giant cantilever fitting-out crane under construction on the west side of the fitting-out basin in 1907. This crane was designed and built by Sir William Arrol & Co. of Dalmarnock Glasgow and was the first of many to be built by Arrol for shipyards and ports around the world.

Above
A row of staging around the upper part of Lusitania's *hull indicates final touches of paint prior to her launch.*

Right
7 June 1906 and the largest ship in the world slips into the Clyde.

Above
*A magnificent view over the
forward part of* Lusitania *from
the 150 ton crane shows work
well advanced.*

Left
Lusitania *dressed overall prior to
running trials. The 150 ton
cantilever crane has recently been
commissioned.*

Cunard had consulted Charles Parsons, inventor of the reaction marine steam turbine, in December 1901, over the use of turbines in large steamers. As this novel form of propulsion was untried, Cunard decided it would not be appropriate for the new ships and thus early designs specified reciprocating machinery. In August 1903 however, with some evidence of the potential of turbines now available,

mountings were fitted on the forecastle and shelter decks and provision made for sighting ports and magazine spaces.[383]

The Turbine Committee inspected a number of land and marine turbine installations. As there were very few turbine powered vessels in service, two Denny-built steamers the turbine driven *Brighton* and the reciprocator *Arundel*, were used for comparative trials

Lusitania was a magnificently appointed ship. This view shows a less well known view of the standard of accommodation in the 3rd Class Dining Room.

Cunard changed its mind. Parsons was again consulted together with Leslie Denny, whose Dumbarton shipyard had fitted the first turbine into a sea-going ship, *King Edward*, in 1901. Cunard then decided to form a committee to consider the question of propulsion. Known as the Turbine Committee, membership included the most eminent marine engineers in the country, among them was Thomas Bell of John Brown.[382] The secretary to the committee appointed by the Admiralty was Engineer Lieutenant W H Wood RN, who later became manager of the engine works at Clydebank.

The Admiralty maintained keen interest in the development of the ships and the builders liased with Sir Philip Watts, Director of Naval Construction, over their design. Twelve gun positions for 6-inch

on the English Channel. On 24 March 1904, the Turbine Committee took the bold step of recommending the adoption of steam turbines. This was a great leap forward in deploying a technology of such recent origin. With the choice of machinery finally settled, the design of the hull could now be completed and an exact specification prepared.

John Brown and Swan Hunter approached this aspect of design in different ways. At Clydebank, the Board had approved the building of an experiment tank and model shop at an estimated cost of £15,000. Here, accurate models of vessels would be made and tested under simulated sea conditions to determine the most effective design of hull form.[384] Swan Hunter approached the same task by making a 47 foot long self-propelled experimental launch which was tested exhaustively in the Northumberland Dock adjacent to the River Tyne.

The new experiment tank at Clydebank was not ready until late 1903 and, in the interim, both John Brown and Swan Hunter were able to access the results of model tests at the Admiralty tank at Haslar and the Denny Ship Model experiment tank at Dumbarton. The Clydebank Company paid Denny the sum of £1000 guineas for this work.[385] By April 1904, tank testing was completed and the dimensions of the ships fixed at 760' x 87.75' x 32.5' and 36,500 tons displacement.

To provide some experience in the operation of turbine machinery on a large ship, Cunard asked John Brown to complete *Carmania*, the second of two 21,000ton ships recently ordered, with turbines in order to compare her performance with the quadruple expansion engines in *Caronia*. Much later, Sir Thomas Bell recalled the reluctance felt at Clydebank:

> '. . . to our horror, they (Cunard) thought a very good way of further testing this would be to stop the reciprocating engines they had commenced for Carmania and to fit turbine engines instead. They thought it would make excellent experience for them. Well, we could not refuse or say anything about it seeing we had agreed to put turbines in the two much larger vessels, so, with the best grace we could muster, we set about designing these turbines - at least Parsons did that, working in conjunction with us and finally - I may tell you after some hairbreadth escapes and troubles - we finished the turbines and got them on board, and on the sea voyages she actually kept level with the Caronia, the reciprocating ship, and the most of the trouble was due to the numbers of ill-designed auxiliaries and how serious a matter their consumption of steam was which really did away with any saving the turbines themselves had over the reciprocators'.[386]

To acquire experience in constructing *Carmania's* engines, a design for triple screw turbine machinery of 1,800 horsepower, was obtained from Parsons. At Clydebank, work continued round the clock to build these engines which, on completion, were subjected to six months of exhaustive shop tests. Only after this, in August 1904, could work on *Carmania's* turbines begin. By this time, construction of *Carmania* was well underway and *Lusitania* had been laid down. The small set of experimental turbines was later fitted into the Glasgow & South Western Railway Company's *Atalanta*, launched in April 1906.

The largest ships built at Clydebank hitherto were the previously mentioned *Caronia* and *Carmania* of 19,594 grt.[387] The increase in size from the *Carmania* to the *Lusitania* was significant and represented a hull over 100 feet longer and a tonnage of over half as much again. Construction of *Lusitania* forced a number of alterations to facilities and plant at all stages of the construction process, at a cost of £61,000.[388] *Lusitania*

One of Lusitania's *1ˢᵗ Class Cabins*

was laid down on 17 August 1904. Paradoxically, her construction coincided with a reduction in employment caused by a dwindling order book. In September 1904, 4,735 men were employed in the shipyard. One year later there would only be 2,841. *Lusitania* was launched on 7 June 1906. As a mark of respect for the late Lord Inverclyde, who had died in 1905, Lady Inverclyde christened the ship. On a magnificent summer's day, the launch of the world's largest ship attracted a record crowd. All 7,500 employees in the shipyard and engine works were given the day off to watch the spectacle and thousands of others filled the yard and lined the south bank of the Clyde:

> 'They came by train, motor and tramway car and

cab from Glasgow, surrounding districts, from many towns in the West of Scotland and by special trains the previous night from London, Liverpool and Sheffield while residents of Clydebank itself turned out almost as a body'[389]

Among the 550 invited guests were many officials from Cunard, John Brown, the Admiralty, and the Government. The Deputy Chairman of John Brown, Charles McLaren, stood in for 82 year old John Devonshire Ellis who was too unwell to attend.

'The launching platform itself was a blaze of colour, the crimson of the carpeting and railings mingling with the white dresses and parasols of the ladies and the black coats of the gentlemen'[390]

At 12.30, the christening bottle was despatched by Lady Inverclyde. At first, it seemed as if the ship was not going to move. Then, almost imperceptibly, she gathered speed and slid majestically into the Clyde entering the mouth of the River Cart to the accompaniment of the Clydebank Burgh Brass Band. Over the following year, an army of craftsmen descended on the ship to bring her to completion. At the peak of fitting-out, nearly 440 carpenters and 980 joiners were employed in the yard. As work proceeded, Cunard became increasingly concerned at the escalating cost of *Lusitania* and her Tyne built sister *Mauretania*. It was clear that the rate of monthly drawings would exhaust the Government loan of £2.6 million long before the ships were completed. At one stage, relations between builders and owner deteriorated sharply. Cunard demanded to know why the cost of the ships had escalated and suggested that they had been deceived into ordering the ships by the builders who deliberately submitted low tenders.[391] In reply, both builders argued that Cunard's auditors and technical staff assigned to both yards had checked and approved expenditure on a monthly basis.

The final cost of *Lusitania* was £1,651,870.16s. 1d, greatly in excess of the £1.3m estimated in 1903. This total was made up of the following elements:

Materials	£924,511 15s 8d
Wages	£445,907 12s 8d
Charges and Profit	£281, 451 7s 9d.[392]

With a final cost of £1,812,251, the situation with *Mauretania* was more serious, forcing Cunard to suspend payments to Swan Hunter.[393] Cunard estimated that *Lusitania* had cost and additional £230,000 while *Mauretania* had cost an additional £400,000.[394] Cunard asked both builders for a rebate on the final price. In agreeing to pay Cunard £30,000[395], John Gibb Dunlop wrote to Cunard's secretary, Watson:

'having regard to the close and friendly relations that have so long existed between the two companies, they [the John Brown Board] agreed that the sum of £30,000 should be deducted from the amount owing by the Cunard Company to ourselves. I informed my colleagues of my private conversation with you and they feel that you will do your best that we shall be ultimately rewarded for the very large pecuniary sacrifice we are now making'[396]

LUSITANIA'S TRIALS

Ship trials were run to ensure that the ship fulfilled the technical conditions set out in the building contract, principally with regard to horse power, speed and fuel consumption. Representatives of the owners and builders were present, with the latter still legally responsible for the vessel. Surveyors from both Lloyds and the Board of Trade were also in attendance. Successful completion of trials would result in the official hand over of the vessel to Cunard.

The *Lusitania's* acceptance programme started on 27 July 1907 with progressive trials. Immediately prior to the trials, her hull had been inspected and cleaned at the Canada Dock in Liverpool[397] there being no dock on the Clyde capable of accommodating such a large vessel. Fourteen separate trial runs were made on the Skelmorlie measured mile, the first two of which averaged a speed of 25.63 knots. Twelve other runs were made at varying speeds to determine fuel consumption. At the end of the day, the ship anchored at the Tail of the Bank to await the arrival of invited guests before making a cruise around Ireland. *Lusitania* left the Clyde that evening and arrived at the Liverpool Bar light-ship on the morning of the 29th. Speed trials then took place on the Firth of Clyde from 30 July until 1 August. The first of the speed trials comprised four runs between Corsewall Lighthouse off Galloway and Longships Lighthouse at Land's End, a distance of 304 miles. Two runs with the tide recorded 26.4 knots and 26. 32 knots. Two runs against the tide recorded 24.32 knots and 24.65 knots. The next trial comprised two runs from Corsewall Lighthouse to Chicken Rock, a distance of 59.75 miles. The run north was completed at a speed of 26.7 knots and the run south at 26.5 knots. The third and last set of speed trials comprised six continuous runs between Ailsa Craig and Holy

Island, a distance of 16 miles, during which *Lusitania* maintained a speed of 25.75 knots throughout. The trials were very successful and the report produced later noted that 'during the whole series of runs the main and auxiliary machinery worked very satisfactorily and without a hitch'[398]

Before *Lusitania* left Clydebank for the last time, she was opened to the public. The sum of £800 was taken in the form of admission charges and donated to charity.[399] *Lusitania* was handed over to her owners on 26 August 1907 and her maiden voyage from Liverpool to New York was begun on 7 September. However, it was not until the following month that she took the Blue Riband at an average speed of 23.99 knots on the east-west passage. On the return voyage she broke the west-east record at 23.61 knots.[400] The Blue Riband was again safely in British hands.

Lusitania's record was later taken by her sister *Mauretania* which proved to be the slightly faster of the two.[401]

Cunard's decision to build giant ships with steam turbines paid off handsomely. It also placed John Brown at the forefront of turbine technology. This was to prove a tremendous asset to the Company and contributed greatly to success in winning further contracts for ships with powerful machinery installations. However, much of this success would not be achieved with Parsons' turbines but with those of an American competitor by the name of Charles Gordon Curtis.

A QUESTION OF TURBINES

By the end of the 19th Century, triple and quadruple expansion (reciprocating) engines powered most of

Built to reassert British supremacy on the North Atlantic, Lusitania's trials started on 27 July 1907. Her maiden voyage from Liverpool to New York began on 7 September although she did not take the Blue Riband for the fastest crossing until October.

117

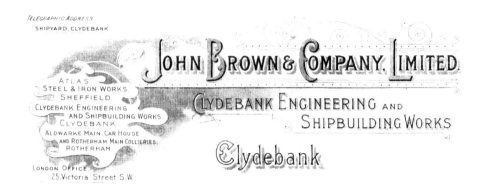

ATLAS STEEL & IRON WORKS SHEFFIELD
CLYDEBANK ENGINEERING AND SHIPBUILDING WORKS CLYDEBANK
ALDWARKE MAIN, CAR HOUSE AND ROTHERHAM MAIN COLLIERIES, ROTHERHAM
LONDON OFFICE, 25 Victoria Street S.W.

TELEGRAPHIC ADDRESS
SHIPYARD, CLYDEBANK

JOHN BROWN & COMPANY, LIMITED.
CLYDEBANK ENGINEERING AND SHIPBUILDING WORKS
Clydebank

The company letterhead which was in use during the early years of the 20th Century.

the world's steamships. The prospect of a new form of propulsion harnessing steam was first demonstrated in 1897, when Charles Parsons, in a spectacular display of showmanship, dashed up and down the serried ranks of the British battlefleet at the Spithead Naval Review in his launch *Turbinia*. The motive power that enabled him to propel this craft at speeds up to an unprecedented 34 knots was the marine steam turbine. The turbine was not a new idea, but Charles Parsons was the first to apply it successfully to marine propulsion. With such a vivid show of capability, the Admiralty could not ignore the potential of this engine, and in the following year ordered the turbine driven torpedo boat destroyer, *Viper*, from Parsons.[402] The turbine was conceptually more sophisticated and mechanically simpler than previous marine engines. Steam filled cylinders, driving piston rods up and down on the crankshaft three or four times a second, were replaced by a quiet, rapidly rotating turbine inside a cast steel casing. Inherently better balanced and more compact, the turbine generated less vibration. Importantly, where a large reciprocating engine extended upwards through several decks, the turbine could easily be accommodated on one. After their adoption in the battleship *Dreadnought* in 1905, turbines displaced reciprocating machinery in the Royal Navy for every significant class of warship from destroyers up. Within a few years, the turbine was the only type of machinery employed in British warships from destroyer size upwards. Charles Parsons erected works at Wallsend on the North East Coast to construct marine turbines but it was clear that demand would soon outstrip his ability to supply. Licence agreements with shipyards followed and in October 1903, John Dunlop, Clydebank's managing director, negotiated with Parsons to become one of the first shipbuilders to sign a manufacturing

agreement.[403] This permitted the construction of turbines at Clydebank from 1 January 1904 for a period of 15 years. The licence cost £2,500 with a royalty of 2s 6d (12.5p) for every unit of horsepower developed by the engine during full power trials.[404] In 1904 it was decided that an experimental turbine would be constructed at a cost of £7,000 to provide manufacturing experience, and in the hope that this turbine could later be fitted into a ship.[405]

By 1905, John Brown had particular reason to be well satisfied with Charles Parsons and his marine turbine. *Carmania*, the first large turbine driven passenger liner was nearing completion; *Lusitania*, the largest ship in the world, was to be turbine powered and the Admiralty had issued invitations to tender for the turbines for the battleship *Dreadnought*.[406] Parsons was not alone in producing designs for a marine steam turbine and at least four others, Curtis, Rateau, De Laval and Ljüngstrom, had patented turbine designs. Curtis had patented his in 1896, and by the following year, had reached an agreement with the General Electric Company, to whom the commercial rights were sold and development facilities secured at its Schenectady works in New York. In 1902, the German Allgemeine Elektricitäts Gesellschaft (AEG) company acquired rights to the Curtis turbine. The Hamburg Amerika liner *Kaiser*, built in 1905 at the Vulkan Works, Stettin, was the first to sail with AEG-Curtis turbines. The Curtis turbine differed in principle from Parsons'. It required less rigorous tolerances between fixed and moving blades, and was more compact and generally more robust. Almost certainly the Admiralty encouraged John Brown to pursue the Curtis turbine which, in 1907, had been selected to power the US Navy battleship *North Dakota*, building at the Fore River shipyard. Thomas Bell, Clydebank's engine works manager had more experience of building turbines than any other marine engineer in the UK. In 1907, Bell travelled to the United States to meet Curtis. They met at the Schenectady Works where he was shown Curtis land turbines under construction. While there, he was introduced to Curtis's assistant, Stephen Joseph Pigott, a talented young graduate engineer. Although Bell was impressed by what he had seen, he was unsuccessful in securing manufacturing rights.[407] By January 1908 negotiations were again underway, and in May, agreement was finally reached between John Brown & Company and the International Curtis Marine Turbine Company.[408] John Brown became the second European company, after AEG, to acquire manufacturing rights.

The Admiralty were quick to investigate the potential of the new turbine. In June 1908, they approved expenditure of £14,000 for the construction of a demonstration turbine of 2,500 shp.[409] Part of the arrangement with the Curtis company was that Stephen Pigott should come to Clydebank for a period of one year to assist in the development of the turbine. Charles Curtis booked a passage on *Lusitania* for Pigott, his wife Mary and their four month old son writing to Thomas Bell:

> 'We have thought it desirable that our Mr Pigott should cross on the Lusitania, both to see the ship and to save time. Owing to the fact that he is very susceptible to sea sickness, and that his wife, who has been quite delicate, is also extremely prone to sea sickness and is taking the baby with them, we have wanted Mr Pigott, to have a comfortable stateroom.'[410]

Pigott arrived in Clydebank in July 1908 and remained there for the rest of his working life despite attempts by Curtis to entice him back with lucrative offers of employment.[411] The development work on the turbine was highly successful and the turbine became known as the Brown-Curtis turbine.[412] To test the turbine, the Admiralty decided to instal it in two Town Class cruisers, *Bristol* to be built by John Brown and *Yarmouth* to be built by the London & Glasgow Company at their Govan shipyard. Admiralty approval resulted in a demand for manufacturing rights from other builders. At first, sub-licences had to be acquired from AEG, but the costs were so prohibitive that John Brown cabled Charles Curtis telling him that his presence here for an urgent meeting was 'absolutely necessary in view of the trend of opinion on the continent'.[413] The result of this meeting was that John Brown would be the UK licence provider. Royalties paid to John Brown by anyone purchasing a licence, were split equally between the John Brown and Curtis Companies.[414] By October 1909, sub-licences were in preparation for Fairfield, Yarrow and Thornycroft followed by Hawthorn Leslie and Wallsend Slipway in March 1910.[415] In October, after the Admiralty issued tenders for destroyers with Brown-Curtis turbines, John Brown was inundated with requests for estimates to build this machinery from most of the major engine builders in the UK.

The Imperial Japanese Navy, with plans to build a major fleet, took great interest in the Brown-Curtis turbine. In August 1910, Thomas Bell was in discussion with their representative, Captain Fuji who had asked for information on the turbine which they hoped to evaluate. In a letter written after this meeting, Bell said:

> 'What I would like to explain to you is that this information represents the whole of the results and experience acquired by us at great cost, not only from the Curtis Co. but as the result of over 12 months of experiments with turbine buckets and nozzles in the 2,500hp experimental turbine which we designed, constructed and erected in our yard at the request of the British Admiralty, who, in return for same, have awarded us with the contract for the machinery of the cruisers Bristol and Yarmouth and of 4 torpedo boat destroyers . . .'

Bell explained to Fuji that he had decided not to give this information to the Japanese Navy noting however, that should the order for this machinery be placed at Clydebank, 'we should be delighted to place the whole of our information and experience at the services of the Japanese Admiralty'[416]

DREADNOUGHT

Battleships were technically complex and expensive to build. They were formidable fighting machines equivalent in importance, if not in destructive power, to the ballistic nuclear submarine of the late 20th century. British naval supremacy was based on a fleet of fifty battleships. Unchallenged for almost 100 years, in the first decade of the 20th century, the Royal Navy was confronted with technical change and a new threat.

Germany naval policy, enshrined in the Naval Laws of 1898 and 1900, directed efforts towards the creation of a major battlefleet of which the British would have to take account. British response was initially half-hearted because of the crushing superiority of the Royal Navy. And so it might have remained had not the revolutionary battleship *Dreadnought*, been constructed at Portsmouth Dockyard in 1906. This battleship was a great advance on existing types. This had been achieved by mounting an unprecedented number of heavy guns of uniform calibre on a hull propelled by steam turbines. *Dreadnought* was hard hitting and fast. The man responsible for the creation of *Dreadnought* was Admiral Sir John Fisher, the remarkable and controversial, First Sea Lord. While Fisher had unquestionably stolen a technical first over the other maritime powers, it was the Royal Navy that had most to lose. All fifty existing battleships in the British fleet, later classified as Pre-dreadnoughts, were relegated to the second rank. The British preponderance in numbers had evaporated.

Three views of the battlecruiser Inflexible *during trials on the Firth of Clyde in 1908.*

Above
Work progressing fixing fittings to the ship.

Opposite page top
Looking forward over 'A' turret from the port bridge wing.

Opposite page bottom
Inflexible *working up on full power trials. She developed 43,390 shp for a speed of 25.5 knots.*

Thus, Fisher resolved that *Dreadnought* and her successors would have to be built quickly. Ironically, the opportunity had now arisen for Germany to match the British in numbers. The Admiralty took comfort in the knowledge that German shipbuilding capacity was not equal to the British. For shipbuilders, battleships were prestigious and lucrative contracts. Moreover, shipyards, including John Brown, had flourished under a succession of Admiralty orders. The impact of the political situation on naval procurement encouraged fresh investment in large new naval yards like Beardmore on Clydeside (completed in 1906) and Armstrong's on the Tyne, (completed in 1913). Fisher was not content with the dreadnought battleship alone and promoted another type of warship based on a merger of the tactical roles played by the battleship and the armoured cruiser. The warship that emerged was the battlecruiser.[417] Longer

than battleships, battlecruisers carried fewer heavy guns on a less heavily armoured hull. The reduced armament and armour was offset by more powerful propelling machinery to give high speed. Speed would be protection and battlecruisers were fast. Whether by accident or design, John Brown was destined to play a leading part in the construction of the battlecruiser.

To re-establish the superiority of the British battlefleet, nine dreadnoughts were laid down soon after *Dreadnought* was completed, of which three were battlecruisers. Every succeeding class was bigger than the last with more or bigger guns, greater speed and heavier armour. This was very much in line with Fisher's dictum 'Build first and build fast, each one better than the last'. In placing these contracts, care was taken to ensure that the private yards were included in addition to the main naval dockyards at Devonport and Portsmouth. Armstrong received

orders for two dreadnoughts, and John Brown, Fairfield and Vickers for one each. The John Brown order was for *Inflexible*, a battlecruiser of the Invincible Class, which was laid down on February 1906, a few days before *Dreadnought* was launched at Portsmouth.

The creation of this dreadnought fleet sat uncomfortably with efforts made by Balfour's Conservative Government to reduce naval expenditure. In January 1906, the Liberal Government took office on a mandate of social reform. The Naval Estimates fell from £42 million in 1904/5 to £36 million in 1906/7 and did not rise again until 1909/10. Between 1907 and 1910, an acute depression in merchant orders hit the shipbuilding industry. Unemployment in shipbuilding rose sharply and several yards, including Beardmore's new works at Dalmuir, were on the point of closure.[418] The order book at Clydebank began to dwindle. Only three

vessels were laid down in 1908, the largest of which was the 12,000 grt *Orsova* for the Orient Line. The slump was evident as early as May 1907 when John Dunlop, works manager, noted that unless new orders were booked, prospects for the yard looked bad.[419] On 29 September 1907, ironworkers went on strike after management refused an increase in pay rates. In the middle of a trade slump, this was not an

The Orient liner Orsova *on trials in 1909.*

Montrose Street, Clydebank showing terraced houses on the left for managers and foremen and tenements on the right for workmen.

opportune moment and the men were forced to return without the increase on 21 November. In the same month, Dunlop noted in his report: 'I regret exceedingly to report that no new work of any description has been received during the past month and in consequence the shipyard is almost at a standstill.'[420] In a strong position, the employers acted

to regulate wage levels on 28 December, when a notice was posted in the yard announcing a general reduction for all trades of 5% on piecework and a farthing (0.1p) on time rates. On return from the New Year holiday, sheet ironworkers held a meeting at lunchtime to discuss the reductions and quickly decided that they would strike. On the following day, coppersmiths and tinsmiths struck. By 2 March, the coppersmiths had returned, followed by the sheet ironworkers two days later. They had little option but to accept the employer's conditions.[421] Between November 1907 and January 1908, one quarter of John Brown's workforce was paid off, reducing in number from 5,741 to 4,472.

Admiralty contracts, which had been a permanent feature of the order book since the mid 1880s, came to an end. With the exception of a small naval paddle tug *Rambler*, the battlecruiser *Inflexible* was the last ship to be laid down for the Admiralty until July 1909, an interval of over three years. While John Brown's association with the Admiralty languished, a working partnership with an important shipbuilder was formed. This was initiated in May 1907[422] when Lord Pirrie, Chairman of Harland & Wolff, proposed an exchange of shares with John Brown. The Belfast Harbour Commission had refused Harland & Wolff's request for additional ground on which to lay out new berths. The volume of orders flowing into the yard was greater than it alone could handle prompting amalgamation with Clydebank, which had capacity to spare.[423] The arrangement had the additional advantage of giving Harland & Wolff access to Brown's turbine technology which they had not yet developed. In addition to accessing the Morgan syndicate's requirement for high-class merchant tonnage, John Brown's Atlas Works at Sheffield would benefit in orders for steel castings and forgings for ships under construction at Belfast. The first fruit of this arrangement was the turbine order for the White Star liner *Laurentic* under construction at Belfast.

BATTLESHIPS FOR THE TSAR

After defeat by the Japanese at the Battle of Tsushima in 1905, Russia was reduced in importance as a naval power from third position to sixth. Initially unwilling to spend large sums on what was regarded as a defeated force, a major programme of new construction was put before the Duma together with plans for capital investment in Russian shipyards. Reluctance to authorise new ships in the aftermath of Tsushima was also the result of severe financial difficulties caused by that conflict. In building new ships, it was recognised that technical assistance, together with the supply of components, particularly propelling machinery, would have to come from abroad.

Since the construction of the torpedo boat *Wiborg* in 1886, the Imperial Russian Navy had not contracted Clydebank shipyard. However, two training ships, *Kiev* and *Moskva* had been built for the Russian Volunteer Fleet. The first sign of renewed contact with the Russian Navy took place in May 1906, when a letter was received at John Brown's London office in Victoria Street from a source within the Russian Naval Ministry. This letter stated that an agency with a large British shipbuilding yard was sought to assist in the rebuilding of the Russian fleet, following the raising of a new Government loan.

> 'It is a preconceived opinion here in the best informed circles, that a large part of the orders for new men of war will have to go to England, as the only country which is able to complete such orders within a short time. Germany, which would have counted as a serious competitor a month ago, is not favourably looked upon now after the failure of German bankers to take part in the recent loan. The friendly feeling towards England is now on the increase here, and the time is coming when England will rank equally with France in the distribution of Russian Government orders'[424]

The first minuted contact between John Brown and Russian interests took place in January 1907 when John Dunlop reported to the Board that an intermediary called John F Wake of Darlington had suggested that John Brown should purchase the Nevskii Shipyard at St Petersburg.[425] The minutes record no discussion of this other than to note that it was turned down. In October of the same year, a letter was received from the Franco Russian Company's Galernii Island shipyard in St Petersburg, acknowledging an offer to undertake model testing in the Clydebank experiment tank. In the same year, construction of the Gangut Class battleships was authorised by the Russian Government. At first the contract was to be given to Vickers Son & Maxim at Barrow who were already building the large armoured cruiser *Rurik*. However, Vickers had fallen out of favour[426] with the Ministry of Marine and the design for the ships was put out to international competition. John Brown prepared to enter the contest. At the same time, they also tendered for the battleship's turbines.[427] John Sampson, a director on

the main John Brown Board, handled negotiations between the Russians and John Brown. Sampson wrote to the company's Russian agents, Messrs Gustav List of St. Petersburg, suggesting that John Brown might collaborate with the state-owned Baltic Works on the preparation of designs for the battleships. This was put to the managing director of the Baltic Works, General Vershsortzoff, who was keen to act on this proposal. Gustav List replied to John Sampson quoting the General; 'John Brown & Co. is reckoned the only specialist who can give information upon which one can implicitly rely'[428] With Vickers out of the running, John Sampson had cleverly positioned John Brown in the competition that lay ahead.

Specifications and an outline of the ships to be built were prepared by Russian naval architects and passed to the 23 competing shipyards.[429] When the various designs were examined, two were selected, the German Blohm & Voss[430] proposal and that of the John Brown/Baltic Works consortium. The Russians preferred the shipbuilding details of the John Brown proposal although the armament solution in the Blohm & Voss design was preferred. The German yard was paid 200,000 roubles for its design, which was never used, and the contract was awarded to John Brown/Baltic Works consortium.[431] This was significant recognition of John Brown's expertise at the forefront of the shipbuilding and marine engineering industries.

THE COVENTRY SYNDICATE

The major programme of battleship construction initiated as a consequence of *Dreadnought*, created an unprecedented opportunity for British armaments companies. John Brown and its associated group of companies was deficient in certain areas of armaments manufacture, principally that of guns and gun mountings. Of the large armament companies, only two, Armstrong Whitworth and Vickers Son & Maxim, already possessed this capacity. These complex mechanisms were key elements in warship construction and consequently gave both companies a competitive advantage.[432] To counter this, in 1905, John Brown & Co., and the Fairfield Shipbuilding & Engineering Co., acting jointly, acquired the capacity to manufacture gun mountings by taking a share in the Coventry Ordnance Works which had recently been acquired by Cammell Laird. By 1907, the Coventry Ordnance Works had been restructured with John Brown taking a 50% interest and Fairfield and Cammell Laird 25% each. The John Brown Board allocated the sum of £300,000 towards the equipment of the new works.[433] Large works at Coventry were extended while new shops were laid out at Scotstoun on the Clyde. Building new works was only part of the difficulty in drawing level with Armstrong's and Vickers. Over the years, both companies had patented the machinery which formed the basis of the mountings used by the navy. The Syndicate had to spend much time circumventing these patents by designing their own mechanisms. The Coventry works, of about 60 acres in extent, manufactured a large range of military hardware including naval guns and mountings of all sizes. The Scotstoun works, covering an area of 16 acres, were erected to supply John Brown and Fairfield on the Clyde with naval ordnance although this was also supplied to Beardmore's yard at Dalmuir. Heavy components for the main armament turrets were manufactured at Scotstoun and the entire turret and mounting, including parts made at Coventry, were assembled and tested in gun pits. Thereafter, these mountings were taken to a dock adjacent to the works, lifted onto a vessel, and taken to the yard in which the warship was building.[434]

The Syndicate was not initially successful in attracting work. When the Admiralty rejected designs for 12" gun mountings in March 1908, an internal memorandum to Syndicate members noted that unless they were accepted as suppliers to the Government, part of the works would have to be shut.[435] Events would conspire to make closure unnecessary.

THE 1909 NAVAL SCARE

The period up to the First World War was one in which the muscles of British industrial power were flexed to the limit but it took the naval scare of 1909 and a public outcry to open Treasury coffers. The Admiralty had planned for the construction of four dreadnoughts every year to guarantee naval supremacy. By 1908, Government cuts in the Naval Estimates meant that instead of sixteen dreadnoughts built or on order, there were only twelve. During 1908, only one keel, for the battleship *Vanguard*, was laid down. The 'Naval Scare' had its origin in 1906 when the Managing Director of the Coventry Ordnance Works, HH Mulliner, became aware that capacity in gun mounting facilities were being greatly increased at the Krupp works in Germany. As this was the most complex and time consuming element in battleship building, he concluded that the Germans were attempting to accelerate their construction

programme by taking advantage of British reductions in spending. Mulliner informed the Admiralty, the War Office and numerous other high ranking officials in the expectation that action would be taken. By the end of 1908 the Parliamentary Opposition and the Press were agitating for Government response. In March 1909, news of the alleged German attempts to outbuild the Royal Navy became a national issue. Figures were produced to show that, by 1912, Germany would have the same number of dreadnoughts as Britain. On 16 March, the First Lord of the Admiralty, Reginald McKenna, introduced the Naval Estimates in the House of Commons and made a strong case for increasing the number of dreadnoughts to be built. The following day he said of the Krupp Works:

> ' . . . their output of guns, gun-mountings, turrets and some other essentials of that kind exceeds that of Armstrong, Vickers-Maxim, Coventry Works, Woolwich Arsenal and our whole national resources put together.'[436]

The Prime Minister H H Asquith and others, including Winston Churchill, refuted the notion that the Germans had embarked on an accelerated building programme. Nevertheless, such was the sentiment in the country that it was decided that four dreadnoughts would be laid down in 1909 and that four additional or 'contingent' ships would follow, if warranted by events in Germany. This compromise proved unpopular and the Government remained under continued pressure to build eight. The campaign for more battleships was characterised by the Daily Mail's slogan 'We want eight and we won't wait'. On 26 July, the Government relented and announced that the four contingent dreadnoughts would also be built. Although none of the orders for the eight ships came to John Brown's,[437] concern over the dreadnought building programme prompted the New Zealand and Australian Governments to offer finance for the construction of one dreadnought battlecruiser each. This offer was accepted and *Indefatigable*, the only battlecruiser planned for the 1908 Programme was supplemented by two sister ships, *Australia* and *New Zealand*, the orders for which went to John Brown and Fairfield. Presiding over the distribution of these contracts, the Admiralty regulated the supply of warship orders to ensure that industrial capacity was maintained across the armour, armament and shipbuilding firms. Thus, although firms tendered for all available Admiralty work, it was in the knowledge that failure in one round would probably be followed by success in the next.

While the above events were in train, the slump continued to exacerbate industrial relations in the shipbuilding industry. On 2 May 1908, woodworkers on the North East Coast refused to accept reductions in wages with the result that woodworkers were locked-out in shipyards throughout the country. Although this dispute had little to do with Clydebank, workers there were solidly behind the dispute but after one month they returned under employers' terms. In December, John Brown management moved to cut their costs. All employees in the shipyard and those from the engine works engaged on fitting-out ships were put on short time working. These conditions were not lifted until 17 March 1909 when normal working was resumed.[438] The effect of the slump had less impact on the engine works. In addition to constructing the machinery for vessels building at Clydebank, it also commenced or completed the machinery for the cruisers *Boadicea*, *Yarmouth*, and for the battlecruiser *Indefatigable*, all of which were building elsewhere. In 1909 the association with Harland & Wolff worked in John Brown's favour when the former switched the order for Hamburg Amerika cargo liner *Preussen* to the Clyde yard. At the same time, the machinery for the battleship *Neptune* was awarded to Harland & Wolff and the turbine work sub-contracted to Clydebank. Under the same arrangement, turbines for the White Star liners *Laurentic*, *Olympic*, *Titanic*, *Demosthenes* and *Arlanza* were also sub-contracted to Clydebank. Harland & Wolff were evidently sensitive about their reliance on John Brown for turbines. In a letter to the editor of 'Engineering', regarding progress photographs taken of *Olympic's* turbines under construction at Clydebank, Thomas Bell advised:

'We have sent some photographs of the turbines to

A view of the fitting-out basin in 1910 showing from left the passenger ship Zealandia, *the destroyers* Bulldog, Beagle, *and* Foxhound, *the steam yacht* Doris *and the cruiser* Bristol.

The essence of seapower, the 12-inch gunned 'P' turret on the battlecruiser Australia *in June 1913. The money to build* Australia *was gifted by the Australian government as a direct consequence of the naval scare of 1909 when it was thought that Germany might outbuild the British in dreadnoughts.*

H&W but please do not refer to them unless they furnish them to you, nor make any reference whatever to our name, as this is a sore point with them!'[439]

In January 1908, David McGee, Shipyard Manager, died at his home, Melbourne House in Dalmuir, and his place was filled by naval architect, William Luke. In turn, John Paterson, previously Luke's deputy, was appointed naval architect. As a mark of respect for McGee the Works closed at noon on the day of the funeral.[440] The Board agreed that his widow should be awarded an annuity of £250 for seven years.[441] The most significant appointment was in June 1909 when,

as a result of John G Dunlop's retiral, Thomas Bell was appointed managing director. Bell's ability in managing the engine works particularly during the introduction of turbine technology, had not gone unnoticed and in January 1908 he had been invited to join the main Board at Sheffield, a position hitherto taken only by the managing director at Clydebank.[442] In Bell's absence, management of the engine works passed to Engineer Commander W H Wood who joined the Company in 1909 following retiral from the Royal Navy.

THE BALTIC WORKS

At the start of 1908, the collaboration between John Brown and the Baltic Works at St Petersburg[443] began to bear fruit. On 30 January, an agreement was signed between the two companies for technical assistance in the design of the Gangut Class battleships, which were to be laid down in the following year. By May, John Brown's noted that nothing had transpired from the warship designs which had been sent out. It seems likely that the delay was caused by the impending merger of the Baltic Works and their near neighbour, the Admiralty Yard, both of which would share construction of the battleships. On 27 January 1909, a further Technical Collaboration Agreement was signed with the Baltic Works and the Admiralty Yard, for the design, and supervision during construction, of four battleships. Two, *Petropavlovsk* and *Sevastopol* were to be built at the Baltic Works and the others, *Gangut* and *Poltava*, at the Admiralty yard. This contract also included the design of Parsons' turbines for the main propelling machinery for which drawings and calculations were to be supplied. Payment was calculated at three roubles for every displacement ton worked and eight roubles for each unit of horsepower developed by the turbines.[444] In the same month, model testing to determine hull characteristics was in progress in the experiment tank at Clydebank. The results were sent to St. Petersburg in the form of a lines plan. In March 1909, William Luke and his assistant, John Black, visited the Russian shipyard, the latter remaining as resident shipbuilder and naval architect. Another Clydebank representative, James Gorrie, who acted as resident marine engineer, joined Black. There was disagreement over the general design of the vessels which prompted the Managing Director of the Baltic Works, General Vershsortzoff, to visit Clydebank in May. This probably concerned John Brown's desire to alter the ships lines against opposition from the head of the Russian Shipbuilding Committee, A N Krylov.[445] The form of hull used would have been of great concern to John Brown as an important element in ensuring the ships were able to make the required speed. In the event, the lines were not altered and detailed work on the battleships began in June.[446] At the same time, aware of sensitivities surrounding the sale of advanced defence technology abroad, John Brown informed the British Admiralty of its activities with the Russian Government.[447] Differences of opinion again arose between technical staff at St Petersburg and Clydebank. When Russian engineers wanted to remove 21 tons of steelwork from turbine

seatings, Thomas Bell insisted that John Brown be relieved of responsibility for the outcome as this would depart 'from known and tried scantlings'[448] All four Gangut Class battleships were laid down on 16 June 1909. By December 1909, calculations and drawings for launching arrangements had been sent to St Petersburg.[449] When the turbine designs were sent to St Petersburg for manufacture there, Russian engineers were quick to notice that they could be boosted from the specified 32,500shp to 45,000shp without alteration. To take advantage of this, the intended Belleville boilers were replaced with the Yarrow small-tube type, which were capable of producing the extra steam required.[450] The Russian battleships thus promised to be among the fastest yet built.

BROWN CURTIS TURBINES

Recognition of the advantages inherent in the Curtis turbine was to be well rewarded by a succession of Admiralty orders. Later, Thomas Bell attributed the success of the Company in developing 'a special standing with the Admiralty' to this turbine, adding that the contracts for the large battlecruisers *Tiger*, *Repulse* and *Hood* were won as a result.[451] Bell did not foresee that the licence agreement of 1904 and 1905 between Parsons and John Brown would include all marine turbines manufactured at Clydebank. This meant that royalties for Curtis turbines constructed at Clydebank would have to be

The experimental Brown-Curtis turbine in the engine shops at Clydebank in August 1909 which was later fitted into the cruiser Bristol. It had advantages over the Parson's type prompting its use in many warships.

paid to both Parsons and Curtis. John Brown took advice on how it might get round this expense but finally reconciled itself to paying royalties twice.[452] Throughout 1912 and 1913, Stephen Pigott, now an employee of John Brown, maintained strong links with Charles Curtis. When the contract for the battlecruiser *Tiger* was won in 1912, Curtis wrote to Pigott from New York:

> 'I am requested by the directors of our company to say that they wish to congratulate you most heartily on the admirable work you have been doing on behalf of the John Brown company, but which has resulted largely for the benefit of our company, and particularly to congratulate you upon getting the award (contract) for the large battleship cruiser the references to which we saw in the papers here some weeks ago. The directors all think, as I do, that your work and the part you have played in the matter has shown not only excellent engineering ability, but has shown tact and capacity to deal with practical matters and with individuals under very difficult conditions. In view of this the directors have voted to give you a present of $900 . . . '[453]

However, Curtis was evidently unhappy that Parsons should receive royalties for Curtis turbines built at Clydebank as this increased the cost of his turbine. He wrote to Bell expressing his concern and received the following reply, which illustrates the regard in which Charles Parsons was held:

> 'As regards paying royalties to Parsons, I would tell you, for your private information, that people in very high positions in the British Navy were so impressed with the wonderful additional tactical advantages obtained in ships fitted with turbines and oil fired boilers that they felt a big debt of gratitude to Sir Charles Parsons, and I was given to understand that, if we agreed to pay Parsons' turbine royalty during the continuance of our licence whether the turbines were his or other types, all opposition would be withdrawn to the introduction of your turbine into the British Navy. In view of this, and also in view of the fact that our Company was not prepared to carry out a wearisome and expensive law suit with the Parsons Company over the matter, we thought it well to agree, and I am sure that you will not be the losers by this'.[454]

Curtis watched the British capital ship programme with great interest. In the correspondence conducted between Curtis and Pigott over many years, technical details of the machinery of both British and American battleships were exchanged. Notwithstanding security implications, Curtis sent Pigott blueprints and details of the battleship *Pennsylvania's* turbines, to be built at Newport News Shipbuilding & Drydock Co., adding that:

> 'there is not the slightest question in (my) mind that you ought to bring down your revolutions far below what you have been working with in England. The revolutions you have been using and the Parsons people have been using, are far too high, both for propeller efficiency and for holding power'.

When the Chief Engineer of the Newport News Company, Mr Bailey, visited Clydebank in the spring of 1913, Curtis asked Pigott to treat the blueprints with the utmost confidentiality. On the other hand, Curtis wanted Bell to be appraised of the data so that he might 'grasp the merit of these new designs as quickly as possible.'[455] This was probably a reference to the turbine machinery intended for the Queen Elizabeth Class battleships, *Barham* and *Valiant* which were ordered early in 1913, with Brown-Curtis machinery. When the order for these battleships was announced, Curtis immediately rewarded John Brown by reducing royalty payments from 1-shilling (5p) per horsepower to 9 pence (3.75p)[456] Further inducements were offered. In March 1913, Curtis urged Bell to further expand this business offering John Brown a special commission of 15% on any new licences.[457]

The extent of the business generated by Brown-Curtis turbines can be gauged by the number of leading firms who, by June 1916, had taken out full licences – Harland & Wolff, Yarrow, Fairfield, Beardmore, Wallsend Slipway, Hawthorn Leslie, Wm. Denny, Scotts, Thornycroft, Stephen, J S White, Cammell Laird and Dunsmuir & Jackson. By the same date, no fewer than 175 ships had been completed with Brown-Curtis machinery. Shipping lines using these turbines included, Orient line, Cunard, Federal Steam Navigation and the Great Eastern Railway Co. In June 1916, it was hoped, with Lord Pirrie's recommendation, that Canadian Pacific would also adopt them.[458] The first merchant ship built at Clydebank with Brown-Curtis machinery was the Orient liner *Ormonde*, laid down in October 1913.

The success of the Brown-Curtis turbine was such that it was selected for the battlecruiser, *Queen Mary*, the battleships *Almirante Latorre* (later named *Canada*), *Almirante Cochrane* (later the aircraft carrier *Eagle*), and the Russian battleships *Imperator Aleksandr III* and *Imperatritsa Mariya*, all of which were building at other shipyards.

By 1910, the great volume of Admiralty work swamped the drawing office, and draughtsmen and tracers could not meet demands. As there was no accommodation to employ additional staff, the work was sub-contracted to firms in Glasgow. This resulted in a strong objection from the Admiralty, on the basis that this work was highly secret. Increasing numbers of Admiralty Inspectors, both hull and engineering, also led to complaints about poor accommodation and overcrowding at the yard. The Company was forced to redress this by building new offices at a cost of £3,000.[459] The 65 tenders for ships and machinery prepared in 1910 indicated the end of the shipbuilding slump. For one of these, to the Hamburg Amerika line, an interesting illustration of capacity at Clydebank was included:

Greatest number of men employed in shipyard	5,000
Greatest number of men employed in engine works	3,500
Greatest tonnage launched in one year	75,000
Greatest amount of horsepower produced in one year	129,000
Area of works	80 acres
River frontage	3,200 feet
Size of dock	800 feet x 330 feet
Total tonnage on order at June 1910	74,700 tons
Total horsepower under construction at June 1910	203,000
Berths	7 large and 2 small[460]

In the same year, a serious dispute occurred between the boilermakers and employers which resulted in a prolonged lockout. Although in many ways part of the industrial relations continuum, this dispute had a specific context. In March 1909, the Shipyard National Agreement was signed by employers and 18 shipyard unions. The Agreement established machinery whereby highly disruptive ad hoc stoppages could be contained through a process of negotiation. In particular, it was agreed that, where a disagreement arose, work would continue while negotiations were in progress. The Agreement, however, failed to have any significant effect in preventing men from doing what they considered to be their right. An example of this occurred in June 1910 when 200 riveters struck at John Browns in protest at pay rates on certain classes of work carried out on warships. The dispute concerned interpretation of the riveters' pricelist. This price list, in which a price was given for each of 664 tasks, was the means by which riveting work was calculated by riveters and by the company. The Clydebank men argued that they should be guaranteed a wage of 4s per hour per squad for shell work and 3/6d for inside work. Calculated by the

pricelist, their wages frequently fell below 2/9d while their average was not much more than 4 shillings. Although pieceworkers, the riveters were making the point that in certain classes of work, a time rate should apply below which their wages should not fall.

By September 1910, 35 strikes had taken place in various yards since the signing of the Agreement, of which 28 had been down to the boilermakers.[461] The event which precipitated the national lockout of boilermakers was the strike of riveters at Armstrong's Walker shipyard on the Tyne and D & W Henderson's on the Clyde. Although the dispute was localised, the employers acted swiftly to impose a national lockout of boilermakers starting on 3 September. The lockout generated strong feelings and it was not until over two months later, on 8 November, that a vote was taken on Clydeside concerning the settlement terms worked out by employers and men's representatives. The result was 15,563 against and 5,650 for a return to work. By 30 November, with the lockout still in operation, the situation at John Brown's forced management to place all remaining shipyard trades on three quarters time. On 14 December, the boilermakers were again balloted on a return to work and, on this occasion, voted 13,715 for and 1,290 against the motion. On the following day the lockout notice was withdrawn. Full time working in the shipyard resumed on 19 December 1910.[462] The basis of the return to work was described as providing 'an equitable means of dealing with and settling sectional disputes' centred on a supplementary agreement to be added to the national agreement of 1909 whereby smoother working would be ensured.

While the above events were unfolding, a 1,056 ton 268 foot long floating palace left Clydebank. This was the steam yacht Doris complete with 'enamelled walls with silk panels and furniture of inlaid satinwood'. Doris was built for SB Joel, head of the South African firm Bernato Bros., which controlled some of the largest mining properties in the Transvaal. The vessel was built in only nine months, which was considered to be a record for a yacht of this size.[463]

FOREIGN CONTRACTS

The effects of Anglo-German naval rivalry were seemingly infectious and many lesser naval powers aspired to include a dreadnought battleship in their fleet. In pursuing foreign contracts, British armament companies often acted in consortia where contracts could be divided out among them. The contracts for Turkish battleships, in which John Brown acted with the Vickers and Armstrong companies, serve as an example. Having advised Armstrong that Clydebank could not accommodate any of the ships because there were no berths available, a combined tender was put forward on the basis that Vickers would build the hull and machinery, with the armour and armament divided among all three.[464] Late in 1908, an arrangement was entered into between John Brown,

Above and Right.
The Russian battleship Gangut *at the Baltic Works in St Petersburg during 1911. Together with her three sisterships* Gangut *was built under the technical direction of John Brown & Co.*

Armstong Whitworth and Vickers to provide technical management for the construction of Spanish warships. A company was established, Sociedad Española de Construccion Naval, in which the British firms held a 40% interest. Dockyards at Bilbao, Cadiz, Cartagena, Ferrol and Santander were taken over and new shipyards, engine works and gun factories built. The consortium supplied management, skilled labour and materials to enable the design and construction of three battleships authorised under the Spanish Navy Law of 1908. John Brown also collaborated with

Palmers, Fairfield and Cammell Laird to build battleships for the Portuguese Navy[465] and to build 'Bristol' type cruisers and coastal battleships for the Chinese Navy.[466] In November 1910, a price of £2,330,000 was quoted to the Chinese for a battlecruiser.[467]

From 1910 onwards, the Board at Clydebank considered or put forward battleship tenders for China, Chile, Argentina, Brazil, Turkey, Japan, Spain, Portugal, Sweden, Norway, Holland, Greece and Russia. Most of these countries either ordered from British yards or employed British expertise to build warships at home. In 1912, the pressure of work at Clydebank forced the Company to withdraw from tendering for Norwegian coastal battleships. They urged the other members of the Coventry Syndicate, Fairfield and Cammell Laird, to give the Coventry works the opportunity to tender.[468] Unlike their main competitors, Armstrong and Vickers, John Brown did not succeed or did not require to bring foreign warship contracts to Clydebank. However, their expertise in marine engineering attracted a very significant customer.

In July 1911, contacts established the previous year with Captain Fuji of the Imperial Japanese Navy bore fruit when designs of Brown-Curtis turbine installations for the battlecruiser *Haruna* and the cruisers *Hirado* and *Chikuma* were sold together with manufacturing rights to the Kawasaki Dockyard Co.[469] This was an important transfer of advanced technology to a rapidly expanding naval power. The relationship with Kawasaki continued and led to the sale of further machinery designs for the battleships *Fuso*, *Yamashiro* and *Ise*. The cruising turbines and gearing for *Ise* were manufactured at Clydebank in 1915.[470]

In Russia, all four Gangut Class battleships were launched in 1911 although none would be completed until late 1914, a much longer building time than would have applied in Britain. In 1911, the Ministry of Marine was contemplating the construction of four large Borodino Class battlecruisers to be built at the Baltic and Admiralty yards. In response to the Russian specification which was sent to them, John Brown's calculated that ships of 35,000tons and a length of 780 feet would be required. In June 1912 when asked to supply drawings of Brown-Curtis turbines of 85,000 shp, for these vessels, Brown's were reluctant to do so, explaining that it had as yet no experience of building machinery of this type beyond the 27,000 shp of the cruiser *Bristol*.[471]

In 1911, with work underway fitting-out the four

battleships at St Petersburg under the supervision of John Brown personnel, discussions were opened with the Russian Shipbuilding Company (Russud) concerning a technical collaboration at their yard at Nikolaev on the Black Sea. This shipyard had been selected to participate in the construction of the Imperatritsa Mariya Class battleships and Admiral Nakhimov Class cruisers for the Black Sea Fleet. An agreement, similar to the one in operation with the Baltic Works, was signed on 27 November 1911[472] although the three battleships had been laid down on 30 October. Clydebank personnel, including John Black, were then transferred from St Petersburg to Nikolaev. John Brown was also awarded the contract for the design and construction of Brown-Curtis machinery for two of the battleships, Imperatritsa Mariya and Imperator Aleksandr III. The contract was signed on 14 September 1911 at a price of £96,000 for each set of machinery.[473] On completion, the machinery for the Imperatritsa Mariya left Clydebank for the Black Sea in April 1914[474] while the machinery for the second battleship, Imperator Aleksandr III, was held in storage until the ship was ready to receive it in 1916. The four Borodino Class battlecruisers, about which John Brown had been consulted in 1911, were laid down at the end of 1913. With eight battleships being built under the technical supervision of John Brown, the Russians felt able to go it alone with the Borodino's and no assistance was requested from any foreign shipbuilder.

The naval consultancy work undertaken for the Russian Government was paralleled by a contract for four merchant ships for the Russian Steam Navigation & Trading Co. of St Petersburg and Odessa, to be built jointly with William Denny, the Dumbarton shipbuilder. The contract for the 380 foot twin screw steamers was signed in London on 26 March 1912[475] and the two Clydebank ships, Emperor Peter the Great and Emperor Nicholas 1, were laid down in Autumn 1912 and delivered to the Russians at the end of 1913. Under the terms of the contract, payment was extended over a five-year period. Following the Russian Revolution, exchange rates and Bolshevik control of the shipping industry combined to make continued repayments impossible and in February 1918, both John Brown and William Denny were informed that the Russian Steam Navigation & Trading Co. could not meet its obligations.[476] In November 1918, both shipbuilders lodged a claim for payment through the Foreign Office stating that, 'our arrangements (of 1912) were conditioned by very keen competition from German shipbuilders and

included terms of payment with credit for five years secured on six month acceptances'.[477] Both companies considered the seizure of the four ships but agreed that a representative, John Crookston, should be sent out to Odessa on the Black Sea to find what he could about the defaulting company. This produced a payment of £25,000 which was split between Denny and John Brown. Some of the assets of the Russian company had been transferred to France and it was to Paris that Crookston went next. It was not until October 1921, however, that French administrators in settlement of claims made a payment of £270,000.[478]

AQUITANIA

After the completion of Lusitania in 1907, the position at Clydebank had deteriorated partly as the result of the failure to win further orders from Cunard. A tender for the 18,000ton Laconia at £397,700 was unsuccessfully submitted in April 1910. The contract for this ship and her sister Franconia went to Swan Hunter, at a price of £374,000 each.[479] The distinction of being the largest ships in the world, which Lusitania and Mauretania enjoyed, ended with the launch of Olympic and Titanic for White Star in 1910/11. At the same time, the Hamburg-Amerika line was planning the even larger ships of the Imperator Class. In response to the big White Star ships, Cunard decided to build an equally large ship and in December 1909, outline designs were prepared. Luxury of appointment was to be the key feature of this ship and although she had to be swift, she was

Shipwrights aligning the massive baulks of timber on which Aquitania's keel will be laid.

A completely new berth was prepared in the East Yard to build the 900 foot (274.5 metres) long Aquitania. The company considered a berth gantry system but opted for a large number of 5-ton steel derricks instead. Rebuilding the berth cost a total of £27,750. This view showing the ground being levelled after driving in new piles was taken on 19 May 1911.

not intended as a record breaker. By March 1910, plans had been prepared for consideration and, in July, the Cunard Chairman, Sir Alfred Booth, had preliminary discussions with representatives from Swan Hunter, Vickers Sons & Maxim and John Brown. On 9 September, the builders were asked if they were prepared to tender for the new ship at a fixed price and with a definite delivery time. However, John Brown's favoured position with Cunard can be seen in a letter to Booth, in which it states 'that as the specification for the big ship will be sent out in a fortnight, they could be stretching a point and, in strictest confidence, make a provisional contract with some of the leading steel makers for the

steel involved.'[480] On 6 December 1910, John Brown submitted a price of £1,414,222. On the 12th, they were informed that the contract was theirs. Three days later, the Cunard Board announced that the new ship would be called *Aquitania*. The contract was signed on 31 January 1911 stipulating a delivery date of 30 November 1913 with penalties for late delivery of £100 per day.[481] As design work began on *Aquitania*, a short distance away in the engine shops, work on the turbine for White Star's *Titanic* was nearing completion[482]

In addition to *Aquitania*, a succession of very large warship contracts was in progress or booked. On 25 October the yard's second battlecruiser, *Australia*, was

launched. At the end of the year the Admiralty invited tenders for a much larger battlecruiser and, on 2 March 1912, John Brown was informed that they had been awarded the contract for *Tiger*. In the same month, tenders were invited for the fast battleships of the Queen Elizabeth Class which resulted in *Barham* being laid down in February 1913. There would be larger ships built at Clydebank, but never again would there be such a concentration of large and nationally important vessels as in 1913. That year recorded the highest output ever for the shipbuilding and marine engineering industries on Clydeside. At Clydebank alone, 82,722 tons of shipping was launched and 239,000 horsepower produced in the engine shops. In rapid succession, rivet followed

plate onto frame. One incident involving *Lusitania* marred an otherwise outstanding year. In January 1913, Cunard's chairman, Sir Alfred Booth, told Thomas Bell that Cunard would hold John Brown liable for defective workmanship carried out on *Lusitania's* starboard low pressure turbine the previous autumn which had resulted in extensive damage. Expensive repairs were required amounting to £62,725 which John Brown had no alternative but to pay. [483]

In time-honoured tradition, full order books and full employment provoked wage demands. If the 'Black Squad'[484] was notorious for its truculence, joiners, the journal Siren & Shipping claimed, were out to take their record. In March 1914, when various items of

A visit by a Japanese naval delegation including Admiral Togo (at centre, not in uniform) on 12 July 1911 standing in front of Aquitania's keel. A number of Japanese technicians worked at Clydebank during the pre-war years principally in connection with turbine technology.

decorative woodwork arrived from a non-union firm in London for fitting in *Aquitania*, Clydebank joiners, a highly organised section of the workforce, refused to handle and fit the work. To make their point, the joiners went on strike. The journal considered this to be 'mean' but added an interesting point about the yard: 'Clydebank, has, in its day, had probably less to say in public about its labour affairs than any establishment in the United Kingdom, and with characteristic reticence it has said nothing about this trouble.'[485]

In March 1914, work was proceeding on *Aquitania* to ensure that she was completed on schedule. Her advertised sailing date was 30 May. Thomas Bell, satisfied with the work undertaken by his own men, commented that the sub-contractors hired by Cunard to work on decorations, lighting and ventilation were having 'a terrific scramble' to be ready on time.[486] On Sunday 10 May, *Aquitania* went down the Clyde to run trials after which she sailed for the Mersey. She

docked there on the 15th and was handed over to Cunard on the 18th. The final cost of *Aquitania* to Cunard was:

John Brown	1,413,152
Public rooms, lifeboats, Blohm & Voss anti-roll system	89,551
Architects fees	8,432
Engine works, general work	70,151
Linen	12,431
Crockery, cutlery etc.	11,340
Legal, travel, provisions	9,025
Interest (at 4.5%)	70,601
Total first cost to Cunard	**1,684,683**[487]

With a terrific scramble of a more sinister nature about to erupt, the Admiralty cabled Clydebank on 31 July, three days before the outbreak of war, asking them to expedite completion of *Tiger*, then the largest warship in the navy, by employing every man available through continuous overtime, night shift and Sunday working. As the last days of peace ran out, John Brown's yard was working to maximum capacity. By August, a record number of 10,729 men were employed in the Works.[488]

DEVELOPMENT OF THE SHIPYARD 1900/1914

The ground acquired in 1897 was intended for new berths but this development had been postponed. In 1900, this proposal was revived and the ground was piled for three small slips with the intention that small vessels would be built in the west yard allowing the east yard to concentrate on large vessels. When John Brown acquired the Clydebank Works, a major programme of capital investment was already underway. As a result of the contracts for *Lusitania* and the battlecruiser *Inflexible*, a further round of

Above
Aquitania's *massive stern dwarfs the three men standing on the other side of the berth on the day of her launch, 21 April 1913.*

Opposite page top
An untypical photograph showing workmen taking a break for breakfast or lunch beside some of the frames towards the aft end of Aquitania in 1911.

Opposite page bottom
A carpenter places a template over a half model of Aquitania's hull to ensure accuracy of form.

expensive alterations to the Works became necessary. Although a significant increase in ship size had occurred over the past fifty years, capacity to erect material on the building berth remained little changed from the early days of iron shipbuilding. The means of lifting frames, beams and plates was the pole derrick, capable of lifting up to three tons. These derricks had the twin advantages of being inexpensive and transportable. The alternative to the pole derrick was the shipbuilding gantry which, although very expensive, enabled many lifts to be made simultaneously. Deck beams could be handled by overhead travelling cranes while, at the same time, frames and shell plates could be handled by cranes mounted on the side of the gantry. A few shipbuilders, such as Harland & Wolff, Beardmore and Vulkan at Stettin, felt compelled to embrace these giant structures. For the construction of *Mauretania*, Swan Hunter erected one to their own design. Despite having spent large sums on the yard or perhaps because of this, John Brown was less ambitious in finding such a solution for the building berth and the well tried system of light pole derricks was retained. John Brown nevertheless was able to complete *Lusitania* to launching stage three months earlier than *Mauretania* building under the new gantry system at Swan Hunter.

The pole derrick evolved into the steel lattice derrick, a more robust version capable of lifting 5 tons. These permitted handling larger plates than was previously possible and, over the next few years, this type of crane was fitted to most of the berths in the east yard. Proposals of a major berth gantry system had not been forgotten. In December 1909, Thomas Bell, the new Managing Director, outlined a £171,000 capital programme of additions 'necessitated by the present demands of shipbuilding to Government and other requirements'[489] The major item was a £100,000 covered building gantry over number 3 and 4 berths in the east yard. The additions were approved with the exception of the gantry. Bell explained that in approving this expenditure of £71,000, an annual saving in Works Charges of £10,000 on unskilled labour alone would be achieved.[490]

Reorganisation of the east yard berths had been completed prior to laying the keel of *Lusitania* in 1904 and had involved reduction in the number of berths from eight to six. One of those berths, number 4, was re-aligned and piled to accommodate *Lusitania*. The *Aquitania* contract required a further reorganisation of the east yard and the building of a completely new berth. Thomas Bell accepted that the berth gantry

system 'undoubtedly made for speed in construction and for greatly reducing the amount of labour requisite for handling the very heavy beams, girders and plates' but added that 'this was quite beyond consideration in the present case, as such a structure could not be erected in less than 12 to 13 months, and the cost, (£130,000) half that of Harland & Wolff's, appeared almost prohibitive'

Bell's solution was to provide 15 additional steel derricks to command the sides and decks of the vessel at a cost of £18,000, and to provide two electric hoists on either side at a cost of £4,950. The cost of creating the new berth including piling was £27,750.[491] The new Aquitania berth was, in time and with a little modification, to hold the 'Queens'.

In 1910 the volume of destroyer orders persuaded the Company to equip one berth in the west yard with a covered overhead gantry for rapid, all weather construction. This gantry system was designed and erected by Sir William Arrol at a cost of £27,000. The provision of better berth facilities, and facilities across the Works generally, was in response to particular contracts. There is no evidence that management created superior facilities in the hope that they would induce contracts as was the case at the adjacent Beardmore works. Consequently, when the order for the battlecruiser *Tiger* was won in March 1912, Thomas Bell told the Board that in order to complete

Above
Emperor Peter the Great, *one of two ships completed for the Russian Steam Navigation Co. in 1913. The shipbuilders had to pursue her owners for their final stage payment following the turmoil of war and revolution.*

Opposite page
A detail from Aquitania's Carolean Smoking Room showing a reproduction of Claud Lorrain's 'Seaport With Figures' set in a carved old-gold frame on solid oak panels.

the ship on time, eight new derrick cranes would be necessary at a cost of £1,200 each. The Committee recommended that the cranes be bought without delay.[492]

Fitting-out was the major area of outside construction in which heavy concentrated loads had to be lifted. Here John Brown provided not one but two 150 ton fitting-out cranes. The first (1905) was a derrick

capacity and one of 20 tons were added to the complement of fitting-out cranes. The fitting-out basin was extended inland several times to accommodate large ships, in particular *Lusitania* and *Aquitania*. In August 1905, the Company submitted drawings of proposed improvements to the fitting-out basin for Admiralty approval as a condition of receiving the order for *Inflexible*. Alterations to the dock totalled

Extensions to the engine works were made to deal with the demand for machinery. Here the new Fitting Shop is seen in 1907 with turbines and casings in various stages of assembly and, on the right, a paddle wheel.

designed by Cowans Sheldon of Carlisle at a cost of £11,000, excluding foundations, and the second (1907) was a giant cantilever crane by Sir William Arrol, the renowned Glasgow firm of structural engineers. Both were provided in response to the contracts for *Lusitania* and *Inflexible*. Cranes of this type gradually replaced the sheer legs which had been in use since the modern era of shipbuilding began in the 1850s. Numerous smaller electric travelling cranes of 5 tons

£60,000 which included the second 150 ton crane at a price of £18,000 excluding foundations.[493] Authorisation to proceed with this work was only given when the contract for *Inflexible* was signed in January 1906.[494] For the latter, £24,000 was allocated to lengthening the dock and renewing wharf piling.[495] The advent of larger ships had a similar effect on the engine works. Heavier cranes were required to lift heavier engines and boilers. The manufacture of

Parsons and later Curtis steam turbines required new machines and shops in which to construct them. In May 1903, following the order for the *Caronia*, £13,650 was spent upgrading the engine works. The contract for *Lusitania* required new boiler and erecting shops.[496] In November 1910, £22,100 was allocated to a new boiler shop bay equipped with two 80-ton cranes and one of 30 tons to enable smoke boxes and uptakes to be fitted to boilers. At the same time, with machinery under construction totalling 216,000 hp, £5,850 was spent on a new lathe and boring machine as machines were 'absurdly congested'.[497]

During the last years before World War One, John Brown's Clydebank yard worked to capacity on highly sophisticated vessels. This view taken in June 1913 shows the quarterdeck of the battlecruiser Australia *with the* Aquitania *on the right.*

1914 - 1918   THE GREAT WAR

War was declared on Tuesday 4 August 1914. On the first weekend of the conflict, A E Pickard's Gaiety Theatre in Elgin Street, Clydebank, billed the Four Killarney Girls 'with up-to-date songs and dances' supported by Bonetti and Corri, 'the funniest of all funny jugglers'. Tickets cost 2 pence (0.8p) for the stalls and 6 pence (2.5p) for the dress circle.[498] On Sunday 9 August, a well attended meeting organised by the Clydebank & District Trades and Labour Council and the Clydebank Branch of the Independent Labour Party was held outside John Brown's main gate. The object was to draw public attention to needed Government regulation of the price and distribution of foodstuffs. A resolution was submitted to the Town Council on Monday, who unanimously agreed to its terms, agreeing also to forward the resolution to the 'proper quarters'. Late on Monday evening, a man steering a motorboat up the Clyde past Dalmuir was shot at twice by soldiers guarding Beardmore's shipyard for failing to stop when requested. On Thursday 13th, an Austrian collier, *Nagy Lagos*, lying at Rothesay Dock adjacent to the shipyard, was seized by Customs authorities and her crew and cargo of coal placed under arrest.[499] Lord Kitchener's appeal for volunteers, at first meeting with a slow response, steadily gathered momentum. By the beginning of September, recruits were enlisting at the rate of 50 to 60 per day encouraged, according to the local newspaper 'since the news of the brilliant fighting of the British Expeditionary Force.' The local Conservative Rooms on Kilbowie Road which served as recruiting offices were inundated - 'many desirous of enlisting have had to call back at a more convenient season.'[500] By the second week in September, over 900 men had enlisted.[501]

The last John Brown Board meeting before the declaration of war was held, not at Clydebank but at the Station Hotel in Sheffield with Thomas Bell, Charles Ellis and John Sampson in attendance. There was little business to discuss; the tender for the Australian depot ship *Platypus* had been accepted and Armstrong Whitworth, with whom the Company was collaborating in the construction of the Chilean battleship *Almirante Latorre*, was two months overdue on instalments for her machinery.[502] The order book included the battlecruiser *Tiger* which was nearing completion, the battleship *Barham*, four months away from launching, and the destroyers *Milne, Moorsom, Morris, Kriti* and *Lesvos* in various stages of construction. The last two were part of an order for the Greek government, which had been secured by the Coventry Ordnance Syndicate at the end of 1913. Two other destroyers, *Mons* and *Marne*, had been ordered but not laid down. Two merchant ships, *Ormonde* and *Stockholm*, were on the stocks. The engine shops were busy with the engines and boilers for the above vessels plus the machinery for two Chilean and one Russian battleship.

The outbreak of War meant the loss of foreign markets to British shipbuilders and the beginning of enormous demand from the Admiralty. For John Brown, already committed to a large programme of warship construction, the most immediate consequence was the understandable Admiralty request to accelerate work. With finite labour resources, this was difficult to achieve. Following near full employment in the industry, there was no pool of labour to be tapped. The only alternative was to suspend work on merchant ships and divert the men onto Admiralty contracts. Work continued all day Saturday and nightshift was worked even on Sundays.[503]

Curiously, the tensions generated between the British and German governments over fleet expansion programmes had largely dissipated in the few years before the war. The 1909 'scare' had proved to be unfounded. Although the Germans had succeeded in building the second largest navy in the world, the Royal Navy's position, expressed by the number of warships in service and under construction, was overwhelming. However, the Two-Power Standard could not be maintained and was abandoned in favour of a 60 % margin in size over the next largest fleet. The great advantage which the Admiralty had was the scale of the shipbuilding industry. Although the Germans, French, Japanese and others possessed or were developing shipbuilding capacity, UK builders commanded 60% of the world market. During the national emergency, a sizeable portion of British shipbuilding capacity was dedicated to war output, with the consequent neglect of the home market. Whatever misgivings might have been expressed at Clydebank in this enforced retreat from traditional markets, still a sizeable portion of its output, some of the most important warships ever built for the Royal Navy emerged from their yard. As the priorities of the naval war shifted, the need for capital ships gave way to destroyers and submarines. However, in response to specific tactical requirements, two of the largest warships ever built for the Royal Navy were to be laid down at Clydebank.

HOUSING WAR WORKERS

In January 1914, serious and continued difficulties in recruiting additional ironworkers came to a head. While it was possible to employ and retain between 2,400 and 2,500 ironworkers, the want of an additional 250 men was making it difficult to 'keep on the right side of the line in our Shipyard Charges' and 'come nearer to Government delivery requirements.'[504] The inability to find these additional ironworkers was attributed to a growing disinclination of ironworkers to travel as they preferred to find employment where they lived, i.e., the outlying districts of Dumbarton, Govan and Partick. In 1911 and 1912, Thomas Bell, Managing Director, had succeeded briefly in retaining an additional 300 men by paying all ironworkers from 10 to 20% more to cover the estimated one hour per day spent travelling to Clydebank. However, he soon found out that many men preferred to work for a fixed weekly amount and that, as a consequence, men produced 10 to 20% less work to take home the same pay as before. This meant that 2,800 men produced the same as 2,500 men while being paid 10 to 20% more. Bell's next solution to the problem was to build houses to accommodate his men. He developed a scheme to provide additional housing for 250 families

Two drillers in a posed photograph taken in 1917.

The battlecruiser Tiger was briefly the largest and fastest warship in the world until overtaken by the succeeding class the following year, such was the pace of construction in the naval race leading to World War One.

Looking aft along the length of Tiger on 20 September 1913. The cavernous spaces are left open for the ship's machinery and main armament to be lowered into the ship once she has been launched. The hazardous nature of working near unprotected spaces like these is obvious, particularly with so many obstructions lying on the deck.

The twin rudders and four propellers of Tiger on the day of her launch, 15 December 1913. The recess area on the side of her hull will later be fitted with armour plate. The Aquitania is in the fitting-out basin on the left.

Another view looking aft over the ship's distinctive funnels and main armament arrangement on 17 August 1914 fourteen days after the start of World War One.

The bridge and forward 13.5-inch guns on 28 August. Someone has written in chalk 'River Bar' over the gun embrasure at bottom left where two men are sitting. To expedite her completion continuous working through the night and all weekend was introduced. She sailed to join the Grand Fleet at Scapa Flow on 3 October 1914.

in Clydebank at rents equivalent to those in Govan.[505] The estimated cost of providing these new tenements was between £28,000 and £30,000.

Bell was also troubled by the predicament of under-foremen who, subject to the fluctuating nature of employment, might well find themselves having to work as mates to the men presently under them. The under-foremen, moreover, had to live in the same tenement blocks as the men with the inevitable consequence that under-foremen became 'reluctant to throw themselves heartily on the side of their employers'. The solution which he engineered was that under-foremen be housed in two storey self-contained terrace flats 'separated by the railway from the working men's tenements'. Bell regarded these

A rivet squad with hydraulic riveter pose for a photograph beside a longitudinal bulkhead on the battleship Barham *on 14 January 1914. The paint marks round the rivets below them were used to count the total number of rivets driven by a rivet squad and formed the basis of payment.*

men as non-commissioned officers and recognised that 'our economic production is largely dependent on them'[506] Consequently, a proposal was put forward to build houses for 50 under-foremen and 12 foremen at an estimated cost of £12,000 to £14,000. The Board sanctioned Bell's proposal and approval was given to build tenements on land already in Company possession and on ground bought from the Caledonian Railway.

In July 1914, approval was given for the construction of fifteen tenements at Whitecrook Street at a cost of £22,500. These accommodated 90 families. In October, twelve cottages were approved for the same street. In January 1915, a further fifteen tenements were sanctioned at a cost of £27,000. These tenements

accommodated 96 families. The builder, Leslie Kirk, agreed to take over three tenements from each group. He also agreed to proceed with accommodation for a further 30 families in 1916 on the basis that the Company would take them over on lease for ten years.[507]

The first of the tenements were ready for occupation in July 1916, but construction of the others was protracted owing to the shortages of labour and materials. To get round this difficulty, Bell proposed that 23 tenements in John Knox Street be purchased and converted from the one room and kitchen type to the 2 and 3 room type. He estimated that this would mean a saving of between 10 and 15% on new building. A further 23 tenements were approved in

June 1916 for construction on Dumbarton Road at the west end of the yard. Between October 1914 and September 1915, 47 cottages and houses for foremen were built in Whitecrook Street, Aberconway Street and near Barnes Street.[508]

BARHAM, REPULSE AND HOOD

In October 1914, following the completion of *Tiger*, the Admiralty asked for work on *Barham* to be accelerated. The phasing of the various trades in the shipbuilding process highlighted the difficulty in keeping the workforce together. Although the Company had plenty of work, the completion of *Tiger* forced the Company to pay off nearly 2,000 men for whom there was no immediate employment. This

August 1915. Some of Barham's crew assembled on her quarterdeck. The covered berths of the West Yard can be seen behind the fitting-out crane.

Four photographs illustrating the construction of Ship No. 443 the battlecruiser Repulse. *This ship was built with great urgency at the demand of the First Sea Lord Admiral Sir John Fisher.*

Right
The forward section of the keel supported over the yard road and railway on 14 April 1915.

Below
Work progressing on machinery spaces on 12 May 1915.

Repulse is launched on 8 January 1916.

A view over her forward turrets on 8 August 1916 at the time of her commissioning.

reduction over a two month period from 10,729 employees in September to 8,650 in October was borne almost exclusively by shipyard trades. Employment in the engine works remained steadier at between 3,200 to 3,500.[509] In an industry in which fluctuating demand made employment notoriously difficult to regulate, expectations that the war would be of short duration compounded the problem.

An American labour mission addressing the men at Clydebank in April 1918.

Nevertheless, management would have viewed the pay-offs with considerable regret in the knowledge that although the men would soon be needed, they would quickly be absorbed into other yards. Within a few months, the loss of these men was to pose a major problem in building what would be the most urgent order of the war period.

In October 1914, Winston Churchill, then First Lord of the Admiralty reinstated Admiral Sir John Fisher as First Sea Lord. His influence on naval building programmes was far reaching and immediate. He set about rectifying what he considered to be shortages of certain warship types, particularly cruisers, destroyers and submarines. Thomas Bell, summoned by Fisher to a meeting of shipbuilders at the Admiralty in November 1914, left with orders for destroyers and submarines. However, it was Fisher's continued interest in the battlecruiser which was to challenge John Brown. After the success of British battlecruisers in action off Heligoland Bight and in sinking Admiral von Spee's squadron at the Falklands, Fisher pressed for the rapid construction of two new battlecruisers. Earlier, in June 1914, orders for two battleships, *Renown* and *Repulse*, had been placed with Fairfield and Palmers. When war broke out, both ships were suspended in favour of vessels that could be completed quickly. When Fisher demanded two new battlecruisers, the suspended battleships, neither of which had been laid down, were changed to battlecruisers. It was Fisher's intention that both ships should be built in the remarkably short time of 15 months in a manner reminiscent of the speed in which *Dreadnought* had been built eight years earlier. To facilitate this, the main armament mountings already allocated to other battleships were transferred to Fisher's new ships. Palmers did not have a slip long enough to accommodate the increased length of the battlecruiser and the contract for *Repulse* was switched to Clydebank in December 1914. Working day and night, Admiralty constructors designed these very large warships in a very short time and both John Brown and Fairfield were provided with sufficient drawings by 21 January 1915 to enable keel laying to take place on the 25th. Full drawings were not received until 22 April.[510] Fisher took great interest in the progress of both battlecruisers. On hearing that work was proceeding less quickly than he would have liked he immediately wired Clydebank on 31 March:

> 'I hear you have nothing like the number of men on Repulse that are required to complete her by the desired date STOP I had hoped that you would have let nothing whatever prevent your pushing her on with the utmost speed possible STOP Please reply'[511]

Bell replied on the same day:

> 'I regret exceedingly that progress hitherto made on the Repulse is not so good as we had hoped for STOP Our foremen have been doing everything in their power to obtain additional men accustomed to heavy type of ironwork during this past two months but the disappointing results of the efforts are entirely owing to the acceleration of mine sweepers and other Admiralty work in merchant shipyards and also to the Captain Superintendent of the Clyde's activity in having commandeered men to help in the acceleration of building of monitors on this river STOP I would venture to suggest that official instructions be issued to Captain Barttelot to commandeer for Clydebank Yard any men still available from the various merchant shipyards STOP With such official assistance in addition to our own efforts we

would then hope to obtain the largely increased number of men required and thus to make quite a different shewing from this time onwards and achieve her completion by the desired time'[512] Within days an interview was arranged between yard management and Captain Barttelot, the Naval Superintendent Clyde. By 6 April, 40 men (15 platers and 25 helpers), 30 squads of riveters, 40 caulkers and 40 drillers had been found. A similar number of men were made available three weeks later and again four weeks after that.[513] Between January and May 1915, 1,400 men were added to the payroll at Clydebank which then stood at 10,668.[514]

In May, the King visited the Clyde in support of the war effort and on the 17th made a tour of the Clydebank Works a visit all the more poignant following the loss of *Lusitania* to the German submarine U20 ten days earlier. On the 18th, Lord Fisher, the former First Lord of the Admiralty, visited the yard possibly as a distraction from events in Whitehall. Fisher's resignation a few days before over the conduct of the Dardanelles campaign had not dimmed his interest in the battlecruiser *Repulse*.[515]

UNREST

By 1915, the peculiar effects of war on workplace and community created the circumstances for serious discontent. Increased war production demanded more labour while, at the same time, the armed services were recruiting heavily in Glasgow and the West of Scotland. Skilled workers were at first exempt from war service. This placed a high premium on skilled men causing wages to rise as a result. To replace the unskilled men who were enlisted, women were introduced in their place under the dilution scheme. Skilled men employed in non-essential work elsewhere were drafted into the factories and yards. These moves to augment the supply of labour were mistrusted and met with resistance by the unions who, understandably, feared that hard won conditions and privileges would be eroded. Suspicions that employers were making vast profits out of Government work, profits that would not be passed on through increased wages, added to a simmering discontent. The shortage of housing in Glasgow and the Clydebank district was aggravated by the influx of workers to the shipyards and munitions plants. Landlords exploited this situation by putting up rents, resulting in the eviction by court order of many tenants unable to pay the increase. This led to a series of protest meetings and demonstrations in which landlords were

denounced.[516] The ensuing agitation posed a threat to public order and industrial output. These events did much to undermine the fragile pre-war balance which had existed between employers and organised labour on Clydeside.

The failure of negotiations in response to a demand for a 2 pence per hour rise in engineering wages at the beginning of 1915 provoked strike action. William

A posed photograph taken in 1917 showing a girl bringing her father's lunch to the yard.

Women workers carrying out light bench work. The chalked message on the wall behind says 'When the boys come home we are not going to keep you any longer girls'.

Beardmore's Parkhead Forge in the east end of Glasgow, by this time swollen to 20,000 munitions workers, assumed an important role in the strike under the leadership of David Kirkwood, chairman of the shop stewards committee. The strike began on 16 February when workers at the Parkhead Forge and the Albion Motor Co., walked out. On the following day, engineers at Clydebank and elsewhere joined the strike. In his report for 3 March 1915, Thomas Bell regretted to note that:

> 'although a mutual recommendation on behalf of the executive of the masters and men was adopted and signed at York on 12 February agreeing to an increase of 3 shillings and 4 $\frac{1}{4}$ pence per week to all engineers and machinemen, the men went out on strike without

a ballot and notification to masters'. The men returned to work on 4 March having won their claim.[517] This strike was instrumental in persuading the Government that control over labour in the production of munitions was essential. The passing of the Munitions of War Act in July 1915 sought to manage output by declaring works engaged on war production 'Controlled Establishments'. On 12 July 1915, Sheffield and Clydebank were brought into this category. Flexibility between trades was encouraged, strikes were made illegal and the 'dilution' of labour was enforced. Infringements were dealt with severely. A strike of shipwrights at the Fairfield shipyard in August 1915 resulted in three men being sent to prison. In March 1916 ten shop stewards at the Parkhead Forge in

The 'John Brown Volunteers' drawn up outside the platers' shed in 1914.

Glasgow were deported to Edinburgh after a brief strike. As a Controlled Establishment, the supply of labour, materials and the flow of work itself to the Clydebank Works came under Admiralty control. In response to the unrest over rent increases, the Government was forced to hastily pass the Rent and Mortgage Interest (War Restrictions) Act in December 1915 which froze rents at August 1914 levels.[518]

THE DUNBARTONSHIRE VOLUNTEERS

The nature of the work undertaken at John Brown's required the permanent presence of a military guard. In October 1915, Thomas Bell proposed that this guard could be returned to more important military duties by replacing them with members of the Dunbartonshire Volunteer Training Corps, which had been set up in the yard. In July 1916, the army recognised this corps and agreed to its replacing soldiers needed for the Front. 130 John Brown employees joined the volunteers at a total cost of £1,000 for clothing and equipment which the Company agreed to finance from excess profits.

The battleship *Barham* was completed on contract on 15 July 1915 although delays in supplying her forward main armament by Vickers prevented her commissioning until 18 August. On trials, she developed over 77,000 shp and made a speed of 25.5 knots. On 4 October, gun trials were carried out. This was the first opportunity to test the operation of main and secondary armament systems and required firing 15" gun salvoes. Such events were often attended by minor damage to ships fittings. *Barham* acquitted herself well; only nine earthenware fittings in the ships lavatories were broken.[519] By December, efforts to speed up work on *Repulse* had taken effect, aided partly by the rapid supply of stern tube castings from the Atlas Works at Sheffield. On 8 January 1916, the battlecruiser was launched. It was clear however that she would not be built in the 15 months which Fisher had hoped for. The twenty months that it finally took to construct such a large ship was nevertheless a remarkable achievement. In August 1916, Thomas Bell made the following comment:

'. . . it is only fair to say that the official date for

Men gathering at the engine works gate waiting for the siren to announce the end of a working day in 1917.

laying the keel - 25 January 1915 was a paper date only to enable some officials to wire Lord Fisher that it had been laid on his birthday. The designs were not sufficiently advanced nor was enough material in the yard to proceed with the work for another six weeks and even then it was with the greatest difficulty that working drawings could be prepared and approved to keep pace with the ship's construction'[520]

Repulse was commissioned at Clydebank on 8 August 1916 and proceeded to the Firth of Clyde to run steam and gun trials. During steam trials, she was worked up to a maximum of 119,250 shp, making a speed of 32.14 knots.[521] Following his resignation in May 1915, Lord Fisher was not in office to see completion of the battlecruisers for which he had pushed so hard. Although very lightly armoured *Repulse* and her sister *Renown* were nevertheless the largest and fastest ships in the fleet. However, they were soon to be eclipsed by the ship which became a national symbol. On 21 April 1916, notification was received from the Admiralty that preparations were to be made for construction of another as yet unnamed battlecruiser similar to *Repulse*. Drawings and particulars were to follow, the message continued, as the matter was not urgent in nature.[522] The battlecruiser was allocated ship number 460. One month later, the long anticipated clash of battle fleets took place. This had a direct influence on the new ship.

ONE DAY IN MAY

The enormous human effort concentrated in constructing machines of war in British and German shipyards since the appearance of *Dreadnought* in 1906, came to a head in May 1916. The spectacle of two rival fleets of dreadnought battleships and battlecruisers, each ship two to three years in the making, bearing down on one another had long been contemplated. Ironically, in building these ships of destruction, a new industrial working elite of unprecedented skill and ability had been created. The clash of seaborn armour took place on 31 May 1916. While the outcome of the Battle of Jutland was a strategic victory for the Grand Fleet, three British battlecruisers were destroyed with the loss of over 4,000 lives. This disaster prompted a re-examination of the design of the new battlecruiser and, in cruel irony, marked her ultimate fate many years later. On 14 June, the Company received a letter from the Admiralty stating that the Treasury had agreed that one of the new battlecruisers, the one allocated to John Brown, was to proceed.[523] On 14 July, John Brown was informed that the new ship was to be called *Hood*. Following keel laying on 1 September[524], work on *Hood* proceeded slowly, as the Admiralty was unwilling to switch men and material from other contracts. However, at the end of February 1917, the Admiralty instructed the yard that work on *Hood* was to proceed 'with all dispatch'. The ship was launched on 22 August 1918 by Lady Hood, the widow of Rear-Admiral Hood who had lost his life on the battlecruiser *Invincible* which had been destroyed at Jutland.

ONE DAY IN JULY

On 1 July 1916, the destroyer *Rowena* was launched at John Browns, at this stage in the war, a routine event. That day was also the start of the Somme Offensive on the Western Front. For several shipyard workers who might otherwise have been present at the launch, but who had rushed to join the forces, the ultimate sacrifice was made:

Private James Wright, 202 Glasgow Road, aged 18, of the Gordon Highlanders, an apprentice carpenter, enlisted June 1915.
Private Andrew Moncur, 104 Kilbowie Road, aged 18, of the Gordon Highlanders, an apprentice riveter.
Private William Goldie, Woodbine Cottage, Hardgate, aged 23, of the Gordon Highlanders, a caulker.
Private Alexander Murray, 47 Alexander Street, aged 19, of the Royal Scots Fusiliers, died on 10 July of wounds received in action, an apprentice caulker.[525]

CONTRACTS FOR THE TSAR

While the emergency war construction programmes were under way, John Brown's Russian contracts were also making progress. In August 1913, the Company, in collaboration with Colonel Sassinovski of the Nikolaev Works, completed designs for Russian cruisers at Clydebank.[526] In November, John Sampson reported regarding joint working of the Russian Shipbuilding Company (Russud) at Nikolaev with the French firm Chantier Navalis.[527]
By May 1915, consultancy work at the Baltic Works had been completed and notice was sent to Clydebank that John Brown personnel could be brought home.[528] However, at Nikolaev work was beginning on the cruisers and in May, men were transferred from St. Petersburg to Nikolaev, thousands of miles away near the Black Sea, to become involved with the cruisers and to assist in the acceptance trials of *Imperatritsa Mariya*. These were successfully completed in July.[529] The Brown-Curtis machinery constructed for the Russian battleship *Imperator Alexander III*, had an eventful journey from Clydebank to Nikolaev in 1916. War restrictions had closed the simplest route through the Mediterranean and the Dardanelles. Weighing 560 tons, the turbines were loaded onto the Russian cruiser *Askold* at

МИНИСТЕРСТВО МОРСКОЕ

НАЧАЛЬНИКЪ
БАЛТIЙСКАГО
СУДОСТРОИТЕЛЬНАГО и МЕХАНИЧЕСКАГО
ЗАВОДА
ПО ДѢЛОПРОИЗВОДСТВУ.

Марта I-го дня 191 5 г.

№ 1955

ПЕТРОГРАДЪ.
Чекуши, Кожевенная линiя, № 18.
Телефонъ № 460-77.

Адресъ для телеграммъ:
„Балтюдъ".

Above.
The heading on a certificate dated 1 March 1915, given to James Gorrie, John Brown's marine engineer in St Petersburg from the Manager of the Baltic Shipbuilding & Engineering Works. Gorrie first went to St Petersburg in 1909. The Certificate (not shown) reads:

'This is given to a British subject - Mr James Gorrie, chief external engineer of John Brown & Company - to prove that on 16 February 1915 he was mercifully awarded with a golden watch by his Imperial Majesty the Emperor of Russia with a representation of the State Emblem of Russia - for his special diligence in the building of military ships at the Baltic Shipbuilding & Engineering Works of the Ministry of Marine'.

The Orient liner Ormonde *fitted out as an Armed Merchant Cruiser and sporting a disruptive camouflage scheme leaves Clydebank on 27 October 1917. She was the first Clydebank merchant ship to be fitted with Brown-Curtis turbines.*

153

Clydebank on 16 May 1916. *Askold* sailed for Archangel where her cargo was unloaded onto six large barges and taken by the rivers, Dvina, Suchona and Volga as well as numerous lakes and canals, to the village of Sarepta near Tsaritsyn.[530] Here the machinery was transferred onto railway carriages and the journey continued to Rostov-on-Don, a distance of 2,500 miles from Archangel. Loaded onto

The Medea Class destroyer Medusa test firing a torpedo in the basin in July 1915. Originally laid down as Kriti *for the Greek navy, she was taken over after the outbreak of war.*

Right
Turbines for the Russian battleship Imperator Alexander III *under construction in the Black Sea, waiting to be shipped on the cruiser* Askold *on 16 May 1916.*

another steamer, the final voyage was made to Nikolaev across the Sea of Azov and the Black Sea. Throughout this journey of nearly 5,400 miles, R Hood, an engineering draughtsman from Clydebank, accompanied the shipment.[531] In October 1916, *Imperatritsa Mariya* capsized and sank at Sevastopol with the loss of 225 lives after unstable propellant caused a massive internal explosion. Although no John Brown personnel were on board, the Company's close association with the ship prompted the Board to vote for the sum of 10,000 roubles (£660) to be sent to the relief fund for the families of those lost.[532]

In February 1917, fresh enquiries were received from Russud for the construction of turbines for four torpedo-boat destroyers and for designs of geared turbines for twin screw submarines. By April, the latter had been supplied.[533]

With World War One approaching its climax, Russia was on the precipice of revolution and civil war. The revolution of November 1917 and armistice followed the exhaustion of the Russian armies in the field with Germany in December. The principal concern at Clydebank was the safety of the six men still in Nikolaev. In February 1918, John Black wrote from the Black Sea:

'Mr Dimitrieff, who still has some connection with the Works through the Head Office at Petrograd, left here yesterday for the purpose of discussing with the Government the question of 'Nationalisation' as they call it, of all the Works at Nicolaieff. Although it is very difficult to get reliable information concerning the doings in Russia, I am making all enquiries necessary in case we must leave. The conditions at Nicolaieff are still good in a sense, but as we hear almost daily of some new excesses in surrounding districts it makes us think of what may happen at any moment here. We are kept informed by the Consul regarding the situation in the North, especially with reference to the chances of leaving the country, but unfortunately the information received is generally about 10 days old, and telegrams at the present time are being sent by post. Since the month of October, on three occasions advice has been received warning Britishers not to come to Petrograd in the hope of getting away'.[534]

This letter was followed by one from Alex Hutcheson, a Clydebank engineer:

'Since the eruption of last year there has been a gradual process on the part of the workers to acquire the full control of the works and they have from time to time forced up wages to an enormous extent and their demands have to be complied with whether or not it means ruin to the various undertakings. These demands have in turn forced up the cost of living so that the process of increase goes on without control or check and for many months now the price of food and clothing has been over nine times pre-war prices'.[535]

No further letters were received and enquiries about the men's safety were made to the Foreign Office. On 20 March 1918, the Foreign Office stated that they had been in touch with the British Consul in Petrograd (St. Petersburg) regarding John Brown representatives in Nikolaev but that no replies had been received and that 'owing to the advance of the enemy (the Bolsheviks) in South Russia, nothing further could be done'. In fact, the Clydebank men, including John Black, had a journey home even more circuitous than that taken by the turbines for *Imperator Aleksandr III*. By early March, they had succeeded in reaching Moscow. On 28 March, they set off for Vladivostock on the trans-Siberian railway. From there, they sailed for Kobe in Japan, arriving on 30 April. The next stop was Vancouver and the journey across Canada. Finally, on 10 July, the men arrived home in Clydebank after a journey round the world that took over five months.[536]

Final accounts for the Black Sea contracts show that £142,000 was paid to John Brown for technical assistance on the battleships and £101,000 for the cruisers.[537] The last act in the Russian contracts was the Board's decision that, in light of cancelled work on destroyers and submarines, an account for £1,500 should be sent for payment.[538]

NEW TECHNOLOGY: NEW HOMES

By June 1916, a large number of houses for war workers were under construction in Clydebank. Prices were rising rapidly prompting local builder, Leslie Kirk, to write to management at Clydebank listing increases in building material costs which had taken place since June 1914:

Timber 155%, Plumber work 72.5%, Bricks 33.3%, Tiling 17.5%, Slater work 15%, Stone 10%, Wages 10%, Cartage 30%[539]

Another reason for the urgent provision of new housing was the introduction of dilution. In November 1916, Thomas Bell noted in his monthly report that:

'the Admiralty most seriously continue to impress upon us the importance of dilution and of

employing as many women as possible. Whilst we have been able to effect considerable dilution in the manning of smaller machines in the Engine Shops and in clerks in the Counting House . . . it has not been easy to effect dilution in the Shipyard.[540]

One process which promised a more productive use of skilled manpower was the adoption of pneumatic riveting. Riveting was an operation which typically

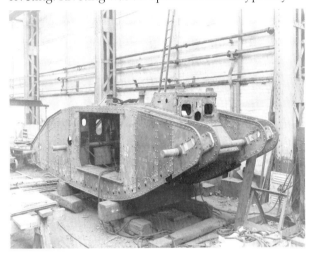

In March 1917, the company undertook to build 50 Mark IV tanks. Bottlenecks in production caused delays and it is likely that only a fraction of this number was constructed. The hull of a tank is seen here on 8 May 1917.

Below.
Clydebank's senior managers pose with two naval officers outside the office on 29 October 1918. From left, John Paterson (Naval Architect), W H Wood (Engineering Manager), Commander Fox, A Williamson, John Spiers, JB Henderson (Secretary) and William Luke (Shipyard Manager)

required four men, a left and a right handed riveter, a rivet heater and a rivet holder. The left and right handed riveters alternately struck the rivet with a rivet hammer until the rivet was closed. In the United States, a tool had been developed which dispensed with traditional rivet hammers and required only one riveter to operate it. This heavy tool, approximately the length of a man's forearm, was connected by hose to a compressed air supply and, when activated, delivered a rapid series of heavy blows to the white hot rivet. Thomas Bell had found it impossible to initiate pneumatic riveting among men in the yard. Because of the extreme urgency surrounding construction of *Repulse*, he had been forced to find

Three women at the stern of a steamer look over to John Brown's shipyard and the hull of the battlecruiser Hood *in 1918.*

Asbestos was one of the greatest hazards in shipbuilding. Here, two men are making an asbestos paste.

labour elsewhere. In April 1915, forty squads of pneumatic riveters were brought to Clydebank from Swindon and locations in the north west of England. These men insisted that they would only come if houses were built for them in Clydebank equivalent to those they were leaving. When the new riveters had been accommodated, Bell found that he had to offer similar inducements to his own hand riveters who performed 80% of all riveting work, to persuade them to change to pneumatic tools. Consequently, he had to proceed with a further twenty tenements to house 160 families. Moreover, the cost of building materials had risen by more than 40% since autumn 1914, making the total cost of the twenty tenements £52,700, £16,700 more than the estimate. In what might be termed 'creative accounting', Bell wrote to the Ministry of Munitions making the ingenious suggestion that the houses be considered 'a constituent of our pneumatic power plant' and that the excess amount be written down out of excess profits allowed under the Munitions of War Acts 1915 and 1916 (Limitation of Profits).[541]

The overwhelming volume of Admiralty work had inevitably displaced other customers and, with few exceptions, prevented the development of commercial links with shipping lines. Nevertheless, given the restrictions of war building programmes, the Company did what it could to keep other commercial interests alive. Late in 1916, with no end to the war in sight, John Brown, Fairfield and Harland & Wolff, secured a building agreement with Canadian Pacific for the construction of new tonnage over a ten-year period. This agreement, which did not come into effect until the termination of hostilities, was recognition that warship building would inevitably come to an end.[542] Time was found to pursue foreign warship work and tenders were prepared for coast defence ships for the Chinese government in association with Palmers. Throughout 1916, the company was involved, through its interest in the Sociedad Española de Construccion Naval, in the design of new cruisers, destroyers, submarines and gunboats for the Spanish Navy. Fresh capital of £27,000 to further develop the business at Bilbao was approved in December 1916. [543] In May 1916, Lord Pirrie, Chairman of Harland & Wolff, arranged for the construction of a large Union Castle liner at Clydebank. This ship, *Windsor Castle*, was not laid down until June 1919.[544]

One consequence of the loss of *Lusitania* in May 1915 was an enquiry from Cunard in November 1916 for the price of a replacement ship for insurance purposes. Based on prices applying at the time of the loss, John Brown estimated the price of a new vessel at £2,260,000.[545]

DEPARTURE OF THOMAS BELL

In May 1917, Thomas Bell was asked by the Government to fill the post of Deputy Controller of Dockyards and War Shipbuilding, a position which reflected the high regard in which he was held. Taking this position required his resignation from John Brown and departure from Clydebank. In his absence the shipyard manager, William Luke, and the engineering manager, W H Wood, had joint responsibility for running the works.[546] John Sampson, like Bell a director on the main John Brown Board, chaired the monthly Committee of the Board meetings at Clydebank. In August 1917, soon after his appointment as Deputy Controller, Bell was given a Knight Commandership of the Order of the British Empire.

Sir Thomas Bell KBE, returned to his position as Managing Director in January 1919. At a luncheon organised by local directors in honour of their chief's return, Sir Thomas attributed his recent appointment to Government office to the fact that he was:

> 'fortunate enough to be the director-in-charge of this great concern' adding that 'Clydebank stood in the Admiralty records easy first, not alone for excellence of work but what was at that time of still greater importance, viz. absolute fidelity to their promises for dates of delivery.'[547]

The priorities of the naval war shifted from capital ships to destroyers and escorts urgently needed to protect merchant shipping in the Atlantic. This view over the new West Yard shows four destroyers under construction during 1918. Beardmore's yard can be seen at top left with the carrier Argus *fitting-out.*

HORSEPOWER

The development of marine propelling machinery as expressed in the pursuit of speed was mainly in the context of the North Atlantic, the Blue Riband and the great liners. The most powerful passenger liners afloat were the German ships of the Imperator Class. The fastest of these, *Vaterland*, developed 90,000 shp although the smaller Cunard liner *Mauretania* remained the swiftest although she developed only 78,000 shp. The war created the need for large warships capable of high speed and there was no better example of this than in the tactical role assigned to the battlecruiser. British battlecruisers of this period pushed the power of turbine machinery to new limits. *Tiger* became the first ship in which the power developed by steam machinery exceeded 100,000 shp. On trials in October 1914, 109,000 shp was recorded for a speed of 29 knots. In August 1916, *Repulse* developed 119,000 shp for a speed of 31.5 knots.[548] During trials in March 1920, *Hood's* machinery developed over 151,000

Five standard ships were built during the First World War including War Hermit *seen here leaving Clydebank on 26 April 1918.*

shp to propel her at a speed in excess of 32 knots. These were performances far in excess of those of any ocean liner. While the machinery in each of these battlecruisers was larger than in preceding classes, advances in marine technology accounted for some of the improvements. The machinery installed in *Hood* weighed the same as that in *Repulse*, despite developing almost one third more power. This was due to the adoption of small tube boilers in preference to the previously standard and heavier large tube boiler.

In *Repulse* and all capital ships before her, the machinery transmitted power from the turbines directly to the propellers. This was an arrangement which led to higher propeller speeds than desirable for maximum propulsive efficiency. The introduction of gearing between the turbine and the propeller shaft enabled the shaft to turn at more efficient speeds. The first large ships to be fitted with geared turbines were the light battlecruisers of the Courageous Class completed in 1916. In *Hood*, gearing had the effect of reducing propeller revolutions at high speed to a maximum of 210 per minute, in comparison with 280 for *Repulse*. For many years, *Hood* was the most powerful warship in the world in terms of both propulsive and offensive capabilities. Clydebank's contribution to the development of turbine machinery remained of outstanding significance. This experience was to prove invaluable when tendering for a new class of super-liner ten years later.

WAR PRODUCTION

Clydebank's wartime output stood highest on Clydeside. 47 vessels of 155,153 displacement tons in total, excluding *Hood*, were produced together with machinery totalling 1,563,500 horsepower. *Pegasus*, which had been laid down as the ferry *Stockholm* in May 1914 was taken over by the Admiralty in February 1917 and completed as a seaplane carrier. The submarine depot ship *Platypus* ordered in July 1914 was completed for the Royal Australian Navy in 1917. A further five destroyers were ordered in 1918 but cancelled at the end of the war without being laid down.

Understandably, output of merchant ships declined significantly during the war. The completion of *Repulse* in June 1916 enabled work on the Orient liner *Ormonde* to be resumed.[549] *Ormonde* was completed as an Armed Merchant Cruiser in November 1917. By that year losses of merchant ships to the U-boat campaign had risen to a critical level. To decrease the time in which merchant ships could be built, a standard merchant ship design was prepared, based on easily manufactured hull and engine components. To supplement production, National shipyards were planned and one completed at Newport in Monmouth, where ships of this type could be batch produced. Spare capacity in existing yards was also utilised. In January 1917, berths became available and the Controller of Merchant Shipping placed an order for two standard ships, *War Thistle* and *War Hermit*. This was quickly followed by the order for two further standard ships, *War Rider* and *War Bodnant*.

The latter ship was placed at Clydebank at the suggestion of Lord Pirrie.[550] The order for a fifth standard ship was placed in November 1918 and completed as the *Bata* for Elder Dempster Lines. Every effort was made to keep the Works at peak production and employment during the war and any excess capacity in the manufacturing and construction programmes was immediately filled. In

despatching tanks already constructed congested production facilities and prevented others from being built.[551] In April 1917, the order for five sets of boilers for standard ships was received from Harland & Wolff. In February, machinery for the destroyer *Tormentor* building at Beardmore's yard and the SS *Princesa* at Stephen's yard was awarded. In August 1917, the machinery contract for the destroyer *Sesame*,

July 1916, turbines for fleet submarines *K1* and *K2*, under construction at Portsmouth Dockyard were awarded to John Brown and, in November, the machinery for patrol boat *P33* building at Napier & Miller's shipyard was constructed.

In March 1917, agreement was given to construct fifty Mark IV tank hulls for the Ministry of Munitions. In May, the first nine tanks were despatched to the Glasgow firm of engineers Mirlees Watson for completion. Clydebank had capacity to build five tanks per week. Unspecified difficulties in

building at Denny's was awarded to Clydebank. Sixteen water tube boilers of the 3-drum type and two sets of turbines each of 4,000 shp were constructed for patrol vessels building in other yards. A considerable amount of component part manufacture was also carried out, including diaphragms and nozzles for Brown-Curtis turbines amounting to a total of 750 tons. Machinery refits were completed on the destroyers *Alarm*, *Mameluke* and *Ossory*; the submarines *K2*, *K7* and *K8*. The cruiser *Crescent* was partially refitted.[552]

Hood, the longest British warship ever built, straddles the East Yard on 21 August 1918, the day before her launch.

Right
One of Hood's *four poppets
which would take her weight on
the sliding ways during her
launch.
The recess in the battlecruiser's
hull where armour will be fitted
can be clearly seen.*

Opposite page
*Flying the Union Jack and John
Brown's company flag,* Hood *is
launched on 22 August 1918.*

160

SUBMARINES

Despite its position as a major warship builder, John Brown's expressed little interest in building submarines. Whether this was through lack of foresight or because there were ample contracts for conventional vessels is not clear. John Brown did have the opportunity to become involved in building what would eventually become the capital ship of the future. In the early years of the 20th Century, great interest surrounded the submarine, which had evolved from a novelty into a vessel with great military potential. A number of leading British shipbuilders already involved in warship work expressed interest in their construction including Beardmore, Scotts, Thornycroft, Armstrong and Vickers. Although the Admiralty opted for the Holland type in 1900, awarding Vickers sole rights to private manufacture, a number of other submarine designs were in circulation.

John Brown's first opportunity to become involved in submarine construction took place in May 1905 when discussions were held at Clydebank with Thorsten Nordenfelt, the Swedish millionaire engineer. Nordenfelt had been closely associated with the Barrow Shipbuilding Co. where a number of unsuccessful submarine designs had been produced in the late 1880s. However, the Clydebank Board decided not to proceed as the principal features of Nordenfelt's submarine had 'been placed before the public by other parties'[553]

In September 1907, Commander Boselli from La Spezia met John Dunlop at Clydebank with the proposal that John Brown consider construction of a new submarine type. Boselli was almost certainly working for Cesare Laurenti, an ex Lt. Commander in the Italian Navy, who became manager of the Fiat San Giorgio shipyard at La Spezia in 1906.[554] Laurenti had prepared a number of submarine designs based on French naval engineer Laubeuf's Narval of 1897.[555] John Brown was interested enough to send John Sampson to La Spezia, although it was decided not to proceed because of restrictions incorporated in Boselli's proposal.[556] In March 1909, Boselli renewed contact with the Company by letter stating that more favourable terms could now be made for the purchase of manufacturing rights.[557] As before however, the Board decided not to pursue rights.[558] In 1909, another Clydeside yard, Scott's Shipbuilding & Engineering Co., decided to acquire a licence and had laid down four Scott-Laurenti submarines before 1914. John Brown stuck to what it was good at and resisted submarine building. It was only when pressed by the

First Sea Lord, Lord Fisher, in 1915, that three submarines were built at Clydebank. Despite successfully launching the largest ships in the world, John Brown struggled with submarines. Of the three, *E36* fell off her launching cradles after the launch ways collapsed. She was later righted and successfully launched.

SHIPYARD EXTENSIONS 1914 - 1918

Apart from numerous small extensions to shops and facilities, the east yard received little attention during the war. All five berths were capable of building warships of battleship size. Cranage on these berths was suitable for lifts of five tons and steelwork prepared in the shops observed this limit. A small amount of sub-assembly work was undertaken in the shops where frames, for example, might have brackets or webs riveted in place before transfer to the berth for erection. Ship construction remained a matter of transferring relatively light pieces of steel, cut to size, bent to shape and punched for rivets, to the berth for assembly. In re-equipping the west yard however, it was decided to double berth handling capacity to ten tons, enabling a greater degree of sub-assembly work to be completed in the shops. One of the three west yard berths had already been equipped with a covered gantry capable of lifting riveted assemblies of up to ten tons capacity. As destroyers were urgently needed in large numbers to protect the battleships of the Grand Fleet, the west yard at Clydebank became, in effect, a specialised destroyer building facility. The order to construct a second covered berth was placed with Sir William Arrol in November 1914 and completed in the following April. The plater's shed was extended and equipped to improve steel throughput to the new berth facility. In 1917, the remaining berth in the west yard was equipped with two tower cranes of ten tons capacity, one fixed and one travelling.

Works extensions had to be sanctioned by the Ministry of Munitions under the simple criterion that output must increase as a consequence. A typical application made during 1916 for relatively small works for female dilutees costing £1,380 was worded: *State the product the output of which the Company is asked to increase.*

> 'These alterations are in connection with dilution of labour, and consist of modifications to a shop for installation of a room where women can sit down and eat their meals and also [for] fitting up 21 lavatories. The expenditure is solely in connection with the dilution of labour and will not

The stamp applied to drawings signifying that they are complete and accurate.

increase the output of this particular product, viz. - the machining of blading and small brass' finishing duplication work.

State which Government Department asks for the increased output:

'The women are employed entirely on Admiralty work'.

Will the proposed extensions be of any service after the war?

'In view of the Governments declaration to gradually reinstate, after the War, all the men thus displaced, the alterations will be of no service whatever'.[559]

In the year ending March 1916, a total of £57,200 was expended on new plant and facilities.[560] A further scheme of extensions affecting several parts of the Works was not completed until September 1919 and reached a total of £174,000.[561] This work was done through grant-in-aid and allowances from excess profits to cover 40% of cost.

A plan of the yard in 1919 showing the full development of the site. Two yards, east and west, are separated by the fitting-out basin. The latter is exceptionally well served with two 150 ton fitting-out cranes. Both yards had separate steel working facilities but other shops, joiners, brass, copper, electrical etc., were shared.

John Brown & Co Ltd 1919

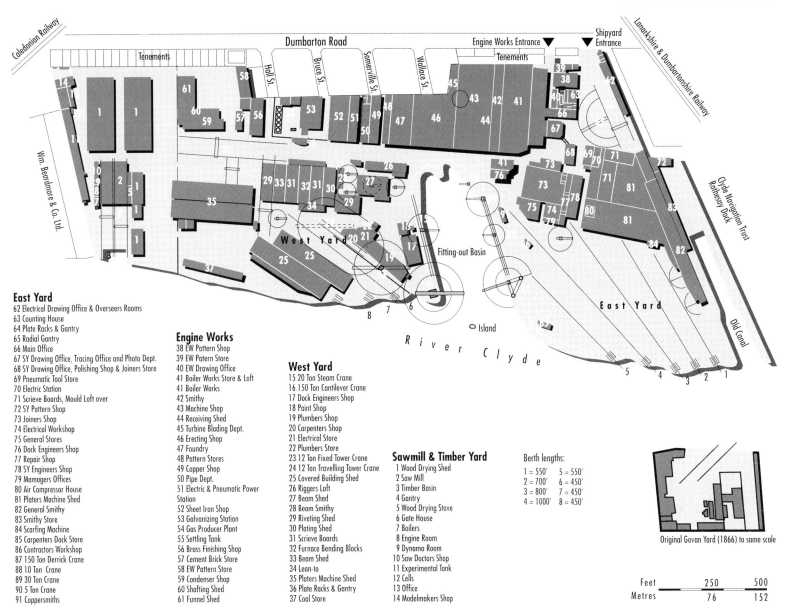

East Yard
62 Electrical Drawing Office & Overseers Rooms
63 Counting House
64 Plate Racks & Gantry
65 Radial Gantry
66 Main Office
67 SY Drawing Office, Tracing Office and Photo Dept.
68 SY Drawing Office, Polishing Shop & Joiners Store
69 Pneumatic Tool Store
70 Electric Station
71 Scrieve Boards, Mould Loft over
72 SY Pattern Shop
73 Joiners Shop
74 Electrical Workshop
75 General Stores
76 Dock Engineers Shop
77 Repair Shop
78 SY Engineers Shop
79 Mamagers Offices
80 Air Compressor House
81 Platers Machine Shed
82 General Smithy
83 Smithy Store
84 Scarfing Machine
85 Carpenters Dock Store
86 Contractors Workshop
87 150 Ton Derrick Crane
88 10 Ton Crane
89 30 Ton Crane
90 5 Ton Crane
91 Coppersmiths

Engine Works
38 EW Pattern Shop
39 EW Patern Store
40 EW Drawing Office
41 Boiler Works Store & Loft
41 Boiler Works
42 Smithy
43 Machine Shop
44 Receiving Shed
45 Turbine Blading Dept.
46 Erecting Shop
47 Foundry
48 Pattern Stores
49 Copper Shop
50 Pipe Dept.
51 Electric & Pneumatic Power Station
52 Sheet Iron Shop
53 Galvanizing Station
54 Gas Producer Plant
55 Settling Tank
56 Brass Finishing Shop
57 Cement Brick Store
58 EW Pattern Store
59 Condenser Shop
60 Shafting Shed
61 Funnel Shed

West Yard
15 20 Ton Steam Crane
16 150 Ton Cantilever Crane
17 Dock Engineers Shop
18 Paint Shop
19 Plumbers Shop
20 Carpenters Shop
21 Electrical Store
22 Plumbers Store
23 12 Ton Fixed Tower Crane
24 12 Ton Travelling Tower Crane
25 Covered Building Shed
26 Riggers Loft
27 Beam Shed
28 Beam Smithy
29 Riveting Shed
30 Plating Shed
31 Scrieve Boards
32 Furnace Bending Blocks
33 Beam Shed
34 Lean-to
35 Platers Machine Shed
36 Plate Racks & Gantry
37 Coal Store

Sawmill & Timber Yard
1 Wood Drying Shed
2 Saw Mill
3 Timber Basin
4 Gantry
5 Wood Drying Stove
6 Gate House
7 Boilers
8 Engine Room
9 Dynamo Room
10 Saw Doctors Shop
11 Experimental Tank
12 Cells
13 Office
14 Modelmakers Shop

Berth lengths:
1 = 550'   5 = 550'
2 = 700'   6 = 450'
3 = 800'   7 = 450'
4 = 1000'   8 = 450'

Original Govan Yard (1866) to same scale

Feet	250	500
Metres	76	152

1919 - 1938   AN EMPRESS, TWO QUEENS AND A DUKE

The optimism which followed the end of the war was short lived in what would be the most difficult decade for shipbuilding since the 1870s. Admiralty work, for so long the backbone of Clydebank's order book, stopped more or less immediately while some warships from the war building programme, already in an advanced state of construction on the building berths, were cancelled and the material dismantled. Spiralling material and labour costs made ship owners reluctant to place orders for new ships and the order book dwindled. To win the orders that were available, shipbuilders were forced to tender at little or no profit. As the situation worsened, some contracts were suspended or cancelled outright. In an effort to reduce costs, employers forced wages down with a consequent deterioration in labour relations. These events, damaging enough in themselves, were set against a background of more effective competition from foreign shipbuilders. Throughout 1919 and into the early 1920s, labour unrest became a significant factor, as expectations of a new and fairer society clashed with economic reality. By 1921, the number of unemployed had accelerated beyond one million, forcing the government to amend the Unemployment Insurance Act, increasing unemployment benefit from 15 shillings to 18 shillings per week.

During the period until his resignation in 1935, Sir Thomas Bell, managing director at Clydebank, used the vehicle of monthly works reports to comment widely on the vagaries of shipbuilding, labour and the cost of living. His reports also reveal his attitude towards the numerous difficulties of the time and of the hardship forced on many thousands of working people.

At the cessation of hostilities in November 1918, four destroyers, one cruiser, one battlecruiser and three standard ships remained from the emergency war building programmes. As these contracts were well advanced, work was allowed to continue, although five other warships, on which work had begun, were cancelled. The problem facing the Company was the relatively few commercial links remaining with

shipping lines - the price to be paid for consorting with the Admiralty. Nevertheless, Bell, in common with other shipbuilders, initially took a positive view of the immediate future. Rebuilding depleted merchant fleets which had suffered through war losses was the new priority, set in a general feeling of optimism. Commenting on the installation of a new frame-bending furnace at Clydebank, Bell said this would

> 'enable the output of framing and consequently merchant work to be doubled, and this will be most
>
> essential in the forthcoming 18 or 20 months, during which we have every prospect of
>
> continuity of work for the whole of our slips'

Bell's strategy for winning new merchant contracts placed great reliance on Lord Pirrie, whose Belfast shipyard had suffered less disruption through Admiralty work than Clydebank.[562] To meet anticipated demand, Pirrie booked all three berths in the west yard and one large berth in the East.[563]

At first, there was a rush of orders. In January 1919, the agreement made with Canadian Pacific in 1916 came into effect with a three ship order divided between John Brown (*Montcalm* and *Montclare*) and Fairfield (*Montrose*). First to be laid down was *Montcalm* in January 1919, followed by *Montclare* in September. Despite the end of the war, both ships were completed with gun positions.[564] Early in 1919, Pirrie's promise of work was realised, first with two ships, the 6,700 ton *Ekari* for the African Steamship Co. laid-down in March, and the 19,600 ton Union Castle liner *Windsor Castle* which was laid down in June. In May, he directed two 9,000ton Elder Dempster refrigerated cargo ships, *Calgary* and *Cochrane*, to Clydebank, followed by two further vessels of the same type, *Calumet* and *Cariboo* later in the year. Pirrie's supply of orders was by no means exhausted and more followed, including six sets of turbines, gearing and shafting for Dutch owners, a large number of cabin fittings for a P&O liner building at Belfast, and up to twenty-five tons of steel work a month from Harland & Wolff's yards for

Clydebank's galvanising shop.[565]

In the spring of 1919, the Great Eastern Railway Co. returned to John Brown's placing an order for two channel ferries, *Antwerp* and *Bruges*. Cunard, John Brown's most important customer after the Admiralty, ordered the 21,000ton *Franconia*, which was laid down in August followed later by the 14,000ton *Alaunia* which was laid down in the following year.

Clydebank's transition to peacetime activities appeared to be fulfilling post-war expectations. With eleven ships in various stages of construction, the yard also secured the reconditioning of *War Angler, Archangel* (previously built in the yard as *St Petersburg*) and the Clyde passenger steamer *Queen Alexandra*.

No sooner had the shipbuilding and engineering industries been released from Government control in 1919, than the first of several strikes to affect the shipbuilding and marine engineering industries took place. Labour relations, kept in check by the Munitions Act of 1915, had simmered throughout the war period fuelled by the suspicion that huge profits were being made by employers. Now, with the demobilisation of thousands of soldiers, the job market began to flood. The position was further compounded by the layoffs resulting from the termination of munitions work. On Clydeside, the trade union response was to call for a reduction in working hours, to enable a greater number of people to remain in employment. On 1 January 1919, as a result of a national agreement between employers and workers, the 47-hour working week replaced the 54-hour week. The Scottish Trades Union Congress and the still active Clyde Workers Committee pressed for a further reduction to 40 hours. Thus the '40 Hours Movement' was formed. Events moved quickly and unofficial strike action followed accompanied by the call for a general strike.

On Monday 27 January 1919, the majority of shipyard workers at John Brown's went on strike followed by the men in the engine works the following day. On Tuesday, only 220 men were left in the entire works, together with a similar number of women. For the latter, there was no possibility of retaining employment as this would terminate on the return of soldiers from military service.[566] Mass picketing of the Beardmore and John Brown works took place 'The result was that in each case only about a third of the willing men were able to get to their work.'[567]

David Kirkwood, the prospective Labour candidate for Dumbarton, in which constituency Clydebank

was a ward, spoke at a mass meeting of workers, urging them to 'stand shoulder to shoulder and not to return to work until the 40 hours was granted.'[568]

By the end of January, 40,000 men were on strike in the Glasgow district, raising the spectre of Bolshevik revolution in the minds of the authorities. The issue was brought to national prominence on Friday 31 January, thereafter referred to as 'Bloody Friday', when thousands of strikers, crammed into George Square in the centre of Glasgow and were charged by riot police. The events in George Square did not signal the end of the campaign and it was not until 12 February that work resumed at Clydebank. The events of January 1919 were responsible for attracting the name 'Red Clydeside', a title which proved to be remarkably enduring.

In February 1919, Sir Thomas Bell wrote of the above events:

> 'As far as one can judge, the movement received the maximum support from the ironworkers, the electricians and the moulders; the ironworkers because of the alleged injustice to men working on lieu or time-and-a-bit rates, and they had a certain amount of justification for their contention. The electricians and moulders had no special grievance to complain of, but showed up more prominently than any other trade during the strike, evidently being dominated by their Bolshevik members . . . Very great credit is due to the police in Glasgow for their fearless and prompt action on Friday, 31 January, when they showed that the City of Glasgow was not to become the defenceless prey of a gang of Bolsheviks, and practically paralysed the strike by locking up the extremist leaders.
> Superintendent McLean and his men of the Clydebank Police Force were also of very great assistance in protecting all men who desired to return to work, and thus counteracting the terrorising tactics of the Bolshevistic in the Burgh'[569]

In March, 300 demobilised men returning from the services forced management to release most women dilutees, many of whom had been in employment at the Works for over four years.[570] There were few other disputes in 1919 although what Thomas Bell described as 'minor irritations' were numerous.[571] The volume of work on hand in 1919 persuaded the Company to make a number of additions to buildings and plant. In October, Bell, reviewing output over the past eleven months said that:

> 'drastic measures will have to be taken to enable

the Works to adjust to present day wage and labour conditions. Prices for ships and engines are only obtainable after severe competition, only those firms equipped with every type of labour saving appliance and the most advantageous arrangements for transport and materials can hope to hold their own'

Bell calculated that the average weekly wage per man was 84 shillings in comparison to a figure of 34 shillings and 6 pence before the war. Although Clydebank benefited from re-equipping carried out under war programmes, Bell pressed ahead with further improvements. Expenditure totalling £71,000 for the engine works and £96,000 for the Shipyard was proposed. Bell justified this commenting 'I am strongly of the opinion that only by such expenditure shall we be able to successfully cope with competition two years hence'.[572] Bell's approach of investing in existing facilities was better founded than his principal Clydeside competitors, Fairfield and Beardmore, both of whom committed more capital in expanding capacity by adding new berths to their existing yards. As events would prove, these berths would see very few hulls.

HOOD

On 22 August 1918, *Hood* was launched. At this stage in her career, she was relatively unknown: 'very few people have hitherto been aware of her existence, and yet the *Hood*, is a far more wonderful vessel than the Hush! Hush! ships [*Glorious, Courageous* and *Furious*] which made such a sensation'[573] However, work on *Hood* served as a reminder that shipbuilding was a hazardous activity. On 19 May, a serious explosion ocurred on board in the vicinity of the ships carpenter's store which killed two men and injured six others. The men were working in an airtight compartment which had been sealed for a period of three weeks. Despite opening the manhole cover to vent the compartment several days in advance of the men working there, a build-up of gas was ignited although the Fatal Accident Inquiry held in July could find no obvious cause for the explosion.[574]

By October 1919, *Hood's* after main armament mountings, turrets and guns were in place, enabling her engines and shafting to be lined up without danger of the hull flexing through added weight. On 8 August, the yard was visited by the Third Sea Lord Sir William Nicholson, and the Controller of Merchant Shipbuilding, Sir Joseph Maclay, to determine the amount of labour necessary for the completion of *Hood* and the cruiser *Enterprise* without compromising construction of new merchant tonnage. As a result, work on *Enterprise* was suspended, causing a large number of men in the engine shops to be laid off. Work on this contract did not resume until October when the Admiralty permitted work to proceed, as the berth was earmarked for the Cunard liner *Alaunia*.[575] *Hood's* forward turrets were erected on board at the beginning of December, while the basin trials of her machinery took place on the 9th and 10th of that month. The battlecruiser left Clydebank on 9 January 1920 never to return and sailed to Rosyth Dockyard where she was dry docked and adjustments to her armament were made. In March, she returned to the Firth of Clyde for official trials. On the 18th, during full power trials, her machinery developed 151,000 shp, driving her at a speed of 32.07 knots on the Skelmorlie measured mile. *Hood* was not only the largest warship in the world, her engines were also the most powerful. In addition to a full complement of Clydebank personnel, onboard during her trials were Vice Admiral Sir Roger Keyes, Commander of the First Battlecruiser Squadron, and the man responsible for the ship's design, Sir Eustace d'Eyncourt of the Royal Corps of Naval Constructors.

STEEL SHORTAGES

Early in 1920, steel supplies from the Steel Company of Scotland, Brown's main supplier, failed to meet the quantity ordered because of exceptional demand. This had an immediate effect on production and the number of ironworkers on the books had to be reduced from 3,000 to 2,500.[576] The crisis in supply appeared to be over when Lord Pirrie suggested that David Colville & Son, the Lanarkshire steelmaker which Harland & Wolff had acquired in 1919, would guarantee Clydebank's supply of steel.[577] Pirrie assured Sir Thomas Bell that Colville's would treat Clydebank equally with Belfast and supply all of their needs.[578] In the event, Colville was unable to maintain supplies and, with production at the yard seriously threatened, the Company was forced to look elsewhere. The solution, found in May, was to purchase American steel which, at £25.50 per ton, was £1.50 cheaper than British steel. An order was cabled across the Atlantic immediately for 600 tons followed by a written order for 2,000 tons. Bell left nothing to chance and sent a representative to the American steelworks to confirm the quality of the steel. On confirmation of suitability a further 4,000 tons was ordered.[579]

In 1920, changes in John Brown's management were

Looking over the Channel steamers Antwerp *and* Bruges *at the forward part of* Hood *on 2 December 1919. The armoured gun houses of her 15-inch turrets are being fitted.*

Hood *running trials on the Firth of Clyde in March 1920. She had the most powerful machinery installation afloat and developed 151,000 shp for a speed of 32.07 knots.*

made possible when Commander Wood, the Engine Works Manager, and William Luke, the Shipyard Manager, retired. Luke's position was taken by Donald Skiffington while Wood's was divided into two posts, one of which went to Stephen Pigott, who was made responsible for design, estimates and technical correspondence. The other post went to Arthur Rankin who was responsible for engine works

JOHN · BROWN & · COMPANY · LIMITED.

THE extensive works of Messrs. John Brown & Co., Ltd., at Clydebank are particularly well equipped for the construction of Passenger and Cargo Steamships up to the largest size and power.

The Atlas Works at Sheffield, covering over 40 acres, are in an unique position to execute either large or small contracts in the shortest possible time for the manufacture of

TURBINE FORGINGS
for Marine Engines.

BOILER FURNACES
Corrugated or Plain.

SHAFTING
Crank and Straight, Hydraulic Pressed, Solid or Hollow, Rough or Finished Machined.

GEAR WHEEL RIMS
Manufactured by the Patent Hollow Rolling Process.

London Offices:
8, The Sanctuary, Westminster, S.W. 1.

management. Pigott's job was more senior, attracting a salary of £2,000 against £1,600 for the other.[580]

HARD TIMES

There were numerous small-scale disputes in the yard during the 1920s. Typical of these was the dispute of May 1920, when plater's helpers struck in an expression of support for helpers in shipyards on the lower reaches of the Clyde. Platers were organised into squads of around ten skilled and twenty unskilled men (helpers). The squad was paid a lump sum weekly for work completed. This sum was usually divided out by the squad leader in proportions previously agreed upon. The helpers were aggrieved at the platers for not paying them an agreed 7.5% increase in their wages and wanted the employers to pay them direct. The helpers' strike prevented any plating work being done and within days, the riveters, with nothing to rivet, were also at a standstill. After two weeks, the men returned pending the decision of an industrial court.[581] Clydebank platers agreed to pay their helpers the 15% in dispute.[582]

Bell, in his monthly report for May, noted wryly:

'The continued prosperity of the past few years appears to have been too much for some of the Trade Unions. For example, we have a demand today by the moulders for an increase of 24 shillings per week for their men and 12 shillings for the apprentices; also a request from the ASE (Amalgamated Society of Engineers) for an increase of 47 shillings per week per man. The natural sequence of such demands, if they are persisted in by the men, can only be stoppage of work, which may further hasten the coming trade slump.'[583]

By the middle of 1920, the cost of shipping and shipbuilding had reached levels that shipowners could not sustain. Cunard approached John Brown over the payment of instalments. Instead of paying cash at the appropriate stage, Cunard wanted to issue bills redeemable at a later date. In other words, the shipbuilder was forced into offering extended credit. Worse was to follow. Sir Alfred Booth, Cunard's chairman, asked for work on *Alaunia* to be suspended. Sir Thomas Bell and Sir Charles Ellis, the John Brown Chairman, met with Booth to discuss the matter and agreed that, for the sake of preserving future relations with Cunard, the berth contract agreed in 1919 would be relieved for a period of two years after *Franconia* and *Alaunia* were launched. The severity of the depression ensured that *Franconia* was not completed until 1923 and *Alaunia* until 1925.[584] At the same time, increased costs forced the New Zealand Shipping Company to cancel a recently placed order for a large refrigerated cargo vessel. Bell calculated that a ship now cost four times as much to build as a pre-war equivalent.[585] Estimates given to Dutch and New Zealand ship owners had 'frightened them off business'[586]

With a trade depression in the making, Sir Thomas Bell acted with sensitivity when the local railway company announced an increase in fares in August 1920. Bell sought to cushion the impact on the 4,000 employees affected by purchasing a block of tickets at the new price to sell to employees at the old. At the same time, he made a contribution to the local golf club to enable them to extend the course from nine to eighteen holes on the basis that the two other major Clydebank employers, Beardmore and Singer, followed suit. More unusually, he provided the golf club with a £2,000 loan at a rate of 5% per annum despite the unlikelihood that many of the men employed in the yard would have been members of this club[587].

The continuing rise in living costs resulted in a six pence per hour wage demand being pressed by all shipyard and engineering trades in September 1920. At the same time, the Shipbuilding Employers Federation warned joiners that the 12 shillings a week bonus given them in May 1920 would be withdrawn in December.[588] In October 1920, a coal strike threatened to have serious national implications. Stocks at Clydebank allowed for five weeks production, while the Company's electricity suppliers, Clyde Valley Electric Co. had stocks for a period of three to four weeks.

By the autumn of 1920, the order book had deteriorated significantly as predicted. To help the yard through this period, Lord Pirrie placed the order for the oil tanker *Invergordon* at Clydebank and she was laid down in August. Pirrie later wrote to Bell in October 1920 promising him an order for another tanker should his 'friends' order one.[589]

The only satisfactory area was the engine works, where, demand remained high. Here, the order book stood at £700,00, which included profit of £46,000 and charges of £92,000. Of this, £307,000 was for Brown-Curtis turbines and gearing ordered by the Kawasaki Dockyard Co. for destroyers, battleships and merchant vessels. Machinery designs for the same company accounted for a further £35,500.[590] Bell neatly describes the trading problems confronted by shipbuilders at the end of 1920 in his monthly report

Ordered groups of men. From top to bottom; John Brown Male Voice Choir in 1918. The football team at the beginning of the 1919 season. Riveters in February 1927

for December:

'When I have lately been in the City I have received many verbal enquiries from shipping friends for ships in which they asked for a fixed price contract. This is most difficult to give, for although the price of steel plates has dropped from £27 to £25.50 this is still £1 dearer than the North East Coast price, and it is difficult to know when any other fall will take place. The same applies to castings, forgings and all other particulars, so even if one quoted a price for ships at present day cost of materials, labour and general charges, without any profit at all, the resulting figure would I fear frighten off many shipowners, being nearly 3.75 times the pre-war cost. One cannot at present, however, risk relying on more than a further reduction of 5% on materials during the next six months, which would have to constitute our profit on the work. As regards any reduction in wages; at present there is no reduction in cost of living for the reduction in wheat has made no reduction in the cost of a 4lb loaf, and the reduction in sugar is more than balanced by the slightly increased cost of bacon, butter and eggs; also, seeing the Board of Trade Index figures are still going up, I rather fear that in arbitration the latest demand for increased wages by all classes of men may receive a certain amount of favourable consideration, and if so, the increase might easily amount to the 5% notwithstanding the suicidal consequence of such action.

Taking all things into consideration, it appears to me worth taking the risk of sending in a fixed price tender for a cargo ship or two for delivery in February/April 1922, the price to be based on the present costs of labour and materials and charges, without any profit, but I would hesitate to recommend any further reduction!'[591]

On 1 December 1920, joiners went on strike in protest at the proposed removal of their bonus. This strike involved 4,000 across the country and did not end until 24 August 1921 when the joiners returned on employers' terms. Six shillings were deducted from their wages immediately, followed by three shillings in October and a further three shillings in December.[592] Bell saw no alternative to the defeat of the joiners:

'the principle at issue is so important that it is worth it, for it is quite plain that until there is considerable unemployment, and until wages are reduced, the cost of living will continue at its ridiculously high rate, for all shops and stores seem able to sell all they have without reducing prices'[593]

As the recession intensified, shipowners were forced to take further action. In April, Royal Mail asked for work to be suspended on *Loch Katrine*. Elder Dempster requested a slow-down on two ships and Cunard wanted to cancel *Alaunia* outright. With their workload collapsing around them, management made strenuous efforts to reduce charges by eliminating non-productive labour throughout the Works. Timekeepers, repair squads, crane and locomotive men and personnel from the drawing offices were paid off. In the engine works, the shafting, condenser and funnel shops were shut, while in the shipyard the central pneumatic station, west yard angle smithy, jobbing platers bay and patternmakers shops suffered the same fate.[594] These measures resulted in charges (overheads) being reduced by a substantial one third. Other ways in which the impact of impending layoffs could be minimised were explored. At the end of April, management received agreement from workers to their proposal that in some departments where layoffs were unavoidable, working alternate weeks by half the staff would sustain all the staff.[595] By mid-May, the miners strike began to take effect, putting some departments on a four-day week through shortage of power. In the town of Clydebank, firewood was the only source of fuel; coke and charcoal were unavailable and gas was much reduced.[596]

Although the yard appeared busy with all eight berths occupied, *Montclare* was the only vessel on which work proceeded at anything like the normal rate; the others were either suspended or proceeding at much reduced pace. In May 1921, the bills outstanding for vessels under construction exceeded £2m:

Elder Dempster	£553,750
African Steamship Co.	£370,000
British & African SS Co.	£263,750
Cunard SS Co.	£368,308
Union Castle	£455,000
Royal Mail	£115,000

In May, electricians struck in protest at the proposed removal of six shillings per week from their wages. The strike lasted two weeks after which the men returned on employers' terms to a reduction of three shillings in June and three shillings in July. While the men were on strike, management assessed their jobs which resulted in numbers being considerably reduced.[597] The apparent callousness of this action is in contrast to Sir Thomas Bell's paternalistic concern over staff:

'I regret to report the death of our foremen joiner Mr William Slater . . . It was a case of an internal malignant tumour, the progress of which the doctors were powerless to correct. I am glad to say that we were able to secure the services of his son as our new foreman joiner, which is doubly happy in that not only is he an excellent man, but being unmarried, it enables Mr Slater's widow and his large family to remain in their present house for the next year or so thus tiding over an awkward difficulty. Until the beginning of July he was foreman joiner with the Ailsa Shipbuilding Co. where he acquitted himself so well that he was approached by Fairfield last year, and this year by Swan Hunter to join their establishments as foreman joiner, but refused both on his fathers advice.

I also regret to announce the death of our gateman John Beaton. Beaton was a remarkable success at the gatehouse for many years, but during the past two years he suffered from a slight shock and seemed to have lost all interest in life, acting practically as supernumerary in the gatehouse. He used to accompany our cashier to the bank carrying a loaded revolver and by some means he obtained possession of this last Saturday morning 9 July and while he was examining it he met with a fatal accident'.[598]

Any work was considered if it kept men and machines busy. To ensure that apprentices in the boiler shop were occupied, an order for 45 cylindrical oil tanks for railway wagons from Cravens Ltd, a member of the John Brown group, was accepted. By August 1921, the weekly wage bill had dropped to £17,500 against £39,000 the year before. Some departments were reduced to working four days out of two weeks. In September, the Shipbuilding Employers Federation announced the removal of 12.5% bonus from time workers and 7.5% off piece rates. By October 1921 the rundown in work resulted in only 300 ironworkers remaining in the yard - the lowest number since the slump of 1909.[599]

RENT STRIKE

The growing number of unemployed persons in Clydebank aggravated the already contentious issue of rent increases. The rent strike of 1915, in which

attempts to raise rents were resisted successfully by working people in Glasgow, resulted in rents being frozen at 1914 levels. Moves to permit rent increases were authorised under legislation in 1919 and 1920 when the Rent and Mortgage Interest (Restrictions) Act was passed. This Act allowed an immediate rent increase of 15% on the 1914 rent and, where repairs to property were made, a further increase of 25%. This

caused widespread opposition in which Clydebank tenants became increasingly active. A 24-hour general strike, called in protest by the Scottish Labour Housing Association on 23 August 1920 at Glasgow Green, was backed solidly by workers at the John

A detail of 'Tamson's Buildings' - the tenements erected beside the shipyard in 1872/3. They survived until the 1980s.

Brown and Beardmore shipyards. Non-payment of rent gave rise to what was termed the Clydebank Rent Strike during which many tenants were evicted. The focus for organised response to the Rent Acts was the Clydebank Housing Association, which successfully prevented many tenants paying more than the 1914 rent.[600] In November 1921, a deputation of unemployed shipyard workers living in John Brown accommodation met with works management. The men, already in debt over defaults in rent payments, gave notice that they were unable to pay rent until they were in employment. After the John Brown Board discussed the matter, the following offers were made:

'1. That in the case of all men who did not make a contribution of at least 2/6d per week towards outstanding arrears of their rent, and also payment of the rent, summonses would be taken out against them, and they would be ejected from their houses.

2. All who restricted their contribution to the sum of 2/6d per week would be required to give the Firm an undertaking agreeing to repay the balance outstanding at the rate of 17/6d per week immediately after work was obtained by them, otherwise the Firm would take out an arrestment for payment of this sum.'

Two additional offers were made similar to point 2. in which the contribution was changed to 5 shillings and 10 shillings.[601]

The general reduction of the order book and thus employment continued unchecked. In February 1922 the weekly wage bill amounted to only £14,000.[602] To deal with the difficulties facing the shipbuilding industry, the Employers Federation moved to reduce costs by removing employees war bonus of 26/6d per week. Having already accepted wage reductions, the unions understandably rejected this move and the lines were drawn for a further round of disputes. At John Brown's, 634 engineers were locked out on 11 March and did not resume work until 15 June. On 28 March, shipyard workers went on strike and did not return until 8 May although the boilermakers held out until 21 June. Phased reductions of 3 shillings per week were implemented in May followed by further reductions in June. The latter reduction enabled work on Franconia to be restarted although the vessels machinery had to wait until the return of the engineers at reduced rates.[603] Complete removal of the 26/6d bonus was effected by January 1923. As different sections of the workforce held out longer than others, wage anomalies arose. For a brief period

in June 1922, a labourer working in the engine works was receiving the same pay as a skilled shipyard worker.[604]

Some much needed work was found in May 1922, when Canadian Pacific sent the 21,000ton ex Hamburg Amerika liner *Tirpitz* to Clydebank for completion of a refit which had begun at the Vulcan Works in Hamburg. The refit included conversion to oil burning (largely carried out in Germany), deck and paint work. On completion, the vessel was renamed *Empress of Australia* and left the Clyde on 16 June.

Although the Employers Federation had succeeded in making a major reduction in wage rates, the general level of demand in the industry remained depressed. In Clydebank alone, an estimated 6,000 men were unemployed. In July, the Company tendered for two cable-laying ships at cost of materials and labour only. Sir Thomas Bell commented: [it is] 'absolutely essential, at the present time, to do everything in our power for old and tried employees of the Company who live in this district, and who form a really dependable nucleus'[605]

THE WASHINGTON CONFERENCE

At the end of 1921, an event of far reaching consequence for the armaments industry in the United Kingdom occurred. This was the first serious attempt by governments to limit the manufacture of armaments. The cessation of Admiralty orders in 1919 undermined the foundations of the heavy armaments industry in Britain. Government policy regarded a major war unlikely for a period of ten years giving rise to the 'Ten Years Rule'. Major cuts in defence spending followed, in the expectation that exports and manufacture of peacetime products would take up the slack.

The Royal Navy emerged from the First World War retaining premier position in the fleets of the world. However, despite a preponderance in numbers, many of the capital ships in the Royal Navy were now old and worn out - the inevitable consequence of being first to sea with new warships. Moreover, in the last years of the war, the United States and Japanese governments both funded vast new naval shipbuilding programmes reminiscent of the Anglo-German race a decade earlier. British response to US and Japanese intentions lay in the design of large battleships and battlecruisers. In September 1921, tenders were invited from the leading shipyards for four new 48,000ton battlecruisers referred to by their design prefix 'G3'. The outcome of this process was the placing of major contracts on the Clyde and on the Tyne and in armaments plants throughout the UK. By far the greater share of the work came to Clydeside with John Brown, Beardmore and Fairfield awarded one ship each while Swan Hunter on the Tyne won the fourth. Large and complex, these ships promised years of work for the builders. A lifeline had been thrown to the armaments companies. Brown's order was received by letter on 24 October and the advance ordering of materials commenced soon after. On 16 November however, before any meaningful work could be undertaken, the Admiralty requested, that the builders suspend work.

The reason for the suspensions lay in a United States government invitation to the leading naval powers to explore limiting the massive warship building programmes in progress and in prospect. The conference venue was Washington where the first meeting was held in November 1921. By the following February, international agreement had been reached and the Washington Treaty signed. The primary outcome was the determination of fleet size by fixed ratios such that the British, American and Japanese fleets would be maintained at a ratio of 5, 5, 3. The long-term significance of this was the eclipse of British naval supremacy which was now shared equally with the United States Navy. Moreover, the Treaty called for a moratorium on battleship building for a period of ten years. These events significantly hastened the step towards turmoil and ruination in which the British armaments industry would find itself before the end of the 1920s. The immediate outcome for British shipbuilders was the cancellation of all four G3 battlecruisers on 21 February 1922. For the Clydebank district, the loss to John Brown and William Beardmore of such major orders was a heavy blow, more especially for Beardmore, which was moving rapidly into financial difficulties. The Treaty did, however, provide the opportunity for the Royal Navy to build up to a position equal to the United States Navy in new battleships and thus, the construction of two battleships, *Rodney* and *Nelson*, was authorised. At least one of the two orders was expected to come to the Clyde in compensation for the cancellation of the G3's although, in the event, the orders went to Cammell Laird and Armstrong Whitworth both of whom, unlike the Clyde yards, had tendered at a loss.[606]

LOSS MAKERS

In 1921, no orders were booked and not one keel was laid down. As construction progressed on those

contracts which owners had not suspended, the search for new work decided Bell that tenders would have to be made at a loss. Even then, it was not until July 1922, nineteen months since the last keel had been laid, that the contract for the 274 ton steam yacht *Restless* was won. This small vessel was followed by two further loss making contracts, the 1,800 ton cable-laying ships *Mirror* and *Norseman*, both of which were laid-down in November.

Throughout 1923, the general trade position remained one of acute depression. Despite attempts to improve competitiveness at Clydebank through reduced labour costs and other savings achieved throughout the Works, only two orders were taken, the intermediate Orient liner *Oronsay*, and the steam yacht *Thalassa*. Shipbuilding employers sought a further reduction in wages, making confrontation inevitable. On 30 April, the boilermakers (ironworkers) were locked out over this issue. With little work in the yard, the men were in no bargaining position but nevertheless lasted until 26 November. During this seven-month stoppage, not one rivet was driven.[607] Some refit work was undertaken when the Orient liner *Ormonde* returned to the yard for conversion to oil burning. The work provided employment for 600 men and was completed by July 1923.[608]

To illustrate the severe nature of competition from continental builders, Sir Thomas Bell cited the case of 23 tenders which had been opened at Helsingfors for a Finnish icebreaker. John Brown was nineteenth and Armstrong Whitworth, who had built the previous icebreaker for these owners, was twentieth and that was without charges.

By September 1923, with the boilermakers still locked out, only 234 men were in the shipyard half of whom were employed in the joiner's shop. The position in the engine shops was marginally better with employment at one quarter of capacity. Wage and material differentials, even within the UK, were marked resulting in tenders 12.5% lower from the North East Coast. When Cunard Chairman, Sir Thomas Royden, offered Bell a contract at 5% above the lowest price quoted by another builder, Bell had to 'regretfully tell him that we could not afford to take it.'[609]

The commercial relationship with Harland & Wolff had delivered eight ships to Clydebank since the Preussen of 1910. The bulk of these contracts had been in the immediate post-war boom and as orders became more difficult to find, Pirrie's obligation to Clydebank waned. Nevertheless Sir Thomas Bell continued to press him for work. On 10 May 1923, he wrote:

> ' . . . I am venturing to approach you at the present time to let you know that things are getting pretty desperate with us . . . Now that times are so bad, I am wondering whether there is any chance of your group of Companies being able to spare even one contract in the near future for us, at whatever prices are obtainable . . . '

Eight days later, Pirrie replied:

> 'I know that you have not very much work at present, and you can rely on me to bear you in mind if anything turns up, but I still think the time before us will be very bad . . . '[610]

Despite Lord Pirrie's good intentions, the oil tanker *Invergordon* proved to be the last ship which Pirrie gave to Clydebank. On 7 June 1924, Pirrie died at the age of 78. Like most other shipbuilding companies, Harland & Wolff, was in difficulties following the decline of the shipbuilding market. In addition to the Belfast shipyard, then the largest private yard in the world, Harland & Wolff had to find orders for five other shipyards on the Clyde[611] all wholly owned subsidiaries. Keeping this number of shipyards employed in addition to finding orders for Clydebank gives a clear indication of the shipbuilding interests alone, which Pirrie had to support. Pirrie's other creation, the Royal Mail Group of which Harland & Wolff was a part, was in parlous financial condition and soon to face its demise. Pirrie's passing was effectively the end of the relationship between John Brown and Harland & Wolff, at least in shipbuilding orders, although financial arrangements between the two companies were not fully untangled until 1935.[612]

THE MARINE OIL ENGINE

Despite the chronic order position, Bell shrewdly took advantage of the lull to investigate the manufacture of marine oil (diesel) engines which promised favourable economies in operation. In this, John Brown was largely reactive. The principal technological developments in marine propulsion systems since the beginning of the steam era had been exclusively British. J&G Thomson played an important part in the development of reciprocating machinery in the nineteenth century while their successors, John Brown, played an equally significant role in advancing steam turbine technology. The benefits that accrued from leadership in marine engineering were an obvious asset to the British shipbuilding industry. Before the First World War, a new marine engine was developed abroad, based on the internal combustion principle. The oil engine, or diesel as it became more popularly known, was first used to power a variety of small river and coastal craft at the turn of the twentieth century. In 1912, the 5,000ton *Selandia*, built by Burmeister & Wain in Copenhagen, became the first ocean-going motorship. She was driven by a four-stroke engine of 2,500 BHP also constructed by Burmeister & Wain.[613] With massive investment and great market share in steam technology, few British engine builders developed oil engine designs. Similarly, many shipping lines were reluctant to change from time honoured propulsion systems. Initially, John Brown expressed little interest in diesels primarily because the liners and battleships in which they specialised were propelled by steam turbines, a technology which was in itself still in the early days of development. However, as early as October 1910, Thomas Bell, conversant with the latest developments, had been corresponding with the MAN works at Nürnberg advising them that: '. . all you are doing seems perfectly in order, and leaves nothing for me to suggest. Hope to visit your works this December or January.'[614] While Bell had taken the initiative over the Curtis steam turbine, and clearly had an interest in the MAN engine, to gain experience in diesel engines, he had turned to Lord Pirrie as Harland & Wolff had entered into agreements with Burmeister & Wain for the manufacture of their diesel as early as 1912.[615] Pirrie placed the contract for the Royal Mail motorship *Loch Katrine*, at Clydebank. The engine for this vessel was of the Burmeister & Wain type built under sub-licence by Harland & Wolff at Finnieston in Glasgow. John Brown engineers observed the manufacture of this engine and were involved in the installation when *Loch Katrine* was taken up-stream to Glasgow to have her engine fitted. Nevertheless, Bell chose the Sulzer and the Cammell Laird Fullager types as most appropriate to John Brown's needs. In 1923, licences to build both engines were taken out. At the same time, an area was prepared in the boiler shop to serve as a diesel erection bay. The only additional machine required to construct diesel engines was a large planer at a cost of £8,600.[616]

The Cammell Laird Fullagar was a two-stroke opposed piston oil engine. In May 1923, two engines of this type were built at Clydebank for the Kawasaki Dockyard Co. for installation in *Florida Maru* and *Cuba Maru*. Despite defective air compressors which had to be redesigned, Kawasaki engineers accepted the engines. No further engines of this type were

manufactured at Clydebank and the Fullagar was neither a commercial or technical success.[617]
The performance of the Union Steamship Co.'s *Aorangi*, built by Fairfield in 1924 with Sulzer diesels, was watched with some interest at Clydebank as she was the first large passenger ship to be powered by diesels. *Aorangi* was the type of ship which might be built at John Brown's and information received at

completed in 1944, the quadruple expansion machinery constructed for two ships building at Napier & Miller's shipyard at Old Kilpatrick in 1926 and 1927, were the last to be constructed at Clydebank.
In 1924, orders were taken for four ferries. Two, *Princess Kathleen* and *Princess Marguerite*, were for Canadian Pacific and *St Julien* and *St Helier* were for

Clydebank following her maiden voyage to Vancouver, indicated consumption half that of a geared turbine installation at service speed. The first diesel driven ship built at Clydebank was the tanker *Lumen* completed in 1925 for H E Moss. Building diesel engines was not to be without its problems. During *Lumen's* maiden voyage in March 1926, all eight pistons cracked.
The emergence of the diesel engine did not immediately replace steam reciprocating machinery which continued to be manufactured for many years. However, Clydebank's long and very successful association with machinery of this type was almost at an end. With the exception of the frigate *Loch Fada*

the Great Western Railway Company. The notable event of the year was the launch of the 20,000ton Orient liner Oronsay on 14 August. Shipyards were at times places of remarkable contrasts perhaps none more so than when a ship was launched bringing together people from very different ends of society. While the yard was slowly finding its way out of recession, endeavouring to offer employment to many thousands of people, the Chairman of the Orient Line, Sir Kenneth Anderson, wrote to Bell with a preoccupation of another nature:

> 'My Dear Bell, I wrote to Lady Novar the other day, asking whether she would pay us the compliment of christening the Oronsay on 14

The oil tanker Lumen, *the first diesel engined ship built at Clydebank.*

August. I confess I wrote in fear and trembling lest proximity of the date to the sacred 12th [of July][618] would be a fatal obstacle, but I am glad to say I have now heard from Lady Novar consenting to our request . . .'[619]

After *Oronsay*, the Orient line ceased to be a customer of John Brown's despite the satisfaction with which the ship was received.

Above
The distinguished launch party gaze up at the liner Duchess of York *as she prepares to enter the Clyde.*

Right
Sir Thomas Bell accompanies the Prince and Princess of Wales into the shipyard to perform the launch of the Canadian Pacific liner Duchess of York *on 28 September 1928.*

CONTINUITY OF LABOUR

By the end of the year, when *Oronsay* was in an advanced stage of fitting-out, difficulty was encountered finding sufficient joiners for this class of work. In his report for 1 December 1924, Bell records:

' . . . owing to a large number of the best Clyde joiners being decoyed away to London and elsewhere, we are greatly dependent on Roman Catholic joiners from Belfast of whom we have over 200. Unfortunately their standard as regards output and sticking to work is by no means very high'[620]

Apart from revealing Bell's prejudices his comment reflects the great difficulty in having the right number of persons of the requisite skill employed to do the work at the appropriate time. When work was scarce, this was all but impossible. Retaining skilled workers was sometimes eased by the success of neighbouring yards in winning contracts, thereby keeping men in the district. Unofficial contact between the management of different yards would often operate in favour of keeping skills in the district. In this respect the commercial rivalry normally existing between competing companies was set aside. By the end of 1924, work for the iron trades at John Brown's was coming to an end as the few ships on hand were launched. Many men paid off as a consequence found employment, literally next door, at Beardmore's yard where the 24,400 ton intermediate liner *Conte Biancamano* had been laid down in June. To ensure that these men did not leave the district altogether when *Conte Biancamano* was launched, Bell proposed, with the consent of John Brown's Chairman, Lord Aberconway, to lay-down a repeat *Lumen*, to the Company's own account, in the belief that a buyer would readily be found.[621] When *Conte Biancamano* was launched on 23 April 1925 at Beardmore's, the ironworkers paid off as a result were immediately taken on at John Brown's, where Bell laid-down *British Diplomat* on the following day. The ready market for this ship did not materialise and she was later sold at a loss of £10,000.

When the Cunard liner *Alaunia* was launched in February 1925, Bell took the opportunity to refer to the damage done to the shipbuilding industry through lack of direct Government support. He compared the 'assistance and encouragement' shown by the French and Dutch governments to their industries and pointed to future shortages of skilled men because the number of apprentices recruited into the industry had halved over the past four years. Bell further described the important role which warship building had previously played in alleviating depression in merchant shipbuilding. He added that warship construction paid wages for hull and machinery fully five times as much per ton as for normal merchant work did. As a consequence, 50,000 tons of warship work provided as much employment as 250,000 merchant tons.[622]

In setting out his position publicly, Bell was well aware of the impending Admiralty contracts for 10,000ton cruisers. Although the Washington Treaty had placed a moratorium on battleships and other classes of warships, the construction of cruisers was permitted up to a certain tonnage. In taking

areas. By May 1925, there was no work for 100 experienced turbine bladers in the engine shops, all of whom had fifteen years experience with the Company. As work on the cruisers' turbines would not start for nearly three months, strenuous efforts were made to retain the turbine bladers by finding them a variety of odd jobs throughout the Works.[624] When the Cunard liner *Alaunia* was finally completed

The fitting-out basin on 16 January 1929 showing from left, Canadian Pacific's Duchess of York, *the New Zealand Shipping Co's* Rangitiki *and Cunard's* Carmania. *The elderly* Carmania *had returned for a refit and makes an interesting comparison with the design of the newer ships.*

advantage of this, the Admiralty had planned eight cruisers under the 1924/25 building programme, although the incoming Labour government reduced this figure to five. The Admiralty did what it could to distribute these orders among the major warship builders although, in the first round, Brown's were not successful. Quite unexpectedly, the Royal Australian Navy indicated their desire to build two cruisers of this type, *Australia* and *Canberra*.[623] Although John Brown's tender was the second lowest after Vickers, the contract for both ships was placed with Brown's as Vickers had already been given a cruiser contract.

Nevertheless, with major gaps in the flow of work, continuity of employment could not be maintained for all trades and layoffs became inevitable in certain

in June 1925, 1,200 men of the finishing trades were paid off. By the middle of July, employment in the shipyard was down to 940 compared with 3,020 in May. The engine works fared a little better with the corresponding figure of 1,569 compared to 2,300.[625] The prospect of fitting diesel engines in a passenger ship presented itself in 1926, when the New Zealand Shipping Co. and the Federal Steam Navigation Line,[626] discussed construction of large diesel engined ships. Orders for two large motorships were placed, assisted by guarantees from the Trade Facilities Act. This Act, the government's response to foreign subsidies, assisted shipowners in buying ships from British shipyards. However, almost immediately the orders were deferred awaiting design alterations by Lord Inchcape, Chairman of P&O, who had a controlling interest in both shipping lines. In July, both contracts were cancelled because freight rates in New Zealand had risen. This blow was softened by the knowledge that smaller vessels might be built at a later date.[627] In 1926, Blue Star Line placed an order at Clydebank for two geared turbine driven A Class ships, *Avila* and *Avelona*.

In the last half of the 1920s, Canadian Pacific set about a major fleet expansion programme. John Brown was successful in winning four major contracts. The first of these was for the 20,000ton intermediate liner *Duchess of Bedford*, secured at a contract price of £910,000. Competition for this contract had been stiff and only one third of establishment charges were recovered in this price. In May 1926, the miners went on strike prompting the

The steam yacht Nahlin *leaves the yard for trials on 2 June 1930.*

The marble lined panels and fittings of one of Nahlin's *bathrooms.*

first general strike in British history. Although the general strike was of relatively short duration, the miners held out for nine months eventually bringing steel production to a halt. By June, shortages were starting to take effect, forcing the progressive lay off ironworkers. By October, both the west and east yards were at a standstill. In an effort to maintain the inflow of cash into the business, stage payments had to be maintained. To earn the £76,000 due on the launch of Blue Star's *Avelona* in December 1926, Sir Thomas Bell brought three shell plates over from Germany to complete her hull. In the same month, Colville's Clyde Bridge steel works was back in operation with an urgent request to deliver 100 tons of keel plates to Clydebank. Delivery enabled the keel

laying stage payment of £175,000 for *Duchess of Bedford* to be made from Canadian Pacific.[628]
In the following year, two sister ships, *Duchess of Richmond* and *Duchess of York*, were laid down. These ships were notable in being the first merchant ships fitted with water tube boilers of the Yarrow type, working at comparatively high steam pressures.[629] The order for three 16,700 ton R Class motorships,

shipbuilders could no longer look to the continent for orders. Referring to the ships currently building for Australian, New Zealand and Canadian interests, he foresaw a growing Empire trade.[630] He had every reason to be optimistic, as Canadian Pacific were planing two large liners, one for their Atlantic and one for their Pacific service. During 1927, Canadian Pacific identified the need for a large and well

A group from Canadian Pacific watch as a Clydebank manager operates the hydraulic riveter on the bottom plates of Empress of Britain.

Launch of
Canadian Pacific Railway Steamer
"Empress of Britain."

His Royal Highness The Prince of Wales has intimated that it is his intention, on this occasion, to wear a Lounge Suit and Bowler Hat.

Rangitiki, Rangitane and *Rangitata* for the New Zealand Shipping Co., was finally agreed in 1927, permitting two to be laid down that year and the other in 1928. Throughout 1926 and 1927, John Brown worked steadily through what might be termed a typical Clydebank order book - warships and passenger liners. By December 1927, 7,145 employees were on the payroll.

EMPRESS OF BRITAIN
Mrs Baldwin, wife of the Prime Minister, Stanley Baldwin, who was also in attendance, performed the launch of *Duchess of Bedford*. At the luncheon which followed, Sir Thomas Bell, noting changes in the shipbuilding market since the war, said that

appointed flagship for their North Atlantic summer service, in addition to providing capability as a cruise ship. In June 1927, Captain Gillies, General Manager of Canadian Pacific Steamships, wrote to various shipbuilders with outline details of a large ship with a service speed of 24 knots and capable of operating as a cruise ship. This process gave shipbuilders the opportunity to consider designs prior to tendering. At Clydebank, James McNeil, John Brown's assistant naval architect, spent several months on this project. Models were made and tested in the experiment tank to determine hull dimensions and efficiency. Invitations to tender were issued in September 1928. With a quote of £2,096,500, John Brown won the contract on 29 October. The price quoted included

A note attached to the launch invitation concerning sartorial issues

179

Vertical keel plates for Empress of Britain *erected on the berth in December 1928.*

Opposite page
The completed ship in April 1931

charges rated at 50% - in effect, reduced profit. *Empress of Britain*, as the ship was to become, was the largest passenger ship built in the UK since the pre-war *Aquitania* and *Olympic*.

With *Empress of Britain*, the three Duchess liners and the ferry *Princess Elaine*, John Brown now had no fewer than five vessels under construction for Canadian Pacific. Relations between both companies were understandably strong. When the completion of *Duchess of Atholl*, a fourth Duchess liner under construction at Beardmore's yard, was delayed when a 35 ton steam turbine fell twenty feet into the double bottom of the ship, Brown's accelerated work on *Duchess of Bedford* to ensure that Canadian Pacific was able to operate their advertised service. The shipping

line asked what the extra cost of putting more men on the contract would be. Sir Thomas Bell replied with a net figure of £9,300 which, in effect, represented a loss of £2,500. Bell considered that this would:

'increase still further the confidence of Canadian Pacific in our resources and ability to carry out work, and this should prove a very valuable factor in the allocation of fresh orders . . . '

Throughout the last years of the 1920s, the yard became increasingly busy. Three train ferries, *Vienna*, *Prague* and *Amsterdam* for the London & North Eastern Railway Co. and four destroyers *Acasta*, *Achates*, *Basilisk* and *Beagle* for the Admiralty were supplemented, in 1929, by the order for the magnificent G L Watson designed steam yacht,

Nahlin, for Lady Yule. *Nahlin* was one of the largest and finest appointed yachts afloat. As big as a destroyer, she was powered by Brown-Curtis turbines capable of driving her at over 17 knots. The staterooms, guest cabins and public rooms were designed by Sir Charles Allom who had undertaken interior decorative work for the Royal Family.[631] In 1929, the contracts for the three R Class motorships under construction for the New Zealand Line turned out to be almost as troublesome as had the Spanish torpedo boats built thirty years earlier. Almost from the start, the contract was soured when the consultant naval architect from Esplen & Company and the assistant manager of the New Zealand line in what Bell described as 'one of the most disagreeable incidents I can remember in the whole of my time at Clydebank' insisted on contract details 'which could never be sustained if taken to a court of law or arbitration.' The chairman of the New Zealand Line evidently held the view that he had agreed on a price for the ships which was too generous and was determined to get everything he could out of the shipbuilders.[632] In the midst of this rancour, *Rangitiki*

was completed and made ready for trials in January 1929. The first difficulty occurred when the liner in number three cylinder of the port engine fractured. In this instance, Bell was pleased to note that the managing director of the New Zealand Line, was 'reasonable and considerate' given the history of the contract. However, a far greater problem was set to overtake this contract. The original design was for refrigerated cargo ships but after work had started, the owners decided to amend the design and add passenger accommodation involving additional superstructure. On *Rangitiki's* completion, it rapidly became clear that a basic error had been made in her stability calculations. Correcting this required 1,200 tons of pig iron ballast to be placed in the bottom of the ship resulting in a 25% loss in cargo space. This could only be considered as a temporary measure until more satisfactory alterations could be made. *Rangitiki* had to return to Clydebank in the summer of 1929 to have some of her superstructure cut down to reduce top weight, thereby making it possible to remove the pig iron ballast. Similar modifications had to be carried out on *Rangitiki's* two sister vessels,

The tennis courts on Empress of Britain.

which resulted in a total loss of £200,000 on these contracts. It might reasonably be assumed that Bell was extremely unhappy with the outcome:

> 'the error in stability calculations is certainly proving a most costly blunder besides the slur it has put on John Brown & Company's reputation. Steps have been taken to prevent the possibility of the head of a department presuming to take such risks and to hide such important information from the managing director'[633]

The naval architect at Clydebank, John Black, as head of the department concerned was blamed although he had, in any case, left the Company in 1928 to join Beardmore's as shipyard manager.[634]

The three Duchess liners built for Canadian Pacific were also not without their problems. Soon after entering service, the main gearwheel on the port engine of *Duchess of Bedford* became 'loose,' a term which, in this instance, almost certainly indicated premature wear of the bearings.[635] In response to this, Canadian Pacific's Superintendent Engineer, John Johnson, issued specifications for all future main gear wheels to be installed in CP ships. To preserve John Brown's reputation, Sir Thomas Bell felt it was essential that new gear wheels be cut and installed in all three Duchess liners at a cost of £9,000 each.[636]

By mid 1929, work in the yard began to thin out and the immediate future began to look bleak. Recent customers, notably the Blue Star Line and the Orient line, were not in the market for new tonnage. Nevertheless, when the New Zealand Shipping Co. issued new invitations to tender, Bell looked the other way considering it wiser, given the experience of the R Class ships, to let the ships be built elsewhere.[637] Throughout 1929, good progress was made on *Empress of Britain*. The design of the public rooms on this ship was not the responsibility of the builder. In this instance architects appointed by Canadian Pacific, Messrs Staynes & Jones, co-ordinated the work of well known designers who had been given individual interiors to create. The principal areas of the ship were given to the following designers: M. Poiret the Swimming Pool and Turkish Bath; Frank Brangwyn, the First Class Dining Saloon; Edmund Dulac, the Smoking Room; Sir John Lavery, the Empress Ballroom and Sir Charles Allom, in conjunction with Messrs Waring & Co., the Mayfair Lounge. The budget for the above work was £250,000, which was additional to the price quoted for the ship. Bell's expectation that there would be trouble in providing for the above within the budget allocated was amply justified when M. Poiret's design for the

swimming pool worked out at twice the amount allocated. This resulted in his eventual removal from the project and the appointment of Staynes & Jones in his place.[638]

At the end of 1929, Bell compared the valuation of the works with that of the valuation for 1899, the year of the take-over by John Brown:

	1899	1929
Machinery in SY and EW	297,220	260,044
Buildings in SY and EW	208,460	361,348
Ground	112,790	123,218
Dock	55,000	69,597
Railways	15,500	23,387
House property	39,447	149,167
Total	**728,417**	**986,761**

The major increase in buildings throughout the Works is consistent with the additional shops and berth structures erected during the period. The rise in the number of houses owned by the Company shows the length to which it had been obliged to go to control accommodation in order to discourage workers from leaving the district. While many of these properties were in excellent condition, Bell was concerned with the condition of the 24 tenements in John Knox Street. It had originally been intended to modernise these 73 flats contained therein with inside lavatories. Bell's minuted comment made in December 1929, reveals his attitude to the inhabitants

Empress of Britain going down the Clyde to run trials.

of John Knox Street:

'Unfortunately for us, as soon as the war ended and we proposed getting rid of the Irish dock labour class who constitute the majority of the tenants, the Rent Restriction Act was passed, which precluded any evictions, unless you could offer the families evicted equivalent accommodation elsewhere'.

Bell estimated that the tenements which were valued in Company books at £13,000 would only fetch £3,000 on the market. He balanced this potential loss with the damage to John Brown 'through the odium of owning what really has now become disreputable slum property, the class of tenants being such that no respectable people would think of going to these houses.'[639]

EFFECTS OF DEPRESSION

The record of profitability at Clydebank during the 1920s was understandably poor given the trading circumstances. Of 23 contracts taken between 1922 and 1928, eight were taken at a substantial loss, twelve at a profit of less then three per cent and the remaining three at less than six percent.[640] The economics of sustaining a shipyard capable of building eight ships when only one or two ships could be obtained concentrated all the overheads on these ships, making them more expensive to build. When these ships were taken on a break-even basis or at a loss as was often the case in depression, the overall effect would, in time, prove ruinous. Only the fittest companies with adequate financial reserves, survived. By the end of the decade, the position was serious enough to prompt a number of shipbuilders[641] to propose a radical programme of rationalisation to reduce excess capacity, which had been created during and immediately after the First World War.

The means to achieve this end was realised through the formation, in 1930, of National Shipbuilders Security Ltd., under the chairmanship of Sir James Lithgow. A list of ailing or redundant shipyards was drawn up and negotiations entered into with the owners for purchase. Once control had been acquired, the plant and equipment was sold off and fixed structures such as shipbuilding gantries, demolished. Inevitably, the closures which followed were controversial, particularly when the largest yard on the Clyde, Beardmore's Naval Construction Works at Dalmuir, adjacent to John Brown's, was one of the first to be acquired and dismantled.

The Clydebank district was particularly affected by this measure. Napier & Miller at Old Kilpatrick, was eliminated as was Archibold Macmillan in Dumbarton. From a total of 39 shipbuilding berths from Clydebank to Dumbarton, only 17 remained after rationalisation.[642] John Brown's emerged weak but intact from this process finding themselves to be the only yard in the district once more as it had been in 1871.

A STATELY LIFELINE

The building of *Queen Mary* was undoubtedly one of the great technical achievements in British shipbuilding. For John Brown & Company, the order for this ship was more important for its survival than was generally known at the time. The progressive collapse of the armaments industries in Britain after 1918 resulted in the bankruptcy of many armaments manufacturers including Beardmore's and Armstrong's. Government inspired restructuring resulted in the survival of a much reduced Beardmore company and the amalgamation of Armstrong with the financially stronger Vickers. By the end of the 1920s, the John Brown Company was also facing a serious financial crisis. The solution was found in a merger of the steel interests of John Brown with the neighbouring Sheffield firm of Thomas Firth & Sons Ltd., which resulted in the formation of a new company, Thomas Firth & John Brown Limited, The original John Brown Company continued as shipbuilders and colliery owners.[643] By 1930, the full effects of the recession hit the Clydebank subsidiary. The difficulties of dwindling orders and the capital restructuring of the parent company were eased when the order for *Queen Mary* was received. This highly prestigious order provided vital security and confidence for John Brown & Company and their bankers.[644]

ORIGINS OF QUEEN MARY

The details of the preliminary negotiations leading to the placing of the contract for *Queen Mary* are rather obscure. From an early stage in the development of the design, Cunard consulted Clydebank and it is likely, given the long-standing relationship between builder and owner, that John Brown was intended from the outset as the eventual builder. John Brown was already the most well known shipyard in Britain as builders of the largest merchant and naval vessels. This contract would embed the Company even deeper in the national consciousness. With the exception of the period, 1884 - 1901, when Cunard had gone to Fairfield, the commercial relationship existing between Cunard and Clydebank, stretching back to 1851, had been mutually beneficial. While Cunard distributed many ship contracts among the principal British builders, J&G Thomson and later John Brown, could certainly claim to be the preferred builders on the basis of tonnage alone. In addition, both *Lusitania* and *Aquitania* were exceptional ships, each the largest so far constructed

'The Cunard Company has been striving for some ninety years to keep its flag well in the forefront on the Atlantic, and it is a race which has no end; it is its business to be in that race. If it had not kept that object always before it, the Cunard Company would not be afloat today'

There were two reasons why new ships were essential; the age of Cunard's existing ships and

for Cunard. The only other vessels of comparable size built in the UK were the Olympic Class ships *Olympic*, *Titanic* and *Britannic*, built for White Star by Harland & Wolff. There is no question that Cunard wanted to regain the premier position on the North Atlantic which they had held for so long. The following extract from the 1931 Shareholders Report makes their position abundantly clear:

foreign competition. Cunard's trio of large North Atlantic liners currently operating the weekly service to New York were *Mauretania* (1907), *Berengaria* (1913, ex German *Imperator*) and *Aquitania* (1914). If twenty years is taken as the average life of a ship, then these ships were in or approaching their old age. At the end of the 1920s, after a long period of stability on the Atlantic, strong competition was again emerging

The 534 on 21 February 1931. This view shows frames erected near the stern through which the inner propeller shafts will later pass.

from other shipping lines. North German Lloyd was completing the 50,000ton *Europa* and *Bremen* and the Compagnie Générale Transatlantique was known to be considering a ship larger than the 43,000ton *Ile de France*. This ship later became the *Normandie*. The Italians were also examining the possibility of building two express liners which eventually materialised as *Conte di Savoia* and *Rex*.

In July 1929, the *Bremen* brought the *Mauretania's* remarkable 22-year retention of the Blue Riband to a close, with a westward run at an average speed of 27.83 knots. Both *Bremen* and *Europa* made a great impact on the North Atlantic route and attracted large numbers of passengers away from Cunard. A response was essential.

Cunard first examined the possibility of new construction in 1926 when the broad requirements for such a vessel were drawn up. From the outset, it was proposed to replace the existing three ships with two. As a consequence, the two ships would require to be large, fast and with lower operating costs than the three. Confronted with an estimated £10 million for both ships, Cunard considered that their North Atlantic rival, White Star, might build and operate one of them.[645]

In planning the new ships, operational characteristics had to be balanced carefully to provide vessels which would prove commercially attractive and profitable. By virtue of their great size, such vessels would inevitably become symbols of national pride, raising expectations that they would reassert British dominance on the North Atlantic as had *Lusitania* and *Mauretania* three decades earlier. In this, speed would be of the essence. Cunard made little public expression of interest in the Blue Riband viewing the issue purely as a facet of winning business. Later, the Cunard Company, sensitive about the term 'luxury' used to describe the *Queen Mary* went to some length to explain that the great size of the ship was fully justified on commercial grounds and not the result of one-upmanship or indulgence on its part.

> 'She is no haphazard ship produced by accident or in a hurry to meet some fancied need; her form is the result of numberless tank experiments simulating with great accuracy every sort of weather which she may expect to meet in the Atlantic. Blue Ribands are pretty ornaments but their revenue value is indirect and comes within the field of advertisement. It would be easier to design a faster ship, but what your board has had continually in mind is regularity of service in all weathers combined with the last word in safety

and comfort for passengers. No 534 may win a blue riband, but her speed is no greater than in the judgement of both your board and of your experts, is necessary to make her a paying ship. . . The . . . No 534 is being built because the Cunard Company will need such a ship and for no other reason whatsoever. She will be such a ship because, being needed, no other sort of ship is wise to build. In other words, for the Cunard Company she is the inevitable ship, and therefore we ordered her.'[646]

THE 'INEVITABLE' SHIP

In 1926, having decided to explore the design of new ships, Cunard approached John Brown and sought their collaboration and experience. Cunard's naval architect, G McLaren Paterson, and his assistant, Lewis McEwan, provided their counterparts at Clydebank with an outline sketch design which the Cunard Board felt appropriate to its needs at that time. The naval architect at Clydebank was John Black and his assistant, was James McNeil. It was decided that two junior naval architects, John Brown[647] and Norman Gemmell, under the direction of Black and McNeil, should be put to work on developing the Cunard sketch designs These naval architects were normally employed in the design section of the main shipyard drawing office. This area was known as the Scientific Section. Such was the requirement for secrecy that the two designers were detached from the department and placed in a separate room and left in no doubt that no-one, apart from their superiors, was to be told about the work they were carrying out. The door of the room was to be kept locked at all times, even when they were working within. Every few months, Paterson and McEwan made the journey from Liverpool to confer with their counterparts at Clydebank and brought with them any modification to the specification, particularly passenger accommodation. From 1926 onwards, the design section worked intermittently on the new ship and by 1927 tank testing had begun. In 1928, John Black left the yard under a cloud following the debacle over the New Zealand Line ships and became Shipyard Manager at the neighbouring Beardmore yard. James McNeil was appointed Naval Architect and John Brown, on his return from a two-year secondment with the Sociedad Española de Construccion Naval at Bilbao in October 1929, became his assistant. At the height of activity in the secret room, three draughtsmen were employed on the giant Cunarder, together with the staff of the experiment tank.

Despite the long gestation period of the design, the fundamental issue of propulsion and steam plant was not decided until 1929 and then with some difficulty. In December 1928, Cunard set-up an 'Expert Committee' including, in addition to Cunard technical staff, Admiral Skelton (Admiralty), Andrew Laing (Wallsend Slipway), Sir Thomas Bell (John Brown), Charles Craven (Vickers), Alexander Hamilton and Sir Charles Parsons. These men were the most eminent marine engineers in the UK and, in the case of Bell, Laing, Craven and Parsons, represented the leading marine engine-building firms. Irrespective of who might eventually win the contract, all agreed it was in the national interest to give freely of their experience and know-how. All were asked to observe strict secrecy over their deliberations and findings. The committee was chaired by Sir Aubrey Brocklebank, a Cunard director, who took particular interest in the development of the new ship. The task presented to the Committee was to consider the most suitable type of propulsive plant, namely diesel, turbo electric or steam turbines. The unanimous decision was the adoption of single reduction geared steam turbines. However, the issue of which type of boiler would be employed to raise steam became a problem and a source of delay as Sir Thomas Royden, Cunard Chairman, explained to Sir Ashley Sparks, Cunard's New York director, in a letter written on 10 July 1929:

> '. . . I had hoped to have made some real progress with the plans of our ship, but a difference of opinion has developed between our expert advisors as to the type of boiler to be used. This originally was to be the Scotch boiler type, but recent developments (which are supported by our experience of the Berengaria's behaviour under the new conditions of water softening, etc.,) indicate that water-tube boilers are the right thing, which is further supported by the fact that all the modern big ships on the North Atlantic are water-tube jobs. As you know, stability is largely affected by the fact of whether one has water-tube or Scotch boilers, and as the lay-out of the proposed ship was based on the assumption that the boilers would be Scotch, this latest change of view has thrown us all back again almost to where we started. . .'[648]

In another letter written to Sparks on 31 July, Royden went further:

> 'The Committee of Experts that sat to discuss the propulsion question seems to me to have been of doubtful value - if not indeed a positive embarrassment . . . our technical people gave such a strong lead that the other members of the Committee (with the exception of Parsons, who dissented from this view) fell in with the Scotch boiler idea. On the strength of this, the Naval Architect's Department went ahead and we have now drawn up a fairly complete set of plans. The Superintendent Engineer now leans towards water-tube boilers, and if his view is adopted, the alterations involved in the dimensions and whole lay-out of the ship are so considerable that it is necessary to begin practically de novo. This is a rather shattering denouement, and I am now considering in what way best to expedite matters so that we can have an alternative scheme for consideration without too much delay . . .'[649]

With water-tube boilers confirmed as the steam generators, the final hull form could now be decided on. This was important to the economics of operating the ship. The object was to provide engines of the minimum power and size capable of pushing a hull with the least resistance through the water while maintaining the required speed. The new Chairman of Cunard, Sir Percy Bates, later described the *Queen Mary* 'as the smallest and slowest ship that could form one half of a weekly service (to the USA) and that is all any sane company could build for the job.'[650] The original choice of Scotch boilers reveals an innate conservatism on the part of Cunard in complete contrast to the pioneering decision to fit steam turbines in *Lusitania* and *Mauretania* thirty years earlier. This conservatism, manifest generally in the design of the ship, was to be the subject of criticism later.

The order book at Clydebank had begun to dwindle as the three Duchess Class Canadian Pacific liners and the three New Zealand motorships went through the final phases of fitting-out. Last to complete were *Duchess of York* and *Rangitane*. The pressure to complete these vessels on time required 1,600 men of the finishing trades, while 983 men stood as an all time record for the joiner's shop.[651] The LNER railway ferries *Vienna*, *Prague* and *Amsterdam*, together with the destroyers *Achates* and *Acasta*, were well advanced and all would be completed by the spring of 1930.

Sir Thomas Bell maintained a crucial interest in the development of the big ship and noted regretfully, in May 1929, that the death of Sir Audrey Brocklebank had lost Clydebank a 'warm friend and upholder,' adding that he thought it now unlikely that Cunard

Sir Percy Bates, Cunard's chairman throughout the complicated and protracted building of Queen Mary.

would be in the market for new tonnage for some considerable time.[652] The following month, Bell reached the conclusion that Cunard had definitely postponed any addition to their fleet and that the outlook for the east yard was now bleak, with only the *Empress of Britain* on the stocks.[653]

Bell was undoubtedly concerned about the financial crisis engulfing the international money markets and its effect on passenger traffic on the North Atlantic. In the first half of 1930, traffic improved and Cunard, satisfied that the design of the new ship fulfilled all their requirements, invited tenders from John Brown, Vickers Armstrong and Swan Hunter & Wigham Richardson. On 12 March 1930, John Brown received an official enquiry for a ship with a service speed of 28 knots. On 10 May, John Brown submitted its tender for a ship capable of 28.5 knots in average Atlantic weather and capable of more than 30 knots on trials. The tender price was £4,500,000 and the ship was to be ready for service in October 1933.[654] On 21 May, Cunard's Chairman, Sir Percy Bates, wrote to Sir Ashley Sparks:

'We received three tenders for this ship, varying by £1 million. Naturally one starts to negotiate first with the cheapest, and while I am hopeful the cheapest will also prove the most suitable, I cannot afford at this stage to disregard the others entirely - much less to add to the risk of embarrassment which would occur should any one builder get to know what his competitors quoted. For what the ship is, no-one can say that any one of the prices quoted is really unreasonable or beyond the ability of the Company to deal with, but before committing the Company at all to any ship, it is necessary to have an agreement with the Government on three points - the most important of which is insurance . . . The Cunard Company cannot build a ship which it cannot insure, so the Government have got to step into the breach, and I am confident that they will do so'[655]

Although the ship was to be paid for entirely out of Cunard's resources, it was necessary to obtain the Board of Trade's willingness to offer insurance for the ship both during construction and in operation, as the sums involved were too large for the open market to arrange. The Board of Trade's approval was confirmed in the Cunard Insurance Agreement Act of 1930.

Of equal importance was the provision of a dry dock capable of accommodating such a large ship as, without this, the vessel could not be docked or repaired in the UK, an unthinkable prospect. The operators of the Port of Southampton, the Southern Railway Company, were actively considering port extensions, part of which was the construction of a new graving dock. However the dimensions of the proposed new dock were 1,200' x 120' while Cunard required 1,070' x 124' for the new ship. Furthermore, the Southern Railway Company intended to build new ocean quays before building the graving dock. Negotiations between Cunard and the Southern Railway were opened to bring the latter's intentions in line with Cunard's.[656]

On 28 May 1930, the announcement that John Brown had won the order was made public although it was to be quite some time before the contract was signed. The delay largely turned on the issue of the new dock, as the Southern Railway Company was less than anxious to accelerate the building of a dock designed to accommodate just one ship. Both Bates and Bell brought what pressure they could to bear on the reluctant General Manager of the Southern Railway, Sir Herbert Walker. Finally, after much deliberation, Walker informed Bates on 1 December 1930, that the Southern Railway Company would definitely build the dock to be ready for October 1933. On the same day the contract for what was now ship number 534 was signed by John Brown's Chairman, Lord Aberconway and Sir Percy Bates. For Sir Thomas Bell, the delay in signing the contract must have given rise to some anxiety as quantities of steelwork had been prepared in the sheds and expenses accumulated. The role of Bell in ensuring that this order came to Clydebank was crucial and from the evidence of surviving correspondence, it is clear that both he and Sir Percy Bates and Sir Thomas Royden before him, enjoyed a most cordial relationship. On receiving the telegram telling of the contract signing on 1 December, Bell wrote the following letter to Bates:

'Many thanks for your kind thought in at once wiring me that Agreement for your proposed new Steamer had been signed and sealed.
Your telegram arrived at 2.15, and it was with a feeling of immense relief that I despatched a message to our shipyard manager that he could make arrangements to lay the keel forthwith.
This is now stopping time (5.15pm) and I have just returned from seeing nearly 400 feet of bottom keel plates faired up in position on the building berth.
If I may venture to say so, I do think you can look back with justifiable pride on this past six months'

work the last days of which have seen the successful termination of these anxious and lengthy negotiations, all of which have been additional to your other heavy responsibilities and work.'[657]

On 3 December, Sir Percy Bates replied:

'I greatly appreciate your kind letter of December 1st and can well imagine your feeling of relief when you got our telegram. I am afraid that I have given you a great deal of trouble this last month or so, but I think you are aware that it was not of my making. It has been a most difficult negotiation to get these different interests into line and at one time, and I am very thankful that stage of the proceedings is over. In case it should be any consolation to you, I would like to say that I doubt very much whether in the circumstances of the last few weeks a contract would have been signed but for the extraordinarily pleasant and tactful manner in which you dealt with the situation. I think this is a good augury for the years of work which lie ahead of us and I hope that the ship when finished will be a real credit to both our Companies'[658]

The great size of the ship - she was the largest moving man-made object at the time - required careful planning and many preparations were made to ensure that she could be physically accommodated, firstly, on the building berth, secondly, on her launching run into the River Cart and thirdly, in the fitting-out basin. Number 4 berth was the only choice for 534, as it had been specially constructed in 1910 to take *Aquitania* and required very little additional piling and preparation to take the new ship. The order for 534 came in time to prevent possible closure of the shipyard, as by April 1931, the yard was without any other work. The two destroyers *Basilisk* and *Beagle* had been completed and *Empress of Britain* was running trials. Indeed, it has been suggested that the *Queen Mary* contract was pivotal for not just the Clydebank yard but the John Brown Company as a whole.[659] Rapid progress was made on building the hull and the machinery and by the end of 1931, the ship was only five months away from launching. Throughout this period, the financial position of the western world was in turmoil as a result of the stock market crash and the deepening of the depression. As a result, trade worldwide and passenger traffic on the North Atlantic dropped significantly. Although Cunard was not in financial difficulties, it could not raise the funds on the market to pay for the ship.[660] The method of financing the new ship was long

established. Payments to the builder were made by the latter drawing on bills of exchange, which the Cunard Company raised on the London Money Market. At that time, this credit was usually charged at a rate of between 2% and 4%. Usually, Cunard paid off these borrowings partly from their reserves accumulated out of the previous years trading and partly out of the ship herself through projected profits earned in her first years of operation. When work on 534 began at the end of 1930, this system operated normally and John Brown was able to draw money weekly as required. However, in July 1931, the interest rate which had stood at 2.25%, rose to 5% and was later to reach 6%. In other words, the cost of borrowing began to rise unacceptably. In the middle of August, amidst fears of an international crisis on the money market, UK companies were unable to find any market lenders at economic rates and Cunard had to rely on its own cash resources, in the hope that normal trading conditions would be restored. This did not happen and the Company, with finite resources, made the decision to suspend work on 534.

On 1 December 1931, Bates wrote to Bell:

'I wrote you not so long ago that in certain circumstances we might ask you to stop all work on No 534 and now I have to make that request for those reasons and with others added. It is the others perhaps which weigh with me the most, for though the Government-supported White Star competition is now practically certain, it is the failure of the Discount Market which brings matters to a head. The Discount Market is out of action and apparently it is expected to remain so, for our Banks are unwilling to take its place, even though we could go on for a bit on our own. . . It is I think a year to the day since we signed the Contract and you can understand how bitter it is to me to have to write like this, but there is no help for it when the whole financial background of England goes wrong, and the best chance of the ultimate completion of No 534 lies in postponement. At the insistent request of the Midland Bank I am reporting the situation to the Treasury, but I do not in the least expect any move from that quarter.'[661]

It was agreed by John Brown and Cunard that the news of the suspension would be delayed until 11 December, when the President of the Board of Trade, Walter Runciman, would make a statement in the House of Commons. Soon after, rumours of the stoppage of work were rife in the press and Bates, anxious to keep the decision secret until the 11th, asked Bell if the shipyard had been the source for press reports. Bell replied on the 10th, assuring him that the 'leak' about the suspension had not been initiated at the shipyard. Meanwhile the notices to be posted on the yard gates were being prepared through the night of the 10th to be ready for posting in the morning before the men turned up for work. Bell's opinion on the suspension was expressed characteristically:

'As regards tomorrow's wholesale publication there is no doubt of the stir it will make. It now rests with the British public (whom the Government are supposed to represent) as to whether they are really proud and jealous of Britain's Maritime Supremacy and whether the Government Authorities concerned will be allowed to maintain their present apathetic attitude'[662]

When the announcement was made, it created headlines throughout the country and there was an immediate clamour for the National Government to assist in getting work on the ship restarted. At Clydebank, the following notice greeted men on the morning of the 11th:

'Notice is hereby given to employees in Clydebank shipyard, engine and boiler departments that all work in connection with contract 534 is to be stopped as from noon on Saturday, December 12. The services of all employees will therefore terminate at noon tomorrow. The owners express their profound regret that special circumstances have necessitated this total suspension of all construction work on the hull and machinery of this important contract. Wages will be paid this evening as usual. Lying time will be paid to time workers tomorrow on ceasing work, and to piece workers on Monday, 14 th inst., at 3pm.'[663]

It was a severe blow for Clydebank district coming just a year after the closure of the Beardmore shipyard. Employment at the yard, which had normally been averaging 5,000, had already been reduced to 3,000 in line with the shrinking order book. Most of these workers were immediately redundant. Additional staff at Clydebank Labour Exchange were required to deal with the long queue of 2,000 local men who applied for dole on Monday morning.[664] In the House of Commons on 11 December, David Kirkwood MP, whose constituency included Clydebank, asked the President of the Board of Trade, Walter Runciman, if Cunard was going to

stop construction of the new liner and if the Government would intervene to prevent this. Runciman replied that the Board of Trade had been informed a few days previously by the Cunard Company of its decision to suspend the contract and that the Board of Trade was satisfied that Cunard had left no stone unturned in trying to avoid the suspension. Runciman stated: 'The question of direct Government aid was not raised, and if it had been raised, it would not have been possible to give financial assistance'.[665]

During the Adjournment, Kirkwood argued against the House going into Christmas recess at such a crucial time and continued with an impassioned plea over the plight of the working class on Clydeside and elsewhere:

'There were two of the greatest shipbuilding yards in the world at Clydebank, and the Labour Government closed down one of them [Beardmore]. They scrapped it. They not only scrapped Dalmuir, but they scrapped Miller and Napier's the adjoining shipyard, and now practically the only job on Clydebank has been stopped'[666]

In the event, the House did go into recess and it was not until 2 February 1932, the first day of the new session, that Kirkwood was again able to press the Prime Minister, Ramsay MacDonald, over the issue of Government assistance to enable Cunard to restart work on the ship. MacDonald reiterated Runciman's previous statement that the Government accepted Cunard's commercial decision to halt work on the ship; that the Government had not been approached for assistance; that if they were, they would give careful consideration to any proposals made but that no direct financial assistance could be given.[667] Kirkwood wrote to Bates the following day saying that following private conversations with Ramsay MacDonald and Walter Runciman, he felt confident that something would be done by the Government and that the next move was up to Cunard. On the 6th, Bates replied to Kirkwood saying that he agreed the next move was theirs and that he was 'considering with my colleagues how best that move can be made.' Sir Thomas Bell applied what pressure on the Government he could and co-authored a letter with the editor of the Glasgow Herald, Sir Robert Bruce, to Stanley Baldwin, President of the Council, of whom Bruce was a long standing friend. The point of this letter was that the Government should step in, not with money, but to undertake to discount bills at the current bank rate whatever that might be. The letter

As a member of the Clyde Workers Committee, David Kirkwood was one of the original 'Red Clydesiders' involved in the 1916 dispute at the Parkhead Forge over dilution which saw him and several others deported to Edinburgh. In 1922 he won the Dumbarton Parliamentary seat for the Independent Labour Party. Acutely aware of the effects of unemployment, he campaigned tirelessly throughout 1932 and 1933 to have work on the 534 re-started.

ended by raising the spectre of French competition for the new Cunard ship in the form of a request to the French Government to lend £2,400,00 to CGT to build a rival ship for the North Atlantic.[668] Bell also sought the willing help of the Duke of Atholl, Chairman of the Union Bank, who unsuccessfully petitioned Baldwin.

On 15 February 1932, Bates wrote to the Prime Minister, Ramsay McDonald, asking for the help of HM Government in the early resumption of work on *No. 534*. Bates wanted the Government to provide financial facilities for 534 in the same way that the Government of 1905 had put up the funds for *Lusitania* and *Mauretania*. In reply, Sir Charles Hipwood of the Board of Trade, said that the Government saw no comparison between the *Lusitania* and 534 and that while the Admiralty had been interested in the use of the former as an armed merchant cruiser, it had no interest in 534 at all. Hipwood added that the Government's main interest was in unemployment. Any hope of Government assistance was finally extinguished when Neville Chamberlain, Chancellor of the Exchequer, wrote to

Bates on 1 March saying that no assistance would be available.[669]

During the first few months of 1932, the press took up the issue of Government support, citing the example of the Ulster Government's assistance to Harland & Wolff through the Loans Guarantee Act and the Government's loan of £206,000 to the North Wales Power Company. Nothing came of any of these moves and Clydebank shipyard and 534 settled down for what was going to be a long wait. At Clydebank, the view was initially taken that work would resume after the New Year holidays. Cunard's naval architect, G W Paterson, asked the builders to re-engage 6 men to- paint parts of the bottom plating; 6 men to continuously inspect shoring, keel blocks and the sighting of the hull for alignment and sinkage; ten men for internal hull inspection and cleaning, removal of rubbish and dirt including coke from riveters' fires, clearing of drain holes and removal of rain water that finds its way into the ship'[670]

In the event, only twelve men were employed. Fire risks, especially that to the timber supporting the ship, were addressed by laying an insulated fire main

Queues of unemployed face an impossible search for work at Clydebank's employment exchange in 1932.

along each side of the berth.

At the time of suspension, hobbing of the third main gearwheel and the third pinion of the second set were in progress and could not be stopped without causing inaccuracies in the teeth. Apart from the men required to continue this work, all engine works employees, with the exception of the head foreman, had been paid off.

At the end of the first week of suspension, the twelve men were employed in the shipyard with the following tasks: two head foremen shipwrights to attend to the bilge and keel blocks and sighting of the keel; four firemen on day patrol and four firemen on night patrol; one heating engineer to attend to steam heating in connection with timber for passenger and crew cabins and one detective on ship and on yard patrol to look out for pilfering. Additionally, all head foremen of the various shipyard departments were in attendance to look after the work for which they were responsible. The entire shipyard drawing office was retained for a time to develop a variety of working plans for the ship.[671] By February 1932, Cunard owed John Brown £1,611,383 for work done on *534*. This sum was reduced by paying off bills at £75,000 per week.[672]

RHUBARB FOR RIVETS

Apart from the routine work carried out by a few foremen on 534, the shipyard had no work whatsoever. The engine works fared little better, employing between 50 and 60 men on the manufacture of replacement parts for machinery. Most of the draughtsmen lost their jobs within the first few months of 1932 but a small nucleus was retained to work on the ship.

In his report to the Board for June 1932, Bell said:

> 'The streets of Clydebank make a terribly depressing sight with the crowds of men loafing about the whole day long, so, after digesting Mr. Hore-Bellisha's refusal, on behalf of the Government, to give any assistance to Cunard, at the end of April we approached one of the local land owners to lease a suitable plot of ground to employ 150 of our skilled men'

The ground was divided into 160 plots to form allotments of 165 square yards each. Seeds and gardening utensils were supplied by the English Allotment Association of the Society of Friends who opened a branch in Scotland. Bell was one of a number of people from Clydebank who joined the Association.

In June, Cunard officials visited the yard, making a minute examination of 534 to decide what painting would be required to prevent deterioration of the structure. It was agreed that £17,000 would be necessary to carry out this work and as a result most of the under-foremen were employed to paint the ship at labourer's rates, 40 to 45 shillings per week. This work was expected to be completed by the end of September.

Although the works were without any employment, the Company did what it could to keep a nucleus of foremen together. While shipyard foremen were painting, foremen from the engine works were employed overhauling machinery throughout the yard. In June, tenders to the Admiralty for cruisers and cruiser machinery were prepared but were unsuccessful.

WARSHIPS AND WELDING

Despite the lack of activity in the yard, Bell took the opportunity to put in hand a number of progressive initiatives - the introduction of welding and the acquisition of manufacturing rights for the Doxford slow speed diesel engine. In August 1932, the Shipyard Director, Donald Skiffington, was sent with the Electrical Outside Manager to visit the works of Murex Ltd., who manufactured welding equipment. They also visited two firms on the North East Coast, Dorman Long and Smith's Dock, to assess the extent and success of welding employed there. Having consulted the English Electric Company, a small corrugated iron shed was erected in the west yard with two transformers, and provision for four additional machines, each capable of supporting twelve welders. The cost of providing this welding station was £7,685.[673]

In September 1932, Bell deliberated between either a Sulzer or Doxford diesel engine manufacturing license as the propulsion unit for future Clydebank merchant vessels. On the basis that the Doxford was cheaper than the Sulzer and occupied less room in the ship, negotiations were started with Doxford.[674] The licence was contingent on a lump payment of £10,000 to Doxford, which, under the prevailing circumstances, posed a problem for Clydebank. This was neatly circumvented in the following way. A cheque for £10,000 was paid to Doxford, who then made out a cheque for £9,500 to the Clydebank works to be repaid, with 5% interest, in instalments of £1,000 on each order for Doxford diesels received at Clydebank.[675] The inability of the yard to attract merchant orders from established customers in the difficult years of the early 1930s was the first real indication that sophisticated merchant ship and warship orders were no panacea for survival. The naval treaties had severely circumscribed naval orders. Now, the serious decline in shipping and the Atlantic trade in particular, removed the other plank in the Company's building strategy. While many yards closed down temporarily during these years others, relying on established customers, were able to keep going. This applied particularly to the builders of unsophisticated merchant vessels.

In June 1933, John Brown's was invited to tender for two large refrigerated cargo ships for the New Zealand Shipping Co., but came well down the list of potential builders on the basis of cost. The Clydebank tender included no charges yet the winning tender was 10% cheaper than theirs.[676] When the order for a merchant vessel was eventually secured, for *Port Wyndham*, laid down in February 1934, she was taken with no charges. This was the first merchant order, excluding 534, since *Empress of Britain* in 1928. Orders for small Admiralty vessels relieved the gloom and despair at Clydebank. Tenders for sloops and destroyers submitted to the Admiralty were

Work restarted once again on the 534. This view taken on 24 August 1934 shows the immense bulk of the ship almost rising to touch the jibs of the cranes which built her. The launching run into the mouth of the River Cart is clearly seen.

This view shows the ship's towering relationship to the town of Clydebank and in particular Singer's vast sewing machine factory.

rewarded in September with an order for two 800 ton sloops, *Halcyon* and *Skipjack* although neither ship was laid down until March of the following year. These vessels appear to have been the first on which electric welding was carried out at Clydebank although, almost certainly, this would have been restricted to unstressed parts of the hull. Much of the work on these vessels was done by foremen and under foremen, the only other workers in the yard being apprentices.[677] On 18 March, the order for two

destroyers, *Fortune* and *Foxhound* was received and James McNeil, the Company's naval architect, was sent to Swan Hunter, Scotts and Denny to collaborate on the design work for the hulls in an attempt to cut costs.[678]

The order book slowly picked up bolstered by the contract for another small Admiralty vessel, the sloop *Enchantress*, which was received on 6 October. By November 1933, approximately 700 men were employed between the shipyard and engine works. In

November 1934, the keel of the cruiser *Polyphemus*, (later *Southampton*) was laid on No 1 berth in the east yard. The order for this ship had been received the previous May and Bell set about re-equipping No 1 berth with three ten ton tower cranes purchased at the sale of plant and machinery from the redundant McMillan's yard at Dumbarton, which had been closed by National Shipbuilders Security Ltd. The cost of the cranes erected on site was £9,600 in addition to the cost of £4,800 for welding plant for that berth. A considerable amount of welding was carried out on Southampton, particularly bulkheads and decks most of which were in ten ton sections.[679] This was a significant development in the move to welded construction in British shipyards, the majority of which did not embrace welding until after 1945.

RESUMPTION OF WORK

Throughout the deliberations leading to the building and subsequent suspension of 534 lay an issue which eventually held the key to resumption of work on the great ship. This was the covert bankruptcy of the Royal Mail Group in 1929. This group, under the chairmanship of Lord Kylsant, owned 15% of the British merchant fleet, which translated into something in the region of 700 ships.[680] At that time, this fleet accounted for over half of the world's total. The Group owed the British government alone guarantees worth £10 million. As receivership was too grim a prospect to contemplate, the Treasury and the Bank of England sought to restructure the Group and much of British shipping in similar fashion to the restructuring of other sectors of the economy, the armaments, steel and shipbuilding industries. This

Another view taken on 24 August 1934 shows men planing the slipways where the forward poppet will be fitted.

LAUNCH OF
Nº "534"
in the presence of Their Majesties
THE KING & QUEEN
Wednesday, September 26, 1934
at Clydebank

Top
4 September. Visible for miles around, and something of a fixture after three years of suspension, the final touches of paint are applied to 534's hull.

Left
The crest from the launch brochure.

Far left
Taken in July, this aerial view shows an empty East Yard apart from 534 and only Port Wyndham in the West Yard.

Opposite page
5 September. With only three weeks to go until launch, staging is cleared from the hull while scaffolding for the launching platform is erected.

Right
An invitation to one of the best seats and a river view of the launch – on board the Clyde steamer King George V.

Above
The Queen, King and Sir Thomas Bell watch in awe as the newly named Queen Mary *starts to move down the ways.*

Opposite page
The launch, the one event which caused hearts to skip among shipyard management. Watched by 25,000 people in the rain, Queen Mary, *weighing a staggering 35,500 tons, slips into the Clyde.*

restructuring process was complicated, protracted, and required the exercising of great care to avoid collateral damage to other industries and the business confidence of the country generally. Cunard and ship number *534* were unavoidably to play important roles in this restructuring in a situation not of their making.

White Star, Cunard's British rival on the North

CUNARD WHITE STAR LIMITED AND JOHN BROWN & COMPANY, LIMITED **"A"** AND STEAMER

LAUNCH OF S.S. No. 534

from Clydebank Shipyard
on Wednesday, 26th September, 1934,
at 3 p.m.

This card entitles ONE PERSON to go on board the Turbine Steamer "KING GEORGE V" at Bridge Wharf (South Side), Glasgow. The Steamer will leave for Clydebank Shipyard at 1.35 p.m.
The Card should be shewn on entering Stand **"A"** and at the gang-way on returning to Steamer after the Launch.
The Turbine Steamer "KING GEORGE V" will leave Clydebank at 4 p.m., and Tea will be served on the return journey.

DRESS: Ordinary Dress.   **NOT TRANSFERABLE**

Atlantic, was part of the Royal Mail Group as were Belfast shipbuilders Harland & Wolff. Cunard had already made several attempts to acquire the North Atlantic interests of the White Star Line. These attempts were, naturally, framed in Cunard's interest, based on their view that White Star, debt laden, was effectively a worthless asset. Initially, no progress was made and lengthy negotiations were carried on throughout 1932. In October of that year, the Government, advised by Walter Runciman and Sir William Mclintock, trustees of the bankrupt White Star and Royal Mail lines asked Lord Weir to examine the whole question of British shipping lines operating on the North Atlantic and to consider the level of subsidy which foreign lines were receiving from their governments. Lord Weir's report of March 1933, recommended that Cunard take over White Star, a position which Cunard readily accepted. However, White Star's chairman, Lord Essenden, could not agree to this. Under Lord Weir's arbitration, an agreement was finally reached in December 1933 whereby Cunard and White Star would amalgamate in proportions agreed between the two Companies of 62:38 in Cunard's favour. On 13 December 1933, Neville Chamberlain stated in the House of Commons that as an effective merger of the North Atlantic fleets of Cunard and White Star would soon be a reality, 'It is the intention of the Government in that event shortly to lay before the House proposals for furnishing the necessary financial facilities for the

completion of the new Cunard liner known as No. 534'. White Star had been rescued at the cost of great delay to both Cunard and John Brown's.

The company which emerged, Cunard White Star Ltd., was brought into being on 17 January 1934, together with loans from the Treasury of £3 million, to be repaid by 1975, to cover the cost of completing *534*; a further £5 million for the cost of a second ship and £1.5 million working capital for the new company. Legislation to permit this was later passed in the form of the North Atlantic Shipping (Advances) Bill on 27 March 1934.

For Clydebank shipyard and town alike, the resumption of work on *534* was greeted with rejoicing. The ship, for two years a symbol of depression, now signalled a return to better times. In the most celebrated of returns to work, the first shift to start on *534* was piped into the yard by the Dalmuir Parish Pipe Band on 3 April to the tune of 'The Campbells Are Coming.' By 25 April, nearly 1,550 men had been re-engaged in the shipyard and engine works. Had it not been for the re-casting of the passenger accommodation throughout the ship, this figure would have been higher. In his bi-monthly report, Sir Thomas Bell noted that it was 'a great relief to have work once more going on in an ordinary fashion and to have the big whistle once more heard at starting and stopping time after a silence of two years and four months.'[681] Formal resumption of the contract was authorised in a letter from Sir Percy Bates to John Brown on 26 May 1934. By the end of that month the number of men employed on *534* and her machinery had risen to 1,900.

The Chairman of John Brown, Lord Aberconway, did not live to see this event. He died in January 1934 after 51 years on the Board 27 of which were as Chairman. His eldest son Henry Duncan McLaren who, like his father, had a legal background succeeded him.

LAUNCH

As the great size of this ship was far in excess of anything so far built on the Clyde, preparations for launching were extensive and required further alteration to the river as well as the fitting-out basin. This basin had been extended landward as far as was possible which meant that the stern of the ship would project into the river. To ensure that the navigable channel was not reduced, the Clyde Navigation Trust undertook to widen the river by 100 feet over a distance of nearly three-quarters of a mile opposite the basin. The mouth of the River Cart was widened

on the west bank as was the Clyde at Dalmuir. It was calculated that during her launch the stern would be immersed to a maximum of 38.7 feet. To allow the ship to enter the river without damage, a trench was deep-dredged along the launching run which required the removal of half a million tons of spoil. In the fitting-out basin, the deep water berth on the eastern side required to be deep-dredged to a level

coming to rest in the water and his calculations proved to be remarkably accurate. She came to a halt after travelling a total distance of 1,196 feet.

Queen Mary was taken into her specially prepared berth in the basin for completion, a process that would take another eighteen months. As the ship already projected 38 feet into the river with her stem hard against the head of the fitting-out basin, she

Queen Mary on 18 January 1935 dwarfs the destroyers Fortune *and* Foxhound, *the sloop* Enchantress *and the cargo vessel* Port Wyndham.

In the engine shops work proceeding on two of Queen Mary's *turbines.*

lower than the deep channel in the river to ensure that the ship had water under the keel at all states of the tide. To stop this berth filling up with silt as the ship lay fitting-out, an underwater curtain of steel plates was constructed around the stern of the vessel. On the surface, a boom held in position by two hoppers also protected the stern of the ship from collision with river traffic. In the dredging work carried out in the river and fitting-out basin, a total of 5 million tons of excavate was removed.[682]

The ship was successfully launched by her namesake under a thick cover of grey sky and driving rain on 26 September 1934. An estimated crowd of 250,000 people, mostly clutching umbrellas, watched as the great ship made her entry into the river. The launching weight at 35,500 tons[683], was the heaviest ever. Donald Skiffington, the Shipyard Director, fussed over launching details to ensure that everything went as planned. James McNeil had calculated that the ship would move 1,194 feet before

could not be moved in and out under the heavy fitting-out crane to have her boilers and machinery installed. Therefore, to ship her boilers, a 600 foot long internal runway was constructed from the forward engine room to the forward boiler room through apertures made in the bulkheads. This way, all twenty-four boilers were lowered into the hull through an opening in the deck and then slid into their final positions.

The ship proved to be a great attraction and although management did not encourage visits, they were more sanguine where it might generate publicity for the Company. Many visitors were, in any case, difficult to resist. In April 1935, the Duke of York and the Duke of Montrose were met in the yard by the Lord Provost of Glasgow and directors of John Brown to tour the ship. Visits for July 1935 included the Duke of Portland and friends; an excursion by Sheffield workers; the South African Prime Minister; the Duke of Hamilton; many other Prime Ministers from the Dominions and Members of Parliament.[684] As work on the ship continued, records for the quantity of items fitted, cables, pipework, light bulbs, paint, etc. were broken regularly.

On 31 March 1935, Sir Thomas Bell retired after sixty years of service at Clydebank. While relinquishing the Managing Directorship at Clydebank to Stephen J Pigott, he retained his seat on the main John Brown Board and did not fully retire until 1946. Bell's association with Clydebank had begun in 1886 and his rise through the Company coincided with the continuing ascent of the British marine engineering and shipbuilding industries to which he made a significant contribution. Under his control, first as Engineering Director and then as Managing Director, some of the most magnificent and important ships in British maritime history were built and engined at Clydebank. *Lusitania, Tiger, Aquitania, Barham, Repulse, Hood, Empress of Britain* and *Queen Mary* all owed something to this remarkable man. After Sir Thomas's death in 1952, a plaque was unveiled in the shipyard as a small tribute to him.[685] At this event, Lord Aberconway said:

> 'Sir Thomas Bell witnessed the tremendous growth and development of the Clydebank shipyard. When he came to it, it was a relatively small yard not larger than 20 or 30 other yards in this country. When he left it, it was not the largest in size, but in reputation it was the greatest yard anywhere in the world. That was due to his ability and personality. Only a really great man could have made the yard rise in the way that he achieved.'

Retiral did not prevent Bell from making regular visits to the yard. He was there on 5 March 1936 when King Edward VIII visited the yard to inspect *Queen Mary* and again on 24 March when the ship made her only passage from Clydebank to the Firth of Clyde. On that occasion, despite great care taken with dredging, the ship was blown off the narrow channel and grounded at Dalmuir Bend causing anxious moments on the bridge. With the tide about to fall, Sir Thomas was only too aware of the potential for disaster. His countenance displayed his concern prompting a Cunard steward to ask if he would have a drink. 'I think I will' was the economical reply.[686] The ship was pulled from the sandbank and reached the Tail of the Bank unscathed.

Queen Elizabeth

Under the terms of the Cunard Insurance Act, the Cunard Company was obliged to build the second ship before the Act expired in 1936. From the outset, the intention had been to operate a two-ship service on the North Atlantic. On 25 November 1935, Sir Percy Bates wrote to Swan Hunter, Vickers Armstrong, John Brown and Cammell Laird advising them that, although his Board had not reached any final decision, they might decide to build a vessel to run alongside the *Queen Mary*.[687] With White Star now under Cunard's wing, Harland & Wolff were invited to tender, a position not previously open to them. In a further letter to Swan Hunter and Vickers Armstrong, Bates asked if they would be prepared to consider a combined tender, as the only berth on Tyneside capable of accepting such a large ship was at Vickers Armstrong's Walker Naval yard. Bates estimated that Swan Hunter would have to lay out £150,000 to build a suitable berth.[688] Both firms agreed to comply with this proposal although in the event, they submitted separate tenders. In writing to Hitchins of Cammell Laird, Bates said that he was not entirely confident that they could deal with such a large ship and that in particular, they might be unable to move the ship into their fitting-out basin. Harland & Wolff found itself in a peculiar situation. The wording of the Cunard Insurance Act, provided for the construction of two vessels in Great Britain, which precluded the Belfast yard from tendering as, Belfast, although in the United Kingdom, was not in Great Britain.

Lord Essenden, writing to Bates on 12 December 1935, said he thought it best if the new ship was built in a 'Scotch or English shipyard' because 'I appreciate from a Government point of view it would be intolerable that they would put up the money and not having the effect of providing employment in these two countries'. Harland & Wolff were, in effect, barred from tendering. Sir Frederick Rebbeck, Harland & Wolff's Managing Director, was justifiably

Donald Skiffington, the Shipyard Director, fussed over the launching details for Queen Mary. *Skiffington invariably performed his tours of inspection around the yard in bow tie and with a rolled-up umbrella.*

concerned about the potential damage to their reputation when it became known that his firm was excluded from tendering. In accepting the position however, he asked Bates to look favourably on Harland & Wolff 'when it comes to maintenance work at Southampton'.[689]

Cammell Laird were unimpressed with the limited timetable laid down for tendering, prompting Robert

retirement in March 1935[690], wrote to Bates saying that Bell was recovering from an illness but that he was now able to participate in the discussions for the new ship. Pigott added that he noted 'feelings of mutual confidence between Sir Thomas Bell and Sir Percy Bates'.

While the shipbuilding firms were working on designs for the new ship, the Daily Telegraph touched

Johnson to write to Bates saying that they wanted full access to details of *Queen Mary's* design, including drawings and test tank calculations as otherwise they would be unable to design a ship this size in the time given them (until the following Easter). He also noted that John Brown had accumulated considerable experience in building *Queen Mary* and that Brown's had also benefited from Cunard's experience and were, as a consequence, well placed to build the next ship. Bates replied that he (Johnson) had missed the point. Cunard had supplied the design of *Queen Mary* to Brown's and asked them to quote for building the ship whereas this time, Cunard were asking the builders to design and quote for building the new ship.

Correspondence between Bates and Clydebank was more cordial. On 28 November, Stephen Pigott, the new Managing Director at Clydebank following Bell's

on Cunard sensibilities by describing this ship as being much larger than the *Queen Mary* and probably in the region of 90,000 tons. Writing to Lord Camrose soon after, Bates expressed irritation at this report, commenting that he hoped that the second ship might even be smaller than the first but that this would have to await the outcome of the shipbuilder's designs.[691] On 31 March, Pigott wrote to Bates saying that, despite the requirement for more passenger accommodation, the new ship would definitely not be bigger than *Queen Mary*.

In May, tenders were opened from John Brown, Cammell Laird, Vickers Armstrong and Swan Hunter. John Brown submitted two proposals, Design A, for a ship slightly larger than *Queen Mary* and Design B, of 58,000 tons and a length overall of 962' 6" and a completely new machinery arrangement. The 'A' proposal was slightly heavier and longer than *Queen*

Queen Mary nearing completion. The task of painting her hull black has started at the stern.

Opposite page
One of the ship's condensers, on its own a formidable structure.

Mary but relied on virtually the same machinery installation to provide 158,000 shp with an overload of 181,700 shp. The only difference was the use of 12 water tube boilers of a larger type than the 24 installed in *Queen Mary*. This meant that the new ship would require only two funnels. Further tank testing had resulted in a modified hull form which, it was calculated, would enable the ship to achieve an extra

Appart from office jobs, very few women were employed in the shipyard. This photograph of polishers probably accounts for most.

half-knot over *Queen Mary* for the same power and fuel consumption.[692] The adjusted tender prices submitted by the four firms were John Brown 'A' £4,293,000; John Brown 'B' £3,595,000; Vickers Armstrong £3,915,000; Swan Hunter 'A' and 'B' £4,845,000; Cammell Laird £4,863,000.[693] Despite Vickers Armstrong's lower tender, Cunard placed the order with Clydebank. The difference between tenders, Vickers Armstrong price was £378,000 less than John Brown's 'A' proposal, was hardly insignificant. Clearly, Cunard preferred John Brown's design and, as importantly, were confident in its proven ability to build and complete a ship of this size. At a preliminary meeting held between Bates, Bell and Pigott on 27 May, the Clydebank men were told they had the order.[694]

Early in July 1936, a revealing event occurred. Stephen Pigott wrote to Bates saying that Sir Thomas Bell had reserved the ship number 535 (*Queen Mary* had been ship number 534) for the new ship in the belief that Bates would appreciate the gesture. On 11 July, Bates replied asking Pigott to 'think of another good one'. The reason was the Chancellor of the Exchequer's apprehension at what might be asked of

him by his critics when making the announcement of the order in the House, namely, 'that this tender business was all a farce and that the order was in Brown's pocket from the start'.[695] On the 28 July, the Chancellor of the Exchequer told the House that the order for the new ship was to be placed with John Brown.

The contract was signed on 6 October 1936, and the keel of ship number 552 was laid on 4 December. By this time, *Queen Mary* had been in service for six months, providing opportunity for her performance to be evaluated and the lessons incorporated into the design of the second ship. Her trials had been successfully completed on the Firth of Clyde over the month of April and she was officially handed over to Cunard on 11 May 1936. Her maiden voyage to New York later that month had been a great disappointment as she was unable to beat the record established by *Normandie* in the previous year. The reason for her inability to put up a better performance was down to the little known fact that she suffered damage to her turbines during the voyage. After her trials, Cunard had not taken up its option, under contract, to open-up the ship's turbines for inspection. During her maiden voyage when full service power was developed, it was noticed that the steam pressure distribution throughout the turbines was not as designed or as obtained on full speed trials. As the trouble developed, Stephen Pigott and John Austin, Cunard's Superintendent Engineer, contemplated what to do. As there was no immediate threat to the turbines, it was decided that the voyage to New York, and a tumultuous reception, should continue and the trouble be investigated there. On opening up the turbines, it was found that the first row of impulse blades had been damaged. The blades were removed and the turbines closed up. As the ship was perfectly capable of making the return passage to Southampton, albeit at slightly reduced speed, her schedule was maintained. Under the circumstances, her average speed of 29.13 knots was highly creditable. Corrective work was undertaken at Southampton. Unlike the unfortunate plight of *QE2* thirty years later caught in a blaze of hostile publicity, this event was quickly rectified without comment from either Cunard or John Brown.[696]

QUEEN MARY, NORMANDIE AND THE DESIGN OF QUEEN ELIZABETH

When *Queen Mary* went into service, inevitably, comparison with *Normandie*, flagship of the Compagnie Générale Transatlantique was made.

While it is not the intention to re-examine that issue in detail, it is necessary, as far as it concerns the work undertaken by John Brown, to consider a few of the criticisms, stated or implied, which were made of the British ship. In Britain, *Queen Mary* was considered to be the finest achievement of the British shipbuilding and marine engineering industry, at a time when that industry enjoyed international pre-eminence. In

characteristics, other criticisms made of *Queen Mary* had a technical basis. The principal criticism concerned the shape or form of the ship's hull. The challenge confronting the naval architect was to design a form which would enable the ship to be driven through the sea at a given speed using the least amount of power. As power was equal to the amount of oil burned in the boilers, form affected

relative terms, the French industry enjoyed neither the prestige nor the scale of its British counterpart, yet, in *Normandie*, they had produced a magnificent vessel. The external and internal design of *Queen Mary* was evolutionary, based on accumulated and unrivalled experience. *Normandie's* appearance was more strikingly modern, reflecting the desire to break with tradition. While this can be attributed to aesthetics, taste, or a reflection of national

running costs. It was claimed that *Normandie's* hull was superior in form to the *Queen Mary's* resulting in better sea-keeping qualities and that her machinery required less power to drive her at the same speed. This questioned the assumed superiority of the Clydebank design.

Throughout the 1920s, a number of theories, originating outside the UK, were advanced purporting to improve the performance of ships

John Brown's prepare to do it all over again only this time a little bigger. The hull of Queen Elizabeth *taking shape on 2 June 1937. Five hundred tons of steel were consumed weekly in the construction of this ship.*

through better hull design. In designing *Normandie*, the Russian naval architect Vladimir Yourkevitch was employed to apply his theories of hull form, known simply as Yourkevitch-form. The North German Lloyd liners *Bremen* and *Europa* also incorporated advanced design features in hull form. Were British naval architects as well informed in important elements of ship design? Part of the answer lies in a report sent from Clydebank to Cunard on 13 March 1934, in response to a request from the latter 'to make an official statement, on behalf of John Brown, to Cunard about the Maier-form'. Maier-form, like Yourkevitch-form, was one of a number of new hull forms designed to achieve a given speed using less engine power. Historically, this was no more than a continuation of the efforts made by engineers and naval architects over many years to reduce the operating cost of ships. Bell wrote to Bates in reply to their request stating:

> 'Although we had previously tried the Maier-form to an extent applicable to the present form of the 534, we thought it better, under the circumstances, to at once make an entirely new model going the 'whole hog' of the Maier-form requirements. It then struck me that it would be best to incorporate in our report on this, our other tests of models based on the theories of Bulbous Bow form, Yourkevitch form and Maier-form respectively'

The report makes interesting reading and explains the decrease (or increase!) in horsepower needed for a given speed by adopting a different hull form:

> 'Bulbous Bow: same as 534 up to 28 knots but above that speed, a gain equivalent to .2 knots at 30 knots.
> Yourkevitch form: 1% more power needed for this form at 29 knots but at 30 knots, required 1.5% less power, or, with the same power, an increase in speed of .15 knots.
> Maier-form: at 29 knots 4% more power required over 534, while at 24 knots 7% more power required.'[697]

Most of the tests conducted at Clydebank in connection with the above appear to have been made after 534 was laid down and, although Bell refrained from making any judgement in his report, it seems that Bulbous-bow and probably Yourkevitch-form offered an advantage not apparent in *Queen Mary*. This advantage was small but important over the course of thousands of miles steamed at high speed. In May 1935, *Normandie* took the Blue Riband in both directions from the Italian liner *Rex*. On trials in March 1936, *Queen Mary* attained a speed of 32.84

knots developing over 210,000 SHP. This compared with the *Normandie's* best performance to date of 32.12 knots. In August 1936, *Queen Mary* took the westward crossing from *Normandie* only to lose it the following year. In August 1938, *Queen Mary* won the Blue Riband decisively retaining it until July 1952[698]. Whatever the merits of Yourkevitch-form, Cunard and John Brown engineers had made sure that their ship had adequate reserves of power and an efficient hull form.

The race across the Atlantic generated enormous media attention and public interest. Fearing that *Queen Mary* might not prove to be quicker than *Normandie*, Cunard White Star received many letters from the public with offers of shipbuilding and technical advice. Inside a Cunard folder marked 'Cranks and Inventors' now held at Liverpool University Archives, there is a series of letters addressed to Sir Percy Bates ranging from the plausible to the bizarre. In one of them, a Mr Anderson from Wallasey wrote in March 1937:

> 'Dear Sir,
> The Normandie v. Queen Mary.
> You should alter the Queen Mary No 2 like sketch enclosed. The SS Queen Mary at 30 knots windage is like pushing the Liverpool Town Hall fitted on a barge through the water - 20% loss of speed and horse power. Even loco's have to be streamlined now.'

The sketch enclosed was a newspaper photograph of the *Normandie* over which Mr Anderson had crudely drawn in pencil a massive turtledeck extending from the bow to the top of the bridge. Written under this, the correspondent urged Sir Percy Bates to 'Put your head out of a railway window at 60 mph for half an hour, you will know what wind resistance is'

Like all the letters sent to him, Sir Percy replied:

> 'I am much obliged by your letter of 25 March, and thank you for the suggestion you make as to the fore part of a sister-ship to the Queen Mary'

In August 1936, Tennyson d'Eyncourt, formerly Director of Naval Construction and responsible for the design of many warships including *Hood*, wrote to Bates, offering to improve the form of the second ship. In November, following reports that *Queen Mary* had rolled badly in a gale, unlike *Normandie*, Joseph Isherwood, a prominent naval architect, wrote with a similar offer extolling the advantages of Arcform[699]. In the same month, Lord Strabolgi, concerned about the rolling, wrote to Bates advising him to consider Yourkevitch-form.

> 'Yourkevitch is ready to work quite anonymously

if it would hurt the feelings of our fellow patriots if a Russian naval architect was known to have assisted. I do beg of you to reconsider this matter as I, like you, want to see the best results from British shipbuilding'

Bates rejected all three offers and wrote to Lord Essenden in the same month:

'We have known right from the start that the Normandie is an easier model to propel, but only in smooth water with waves not exceeding 3 feet in height. Beyond that point the Normandie's model becomes a disadvantage and the Atlantic is rarely smooth enough to make the Normandie's form worth while month in and month out.

As regards 552 a complete study has been made of the Normandie and her performances and partly

Above
Sir Percy Bates and Queen Elizabeth looking up at the ship which bears her name.

Launch of Queen Elizabeth *on 27 September 1938. The Munich crisis prevented the King's attendance*

Over
By 1937, re-armament was well underway. Here the cruiser Southampton nears completion early that year.

as a result of this the model of 552 will differ from that of 534 but will still not be of such an extreme type as the Normandie. As you know we expect to get another half knot out of this change.[700]

In a letter to Cunard, the Clydebank firm stated:

'As a result of further extensive research in our Experiment Tank, where we have specialised in models of this type during the last few years, we have now evolved a form (based on orthodox principles) which shows a further improvement in propulsive performance over that evolved for the Queen Mary to the extent of improvement in speed by about one third knot at 29 knot service speed, and improvement of about one-half knot at somewhat higher speeds. With the same propulsive power this provides a further margin for ensuring the maintenance of the speed required in all conditions of weather that may be expected in the North Atlantic, and we are confident that, from all considerations, the properties of our new design will bear favourable comparison with any liner form yet built, and should enable large economies to be effected in operation in service'[701]

Work on *Queen Elizabeth* proceeded rapidly and by February 1937, Colvilles Ltd. were supplying steel to Clydebank for this ship at the rate of 500 tons per week.[702] As the ship's launch day in 1938 approached, international events were increasingly dominated by the crisis surrounding German ambitions for the Sudetenland in Czechoslovakia. On 27 September, Queen Elizabeth, accompanied by Princess Elizabeth and Princess Margaret, arrived at Clydebank to give her name to the ship. Unlike the naming of *Queen Mary*, there was no secret about the name of the new ship. As head of state, King George VI was detained in London, awaiting the outcome of Neville Chamberlain's negotiations with Hitler. As the Queen approached the end of her launching speech, the ship, suddenly began to move. At her side, Stephen Pigott said 'quick Ma'am, she's going; launch her please' The Queen instantly cut the string which sent the bottle of Australian wine crashing onto the bow of the rapidly receding liner. It had been a close call.

THE 'WORLD'S BUSIEST SHIPYARD'

The trickle of Admiralty orders in the early part of the 1930s grew into a torrent by its end. No fewer than twenty-two warships were laid down compared to only eight merchant vessels including the two Queens in the same period. Among the warship contracts were two destroyers built for the Argentine

Navy, *San Juan* and *San Luis*, the only warships to be built for foreign owners at Clydebank since the *Asahi* of 1899. Also built were the submarine depot ships *Maidstone* and *Forth*. The latter was the last large ship to be fitted with Brown-Curtis machinery. Advances made to Parson's turbines set against the inability of John Brown to further develop the Brown-Curtis type eliminated any advantages which the latter had to offer.

JOHN BROWN & CO. LTD.
CLYDEBANK
2nd November, 1939.

ON THE WORKING OF KEELS.

No flat keel plate or vertical keel plate, top or bottom angles must be drilled until a sample of each, incorporating all features, has been marked off, examined by Head Loftsman, Head Ironworker and the Foreman in charge of the work. After which, the Manager in charge of the contract must inspect same, and it will be his prerogative as to whether the Overseer on the contract be invited to scrutinise same before drilling takes place.

Under no circumstances may a keel be worked without all bars, including angle butt straps and bosom pieces, being worked. Same must have holes in and drilled through all plies.

Head Loftsman ....
Head Ironworker ....
Foreman Plater ....

Plates which are knuckled must have ends planed, corners filed and must be annealed before this work is carried out.

The way it has to be done. An instruction concerning the working of keels by Head Loftsman Samuel E Bebbington, November 1939.

The increase in international tension was eloquently expressed by the growth in Naval Estimates which rose from a low of £51.5 million in 1930/31, to £96 million in 1938/39.[703] While the years before the First World War saw unrestricted battleship building, the period prior to the Second World War was limited by international agreement. However, the expiry of the Washington and London Naval Treaties at the end of 1936, signalled the resumption of battleship construction. The Admiralty moved quickly to lay down the battleships of the King George V class. In November 1936, the Controller of the Navy telephoned Stephen Pigott directly to tell him that Cabinet approval for a battleship to be built under the 1937 Programme at Clydebank had been given. This ship, initially called *Anson*, was later renamed *Duke of York*. Foreseeing Clydebank's increasing preoccupation with naval work, Pigott's first reaction was to write to Sir Percy Bates urging him to press on with *Queen Elizabeth* while he still could.[704]

The failure of the Japanese to sign the Second London Naval Treaty in April 1937, and their later failure to provide assurances over the size of their new battleships. made it necessary for the Admiralty to propose the Lion Class battleships. These were bigger and more powerful versions of the King George V Class. In 1938, contracts for the first two ships were awarded to Vickers Armstrong and Cammell Laird. In 1939, two further orders were placed, one with John Brown (*Conqueror*) and one with Fairfield (*Thunderer*). Brown's tender was submitted on 17 July and accepted on 16 August with a delivery in 1944. A tender submitted on 8 May 1939 for a fleet aircraft carrier (*Indefatigable*) was accepted on 19 June 1939 to be completed in 36 months. This order brought the value of naval work alone to a figure of almost £17 million and a total order book of £28 million.[705] As shipyard capacity for large warships was stretched, competitive tendering ceased to apply and orders were simply placed by the Admiralty. In the case of the aircraft carrier, the contract was awarded to John Brown based on a reasonable machinery price being subsequently agreed.

As the political situation in Europe continued to deteriorate throughout 1939, the design office at Clydebank worked on what would prove to be their last peacetime projects among which were merchant ships for the Soviet Union. In February, twelve firms, including John Brown, were approached by the Admiralty, asking them to participate in designs for a new Royal Yacht to replace *Victoria & Albert*. The basis of the approach was that the best elements of each shipbuilder's design would be incorporated into a final design. Of the original twelve builders, Stephens, John Brown and Vickers Armstrong were considered most acceptable and a final design prepared. Tenders were due to be invited on 1 August with the expectation that the vessel would be laid down during the autumn.[706] It would be almost fifteen years before that event became a reality.

When the first air raid siren sounded over Britain in September 1939, John Brown's shipyard was in full employment with an order book which earned it, at least in the columns of a local newspaper, the title 'The World's Busiest Shipyard'.[707]

Looking over the East Yard at the 1,031 foot long (313.5 metres) Queen Elizabeth *shortly before her launch.*

A wonderfully atmospheric photograph of Queen Elizabeth *being manoeuvred into the fitting-out basin after launching.*

1939 - 1945   THE SECOND WORLD WAR

After the declaration of war on 3 September 1939, one of many fears preoccupying Clydebank Town Council officials and public alike was that of air attack. Answering criticisms that the Council had been tardy in providing for air defence, the Provost explained that it was only on 15 April 1939, that the Home Office had told the Council what they knew already - Clydebank was highly vulnerable. Nevertheless, official recognition, albeit unpalatable, entitled the Council to implement a series of measures concerned with the air defence and protection of the town. This included the distribution of gas masks, evacuation of children and the provision of air-raid shelters. 'Anderson' shelters were installed in houses where garden space permitted. Much of Clydebank's working population had been accommodated in high-density tenements, each housing up to twelve families. Providing adequate protection for them was a problem because of the limited space around the tenements in which to erect shelters. Measures taken by the Council to

The Fairfield built Anchor liner Cilicia *leaving the basin at Dalmuir in October 1939 after conversion to an Armed Merchant Cruiser by John Brown.*

minimise the effects of war on the town were reflected in the shipyard where five steel pillboxes were erected along the river frontage manned by a volunteer ARP (Air Raid Protection) unit. Later, a John Brown Home Guard company was formed, in reality a branch of the Dumbarton Home Guard, which took over ARP duties. James McNeill, Clydebank's naval architect who had been a major in the artillery during the First World War, commanded this Company.[708]

In September 1939, ships representing an immensely valuable national asset were under construction at Clydebank: the Cunarder *Queen Elizabeth*; the battleship *Duke of York*; the aircraft carrier *Indefatigable*; the cruisers *Fiji* and *Polyphemus* (later *Bermuda*); the destroyers *Nizam* and *Nerissa*; the frigates *Garth* and *Fernie*; the depot ship *Hecla*; an as yet un-named merchant ship for the New Zealand Shipping Co. The motorship *Suffolk* was at Elderslie Dockyard, further up the River Clyde, for hull inspection prior to running trials. The engine works were busy on a remarkably wide variety of contracts in addition to the machinery for these ships.[709] Industries essential to the war effort were organised in a manner similar to that during World War One. On 10 June 1940 a letter from the Ministry of Supply declared the company a Controlled Undertaking stating that 'powers of competent authority will be exercised by the Admiralty'.[710]

Local administrations were organised under a senior Admiralty appointment (Flag Officer Clyde) to monitor supply of materials and labour.[711] The industry was, in effect, treated as one organisation and, when necessary, contracts, materials and labour were diverted to wherever the effort would be most productive. Absenteeism was closely monitored and figures for each yard were published at regular intervals. Following negotiations with the Clyde Shipbuilders Association and the Confederation of Shipbuilding and Engineering Unions, the weekly number of hours to be worked was fixed at 56. This figure was made up of the normal week of 47 hours plus a minimum of 9 hours to be worked as overtime.[712]

At the outbreak of hostilities, John Brown's was asked by the Admiralty to undertake the conversion of merchant ships to Armed Merchant Cruisers (AMC). Additionally, the yard was designated an Emergency Repair Centre to repair battle damaged ships an activity which was given the highest priority. The presence of the *Queen Elizabeth* and the expected launch of the battleship *Duke of York* in September 1939, meant that the fitting-out basin would be unable to accommodate many other ships. The programme of new construction was already stretching the Clydebank yard to the limits. John Brown asked the Admiralty if it could make use of the basin at Dalmuir assuming it could be secured from Arnott Young who, in any case, were unlikely to be breaking ships in time of war. Arnott Young agreed to make their side of the basin available for the sum of £2,000 for disturbance to their activities

and a £100 weekly charge thereafter.[713] The Anchor Line ship *Cilicia* was the first AMC conversion and was well advanced when war broke out. On 4 September, the Third Sea Lord and Controller of the Navy, Admiral Sir Bruce Fraser, informed the yard by letter that there was little point in launching *Duke of York* on 16 September as planned, because the supply of her main armament would now be up to one year late. The manufacture of these complex mechanisms, a critical bottleneck in the completion of many warships, delayed *Duke of York's* delivery from January to August 1941. With this contract now delayed, management decided not to launch her until *Queen Elizabeth* had left the yard, thereby easing accommodation in the fitting-out basin. However, an important building berth would now be out of commission until *Duke of York* could be launched.

There was great concern that the sheer bulk of Queen Elizabeth *lying at Clydebank would be an unmissable target for German bombers. It was decided that she should be brought to a condition that would enable her to sail to New York and safety as soon as possible.*

A VULNERABLE QUEEN

Undoubtedly the greatest dilemma facing John Brown's was the incomplete liner *Queen Elizabeth*. This ship sat like a giant beacon in the middle of Clydebank, visible for miles around. There was now no hope of her entering service as the jewel of the British merchant marine. During the first weekend of the war, her newly erected fore funnel, resplendent in Cunard red and black, was hastily overpainted in grey.

The possibility of air attack on the shipyard was taken very seriously and the Managing Director, Sir Stephen Pigott, arranged to have *Queen Elizabeth* prepared as an air raid shelter. All 3,500 men on the day shift working on this ship were to be accommodated on the lower decks while an additional 1,000 men employed elsewhere in the yard could also be provided for. To combat fire on board, the following precautions were put in place: several shipyard engineers stood by pumps and sprinkler systems day and night; six firemen patrolled the ship; 39 sprinkler sections were coupled to the water supply; 231 hydrants were available on decks; 224 separate lengths of hose were positioned throughout the hull; 158 chemical extinguishers were placed on decks; 405 buckets of water were distributed from the Sports Deck to shaft tunnels and finally, 40 barrels of water were placed between the Sports Deck to C Deck.[714]

At first it was proposed that work on *Queen Elizabeth* would gradually be brought to a standstill as men transferred to warship work. However, Sir Percy Bates, Cunard Chairman, dismayed at this prospect, wrote to the Chief of Naval Staff, Rear Admiral Burrough, for a decision on the ship's future. Bates wrote to Stephen Pigott on 26 September saying that, as Cunard White Star were being paid at the rate of £30,000 per week for work on the ship, he 'felt on delicate ground continuing to draw all this money from the Treasury in present circumstances'. By the end of September, a total of £3,829,624 had been spent on a ship with no obvious role. On the 29th, both Pigott and Bates were invited to a meeting at the Treasury with the Third Sea Lord and Controller, Admiral Bruce Fraser. A proposal to dismantle her superstructure and convert her into an aircraft carrier was considered. Sketch designs, prepared at Clydebank, showing the converted ship with a capacity of 40 aircraft were produced. Bates noted 'I regret to say that Admiral Fraser evinced very little interest'.[715] Earlier, Rear Admiral Burrough, Chief of Naval Staff, had written to Bates saying that neither

Queen would be needed as aircraft carriers but that *Queen Mary* would probably be used as a fast transport and work on *Queen Elizabeth* stopped.[716] However, it was decided that the ship should be completed and removed from Clydebank as soon as possible. The Clyde Navigation Trust indicated that the dredged channel in the Clyde would not be ready before the end of February 1940, giving a period of five months in which to complete work on the ship. The schedule for completion recognised that all main systems must be operational, that decorative work was not essential and that trials in open water would not be possible. The intention was to sail the ship across the Atlantic to either a port in the USA or to Bedford Basin, Halifax, Nova Scotia, for lay-up[717]. At this time 600 men were working on her machinery, 430 in the shipyard shops and 340 on the ship itself. In preparation for lay-up, the ship was shorn of many of her decorative fittings while others, which had never been fitted, were to wait in a shed at Clydebank until the end of the war. In stark contrast to the pomp and circumstance which attended her smaller sister's debut on the Atlantic four years earlier, *Queen Elizabeth* had an ignominious start to her career. In great secrecy, she left her berth in the fitting-out basin at Clydebank on Monday, 26 February 1940. The process of moving the ship began at 12.32pm, all ropes were cast off at 12.58. By 1.05, the ship was straight in the river. The mean draught on leaving Clydebank was 35' 5/16". The passage down the river was without incident. The bends at Dalmuir and Rashilee were successfully negotiated without touching the mud or the banks as, at each of these bends, the ship was manoeuvred into position for turning by going astern. She was anchored between Ashton and Kilcreggan at 5.20pm. The oil tankers *War Bharata* and *British Lady* came alongside on the 26th about 10pm and 6,012 tons of oil fuel were taken on board.

Men from John Brown's remained on board until Tuesday evening in order to tidy up and make the ship safe. *Queen Elizabeth* was taken over from the builders at 3pm on Tuesday 27 February. Adjustments to the compass were made with difficulty because of restrictions in the manoeuvring area inside the protective boom which had been placed across the Firth of Clyde. The ship's machinery, therefore, had no opportunity of being tried under anything approaching working conditions before the vessel proceeded out to sea. The only occasions in which the machinery had been turned were in static dock trials at Clydebank and during the passage down the

Queen Elizabeth's *makers plate.*

Clyde. Steam was raised on all boilers on 1 March and the vessel left her anchorage at 7.45am the following day, with a mean draught of 37' 9". To limit the extent of any damage caused by enemy action, it was decided that the ship would proceed to sea with each of the four main engines working as separate units, each supplied with steam from three boilers. After passing through the boom at about 8.15am, four

Queen Elizabeth sailed unaccompanied to New York. On 5 March, the machinery was run at about 173 revolutions, which, it was estimated, would produce her designed service speed of 28.5 knots. She arrived at New York on 7 March having steamed a total of 3,118 miles and consuming 3,506 tons of oil fuel.[718] There is no doubt that the effortless performance of this ship in crossing the Atlantic without mishap and

destroyers and a seaplane formed an escort, and thus the largest ship in the world proceeded to the open sea. Over a two-hour period, engine revolutions were increased from 100 (equal to 28,500 shp and 17 knots) to 154 (equal to 96,000 shp and 26 knots). When a speed of 25 knots had been reached and maintained for one hour, the escort was informed that the 'engine trials' were entirely satisfactory and that there was no objection to the escorting vessels discontinuing their services at the time and position previously arranged. At 2 am on the 3rd, her escort turned for home and

without trials reflected credit of the highest order on the engineering staff at Clydebank. Sir Percy Bates said 'that the supreme confidence on the part of the men who built the liner and those who had to run her as to the satisfactory state of her machinery was one of the highest testimonials ever paid to British shipbuilding'[719]

Nevertheless, the fate of the ship and her running mate *Queen Mary*, remained unclear. On 28 February 1940, the First Lord of the Admiralty, Winston Churchill, attended Clydebank for the launch of *Duke*

Painted in wartime grey, Queen Elizabeth *is taken down river to the Firth of Clyde on 26 February 1940 from where, without any trials, she sailed without mishap to New York. This was a remarkable achievement given the complexity and extent of the electrical, mechanical and propulsion systems onboard.*

of York. At this time the possibility of converting *Queen Elizabeth* into an aircraft carrying ship was again discussed with Lord Aberconway and Stephen Pigott. By April, with the vessel safely berthed in New York harbour, three possible uses for her had been identified; a troop-ship, an aircraft carrying ship or as a combined plane and troop carrier. As an aircraft carrying ship, James McNeil, John Brown's

The John Brown Company of the Home Guard under the command of James McNeill assembled on board a ship at Clydebank during 1940.

Queen Elizabeth, King George VI, Winston Churchill and Sir Stephen Pigott make their way to the East Yard to launch the battleship Duke of York *on 28 February 1940.*

naval architect, calculated that she was capable of accommodating 270 aircraft dispersed throughout various decks. Had this option been adopted, work would have been carried out at Halifax under the direction of John Brown's and the ship later dry-docked in Southampton. The final decision was to fit

her out as a troop carrier and *Queen Elizabeth* sailed from New York in November 1940 to Singapore for conversion. Her subsequent war and service careers together with other large ships at Clydebank have been well documented.

The sudden and secret departure of *Queen Elizabeth* from the Clyde in February 1940 gave rise to the story, still prevalent in Clydebank, that several John Brown workers had turned up for work on the ship one morning only to find themselves whisked off to New York leaving irate wives and spoiled dinners behind. Unfortunately, surviving records make it clear that this did not happen. The origin of this story is likely to be found in the conversion of *Queen Elizabeth* to a troopship at New York later in 1940. For this, John Brown loaned Cunard White Star two plumbers, two electricians, two joiners, one shipyard engineer and one sheet ironworker. The men sailed from Southampton to New York on 23 September on the *Scythia* and *Samaria*, signed on as crewmembers.[720] Three of these men later accompanied the ship to Sydney.[721]

In recognition of their efforts in building the two Queens, Stephen Pigott was awarded a knighthood, Donald Skiffington, shipyard manager, a CBE and four foremen the OBE.[722] At the award ceremony in Edinburgh, the Secretary of State for Scotland, John Colville, said

> 'We have had reason to be proud in the past of Scottish shipbuilding, and I believe we will yet have reason to be proud in the future. It must give a thrill of pride to any Scotsman, and especially anyone who is associated with the construction of these great vessels, to know their excellence carries Scottish worth and fame across the world'[723]

James McNeill, the man largely responsible for the detailed design of both Queens, was awarded the honorary degree of LLD at Glasgow University in June 1939.[724] In the following year, his fellow countrymen honoured Sir Stephen Pigott when the American Consul General presented him with a gold medal on behalf of the American Society of Mechanical Engineers.[725]

As the war at sea unfolded, many John Brown ships held in special regard by the nation were sunk. The first major passenger vessel to be lost was the *Empress of Britain* sunk in November 1940. Sir Stephen Pigott sent a message to Sir Edward Beatty, Chairman of Canadian Pacific in Montreal 'from all those who had a part in her building' deploring her loss.[726]

Making repairs to damaged warships was given top

priority by the Admiralty. The private yards took their share of this repair work which invariably created havoc with work on existing contracts. Typical of this was the work carried out on the cruiser *Fiji*. On completion at Clydebank she had entered service in May 1940 only to be damaged in July while serving in the West Indies. The Admiralty ordered her return to the Clyde for repair. Sir Stephen Pigott noted in his report 'we have no choice but to undertake this work although we are not glad to again have this vessel on our hands'[727] *Fiji* arrived on 27 July and left on 2 August. Pigott's irritation was directed at the dislocation to the shipbuilding programme caused by transferring large numbers of men from urgent construction work.[728] Soon after *Fiji* had been despatched to sea for the second time, she was torpedoed in the North Atlantic. The ship managed to limp back to the Clyde for extensive repairs at Govan dry docks. This work lasted between September 1940 and February 1941 when *Fiji* again put to sea. The cruiser was bombed and sunk off Crete on 22 May 1941. At the end of 1940 an order for four tank landing craft (LCT) was received These 370 ton vessels were built over two months in four sections and transported to the Mediterranean in support of General Wavell's North African campaign. John Brown's designed a type of landing craft intended to offer on-shore gunnery support to advancing troops. Designated LCG (M) they mounted two 25pdr or 17pdr field guns. Eight were built at Clydebank.

THE 1941 APPRENTICE STRIKE

In February 1941, apprentices in the shipbuilding and engineering industries on Clydeside went on strike in defiance of legislation which specifically banned strikes in wartime. Within a very short time, 15,000 apprentices had struck throughout the main industrial centres in the UK. The origins of this strike lay in 1937, when a strike was called in support of dissatisfaction over apprenticeships and in particular the very low rate of pay. The settlement to the 1937 dispute resulted in a modest award but did not fully allay feelings of exploitation. The 1941 dispute started at the Glenfield & Kennedy engineering works in Kilmarnock. However, it was a 21 year old Clydebank apprentice fitter from John Brown's, Johnny Moore, who led this highly organised dispute to a successful conclusion. The introduction of dilution had exacerbated apprentice grievances, particularly where a 4th or 5th year apprentice was working alongside a dilutee who might have received a training

programme of just six weeks duration. While the apprentice might be paid 18 shillings per week, the dilutee would be paid journeyman rates of about £4 per week. Moore was the secretary of the Clyde Apprentice Committee, an unofficial organisation which stood outside the Trade Union movement. The Government moved very quickly to contain the strike and within three weeks, a public inquiry was set up

THE CLYDE APPRENTICE № 60
VICTORY BALL
In the GAINSBOROUGH, on Friday, 9th May, 1941
SOUVENIR PROGRAMME - 1D.

APPRENTICES EVERYWHERE, ORGANISE! UNITE!

The 1941 Victory was the greatest in Apprentice History!

Johnny Moore

Let Yourself Go!

A ticket to the Victory Ball in celebration of hard won but improved conditions of employment for apprentices. The strike was lead by Johnny Moore, a John Brown engineering apprentice, whose picture is on the ticket.

in the Central Hotel, Glasgow under Sir John Watson KC, to hear evidence. The first day of the inquiry followed the night bombing of Clydebank during which the Moore family home was destroyed. Nevertheless, Johnny Moore put forward a strong and successful case in support of apprentice demands. As a result, wages were pegged, by a fixed percentage, to those of journeymen. Moore's occupation was 'reserved' i.e. important in the national interest, ensuring that he would not be called up. Employers were obliged to routinely confirm reserved status for employees thus categorised. When Moore returned to work at John Brown's however, his reserved status was allowed to lapse and he automatically received call up papers for the Royal Marines. When this became known to shop stewards in the Clyde area, industrial action was threatened. Moore's call up papers were quickly withdrawn.[729]

THE BOMBING OF CLYDEBANK

As early as October 1939, German reconnaissance aircraft had made a detailed photographic survey of the River Clyde, marking important industrial targets. The first bombs to fall in the Glasgow district were dropped in July 1940 by aircraft operating singly. This pattern continued until the end of the year. There was no doubt that Clydeside, one of the single most important centres for armaments' manufacture in the UK, would be a priority target for a mass attack. In addition to John Brown's, Clydebank had a number of large works dedicated to the war effort including the Royal Ordnance Factory at Dalmuir and Singer's sewing machine factory now

'So far the continuance of work has had virtually no interruption through the effects of air raids. It is, however, fully recognised that much interruption may yet be experienced and, with a view to our having more immediate warning, we have agreed to participate in a system of local control which may possibly be augmented by roof watchers with the object of minimising the

Clydebank ablaze during the night of 13 March 1941. With the exception of a few bombs, the Luftwaffe completely missed the shipyard but severely damaged the town of Clydebank killing 448 people.

working on munitions contracts. Management at Clydebank were well aware of the target the works presented and in November 1940, the following comments were recorded at the Committee of the Board Meeting:

> 'We have pressed the Admiralty and the Home Defence for fuller protection than that now confined to batteries placed throughout Clydeside. We are now told that the Admiralty intends the manning of the lighter guns which will shortly be mounted on ships nearing completion and that the Home Defence will place within our shipyard several batteries of a new type of gun designed especially for use against diving bombers and apparently useful only against day-time air raids.'

length of time which would be spent in shelter and the corresponding stoppage of work.'[730]

On the eve of the Clydebank Blitz, the 'fuller protection' desired by the shipyard management was not in place and it is doubtful whether, even if it had been, the pounding of Clydebank would have been lessened. On the morning of Thursday 13 March 1941, German radio navigation beams were detected intersecting over Clydeside.[731] Shortly after 9pm, the first incendiaries began to fall on Clydebank as air raid sirens broadcast their compelling message to the public. The raid which followed was devastating. Severe damage was inflicted to the Singer works and the Royal Ordnance Factory. John Brown's, perhaps the target most urgently sought by the bombers, received light damage. With one exception, none of the warships in the yard was in a position to open fire on the attacking German aircraft. The exception was the Polish destroyer *Piorun* which had been laid-down at Clydebank as the *Nerissa* and handed over to Polish naval forces on 4 November 1940. *Piorun* had completed trials and made a number of short voyages on convoy protection duties. She arrived back in Clydebank on 2 March for repairs to her oil tanks.

and 00.55 hours from a height of 2800 - 3400m. with 12 SC500 (500 kilo high-explosive bombs), 6,912 B1El (incendiaries). Dropped with visual reference to ground. Bomb positions on target with resultant explosion identified. Direct hits on target Glasgow - Clydebank. Brown shipyard. Intense incendiary effect observed.'[734]

After a respite of sixteen hours, the bombers returned

The aftermath of the Clydebank Blitz, gutted tenements in the 'Holy City' district of the town.

When the German attack developed, *Piorun's* Commanding Officer and many other officers were on shore leave. The young crew that remained on board could not resist the opportunity to engage the enemy and a spirited reply was made using the destroyer's anti-aircraft guns. [732]

Potentially the most damaging of bombs dropped was the land mine which floated down over the fitting-out basin and snagged on a crane. Had the mine detonated it would have severely damaged the battleship *Duke of York*. As it was, a number of small fires broke out on her decks, caused by incendiaries setting alight timber and loose material. It was the town however, that bore the brunt of the attack.

On the first night of the raids, a total of 236 aircraft carrying 272 tons of high explosive and 1,650 incendiaries attacked Clydeside.[733] On their return to base in northern France, German pilots filed action reports. One such report completed by men of the 26 Squadron of the Third Airfleet reads:

'III./KG 26   with 12 Heinkel 111 between 00.20

to continue the carnage. Of 12,000 houses in the town, 4,300 were totally destroyed or were beyond repair. Only eight survived without damage of some sort. 448 people lost their lives. Of a population of over 50,000, about 40,000 had left Clydebank by the evening of the 15th. While the shipyard had brought the town of Clydebank into being, over two nights in March 1941, its presence brought the town to its knees. An internal John Brown report noted the events of 13 and 14 March:

'Thursday 13 March 1941

Sirens sounded at 8pm and the attack commenced at 9.40 and continued until 6.15am. Within four minutes of alarm First Aid Post was manned and Fire Fighters and Home Guard were on duty. During the night large numbers of incendiary bombs were dealt with and damage was done to gate house and National Insurance Office. Both were partially wrecked by high explosive bomb which fell in roadway.

All GPO phones were put out of action and the

Messenger System had to be put into force. A serious fire broke out in the Drying Sheds and all Forces had to be concentrated at the west yard fire. The water pressure was low due to damaged water mains in the town. Water had therefore to be drawn from the Experimental Tank which has been kept filled in case of emergency.
The Shaft Shop, Funnel and Drying Sheds

Sirens sounded at 8.35pm and the attack commenced quickly thereafter. There was a lull about 2am and the 'Raiders' Past' signal sounded at 2.25am. Bombing was continuous during this period. Further alarms sounded at 4.10am followed quickly by the attack which was continuous, and the "Raiders' Past" signal sounded at 5.30am Large numbers of mines and

The fitting-out basin a few months after the bombing of Clydebank. The Luftwaffe missed a veritable fleet of warships including the battleship Duke of York *seen here on the left and the monitor* Roberts *in the foreground. The fleet aircraft carrier* Indefatigable *and the cruiser* Bermuda *and numerous destroyers were also under construction in the yard.*

received direct hits by high explosive bombs and the Brassfinishing Shop suffered severely from blast. The ARP, Fire Fighters, Fire Watchers and Home Guard all rendered valuable work, and the co-operation between these services was excellent. Owing to the fall of water pressure help was given in the west yard by three AFS units - two from Glasgow and one from Falkirk.
Friday 14 March 1941

high explosive bombs were dropped around but not in the Yard.
The forces available on the Friday night were very much reduced owing to the large number who were bombed out of their homes. The Home Guard and nucleus ARP personnel bore the very heavy work well.
Fire broke out in the Drying Sheds and Pattern Store in the west yard and outside AFS assistance

was requested to deal with and subdue this fire. Again the collaboration between the nucleus ARP personnel and Home Guard was excellent, and these services rendered valuable assistance. It is most difficult to select any individuals for particular acts of outstanding work, as all had a very heavy and arduous task to perform.[735]

The first Board meeting at Clydebank following the

Two further air raids caused some damage to the yard. The first, on 7 April, destroyed the mould loft, while in the second, on 7 May, two land mines caused serious damage to the fitting-out basin and damaged the superstructure of the destroyer *Onslow*. In the same raid, four bombs fell on number 2 berth two of which exploded, dislocating timber arranged for receiving the keels of two destroyers. A Royal

With a Royal Marine band playing on her quarterdeck, the battleship Duke of York *leaves Clydebank on 4 September1941.*

bombing, took place on 31 March. The meeting was well attended - Sir Stephen Pigott (Managing Director and Chairman of the meeting), Lord Aberconway (Chairman), Sir Thomas Bell (Consultant), Sir Holberry Mensforth (Director), Sir Gerald Talbot, Mr S Rawson, Hon. Charles McLaren, Captain E Smith, Donald Skiffington (Shipyard Director), Dr. James McNeill (Technical Director), Tom Crowe (Engineering Director), J Bridge and J Beck (Secretary). The minuted reference to the catastrophe which had engulfed the town was brief: £5,434 was voted for the construction of a duplicate air raid shelter in the shipyard for employees and £5,000 was to be paid to the Clydebank Air Raid Distress Fund. The main item of business was the order for the battleship *Vanguard* together with four destroyers.

Engineer was killed when one of the two bombs he was attempting to defuse went off.[736]

In the immediate aftermath of the March 1941 blitz on Clydeside, Vice Admiral Troup, Flag Officer Clyde, issued the first of a series of Shipyard Letters which advised yard management on current regulations and measures to be taken in the interests of the war effort. The 'measures' reflected the continuing vulnerability of industrial targets in the face of sustained attacks. The first such letter, issued on 18 March 1941, asked shipyards to provide details of completion dates of HM ships, which may have been delayed following damage to their works. The second letter urged yards to generate as much smoke through industrial processes as they could on moonlit nights to obscure the view from the air.[737] To protect shipyards from

223

possible attack from the river, the Clyde River Patrol was formed and regular patrols maintained. As a measure against aerial mines, shipyard management were told to ensure that the water adjacent to building berths was swept prior to launchings.[738] The Luftwaffe never appeared again over Clydebank in any numbers. However, there was to be one further tragic consequence of the Clydebank Blitz. On 15

twenty years earlier, had brought these great ships into existence. Following the loss of *Hood*, Sir Stephen Pigott recorded the following in his report to the Board:

'The loss of this great Clydebank-built ship has caused genuine depression and regrets with all at Clydebank, and through the medium of the shop stewards we are endeavouring to exhort the

The keel of Vanguard *was laid down on 2 October 1941. Initially it was hoped that she could be completed by 1944. On the left is part of the stern casting which will hold the ship's rudder.*

September, a mine exploded in Dalmuir basin destroying a tug which was assisting the departure of *Athene*. All hands bar one were lost. Six John Brown riggers standing on the jetty were also killed and four others seriously injured.[739]

1941 was a hard year for John Brown's and Clydebank. To the devastation inflicted from the air was the added sadness when three John Brown built capital ships were sunk with heavy loss of life. The first was *Hood*, lost in engagement with *Bismarck* in May, then *Barham* torpedoed in the Mediterranean in November and lastly, *Repulse*, sunk by the Japanese off Malaya in December. The sinking of *Hood*, regarded by many as the very embodiment of British naval might, ranked as a national disaster. Who can guess at the feelings experienced by men who, over

workers to give expression of their feeling by increased effort on the work in progress, and more especially to the earliest possible completion of HMS Duke of York. A letter expressing sympathy and regret at the loss of HMS Hood has been sent to the Controller of the Navy.[740]

The sense of loss was offset in small degree when it became known that the destroyer *Piorun*, launched in the yard a year earlier, was the first ship to sight and engage the *Bismarck* on the evening of 26 May.

NEW CAPITAL SHIPS

Of the five capital ships under contract at Clydebank during the war, only *Duke of York, Indefatigable*. and *Vanguard* were built. Admiralty indecision over design combined with insufficient capacity to manufacture ordnance and an acute shortage of skilled labour caused the cancellation of the Lion Class battleship (*Conqueror*) and the Malta Class fleet aircraft carrier (*Malta*). Nevertheless, these contracts occupied time and played an active part in scheduling work through the yard.

The day after war was declared, the Admiralty suspended all four Lion Class battleships in favour of more urgently required ships. *Duke of York* had been subject to delays because of the failure by Vickers Armstrong to supply her main armament on time. As a result, her launch was postponed until *Queen Elizabeth* was out of the yard thereby easing congestion in the fitting-out basin. On 28 February 1940, two days after *Queen Elizabeth's* departure, *Duke of York* was launched by Her Majesty Queen Elizabeth with King George VI and Winston Churchill in attendance. To enable *Conqueror* to be laid down on the same berth in January 1941, this berth, the second largest, would be out of commission for a year. However, the Assistant Director of Naval Construction, Sir Stanley Goodall, proposed that the monitor Roberts be allocated to this berth as she could easily be built within the time available.[741]

While the Lion Class ships awaited their fate during the summer of 1939, another battleship began to assume form. The First Lord of the Admiralty, Winston Churchill, accelerated plans to build this ship utilising the main armament from the World War One battlecruisers *Courageous* and *Glorious*. In February 1940, the Admiralty notified John Brown that they 'may be asked to accept in lieu [of *Conqueror*] a vessel of approximately equal size for taking existing 15" armament reconditioned'[742] The ship to which this notice referred was *Vanguard*. Although *Vanguard* was not intended as the last battleship to be built for the Royal Navy, indecision over the four ships of the Lion Class and their subsequent cancellation gave *Vanguard*, by default, the distinction of being the last of her type to be built in Britain. From a peculiarly Clydeside point of view, this was appropriate since one of the first two British ironclad battleships, *Black Prince*, sister ship of the preserved *Warrior*, was built on the Clyde by Robert Napier in 1860. While the Admiralty deliberated over *Vanguard's* details, calculations and preliminary work were carried out at Clydebank throughout much of 1940. In a private letter dated 26 October 1940, Goodall indicated to Pigott that *Vanguard* would definitely proceed.[743] To expedite the design, 6 Clydebank draughtsmen were sent to Bath to work

alongside Admiralty constructors.[744]

Shortages of labour, which had been experienced by John Brown's also, caused great difficulty and embarrassment to another Clyde shipbuilder. With fewer workers than John Brown, the Fairfield Shipbuilding & Engineering Co. at Govan, had contracted for as much work as the Clydebank yard and had taken on a similar amount of emergency

Vice-Admiral Lord Louis Mountbatten accompanies his mother the Dowager Marchioness of Milford Haven (out of shot) who will shortly launch the aircraft carrier Indefatigable.

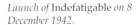

Launch of Indefatigable *on 8 December 1942.*

repair work. By January 1941, the Admiralty had become alarmed at the slow progress of contracts at Fairfield where the battleship *Howe*, sister ship of *Duke of York*, and the aircraft carrier *Implacable*, sister ship of *Indefatigable*, were under construction. The Director of Navy Contracts, Mr Hanniford, wanted *Howe* to be transferred to John Brown for completion, as Fairfield could not do so before mid-summer 1942. Fairfield management naturally resisted this move because of the loss of prestige that would result. John Brown was similarly reluctant because of the dislocation this would have on their construction programme. Labour shortages lay at the heart of the problem. However, Clydebank management agreed to assist their Clydeside competitors and two

during the depressed years of the 1920s and 30s. Depending on their trade, these men were liable to be directed to the nearest shipyard under the terms of the Order.[746] By April 1942, 5,147 were employed in Clydebank shipyard (excluding engine works) of which 143 were women[747]. Of these women, 43 were employed as polishers and the rest were classified in other trade categories including labourers.[748]

A group of women dilutee electricians pose for a 'snap' in 1943. (courtesy of Isobel Downie)

Harry Lauder entertaining shipyard workers at a launch during the war.

destroyers were transferred from Fairfield to Clydebank. In compensation, John Brown pressed the Admiralty to authorise construction of *Vanguard*, as it looked probable that none of the new 16" gunned battleships would be built. *Vanguard* was ordered on 14 March 1941 and Fairfield kept *Howe*.[745]

LABOUR SHORTAGES AND ADMIRALTY PRIORITIES

The shortage of skilled workers proved to be one of the greatest impediments to production. In 1941, the Ministry of Labour, under the Essential Work Order, compelled all men aged twenty or over who had been employed in a shipyard during the last fifteen years to register. This revealed the great potential of those who had left or been forced out of the industry

Progress on construction of the battleship *Vanguard* was a symptom of two effects: Admiralty vacillation and lack of manpower. In an impossible situation, John Brown was criticised for lack of progress by the Admiralty and yet, at the same time, denied the men to work on her by the same authority. At a meeting on 30 December 1941, following the loss of *Prince of Wales* and *Repulse* in the Far East, the Controller asked for *Vanguard* to be completed urgently, although the ship was not given the highest priority. To put more workers on *Vanguard* and *Indefatigable*, the cruiser *Bellerophon* was suspended and the sloops *Snipe* and *Sparrow* were transferred to Devonport Dockyard.[749] Progress on the Port Line ship, which had been laid down in November 1941, was decelerated. In March 1942, Sir Stephen Pigott advised the Admiralty that even given Priority A1, completing *Vanguard* by September 1944 would be a 'notable achievement'. At that time, *Indefatigable* was fully manned and *Vanguard* manned as fully as material available allowed. The only outcome of pressing the Admiralty for additional labour was the voluntary transfer of one squad of platers from Stephen's shipyard further up the River Clyde. Pigott had no alternative but to tell the Admiralty that *Vanguard* would not be completed in 1944.[750] In a letter of 4 April, 1942, the Admiralty nevertheless complained about lack of progress on the ship. When Admiral Lord Chatfield made further criticisms of the battleship building programme, Pigott met with the Controller, Admiral Bruce Fraser, on 23 April 1942. At this meeting it emerged that *Vanguard* was intended to have priority only over the Lion Class battleships and that it was still the Admiralty's view that *Indefatigable* was more important than *Vanguard*. Pigott was told that Admiralty priorities for Clydebank in 1942 were in the following order of importance: repairs to naval ships already in service; destroyers to fullest capacity of number 7 and 8 berths; the light cruiser *Bermuda*, then *Indefatigable* and lastly *Vanguard*.[751] The pressure to complete emergency repairs to ships damaged in service and warship contracts made it difficult for work on the refrigerated cargo ship for the Port Line to be maintained. Despite the circumstances of the day, the Port Line took an uncompromising view[752] and in June 1942 moved to hold John Brown responsible for delays in completing their ship.[753] In the following month, the Ministry of War Transport resolved the situation by acquiring this ship, then known only by its yard number 577, for 'Admiralty Special Service'. This meant conversion into an Escort Carrier for trade protection duties.[754] Plans to convert the vessel, which was not very

advanced on the building slip, were prepared and she was later given the name *Nairana*.[755] The manpower required for this would further delay completion of *Vanguard* until June 1945. Pigott met with District Shipyard Controller, Vice Admiral Troup, on 2 July 1942 to discuss the implications. Troup claimed that the Admiralty was hopeful of getting 2,000 skilled men, who had been out of the industry for some time,

Princess Elizabeth receiving instruction from Sir Stephen Pigott on how to launch the battleship Vanguard *in 1944.*

to return and that *Vanguard* should benefit from this.[756] At a further meeting at St Enoch's Hotel, Glasgow, on 9 July 1942, Pigott submitted that representation should be made to Mr Bevin, Minister of Labour, for the complete interchange of labour within and between all establishments as the most meaningful way in which production could be accelerated.[757] At the John Brown ordinary general meeting in July, the Chairman, Lord Aberconway, summed the situation up: '. . . it would appear that manpower is now the measure of output.'[758]

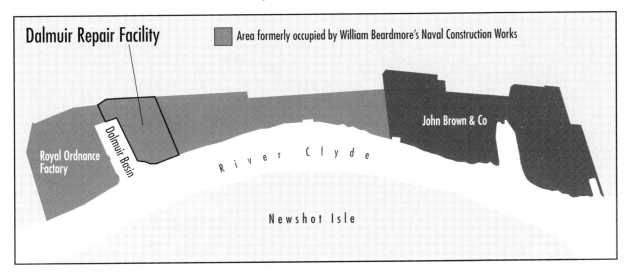

Dalmuir Repair Facility

Area formerly occupied by William Beardmore's Naval Construction Works

Royal Ordnance Factory

Dalmuir Basin

R i v e r   C l y d e

John Brown & Co

Newshot Isle

Part of William Beardmore's redundant shipyard at Dalmuir was managed by John Brown as an emergency repair yard.

Nevertheless, in December 1942, the best that could be provided for *Vanguard* was an additional 500 ironworkers although a further 500 were still needed. The deficiency of aircraft carriers in the fleet following war losses ensured that *Indefatigable*, required for the eastern theatre of operations, and *Nairana*, destined for Arctic service, were subject to special efforts to ensure the earliest completion.

the Admiralty transferred men to *Indefatigable* and *Nairana*.[760]

Percentage of total John Brown labour force applied to various contracts in 1942/43

	1942	1943
Destroyers	34	20
Nairana	2	13
Indefatigable	25	24
Repairs	23	30
Bermuda	10	-
Loch Fada and Bellerophon	-	1
Vanguard	6	12
Total	**100**	**100**[761]

The four twin 15-inch turrets for Vanguard *undergoing modification at Harland & Wolff's Scotstoun works in 1945, formerly the Coventry Ordnance Works. These turrets had been landed from the large cruisers* Courageous *and* Glorious *during the 1920s and put in store. The turrets were fitted with thicker armour and modernised including increased elevation of the guns from 20° to 30° to provide greater range.*

Indefatigable was launched on 8 December 1942, three weeks ahead of schedule, by the Dowager Marchioness of Milford Haven accompanied by her son Vice-Admiral Lord Louis Mountbatten. The latter, on leave from active service, agreed to address the workers:

> 'He told, in a marvellously graphic and moving way, how he had been in command of HMS Javelin, a Clydebank built destroyer, in the Channel one dirty night and had been hit simultaneously by two torpedoes; one had blown off the bows immediately in front of the bridge, while the other had blown off the stern. Thanks to the workmanship, the quarter inch plate had held, and with air cover and sea escort she was towed back to harbour the next day, and, with her valuable engines intact, had a new bow and stern put on.'[759]

The troubled history of *Vanguard's* construction continued into 1943 when, in August and September,

THE DALMUIR SCHEME

As in the First World War, one of the greatest challenges of the war at sea was the protection of merchant shipping from U-boat attack, particularly on the North Atlantic. Building destroyers and escort ships, the vessels most needed in this struggle, became first priority. Again, the difficulty was how best to achieve this aim without crippling other shipbuilding programmes. Even with John Brown's working at full capacity, only four destroyers were laid down throughout 1942[762] followed by six in 1943. One solution was to build these vessels elsewhere. Thus, the Admiralty had large numbers of convoy escort vessels built in Canada and Australia. However, John Brown's was earmarked to become closely involved with plans which the Admiralty drew up in 1942. These plans involved the mass production of around 90 anti-submarine frigates of the Loch Class, the design of which was intentionally unsophisticated to permit prefabricated construction in British shipyards more usually associated with merchant tonnage. Details of the prototype prefabricated frigate *Loch Fada* were entrusted to Clydebank and the ship laid down on 8 June 1943 and launched on 14 December. The scheme for mass production envisaged hulls constructed by merchant yards being sent to two separate fitting-out facilities where squads of finishing trades could be concentrated on their completion. One facility was developed at the Hendon Dock, Sunderland, on the river Wear and the other at Dalmuir on the Clyde under the management of John Brown. It was anticipated that more than 1,500 persons, a very optimistic figure given labour shortages, would be employed at Dalmuir once the frigate programme was fully under way. Dalmuir's attractiveness lay in a fitting-out basin and cranage which had been completed in 1906 as part of William Beardmore's large Naval Construction Works. The Dalmuir basin had been used by John Brown since the beginning of the war for merchant ship conversions and repair work. In November 1942, the Admiralty first raised the issue of completing 60 corvettes at Dalmuir with John Brown.[763] On 9 February 1943, it requested that John Brown operate Dalmuir on commercial lines with

adjacent shops had been destroyed during the bombing of March 1941. To rectify this and provide new machinery it was estimated that expenditure of £403,000 was necessary.[764] In the summer of 1943, the Admiralty advanced £100,000 to get the scheme under way.[765] Before Dalmuir could be brought on line as a corvette fitting-out facility, however, the Loch Class frigate programme was drastically

new plant and facilities to be financed by an Admiralty advance. However, the Clydebank Board was not interested in this form of operation and it was agreed that Dalmuir be operated on Admiralty account with John Brown providing management expertise for a fee of £10,000 per annum. However, the existing facility at Dalmuir was in poor condition. The wharfage required a great deal of repair work to stop it falling into the river while many of the

curtailed with 50 out of 60 corvettes cancelled. The reason was the successful outcome of the Battle of the Atlantic in the summer of 1943 in which the U-boat offensive had been checked. Nevertheless, Dalmuir was used extensively as an overflow for Clydebank and other shipyards. Manpower never approached anything like the projected figure and it seems more likely that between two and three hundred men were employed there.

Men leaving Vanguard *at the end of a shift in the summer of 1945. The completion of the battleship was the subject of much debate and not a little acrimony between shipbuilder and Admiralty although the latter consistently placed her at the bottom of yard priorities. In March 1944* Vanguard *was given A1 priority but by then there was no chance of completing her until 1946.*

MALTA

With the war building programme at Clydebank under way and Dalmuir being brought into operation, John Brown was selected to be the lead yard for the construction of the very large Malta Class fleet aircraft carriers. The contract for *Malta* was placed on 15 July 1943, although design details of the ship were and would remain vague. First indications suggested a ship driven by five shafts generating 190,000 shp in a hull 950 feet in length - only 70 feet shorter than *Queen Mary*. Such was the nature of placing contracts in wartime, that it was not until the following September that John Brown performed the curious task of tendering for a ship it already had on its books.[766] As design work at Bath was slow, five draughtsmen were sent from Clydebank to speed up the process. When it looked as if only one of the three projected carriers would be built, the Board took 'such action as is possible to encourage that *Malta* is selected'.[767] Meanwhile the shipyard was advised that a great deal of welding would be incorporated into her construction and that building drawings were expected from Bath during the middle of April 1944. Provisional contracts were drawn up with William Beardmore & Co. Parkhead, for the main hull castings.[768] However, in reality, the Admiralty was far from making a decision. 'We are told in great confidence that the actual building of this ship is yet a matter of difference of opinion between Cabinet, Board of Admiralty and the First Sea Lord'[769] By June, the project was undergoing a major redesign, further delaying any possibility of work beginning.[770] To provide continuity of employment in the engine works and to ensure sufficient men in place to build *Malta's* machinery, the yard applied for licences to build merchant ships in June 1944. By September John Brown had eight draughtsmen seconded to Bath assisting with Malta while Assistant Controller, Sir Stanley Goodall, assured Stephen Pigott that *Malta* would not be stopped but would proceed slowly.[771] With the end of hostilities in Europe in sight, the Admiralty issued instructions to builders that only ships capable of completion by June 1946 should proceed. However, at first *Malta* was an exception. As late as June 1945, James McNeill, John Brown's naval architect, visited Bath to discuss details of *Malta* and it was not until 21 December 1945 that the contract was cancelled.[772] Curiously, two small hull sections based on the aircraft carrier design were built. These sections were constructed at the bottom of the new building berth which had been prepared for the carrier. Referred to as target vessels, they were launched in June 1945 and taken to Loch Striven for target practice.[773]

In March 1944, construction of *Vanguard* was finally given Priority A1, if only because other more important vessels had been completed. With planning for the British Pacific Fleet in progress, of which *Vanguard* would be a part, much work was required to 'tropicalise' the battleship and completion was now projected to December 1945.[774] To ensure that sufficient numbers of the finishing trades were retained at Clydebank to work on the battleship after launching in November, John Brown entered into negotiation with Harland & Wolff to complete four frigates which they had launched.[775] In the event, two arrived from Belfast (*Loch Gorm* and *Loch Craggie*) and one from Barclay Curle (*Loch Alvie*). After an agonisingly long time on the building slip, Princess Elizabeth finally launched the battleship *Vanguard* on 30 November 1944.

With the end of the European war in sight, the emphasis of war production began to change. In October 1944, Stephen Pigott met with the Director of Naval Construction, Sir Stanley Goodall to discuss the completion of Admiralty contracts. It was agreed there would be no slowing down of naval contracts for ships that could be completed by June 1946. For ships likely to be completed after that date and for new ships of the 1944 building programme, progress would be dependent on the availability of tradesmen. In October, preparations for the resumption of merchant shipbuilding were made. John Brown applied to the Admiralty for licenses to construct ships for the New Zealand, Port and Cunard White Star lines. By November, two orders had been booked, one for the refrigerated cargo ship *Port Wellington* at an estimated cost of £785,000 including establishment charges and a profit of £140,000, and the other for the small Cunard passenger cargo ship, *Media* at an estimated price of £865,000, including charges and profit of £150,000.[776] At the beginning of 1945, transport ferries to be used in the planned invasion of Japan, were given highest priority.[777] Eight of these vessels, which had been launched elsewhere, were sent to the Dalmuir and Clydebank yards for completion. These contracts were, in effect, the last to be urgently required under the war programme.

In April, the Company was in negotiation with the New Zealand Shipping Co., Port Line, LNE Railway and Cunard for new tonnage. Mindful of the slump that rapidly overtook the boom which followed the end of the First World War, the first steps towards diversifying output from the engine shops were taken with the submission of a tender to the Hydro Electric Board for water turbines for Clunie Power Station. Elaborating on this theme, Lord Aberconway said that in addition to water turbines, the Company would also pursue contracts for gas turbines and machinery for heavy presses.[778]

On 8 May 1945 at 3pm, the Prime Minister, Winston Churchill, announced the end of the war in Europe. In Clydebank, bunting and flags of the Allies adorned the Municipal Buildings which also sported an illuminated sign reading 'V DAY'. The local newspaper reported:

> 'It was only after dark however, that celebrations seemed to get under way properly. Groups of people paraded the streets arm-in-arm singing lustily, mostly songs of last war vintage. The interiors of brilliantly lit houses could be seen, and with windows open, the radios, gramophones, piano accordions and even bagpipes mingled with the singing from the streets . . . Perhaps the biggest feature of the night were the countless bonfires which sprang up in almost every street. The glare in the sky reminded one of the less happier times during the raids of 1941. '[779]

At the ordinary general meeting of John Brown & Co. Ltd in London in July 1945, Lord Aberconway, Chairman, summarised the wartime output of the Clydebank Works.

Ships launched or completed at Clydebank during the war totalled 58 with an approximate displacement of one third of a million tons. The machinery for these ships totalled 2 million horsepower. 116 warships were modified or repaired, and 11 merchant ships converted for war service. Additionally, 38 sets of machinery totalling 170,000 hp were built for ships constructed elsewhere while a further 10 sets of machinery for other shipyards totalling 130,000 hp were under construction in August 1945. A large volume of miscellaneous engineering work including boilers and twin barrelled anti-aircraft guns were also produced.[780]

Looking to the future, Lord Aberconway said

> ' . . . while the future of the shipbuilding industry may be influenced by the large amount of existing tonnage resulting from wartime activity, we are confident that there is and will continue to be a large demand for the types of ship upon which we specialise at Clydebank.'

On the 14 August, the Second World War came to an end with the acceptance of Japanese surrender. This time the task of informing the nation fell on the newly elected Labour Prime Minister, Clement Attlee. In contrast to VE Day, the mood in Clydebank on VJ Day was described as one ' . . . of relief, but this time, with the dark shadow of war completely gone, a general happiness was apparent in the populace of the worst hit burgh in Scotland.'[781]

Throughout the war years, John Brown maintained high levels of profitability peaking in 1941 with a

Work proceeding in November 1945 at a less urgent pace to complete Vanguard, *a destroyer and the cruiser* Tiger

trading profit of £996,727. This figure reflected the final profit on *Queen Elizabeth* which, unlike the modest profit of £157,413 made on her smaller sister, recorded £276,574 representing a profit of 5.6% on cost. By comparison, the cruiser *Southampton* made a profit of £160,252 which represented a 17% profit on cost.[782] The combined trading profit for the years 1939 to 1945 was £3,442,875.[783] There was a distinction between commercial and Admiralty contracts which made the latter so attractive. Commercial contracts were based on the tender price calculated by the firm. This price was made up of the cost of labour, material and overheads (establishment charges). To this, a profit was added. In prudent

A view of Dalmuir basin shortly after the war. The Admiralty retained the use of the west wharf and the large 150 ton crane where the cruiser Tiger *has been moored. The east wharf, which had been rebuilt for the frigate programme during 1943/44, has now returned to Arnott Young & Co., shipbreakers, where the Fairfield built diesel driven passenger cargo liner* Aorangi *is about to be demolished.*

fashion, escalator clauses to protect the builder from unforeseen inflationary rises in the cost would normally be incorporated in the contract. As ever, Admiralty contracts were highly profitable principally because they were awarded on a cost plus basis. Although initially determined by tender, they were settled on the basis of what the ship actually cost to build plus a fixed profit of say 10%. Full charges and profit were thereby guaranteed irrespective of whatever fluctuations might adversely affect the cost.

SHIPYARD DEVELOPMENTS 1939/45

At the start of the Second World War, the volume of orders awarded to the yard placed the fitting-out basin and its facilities under severe strain. Although this basin could accommodate many smaller vessels, it could accommodate only two large vessels at one time. By the end of 1939, three capital ships were on order - two battleships, *Duke of York* and *Conqueror*, and a large fleet carrier, *Indefatigable*. In addition to

Queen Elizabeth and orders for cruisers, destroyers and the prospect of yet another fleet carrier, the fitting-out basin was inadequate. Late in 1939, a plan was revised to create a riverside fitting-out wharf at the west end of the yard. It was proposed that the 150 ton derrick crane on the east wharf of the fitting-out basin be moved to serve this new quay.[784] This crane would be replaced by a new 250 ton giant cantilever crane which would have been necessary to handle the turntables for the triple 16" turrets of the Lion class battleship *Conqueror*. In the event, the order for *Conqueror* was cancelled and the riverside development did not take place. Nevertheless, the promise of this battleship contract motivated the management to uprate the existing 150 ton cantilever crane on the west wharf, built by Sir William Arrol in 1907, from 150 to 200 tons capacity in 1938 at a cost of £10,000.[785]

In September 1942, the Machine Tool Controller made a study of shipyards on the Clyde to determine what additional plant they required to ensure efficient production. At John Brown's, the figure of £125,000 was considered necessary for the purchase of cranes, shipyard and engineering machinery.[786] While minor extensions to both west and east yards had taken place during the inter-war period, no major investment had occurred since the west yard scheme of 1919. As was the case in 1914/18, the war provided the impetus for major capital renewal schemes to be partly financed by the Admiralty. As early as February 1943, the issue of modernising the shipyard to take advantage of post-war shipbuilding was under discussion at monthly Board meetings. In July 1943, Stephen Pigott told the Board that a committee of shipbuilders and ship owners had been formed to consider the future. At the same time, the Board recommended an investigation into his view that the engine works should consider moving into the market for land boilers, pulverising fuel plant and mechanical stokers.[787]

Of principal concern was the condition of the east yard. With the exception of number one berth, its remaining four berths were equipped with five ton derrick cranes. These derricks were first installed in 1905/6 for the construction of *Lusitania*. Many more were added for *Aquitania* in 1911. Number one berth had been equipped with three fixed tower cranes of 10 tons capacity purchased from the redundant Dumbarton yard of Archibald McMillan in 1932. Thus, the majority of ships built in the east yard, including the two *Queens*, *Duke of York* (1940) and *Vanguard* (1944), were constructed using the same facilities that had built *Lusitania* and *Inflexible* during the first years of the century.

Welded prefabrication and the need to provide the heavier berth lifts, provided the impetus for change. In February 1942, the Board discussed the impact which welding and prefabrication was making on US and Canadian shipbuilding programmes. Pigott noted that 'Shipbuilders in this country must give serious consideration to this post-war' although he thought that 'British shipbuilders [would be] less likely to introduce welding on the US scale although prefabrication will obtain to a greater degree post-war'.[788]

The order for the aircraft carrier *Malta*, which would incorporate more welding than hitherto, highlighted the inadequacies of the east yard. The five ton limit would have seriously reduced the amount of prefabrication able to be undertaken. Application was made to the Admiralty for reconstruction of the yard with seven tower cranes each capable of lifting twenty tons. The estimated cost of reconstruction was put between £200,000 and £300,000 for which the Admiralty would contribute 60% of the cost. The breadth of *Malta* required the realignment of the one thousand foot long number four berth as, at 135 feet wide at flight deck level, *Malta* would overhang number 3 berth on which *Vanguard* was building. In September 1942, Pigott wrote to the Admiralty asking their permission to realign this berth prior to laying down the carrier. This was duly granted and the Admiralty agreed to pay 50% of the final cost of £86,000. This work was not completed until after the war.[789] The installation of the new east yard cranes started in 1945 and was completed in the following year.

In the summer of 1946, the battleship Vanguard, *the cruiser* Tiger *and the passenger cargo ship* Port Wellington *occupy the fitting-out basin. Work on* Tiger *will shortly come to halt and not restart until almost ten years later and then to an entirely new design.*

The re-equipping of the East Yard with new 20-ton tower cranes can be seen on the left where Media *for Cunard White Star is well advanced on the left.*

1946 - 1972   POST WAR BOOM AND BUST

Rebuilding war-depleted merchant fleets augured well for John Brown's and British shipbuilding generally although the short-lived boom following the First World War urged caution. The UK remained the world's first shipbuilding nation, a position consistently held since the advent of the steamship over 100 years earlier. Moreover, important foreign competition had been reduced to scrap, if not eliminated. In August 1945, a report was prepared by the Shipbuilding Committee for the Minister of War Transport and the First Lord of the Admiralty, assessing the prospects for the industry over the next ten years.[790] The report concluded that the British mercantile marine should be restored to at least the pre-war figure of 18 million gross tons from the present 14 million, excluding 3 million tons of Lend-Lease and Mutual Aid vessels. In the ten year period

in prospect, 10 million tons of new shipping was expected to be placed with UK shipbuilders, peaking in 1949/50. Employment in the industry was expected to drop from the 1945 figure of 163,000 to 90,000 after 1950.[791] Of the 50,000 men employed on warship construction in 1945, 20,000 were envisaged for this sector one year hence. The output figures quoted in the report were conservative in what would prove to be a long, profitable but deceptive boom.

John Brown's emerged from the war with a large order book comprising ships left over from the war programme, new merchant vessels and contracts to recondition *Queen Mary* and *Queen Elizabeth*. The yard was about to enter the post-war era with a flying start.

Refurbishing the Queens had been contemplated as

A picture which says it all for John Brown & Co. En route to her trials, Britain's largest and last battleship Vanguard, *passes by the largest ship in the world,* Queen Elizabeth, *which is being refitted and painted off Gourock in the summer of 1946.*

early as June 1942, when Sir Percy Bates indicated to Sir Stephen Pigott that Cunard White Star wanted absolute priority given to the refitting of *Queen Elizabeth* for commercial service after the war. Pigott was only too pleased to give this assurance.[792] On 8 July 1944, Pigott met with Cunard White Star's new Chairman, Sir Thomas Brocklebank on board *Queen Mary*, on the Firth of Clyde at the end of one of her trooping runs. The subjects under discussion were he conversion of *Queen Mary* to commercial service after the war and Cunard's post war shipbuilding requirements. At this meeting, the possibility of building a 10,000ton cargo passenger ship after the war was discussed.[793] In January 1945, Cunard asked John Brown's what the approximate cost of a vessel similar to *Mauretania* would be. To assist Cunard in developing plans for this ship which would become *Caronia*, two draughtsmen were seconded in June 1945. The relationship existing between the two companies could not have been more amicable. Tenders were considered unnecessary and prices were approximate. Brocklebank told Pigott 'if your detailed estimate does not exceed our earlier rough estimate, the ship is yours'. The price submitted for Caronia was £3,425,000 which included full establishment charges and profit of £475,000. A

margin of £250,000 was agreed to cover increases in labour and materials.[794] This contract would later prove to be financially disastrous. With *Queen Elizabeth* about to be released from Government service at the end of 1945, senior John Brown men were invited to join the ship on a round trip to New York to assess the work needed to be done in bringing the ship back to her planned original condition.[795] In September 1945, a contract for another of Clydebank's specialisms was taken, when the British Transport Commission placed an order for the ferry *Arnhem*, at a price of £632,000.[796] With the war over, work on *Vanguard* could be undertaken without undue pressure. Completing the battleship was not without incident. In September 1945, three engine fitters were killed and eight others injured in a violent explosion which occurred in a compartment deep within the ship. At the public enquiry, the cause of the explosion was attributed to methane gas from decomposing organic matter at the bottom of the fitting-out basin seeping into the ship through sea valves, which, although watertight, were not gas tight.[797]

The reconditioning of *Queen Elizabeth* was estimated at £1,300,000 of which £210,000 was for charges and profit. In March 1946, *Queen Elizabeth* arrived in the

Vanguard, last of an illustrious line of British battleships, steams at full speed on the Arran measured mile in July 1946. At a deep displacement of 51,070 tons, the ship developed 132,950 shp for a speed of 30.37 knots.

Firth of Clyde to have her machinery overhauled and complete the fitting-out that had been postponed in 1940. During her wartime career, the ship had sailed 500,000 miles and transported more than 750,000 men to and from battlefields all over the world.[798] As there was no room for her in the basin at Clydebank, and as the state of the River Clyde would not have permitted the passage upriver, the liner spent three

approached the designated area at full power to commence her run, there was no sign of the white poles, much to the consternation of those on the bridge. Investigation revealed that a Polish army camp had been stationed nearby until recently. When the camp was dismantled, the white sighting poles had been cut down as they were assumed to be part of the camp.[800] On replacing the poles, *Vanguard*

The 34,000 ton Caronia, *sailing down the Clyde in December 1948, represented a return to the liner market on which the Company pinned much of its future, particularly in the likely absence of warship work.*

months moored at the 'Tail of the Bank' while men from Clydebank travelled daily to work on her. In the summer of 1946, the newly completed *Vanguard* slipped quietly past *Queen Elizabeth* to undergo acceptance trials on the Firth of Clyde. This meeting of the world's largest ship and the largest British battleship was eloquent testimony to achievement at Clydebank.

In the normal course of events, *Vanguard's* trials programme would have included a number of full power runs on the measured mile off Arran on the Firth of Clyde to determine speed and fuel consumption. The measured mile[799] was delineated by sets of white sighting poles arranged on high ground exactly one mile apart. When *Vanguard*

made 30.37 knots developing 132,950 shp on full power trials in July 1946. Her displacement was 51,070 tons.

In mid-June, having completed her overhaul, *Queen Elizabeth* moved to Southampton for refurbishment of her accommodation. At the peak of this contract, 1,000 Clydebank men of the finishing trades went south to work on the ship.[801] They were accommodated at Velmore Camp, a former American military base outside Southampton. Higher bonus rates paid to Southampton workers carrying out the same tasks as Clydebank workers caused the latter to hold a one hour token strike in July.[802] On 7 October, *Queen Elizabeth* returned to the Clyde. Over the next few days, with the Queen and Princess Elizabeth on board, the liner undertook highly successful trials. Returning to Southampton on 9 October, *Queen Elizabeth* became the British ship to inaugurate the post-war trans-Atlantic passenger service, leaving for New York on the 16th.[803] *Queen Mary* continued repatriating American servicemen and was not taken out of service for refurbishment until September 1946. Although the possibility of carrying out this work at Faslane was discussed, work began at Southampton providing further work for the Clydebank men still based there. *Queen Mary* entered service with Cunard in August of that year.

The last ship to be refitted by John Brown at Dalmuir under the terms of the management agreement negotiated with the Admiralty was the submarine depot ship *Maidstone* which arrived in January 1946. Thereafter, the repair facilities which had been created at Dalmuir were surplus to John Brown's needs and termination of the management agreement took effect on 30 June 1946. Dalmuir basin was used to berth several cancelled destroyer hulls including *Talavera* and *Trincomalee* prior to their scrapping.[804] After completion of *Barrosa* and *Matapan* in 1947, the last ships of the war programme, only two warship contracts remained, the destroyer *Daring* and the cruiser *Tiger*. Both would suffer prolonged delays as the Admiralty vacillated over their design. *Tiger* was moved to Dalmuir basin in December 1946 where work continued on her slowly until March 1948. After the tremendous flood of naval work over the war years, it would not be until 1953 that another warship, ordered post-war, would be laid-down at Clydebank. In December, the New Zealand Shipping Co., asked John Brown's to reserve one building berth for them immediately and two others during the first half of 1947.

In January 1947, the Essential Work Order which had been implemented in 1941, was withdrawn, restoring choice in employment to thousands of shipyard workers. The severe winter of 1947 was one of the worst on record and imposed demands on power supply which greatly affected national life. The unprecedently cold weather in January, February and March forced stoppages and caused delays throughout the manufacturing and service industries. Power cuts and shortages of steel brought additional delays. While work at Clydebank never came to a standstill, progress on contracts was severely dislocated. No fewer than nineteen ships in various stages of construction or on order at Clydebank were affected. Because of the extreme weather conditions, men in both the shipyard and the engine works

refused to work on Saturday mornings. Reduction of the working week, was, in any case, under discussion. Following agreement between the Shipbuilding Employers Federation and the Confederation of Shipbuilding and Engineering Unions, the working week of 47 hours was reduced to 44 hours from March 1947.[805]

In June, the Government White Paper 'Industry and Employment in Scotland' was published. This indicated the contribution which Scottish industry was making to the UK economy. Several shipbuilding statistics were highlighted: 1,150,000 gross tons of merchant ships were on order in Scottish yards which, in 1946 had produced 38% of the UK total. Employment was currently 47,200 persons, compared with the peak wartime figure of 65,700 in December 1943.[806] The importance of the shipyard to the John Brown Company was revealed in the annual statement of profits for the year to April 1947. Of a net profit of £508,795 for the group, Clydebank's contribution was £404,350.

GAS TURBINES

The main activity in the engine works continued to be the manufacture of diesel and steam machinery for marine propulsion. Licenses were held for Doxford and Sulzer diesels and also with Parsons for steam turbines. The need to retain a large engineering design section had been reduced since the days of Clydebank's Brown-Curtis turbine. The manufacture of diesels required very little design effort by the

The plater is directing the craneman above as a plate is manipulated through the large plate rolls to form the correct curvature in this photograph taken in 1948.

shipbuilder, as the patent holder provided the necessary drawings. To further simplify design and manufacture, diesels were built to standard designs based on power. Steam turbines were designed on an individual basis. Parsons supplied basic design drawings for the turbine contract, but much detailed design work still required to be undertaken by the engine builder. To reduce the design load on those

A room laid out for an after-launch reception in September 1948.

firms involved in the manufacture of steam turbines, industry wide agreement was reached in 1944, to centralise research and development as well as design functions in one company. This company was Pametrada (Parsons Marine Turbine Research and Development Association). Henceforth, John Brown was able to operate with a much reduced engineering design section under a Chief Engine Designer and a small number of engineers.

Mindful of the slump which overtook the brief boom at the end of the First World War, Lord Aberconway outlined a diversification strategy, in April 1945, to help maintain employment in the engine works. The areas to be pursued were gas turbines, water turbines and machinery for heavy presses.[807] Manufacturing rights were acquired from Messrs Boving & Co. Ltd., specialists in water turbines, and preparations put in hand to tender for hydro-electric schemes. Manufacturing these turbines was a very appropriate diversification into non-marine work and well within the technical capability of the works. No design expertise was required as Boving provided this. More interesting, although decidedly less profitable, was the move to explore the gas turbine. By October 1945, Pametrada had prepared two designs for manufacture at Clydebank, a small 500 hp turbine and a 3,500 hp open cycle gas turbine. At the same time, Clydebank engineers investigated the availability of other gas turbine technologies. In June

1946, a manufacturing license was negotiated with the Escher Wyss Company of Switzerland for their closed cycle gas turbine. However work on this turbine moved slowly as it was discovered that for their purposes, John Brown's had to become involved in a partial redesign. It was not until 1948, that significant progress was made in the construction of the Pametrada turbines and the first Escher Wyss turbine was built. By this time, eight water turbines for various hydro-electric power stations were under manufacture.[808] In June, the contract for the first commercial gas turbine was received from the North of Scotland Hydro Electricity Board. This 12,500kw unit, of the Escher Wyss type, was for a power station in Dundee. Orders followed for three more units at Coventry, Rothes and at Altnabreac near Thurso. To reduce operating costs, the gas turbines were to run on cheap fuels, coal slurry in the case of Rothes, heavy fuel oil in Dundee and waste gas in Coventry. Difficulties in making the turbines work satisfactorily were compounded when the Ministry of Fuel and Power required peat to be used as fuel. The objective behind this initiative was twofold; to establish gas turbine power stations to supply remote areas burning peat, and to reclaim, for useful purposes, the bog from which the peat was dug. Altnabreac was selected to burn peat. John Brown's bravely rose to the challenge.[809]

However, this particular excursion into gas turbines was not a success. Peat and coal slurry proved to be unsuitable fuels and refined oil had to be burned instead of heavy oil. Numerous other technical problems beset the Clydebank engineers and when Rothes and Altnabreac were eventually commissioned, it was for a brief time only, as they were too expensive to run given the small output of around 2 megawatts. The order for the first gas turbine for Dundee proved to be the most difficult of all. By 1960, with no prospect of commissioning, it had to be written off and scrapped. That year, after sustaining heavy losses, all gas turbine work was terminated.

STEEL SHORTAGES AND SLUMP

In 1948, Sir Stephen Pigott retired as Managing Director and was replaced by James McNeill, the Technical Director, and the first naval architect to hold this post. McNeill's old post was taken by John Brown, who, like McNeill before him, had spent his working life with the Company. During that year, it became clear that a major error had been made in the estimate for *Caronia*, blighting an otherwise successful return to merchant shipbuilding. Delivered on 17 December 1948, Caronia recorded a massive loss of £787,595 in the year 1948/49 equal to the combined profits made on *Queen Mary, Queen Elizabeth* and *Vanguard*. Signed in 1945, the contract had not sufficient allowance for escalating labour and material costs, both of which rose sharply. The profit for that year on other ships would have been in the region of £500,000. Profitable business was resumed in the following year with a positive £630,200.[810] Throughout 1948, shortage of skilled labour delayed a number of contracts including *Caronia* and the refrigerated cargo ships *Sussex* and *Hinakura*, both of which were laid down in 1947. During the first quarter of 1949, steel supplies to the yard fell to 5,150 tons in place of the 8,000 tons required. This reflected increased demand across the manufacturing and construction sectors and the inability of British steel makers to cope. The outcome was a slowing down in the building of ships and a predictable increase in the price of steel which rose by £3 per ton.

By January 1949, the yard was employed on the following contracts: *Nottingham* for Federal Steam Navigation Co., *Vikfoss* and *Vikland* for Tanker Corporation of Panama, *Rangitane* and *Hinakura* for the New Zealand Ship Co. The refitting of *Rangitiki* had been completed while that of *Rangitata*, along with the Cunarder *Franconia*, were in progress. *Amsterdam*, a train ferry for the British Transport Commission and the destroyer *Diamond* were laid down in March. The latter was to be the first all-welded ship built by John Brown's.

A drop in the number of enquiries for ships followed the rise in the cost of steel announced in March 1949.[811] To sustain the order book, contracts were taken at a fixed price including two 19,000dwt tankers for the Alva Steamship Corporation *Almak* and *Algol*. Speaking at the 86th Annual Meeting of John Brown & Co. in London, Lord Aberconway blamed rising costs for the poor order position. He also noted that Germany and Japan had actively resumed shipbuilding. [812]

Within a year however, the position had been radically transformed with the start of a prolonged boom in merchant shipbuilding. Naval work was also revived when, in August 1951, the Admiralty asked Clydebank to build the first of a new class of frigate of the Leopard Class. By the end of that year, Clydebank had no less than 26 ships on order, 21 of which had still to be laid down. Among these was the contract for the 29,000ton *Arcadia* for P&O. At the same time, expenditure of over £500,000 was announced on various improvements throughout the yard.[813] The year 1951 also marked the centenary of the commencement of shipbuilding by J & G Thomson at Govan.

LAND BOILERS

In February 1950, Atlee's Labour Government was returned on a much reduced majority. With

Men from the Boiler Shop in March 1950

Clydebank's first all-welded ship, the destroyer Diamond, *running trials in February 1952.*

nationalisation a distinct possibility, John Brown & Co. acted to protect itself by diversifying. This took two routes, investment into companies including Wickman Machine Tools and Westland Helicopters

241

and the formation of a separate company to manufacture boilers for power stations. At Sheffield, Firth Brown already manufactured forged steel drums - an important boiler component and the decision was taken to establish new works at Whitecrook in Clydebank. The origins of this decision lay with Lord Aberconway and a discussion with Lord Citrine, Chairman of the CEGB in which

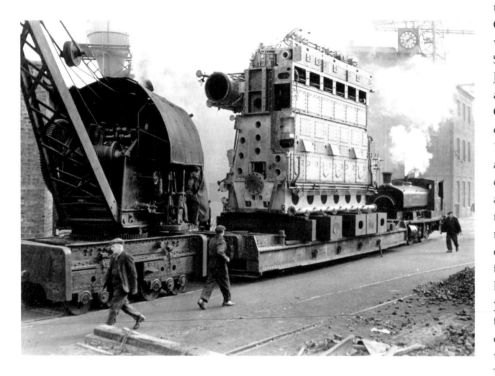

A John Brown Sulzer diesel engine for Otaki *being taken from the engine shops in March 1953.*

the latter indicated that 10% of CEGB's allocation of boiler work would go to John Brown. As these boilers were considerably bigger than marine boilers, John Brown approached Mitchell Engineering Ltd., to assist in their design and manufacture. This collaboration proved unsatisfactory however and the Riley Stoker Corporation, American boiler specialists, entered into agreement with John Brown taking over Mitchell's role. Large shops were erected at Whitecrook in 1951 where about 500 men were later employed.[814] Like Clydebank shipyard, John Brown Land Boilers Ltd was a subsidiary of the parent John Brown company and had nothing to do with the former.[815]

In March 1952, orders for more intermediate liners for Cunard followed, when contracts were signed to build *Saxonia* and *Ivernia*, the first of four 20,000ton liners for the Liverpool - Montreal service. During the same month, a delegation from Canadian Pacific visited the yard to discuss the possibility of building new Empress class intermediate liners for their Canadian service and cargo ships for their Pacific

service.[816] Although John Brown's had built many Canadian Pacific ships they were unsuccessful in winning any of these orders.

BRITANNIA

Plans to replace the Royal Yacht had been interrupted by the outbreak of the war in 1939. In 1951, these plans again rose to prominence. Initially, there was urgency over the construction of the yacht, as King George VI was ill and it was hoped that the new vessel would be available for convalescent purposes. Seven shipbuilders were approached and of these, John Brown was best able to meet the specification and short timetable. The Company wrote to the Controller of the Navy on 24 November 1951 with details of construction and delivery. On 5 February 1952, the Director of Navy Contracts replied authorising construction. The letter stated 'Very early completion of the ship is of the utmost importance and the estimated date for completion should be reported as soon as possible'.[817] Meeting this requirement was possible because the recently built channel ferry, *Amsterdam*, had a hull form similar to the proposed yacht. By adapting this design, John Brown was in a unique position to build the King's yacht quickly. However, the King died on 6 February the day that John Brown received the letter confirming the contract. The original tender price was £1,615,000 which included a profit of £125,000.[818] Throughout the early planning stages of this ship, the Admiralty, with due regard to political sensitivities of the day, referred to her as a hospital ship. This was euphemistic in part only, as the ship was indeed designed for ease of conversion into a hospital ship should events require it. A considerable amount of work on the design of this vessel had already been completed by this time, with only details of the hull form to be finalised. By April 1952, the ship was openly referred to as the Royal Yacht.[819] By July, Queen Elizabeth had agreed decorative arrangements with designer J Patrick McBride. The ship was, of course, *Britannia*.

Throughout this period, steel shortages continued to delay work in the yard and requests were made directly to Sir John Craig at Colville's, the yard's principal supplier of steel, to improve matters. In the interim, it was decided to ensure that steel supplies for the Cunard and P&O ships together with the Royal Yacht would not be affected. In the case of the two shipping lines, this decision was taken to minimise losses which they would otherwise suffer through late delivery of their ships.

Perhaps because of John Brown's reputation, enquiries were received for vessels of various descriptions. In April 1953, Khalil Abdulla & Sons of Bahrain, wrote asking if John Brown would build them a fishing boat. They were politely requested to approach Robertson's at Sandbank or McGruers at Clynder elsewhere on the Clyde, specialists in this type of work.

completion in 1958. Theoretically, three yards could accommodate the ship within their existing building programmes: John Brown, Cammell Laird and Harland & Wolff. At Clydebank, the 1,000 foot long berth in the east yard would be available in January 1954.[823] In March 1953, the Admiralty advised John Brown that their 'allocation under the new programme [of naval construction] is likely to

The keel plates for Britannia *lowered onto the building berth on 16 June 1952.*

The full order book gave rise to difficulties in quoting acceptable delivery dates. In July 1952, an enquiry from the Burmah Oil Company for a 30,000 dwt.[820] tanker was given a hopelessly unrealistic delivery date of late 1959. In 1953, the vagaries of the shipbuilding industry were reflected in falling demand just as the yard was benefiting from a programme of full production. By mid 1953, the number of orders placed in UK yards was 35% down on the corresponding period in 1952.[821] By the end of 1954, the slump forced the cancellation of four tanker contracts.[822]

Throughout 1952 and early 1953, it seemed highly probable that a large fleet aircraft carrier for the Royal Navy would be authorised. Tentative building schedules foresaw keel laying in late 1953 and

include all the machinery for the capital ship'.[824] In April, the preliminary design contract for this machinery was awarded to the Yarrow Admiralty Research Department (YARD) in Scotstoun, Glasgow. In July, the entire project fell victim to a Government defence review without invitation to tender being issued. James McNeill's big aircraft carrier was proving to be every bit as elusive as *Malta* had been some years earlier.

In 1953, the corporate structure of John Brown & Co. Ltd., was changed. The divisions, of which Clydebank was the major one, were spun off into separate companies under the overall control of the parent which then became a holding company. This move was prompted by the desire to limit the impact of the Labour Government's commitment to nationalisation of the steel industry and to stimulate further diversification. The Clydebank subsidiary became John Brown & Co. (Clydebank) Ltd., with capital of £5 million. Of the 5 million £1 shares issued, each of the directors of the new company was allocated one share only, while the parent company held the rest. The first board meeting of the new company was held on 27 March 1953 at Clydebank.

John Brown, John Rannie, and George Strachan. On 16 April, the Queen launched the Royal Yacht. The name of the ship had been kept secret until then although John Rannie, Shipyard manager, had dropped a hint by asking the Clydebank Burgh band to play Rule Britannia.

May 1953 was an eventful month. The Clyde Navigation Trust approached John Brown's looking

The new board comprised Lord Aberconway, Chairman; his son Charles McLaren, Vice Chairman; Dr James McNeill, Deputy Chairman and Managing Director; S W Rawson; Eric Mensforth; J W Beck,

for support in building a large graving dock either in the vicinity of the King George V Dock in Glasgow or at Newshot Isle directly across the river from Clydebank shipyard.

John Brown's response, in common with other shipbuilders was that they would support the initiative if the dock were of the largest dimensions and situated on the lower reaches of the Clyde for easy access from the open sea. Furthermore, John Brown's agreed to participate only if the scheme received general support.[825] May 1953 also marked the end of steel rationing, a measure previously adopted to regulate the supply of steel, although shortages continued to plague production schedules for some time to come. On 14 May, the 29,000 grt P&O liner *Arcadia* was launched. At the same time, sheet ironworkers went on unofficial strike over demarcation with shipwrights concerning insulation work on Arcadia. On 23 May, Lord Aberconway, Chairman of John Brown & Co. Ltd., died and was succeeded by his son, Charles McLaren, the third

Lord Aberconway.

The year 1954 opened with the delivery of *Britannia* but was otherwise marked by a dearth of orders. Nevertheless, with a large volume of work already in production, employment at the Company peaked when, in February a total of 7,759 was recorded. Of these, 6,876 were employed directly in the shops. 112 were women. In the offices, 883 were employed of

laid up in Dalmuir basin since the end of the war. With two additional Tiger class cruisers undergoing similar rebuilding, John Brown's was made lead yard for the conversion and given priority in the supply of armament.[829] As *Tiger* was to be rebuilt to a completely new design, she was dismantled down to the weather decks in preparation for the new superstructure.

Britannia *enters the water on 16 April 1953.*

whom 167 were women.[826]

Early in 1954, Sir James McNeill, knighted in the New Year's honours list, commented on the difficulty of attracting new orders referring in particular to Dutch and German yards where, in the case of the latter, subsidies would enable them to undercut British prices.[827] In the same month, McNeill rejected an offer to tender for the 23,000ton Swedish America Line passenger ship *Gripsholm* as he thought the purpose of the request was only to act as a price check against what he termed 'their own shipyards'.[828] In fact, the *Gripsholm* was awarded to the Italian shipbuilders Ansaldo at Sestri-Ponenti. In 1955, the market recovered and orders began to flow. In May, work began on the £3 million contract to rebuild the cruiser *Tiger* which had effectively been

Some of the many thousands who packed into the yard to see the Queen *and* Britannia.

In the same month an enquiry from Esso for a 35,000ton tanker was declined as it would have required one of the two large berths which had been reserved for other contracts.[830]

ORDERS GALORE
In 1956, John Brown tendered for four large passenger ships: two for P&O, and one each for Canadian Pacific and Union Castle. The P&O vessels in particular would prove to be innovative in design and construction. The first of these, *Oriana*, was awarded to the Vickers Armstrong yard at Barrow who had acted as design consultants to the Orient Line.[831] In the early part of 1956, designs and estimates for the second P&O vessel were in preparation at Clydebank when the shipping line

Britannia fitting out under the cantilever crane. Great care was taken to achieve a smooth high gloss paint finish on her hull. Note her funnel on the quayside waiting to be lifted on board.

The P&O liner Arcadia *takes to the water on 14 May 1953.*

decided on a drastic redesign in which the ship's machinery was placed aft. Four yards tendered for this contract, John Brown, Vickers Armstrong, Cammell Laird and Harland & Wolff. Tenders based on the new design were submitted on 14 October. In January 1957, Harland & Wolff was awarded the contract for the ship later named *Canberra*. The Canadian Pacific tender was similarly unsuccessful with this contract, *Empress of Canada*, being placed with Vickers Armstrong on the Tyne. The final tender of the quartet was for the Union Castle liner *Transvaal Castle*. The contract for this ship was won in July 1957, at the price of £10,185,900 including a profit of £1,482,240 with a delivery date of March 1962. In June, Cunard reserved a berth for a 30,000 gross ton liner to replace *Britannic* on the Liverpool/New York service, to be delivered in March 1961. Work on this design was postponed in 1957 and the ship cancelled outright in 1958.[832]

In the year to March 1956, the yard had won orders for ten ships aggregating 160,000 gross tons at a value of over £20 million.[833] All berths would be occupied until 1962. In September, platers, welders, caulkers and burners went on strike for two and a half weeks for a guaranteed wage. The men returned to work with little change to their conditions.[834]

The supply of skilled labour, particularly boilermakers, remained a problem. This was threatened in 1957 when it became known that the nearby Royal Ordnance Factory at Dalmuir was to be sold to Babcock & Wilcox, the Renfrew boilermakers. George Strachan, John Brown's Engine Works Manager, wrote to James McNeill that this development will be 'a menace to us from the point of view of labour'[835]

TANKER YARD

By 1956 the market for new merchant tonnage in the United Kingdom was calculated as follows: tankers 51%, cargo 35%, ore 6.4%, passenger cargo 3.7%, passenger 0.8% and the remainder miscellaneous.[836] The enormous demand for tankers persuaded John Brown's to concentrate on this type of ship in addition to building for their traditional market of passenger and naval vessels. The increasing size of tankers meant that very few of the seven berths in the yard could accommodate them. The west yard berths, largely unaltered since 1919, were too small while the east yard berths were earmarked for large passenger ships or warships. Nevertheless, the east yard was used for tanker construction and as a consequence became overtaxed while the west yard was under-employed. The continued demand for tankers of ever increasing size provided the incentive to restructure the west yard. Early in 1956 the main John Brown Board gave approval to completely rebuild the west yard at an estimated cost of £495,000.[837] This scheme would provide for two new berths able to build ships up to 30,000 gross tons, new berth cranes of 40 tons capacity and a new fabrication shop with overhead cranage of 40 tons. At the same time, approval was given for expenditure of £66,905 on new machinery for the engine works. However this scheme was overtaken by events in the Middle East. In July 1956, President Nasser of Egypt nationalised the Suez Canal. Following the Anglo-French invasion of Egypt and the subsequent closure of the Suez Canal, oil companies were forced to transport oil around the Cape of Good Hope

Prior to the Suez crisis, the P&O Group including the New Zealand and Federal Lines, had committed themselves to a major tanker building programme. A committee was appointed to deliberate on the size of tanker most likely to offer the best operating costs. This resulted in the recommendation that tankers of 36,000tons deadweight would be built by a group of British builders including John Brown, Vickers, Swan

Sylvania, last of four Cunard intermediate liners leaves Clydebank to run trials in May 1957.

Hunter, Smiths Dock and Charles Connell. Following the closure of the canal, the Committee recognised that it now made economic sense to build much larger tankers to make the longer and more expensive trip round the Cape of Good Hope. On 20 August 1956, a further meeting was called at Clydebank to consider the tanker building programme in light of changed circumstances. The outcome was that John Brown and Vickers would be

The cruiser Tiger working up to full speed during trials on the Firth of Clyde in 1958.

asked to build tankers of 49,000tons deadweight for the P&O Group. British Petroleum, who had two berths reserved at Clydebank, wished to proceed with two tankers of similar size and asked the yard to investigate the possibility of building tankers of between 60,000 to 80,000tons deadweight.[838] Fortunately, plans to rebuild the west yard were in the early stages. Proposed west yard berths capable

The third Lord Aberconway who succeeded his father as Chairman of John Brown & Co. in May 1953.

No shortage of work. The East Yard on 16 April 1956 showing three ships under construction on the building berths from left, British Industry, British Trader *and* Salmara. *The frigate* Lynx *can be seen in the fitting-out basin at right.*

of building ships 750 x 105 feet were increased to 800 x 107 feet. Steel production in the proposed fabricating shop was increased to units of 60 tons which demanded a corresponding increase in capacity for berth cranes. On 28 August 1956, Sir James McNeil wrote to Lord Aberconway seeking approval for an enlarged scheme of reconstruction:

> 'My Dear Charles, Since this scheme was first approved the demand for the larger type of tanker has expanded rapidly . . . In order to deal with the larger sizes which are likely to be repeated, it will now be necessary to enlarge on our previous reconstruction of the west yard. The members of the Local Board resident at Clydebank are unanimously of the opinion that such a scheme as now submitted is necessary for

the future of the yard, and I shall be obliged if approval could be given to it pending final approval of the Board.'[50]

The cost of the scheme had rocketed to £1,028,000. Calculations made in 1957 indicated that a profit of £1,339,600 after tax would be made on nine ships already on order and earmarked for construction on the new berths. Expenditure on the west yard would be recovered after six years by profits earned by the new berths.[51] The difficulty of keeping up with tanker sizes was clear in December 1956 when BP indicated that 65,000tons deadweight tankers of 775 x 110 feet would be built. The breadth was three feet wider than the new berths for which adjustment to civil engineering works had to be made. In the summer of 1957, a Lloyds ship surveyor, Fred Reid, was sent to Clydebank.[52] On his first day, he was introduced to John Rannie, Clydebank's Shipyard Director who had also been a Lloyds surveyor. Rannie asked him what yard he had trained in. When the surveyor replied the Blythswood shipyard, Rannie said, 'I'm going to be very frank with you, do not expect the same quality of steelwork at this yard'. Given that John Brown's was widely considered, with every justification, to be one of the finest yards in the UK and that John Rannie was heart and soul a John Brown man, his comment requires explanation and perhaps offers insight into the dilemma facing John Brown in entering the competitive market for oil tankers.

John Brown's traditional work was, typically, the passenger liner and warship. The internal complexity of these ships required long building periods. They were more often than not subject to continual detail changes on the part of the owner. Consequently, there was a greater emphasis on fitting-out and fitting-out organisation. At the Blythswood shipyard, where tankers were the main product, steelwork was the principal element in construction as there was little involved in fitting-out. For this yard, competitiveness lay in efficient processing of steelwork. As a result, Blythswood had acquired a reputation for good steelwork. When John Brown entered the tanker market, they had to consider steelwork as the single largest element of the contract. Rannie's comment was not a condemnation of John Brown's steelworking *per se* but recognition that it was not the particular strength of the yard.

Nevertheless, as the 1950s drew to a close, John Brown had acquitted itself well in its preferred market obtaining a large share of orders for British passenger liners. In the UK alone, British owners contracted 24 passenger liners of 20,000tons and over. Of these contracts, Harland & Wolff headed the table with eight, John Brown and Vickers Armstrong (with yards at Barrow and Tyneside) each won six. Naval work, although much reduced by comparison with former years nevertheless produced contracts for the Rothesay Class frigate *Yarmouth* in 1957 and the County Class cruiser *Hampshire* in 1959. Conversion of the cruiser *Tiger* had been completed in 1958. The demand for tanker tonnage had been recognised and a new west yard created specifically to win a share of this market. During the late 1950s, building a nuclear powered merchant ship seemed inevitable. In July 1957, with this in mind, John Brown's and Hawker Siddley each subscribed £0.25 million to form a company under the name of Hawker Siddley John Brown Nuclear Construction Ltd. This was seen as a natural development of John Brown's marine engineering and land boilers activities. Eric Mensforth, a director on the main John Brown Board stated:

> 'As builders of the world's largest ships, John Brown's believe that this experience coupled with the technical resources of the new company, will

enable them to carry out most efficiently the building of Britain's first nuclear merchant vessel, which surely must be undertaken if we are to maintain our position as a leading maritime nation'.[53]

Plans for the construction of a 65,000 dwt. nuclear propelled tanker were under consideration which Mensforth hoped might be sailing by 1963. A British

British Queen, running trials on 18 December 1959, was the largest at 49,000 dwt of the trio laid down at Clydebank during 1958/9 for the BP Tanker Co.

nuclear powered merchant ship never became a reality. American, German and Japanese nuclear merchantmen proved to be costly liabilities.

A view of the experiment tank at Clydebank where models of different form were tested to find the optimum performance characteristics. The tank which was built in 1903 is shown here in May 1955.

OMINOUS SIGNS

The boom in shipbuilding which lasted through most

of the 1950s, masked a reduction in market share and competitiveness. Between the years 1948 and 1958 world output of ships had increased from 2.3 million gross tons to 9.3 million tons.[54] During this period of expansion, British output remained much the same at 1.3 million tons, revealing a serious relative decline. In the same ten year period, British share of the shipbuilding market had dropped from 51% to 15%.

In 1957, for the first time in history, the UK was overtaken as the world's leading shipbuilder. Japan now headed the table. In the following year, the UK was pushed into third position behind West Germany.[55] Shipbuilding capacity had been greatly increased worldwide and the contraction in orders evident from 1959 onwards established fiercely competitive conditions. The heady years of the 1950s,

when work often had been turned away, had come to an abrupt end. John Brown's was now obliged to accept contracts for what it termed 'plain cargo ships' at prices which would give no significant return.[56] Employment in the works, which had stood at 7,759 in February 1954, had fallen to 4,983 by May 1960.[57] The period since the end of the war had been consistently profitable with the exception of the large

Deputy Chairman of John Brown. The task facing his successors would prove to be a difficult one. His successor was the Technical Director, John Brown. At the same time, John F Starks, Chief Constructor at the Admiralty's Submarine Design Section, replaced John Brown as Technical Director.

In March 1960, the frigate *Yarmouth* was handed over to the Admiralty in the record time for the class of 28

Opposite page
The West Yard under reconstruction on 21 May 1959. The old covered sheds, under which Britannia *had recently been built, were pulled down and the berths reduced from three to two. Half way through the scheme, the new berths were lengthened and widened to take account of the increasing size of tankers. New travelling tower cranes with a capacity of 60 tons were built by Sir William Arrol.* British Queen *is well advanced to left with* Kent *in the foreground.*

Left
Looking through the new West Yard fabrication shed at the tanker British Queen *in August 1959.*

loss made on *Caronia* in 1949. In the fourteen years since 1946, Clydebank had earned profits of £6,388,906 averaging £456,000 per annum.[58] Bt the end of the 1950s, over £500,000 had been spent rebuilding the fitting out basin and over £1.5 million spent in building a new west yard. This investment had been made when the downward trend of British shipbuilding was all too apparent. Made earlier, when profits were high, investment in new facilities and methods would have yielded a better return and better prepared the yard for the difficult years ahead. At the end of 1959, Sir James McNeill relinquished executive control of the Clydebank Works to become

The diesel erecting shop in August 1963 with crankshafts in the foreground and the engine on the right.

251

months. This left *Hampshire* as the sole Admiralty contract at Clydebank. In the same month, the Admiralty informed builders that henceforth, tenders would now be placed on a competitive basis in the interests of getting more economically built ships

Q3

Early in April 1959, Cunard announced its intention to replace *Queen Mary*, now 23 years old, and at the

An aerial view of the yard in 1961 with the County Class destroyer Hampshire *and Union Castle's* Transvaal Castle *in the fitting-out basin.*

Transvaal Castle running trials in December 1961.

same time, approached John Brown for preliminary designs and costings. On 9 April, the story made headlines in the national press according to which talks were in progress between Cunard, the Government and John Brown's.[848] Early in 1959,

when Cunard Chairman, Sir Fred Bates, telephoned Sir James McNeill to say that Cunard was considering a replacement for *Queen Mary*. This was the first indication that the big contract for which the yard had been waiting was in the offing. In the Engine Design Office, the Chief Engine Designer[849] dusted off speculative drawings prepared as early as 1947 for this eventuality. Drawings of *Queen Mary's* and *Queen Elizabeth's* machinery spaces were produced which, although overtaken by technical developments, would provide a basis for the new ship.[850] As with the two Queens, Cunard was again dependent on a Government loan. Government involvement and finance brought with it the need to investigate the type of ship required and, in September 1959, a special committee under the chairmanship of Lord Chandos, chairman of Associated Electrical Industries, was set up to advise the Minister of Transport, Ernest Marples, on how the British express passenger service on the North Atlantic could best be maintained. Hopes in Clydebank that the contract might proceed swiftly in their favour were thus dashed. In May 1960, after long discussions, the Chandos Committee recommended that a ship of 75,000 gross tons and an overall length of 990 feet[851] capable of maintaining a service speed of 29.5 knots should be built. The Committee estimated that this ship, which became known as the *Q3*, would cost £30 million, for which the Government would contribute a loan of £18 million. John Brown's was quickly disabused of the idea that the order would be theirs. While they had been exclusively involved in the preliminary design phase from April to September 1959, Cunard was obliged to put the ship out to competitive tender with other major UK shipyards. Invitations were issued, in March 1961, to a Vickers Armstrong/Swan Hunter Wigham Richardson consortium, Cammell Laird, Harland & Wolff, Fairfield and John Brown. Throughout the ensuing period, John Brown's used its excellent relations with Cunard to the full, principally through Cunard's naval architect, Robert Wood, much to the annoyance of the other shipbuilders.[852] Through the decades, the close relationship between John Brown and Cunard resulted in many Clydebank men working for Cunard and both Wood, and his successor, Dan Wallace, were Clydebank trained naval architects. Despite his familiarity and affection for Clydebank, Wood nevertheless conducted himself in a thoroughly professional and evenhanded manner.[853] In July 1961, after months of work by the shipbuilders, the tenders for *Q3* were submitted. In the following month, Lord Aberconway, commenting on the annual report for 1961 said 'the new Queen was vital to Clydebank if continuity of employment is to be maintained and to hold together Clydebank's skilled labour force. If the contract is lost, the yard will be severely underemployed.'[854]

In keeping with tradition, the principals of the tendering shipyards were invited to the opening of tenders at Cunard's Liverpool offices. Before describing the outcome of this meeting however, some reference has to be made to developments in the construction of passenger ships which had taken place in the 1950s. During this decade, aluminium first came to be used in the upperworks of passenger liners. Although more expensive than steel, aluminium was half its weight, which meant that a lighter ship with correspondingly reduced power requirements could be achieved which would still carry the same number of passengers at the same speed. The vessel which took the Blue Riband from *Queen Mary* in 1952, *United States*, had a steel hull and an aluminium superstructure. However, the commercial advantages of her lighter structure were more than offset by her extremely powerful but financially ruinous machinery, which consumed fuel at a prodigious rate. Throughout the 1950s, aluminium became more widely adopted and, in the United Kingdom, the P&O line employed it extensively in *Oriana*, built by Vickers Armstrong in 1960 and *Canberra*, built by Harland & Wolff in 1961. Cunard, perhaps more conservative in outlook, was slow to acknowledge the use of aluminium and the outline specification for the *Q3* was for an all-steel ship.

When the tenders were opened by Sir John Brocklebank, Cunard's new Chairman, both Lord Aberconway and Mr. John Brown, Clydebank's Managing Director, were shaken to find that the Vickers Armstrong/Swan Hunter consortium had submitted the most attractive tender. Moreover, they had submitted two designs, one, the all-steel 4-shaft ship Cunard asked for, the other, a smaller, 2-shaft alloy/steel design. The disturbing news for John Brown was that the consortium's 4 shaft all-steel design was preferred on cost and delivery to their own. It was later found that Clydebank's price was £1.8 million higher than the consortium's. John Brown's hull would have cost £2.15 million more to build although its machinery price was £0.35 million lower.[855] John Brown's hull was a much heavier and stiffer structure than the consortium's and required more power and therefore more expense to propel it.

However it was the consortium's smaller two-shaft design which caused Cunard to pause. Many of the features it embraced were based on the *Oriana*, a ship which incorporated not only an aluminium superstructure but also some novel steelworking features.[856] The Clydebank tender was based almost entirely on steel, in compliance with Cunard's specification. At this time, John Brown's had no practical experience of aluminium construction in

The Federal Steam Navigation Co's Somerset *nearing completion in October 1962.*

merchant vessels. As Roy Turner, Vickers' naval architect put it 'we had just built the *Oriana*, John Brown's hadn't.'[857]

From Cunard's point of view, despite its predilection towards Clydebank, the fact remained that the designs put forward by the Vickers Armstrong/Swan Hunter consortium were cheaper, more interesting and, in the smaller ship proposal, placed an entirely different perspective on *Q3*. For the Clydebank men the experience was a shock. Lord Aberconway in particular was distinctly unhappy at letting the new 'Queen' slip through his fingers. As the meeting progressed, Mr. John Brown, argued that the alternative Vickers Armstrong/Swan Hunter proposal for a twin screw design was very different from that submitted by Clydebank and suggested that John Brown's should be given the opportunity to re-tender on a similar basis. Cunard agreed to consider this proposal although the meeting ended without any decision. Soon after, Cunard decided that Q3 was not the ship it wanted and the process of determining the characteristics of a smaller, slower, twin shaft vessel began.[858]

If Q3 was dead, it was still perfectly clear that a new ship would be built. The experience of tendering for Q3 had highlighted John Brown's relative

declaration, however, made no mention of magnets! In a similar act of 'industrial espionage' Col. Austin Bates, a Cunard Director and brother of the former Chairman, in company with Robert Wood, booked a passage with the object of assessing soundproofing qualities of bulkheads between cabins. Bates, equipped with a hunting horn, blew into the instrument while Wood, in an adjoining cabin,

Looking into the basin from the stern of Somerset *on 26 October 1962. The guided missile destroyer* Hampshire *is nearing completion and the Cunard liners* Ivernia *and* Saxonia *have returned for conversion to cruising.*

inexperience in working with weight saving aluminium. In an inspired, if belated, piece of research, Mr. John Brown in company with Robert Wood, Cunard's naval architect, booked a passage on *United States* on the last leg of her Atlantic run from Southampton to Bremerhaven. With small magnets concealed in their hands, they strolled the upper decks of the liner making frequent stops at bulkheads to admire the view. In a relatively short time, the entire superstructure of the ship had been surveyed providing an accurate estimate of the extent to which aluminium was incorporated in the structure. Many of the details surrounding *United States*, particularly her power plant and speed, were secret and it should be added that, before conducting their survey, both men had declared their interest in the ship. This

measured the sound with a sound level meter.[859] While these events were unfolding, other factors of a more pressing nature were brought to bear on the future of Cunard's new Queen. Four years earlier, in 1957, for the first time more people crossed the Atlantic by air than by sea.[860] As passenger traffic figures on the North Atlantic continued to decline, Sir John Brocklebank announced, on 19 October 1961, that the contract for the Q3 was to be postponed while Cunard reappraised the type of ship it required. Postponement, followed by cancellation, came as a blow to John Brown. Great disappointment was also expressed on Tyneside where Q3 would probably have been built had a contract been awarded.[861] Later, Aberconway wrote to Brocklebank to remind him of the consultancy work which John

Brown's had undertaken prior to the specification for Q3 being issued. Although a fee of £100,000 was suggested, both companies later agreed on £75,000.[862]

UNPREPARED AND UNCOMPETITIVE

By the end of 1961, Clydebank shipyard was becoming increasingly uncompetitive. Although the order for an 80,000ton tanker for the Olsen Line was pursued, the owner's specification could not be met 'at a price acceptable to Clydebank'.[863] A similar ship for Naess Denholm was lost to a German yard whose price considerably undercut Clydebank's, although the latter was reputedly the best British offer.[864] Tenders for a passenger ship for British Railways, for a 53,000ton tanker, and for a second guided missile destroyer for the Admiralty were equally unsuccessful. One of only two orders which did materialise, a 53,000 dwt. turbine tanker for A Ravano & Co., was cancelled in February of the following year.[865] The other, *Centaur*, a passenger cargo ship for Alfred Holt & Co's Blue Funnel Line, was booked at a fixed contract price of £1,685,000. A long period of profitability was drawing to a close. Of the contracts in progress during 1963/4, losses were forecast on *Centaur* (£317,000), on the conversion of *Franconia* (£63,000) and on diesel machinery contracts for the Caledon yard in Dundee (£68,000). The profitable contracts were the 70,000 ton tanker *British Mariner* (£139,000), for a brief period the largest tanker so far built in the UK, and the frigate *Aurora* (£239,000).[866] Significantly, as had been the case with naval work, *Aurora* was the most profitable work on hand. The sudden inability to win remunerative contracts from 1961 onwards highlighted the inherent profitability of contracts booked earlier. Over the four years to 31 March 1963, profits averaging £994,000 per annum were recorded.[867]

In 1962 the Patton Report on Productivity in Shipbuilding was published by the Shipbuilding Conference. This report, one of several produced in response to a general loss of competitiveness, analysed methods in the UK industry in comparison with those abroad. Its main conclusions confirmed that continental shipyard layout and plant was only marginally better than modernised British yards. Double shifting, a desirable feature available to foreign shipbuilders, was not available to their British counterparts. The Report cited the example of highly efficient Swedish yards. Clydebank's response, in the form of a memorandum to the Board, noted that these yards did not build passenger or naval ships but concentrated on limited range of types in which

output was closely related to a steady flow of steel unlike the position at Clydebank where, the report noted 'The light scantling, intricate structure of a destroyer gives no scope for building up a high tonnage of steel throughput, although related to a profitable contract.' In response to the flexibility of labour, the report commented that Clydebank 'suffered the same disabilities as all British yards in

Standing in the snow outside a Soviet ministry, three Clyde shipbuilders try to win orders in the Soviet Union in 1962. From left, Jim Lees of Scotts, John Brown, of the Clydebank yard and Jim Stephen, of Stephens. Of the three, only Stephen's won work.

requiring to observe demarcation practices, but had succeeded better than most others in avoiding major disputes and loss of output from this cause'[868] To redress the impact of dwindling orders in the engine works, the possibility of establishing a commercial organisation to sell the work's capacity was discussed in November 1961. This was tacit recognition that the Company was overly product oriented at the expense of the market. It was agreed that the 'ship first' approach to the future employment of the Works should be dropped.[869] Hitherto, there had been no sales function built into the organisation as, traditionally, work came to John Brown. Keeping abreast with tankers of the largest size was becoming something of a contest. BP was planning ships in excess of 100,000tons. These ships would be impossible to accommodate in the new west yard berths. The only berth capable of handling this size was the big berth in the east yard which was held in reserve for the new Cunard liner. Consequently, the Clydebank Board felt it had little option but to recommend further expenditure of £0.25 million on modifying the west yard to take tankers of 100,000tons.

Following a visit to the yard by a Russian trade delegation, the Managing Director, Mr. John Brown, travelled to Moscow early in 1962 in an effort to win work. This resulted in an unsuccessful tender for a large cargo ship.[870] Yet another unsuccessful tender was for the Norwegian America line passenger ship

255

Sagafjord. Clydebank's quote was £160,000 higher than the best British price which was Swan Hunter's at £5,630,000.[871] Better news was received from the Admiralty with the award of the contract to build *Intrepid*, one of two assault ships. The loss of *Sagafjord* in particular, caused the Board to consider Clydebank's competitiveness. Concerned that they were too expensive because the quality of their work

complex design. George Strachan, Engineering Director, proposed that links be encouraged with either Harland & Wolff or Cammell Laird. It was also agreed that an approach be made to the Admiralty to find out whether John Brown was considered capable of building this ship on their own.[873] It was agreed that John Brown would probably work with Harland & Wolff, with whom they were already sharing work

The West Yard fabrication shed on 29 January 1963 showing a double bottom unit for the assault ship Intrepid *being moved down the shed.*

was unnecessarily high, the Board discussed the desirability of 'cutting down standards'.[872] At the same time, it sought solace in potential profits which would arise from winning one of the large aircraft carriers which were again under discussion at the Admiralty. There was concern that the latter might not be prepared to consider tenders from shipbuilders acting on their own in view of their

on the assault ships, to spread the enormous load which would be placed on the design and drawing offices in preparing tenders for the very large warships. The final element in this strategy foresaw that the two yards would then bid for one aircraft carrier each out of a possible total of three.

The lack of competitiveness continued to preoccupy the Board. In December 1962, the following chart was prepared which examined tenders in comparison with those of competitors:

Ship	Type	JBrown	Competitor	Builder
Avalon	Pass.	2,065,000	1,970,000	Stephen[874]
Cambridge Ferry	Ferry	748,000	700,000	Hawthorn Leslie
Sagafjord	Liner	5,790,000	5,630,000	Swan Hunter
Beaverbrook	Cargo	970,500	720,000	Vickers Armstrong
Orissa	Tanker (55,000dwt)	2,860,000	2,600,000	Lithgow
Ottawa	Tanker (85,000dwt)	3,835,000	3,366,000	Swan Hunter[875]

Management reflected on four themes. Were they quoting like for like? Was their estimating procedure accurate? Were competitors estimating wrongly? Were competitors deliberately tendering unprofitably? The report stated 'that orders are only being taken when the successful firm has accepted an abnormally severe reduction in any possible contribution to charges.' The Board accepted that some of the price difference was due to intrinsically cheaper costs and cited lower wage rates on the Lower Clyde as an example. The report concluded 'It is possible that the limit of 'buying' orders has been reached and that firms will select only special jobs which may offer the opportunity of keeping a limited labour force together, until British shipowners find it possible to resume ordering.'[876]

At the height of Clydebank's difficulties in 1963, the company issued the first of a series of newsletters under the title 'News from Clydebank'. The newsletter was intended to communicate the Company's current achievements to a wider audience. The description of the passenger cargo ship *Centaur*, intended for service in the Far East, is a reminder of the complexities involved in building ships:

'Centaur is an unusual cargo liner, accommodating 200 passengers, 4,500 sheep or 700 cattle, and 50 dairy cows with dairy equipment, as well as general and refrigerated cargo. Alfred Holt & Co. and John Brown's jointly developed the design of the ship for the Australia Singapore run from the owner's original concept.

Passengers and cattle will journey with the utmost comfort, but they will remain happily oblivious of each other. Passengers will enjoy air-conditioned one, two or four berth rooms, executive suites, public rooms and swimming pool. Sample animal pens were built by John

Brown's and sent out to Australian waters for trial. A compact arrangement incorporating feeding, drinking and cleansing facilities was thus developed.

Because *Centaur* will be aground while loading livestock in some Australian ports, her bottom structure required special stiffening. Moreover, a ship for this trade must be fast. After exhaustive

tank tests, a suitable hull form was selected, incorporating a bulbous underwater bow and specially designed bossings and propeller supports. Special machinery ensures that the unusual sanitary services function when the ship is resting on a harbour bed, and in addition,

The passenger cargo ship Centaur for service in the Far East fitting-out on 24 September 1963. The 71,000 dwt tanker British Mariner is in the foreground.

cooling water can be supplied to the diesel generators, thus maintaining electrical power. Her high speed (20 knots) and facilities will enable her to replace two vessels currently operating.'[877]

In an effort to bring tanker orders to Clydebank, John Rannie, Shipyard Director, visited the USA in the spring of 1963, to discuss possible contracts with

The Leander Class frigate Aurora, in March 1964, one of the very few profitable contracts booked at Clydebank during the 1960s.

Texaco, Mobil and Esso. Although pleasantly received, he was left in no doubt that orders would not be placed at Clydebank while Japanese shipbuilders kept their prices low.[878] The unpalatable truth was that the modernised west yard, dedicated to tanker construction, was unable to compete in this intensely competitive market. Foreign yards could put these relatively simple ships together cheaply and quickly. Although John Brown's had made its name building sophisticated specialist ships, investment at Clydebank had favoured a new tanker yard and to the detriment of productive capacity and new methods in its traditional field. To compound matters, by the end of 1963, work on the assault ship *Intrepid* had ground to a halt because of delays in receiving drawings from Harland & Wolff, threatening jobs among the finishing trades. The completion of *Centaur* was described as 'exceptionally difficult'[879] which meant at a large loss. Tenders were submitted for four large oil/bulk carriers and a Leander Class frigate.

A wage increase of 8 shillings per week was negotiated for shipyard workers, linked to a reduction in working hours to 40 hours over two

years. Engineering workers received 10s and 6d per week, with no reduction in hours. The only order received was for the 28,000 dwt. bulk carrier *Vennachar*. As this was Clydebank's first order for a bulk carrier, drawings were purchased from Scott's Greenock shipyard to relieve the pressure on the ship drawing office which was by then heavily involved with a Swedish American liner.

THE LAST NAVAL CONTRACTS

Although the 1953 fleet carrier had never been ordered, the Navy's strategic role still required replacement of the ageing fleet carrier force. On 30 July 1963, the Admiralty announced that one, possibly two, large fleet carriers would be built, although the Navy wanted three. The intended timetable foresaw that tenders would be requested in April 1966 and that the carriers would be completed by 1973.[880] In the Spring of 1963, Scotts' Shipbuilding & Engineering Co. Ltd., Greenock, approached both John Brown and Fairfield about the possibility of forming a joint company to tender for *Renown* and *Revenge*, the last two Polaris ballistic missile submarines to be built for the Royal Navy. John Brown's emerged as Scott's preferred partner, on the basis that a fixed profit of £1,250,000 would go to John Brown out of a total profit of £3,550,000. John Brown would also contribute £350,000 towards the cost of installing necessary heavy plate rolls for hull work. It was agreed that one submarine would be built at each yard, with final fitting-out of both to be undertaken at Scotts'. Despite the previous experience of Technical Director John Starks as Admiralty Constructor with responsibility for nuclear submarines, the bid was unsuccessful and the contract awarded to Cammell Laird.[881] Where recent history would have suggested a major role for John Brown & Co. in building capital ships, the emergence of the submarine as the principal vessel of war highlighted Clydebank's lack of involvement in that market. Naval Contracts placed by September 1963 with Vickers Armstrong, Cammell Laird and John Brown were as follows:

Vickers	Cammell Laird	John Brown
2 nuclear submarines	2 diesel submarines	1 assault ship
1 diesel submarine	1 frigate	1 frigate
1 GM destroyer	2 Polaris submarines	
2 Polaris submarines	2 boom defence vessels	
2 frigates		
1 frigate (export)		

Intrepid proved to be the last warship constructed at Clydebank. Changing conditions of another sort occurred on 1 April 1964 when, as a result of restructuring the three armed services, a unitary organisation, the Ministry of Defence, was created. The Admiralty, so much a feature of activity at Clydebank, had ceased to exist.

As a result of the continued uncompetitive state of the British shipbuilding industry, a number of yards teetered on the brink of collapse. The scene was thus set for the first major contraction of the industry since the 1930s. In 1963, William Gray at West Hartlepool and Denny Brothers at Dumbarton closed, followed by Harland & Wolff at Govan and William Hamilton at Port Glasgow. In 1964, the Blythswood Company at Scotstoun and Short Brothers at Sunderland also ceased trading. By the mid 1960s, the British shipbuilding industry had contracted significantly, world share of output dropping from 50.2% in 1947 to 8.3% in 1964.[882] The tonnage produced in the UK was, however, approximately the same at 1,043,000grt in 1964 compared to the 1947 figure of 1,193,000grt. However, the demand for ships had soared worldwide and was met by foreign yards, particularly in the Far East.[883] The principal difference between the output figures for 1947 and 1964 was that much of the 1964 output had been produced at a loss.

At the start of 1964, Mr. John Brown retired to be succeeded by John Rannie as Managing Director. At the same time, Robin Williamson replaced A N Benson as Financial Director and Secretary while Tom Simpson was appointed as the Company's first Commercial Director.

KUNGSHOLM

With the Cunard liner still in gestation, a gap in passenger ship construction at Clydebank was looming, with the certainty that the fitting-out trades would be paid off. The departure of *Transvaal Castle* in December 1961, to begin her maiden voyage from Southampton to Durban in the following month, accelerated that process. With one eye firmly fixed on the possibility of building the Cunarder to succeed the abortive *Q3*, retaining a large complement of finishing trades was of vital importance. The Swedish America Line's requirement for a passenger ship fitted the timetable perfectly. Concerns over uncompetitiveness almost certainly conditioned the Board's attitude in pursuing the contract for this ship. The process started on 17 December 1962, when the Managing Director wrote to the Swedish America

Line asking that John Brown's be permitted to tender for the new intermediate liner, initially named *Salholm*, to be built for North Atlantic service. The Swedish America Line was known throughout the shipbuilding industry for commercial astuteness. Following intensive negotiations in Gothenburg between John Brown and Swedish American personnel, tenders were submitted on 4 June 1963. It

The assault ship Intrepid *sails away from Clydebank in March 1967 bringing naval work to an end and severed a connection with the Royal Navy that started in earnest with the torpedo cruiser* Scout *in 1884.*

soon emerged that John Brown's tender had been successful at £6,780,000 and with a delivery date of October 1965.[884] To ensure every chance of winning the contract, a price had been quoted based on charges with no profit and with no escalator clauses to protect costs against inflationary rises in labour and material. The ship, later renamed *Kungsholm*, was laid down on 1 January 1964. By the end of that year it was clear that the delivery date could not be met, forcing John Rannie to re-negotiate a delivery date of 19 December 1965. The new contract specified that delivery beyond then would incur penalties of £3,000 per day. As work on *Kungsholm* continued, Cunard prepared to invite tenders for the ship that became *QE2*.

Q4

After *Q3* had been cancelled, Cunard reflected on the type of ship most appropriate in the changed operating conditions on the North Atlantic. Sir John Brocklebank, Cunard Chairman, commented in March 1962, - 'She must be a top flight cruise ship and a revolutionary North Atlantic unit with a concept in advance of any existing ship.'[885] Vickers Armstrong's Q3 design had earned them a contract from Cunard, signed in May 1963, to develop a concept proposal for Q4 at Barrow. Although Cunard maintained a dialogue with John Brown's throughout the development period of the new ship, technically important work had thus been lost to Vickers

Part of Kungsholm's *raked bow being lowered into position.*

Armstrong. The design for the successor ship, Q4, eventually to become the QE2, developed into a ship of 57,000tons with two shafts. Unlike Q3, Q4 was to be capable of negotiating the Panama Canal and therefore able to cruise from ports on either coast of the United States. On 19 August 1964 invitations to tender were issued to Fairfield, Cammell Laird,

Harland & Wolff, Vickers Armstrong/Swan Hunter and John Brown. In October, Cammell Laird dropped out of the competition to be followed by Fairfield in November. The main John Brown Board met at The Sanctuary, John Brown's London office, to discuss and approve the terms of the quotation for Q4. In consideration of the great prestige of the contract, it was agreed to cover full costs, full charges but include no profit although this was kept secret at the time. The Board felt that 'extras' by way of changes to the contract during construction would ensure no loss. It was their view that the contract for this ship must be won.[886] On 30 November the tenders from the remaining three shipbuilders were opened. With a tender price of £25,427,000, John Brown's price was the lowest and its delivery date of May 1968 the earliest. However, Sir John Brocklebank and his staff were shocked to note that all three tenders were in excess of the £22 million set aside for the ship. John Brown was advised that its tender was the lowest but that their price would have to be cut down before a contract could be signed. Cunard asked them to reduce the cost of the ship by approximately £2 million. To qualify in time for the loan under the Government's Shipbuilding Credit Scheme, it was essential that the final figure be reached quickly. A team of Cunard personnel led by Dan Wallace, naval architect and Tom Kameen, superintendent engineer, came to Clydebank to meet with John Starks and George Strachan. Over the course of three weeks, with beer and sandwiches at weekends, the cuts were made. Even at this stage there was some doubt about whether or not the ship would go ahead.[887] The contract for Q4 was signed on 30 December 1964. There was much jubilation in the yard: Work for a large number of people on the world's most prestigious shipbuilding contract had been secured for three years. Cunard, too, was delighted that the old partnership was in business once again. Tom Kameen recalls that John Brown's was held in very high regard by Cunard, based partly on the technical excellence of the two original Queens, and partly on the 'terrific support and assistance given to Cunard in running their fleet'.[888] In December 1964, no one could have foreseen the troubles that would lie ahead.

During the course of 1965, other substantial contracts were booked or in progress. These included the 12,000ton cargo liner *Glenfinlas* for the Glen Line, the 18,000ton bulk carrier *Cape St Vincent* for charter to Lyle Shipping Co., and the partial conversion of *Queen Elizabeth* to be carried out during 1966. The latter contract enabled continuity of employment to be maintained for finishing trades after the departure of *Kungsholm* in 1966. Additionally, three jackup drilling rigs for the North Sea were ordered by International Drilling Co. Ltd. the first North Sea orders to be placed with any shipbuilder in the UK. Work in hand included, *Kungsholm*, the lumber carrier *Vennachar*, the assault ship *Intrepid*, the partial

subjected to no fewer than eight stoppages by finishing trades, principally plumbers and electricians. In a letter to the Swedish American Line, dated 31 January 1966, Company Secretary Robin Williamson sought to explain the position:

'As evidence of the difficult labour conditions prevailing in this period, it is interesting to note that increases in wage rates in the shipyard of

The striking lines of the Swedish America liner Kungsholm *take shape. A section from the jack-up rig* North Star *is in the foreground.*

conversion of the intermediate liner *Sylvania* and a second 70,000ton tanker, for BP, *British Confidence*. *Kungsholm* was launched on 15 April 1965 and taken to the basin for fitting-out to begin. The late arrival of drawings for the Intrepid delayed her completion which meant that both vessels were now in contention for the limited number of men of the finishing trades, a position which management had sought to avoid in their original production schedules.[889] Much to the irritation of the navy overseer at Clydebank, more men were put on *Kungsholm* than on the assault ship. Given the penalties for late delivery on the liner, there was a simple and compelling logic behind this. The Navy could wait. At the same time, the yard was hit by a rash of disputes in which *Kungsholm's* fitting-out was

approximately 20% in nine months were awarded. The excessive demands made by labour in an economy where the demand for skilled and unskilled labour developed to far exceed the supply, were met in an attempt to keep delay to a minimum, albeit at a cost not predicted at the time when extension of delivery was agreed and totally unforeseen at the negotiation of the contract.'[890]

Williamson continued that in conceding to high wage demands, senior management had:

'. . . not only to deal with difficulties as soon as they arose, but also foresee many of them and avoid disruption of work before they materialised. Despite these efforts, from time-to-time the underlying discontent and uneasiness of

the workpeople erupted in overt actions . . . It cannot be too strongly emphasised that these incidents, are only the culmination of day-to-day continuous difficulties the like of which our shipyard has never before experienced'
Knowing that management was vulnerable, claims for higher wages were pressed in the traditional manner. The effect of this was to delay *Kungsholm's*

workmanship which is most costly.'[893] The Swedish American Line was delighted with the ship they received. They had every reason to be. If John Brown's failure to win the Norwegian America Line contract for *Sagafjord* late in 1962 had contributed in some degree to the Kungsholm debacle, management at Clydebank must have been chastened to note that the *Sagafjord* contract had put her French builders out

Kungsholm departs Clydebank in March 1966 leaving behind the greatest loss ever made by the company on a single contract.

delivery until 11 March 1966 resulting in significant penalty payments. More importantly, the actual cost of building the ship had risen out of all proportion to the original tender of only a few years earlier. By 7 January 1966, the loss on *Kungsholm*, excluding penalties, was a staggering £2,474,000.[891] The Company had no option but to swallow this particularly bitter pill. At the end of the contract, losses had accelerated beyond £3 million.[892] Ironically, in *Kungsholm*, Clydebank had produced a magnificent ship equal to the finest traditions of the yard. A comment in the shipyard report for February 1966 offers some explanation and confirms the view that the Swedes were exacting in their demands: 'Inspectors have been most severe ensuring a quite exceptionally high standard of material and

of business.
Attention now focused on *Q4*, the keel for which had been laid in July 1965 with launching planned for mid 1967. *Q4* had been tendered for and laid down before the true scale of losses on *Kungsholm* had been learned. Losses on a similar scale would be catastrophic for Clydebank and the John Brown Company. In his annual report for 1966, Lord Aberconway included the following chilling statement:

'The outcome of this contract, decisive perhaps for the continuance of Clydebank as a shipyard and for the future livelihood of those who work there, depends greatly on how well our team of management, staff and workpeople work. I cannot emphasise to each of them too strongly how much it is in his own interest that he should strain every nerve to make this contract come out on the right side, and not let it come out on the wrong side.'[894]

GAS TURBINES

The Company's second foray into gas turbines was to prove highly successful although, at first, the true potential of the business was not appreciated. In 1965, the General Electric Company at Schenectady, New York State, had perfected an industrial open cycle gas turbine which was selling well. To exploit this development, General Electric was in the process of establishing a number of joint manufacturing agreements with other companies throughout the world. It will be recalled that, in the early 1900s, John Brown and General Electric had collaborated on the development of the Brown-Curtis marine steam turbine. It appears that memories of previous collaboration had been erased and it was to Constructors John Brown (CJB), the civil engineering division of the John Brown Group, that General Electric originally turned as a potential partner. CJB promptly directed the Americans to its sister division at Clydebank. A deputation from General Electric's Gas Turbine Division, led by their Marketing Manager, Whit Ridgeway, travelled to Clydebank to make an assessment of John Brown's suitability and manufacturing capability. From the start, the relationship augured well. When the financial resources of the Clydebank Company were discussed, George Strachan, Clydebank's Engineering Director, was able to produce a Clydesdale Bank £1 note which bore an illustration of John Brown's shipyard. With the quip 'we print our own money' the circumstances were created for a congenial and constructive business relationship. By May 1965, with an agreement signed, John Brown Engineering (JBE) was committed to gas turbine manufacture. The nature of the agreement specified that the turbine design together with the rotors, the sophisticated heart of the turbine, would be supplied by General Electric together with a number of other specified parts. JBE would manufacture or buy in all the remaining components of the gas turbine and assemble them at Clydebank. The agreement brought difficulties, both philosophical and commercial. The Americans conducted business on what they termed an Advanced Ordering Concept in which turbines were manufactured for stock to ensure rapid supply when an order was received. Although the turbine still required to be modified to the particular

requirements of the customer, delivery could then be made within a reasonably short time. This approach was in stark contrast to John Brown's commercial practice where an order was a prerequisite to the manufacturing process. The Advanced Order Concept went against the grain. Moreover, gas turbines required new activities which simply did not exist within the marine engineering structure at

Clydebank. Stores, technical, installation, sales and maintenance organisations had to be created from nowhere. At first there was a degree of scepticism about the merits of entering into this field, particularly when Clydebank began the manufacture of the first three gas turbines as an act of faith in total absence of any orders. If General Electric's unsolicited arrival at Clydebank could be assigned to providence, then management would have been forgiven for interpreting a blackout in New York as divine intervention. On 9 November 1965, much of the north eastern portion of the United States was plunged into chaos affecting 30 million people following a series of power failures which resulted in the progressive loss of all electricity supplies. To provide alternative power systems, public utilities swamped General Electric with orders for gas turbine power units. Unable to meet demand, the Americans immediately looked to their new partners across the Atlantic, bought all three gas turbines under construction at Clydebank and placed an order for a further three at the same time. It was clear to all concerned that the market to support the Advanced Order Concept was viable and that Clydebank had the makings of a highly profitable core business. Plans to diversify into general engineering were now unnecessary. Significantly, the activity which was responsible for the Company's inception in 1847, the construction of marine engines, was about to end. The Sulzer diesel for the bulk carrier *Kyoto Forest* was the last constructed at Clydebank for a John Brown built ship. In 1970, a set of steam turbines were built under a Stal-Laval license for the tanker *Texaco Great Britain* constructed by Swan Hunter. The marine era finally

The Clydesdale Bank £1 note with an engraving of John Brown's fitting-out basin on the back which Engineering Director George Strachan jokingly produced to impress Whit Ridgeway, General Electric's Marketing Manager. (courtesy of the Clydesdale Bank)

263

Below
The launch of British Confidence *in February 1965, the last tanker to be built at Clydebank.*

Bottom
Cape St Vincent throwing her helm over during turning trials in June 1966.

came to an end in 1972 when a Frame 3 gas turbine was built to drive a generator on a Ro-Ro ship building in Australia for the Union Steamship Company.[895]

The ability to manufacture gas turbines was well within Clydebank's grasp. However, to win business independently of General Electric, turbines had to be marketed and sold in the context of a complete power

station. This required a range of skills virtually unknown within John Brown's. To the great credit of the Company, they transformed themselves into an international gas turbine power station contractor - a wholly different business from making engines. In a remarkably short space of time, John Brown Engineering had succeeded in reinventing itself.[896]

RECOGNISING THE PROBLEMS

During the 1950s, the era of riveted ship construction came to an end to be replaced by welding. Welding enabled large sections of a ship's structure to be prefabricated under cover before being transported to the berth for erection by heavy cranes. This technology introduced the concept of 'flow production' in which ships were built in a manner not dissimilar to a production line found in a car plant. This concept was amenable to more advanced methods of production and quality control in which management acted to ensure the maximum throughput of steel. This encouraged a new breed of graduate engineer into the industry, responsible for promoting efficient working practices. In the United Kingdom, this tended to militate against the tradition in which men worked their way up to positions of responsibility through an experiential path. The systemisation of the shipbuilding process enabled some countries in the Far East and Europe, where shipbuilding had not been a major industry, to expand. High labour rates did not imply lack of competitiveness. In Sweden yards such as Gøtaverken's Arendal yard at Gothenburg and Kockums at Malmø adopted highly automated and flexible flow-production techniques to ensure competitiveness despite high labour costs.

The emergence of intense competition from new yards in the Far East and Europe provided British shipowners with choices which would challenge old allegiances to the home industry. In many British shipyards, the shift from riveted to welded construction brought few initial advantages. Changeover required expensive redevelopment of the shipyard site together with new facilities and plant. The unions, recognising the threat to employment strove to preserve jobs and demand manning at the old levels. Compromise resulted. Typically, tasks which required five men under old methods and, which might now be accomplished with two, were performed with three. Productivity gains were thus minimised. Management took little time to consider the future of the industry partly because it was preoccupied with the day to day problems of running the business. One hundred years as the world's most successful shipbuilding nation militated against radical thinking. With loss of market share and consequently loss of jobs, unions could hardly be blamed for trying to preserve what it could. The traditions and attitudes which existed on both sides of the shipbuilding industry did not augur well in the face of the greatest challenge in its history.

factors contributing to the success of overseas builders. Management functions, production control methods, organisation of labour, management/ worker relations, subsidies and low labour costs were positive influences on overall operating conditions. In January 1965, a deputation headed by Roy Mason, Minister of State for Shipping, visited Japanese shipyards and met with the Japanese Shipbuilder's

The handsome Glenfinlas *running trials on the Firth of Clyde on 29 December 1966.*

At Clydebank, the loss of competitiveness resulted in a £1.4 million trading loss for the year 1964, prompting Lord Aberconway to comment that such losses were 'insupportable'. The trend towards ever larger tankers and bulk carriers continued unabated. The 100,000ton capacity of the new west yard at Clydebank was incapable of building the ships now wanted. By 1964, design studies envisaged ships up to 250,000tons. For most of the British builders who constructed ships of the largest dimensions, the huge increase in ship size over such a short space of time presented difficulties in planning future construction strategies.

A modern shipyard was, however, only one of many

Above
A draughtsman drawing a line for a test tank model in 1963.

Left
The new ship drawing office in July 1964.

Association. The eight yards visited were generally larger than their British counterparts and, in the many cases where these yards were new or newly extended, were building in very large docks rather than on slipways. The typical time taken to build a 70,000ton ship was less than half a year, a much shorter period than British practice allowed.

In a memo to John Rannie in March 1965, George Strachan, who met Roy Mason soon after his return from Japan, said that he (Mason) 'took a poor view of our shipbuilding capacity compared with what he saw in Japan' The short report published as a result of this visit to Japan referred to a number of points pertaining to the successful position of the Japanese industry:

- A permanent labour force organised in one shipyard union, paid at marginally lower rates than in the UK.
- A management structure which contained large numbers of men at middle management level with control of individual shops.
- Middle management was invariably technically qualified graduates with practical experience in the work for which they were responsible.
- The widespread use of planning and production control techniques and of computers in these fields as well as in ship design.
- In every case where facilities were being extended, construction docks in preference to slipways.[897]

It was against this background of concern for the industry that the President of the Board of Trade, Douglas Jay, set up the Shipbuilding Inquiry Committee in February 1965, under the chairmanship of Reay Geddes. This was to report on the changes necessary to make the British shipbuilding and marine engineering industries competitive. At company level, John Brown's was similarly motivated to consider what it might do to safeguard its future, and thus the Newshot Isle Project came into being.

NEWSHOT ISLE PROJECT

This remarkable plan envisaged construction of a shipyard at Clydebank comparable with overseas super yards where production costs would be on a par with the best European yards and close to that of the Japanese.[898] For a time, the Newshot Isle Project lifted the collective spirits of the John Brown management. The project appeared to meet three

An aerial view of Newshot Isle showing the proposed diversion of the River Clyde.

separate strategic requirements: a deepened river channel for the Clyde Navigation Trust, a new ore terminal for the steel industry and a super yard for John Brown and Company. For the latter, this project was arguably a defining moment. After sixty five years of largely profitable shipbuilding at Clydebank, a bright future might yet be secured from impending financial failure.

The origin of the Newshot Isle Project lay not with management at Clydebank shipyard but with the Clyde Navigation Trust. The principal engineer, Barclay Braithwaite, was contemplating the same problem shared by shipbuilders: the ever increasing size of ships. A factor of equal concern for Braithwaite was the future trading prospects of the River Clyde following likely British membership of the European Economic Community. Trade with the EEC would surely favour ports on the east coast.

Further incentive to develop the Clyde lay also in the knowledge that the National Ports Council proposed to spend £100m over the next ten years in improving British ports. However, the Clyde Navigation Trust's sensitivity to the shipbuilding industry's need for new facilities was as much a motivating factor, such was the age old interest existing between them. Braithwaite's principal concern was that within a short period of time, large ships would be unable to make the passage upriver to the docks in Glasgow because of the restrictions inherent in the river itself. Larger ships meant lower freight costs. It very much seemed that Glasgow was facing extinction as a port. The River Clyde was essentially canalised and had been modified over a period of two hundred years in a remarkable series of engineering initiatives. The steady increase in ship size, up to and including the Queens of the 1930s, had been matched by a series of measures resulting in selected widening and dredging of the channel. Now, with the comparatively sudden and dramatic increase in ship size during the 1950s and 60s, solutions of a more comprehensive nature were needed. The bend in the River Clyde at Dalmuir, itself partly a creation of river engineering, was one of the most difficult to negotiate, and indeed, on her voyage down river, the *Queen Mary* had stuck on the north bank, blocking the navigable channel.

The Clyde Navigation Trust already had a proposed scheme of river improvement from Greenock to the King George V dock in Glasgow, requiring dredging to permit vessels with five foot greater draught to make the passage. Further dredging was planned to remove yet another five feet from the river. In its natural state, the river Clyde had diverged at Dalmuir into a north and south channel to form what is known as Newshot Isle. In the 1860s, as part of the

series of river improvements, the south channel was closed and the north channel developed into the main navigable waterway. William Girvan, one of Braithwaite's assistant engineers, first proposed the simple solution of reversing this process. As a consequence the river would be straightened and a large amount of land i.e. the old riverbed and the greater part of Newshot Isle, would become available for industrial development. Indeed, the old riverbed would make an ideal shipbuilding dock. Additionally, ground and water would become available for the creation of a new iron-ore terminal to replace General Terminus in Glasgow. The plan had immediate appeal. When Braithwaite asked Clydebank's Managing Director, John Rannie, if he had any possible use for this ground, Rannie, in wholly characteristic fashion, seized the drawing which the port engineer had prepared and rushed

A plan showing the imaginative but abortive Newshot Isle Project. The plan was to divert the Clyde through Newshot Isle thereby making the old river bed available for constructing three large building docks.

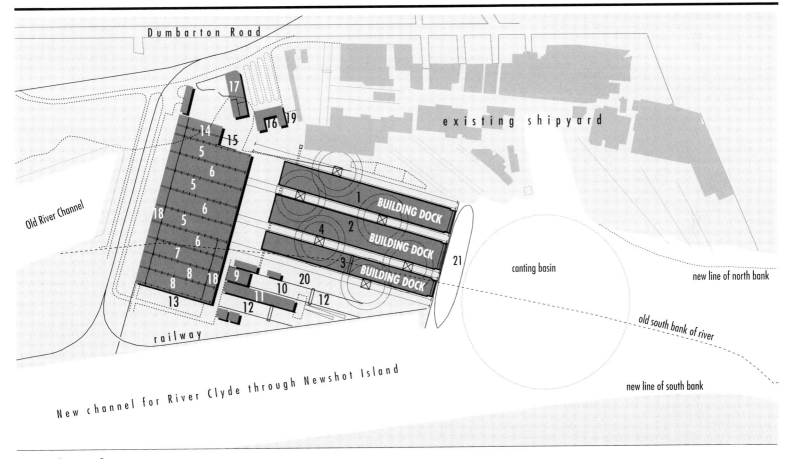

Newshot Isle Project
1965 (3 Building Dock Scheme)

1. No 1 Building Dock 1,300' x 170' at entrance x 25' at HW
2. No 2 Building Dock 1,300' x 190' at entrance x 25' at HW
3. No 3 Building Dock 1,300' x 150' at entrance x 30' at HW
4. 6 Level luffing travelling cranes : 120 tons at 140', 80tons at 190' lift 175'
5. Major Assembly Bay 120' span (2 x 100 tons and 2 x 40 tons)
6. Sub Assembly Bay120' span (2 x 40 tons)
7. Frame Bay 100' span (2 x 20 tons)
8. Plate Bay 100' span (2 x 20 tons)
9. Section Preparation
10. Section Stockyard
11. Plate Preparation (2 lines)
12. Plate Stockyard (1 x 20 tons)
13. Future extension
14. Pipework and Fittings
15. Plate Stockyard
16. Offices
17. Canteen and Welfare
18. Marshalling, Stowage and Cross Transfer area (3 x 20 ton semi goliath)
19. Main Yard Entrance
20. Unit Storage Area
21. Fitting-ot Quay

Existing Shipyard

Proposed Shipyard

Feet   500   1000
Metres   152   304

back to Clydebank. Staff at Clydebank worked in secrecy over the next ten days to develop the scheme. Rannie saw the enormous potential for a new shipyard the equal of any in the world and, after some preliminary work at Clydebank, consulted Lord Aberconway. Aberconway was immediately supportive and wrote to Roy Mason at the Board of Trade on 26 March 1965:

'knowing of your keen interest in promoting the efficiency of the shipbuilding industry, . . I write to give you very early and preliminary information of a highly imaginative scheme whereby a completely modern shipyard on the Clyde, to build ships up to 200,000tons deadweight in building docks, could be constructed, at, we believe, no prohibitive cost.'

Aberconway's letter identified the principal benefits in favour of the scheme:

1. By making the river straighter Glasgow would become more accessible to large ships.
2. A vast new shipbuilding yard would be created
3. Creation of an iron-ore terminal in the basin formed by blocking the old river channel.

He also referred to the wider implications resulting form the proposal:

'A scheme like this could well be the means of achieving on the Clyde a far-reaching measure of rationalisation. I would make it clear that John Brown's would welcome a venture among Clyde shipbuilders, whom we should lead, to set up and operate such a yard comprising both the proposed and existing facilities. We would also hope for Government participation.'

It was clear that such a grand scheme, estimated at £25m, would require considerable justification and support, not to mention a financial commitment which John Brown could not provide alone. A key element would be to persuade other Clyde shipbuilders to join. Letters were sent to William Ross, Secretary of State for Scotland, Lord Bilsland, Chairman of the Scottish Development Council (and a John Brown Director), the Minister of Transport, the Scottish Trades Union Congress and others. Rannie held a meeting at Clydebank on 16 April with Babtie Shaw & Morton, the Glasgow consulting engineers and Tom Craig, Managing Director of Colvilles Ltd.[899]
On 28 April, the Geddes Committee, under the terms of their remit, visited Clydebank for preliminary consultations and discussions with John Brown about the future of the shipbuilding industry. Lord Aberconway and Sir Eric Mensforth from the parent

John Brown Board were joined by Clydebank directors John Rannie, George Strachan, John Starks and Dr. John Brown. The new scheme was presented before the Committee who received it positively and asked to be kept in touch as it developed.
The following day, John Rannie fronted a press launch at Clydebank under the general heading 'Huge Shipyard Extension Plan to Cater for Mammoth Ships'. The press was given the following copies of replies made to Aberconway's original letter as something of a testimonial for the scheme:
Roy Mason, Minister of State for Shipping.

'. . . I welcome the company's initiative in putting forward, as a basis for discussion with all interested parties, this interesting and forward looking idea in the field of shipbuilding techniques new to this country. I quite see that the proposal would have considerable advantages from the company's point of view. A detailed examination will, however, be needed of the benefits of the scheme, not only to John Brown's but also to shipbuilding generally on the Clyde, and of its implications for other interests in the area. The preliminary and tentative nature of the scheme precludes such consideration at the present stage. I will await with interest the results of the further study which the company are putting in hand.'

The Secretary of State for Scotland.

'. . . the Secretary of State has been most impressed by John Brown's initiative in developing the outline of this far-sighted scheme. It is of great importance to Scotland that the Clyde should have the best possible shipbuilding and port facilities. The Secretary of State warmly welcomes the Company's decision to discuss their scheme with the other bodies concerned with it and to put in hand a detailed examination of its feasibility'

Reay Geddes, Shipbuilding Inquiry Committee.

'The scheme has been outlined to the committee who raised a number of questions on which they would like to have further information. The Committee welcomed the Company's initiative in bringing forward constructive proposals for a major development of the industry's facilities on the Clyde along new and imaginative lines'

Tom Craig, Chairman of Colvilles Ltd. was more guarded in his support for the project but promised to give it serious consideration along with any other proposals for a new ore terminal.[900] The Clyde Trust was strongly in favour of the plan and, at the

QE2. *Instructions signalled to the craneman as a prefabricated unit is lowered into position on the berth.*

Far left
The bulbous bow is about to be welded to the rest of the ship.

Left
One of two six-bladed propellers.

Management Meeting of the Trust on 4 May, Thomas Robinson, Chairman, committed the Trust to the project which he said 'must be carried through'. Following a good response from the media, the preparation of a thorough project report was put in motion. Glasgow consultant engineers, Babtie Shaw & Morton, worked on the engineering aspects of the scheme and obtained estimates from a number of firms. [901] A thorough site inspection including an aerial survey and test bores for a soil investigation for the new south channel and the building of the docks was conducted. While the engineering report was underway, John Rannie initiated a wide ranging survey among potential customers including: Texaco Inc., Esso, BP Tanker Co. Ltd., Mobil Oil Co. Inc., Shell International Marine Ltd., with the intention of establishing the maximum size of tanker likely to be ordered in the foreseeable future. The dimensions of existing and proposed docks were listed. Economies expected to accrue from the project together with proposed new working practices and anticipated production costs were investigated. Cooper Brothers & Co. chartered accountants, were asked to examine all financial aspects of the scheme.

On 2 November the general manager of the Clyde Navigation Trust, R Proudfoot, wrote to John Brown's concerning provisional details of the ore terminal at Newshot and of plans to dredge the river for large ships. The new ore terminal would be 2,000 feet long and be capable of berthing two 65,000 dwt. ore carriers, although in the first instance dredging would take place to accommodate 45,000 dwt. vessels. He agreed that existing river depths were sufficient for the safe passage of very large tankers in light condition from Clydebank to the Tail of the Bank, although some river bends would require modification.

Before the report moved into its final stage, draft papers were circulated among various directors within the John Brown group as well as others outwith. Numerous revisions were made. Aberconway fussed over the final form of words and by mid November 1965, the report was ready for limited circulation to the Minister of State (Shipping), Permanent Secretary at the Board of Trade, Secretary of State for Scotland, the Permanent Secretary at the Scottish Office and Reay Geddes, whose committee was also reaching the final stages of its own report. Aberconway was very sensitive to the latter and deliberately played down the Newshot Scheme until such time as the Geddes Report was in the public domain.

On 5 January 1966, Reay Geddes wrote to Lord Aberconway saying that the issues of very large tankers and building docks would be dealt with in his report, although this would be in general terms without reference to any one company's proposals. The thrust of Geddes comment on the Newshot Report lay in two points. Why build the biggest ships foreseen? No economic justification had been given in the report, and, in Geddes' own words:

'one of the main spheres in which a reduction of costs can be achieved in the industry is by better management/labour relations. This is a matter of importance which will have to be tackled by the industry as a whole, whether or not building docks are constructed.'

John Brown's Newshot Report stressed the necessity for Government participation but also invited other Clyde shipbuilders to become involved in the form of a full merger.

While both the Newshot and Geddes reports had been in preparation, there was an event of great significance which added momentum to both. On 15 October 1965, the Fairfield Shipbuilding & Engineering Co. Ltd. collapsed despite a £34 million order book. The news sent reverberations up and down Clydeside and underlined, in the most dramatic terms, the urgency of the task facing the shipbuilding industry and the Geddes Inquiry. John Brown had identified the Fairfield shipyard as the most likely to share in the Newshot Project largely because of the similarity in product. The failure of Fairfield, unwelcome and unexpected, added urgency to Aberconway's scheme. The other shipbuilders, Stephen's, Yarrow's and Connell's, were, however, completely unimpressed and saw it as an attempt to bail John Brown's out. In March 1966, the Geddes Report was published. Two shipbuilding groups were envisaged for the Clyde, an upper and a lower group. There was no mention of the Newshot Isle scheme. John Brown's bid to build and manage a new yard on the Clyde had fallen on deaf ears. When it came, Government investment in a super yard went to Belfast. In September 1967, approval was given to the construction of a large building dock at Harland & Wolff at a cost of £13.5 million of which £8.5 million was in the form of Government grants. [902]

There was more bad news for John Brown. In February 1966, The Secretary of State for Defence, Denis Healey, published the White Paper which sealed the fate of the British aircraft carrier. Healey's strategic priorities excluded the building of aircraft carriers, further reducing Clydebank's prospects for winning profitable naval work. The implications for major British shipyards were obvious: the foreseeable future would be one without very large surface capital ship contracts. Henceforth, new capital ships would be exclusively of the submarine type. Vickers Armstrong at Barrow, and, to a lesser extent, Cammell Laird at Birkenhead, had cornered this

all the UK builders approached. John Brown's were clearly not competitive at building ships of this type, which, historically they had never been interested in. Increasingly, however, it was to this type of ship that they had to turn in the absence of demand for passenger cargo vessels.

In the wake of the *Kungsholm* disaster, in June 1966, Lord Aberconway wrote to John Rannie under the

particular market. It was clear from 1966 onwards, that John Brown's future naval role would be limited and that competition for contracts would be intense. An indication of the trap closing around Clydebank was given in 1966 when the Wearside shipbuilders, Austin & Pickersgill, invited other UK builders to participate in construction of their SD14 standard design. A&P's cost to build an SD14 was £883,000 while, at £1,342,00, John Brown's was the dearest of

heading 'Clydebank Liquidity' to ask for a projection of cash and trading forecasts for the next three years. The letter pointed out what John Rannie knew already - the previous three years had accumulated losses of over £4 million. While these losses had been made good by transfers from the parent company, Rannie was to assume, henceforth, that there would be no further subventions, out of shipbuilding reserves built up in better days, from the parent.

The elegant bow of QE2 *in September 1967.*

'no further moral debt from John Brown to Clydebank remains . . . (and any) remaining indebtedness of Clydebank to John Brown will be in the ordinary course of business. For the purposes of this exercise (forecasting to 1969) that indebtedness should be regarded as having to be repaid at an early date, and the weight of financing deemed thereafter to be placed upon the bank.'[903]

Queen Elizabeth arrives at John Brown's main entrance on the day of the launch.

Opposite page
20 September 1967. Clydebank shipyard's last triumph takes to the water.

Clydebank shipyard was on its own. After much consideration and several reforecasts, Robin Williamson, Financial Director, sent the forecast to Sheffield in handwriting as 'we can't raise a typist this morning' on Saturday 17 September 1966. The projections from 30 September 1966 to 31 March 1968 indicated keeping below the assumed bank overdraft limit of £850,000 but the indebtedness to the parent company would rise from £3,560,000 to £5,860,000. The forecast results of losses were:

Year to 31 March 1967	£269,000
Year to 31 March 1968	£391,000
Year to 31 March 1969	£1,230,000
with *Q4* making no profit and the yard empty.[904]	

The actual loss for 1967 alone was £932,175. It seemed certain that under the terms of Lord Aberconway's letter, Clydebank shipyard would close after the *Q4* had been completed.

In October 1966, the shipyard and engine works were split into two separate businesses. This was in recognition that the shipyard would probably fail or be merged with other Clyde yards, in line with the recommendations of the Geddes Report. The engine works, which a few years earlier had seemed to be in terminal decline through the contraction of marine work, were showing all the signs of making a dramatic recovery courtesy of General Electric and the industrial gas turbine. Renamed John Brown Engineering (Clydebank) Limited, the engine works would remain firmly under the wing of the John Brown parent.

THE FAIRFIELD COLLAPSE

The outcome of the Fairfield collapse had a bearing on subsequent events. Closure of this modernised yard seemed unthinkable. It was one of the classic names in British heavy industry with a history as long as that of Clydebank's. Iain Stewart, chairman of Hall Thermotank, the air conditioning and ventilation specialists, stepped in to take the yard over. He found a willing supporter in George Brown, Minister of Economic Affairs in the Labour Government, who was able to persuade the Government to put up an immediate £1 million to keep the yard going until its future could be determined within the context of the soon to be published Geddes Report. At the same time, Stewart persuaded a number of prominent businessmen and trade unions to contribute towards maintaining the yard. These included Hugh Stenhouse, Harold Salvesen, Isaac Woolfson and Roy Thomson. Stewart's ambition was not limited to sustaining the existing business but to overhauling the manner in which the business was conducted. Labour relations, modern methods of management and production control were the essential elements in what became known as the 'Fairfield Experiment.' In January 1966, Fairfield (Glasgow) Limited started trading.

THE GEDDES REPORT

The Geddes Report, published in March 1966, recommended the creation of large groups on the main shipbuilding rivers and districts. Rationalisation was implicit. Reduction in the number of yards in the 'Warship Group[905]' of which John Brown was a member, was also recommended. Through merger, shipbuilding firms would reduce costs by directing resources such as marketing, design, purchasing, personnel, training, and management services through one organisation. Geddes did not subscribe to the view that large

Opposite page
*Welders at work in the West Yard
on 26 February 1968.*

building docks were necessarily the way forward. The benefits of merger were similar to those of Lord Aberconway's Newshot Isle scheme without the cost of building a new super yard. Thus the scene was set for the creation of two shipbuilding groups on the River Clyde, Scott Lithgow on the lower reaches and Upper Clyde Shipbuilders on the upper reaches. To enable restructuring and modernisation of the industry, the Government established the Shipbuilding Industry Board, (SIB) under Sir William Swallow, to direct groupings and to act as a mechanism through which grants and funds could be funnelled.[906] The SIB was seen as a temporary body which would cease activities once a rationalised shipbuilding industry had been restored to a competitive position. The prospect of substantial Government grants to facilitate merger and re-equipping energised discussion between yards. As early as August 1966, the three family controlled yards, Stephen's, Connell's and Yarrow's, had taken the first steps towards merger. They had no intention of including the two larger yards, Fairfield and John Brown. The radical management controls and Government intervention in the 'experiment' at Fairfield did not accord with either their working methods or ideology. John Brown's was a loss maker with the largest single shipbuilding order on its books. Repetition of losses on anything like the scale of *Kungsholm* would bring the whole group down. At Fairfield, Iain Stewart proposed the merger of Fairfield with John Brown, where his new methods could be applied to the Q4.[907] Discussions between the two firms were held in London. John Rannie resisted the idea of introducing the work study methods in operation at Fairfield on the basis that they would interfere with methods currently in place. For the Fairfield team, the prospect of merger with a company unable to embrace the methods which were virtually their raison d'être was anathema.[908] While these discussions were grinding on to little effect, an SIB working party set about the task of looking at the individual Clyde yards and recommending a merger under the terms of the Geddes Report.

The working party of three was chaired by Anthony Hepper, a director of Thomas Tilling Ltd.[909] The others were Jasper Macmichael, a management consultant and A. W. Giles, from merchant bankers Baring Brothers.[910] In March, Tom Burleigh, Managing Director of Firth Brown Tools Ltd., was made Deputy Chairman of John Brown & Company (Clydebank) Ltd. His immediate task was to negotiate the Company position in merger

discussions with the SIB at the first meeting on 22 March 1967. Back at Clydebank, the Board agreed that orders for container ships would be pursued in recognition that a transport revolution was taking place in which containerisation was replacing the traditional piecemeal movement of goods.[911] This development marked the gradual eclipse of the passenger cargo ship, another type of vessel in which John Brown's had specialised. In July, the SIB working party announced its conclusions. It envisaged that John Brown's, Fairfield's and Yarrow's would form the nucleus of the proposed group and that Stephen's and Connell's would be closed when their order books ran out. Rationalisation on this scale would reduce the existing labour force of 13,000 to 7,500. Curiously, the most recently modernised of all Clyde yards, the Swan Hunter owned Barclay Curle, was not included and closed in 1968.[912] The basis of the merger was calculated on the assets of each yard together with the value of its order book. Fairfield emerged as the largest shareholder with 35% and John Brown second with 30%. Yarrow was allotted 20%, Stephen 10% and Connell 5%.

In the midst of merger discussions, the Q4 was brought to launch on time, 20 September 1967. In the engine shops the ship's turbine machinery and boilers were well advanced. Pametrada, the designers of *Q4's* machinery, ceased to exist in 1967 and John Brown recruited the nucleus of their design team specifically to work on the liner's machinery contract. The many uncertainties surrounding the yard's future were temporarily forgotten on this warm sunny day as thousands of people flocked to the yard and the opposite bank of the river in time honoured fashion. As with the previous Queens, the name of the new liner had been kept a secret. At 2.28, Queen Elizabeth christened the ship *Queen Elizabeth the Second* and pressed the button sending her into the water. At the same time, aircraft from 736 Squadron the Fleet Air Arm flew overhead in an anchor formation.

To prepare for merger, Clydebank shipyard was first de-coupled from John Brown & Co. (Clydebank) Ltd., to become John Brown & Co. (Shipbuilders) Ltd on 25 January 1968. The Board of the new company comprised John Rannie, Managing Director; John Starks, Assistant Managing Director; George Parker, Shipyard Director; Ian McCallum, Technical Director; Tom Simpson, Commercial Director and Robin Williamson, Secretary. The new company was a stepping stone to the wider merger and had an existence of only two weeks. On 5 February 1968,

John Brown & Co. (Shipbuilders) was sold to Upper Clyde Shipbuilders in exchange for 1,199,999 £1 shares in the new company.[913] Lord Aberconway had been relieved of a loss making subsidiary but had gained a major shareholding in the Government supported Upper Clyde Shipbuilders Limited.

UPPER CLYDE SHIPBUILDERS LTD

The John Brown shipyard was now the Clydebank Division of Upper Clyde Shipbuilders Limited (UCS) which had other Divisions at Linthouse, Scotstoun and Govan. The group also had a 51% controlling interest in the Yarrow shipyard at Scotstoun. In a demonstration of even-handedness, the headquarters were located at Fitzpatrick House in the centre of Glasgow. Former John Brown men were well represented on the Board of UCS with four out of fourteen seats. Tom Burleigh, Director; John Rannie, Special Director in charge of QE2; John Starks, Technical Director and Robin Williamson, Financial Director. Anthony Hepper was Chairman with Sir Charles Connell, Sir Eric Yarrow and Iain Stewart as Deputy Chairmen. Within two months, Iain Stewart's role was marginalised by the nascent UCS Board and he resigned.

The task facing the new company was complex and demanding. The five constituent companies had to be forged into a single identity under new management, production and financial controls. Modernisation and re-equipment of the yards would be required. The redeployment of company resources consistent with efficient production had to be implemented. Initially, it was considered that a major reduction in manpower and closure of the Linthouse and Scotstoun shipyards was required. Most importantly, the new management had to stem years of endemic loss making and bring the Company to break even point and thence to profitability. Government policy was to support this fundamental overhaul of what was one of Britain's oldest and hitherto most successful industries. The SIB, set up by the Ministry of Technology, was the instrument through which the finance to mobilise these objectives was channelled. However, SIB funds were not simply there for the taking. UCS had to develop a corporate plan to reconcile the above objectives. Money would not be released for subsequent phases of restructuring if productivity did not rise and losses were not reduced. Once profitability was achieved, Government funds would cease. The formation of UCS, on 7 February 1968, brought with it the first tranche of £5.5 million from the SIB including a £500,000 loan for capital

equipment. UCS management consultants started work on a Corporate Plan to identify the strategies required to release the funds necessary to turn the business round. This plan was to be submitted to the SIB early in the following year.

The first meeting of the Executive Committee took place on 22 April 1968 at Fitzpatrick House. After inauguration, the first progress reports were received from each of the five divisions. Under John Brown management, the workload at Clydebank had shrunk dramatically with only three ships in the yard, Volnay, QE2 and the recently laid down lumber carrier Vancouver Forest. At this level of loading, Clydebank's chances of reducing losses were negligible. Clydebank's priority, therefore, was to secure new work. Three other contracts were brought forward: another lumber carrier, Kyoto Forest, the drill ship Offshore Mercury and the passenger ferry Blenheim for Fred Olsen. Blenheim's contract included severe penalties for late delivery: £1000 for each day beyond 21 February 1970 and £3,000 per day after 1 May 1970.[914]

New orders were not the only problem confronting the management; labour relations were deteriorating as a result of the new productivity scheme put in place under the terms of SIB assistance. George Parker, Clydebank's Divisional Director, reported an 'irresponsible and unrealistic' wage demand from sheet ironworkers. On 6 May the sheet ironworkers went on strike. They returned on the 27th having won an additional 4d per hour.[915] John Rannie reported that finishing trades were working well on QE2 although a strike of sub-contract pipe coverers, insulators and plumbers was threatening progress. More than any, this was the contract which had the potential to create havoc but Rannie was able to assure the Committee that Cunard had agreed to an increase in the ship's price caused by higher wages. Bulk carriers and large containerships were rapidly replacing the general cargo ship, so much a feature of Clyde shipbuilding output in the past. Unable to build ships larger than 80/100,000tons, it was decided they should concentrate on building standard bulk carrier designs of between 18 to 28,000tons. In avoiding ships of the larger size, the UCS Board considered that their competitive position in medium sized ships had been improved because Japanese yards had been swamped with orders for large tankers.[916]

In August, UCS received an invitation to tender for the conversion of Carinthia and Sylvania into cruise liners, following Cunard's disposal of the ships to

Anthony Hepper, Chairman of Upper Clyde Shipobuilders Ltd. His task was to make the company profitable in the space of a few years. It would prove impossible.

Opposite page
Completing the ship. Clockwise from left, caulking the deck with white marine glue; painters abseil down the funnel painting as they go; varnishing the decks.

Fairwind Shipping Corporation of Monrovia. The work on each ship, valued at between £3 and £4 million, had to be turned down because of insufficient labour. *QE2* was consuming every man-hour that UCS had to spare. With a boom in shipbuilding underway, UCS was receiving a large number of enquiries but lacked the technical capacity to deal with the volume. Similarly, shortages in design

Painting the draught load figures on the liner's bow.

and estimating capacity had the effect of reducing steel throughput.[917] By September, the workload at Clydebank was building up, with six ships including *QE2*. Labour shortages and difficulties continued to plague production. The traditional position of a ship nearing completion with delivery dates to be held gave the men the upper hand. Equally traditional was the certainty that once the ship left the yard, a large

number of men would be unemployed. One hundred and fifty boilermakers were urgently required, while, in protest at a letter which had been sent out to the men urging greater productivity, the engineers held a one day strike and cranemen a ten minute token stoppage. The painters were considering a complete stoppage. John Rannie was not finding his position as special director in charge of *QE2* easy. He required an additional 200 joiners to complete the liner. Delays in the completion programme had been caused when the decorative sub-contractors arrived late, causing ventilation contractors to leave for other work. Nevertheless, Rannie confirmed that the ship would leave Clydebank on 19 November as originally planned. However, labour difficulties among the work force and sub-contractors meant that the ship would leave incomplete. At a Board meeting held in September 1968, Rannie put on record that there had been no last minute alterations or additions to the ship and that Cunard were 'helping us all they can'. Importantly, he had informed Cunard that three areas within the ship would be incomplete on departure from Clydebank.[918] In October, 150 joiners were lent from Lithgow's to work on *QE2*. The continuing shortage of boilermakers pushed back delivery times on the other contracts from between four and eight weeks. The best that could be achieved within the Company was the transfer of 68 men from Linthouse. UCS strove to establish centralised production and management systems from those employed by the old companies and, by November 1968, a production control organisation was in place. On 22 November, with the approval of the Department of Employment & Productivity, phase one of a pay and productivity deal was signed with unions representing UCS's 12,000 workforce. In the same month, production targets were set for the Clydebank and Govan yards where 1,000 tons of steel was to be erected weekly on three berths at each yard. Upgrading steelworking facilities and installing 120 ton berth cranes at Clydebank alone would cost £3.5 million. In December, the plan to load Clydebank with a greater volume of work was assisted when orders for four 54,000ton bulk carriers for the Oriental Marine Company of Seoul were announced.[919] With an order book now standing at 25 ships across the Group, UCS appeared to be making progress. In December 1968, the UCS Board agreed to set aside £500,000 from the remaining SIB grant of £2.25 million for replacement machinery and equipment, in recognition that production facilities required to be brought up to European standards.[920]

A TROUBLED QUEEN

On 31 December 1968, John Rannie would reach retirement age and his service with the company would come to an end. However, as finalising the details of *QE2's* contract was likely to take additional time, he accepted the offer of a further six months service for a retainer of £2,500.[921] On 19 November 1968, *QE2* left Clydebank, on time, for the Firth of

of any major difficulty, the ship would be fully manned by 3 December and ready for acceptance trials by 10 December. The Board was told that a large number of items still had to be fitted before 24 December. Expected labour difficulties affecting the final stages were resolved by paying a £20 finishing bonus. Although these payments were outside the Price Variation Agreement, Cunard agreed to make a

Clyde Dry Dock at Greenock with Sir Basil Smallpiece, Cunard Chairman, and Prince Charles on board. About 100 cabins were incomplete and several hundred men were on board working continuously to finish the ship. At Greenock, John Rannie addressed his men exhorting them to do their utmost to carry the work on. On 27 November, the Cunard Board met and Sir Basil Smallpiece confirmed that in the absence

contribution. Because of the incomplete state of parts of the ship, difficulty was anticipated at the press visit on 10 December. Smallpiece thought this would be addressed by a briefing explaining that John Brown men would be working throughout the trials period.[922]

QE2's first technical trials were carried out between 26 and 30 November but had to be abandoned when

Working flat out through the night to complete the ship a task that was not quite finished when she sailed downriver on 19 November 1968.

279

oil fuel contaminated the feed water system because of a faulty non return valve. At a stroke, delivery was delayed for one week while the trouble was located and put right. This required a lengthy period of cleaning out in the dry dock and forced Cunard to cancel a charity cruise scheduled for Christmas. Cunard took these events in its stride and agreed that final acceptance trials would be conducted on a 10

John Rannie, Special Director for QE2, (left) was set to retire on the hand over of the ship. As a tribute to him, he was presented with a citation on the ship signed by all John Brown men on board. John Starks, Technical Director of Upper Clyde Shipbuilders, congratulates him warmly.

day trip to the west coast of Africa, where air conditioning plant would also be tested.

Trials resumed on 17 December. John Rannie, John Starks and Graham Strachan were on the bridge as the liner worked up speed over the measured mile off Arran. Contract conditions for speed and power were 32 knots and 110,000 shp. *QE2* lived up to expectations recording a speed of 32.5 knots at 117,000 shp. It seemed that all was well. The ship returned to the Tail of the Bank from where she sailed to Southampton and then to the Canary Islands. On Christmas Eve, as she steamed southwards, vibrations were felt from the starboard turbine. Within hours, the world knew that the *QE2* had major technical problems. What should have ended well for *QE2*, UCS and John Rannie rapidly became a disaster. Although the turbines were not Rannie's responsibility, media condemnation of their failure also highlighted the incomplete state of the liner. This was compounded by Sir Basil Smallpiece's very public rejection of the ship. In the last hours of his employment, Rannie and the UCS Chairman, Anthony Hepper, argued over the condition of the ship and Rannie's six months consultancy was withdrawn. When *QE2* docked at Southampton on 2 January 1969, John Rannie slipped quietly away and

into retirement. UCS Technical Director, John Starks, took over the completion of the ship.

At the end of 1968, shortages of manpower and continuing unrest among the unions disrupted output at Clydebank. George Parker, Shipyard Manager, argued that the serious position at Clydebank was not being taken account of at UCS headquarters and he urged an immediate review of the yard's commitments. To alleviate pressure on the drawing office and technical departments, he temporarily took men off *Blenheim*, concentrating them on other contracts.[923] UCS's personnel department also contacted the Ministry of Labour in a bid to inform the men at Burntisland shipyard in Fife, which had recently gone into liquidation, of employment on the Clyde.[924]

Senior men from John Brown Engineering were standing alongside when the *QE2* berthed at Southampton. On 5 January, after the machinery had cooled, inspection of the turbines was carried out. The metal debris visible as the turbine casing was lifted off indicated that the damage was considerable. On inspection, it was clear that the rotors would have to be returned to Clydebank for repair. It was equally clear that repair was going to take much longer than a week.[925] The rotors were airfreighted to Glasgow the following day. Graham Strachan, Managing Director of JBE, placed Jim Turner, the director of the marine and general engineering division in charge of co-ordinating the turbine repair. John Brown engineers quickly realised that the cause of the failure was steam excitation. This can develop when the frequency of vibrations set up inside the turbine results in premature metal fatigue of the blades causing them to snap at the root. The most convenient solution was to redesign and manufacture blades with thicker roots. Sourcing the molybdenum steel from which the blades were made began quickly, and manufacturing the redesigned blades was put in hand.

The Clydebank diagnosis was met with scepticism by Cunard's consultants, the Technical Investigation Department at Lloyds. When Cunard discussed the failure with AEI, with whom turbine orders for Cunard container ships had recently been placed, both JBE and UCS threatened legal action. AEI was a competitor. On 5 February, JBE held a press conference to announce an interim report on their findings. This confirmed their initial diagnosis of steam excitation causing blade failure which they attributed to a design error by the now defunct Pametrada[926]. Sir Basil Smallpiece's reaction was to publicly demand an independent assessor. Newspapers ran headlines quoting the Cunard Chairman 'What Reliance Can We Place on John Brown Engineering?'.[927] The national importance of *QE2* and the bitter disagreement between John Brown Engineering and Cunard ultimately required the involvement of the Minister of Technology, Tony Benn. On 10 February, the Minister convened a meeting to appoint an independent assessor with Sir Basil Smallpiece, Tony Hepper and Sir George Gardner, JBE's Managing Director in attendance. Gardner had previously suggested to Benn that Sir Arnold Lindley, President of the Institution of Mechanical Engineers and a former managing director of GEC, should be considered. Lindley was eminently suitable and Benn had little difficulty in obtaining approval. While this meeting was underway in London, a highly encouraging event occurred in Glasgow. Whit Ridgeway, General Electric's General Manager, had arrived to award the Company the title of 'Manufacturing Associate of the Year' as they had delivered more gas turbines than any other of GE's five associates.

On 11 February, Tony Benn arrived at Clydebank to see the damaged turbines for himself, commenting later at a press conference 'I have come here today to take the steam out of the situation and put it back into the turbines', a comment which was greatly appreciated at Clydebank.[928] Meetings between UCS, JBE and Cunard remained difficult in contrast to the friendliness that had existed between John Brown's and Cunard in the past. With the exception of formal meetings, communication between parties was discouraged and only took place after thorough vetting by lawyers.[929] To complicate negotiations, the press made the most of the situation.

Sir Arnold Lindley's report was made public on 28 February and vindicated the Clydebank engineers. At a press conference Sir Arnold said:

> 'Steam excitation is a phenomenon well known to steam turbine engineers not only in Britain but also in Europe and America. In the case of marine turbines which operate under variable speed conditions, this excitation is particularly difficult to avoid.
>
> It should be made clear that there is no reflection whatsoever on the quality of workmanship or of the material used in any part of the construction of the turbines.
>
> The remedial measures proposed [by JBE] were adequate, and when complete, trials could be resumed with every confidence'.[930]

By 21 March, the rotors had been returned to the ship and the turbines closed up. Cunard made the welcome gesture of inviting all those who had worked on the ship on an eight day trial trip to the west coast of Africa. Her first scheduled voyage, a preview voyage for travel agents, was planned for 22 April and her maiden voyage to New York for 2 May. There was no standard, proven design for steam

turbine machinery as was the case with diesel machinery. *QE2* machinery was particularly advanced and in every respect a 'one off'. The design was not tested until the engines were built and run. Problems of the sort that overtook *QE2* were far from unheard of. The circumstances were particularly unfortunate in that they occurred in the world's most prestigious ship under the focus of world attention.

FIRST CRISIS AT UCS

As the above events unravelled, culminating in highly successful trials, the fortunes of UCS plunged. The extra time required to complete *QE2* at Southampton had distorted the programme of work at Clydebank. George Parker was particularly concerned that fitting-out ships at Clydebank had been seriously delayed because senior managers were at Southampton. At the same time, he reported to the Executive Committee that 'a really tight grip has been taken of boilermakers . . . on such items as supervision, timekeeping and general pace of work.'

The Minister of Technology, Anthony Wedgewood Benn, visited Clydebank at the height of the QE2 turbine debacle stating 'I have come here today to take the steam out of the situation and put it back into the turbines,' a comment that was appreciated by beleaguered John Brown Engineering management. He is seen later in the day addressing workers concerned about the future of the shipbuilding industry.

He bemoaned the fact that outfit trades, swollen by the return of men from *QE2* on 3 February 1969, could not be dealt with in the same way because of their numbers. Under the terms of the Productivity Bargain, phase one of which had been signed in November 1968, employment, for men with over nine months service, was guaranteed for a period of two years.[931] Thus, Clydebank was committed to retain surplus workers, although there was no work for them.

By February 1969, UCS was anticipating an annual output of thirteen ships, including oil rigs and dredges, which were considered to be profitable business. Steelwork productivity had shown an increase at Clydebank, was static at Scotstoun and had declined at Govan.[932] Bound by the employment guarantee, Clydebank was carrying 400 workers with more than nine months service for whom there was no work. It seemed the only way forward was to displace those with over nine months service by distributing them throughout the other divisions and making those with less than nine months service redundant. However, at union suggestion, short time working was introduced to preserve jobs.[933] In early February, a crisis of arresting proportions was precipitated when Cunard suspended payments for *QE2* inducing severe cash flow problems.[934] On 7 February, the Company submitted an urgent request for £6 million to the SIB, including £3 million for what were termed 'transitional losses'. £500,000 was needed at the beginning of March because a number of firms, including British Steel, were threatening to withhold supplies if their bills were not paid.[935] UCS was on the brink of collapse. The financial crisis was partly explained by losses of £3.5/4 million in excess of those calculated on contracts at the time of the Company's formation.[936] The Chairman, Anthony Hepper, more fully attributed the cash crisis to:

- a shortage of working capital from the outset
- original profit forecasts not met
- formation expenses had been incurred
- Cunard's stopping payments because of the *QE2* debacle.[937]

Hepper railed that he and his fellow executive directors had been sold a 'false prospectus' at the time of their appointment.[938] By the beginning of March, having studied the UCS plan carefully, it became clear that the SIB would reject it. The SIB made a counter offer of £3 million which an infuriated Hepper considered 'patronising and insulting'.[939] He called an emergency meeting of the UCS Board on 13 March to decide whether or not

they should request a liquidator there and then. Hepper gave an account of meetings held with the SIB and the Minister of Technology which had led to the present position. UCS had asked for £6 million; the SIB had offered £3 million with no guarantees of further support unless the business could be turned around. With weekly losses running at £100,000, the £3 million would be gone by the end of June.[940] Hepper asked each of his directors in turn whether they should liquidate now or accept the SIB's offer. Sir Eric Yarrow expressed the view that the UCS Board had been asked (by the Government) to undertake an impossible task. Sir Charles Connell, on a business trip to Australia, telephoned the meeting to offer his view. After much debate, the Board decided to accept the SIB's £3 million for the following reasons:

- The Minister of Technology, Tony Benn, had sent an urgent message to the meeting to urge that they continue trading and to state that he would do 'everything in his power' to assist.[941]
- The SIB would consider further support if their conditions were met.
- Liquidation would be a disaster.[942]

On 14 March, Tony Benn visited the yards at UCS in a highly public display of support for the stricken Company. During this visit, Tony Hepper told him that he would resign if the SIB did not change its attitude.[943] To ease bruised communications between the SIB and UCS, a Government nominee, Alex Mackenzie, was appointed to sit on the Board. As these events unfolded, Clydebank's order position was weakened when the contract to build four large bulk carriers for Korean owners ran into serious difficulties. UCS was struggling to provide a price suitable to the owners. In the same month, 400 redundancies were made at Clydebank.[944]

The dust had hardly settled from the events of March when, in April, the UCS Board prepared to submit its Corporate Plan, prepared by P-E Consultants, to the SIB. It envisaged a further £12 million for the Company, of which a major feature would be expenditure of £4.2 million at Clydebank to upgrade facilities at the west yard. While the UCS Board had disagreed about this level of investment at Clydebank, the plan was nevertheless submitted in this form. The plan anticipated losses through 1970/71 and 1971/72 with profitability achieved in 1972/73.[945] In the midst of this, Yarrows, the warship division, was awarded the Queen's Award for Industry. Discussion with the SIB and Tony Benn over the first week in May revealed that the £12 million would not be forthcoming. The best that could be expected was £9 million and then only on the basis that the Company found the other £3 million itself. At this point, after a meeting with the John Brown Board, Lord Aberconway wrote to the Minister for Technology offering to sell the Government its shareholding in UCS for £1 on condition that the Government paid-off Clydebank's debts at that time, completed Clydebank's contracts and did its best for Clydebank employees.[946] Asked if John Brown would be prepared to put more money into UCS, Lord Aberconway appeared on television to say 'I cannot conceive that it would be in John Brown's shareholders' interests to put more of their money into UCS.'[947] At the same time he made public the offer to sell John Brown's 33% shareholding to the Government for £1 or a peppercorn.

With the Corporate Plan rejected, the Board again considered its position. At a meeting in May, Anthony Hepper concluded yet again that UCS was 'virtually a bankrupt Company and we must say to the Minister that strictly the Company should liquidate.'[948] With no support for the plan from either the SIB or the Ministry of Technology, the Company was forced into an unpalatable choice: drastically reduce the size of the Company by eliminating a major productive unit. Hepper stated 'if an answer was required today, it would be Clydebank'.[949] A Working Party was formed to examine the effect of closing either the Govan or Clydebank yard.[950]

The SIB's intention was not simply to thwart the UCS Board but to force change in its composition and remove Hepper. By July, five directors had resigned, including Tom Burleigh, the most senior of the former John Brown men, and Williamson, Clydebank's former secretary. Anthony Hepper remained as Chairman but a new post of Managing Director was created, in the hope that a shipbuilding manager of proven record could be found. The nominee of the SIB was Ken Douglas, Managing Director of Austin & Pickersgill's profitable yard on Wearside. By August 1969, staff reductions across the Group since December 1968 amounted to 2,358, saving over £350,000 per annum on the salaries bill.[951] At the same time, the Technical Division produced designs for a 16,000ton general-purpose ship later to be known as the Clyde Class. Throughout September and November, Ken Douglas implemented a Steelwork Incentive Scheme to improve productivity, while a new capital expenditure programme was prepared for the SIB. The short and long term cash position remained serious and threatened the legality

of the Company's trading position. Early in November, Hepper and Douglas met Sir William Swallow. £3 million was needed immediately with a further £3 million by March 1970. This was beyond the SIB's ability to grant and thus Hepper and Douglas made direct approach to the Paymaster General, Harold Lever. Asked if the Company could be made viable, the two UCS men replied yes,

The 38,457 dwt bulk carrier Volnay *built specifically to carry grain, running trials in 1969.*

provided that the finance was forthcoming. While Lever put this to the Cabinet, it was agreed that new orders would not be booked.[952]

Late in 1969, Sir Eric Yarrow, who made no secret of his desire to remove his former yard from UCS, met Conservative MP Nicholas Ridley. Ridley's particular remit was the British Shipbuilding Industry. Yarrow was critical of UCS and suggested how the Company might otherwise be handled.[953] The matters discussed at this meeting were later enshrined in a private memorandum which Ridley circulated to Sir Keith Joseph and two other Conservative politicians. Yarrow's views undoubtedly influenced, or, were at least concurrent with, those germinating in the minds of right wing Conservative politicians. This would later have a significant bearing on UCS.

At Clydebank, the self-propelled drilling rig *Offshore Mercury* was completed on 3 December, the Olsen liner *Blenheim* was launched on 10 January and *Kyoto Forest* was handed over on 10 February. Another self-propelled drilling rig Oceantide was delayed 12 to 14 weeks because of the late delivery of her jackup legs, which had been subcontracted to John Brown Engineering next door.[954] By the end of January, the Company's position was again critical, with creditors pressing for payment from funds which were not there. Hepper wrote to Harold Lever 'extremely concerned about the non-arrival of financial support'[955] The Company was balanced on a knife-edge, with thousands of jobs at risk and the reputation and integrity of the Board in question. On 7 February, the Company was given £7 million as a final payment. There would be no more. The £7 million came with a high cost in jobs. 3,500 were to go before August. The reason given was that simple ships required fewer man-hours to build. The public announcement that large redundancies would be needed solicited the equally public reply from the unions: one redundancy would result in an indefinite stoppage by the entire workforce. If management was compelled to this course of action, the loss of jobs on this scale was anathema for the unions. The UCS Board met on 22 March to decide how to react. In advance of meetings between management and Unions, Hepper sent a letter to union officials. This letter described the progress made since the crisis of last June and referred to the following points: new management structure; sales teams operating around the world bringing in new work; Clyde Class developed; orders for eight 26,000ton bulk carriers and seven Clyde design; productivity rising; improved morale and customer confidence. The letter ended by stressing the importance of the 3,500 redundancies to be split between 2,500 in the finishing trades and 1,000 in steelwork trades.[956] The brunt of these redundancies were to be borne at Clydebank, already secretly identified as the yard to close. The yard manager reported that morale had plummeted and that time had been lost through numerous meetings. Finishing trades went on strike demanding a £50 finishing bonus regardless of performance and police had been called to investigate sabotage on Blenheim.[957] .

On 19 June 1970, a Conservative Government was elected in a surprise victory and Edward Heath became Prime Minister. Tony Benn's Ministry of Technology was dismantled and replaced with the Department of Trade and Industry under John Davies. In August, Sir Eric Yarrow resigned from the UCS Board following the return of the Yarrow warship yard to private ownership in April.

TIMETABLE TO LIQUIDATION

On 27 October 1970, Nicholas Ridley, junior minister at the Department for Trade and Industry, informed UCS that the Government would not provide the Company with trading guarantees under the terms of the Shipbuilding Industry Act, thus provoking another serious crisis. The Minister further stated that if the directors of UCS could confirm that they would trade 'properly' and had sufficient funds to do so, he would provide the guarantees within hours.[958] The Company duly prepared a report on its trading position which indicated that profitability would be achieved during the first quarter of 1972. This report was submitted to the DTI on 18 November. At the end of November, after numerous disputes involving the boilermakers at Clydebank, Douglas had sanction from the Board to recast production schedules to permit the yard to be run down. The gravity of the situation was either not fully communicated to the workforce or it was not believed. The traditional mistrust of management held sway and prevented rational examination of the situation by the unions. That the industry might be facing extinction never entered their minds. Management, aware of the grim situation on a daily basis, had the task of turning a loss-making business around when both time and working capital were impossibly short. Early in December, the DTI asked Hepper 'what reaction would result from his Board being called to London to be told of the disbelief of the Government at the figures presented in the UCS report of 18 November'.[959] On 17 December, John Davies told UCS that although he did not question their report, he would not sign guarantees. The Minister wanted to see at least another £3 million in the balance sheet. With the Company in danger of immediate collapse, Hepper persuaded shipowners with orders at UCS to allow a 6% increase in the order value thereby providing the necessary £3 million.[960] Thus armed, UCS directors met the DTI in London on 23 December 1970 and the Government agreed to provide the guarantees. At this meeting, the closure of Clydebank was confirmed.

Following press speculation on the future of UCS, Hepper released the following statement:

'In view of the speculation as to the continuation of the Company and its activities, the Board of UCS state that there is no prospect of the Company going into liquidation and that the present temporary cash stringency will shortly be resolved. The Company has been aware for some time of the advantage of concentrating the major

Opposite page top
A group of prize winning Clydebank apprentices by the dockside with Training Officer Alex Scullion and Boyd Haining, (second from right) Personnel Manager.

Opposite page below
The Olsen passenger car ferry Blenheim *built for service in the North Sea during summer and the Canary Islands in winter. She is seen here running trials on the measured mile off Arran in September 1970 at least five months beyond her delivery date.*

part of their activities into a single site whilst maintaining and even expanding their share of the shipbuilding market. With this in view, the closure of the older east yard at Clydebank has been in progress for about a year and will be complete during 1971.'[961]

Clydebank had an order book of twelve ships. Closure of the east yard, which was greatly in need of modernisation, made sense although in reality the plan was to reduce UCS down to the former Fairfield yard. The difficulties facing British industry were signalled by the shocking news, announced on 4 February 1971, that Rolls Royce was bankrupt, attracting the epithet 'Lame Duck'. In April, Cunard prepared to press a claim of £2 million against UCS for losses and delays in the QE2 contract. Hepper told Sir Basil Smallpiece that if it persisted it would force UCS into liquidation. The threat of a counter claim from UCS for alterations and delays to the contract brought the issue to a close.

By June, UCS had run out of money and plunged into crisis for the last time. The Directors were convinced of productivity gains being made and 'the certainty of a viable future provided an immediate injection of working capital was made'. On 8 June 1971, Hepper and Alex Mackenzie, made the now familiar sojourn to the SIB to ask for £5 million to keep the Company afloat. The SIB representatives 'were sympathetic and recognised the tragic nature of the situation in view of the recent improving trend which they had noted with approval'. The SIB was unable to assist.[962]

Hepper and Mackenzie went to the DTI to meet the Minister, John Davies, who said that the Cabinet would consider the issue and inform the Company at mid-day on 10 June. However, it was agreed that Anthony Hepper and Ken Douglas would drive to John Davies' Knutsford constituency in Cheshire on Sunday 13 June to appraise him of the situation. Unless the Government stepped in, Hepper would require to petition for a provisional liquidator on Monday 14 June. Nearly 9,000 jobs were at stake, including 3,080[963] at Clydebank.

At the Knutsford meeting, the Minister said that the Prime Minister was now fully aware of the situation and that it would be on the agenda for a meeting at Chequers later that afternoon. No decision had been made but the Cabinet was meeting on Monday morning to decide the fate of the Company. On Monday 14 June, the Board of UCS, Anthony Hepper, Ken Douglas, A Crawford, John Starks, and Alex Mackenzie, met at the Linthouse headquarters to await the decision of the Cabinet. As the Board

waited, Hepper speculated that the Government might consider a reduction in operation rather than outright closure. At 12.30 Hepper was called to the telephone to hear the message from Downing Street. He returned to the Boardroom to quote the following message:

'The Secretary of State said that Her Majesty's Government had now reached the firm conclusion that they cannot put in large sums of

money to save UCS, but that they were seeking to enlist the co-operation of the provisional liquidator so that they could explore what parts of the Company might be saved and that they will be prepared to give him funds to that end. '

Accordingly, a petition was lodged with the Clerk of the Court for the appointment of a provisional liquidator at 3.30pm on 14 June 1971. The Board

15 June 1971, the day after Upper Clyde Shipbuilders went into liquidation. With the bulk carrier Samjohn Pioneer in the background, over 3,000 men employed at Clydebank gather to hear the initial reaction of their shop stewards.

released the following press statement of the two prepared:

'The Directors of Upper Clyde Shipbuilders Limited profoundly regret to announce that in view of the present financial position of the Company as disclosed in the most recent review of its affairs, they have been obliged to instruct an application to be made to the Court for the

appointment of a Provisional Liquidator.

The Company was formed as a consequence of the policy outlined in the Geddes Report and began operating in February 1968. Throughout the three years to the end of 1970, production was mainly devoted to the completion of a variety of unprofitable ships, many of which were inherited from the predecessor companies. During that period, substantial losses were inevitably incurred, which were largely financed by loans and grants from public funds.

By the end of 1970, the initial order book had been superseded by a programme of standard bulk carriers and 'Clyde' ships which, backed by the necessary working capital, would have become profitable.

However, the continuing acute shortage of working capital disrupted supplies and thus seriously retarded the shipbuilding programme with the result that the Company has continued to incur substantial losses for longer than had been forecast. Strenuous efforts have been made to obtain further working capital from various sources without success.

Despite these difficulties, the throughput of steel today, measured in gross tons, is over 1300 tons per week, compared with the average in 1970 of 867 tons per week. This has been achieved by a steelwork labour force 16% less in numbers than in 1970. The overall reduction of the labour force in the past 15 months is 25%. The number of ships delivered from the yards now controlled by the Company is as follows:

Annual average deliveries over 5 years prior to 1968 was 8 ships, in 1968, 3 ships, in 1969, 7 ships in 1970, 12 ships.

It is tragic that this record of achievement, which can be attributed to the support of our customers, and to the performance of our management and men, and which is now forecast to produce a profit in 1972, should be finally frustrated by the current shortage of working capital.

The Directors will give the Provisional Liquidator every possible assistance in his efforts to minimise the loss and hardship which will occur. All employees should continue normal working pending further instructions from the Provisional Liquidator.'[964]

The Provisional Liquidator appointed was Robert Courtney Smith.[965] When the news broke, the shock on Clydeside was palpable. The district was immersed in the shipbuilding tradition. It was what they did. Now it looked as if only one shipyard, Yarrows, would survive on the upper Clyde. At Clydebank the news was received with disbelief. Many questions hung in the air. How could this yard, with its worldwide reputation and which had so recently built what was regarded as the finest ship afloat, be closed? While the town of Clydebank adjusted to losing the industry which had brought it

yards which resulted in the 'UCS Work-in.' Unable to accept closure, the unions, led by Jimmy Airlie and Jimmy Reid, the latter a Clydebank shop steward, galvanised the workforce into a position of dignified resistance, committed to a continuation of labour. The subsequent disclosure of the highly provocative private memorandum written by Nicholas Ridley MP before the election of June 1970, did much to

23 June 1971. At centre, shop stewards James Airlie and Jimmy Reid, link arms with Winifred Ewing, Tony Benn and Bob Dickie, in a march through Glasgow. The fight to save UCS had started to great support not just in Glasgow but throughout Britain.

into being, the few ships left in the yard were completed. The last ship to be built at Clydebank was *Alisa*, a very plain Clyde Class bulk carrier. This ship was launched without ceremony. The ordinariness, which marked the final production at Clydebank, mirrored the start of shipbuilding at Govan 124 years earlier with the equally humble *Jackal*. In a curious irony, *Alisa* was taken from Clydebank following her launch on 5 October 1972, to a fitting out basin at Govan for completion, a stone's throw from J & G Thomson's original yard.

AFTERMATH
The liquidation produced a convulsion within the

characterise the Conservative Government as conniving and unsympathetic. The shop stewards' campaign succeeded in maintaining the issue at national level and won the outright backing of public opinion. The Government was forced to find a solution to the redeployment of the five yards.[966] A Government sponsored report into future uses for Clydebank shipyard claimed it was 'Widely agreed that productivity was 33% below what could be reached without spending anything. Claims of an 85% increase (in productivity) may be true but only serve to show how bad they were.' The Report saw no future for Clydebank as a shipbuilding yard and linked four strengths: established reputation, skilled labour force, technical competence and good launching facilities to seven weaknesses: poor profitability, 90% of plant ten years old, not suitable for flow line production, ineffective production and financial control, poor management, high wage rates/low productivity and a reputation for not meeting delivery dates.[967] Nevertheless a number of companies did express an interest in taking over all or

Above
Varda, *just launched, joins the* Orli *on the left and* Arahanga *in the fitting-out basin on 21 December 1971.*

Opposite page
5 October 1972. Alisa, *the last ship to be built at Clydebank, waits in the mist to be launched. She is standing on an East Yard berth where 100 years previously the* Braemar Castle *had been the first ship to enter the water.*

part of the yard. Breaksea Tankships Inc., wanted to build large gas tankers, for which they would have required £8 million of public money. Harland & Wolff were willing to negotiate a ten year contract for the supply of hull units which would employ between 700 and 800 men.

In January 1972, while a new owner was sought for the shipyard, the plight of Clydebank was heightened when its greatest product, *Queen Elizabeth*, the world's largest passenger ship, was burnt out in Hong Kong harbour. The poignant destruction of this ship seemed to indicate that an era was over.

The shipyard became the subject of a major study to seek a potential buyer. This was successful when the Marathon Manufacturing Company of Houston, Texas, acquired the yard on 8 August 1972 for the construction of oil drilling rigs and platforms. The purchase price was £1,150,000. If the product was less majestic than the ship, employment was nevertheless found for most of the 2,520[968] men still in the

Clydebank Division of UCS in liquidation. Under the circumstances, it was welcomed with open arms. As *Alisa*, the last ship to be built at Clydebank, did not leave the yard until some days after her launch, UCS rented facilities from Marathon until 7 November 1972[969] at which date shipbuilding can truly be said to have ended at Clydebank.

The demise of shipbuilding at Clydebank should not obscure the success which the former engine works, now John Brown Engineering, was enjoying. The entry into gas turbine sales and manufacture was an unqualified success, leading, in August 1972, to the renewal of the manufacturing associate agreement with General Electric for a further ten years.[970] It is a curious irony that the Company which first traded as makers of marine engines in 1847 should remain as makers of engines albeit for land purposes. The more acclaimed and publicly recognised activity of shipbuilding had proved not to be as enduring.

In depressing circumstances, Clydebank had built its last ship. Since the formation of the Company in 1847, the Thomson brothers, their sons, John Brown and Company and various short lived variants, had built over 700 ships. The period traced the expansion of British maritime power through innovation and market domination to its zenith. The gradual decline through two world wars and the Great Depression, tested the Company and the people of Clydebank to the extreme. When it came, the end of shipbuilding and marine engineering at Clydebank, and elsewhere in the United Kingdom, was the result of many factors which can be long debated. Beyond debate however, is Clydebank's contribution to the maritime history of the world and in particular, to those relatively few but superb examples of the naval architect's craft. The names fall thick with history and pride - *Servia, City of New York, Lusitania, Inflexible, Aquitania, Tiger, Barham, Repulse, Hood, Empress of Britain, Queen Mary, Queen Elizabeth, Duke of York, Vanguard* and *QE2*.

The town of Clydebank, which had been brought into existence alongside the building of ships, had lost the product for which it was known throughout the world. On Clydeside, that most innocuous of names, John Brown, signified an immense pride, which, in typical manner, was never well expressed but nevertheless deeply held. British people, wherever they might be, could point to its products and say 'we built that'.

◆

Upper Clyde Shipbuilders Clydebank Division 1971

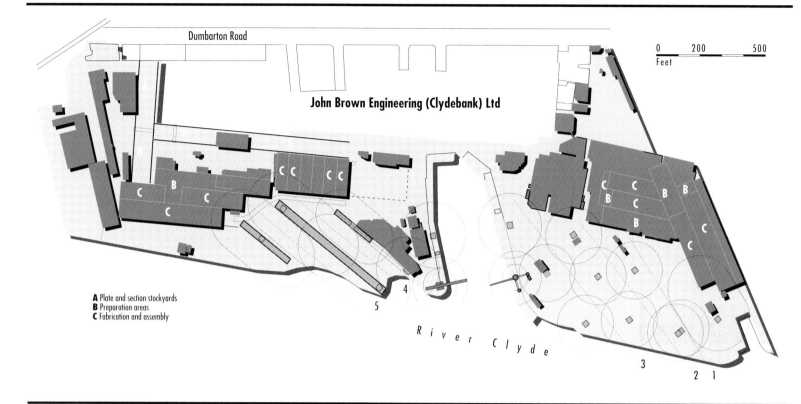

John Brown Engineering (Clydebank) Ltd

A Plate and section stockyards
B Preparation areas
C Fabrication and assembly

Below
Plan showing the final development of Clydebank shipyard with the new West Yard berths and shops. John Brown Engineering, the former engine works, has been separated from the yard.

FINAL DEVELOPMENT OF CLYDEBANK SHIPYARD 1971

In 1971, Clydebank shipyard was organised along flow-line production methods. In essence, plates and sections were brought into the stockyard at the west end of the yard and delivered to the berths in the East and West Yard in the form of prefabricated units ready for erection. The West Yard berths were comparatively modern with travelling cranes of 60 tons capacity. The East Yard was equiped with fixed cranes of between 40 and 20 tons capacity installed at the end of the Second World War.

Throughout the various operations in the production line , steel was handled by electric overhead cranes some fitted with magnetic lifting equipment. Conveyors delivered steel to both plate and section shot blasting machines. Within the limitation of the building available, maximum throughput of steel was achieved. The preparation areas listed the following machines;

Plate levelling rolls
Plate shot blasting machine with power conveyors
Mechanical rotary planing machine
Tenth scale profile cutting machine
Flame planing machines

Section shot blasting machine with power conveyors
Mechanical plane for light bulkheads, decks etc.
Profile cutting machine
Cold frame bending machine
Plate bending rolls
Mechanical plane

At the time of writing, the majority of the buildings of the former John Brown shipyard and engine works still stand and serve a purpose close to that for which they were first built. Under John Brown Engineering, the engine works has manufactured over 626 gas turbines for a great number of customers in countries all over the world. In 1997, the Kvaerner Group acquired John Brown Engineering and renamed the business Kvaerner Energy. In 1999, Kvaerner put the works up for sale.

From 1972, Marathon Manufacturing of Houston, Texas, constructed 14 jack-up drilling rigs and converted the drill ship *Douglas Carver*. In 1982, the French owned UiE Company acquired the yard from Marathon and constructed a number of modules and decks for the North Sea (see page 333).

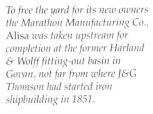

To free the yard for its new owners the Marathon Manufacturing Co., Alisa was taken upstream for completion at the former Harland & Wolff fitting-out basin in Govan, not far from where J&G Thomson had started iron shipbuilding in 1851.

With no obvious use the cranes that served the 'big berth' in the East Yard were pulled over in 1980 to make way for the construction of oil rigs.

FOOTNOTES

[1] Robin A Williamson, company secretary during the 1960s, in a telephone conversation with the author

[2] The order was placed with John Napier & Son of Howard Street Glasgow although the work was undertaken by John's son David.

[3] Millar, W. J. *On Early Clyde Built Steamers*, page 72, transactions of the Institute of Engineers and Shipbuilders in Scotland Volume XXIV 1880-81, Glasgow, 1881

[4] Robert Napier did not build his first marine steam engine, for the paddle steamer *Leven*, until 1823

[5] Riddell, John F, *Clyde Navigation*, John Donald, Edinburgh, 1979, page 56,

[6] Ibid. Page 67

[7] Gifford, P, *Tod and M'Gregor: Atlantic Shipbuilders*, Scottish Industrial History, Volumes 14 to 15, page 43,

[8] The North British Daily Mail on 26 March 1853

[9] Mechanics Magazine, Vol. 58, April 1853 page 314.

[10] Index to the Services of Heirs in Scotland, volume IV 1830 - 1859

[11] Dates supplied by Roderick McConnell, James Roger Thomson's great grandson

[12] Agreement between Robert Napier and James Thomson in Manchester, dated 8 January 1828, Glasgow University Archives, DC90/2/2/1

[13] In 1841, date of the first national, census, the Thomson were living at Greenlaw Cottage beside James's father-in-law. At this time they had a family of four and two family servants. See Census of 1841, Volume 646, folio 4, Govan

[14] This yard, to the east of Water Row had been operated by MacArthur and Alexander since 1839

[15] Smith, EC. *A Short History of Naval and Marine Engineering*, page 145/146, Cambridge University Press, 1937

[16] UCS 1/34/1, Ledger

[17] UCS 1/34/1 Ledger. In both instances, the value of the ground does not appear in company records until 1854. Although James Lumsden was paid out £1,500 in 1854, no further payments were made to either Lumsden or Mathieson until 1863 when both were fully paid off out of profits for that year.

[18] *Memoirs & Portraits of 100 Glasgow Men*, page 321, published by James Maclehose, Glasgow, 1886

[19] Strictly speaking, the name Clyde Bank or Clydebank, as it later became, was in use before the Thomsons took it for their business and at least one company, the Clydebank Printworks at Finnieston Quay, was in existence before 1847

[20] The Glasgow Herald, 10 April 1848

[21] The North British Daily Mail, 16 October 1850

[22] The Glasgow Herald, 28 November 1851, page 7

[23] Cessnock Bank and Hornbank were effectively given to the Thomsons for a period of time, payment being made much later. Cessnock Bank, the larger of the plots, was valued at £8,000 in 1851 by the owner John Russell. Although he received payments of £1,000 in 1851 and 1852, the balance of £6,000 was not repaid until 1855. Hornbank was valued at £4,000 by the owner George Gibson, a merchant, and paid off in June 1863.

[24] Ordnance Survey 1:25000 First Edition Sheet VI. 9 parcel number 1104

[25] Confusingly, various names were used in describing the yard including Cessnock Bank Shipyard, Clyde Bank Shipyard, Bankton Shipyard, the Clyde Shipbuilding Yard and even Clyde Villa Shipyard, the latter taking its name from the plot of ground to the immediate west of the yard

[26] Charles succeeded his brother David when the latter died in 1845

[27] The North British Daily Mail, 23 March 1852, page 2

[28] The North British Daily Mail, 7 June 1852, page 2

[29] The Dumbarton Herald, 19 August 1852

[30] These cranes were owned by the Clyde Trustees, the first of 40 tons capacity erected in 1844 at Windmillcroft Quay, the other, of 30 tons lifting capacity erected in 1848 at Lancefield Quay. See Riddell, op. Cit. page 182

[31] The North British Daily Mail, 17 March 1853, page 2

[32] The North British Daily Mail 8 August 1854, page 2

[33] UCS 1/34/1, Ledger, pages 28/29. This contract made a profit of £396 but did not include foundations or the masonry plinth. Crane manufacture was an obvious diversification for engineering firms. With the growth of industry in Glasgow and the persistent need to lift heavy, concentrated loads such as engines and boilers, crane making was added to the growing list of engineering products made on Clydeside.

[34] The Glasgow Evening News, 12 October 1929

[35] Bourne, John, *A Treatise on the Screw Propeller*, 1857. Both *Bordeaux* and *Frankfort* were built by John Reid.

[36] Seaton, AE, *A Manual of Marine Engineering*, 1904

[37] Guthrie, John, *A History of Marine Engineering*, Hutchinson Educational Ltd, London, 1971.

[38] Guthrie, John, ibid., pages 106/7

[39] Letter from George Thomson to Robert Bowman referenced in an unpublished manuscript by Harry Brown on the history of Clydebank shipyard at Clydebank Central Library, Scotland. Volume 2, reference number 34.

[40] Court of Session Cases, Volume XIV, 1857, page 994

[41] nhp refers to nominal horsepower. The power output of steam reciprocating machinery was generally calculated in units of ihp meaning indicated horsepower. Nominal horsepower power, nhp, was a less accurate means of assessing the power output from reciprocating machinery. The output

from steam turbine machinery was calculated in units of shp meaning shaft horsepower. The power output from a diesel engine was calculated in units of brake horsepower, bhp.

[42] Warship International No 4, 1985, Main Shipyards, Engine builders and Manufacturers of Guns and Armour Plate in the St. Petersburg Area up to 1917. Page 350

[43] The North British Daily Mail, 30 May 1855

[44] The London Illustrated News, 24 October 1857, page 402

[45] Ihp refers to indicated horsepower.

[46] UCS 1/11/1 Letter Books, 16 April 1861

[47] UCS 1/11/1 Letter Books, 24 July 1861

[48] *Warrior* has been preserved and can be seen in Portsmouth.

[49] Return of the Names of Marine Engine Makers, ordered by the House of Commons, 1843 page 356

[50] Amended Report by the Committee on Marine Engines, House of Commons Papers (Parliamentary) 1859 (II) Vol.17 page 97

[51] Amended Report by the Committee on Marine Engines, page 129

[52] Ibid.

[53] Amended Report by the Committee on Marine Engines, page 130

[54] UCS 1/11/1 Letter Books, 10 June 1862

[55] UCS 1/11/1 Letter Books, 24 November 1862

[56] UCS 1/11/1 Letter Books, letter from J&G Thomson to Admiral Robinson, 19 June 1862

[57] The Dumbarton Herald, 9 February 1865

[58] Bulloch, James D, *The Secret Service of the Confederate States*, London 1883, page 48

[59] Warship International No. 4, 1995, page 367

[60] Bulloch, James D, op. cit., pages 271, 380

[61] UCS 1/11/1, Letter Books, 9 May 1862, page 520

[62] Spencer, Warren F, *The Confederate Navy in Europe*, University of Alabama Press, 1983, page 70

[63] UCS 1/11/1, Letter Books, 20 June 1862

[64] Warship International No. 1, 1987, page 14

[65] UCS 1/11/1 Letter Books, 7 July 1862

[66] UCS 1/11/1 Letter Books, 27 August 1862

[67] UCS 1/11/1 Letter Books, 1 September 1862

[68] Parkes, Oscar, *British Battleships*, Seely Service & C0., London 1970, page 77

[69] Bulloch, James D, op. cit., page 273

[70] Spencer, Warren F, op. cit., page 121.

[71] The Dumbarton Herald, 28 January 1864, article attributed to The Glasgow Mail

[72] *Danmark* was too late to have any effect on the dispute which was ended with the Danes losing Schleswig Holstein to the German Confederation

[73] UCS 1/11/1 Letter Books, 19 September 1862

[74] UCS 1/11/1 Letter Books, 10 October 1862

[75] The Dumbarton Herald, 3 December 1863, article headed The Pampero - Alleged Tampering with J&G Thomson's Workmen

[76] Hearn, Chester G, Gray *Raiders of the Sea*, Louisiana State University Press, 1996, page 108

[77] Court of Session Cases, Third Series, 1864 volume 2 page 1032 *Pampero* was sold to Chilean interests secretly at the beginning of 1866 and renamed Tornado. See Warship International No. 1 1987 page 18

[78] North was quoted a price of £56 per horsepower for horizontal direct acting engines while Bulloch was quoted £11,000 each for two pairs of similar engines of 200 horsepower together with tubular boilers. This quotation was accompanied by a drawing which showed the type of vessel to which these engines would be suited. See UCS 1/11/1 13 February 1863 page 640 and 23 February page 654 and 656

[79] Warship International No. 4, 1984, page 386

[80] The Glasgow Herald, 4 October 1862

[81] Luraghi, Raimondo, *A History of the Confederate Navy*, Naval Institute Press, Annapolis, 1966. page 271

[82] To give some indication of present day values, a factor of approximately 100 can be applied to these figures.

[83] UCS1/3/18, Interlocutor submission between George and James Thomson. Dissolution of company 6/8/63

[84] McGrigor Donald, McGrigor Donald & Co. Sederunts 179 George Thomson's Trust Volume 1 page 108

[85] Ibid.

[86] The Glasgow Herald, 16 March 1870 James had six children, four girls and two boys. One of the girls, May, married Isaac Beardmore, uncle of William Beardmore who was soon to rise to prominence at the head of the great armaments company bearing his name. See Glasgow City Archives, Glasgow, Trust of Grace McIntyre Thomson who died at Linnburn 16 May 1883. SRA T-HB/627

[87] Glasgow City Archives, Barclay Curle Minute Books, TD265/1/5

[88] The Dumbarton Herald, 30 April 1863 attributed to The North British Daily Mail. Demand encouraged the expansion of the industry and by 1864 there were no fewer than 31 shipyards on the Clyde, thirteen of which had commenced activities within the past three years.

[89] The Dumbarton Herald, 23 April 1863

[90] The Dumbarton Herald, 24 May 1866, attributed to the Glasgow Morning Journal

[91] The Dumbarton Herald, 31 May 1866

[92] *Memoirs & Portraits of 100 Glasgow Men*, published by James Maclehose, Glasgow, 1886

[93] McGrigor Donald, op. cit. Volume 1, Inventory of Estate of George Thomson, 29 June 1866, page 45

[94] McGrigor Donald, Ibid. Volume 1, Valuations of property by Robert McTear, page 48. The single most expensive item valued by McTear at George's Newton Place home was a rosewood grand piano forte by Erand at £90. This was not the only piano at Newton Place. A walnut cottage piano by Callard was valued at £52.10s. At Dalling Mhor, the most expensive item valued was a billiard table and fittings at £50

[95] McGrigor Donald, Ibid. Volume 1, Report by William Anderson CA, page 105

[96] McGrigor Donald, Ibid. Volume 1, Special Meeting of 7 November 1866, page 72

[97] Griffiths, Denis, *Power of the Great Liners*, Patrick Stephens Ltd., London, 1990, page 29

[98] McGrigor Donald, op. cit. Volume 1, Meeting of 14 September 1866, page 35

[99] McGrigor Donald, Ibid. Volume 1, Meeting of 7 November 1866, page 69

[100] McGrigor Donald, Ibid. Volume 1, Meeting of 19 June 1867, page 93

[101] McGrigor Donald, Ibid. Volume 1, Meeting of 18 December

1867, page 289

[102] name later changed to *Siberia*

[103] McGrigor Donald, op. cit. Volume 1, Meeting of 6 November 1867, page 272

[104] McGrigor Donald, Ibid. Volume 1, Letter from Clyde Bank Foundry to John Burns Esq. 23 November 1866, page 76. Several other exchanges of this sort are detailed in the Sederunt Book. In August of the following year, a similar arrangement was entered into with G&J Burns for the steamer *Samaria* in exchange for which the vessels *Asia*, *Africa* and *Persia* had to be taken for £8,000, £8,000 and £18,000 respectively.

In November, another deal of this sort was struck when G&J Burns offered to place a contract for two vessels *Raven* and *Racoon* on the basis that they take over the *Weasel* for £14,000. The Trustees agreed to this provided that a minimum of £34,000 was paid for the ship and that the *Weasel* was acquired for £13,000 this sum payable over twelve months. By November, the Trust decided that this contract would only be acceptable if the price were not less than £38,000.

[105] McGrigor Donald, op. cit. Volume 1, Meeting of 19 June 1867, page 91

[106] McGrigor Donald, Ibid. Volume 1, Meeting of 19 June 1867, page 92

[107] McGrigor Donald, Ibid. Volume 1, Meeting of 15 April 1868, page 318

[108] McGrigor Donald, Ibid. Volume 1, Meeting of 15 April 1868, page 319

[109] McGrigor Donald, Ibid. Volume 1, Meeting of 1 July 1868, page 323

[110] Ibid.

[111] McGrigor Donald, Ibid. Volume 1, Meeting of 16 February 1869, page 383

[112] McGrigor Donald, Ibid. Volume 1, Letter to G&J Burns 1869, page 388

[113] McGrigor Donald, Ibid. Volume 1, Meeting of 5 May 1869, page 385

[114] Ibid.

[115] McGrigor Donald, Ibid. Volume 1, Meeting of 16 February 1869, page 382

[116] McGrigor Donald, Ibid. Volume 1, Report by William Anderson, 30 June 1869, page 394

[117] Ibid.

[118] McGrigor Donald, Ibid. Volume 1, Meeting of 30 December 1869, page 390

[119] McGrigor Donald, Ibid. Volume 1, Meeting of 30 December 1869, page 392

[120] McGrigor Donald, Ibid. Volume 1, Report by John Grant 30 December 1869, page 412

[121] McGrigor Donald, Ibid. Volume 1, Report by John Grant 30 December 1869, page 414

[122] When the Fairfield works were completed in 1871, they were the finest works on Clydeside. Only Thomson's new works at Clydebank eventually equalled Fairfield in the context of facilities, and scale while Beardmores' works at Dalmuir (1905) exceeded them..

[123] *The Fairfield, Shipbuilding and Engineering Works*, reprinted from Engineering, 1909, page 2

[124] Glasgow City Archives, UCS 2/6/26, Papers relating to construction of fitting-out basin

[125] Elder's pioneering work in the development of the marine steam engine was continued by JLK Jamieson, Alexander Kirk, and Andrew Laing - all successive heads of the engineering department at Fairfield.

[126] Tod & McGregor, Thomas Wingate & Sons, John Shearer and Napier Shanks & Bell had all moved to make way for new docks.

[127] Riddell, op. cit. Page 203. Plantation Quay was the westward continuation of Mavisbank Quay.

[128] George Reith was the great uncle of John Charles Reith, the first Director General of the British Broadcasting Corporation

[129] Glasgow City Archives, T-CN8.63, Clyde Navigation Trust

[130] Ibid.

[131] McGrigor Donald, op. cit. Volume 1, Meeting of 1 February 1870, page 417

[132] McGrigor Donald, Ibid. Volume 1, Meeting of 2 August 1870, page 445

[133] The Illustrated London News, 3 December 1870, page 580

[134] McGrigor Donald, op. cit. Volume 1, Meeting of 7 June 1870, page 439

[135] McGrigor Donald, Ibid. Volume 1, Meeting of 14 July 1870, page 443

[136] McGrigor Donald, Ibid. Volume 1, Meeting of 1 November 1870, page 449

[137] McGrigor Donald, Ibid. Volume 1, Meeting of 1 November 1870, page 450

[138] McGrigor Donald, Ibid. Volume 1, Meeting of 1 November 1870, page 451

[139] McGrigor Donald, Ibid. Volume 1, Meeting of 8 November 1870, page 454

[140] Donald Currie was a native of Greenock. He worked with McIver & Co. in Liverpool later establishing the Leith, Hull & Hamburg Steam Packet based in Liverpool. In 1876, the Castle Mail Packets Co. was formed, controlled by D Currie & Co. In 1900, the Castle Co. and the Union Steamship Co. were merged to form Union-Castle Line with Sir Donald Currie, as Chairman

[141] McGrigor Donald, op. cit. Volume 1, Meeting of 6 December 1870, page 457

[142] McGrigor Donald, Ibid. Volume 1, Meeting of 1 March 1871, page 486

[143] Ibid.

[144] Ibid.

[145] McGrigor Donald, op. cit. Volume 2, Sederunt Book 2, Meeting of 4 May 1871, page 9

[146] McGrigor Donald, Ibid. Volume 2, Meeting of 4 May 1871, page 5

[147] McGrigor Donald, Ibid. Volume 2, Meeting of 6 June 1871, pages 12/13

[148] McGrigor Donald, Ibid. Volume 2, Letter from Robert Thomson 10 June 1871, page 19

[149] McGrigor Donald, Ibid. Volume 2, Meeting of 19 June 1871, page 21

[150] Ibid.

[151] McGrigor Donald, op. cit. Volume 2, Meeting of 3 June, pages 25/26

[152] McGrigor Donald, Ibid. Volume 2, Meeting of 19 July 1871, page 36

[153] Union Bank of Scotland Archives, Board Minute Books, 23 August 1871

154 UCS 1/10/1, Shipyard Diary

155 The Engineer, 24 November 1871, page 360 for a description of the works and comparison with Fairfield

156 UCS1/11/1, Letter Books, pages 72 and 235

157 With the exception of John Scott Russell's 19,000 ton *Great Eastern* built in 1858 at Millwall.

158 UCS1/11/1, Letter Books, page 249

159 Glasgow City Archives, TCN8.63, letter 26 March 1870

160 Glasgow City Archives, Ibid., letter, 5 March 1872

161 Glasgow City Archives, Ibid., Claim for Compensation, pages 114/119

162 Glasgow City Archives Ibid. Valuation of Govan Shipyard, 1 February 1870, page 29

163 The Engineer, 24 November, 1871, page 360. This article provides a good description of the new yard.

164 Glasgow City Archives, TCN8.63, letter 21 August 1872

165 Ibid. Note: it was also intended to build ships number 130 and 132 at Govan

166 Riddell, op. cit. page 205

167 With the decline of shipping on the Clyde, Princes Dock was filled-in during the 1980s returning the south bank of the Clyde to something resembling its former line. The site of the original Clyde Bank Iron Shipyard is adjacent to the area presently occupied by Bell's Bridge.

168 *The Dynamics of Victorian Business: Problems and Perspectives in the 1870s* edited by Roy A Church, Chapter *The Shipbuilding Industry, 1800-1870*, by Antony Slaven, page 107, Rutledge, 1979

169 McGrigor Donald, op. cit. Volume 1, 29 October 1866 pages 203 to 269, inventory of Clyde Bank Iron Shipyard made by James McNaught and Peter Denny

170 Newman, Brian, *Plate & Section Working Machinery 1850-1945*, Centre for Business History in Scotland, 1995, page 1

171 McGrigor Donald, op. cit. Volume 2, page 56

172 McGrigor Donald, Ibid. Volume 2, page 75

173 The Trustees agreed that Andrew Burns, the shipyard manager, should have an increase in salary from £450 to £600 and to ensure that his salary together with commission should be no less than £1,000 per annum. Burns replied that he would prefer to see the £1,000 guaranteed minimum restored and suggested a scale of profits ranging from 5% for profits of £10,000 to 7.5% for profits over £14,000 on the basis that the new works were far larger than the old. He also asked if the Company would build a house for him near the works as there were no suitable houses in the district. He offered to pay rent of 5% based on the cost of this house or, conversely, build the house at his own expense on the understanding that the Company would buy it from him at the end of his contract. Initially the Trust declined to have anything to do with building a house for Burns but on receipt of a rather humble letter from him withdrawing the suggestion, it decided, after all, that as long as the house cost no more than £1,000, it would buy it from him at the end of his employment with the firm. Sederunt Book 2, Meeting of 6 December 1871, page 77

174 McGrigor Donald, op. cit. Volume 2, Meeting of 7 February 1872, page 99

175 Moss and Hume, *Shipbuilders to the World, 125 Years of Harland & Wolff*, Blackstaff Press, Belfast, 1986., page 29

176 Perhaps in recognition of the White Star challenge and sensitivity over ship size, Cunard made a supplementary contract with J&G Thomson for lengthening *Bothnia* and *Scythia* by 38 feet, making them each 420 feet in length.

177 Moss and Hume. op. cit. Page 18. See also UCS 1/11/1 letterbooks 25 February, 3 March and 11 July 1859

178 McGrigor Donald, op. cit. Volume 2, Meeting of 3 January 1872, page 85

179 McGrigor Donald, Ibid., Meeting of 6 March 1872, page 106

180 McGrigor Donald, Ibid. Volume 2. Meeting of 14 June 1872, page 165

181 McGrigor Donald, Ibid., Volume 2, Page 166

182 McQueen, Andrew, *Clyde River Steamers of the Last Fifty Years*, Gowans & Gray Ltd, 1923

183 McGrigor Donald, op. cit. Volume 2, Meeting of 4 December 1872, page 190

184 McGrigor Donald, Ibid. Meeting of 8 January 1873, page 194

185 McGrigor Donald, Ibid. Meeting of 15 January 1873, page 200

186 McGrigor Donald, Ibid. Volume 2, Report by William Anderson CA, page 217

187 At an earlier Trust Meeting, James Roger and George Paul had put forward a proposal for the separation of the business from the Trust while 'securing the rights and interests of the younger members of the family'. This was now revived and it was agreed that disentangling the affairs of the business and the family represented the best solution for both. As if to underline the awkward and conflicting elements which the Trust had to administer, Mrs Thomson wrote in November 1872 requesting £150 of additional allowance for both of her youngest children, Margaret and Robert, as well as a reconsideration of the £200 allowance given to her three unmarried daughters. The Trustees decided that the two youngest children should each receive £150 but that any further increase on present levels of allowance to their siblings must await the decision of the arbiters in the case between the Thomson Trust and the Clyde Navigation Trust.

188 McGrigor Donald, op. cit. Volume 2, Meeting of 20 October 1873, page 239 and minute of sale 29 October 1873, page 244

189 Union Bank of Scotland Archives, Letter from Charles Gairdner to CD Donald, 9 May 1873

190 McGrigor Donald, op. cit. Volume 2, Meeting of 7 May 1873, page 223

191 Glasgow City Archives, T-CN 8.63 Submission between the Trustees of George Thomson and the Clyde Navigation Trust. Speeches of Council page 135

192 McGrigor Donald, op. cit. Volume 2, Meeting of 19 April 1873, page 208

193 McGrigor Donald, Ibid. Meeting of 13 June 1873, page 224

194 McGrigor Donald, Ibid. Meeting of 27 August 1873, page 227

195 Ibid.

196 McGrigor Donald, op. cit. Volume 2, Meeting of 20 October 1873, page 239

197 McGrigor Donald, Ibid. Meeting of 29 October 1873, page 242

198 McGrigor Donald, Ibid. Meeting of 26 November 1873, page 248

199 McGrigor Donald, Ibid. Meeting of 26 November 1873, page 249

200 McGrigor Donald, Ibid. Meeting of 5 December 1873, page 251

201 McGrigor Donald, Ibid. Meeting of 13 February 1874, page 254

[202] McGrigor Donald, Ibid. Meeting of 13 February 1874, page 255

[203] McGrigor Donald, Ibid. Meeting of 18 November 1874, page 261

[204] McGrigor Donald, Ibid. Minute of Agreement 22, 23 and 29 December 1874, page 266

[205] Formerly Marion Paterson Neilson

[206] The Thames Iron Works had won orders for two ironclads which were part of a modest fleet expansion initiated by the Turkish Government.

[207] UCS 1/11/1, Letterbooks, Letter of 1 April 1872, page 305 Letter of 1 April 1872 to Messrs Charles Hansen & Co., Constantinople. The Thomsons asked their agents in Turkey, Charles Hansen & Co. to press for payment.

[208] Ibid.

[209] UCS 1/10/1, Shipyard Diary

[210] The Dumbarton Herald, 5 November 1874

[211] Dumbarton Herald, 23 March 1872

[212] McGrigor Donald, op. cit. Volume 2, Meeting of 6 March 1872, page 107 and Meeting of 26 March 1872, page 126

[213] McGrigor Donald, Ibid. Meeting of 26 March 1872, page 127

[214] Glasgow Herald, 21 January 1941

[215] UCS 1/10/1, Shipyard Diary

[216] UCS 1/10/1, Shipyard Diary

[217] The Baillie, 2 March 1881

[218] From Bridgeton in Glasgow

[219] UCS 1/11/1, Letter Books, letter to Charles Gairdner, Union Bank, 23 November 1875 page 625

[220] UCS 1/11/1, Letter Books, page 631, letter dated 8 December 1875

[221] Inclusive of interest payable to Trust beneficiaries

[222] Dumbarton Herald, 17 August 1876 and 7 September 1876

[223] UCS 1/10/1, Shipyard Diary entry for 24 July

[224] UCS 1/10/1, Shipyard Diary entries for December. Note BST was not introduced until 1916

[225] UCS 1/10/1, Shipyard Diary entry for 1 August 1877. The adjustment between winter and summer working was made locally until moving the clocks back and forward one hour became a national event.

[226] Dumbarton Herald, 12 November 1879

[227] Union Bank of Scotland Archives, Board Minute Books, 19 January 1876 and 3 Dec. 1874

[228] Union Bank of Scotland Archives, Letter from Charles Gairdner to James Roger Thomson 8 August 1877

[229] The Baillie, 2 March 1881

[230] Dumbarton Herald, 21 April 1881

[231] UCS 1/10/1, Shipyard Diary. Entry for 4 May 1881 stating 'Joiners started back at advanced rate of 7.5% on wages'

[232] UCS 1/3/38, Memorandum between J&G Thomson and the South Eastern Railway Company, 26 May 1881

[233] UCS 1/3/41, Report by William McKinnon CA, dated 3 May 1883, on 'The affairs of J&G Thomson with suggestions for a re-arrangement of the finances of the firm and the better management and conduct of business generally.' The balance sheet for the year to 31 December 1882 is attached.

[234] UCS 1/3/43, Report by Kerr Anderson Muir & Main CA and McClelland McKinnon & Blyth CA, 1 August 1882

[235] McGrigor Donald, op. cit. Volume 2, Meeting of 15 March 1882, page 407

[236] Union Bank of Scotland Archives, Board Minutes for 8 February 1883

[237] UCS 1/3/41, op. cit.

[238] Letter from London Office to Charles Gairdner, 14 July 1883

[239] UCS 1/3/8, letter from JP Wilson to J&G Thomson accepting the post as general manager, dated 11 May 1883

[240] UCS 1/10/1, Shipyard Diary, 13 August 1875

[241] UCS 1/10/1, Shipyard Diary, 14 September 1882

[242] Dumbarton Herald, 28 November 1883

[243] UCS 1/22/1, Plant files, September and October 1884

[244] The Machinery Market, 1 March 1884, page 14

[245] UCS 1/10/1, Shipyard Diary, 5 September 1881

[246] Dumbarton Herald, 7 September 1881

[247] Dumbarton Herald, 21 May 1884

[248] Dumbarton Herald, 25 June 1884

[249] UCS 1/10/1, Shipyard Diary, 15 January 1885

[250] Dr James Stevenson, a local GP, was employed on a part-time basis by the company at an annual salary of £350. See UCS 1/4/1, contract of employment

[251] Dumbarton Herald, 2 December 1885

[252] Dumbarton Herald, 17 August 1887

[253] UCS 1/10/1, Shipyard Diary, 4 October 1887

[254] Dumbarton Herald, 12 October 1887

[255] Dumbarton Herald, 19 October 1887

[256] UCS 1/10/1, Shipyard Diary, 13 October 1887

[257] Dumbarton Herald, 2 November 1887

[258] Dumbarton Herald, 8 January 1890

[259] UCS 1/10/1, Shipyard Diary, 22 November 1894

[260] His salary was £250 rising to £375 in the last year of his four year contract. UCS 1/3/8, Agreement between JH Biles and J&G Thomson dated 5 August 1880. Biles actually started work at Clydebank on 29 July 1880

[261] Transactions of the Institute of Engineers & Shipbuilders in Scotland 1913, Obituary of John G Dunlop.

[262] Slaven, A and Checkland S, (editors), *Dictionary of Scottish Business Biography,* Aberdeen University Press, 1986 *Volume* 1, page 207, Sir Thomas Bell by Anthony Slaven.

[263] Skelton, Sir Reginald, Engineer-in-Chief of the Fleet, *The Work of Andrew Laing*, Transactions of the North East Coast Institution of Engineers and Shipbuilders, 1932 – 33, page 6

[264] *Half a Century of Shipbuilding*, James & George Thomson Ltd, reprinted from Engineering, London, 1896, page 10

[265] The letters from Clydebank which solicited these replies have not survived.

[266] University of Liverpool Archives, D42 Secretary's Letter Books S1.4 dated 14 September 1881

[267] University of Liverpool Archives, S1/5 Cunard Letter Books, 8 December 81

[268] University of Liverpool Archives, S1/7 Cunard Letter Books, 6 March 1883 and UCS 1/3/41 balance sheet to 31 December 1882

[269] Union Bank of Scotland Archives, Letter from JP Wilson to William McKinnon 3 Sept. 1883. The cost of the repair to *Aurania* was £4,000. John Burns placed an order for *Skirmisher* for the Belfast trade at a price of £34,000 which included a profit of £10,000. Union Bank of Scotland Archives, letter from William McKinnon to Charles Gairdner 21 Sept. 1883

[270] UCS 1/10/1, Shipyard Diary. Entry for 1 October 1884, 'Works put on short time working 8.30 till 4.30 with one 1 hour

break'

[271] Union Bank of Scotland Archives, Letter from McKinnon to Charles Gairdner quoting James Roger Thomson, 25 February 1885

[272] Ibid. Letter from James Currie to Charles Gairdner, 23 April 1885

[273] *Conways all the World's Warships 1860 - 1982,* Conway Maritime Press, London, 1979, pages 1/2

[274] Union Bank of Scotland Archives, Letter from McKinnon at Clydebank to Charles Gairdner, 14 October 1885

[275] Ibid. Letter from McKinnon to Charles Gairdner, 17 July 1886

[276] Ibid. letter from Charles Ker to Charles Gairdner 13 September 1888

[277] UCS 1/74/1, Tender Books, various dates throughout 1889.

[278] Union Bank of Scotland Archives, op. cit. Letter from McKinnon to Charles Gairdner, 21 October 1886

[279] Ibid. Letter from McKinnon to Gairdner March 1888

[280] Dumbarton Herald, 13 April 1887

[281] Union Bank of Scotland Archives, op. Cit. Letter from David Richie to Charles Gairdner 22 September 1888.

[282] UCS 1/107/1, Report of enquiry into City of Paris accident, dated 24 June 1890

[283] Ibid.

[284] Kludas, Arnold, *Great Passenger Ships of the World*, Patrick Stephens, Cambridge, 1975. Vol. 1 page 12

[285] UCS 1/10/1, Shipyard Diary, entry dated 29 September 1890

[286] Engineering, 17 June 1891, page 71

[287] UCS 1/10/1, Shipyard Diary, entry dated 24 August 1892

[288] Union Bank of Scotland Archives, Board Minutes 12 June 1889

[289] Ibid. 6 July 1889, Letter from David Ritchie to Charles Gairdner. My Dear Gairdner, . . . I am not quite sure that it will be any great disadvantage coming behind Fairfield after all. I hope they will experiment on the public with the ordinary stock. The result would be of service and might stimulate us to bolder measures in the launching of Clydebank.

[290] UCS 1/3/25, Report on liquidation of J&G Thomson and transfer of business to J&G Thomson Ltd, dated 31 March 1891

[291] Union Bank of Scotland Archives, op. cit. Letter from Charles Gairdner to CD Donald 19 June 1891

[292] National Archives of Scotland, Dissolved Companies Register BT2

[293] *Glasgow Contemporaries*, The Photo-biographical Publishing Company, Glasgow, 1901, page 178

[294] UCS 1/3/5, Report on Harland & Wolff 1890 by T Crawford and D Bremner

[295] UCS 1/3/10, Directors report to 31 March 1891 In this report the profit is stated as £41,348 before tax including interest receivable

[296] UCS 1/3/8, Correspondence between J H Biles and J&G Thomson Ltd, dated 24 March 1890.

[297] Transactions of the Institution of Naval Architects, 1934, Sir John Harvard Biles obituary.

[298] UCS 1/3/14, Directors report to 31 March 1895

[299] The agents were:Creswell D Haynes in Spain; Messrs Schultz of Hamburg in China.; Mr Kohnstrom in China; Mr Ratzels in Russia. Bolling & Lowe in Turkey and Mr Buzon in Argentina

[300] UCS 1/3/17, Minutes 2 September 95 and 5 December 1895. Contract with Professor Biles 24 December 1895

[301] UCS 1/1/12, Board minutes, 15 June 1897

[302] The accident occurred at Stanford Hall on 30 September 1899. Pilcher died of his injuries on 2 October.

[303] UCS 1/1/12, Board minutes, 19 August 1891

[304] UCS 1/1/12, Board minutes, 14 April 1896

[305] UCS 1/1/12, Board minutes, 16 November 1896

[306] UCS 1/1/12, Board minutes, 14 July 1896

[307] UCS 1/1/12, Board minutes, 7 January 1896 and 10 March 1896. The minutes simply record the facts as stated here. Unfortunately, any discussion which might have occurred was not minuted

[308] UCS 1/4/1, Agreement between Clydebank Engineering & Shipbuilding Co Ltd and W J Luke NA of Broomwood Road, Wandsworth Common, London, July 1898

[309] Rippon, P M, Commander, *Evolution of Engineering in the Royal Navy,* Spellmount Ltd, Tunbridge Wells, 1988, page 76

[310] Crampsey, Bob, *The King's Grocer,* Glasgow City Libraries, 1996, page 83

[311] UCS 1/1/12, Minutes, 2 May 1896

[312] UCS 1/1/12, Minutes, 1 December 1896.

[313] This company was founded by prosperous chemical manufacturers of Glasgow who owned shares in J&G Thomson & Co. Ltd

[314] UCS 1/4/60, The Case of the Spanish Government against the Clydebank Engineering & Shipbuilding Co Ltd. Petition of Appeal.

[315] UCS1/1/12, Minutes, 4 September 1896.

[316] UCS1/1/12, Minutes, 6 April 1897

[317] UCS 1/1/12, Minutes, 7 September 1897.

[318] UCS 1/1/12, Minutes, 27 July 1897. A figure of £6,000 is mentioned for this vessel.

[319] UCS 1/1/12 Minutes, 1 October 1897. Thomson's naval architect, William Archer, submitted a report stating why he had altered the lines from that of the preceding Rocket type. The cost of altering the two still on the stocks would be £15,400.

[320] UCS 1/1/12, Minutes, 21 September 1897

[321] UCS 1/1/12 Minutes, 1 October 1897

[322] It is difficult to be certain about the outcome of this attempt at circumventing penalties as the Clydebank Board Minutes for the year 1898 are missing

[323] UCS 1/1/13, Minutes, 17 January 1900.

[324] UCS 1/4/60, op. cit. Court Proceedings

[325] UCS 1/4/60, op. cit, Supplementary Statement for the Appellants

[326] UCS 1/1/12, Minutes, 1 October 1897. A figure of £32,900 was mentioned.

[327] UCS 1/1/13, Minutes, 17 January 1900. John Gibb Dunlop referred to an application to the Admiralty to have *Brazen*, *Electra* and *Recruit* accepted at 29.5 knots explaining that this was the best possible and would involve a penalty of £500 per ship.

[328] See *The First Destroyers* by David Lyon, Chatham Publishing, London, 1997, for a full account of the early development of the TBD.

[329] UCS1/1/12, Minutes, various, throughout 1896 and 1897

[330] UCS 1/1/12, Minutes, October 1890 to October 1897. In July 1896 a Canopus Class battleship, broadly similar to the *Asahi*, was tendered for unsuccessfully at the following prices – Hull £317,000, Machinery £124,800, Auxiliary Machinery £10,628,

Profit £30,000 Total £482,428. See UCS 1/1/12, Minutes, 14 July 1896

[331] UCS 1/1/12, Minutes, 7 September 1897

[332] Glasgow City Archives, UCS 2/1/1 Fairfield Director's Minute Books, 23 October 1893

[333] UCS 1/4/9, Annual report and Balance Sheet to 31 March 1898

[334] Based on *Sir John Brown (1816-1896) Steel and armour plate manufacturer*, Sheffield City Archives, reference TWE.BIOG

[335] Parkes, op. cit. chapters 1-6

[336] Grant, Sir Allan, *Steel & Ships The History of John Brown's*, Michael Joseph, London, 1950. page 30

[337] Bellamy, Joyce M, *A Hull Shipbuilding Firm*, Business History, Volume VI, 1963, page 31

[338] Grant, Sir Allan, op. cit. page 32

[339] Ibid. page 37

[340] Since the arrival of Edward J Reed, Admiral Robinson and Sir John Brown on the board, a number of warships for the British and foreign navies had been built including armoured cruisers. Reed resigned in May 1874 to become a member of Parliament. See Bellamy, Joyce M, op. cit., page 33

[341] Ibid. page 40/41

[342] The propeller for the *Gallia* was supplied by John Brown in 1879

[343] Sheffield City Archives, Secretary's Letter Books Private No 4 , letter dated 5 June 1899

[344] Ibid.

[345] Ibid.

[346] UCS 1/3/25, op. cit.

[347] UCS 1/4/1, Letter of 27 June 1899 from McGrigor Donald & Co. to Watt Son & Co. Staff contracts. Letters about JRT and GPT removal from board

[348] Scottish Records Office, CS 318/44/283, Sequestration papers of James Roger Thomson Various dates through 1899 to July 1900.

[349] UCS 1/1/13, Minutes, 18 December 1903

[350] UCS 1/4/1, letter from Watt Son & Co. to Charles Ker, liquidator, dated 7 October 1899

[351] UCS 1/1/13, Minutes, 18 October 1899

[352] UCS 1/1/13, Minutes, 2 May 1905

[353] Grant, Sir Allan, op. cit. page 26/28

[354] The Dumbarton Herald, 23 March 1872

[355] They requested a full explanation of Company intentions noting that the Clyde Navigation Trust held that they had no right to do this. See Glasgow City Archives TCN 8.63 letters 17 and 29 August 1872

[356] UCS 1/11/1, letter Books, letter 21 August 1873, page 377

[357] UCS1/10/1, Shipyard Diary, entry dated 22 April 1875: 'Espirito Santo launched by Miss Finlay Miss Muir cut the dogshores. All machinery on board and steam up. A splendid launch'

[358] UCS1/10/1, Shipyard Diary, entry dated 5 May 1874: ' Saragossa launched at 2.30pm by Miss Thomson. Engines and boilers, masts, yards and sails all fitted, after leaving the ways the vessel made two sudden lurches and was drawn into the river bank for safety and taken to Glasgow next morning'

[359] UCS 1/1/12, Minutes, 16 November 1896. Total cost including fees and boundary wall was £18,000. See UCS 1/22/1, Plant files, 1 June 1897

[360] UCS 1/1/12, Minutes, April and June 1897

[361] UCS 1/22/1, Plant files, 5 November 1897

[362] UCS 1/22/1, Plant files, December 1897

[363] UCS 1/4/10, Valuation of Works by Thomas Binnie and James Barr, dated 3 March 1899

[364] The first *Sheelah* was sold to Gaston Menier soon after completion

[365] UCS 1/1/13, Minutes, 22 September 1899

[366] Tender dated 24 April 1899 – Numerous launches, pinnaces and cutters. Prices from £350 for a 42' launch to £32 for a 13.5' dinghy.

[367] UCS 1/1/13, Minutes, 18 October 1899

[368] UCS 1/10/1, Shipyard Diary, 27 June 1903

[369] The financial records for the years 1900 to 1930 are missing.

[370] Moss & Hume, op. cit., page 108

[371] Hyde, Francis E, *Cunard and the North Atlantic 1840 - 1973*, MacMillan, London, 1975, page 139

[372] University of Liverpool Archives, Cu31, Confidential negotiations with Mr Albert Vickers. Memo of 14 March 1902 from J Moorhouse to Lord Inverclyde. It seems that Cunard were instrumental in proposing this amalgamation.

[373] UCS 1/1/13, Minutes, 22 October 1902

[374] University of Liverpool Archives, D42/B8/1 Cunard Board Meeting 30 May 1901. Even earlier, in November 1899, JH Biles, presumably with much the same in mind, had asked Clydebank to price a twin screw ship of 700 x 71 x 52 feet. The price quoted was £445,000. UCS1/1/13, Minutes, 22 November 1899 and UCS 1/74/3, Tenders

[375] University of Liverpool Archives, D42/B.8/1, Extracts from minutes, Board Meeting of 21 February 1902

[376] University of Liverpool Archives, B1.4 Minutes of Board Meetings. A memorandum was circulated to Cunard shareholders on 30 September 1902 listing eight conditions. Most significant was Cunard's pledge to remain a British undertaking.

[377] In 1903, C S Swan & Hunter amalgamated with Wigham Richardson to become Swan Hunter & Wigham Richardson Ltd.

[378] University of Liverpool Archives, Cu 31, confidential negotiations between Lord Inverclyde and Albert Vickers, letter dated 4 November 1902

[379] University of Liverpool Archives, D42/B.8/1, Cunard Board Meeting, 19 March 1903.

[380] University of Liverpool Archives, Secretary's letters (No 26) Letter from AP Moorhouse to Edwin Hodder, dated 29 December 1892, in which it is stated that these ships were the first to be subsidised by the Government as armed cruisers.

[381] The Fairfield Board told Cunard that they would not state a maximum price but that they would build on the basis of time and material plus 20% for profit and charges. They also wanted payment on a monthly basis rather than the more normal stage payment method. The 20% figure asked for was very high indicating that Fairfield was not that interested in winning the contract. See Glasgow City Archives, UCS 2/1/3, Fairfield Director's Minute Books, 18 November 1902, pages 186, 187.

[382] The full committee was Admiral H J Oram (Engineer in Chief, Admiralty), Thomas Bell (John Brown), J T Milton (Lloyds), James Bain (Cunard), Sir William White (Swan Hunter & Wigham Richardson), H J Brock (Denny), Andrew Laing (Wallsend Slipway) University of Liverpool Archives D42/B.8/

1 Cunard Board Meeting, 20 August 1903

[383] UCS 1/21/137 Outline specifications for Cunard steamers

[384] UCS 1/1/13, Minutes, July 1902

[385] UCS 1/1/13, Minutes, 21 January 1903

[386] Sir Thomas Bell's farewell speech 17 April 1946, courtesy of Michael Bell

[387] Grt. This refers to gross tonnage, a measure of the cubic capacity of a vessel.

[388] UCS 1/22/2, Shipyard expenditure May/June 1904. Equipping the engine works alone cost £10,675 of which £4,300 was for a new lathe to turn the rotor drums and £2,900 was for a special boring machine. See also UCS 1/1/13 Minutes, 23 February 1904. A new erecting shop was proposed at an approximate cost of £10,000

[389] The Glasgow Herald, 8 June 1906, page 11

[390] Ibid.

[391] University of Liverpool Archives, S7. 1/26 letter from William Watson, Chairman of Cunard to John Brown and Swan Hunter & Wigham Richardson dated 15 December 1906

[392] University of Liverpool Archives, D42/S7/1/9, schedule of costs of Lusitania and Mauretania.

[393] Buxton, Ian, *Mauretania And Her Builders*, Mariners Mirror, Vol. 82 No1, February 1996, page 67

[394] University of Liverpool Archives, D42/S7/1/26, Memo dated 30 May 1907, about additional costs of *Lusitania* and *Mauretania*

[395] UCS 1/1/113, Minutes, 19 February 1908 and University of Liverpool Archives, D42/S7/1/9

[396] University of Liverpool Archives, D42/S7/1/26, Letter dated 25 February 1908 from John Gibb Dunlop to Watson of Cunard

[397] The want of a suitable graving dock on the Clyde required large ships built there to go elsewhere for hull inspections and repair work

[398] University of Liverpool Archives, D42/PR3.28/3a Report of Speed Trials of S S Lusitania, 1907

[399] UCS 1/1/13, Minutes, 17 September 1907

[400] Kludas, A, op. cit., Volume 1, p134

[401] In March 1914 *Lusitania* was again able to equal her best trial speed when on passage from New York to Liverpool she covered 618 miles in 24 hours at an average of 26.7 knots. See McCart, Neil, *Atlantic Liners of the Cunard Line*. p64

[402] The hull was sub-contracted to Hawthorn Leslie on Tyneside. Soon after, Armstrong at Elswick constructed *Cobra*, the second torpedo boat destroyer employing Parsons turbines.

[403] UCS 1/1/13, Minutes, 21 October 1903

[404] UCS 1/11/6, Correspondence with Charles Curtis, letter dated 14 November 1905

[405] UCS 1/1/13, Minutes, 23 February and 20 April 1904

[406] The Marine Review, 29 June 1905 page 19. In October 1905, a modified licence with Parsons was received permitting manufacture of turbines for abroad on a greater scale than in original agreement. See UCS 1/1/13, Minutes, 18 October 1905

[407] Bell, op. cit.

[408] UCS 1/1/13, Minutes, 20 May 1908

[409] UCS 1/11/4 Letter Books, letter from Thomas Bell to Captain Fuji of the Japanese Navy 18 August 1910

[410] Unpublished biography of Sir Stephen Pigott in possession of Eleanor Shipp, his daughter

[411] Telephone conversation with Mrs Shipp, 19 November 1996

[412] They were first referred to as Curtis-Brown turbines

[413] Sheffield City Archives, Monthly shipyard report, 21 September 1909

[414] UCS 1/11/6, Letter Books, 14 January 1913

[415] UCS 1/1/13, Minutes, 20 October 1909 and 17 March 1910

[416] UCS 1/11/4, Letter Books, Letter to Captain Fuji 18 August 1910.

[417] The term battlecruiser did not come into use until a few years later. Ships of this type were at first referred to as armoured cruisers

[418] Johnston, Ian, *Beardmore Built, The Rise and Fall of a Clydeside Shipyard*, Clydebank District Libraries & Museums, Clydebank, 1993, page 49

[419] Sheffield City Archives, Shipyard report for 15 May 1907, unlisted documents

[420] Ibid. report for 28 November 1907

[421] Ibid. report for 1 January 1908

[422] It seems likely that the exchange of shares did not take place until September 1908 as indicated by a letter from John Brown's secretary to Pirrie who was staying in a hotel at Braemar at the time. According to this letter, Pirrie was to pay John Brown £835,000 in cash for his shares in John Brown. See Sheffield City Archives, John Brown secretary's letter books, letter to Pirrie dated 16 September 1908.

[423] Glasgow Herald, 17 June 1907

[424] UCS1/4/6, letter from a Russian source sent to John Brown by HJ Stockman & Co. Philpot Lane, London on 8 May 1906Most likely, this letter would also have been distributed to Armstrong's, Vickers and Beardmore

[425] UCS 1/1/13, Minutes, 16 January 1907

[426] UCS 1/21/93, letters from agents Gustav List in St Petersburg to John Brown dated 11 December 1907 describe anti-Vickers sentiment.

[427] UCS 1/21/93, Tenders were sent to the Baltic Works and Franco Russian Shipbuilding & Engineering Co., both of St Petersburg

[428] UCS 1/21/93, letter dated 19 Dec. 1907 from Ing. A de Kuster of Gustav List to John Sampson

[429] UCS 1/21/106, Russian correspondence showing list of competing builders.

[430] Italian shipbuilders Ansaldo had been part of the Blohm & Voss design through the designs of the naval architect Cuniberti.

[431] UCS 1/21/106, See also J N Westwood, *Russian Naval Construction 1905-45*, University of Birmingham, Macmillan Press, 1994.

[432] The only other plant in the UK capable of manufacturing mountings was the naval ordnance works at Woolwich Arsenal although output was restricted to smaller, transportable mountings

[433] The Dumbarton Herald, 20 June 1906

[434] *The Coventry Syndicate*. a book produced by the company for publicity and sales purposes in 1914

[435] Sheffield City Archives, Secretary's Letterbooks, memorandum dated 6 March 1908. Unlisted documents

[436] Hansard, 17 March 1909. By the end of the year, the Daily Mail claimed, incorrectly, that Germany could turn out one super-dreadnought every month. See the Daily Mail, 15 December 1909

[437] On Clydeside, Scotts and Beardmore received one each

[438] UCS 1/10/1, Shipyard Diary, entry dated 17 march 1909

[439] UCS 1/11/4, Letter Books, letter dated 12 October 1912

[440] UCS 1/10/1, Shipyard Diary, 21 January 1908

[441] UCS 1/1/13, Minutes,19 February 1908 When this annuity ran out in February 1915, Thomas Bell explained that as Mrs McGee's two eldest sons were in the Forces, payments should continue until the end of the War

[442] Sheffield City Archives, Secretary's letter books, 29 January 1908. The letter stated that the directors of John Brown had 'much appreciated your past services to the company and trust you may see your way to accept the position now offered as some recognition of their appreciation'

[443] The Baltic Works at St. Petersburg were established in May 1856 by a Scotsman called McPherson. By the turn of the century, these Works had become the largest of the many shipyards in St Petersburg. See Warship International No 4 1985, Main Shipyards, Engine builders and Manufacturers of Guns and Armour Plate in the St. Petersburg Area up to 1917, pages 347/350

[444] UCS 1/1/13, Minutes, 20 January and 25 February 1909 and UCS 1/21/108 contract document

[445] From information supplied by Stephen McLaughlin translated from History of Domestic Shipbuilding, Volume III, Shipbuilding at the Beginning of the 20th Century, Edited by I D Spasskii, St. Petersburg, 1995

[446] UCS 1/1/13, Minutes, May and June 1909

[447] UCS 1/1/13, Minutes, 16 June 1909

[448] UCS 1/13/1, Letter of 19 July 1909

[449] UCS 1/13/1, Letter of 21 December 1909. In October 1910, the launching calculations for Lusitania and Inflexible were sent to John Black at the Baltic Works. See UCS 1/11/4 letter of 2 November 1910.

[450] Stephen McLaughlin, op. cit.

[451] Bell, op. cit.

[452] UCS 1/1/13, Minutes, 18 December 1908/26 April 1909

[453] UCS 1/11/6, letter from Charles Curtis to Stephen Pigott, 7 May 1912. $900 was then equivalent to £184, 4/2d

[454] UCS 1/11/6, letter from Thomas Bell to Charles Curtis, 2 November 1912

[455] UCS 1/11/6, letter from Charles Curtis to Stephen Pigott, 13 March 1913

[456] Under UCS 1/11/8, to UCS 1/11/10, there are numerous letters discussing technical details and drawings of the machinery arrangements of US battleships to be built with electric drive

[457] UCS 1/11/6, letter from Charles Curtis to Thomas Bell, 1 March 1913

[458] Sheffield City Archives, Monthly shipyard reports, 27 June 1916. Unlisted documents

[459] UCS 1/22/3, Minutes relating to yard extensions containing note from Thomas Bell dated 20 April 1910

[460] UCS 1/13/1, Private Letter Books, June 1910

[461] The Dumbarton Herald, 1 June 1910 and 7 September 1910

[462] UCS 1/10/1, Shipyard Diary, 8 and 30 November, 14, 15 and 19 December 1910

[463] Dumbarton Herald, 3 August 1910

[464] UCS 1/1/1, Minutes, 24 July and 23 August 1911

[465] UCS 1/1/1, Minutes, 29 July 1912

[466] UCS 1/1/1, Minutes, 24 July 1911, 22 October 1912 and 19 February 1913

[467] UCS 1/74/6, Tender Books for the year 1910

[468] UCS 1/1/1, Minutes, 24 September 1912. In the event, the Syndicate did not win the work and both ships were built by Armstrong and later taken over by the Royal Navy on the outbreak of war and named Gorgon and Glatton

[469] UCS 1/1/13, Minutes, July 1911, page 29

[470] UCS 1/1/1, Minutes, 23 June 1915

[471] John Brown did, however, explain that the order for the battlecruiser Tiger had been received for machinery of similar power.

[472] UCS 1/21/108 contract details, 27 November 1911

[473] UCS 1/13/1, Letter of 12 December 1911

[474] Sheffield City Archives, Monthly shipyard report for 28 April 1914. Unlisted documents

[475] UCS 1/1/1 25, March 1912

[476] Ibid

[477] Sheffield City Archives, unlisted John Brown documents

[478] UCS 1/1/1, Minutes, October 1919, April 1920, December 1920 and October 1921

[479] UCS 1/74/6, Tender books, tender dated 30 April 1910. Steamer 600 x 71 x 52.25. 12,500ihp. Price £ 397,700

[480] UCS 1/11/4, Letter Books, 15 October 1910

[481] University of Liverpool Archives, File AC14/46 172 605

[482] Sheffield City Archives, Report 16 February 1911 Unlisted documents, According to the report of 24 July 1911, Titanic's turbines had been completed and forwarding instructions from Harland & Wolff were awaited

[483] University of Liverpool Archives, B1.9 Board Meetings 16 January 1913 and 16 October 1913

[484] A term applied to ironworkers - the platers, riveters etc. who assembled the steelwork on the berth

[485] The Syren and Shipping, 25 March 1914, page 727

[486] Sheffield City Archives, Report for 31 March 1914 Unlisted documents

[487] University of Liverpool Archives, File AC 14/46 File 606

[488] Sheffield City Archives, Report for 1 September 1914Unlisted documents

[489] The principal items were: 6 electric derricks £4,500, Electric Drive etc. £24,000, Gantries for stacking and handling plates etc. £4,000, Pneumatic Power Plant £5,500, Smiths Shop and Forge £15,000, Hydraulic Compressors £8,000, 3 extra Gas Producers £10,000

[490] UCS 1/22/3, Plant Files, 31 December 1909

[491] UCS 1/22/3, Meeting, 28 February 1911, and Thomas Bell's paper detailing this expenditure. This paper is at Sheffield City Archives under John Brown, Managing Directors Reports

[492] UCS 1/1/1, Minutes, 25 March 1912

[493] UCS 1/1/13, Minutes, 16 August 1905

[494] UCS 1/1/13, Minutes, 30 January 1906

[495] UCS 1/1/1, Minutes, 17 February 1911.

[496] UCS 1/22/2, Yard expenditure 20 May 1903, 28 March 1904, 21 April 1904

[497] UCS 1/5/9, Report, 1 November 1910, on Engine and Boiler Works by Thomas Bell.

[498] The Clydebank and Renfrew Press, 7 August 1914

[499] The Clydebank and Renfrew Press, 14 August 1914

[500] The Clydebank and Renfrew Press, 4 September 1914

[501] The Clydebank and Renfrew Press, 11 September 1914

[502] UCS 1/1/1, Minutes, 27 July 1914

[503] The Clydebank and Renfrew Press, 14 August 1914

[504] UCS 1/5/13, Thomas Bell's memo 'Shortage of Ironworkers', dated 26 January 1914

[505] Bell notes that current rents in Clydebank are 10 to 20% higher than in Govan

[506] UCS 1/5/13, op. cit.

[507] UCS 1/1/1, Minutes, 20 January and 22 February 1915 and the Building Register of Clydebank Council

[508] Building Register of Clydebank Council. The number of tenements and cottages built is at variance with the numbers stated in John Brown minute books.

[509] Sheffield City Archives, Reports for 1 September and 27 October 1914. Unlisted documents

[510] Raven, Allan and Roberts, John, *British Battleships of WW2*, Arms & Armour Press, London, 1975, page 47

[511] UCS 1/21/29, manpower on *Repulse*, correspondence dated 31 March 1915

[512] Ibid.

[513] Ibid.

[514] UCS 1/5/14, Reports for 26 January 1915, showing 9,270 men, and 27 May 1915, showing 10,668 men

[515] UCS 1/5/9, Report, 29 June 1915

[516] Hood, John (Compiled by) *The History of Clydebank*, Parthenon Publishing, Cranforth, 1988, p69

[517] Sheffield City Archives, Shipyard Report, 3 March 1915. Unlisted documents

[518] Hood, op. cit. p79

[519] UCS 1/5/14, Report, 28 October 1915

[520] UCS 1/5/15, Report, 31 August 1916

[521] Raven and Roberts. Ibid. page 295

[522] UCS 1/1/1, Minutes, 3 May 1916

[523] Four ships of this class were planned although only *Hood* was built.

[524] There is no evidence in the John Brown files to support the widely held view that *Hood* was laid down on 31 May 1916 only to be stopped following the disastrous losses of British battlecruisers at Jutland

[525] The Clydebank and Renfrew Press, July 1916

[526] UCS 1/1/1, Minutes, 28 August and 16 September 1913.

[527] UCS1/1/1, Minutes, 21 November 1913

[528] UCS1/1/13, Minutes, 29 March 1915

[529] UCS 1/1/1, Minutes, 27 May 1915

[530] later Stalingrad

[531] UCS 1/21/105, Report by R Hood See also *Warship International* No1. 1989, British Naval Operations in the Black Sea 1918 – 1920, by David Snook, Page 40

[532] UCS 1/1/1, Minutes, 21 December 1916

[533] UCS 1/1/1 Minutes, 1 February 1917, 24 March 1917 and 25 April 1917

[534] UCS 1/21/107, Letter from John Black from John Brown & Co. Ltd. Nicolaieff, 7 February 1918

[535] UCS 1/21/107, Letter from Alex Hutcheson from John Brown & Co. Ltd. Nicolaieff, 12 February 1918

[536] UCS 1/1/1/ Minutes, 20 March 1918, 2 May 1918 and 1 August 1918

[537] UCS 1/21/107, op. cit.

[538] UCS 1/1/1, Minutes, 22 August 1918

[539] UCS 1/22/4, Minutes relating to yard extensions etc. Quotation dated 5 June 1916, from Leslie Kirk, contractor, for the erection of 20 four-storey tenements in Clyde Street complete with washouses. Total £52,762.

[540] Sheffield City Archives, Report, 2 November 1916. Unlisted documents

[541] UCS 1/22/4, letter from Owen H Smith Ministry of Munitions 'C' Section to John Brown, 4 September 1916 and letter from Thomas Bell to Owen H Smith of 'C' Section dated 5 October 1916

[542] UCS 1/1/1, Minutes, 30 November 1916

[543] UCS 1/1/1 Minutes, 21 December 1916

[544] Sheffield City Archives, Report, 1 June 1916

[545] UCS 1/74/7 Tender Books, 15 November 1916

[546] UCS 1/5/16, Correspondence noting departure of Thomas Bell, June 1916

[547] Clydebank Press, 10 January 1919

[548] Recalling the great competition in horsepower and speed to across the Atlantic in the previous century, her Fairfield built sister *Renown* made 126,300 shp for a speed over 32 knots

[549] Sheffield City Archives, Report, 1 June 1916. Unlisted documents

[550] Sheffield City Archives, Report, 1 February 1917

[551] Sheffield City Archives, Report, 27 June 1917

[552] UCS 1/106/9, work for the Royal Navy completed at Clydebank during the war. Undated

[553] UCS 1/1/13, Minutes, 2 May 1905

[554] UCS 1/1/13, Minutes, 24 May 1909

[555] Warship International, No 2, 1995, Article, *Laurenti Type Submarines in the World's Navies*

[556] UCS 1/1/13, Minutes, 17 September 1907 and 16 October 1907

[557] UCS 1/1/13, Minutes, 17 March 1909

[558] UCS 1/1/13, Minutes, 24 May 1909

[559] UCS 1/22/4, Extensions at Controlled Establishments, Plant & Property extensions from year ending 31 March 1916 to 15 November 1918

[560] UCS 1/22/4, Letter from Ministry of Munitions Of War dated 20 June 1916

[561] UCS 1/22/5, Papers dealing with Admiralty Extension No. 130. Summary of Proposed Extensions and Additions 25 October 1919

[562] UCS 1/5/18, Report, 19 March 1919

[563] UCS 1/5/22, Letter to Lord Pirrie, dated 10 May 1923

[564] Musk, George, *Canadian Pacific*, David & Charles, Newton Abbot, 1981, page 168

[565] UCS 1/1/1, Minutes, 29 May 1919

[566] UCS 1/5/18, Report, 28 January 1919

[567] Dumbarton Herald, 29 January 1919

[568] Ibid.

[569] UCS 1/5/18, Report, 20 February 1919

[570] UCS 1/5/18, Report, 19 March 1919

[571] UCS 1/5/18, Report, 1 May 1919

[572] UCS1/5/18, Appendix to Report, 25 October 1919

[573] Dumbarton Herald, 15 January 1919, attributed to the Pall Mall Gazette

[574] Dumbarton Herald, 24 May 1919 and 9 July 1919

[575] UCS1/5/18, Report, 3 September 1919 and 30 October 1919

[576] UCS1/5/19, Report, 28 January and 20 March 1920

[577] Moss & Hume, op. cit., page 219

[578] UCS1/5/19, Report, 31 March 1920

[579] UCS1/5/19, Report, 20 May and 29 June 1920

[580] UCS 1/1/1, Minutes, 29 April 1920

[581] UCS 1/5/19, Report, 20 May 1920

[582] UCS 1/5/19, Report, 24 August 1920

[583] UCS 1/5/19, Report, 20 May 1920

[584] UCS 1/5/19, Report, 25 June 1920

[585] UCS 1/5/19, Report, 20 May 1920

[586] UCS 1/5/19, Report, 24 August 1920

[587] UCS 1/1/1, Minutes, 24 August 1920

[588] UCS 1/5/19, Report, 28 September 1920

[589] UCS 1/5/19, Report, 21 October 1920

[590] UCS 1/5/19, Report, 21 October 1920

[591] UCS 1/5/19, Report, 1 December 1920

[592] Engineering, 26 August 1921, page 315

[593] UCS 1/5/19, Report, 23 December 1920

[594] UCS 1/5/20, Report, 6 April 1921

[595] Dumbarton Herald, 23 April 1921

[596] Dumbarton Herald, 18 May 1921

[597] UCS 1/5/20, Report, 1 June 1921

[598] UCS 1/5/20, Report, 27 July 1921

[599] UCS 1/5/20, Report, 26 July and 27 September 1921

[600] Hood, op. cit., page 80

[601] UCS 1/5/20, Report, 30 November 1921

[602] UCS 1/5/21, Report, 1 February 1922

[603] UCS 1/5/21, Minutes, 1 June 1922

[604] UCS 1/5/21, Minutes, 1 June 1922

[605] UCS 1/5/21, Report, 26 July 1922

[606] John Brown was asked to tender for the G3 machinery contract by Swan Hunter & Wigham Richardson and Armstrong Whitworth should either win the contract for the hull. The latter placed the machinery contract with Wallsend Slipway who also tendered at a loss to win the business.

[607] UCS 1/10/1, Shipyard Diary, entries dated 30 April and 26 November 1923

[608] Dumbarton Herald, 28 March 1923

[609] UCS 1/5/22, Report, 20 December 1923

[610] UCS 1/5/22, Report, 31 May 1923

[611] The yards were; Cairds, McMillans, D&W Henderson, A&J Inglis and the Harland & Wolff Govan yard

[612] Moss & Hume, op. cit., page 310

[613] Guthrie, John, A History of Marine Engineering, Hutchinson Educational Ltd, London, 1971, page 209

[614] UCS 1/11/4, Letter Books, Letters of 15 August and 13 October 1910. MAN was working on their first double acting reversible oil engine.

[615] Moss & Hume, op. cit. page 156

[616] UCS 1/5/22, Report, 20 December 1923

[617] UCS 1/1/1, Minutes, 28 October 1921 and UCS 1/5/22, Report of 31 May 1923

[618] Start of the grouse shooting season

[619] UCS 1/5/23, Report, 16 June 1924

[620] UCS 1/5/23, Report, 1 December 1925

[621] UCS 1/5/24, Report, 27 February 1925

[622] Dumbarton Herald, 11 February 1925

[623] Raven, Alan and Roberts, John, British Cruisers of World War Two, Arms & Armour Press, London, 1980, page 110

[624] UCS 1/5/24, Report, 29 May 1925

[625] UCS 1/5/24, Report, 30 June and 28 August 1925

[626] Both lines were amalgamated in 1907

[627] Cancellation resulted in a payment to Brown's of £25,490 to cover the cost of work done. UCS 1/5/26, Report, 29 September 1927

[628] UCS 1/5/25, Report, 20 December 1926

[629] Smith, Edgar, A Short History of Naval and Marine Engineering, Cambridge University Press, 1938, pages 305 to 307

[630] UCS 1/107/90 Sir Thomas Bell's toast to the Duchess of Bedford delivered at the time of her launch

[631] Shipbuilding & Shipping Record, 6 August 1936, page 179

[632] UCS 1/5/27, Report, 25 May 1928

[633] UCS 1/5/28, Report, 30 August 1929

[634] The story, probably apocryphal, which circulated at the time was that Black had been asked by the New Zealand Line to look at a ship in London which had accommodation of the type required for their motorships. During his inspection, Black reputedly used his umbrella as a measuring stick to mark off the dimensions of cabins etc. thereby sowing the seeds of later miscalculations. Conversation with Sir John Brown, October 1995

[635] UCS 1/5/28, Report, 26 April 1929

[636] UCS 1/5/28, Report, 24 June 1929

[637] UCS 1/5/28, Report, 23 May 1929

[638] UCS 1/5/28, Report, 1 and 29 November 1929

[639] UCS 1/5/28, Report, 20 December 1929

[640] Slaven, Anthony, A Shipyard in Depression, John Brown's of Clydebank 1919-1938, Business History, Volume XIX, 1977, page 198

[641] On the board of directors were Sir James Lithgow, Lithgows Ltd; A. Ayre, Burntisland Shipbuilding Co.; John Barr, Vickers Ltd.; Commander Craven, Vickers Armstrong Ltd.; J Kempster, Harland & Wolff; Sir Alexander Kennedy, Fairfield; F Pyman, Wm. Gray & Co. Ltd.; Murray Stephen, A Stephen & Co. Ltd.; T Thirlaway, Swan Hunter & Wigham Richardson Ltd.; Norman Thomson, J L Thomson & Sons Ltd

[642] Berths: John Brown, 8; Wm. Beardmore, 13; Napier & Miller, 6; A. McMillan, 3 and Wm. Denny, 9. Scotts of Bowling has not been included. Only John Brown and Denny survived.

[643] Grant, op. cit. page 77

[644] Sorbie, James, John Brown's of Clydebank: Aspects of Accounting Practice and Financial Management Between the Wars., Unpublished Thesis, University of Glasgow, 1983, page 42

[645] University of Liverpool Archives, Secretary's Letters (No 26) letter from Sir Thomas Royden to Sir Ashley Sparks, Cunard's director in New York, 5 March 1928
In June 1928, White Star laid down Oceanic, a 1,000 foot 70,000 ton ship at Belfast. First ordered in 1924, this ship fell victim to the difficulties of the Royal Mail Group of which both White Star and Harland & Wolff were members. This ship was never completed and the contract cancelled in 1930

[646] University of Liverpool Archives, D42/C3.343 54th OGM 8 April 1931

[647] The naval architect referred to, Mr John Brown, was no relation to the John Brown who founded the John Brown Company. The young naval architect later became Managing Director of the Company

[648] University of Liverpool Archives, Secretary's Letters (No 26), letter dated 10 July 1929

[649] University of Liverpool Archives, Secretary's Letters (No 26), letter dated 31 July 1929

[650] University of Liverpool Archives, D42/C3/166-169 A3, Letter from Sir Percy Bates to Lord Camrose, dated 31 March 36

[651] UCS 1/5/27, Report, 18 December 1928

[652] UCS 1/5/28, Report, 23 May 1929

[653] UCS 1/5/28, Report, 24 June 1929

[654] University of Liverpool Archives, D42/C3.347, Figures vary on the actual contract price of Queen Mary. A Cunard document prepared in October 1942 states the contract price as £4,283, 750 and the actual cost as £5,614,734. See Liverpool Archives D42/C3.283. John Brown's tender dated 10 May 1930 was for a price of £3,992,000

[655] University of Liverpool Archives, Secretary's Letters (No 26), letter dated 21 May 1930

[656] University of Liverpool Archives, Secretary's Letters (No 26), letter from Sir Percy Bates to Sir Frederick Lewis, 27 May 1930

[657] University of Liverpool Archives, C3/286 Queen Mary Building Contract, letter dated 1 December 1930

[658] Ibid

[659] Hood, op. cit., page 112

[660] Hyde, Francis E, op. cit. page 206

[661] University of Liverpool Archives, D42/C3.342, letter from Sir Percy Bates to Sir Thomas Bell dated 1 December 1931

[662] Ibid. letter from Sir Thomas Bell to Sir Percy Bates dated 10 December 1931

[663] Dumbarton Herald, 16 December 1931, telegram from Sir Thomas Bell to David Kirkwood MP quoted from article entitled 'Clydebank Yard Closed Down'

[664] Ibid

[665] Hansard, 11 December 1931, page 2229

[666] Hansard, 11 December 1931, page 2285

[667] Hansard, 2 February 1932, page 27

[668] University of Liverpool Archives, D42/C3.342, Letter from Sir Robert Bruce to Stanley Baldwin, 11 December 1931

[669] Hyde, op. cit., page 207

[670] University of Liverpool Archives, D42/C3.342, Memo to Chairman of Shipbuilding Committee, dated 14 December 1931

[671] University of Liverpool Archives, D42/C3.342, Report dated 18 December by M McMillan, Cunard building superintendent at Clydebank

[672] UCS 1/5/30, Reports for January and February 1931

[673] Bell's initial observation on welding was that it was about saving weight and not money although he conceded that the latter would happen in time and foresaw that it would be employed more and more and especially for warship work. See UCS 1/5/30, Report, 25 August 1932 and UCS 1/5/31, Report, 2 February 1933

[674] UCS 1/5/30, Report, 30 Sept. 1932

[675] UCS 1/5/30, Report, 2 December 1932

[676] UCS 1/5/31, Report, 28 July 1933

[677] UCS 1/5/31, Report, 28 April 1933

[678] UCS 1/5/31, Report, 28 March 1933

[679] UCS 1/5/33, Report, 1 June 1934

[680] Green, Edwin and Moss, Michael, A Business of National Importance, The Royal Mail Shipping Group 1902 -1937, Methuen, London, 1982, page 92

[681] UCS 1/5/33, Report, 27 April 1934

[682] Gardner, A. C., River Work for the Queen Mary, Transactions of the Institution of Engineers & Shipbuilders in Scotland, Glasgow, 1936 – 37, page 6

[683] McNeill, J, Launch of the Quadruple Screw Turbine Steamer Queen Mary, Transactions of the Institution of Naval Architects, London, 1935. Including the weight of poppets etc., the total weight on the ground ways was 36,700 tons.

[684] UCS 1/5/53, Report, 31 July 1935

[685] The inscription on the plaque read: Thomas Bell, 1865-1952. Clydebank 1886-1946. Managing Director 1909-1935. Si monumentum requiris circumspice. [If you seek his memorial, look around you]
Earlier, in 1941, Aberconway wrote to Bell urging him to continue as a director of the company: 'I can only reiterate what I have previously stated to you, namely, that both my colleagues and I feel that your presence on the Board is of very great assistance to the Company, for two reasons. Firstly, your advise, if I may say so, on general questions is always most sound, and, on Clydebank questions, is invaluable. Secondly, your presence on our Board is a great asset as regards getting work from shipowners. You must remember, in this connection, that without exaggeration you undoubtedly rank as the most famous of all shipbuilders.' Letter dated 6 February, 1941, supplied by Michael Bell, Sir Thomas's nephew

[686] Telephone conversation with Michael Bell, nephew of Sir Thomas Bell, 26 April 1997

[687] University of Liverpool Archives, D42/C3/166-169 A3, Folder marked 'Negotiations with John Brown', Minutes of Board Meeting 13 July 1936

[688] University of Liverpool Archives, D42/C3/166-169 A3, letter to Lord Essenden dated, 26 November 1935

[689] University of Liverpool Archives, D42/C3/166-169 A3, letter from Rebbeck to Bates dated, 16 December 1935

[690] Sir Thomas Bell remained on the board of John Brown & Co. Ltd.

[691] University of Liverpool Archives, Letter from Percy Bates to Lord Camrose, dated 31 March 1936

[692] University of Liverpool Archives, Chart dated 14 April 1936, showing details of builders proposals

[693] University of Liverpool Archives, D42/C3.236, 13 July 1936

[694] University of Liverpool Archives, D42/C3/166-169 A3, Minutes of Board Meeting, 13 July 36

[695] University of Liverpool Archives, Folder marked 'Negotiations with John Brown', Letter from Sir Percy Bates to Sir Thomas Bell, 11 July 1936

[696] Correspondence with Tom Kameen, former Superintendent Engineer of the Cunard line and conversations with Willie McLaughlin, formerly John Brown's chief engine designer

[697] University of Liverpool Archives, D42/C3.347, letter from Sir Thomas Bell to Sir Percy Bates dated 13 March 1934, enclosing a four page report on various hull forms tested at Clydebank

[698] Queen Mary's record voyage was number 48. On her westward passage she made 206,100shp, with 190.32 revolutions and an average speed of 30.94 knots. On her eastward passage she made 211,552shp, with 193.2 revolutions and an average speed of 31.72 knots. (figures in the possession of Willie McLaughlin, John Brown's chief engine designer)

[699] Arcform, developed by Joseph Isherwood, was yet another approach to the design of an efficient hull form.

[700] University of Liverpool Archives, D42/C3/172, letter dated

12 November 1936

[701] University of Liverpool Archives, D42/C3.167, letter from Clydebank to Cunard, 8 April 1936

[702] University of Liverpool Archives, C3/170-181, Letter from Sir Percy Bates to Stephen Pigott dated 3 February 1937

[703] *Conway's all the World's Warships 1860 - 1982* op. cit., Volume 1922/46 page 3

[704] University of Liverpool Archives, Folder marked 'Negotiations with John Brown', letter dated 26 November 1936

[705] Lennox Herald, 3 June and 19 August 1939

[706] UCS 1/5/37, Minutes, 22 February 1939 and PRO ADM 167/107, courtesy of David Brown and George Moore.

[707] Lennox Herald, 19 August 1939

[708] Interview with Sir John Brown, 12 May 1997

[709] In course of construction were twenty-seven boiler drums for the cruiser *Curacoa* and 18 drums for V&W Class destroyers. Thirty 3.7" AA gun cradles for Vickers, five crankshafts for the Doxford company and boiler drums for Mitchell Engineering Co. Large armour plate rolls for Beardmore and 3.7" and 2 pounder AA gun mountings for Vickers. Gearing for escort vessels building at Yarrow and condenser shells for escort vessels building at Thornycroft were in progress.

[710] UCS 1/5/42, Report, 28 June 1940

[711] His offices were in the St Enoch's Hotel in Glasgow.

[712] Glasgow University Archives, GUA TD1347, papers from Robert McAlister & Son Ltd Shipyard Letter No. 14 , 21 June 1941

[713] UCS 1/22/21, Letter of 14 April 1944 to Director of Navy Contracts

[714] Liverpool University Archives, D42/C3.238, Correspondence between Sir Stephen Pigott and Cunard White Star, September 1939

[715] Liverpool University Archives, D5, Matters Arising out of Wartime Conditions, Letter, 28 September 1939

[716] Liverpool University Archives, D5, Letter, 15 September 1939

[717] Liverpool University Archives, D5, Note of Treasury meeting on 29 September 1919

[718] Liverpool University Archives, D42/C3.273, Reports from Cunard's naval architects and engineering departments in March 1940

[719] Dumbarton Herald, 30 March 1940, Sir Percy Bates at a luncheon for the Institute of Marine Engineers in London

[720] UCS 1/5/43, Report, 27 September 1940

[721] UCS 1/5/44, Report, 1 November 1940

[722] Dumbarton Herald, 7 January 1939

[723] Lennox Herald, 18 March 1939

[724] Lennox Herald, 4 June 1939

[725] Dumbarton Herald, 8 June 1940

[726] UCS 1/5/44, Report, 15 November 1940

[727] UCS 1/5/43, Report, 26 July 1940

[728] UCS 1/5/43, Report, 30 August 1940

[729] Interview with Johnny Moore, 26 February 1997 and transcripts of the Public Inquiry in his possession

[730] UCS 1/5/44, Report, 15 November 1940

[731] Jeffrey, Andrew, *This Time of Crisis*, Mainstream Publishing, Edinburgh, 1993, page 55

[732] Telephone conversation with Jan Rudzinski, in May 1996, who served on ORP Piorun at the time

[733] McPhail, I M M, *The Clydebank Blitz*, Clydebank District Libraries & Museums, 1974, page 16

[734] Based on reports from the Bundesarchiv, Militärarchiv courtesy of Christine Schmitt Mackinnon

[735] UCS1/5/45 1941, Report, 28 March 1941

[736] UCS1/5/46, Report, 30 May 1941

[737] Glasgow University Archives, GUA TD1347, papers from Robert McAlister & Son Ltd

[738] Ibid. notification of 11 November 1941

[739] UCS1/5/47, Report, 26 September 1941

[740] UCS1/5/46, Report, 30 May 1941

[741] UCS 1/5/40, Report, 1 December 1939

[742] UCS 1/5/41, Report, 28 February 1940

[743] UCS1/5/44, Report, 1 November 1940

[744] UCS 1/5/44, Report, Shipyard Drawing Office, 18 December 1940

[745] UCS 1/5/45, Report, 31 January and 1 February 1941. The loss of *Prince of Wales* in December 1941 put additional pressure on Fairfield to complete *Howe* By 19 December 1941, 80 engineers had been transferred from Clydebank to Fairfield

[746] The Lennox Herald, Article 'Back to the Shipyards,' 7 June 1941

[747] One of these women was Isabel Dowie who had been given the option to join the forces or work in the shipyards. With many of her family already in the shipyards, she applied for the latter. After a crash course lasting six weeks in a Glasgow college at the beginning of 1942, Isabel was sent to John Brown's as a dilutee electrician. She recalls being well treated although noted that on occasions men were perfectly content to let women carry out heavy work. Pulling thick cables through bulkheads in lower compartments of the aircraft carrier *Indefatigable* was such a task. Later, as this ship neared completion, her work included the wiring of Morse keys and the firing mechanisms in gun turrets. Interview on 23 November 1996

[748] Glasgow University Archives, GUA TD1347, Papers from Robert McAlister & Son Ltd Shipyard letter No. 41, 17 April 1942

[749] The machinery for all three vessels would continue to be built at Clydebank

[750] UCS1/5/49, Report, 21 March 1942

[751] UCS1/5/49, Report, 21 March 1942

[752] Herbert Corry, Port Line's chairman, complained about this treatment to Sir James Lithgow, Controller of Merchant Shipbuilding.

[753] UCS 1/1/3, Minutes,1 June 1942

[754] UCS 1/1/3, Minutes, 15 July 1942

[755] In September 1942, Port Line asked Clydebank when it would next be possible to lay down another ship similar to 577. The replacement ship, *Port Wellington*, was not laid down until February 1944.

[756] UCS 1/5/50, Notes on meeting, 2 July 1942

[757] UCS 1/5/51, Report, 15 July 1942

[758] Dumbarton Herald, 4 July 1942, By this time, the Admiralty was, in any case, considering converting the battleship into an aircraft carrier. See UCS 1/5/51, Report, 15 July 1942

[759] This is a quote from 'John Brown Anecdotes' compiled by Lord Aberconway for private circulation in January 1985.

[760] ADM 116/4991, Public Records Office, courtesy of George Moore

[761] Ibid.

[762] Two others, *Milne* and *Roebuck*, were transferred to Clydebank from Scotts at Greenock

[763] UCS 1/1/3, Minutes, 9 November 1942

[764] UCS 1/22/21, meeting with Mr Jubb, Director of Navy Contracts, on 8 December 1944

[765] UCS 1/1/3, Minutes, 8 July 1943

[766] UCS 1/1/3 Minutes, 2 September 1943

[767] UCS 1/5/55, Report, 28 January 1944

[768] UCS 1/5/56, Report, 8 April 1944

[769] UCS 1/5/56, Report, 28 April 1944

[770] UCS 1/5/56, Report, 2 June 1944

[771] UCS 1/5/57, Report, 29 September 1944

[772] Friedman, Norman, *British Carrier Aviation*, Conway Maritime Press, London, 1988, page 295

[773] UCS 1/5/58, Report, 30 November 1944

[774] UCS 1/5/55, Report, 30 March 1944

[775] UCS 1/1/3, Minutes, 12 April and 20 July 1944

[776] UCS 1/1/3, Minutes, 30 November 1944

[777] UCS 1/5/59, Report, 17 January 45

[778] UCS 1/1/3 Minutes, for 30 April 1945

[779] The Clydebank Press, 11 May 1945

[780] From Lord Aberconway's speech at the ordinary general meeting of John Brown & Co. Ltd, July 1945. See Lennox Herald, 4 August 1945

[781] The Clydebank Press, 17 August 1945

[782] Figures courtesy of Graeme Smith CA

[783] See Profit and Loss Appendix by Graeme Smith CA

[784] UCS 1/22/9, Letter from Sir Stephen Pigott to RW Rawson dated 4 September 1939

[785] UCS 1/5/35, Report, April 1937

[786] Public Record Office, PRO, BT28/319 179075, Report of the Machine Tool Controller, Cecil Bentham, 1942

[787] UCS 1/1/3, Minutes, 8 July 1943

[788] UCS 1/5/53, Report, 26 February 1942

[789] UCS 1/22/10, Correspondence about Number 4 berth with Director of Navy Contracts, Jubb and Sir Stanley Goodall, Director of Naval Construction. Various letters during 1943 Alterations to number 4 berth were originally to take 6 months but had not been completed by June 1945. The contract was started on 1 December 1943

[790] UCS 1/11/13, report of Shipbuilding Committee, August 1945

[791] In June 1943, employment reached the wartime peak of 180,000

[792] UCS 1/5/51, Report, 15 July 1942

[793] UCS 1/5/57, Report, 20 July 1944. This ship became *Media*

[794] UCS1/1/3, Minutes, 25 October 1945

[795] UCS1/5/60, Report, 29 June 1945

[796] UCS1/5/61 Report, 28 September 1945

[797] The Lennox Herald, 27 October 1945

[798] McCart, Neil, op. cit. Page 196

[799] The Arran measured mile was in fact two miles, one after the other. This location provided the deepest water of any of the British trial runs and was frequently used because shallow water adversely affected performance

[800] Interview with Sir John Brown, 12 May 1997.

[801] The Lennox Herald, 20 July 1946

[802] Ibid.

[803] McCart, op. cit. page 197/8

[804] UCS 1/22/28, Letter from Admiralty to close down Dalmuir Basin and termination of management agreement. The shipbreakers Arnott Young wanted to restart shipbreaking at the earliest opportunity and it was agreed by the Admiralty that breaking the *Empress of Russia* could begin in January 1946

[805] UCS 1/5/ 60, Report, 27 February 1947. The position at mid-February 1947 was as follows; *Tiger*, fitting-out at Dalmuir where about 200 men were employed on the ship and 50 in the engine shops; *Norfolk*, completed 15 February; *Barossa*, completed 14 February; *Matapan*, fitting-out; *Media*, fitting-out; *Diamond*, about to be laid-down; *Haparangi*, about to be launched; *Caronia*, building; *Arnhem*, fitting-out; *Suffolk Ferry*, building; *Patria*, building; *Imperio*, building; *Sussex*, on order; *Hinakura*, on order; *City of Oxford* and *City of Birmingham*, both on order. Work on the reconditioning of *Queen Mary* was in progress at Southampton. In the engine shops 4 sets of machinery and three water turbines were under construction

[806] The Dumbarton Herald, 7 June 1947

[807] UCS 1/1/3, Minutes, 30 April 1945

[808] UCS 1/5/72, Report, 30 April 1948. These were three for Clunie power station, one for Kuusankoski(?), three for Errochty and one for Lawers

[809] Based on an interview with Bill Connell, 1 April 1997. Bill Connell was Project Designer and later the head of the Gas Turbine Department at Clydebank

[810] Figures courtesy of Graeme Smith CA

[811] UCS1/5/75, Report, 30 June 1949

[812] Lennox Herald, 5 August 1950, John Brown & Co., report of annual meeting

[813] UCS1/5/79, Report, 17 December 1951

[814] UCS 1/22/33, Letter dated 26 January 1951

[815] In September 1966, John Brown Land Boilers was incorporated into a new company, Foster Wheeler John Brown Boilers Ltd. in which Foster Wheeler held 61% and John Brown 39%. By this time, the company was operating at Whitecrook and at the former Denny shipyard at Dumbarton

[816] UCS 1/5/80, Report, 13 March 1952

[817] Public Records Office, ADM116/6308, letter from the Director of Navy Contracts to John Brown & Co., 5 February 1952.

[818] Public Records Office, ADM116/6308, letter from John Brown & Co. to the Director of Navy Contracts, 26 August 1952. The eventual price of Britannia as paid to John Brown was £1,948,034 including prime cost of £1,636,380 and establishment charges and profit of £304,530. Letter of 28 March 1958 from John Brown & Co. to Director of Navy Contracts.

[819] Given the uproar caused in December 1996 by the announcement that *Britannia* was to be replaced, one cannot but admire the approach adopted in 1952

[820] dwt. This refers to deadweight, a measure of the cargo capacity of a ship in tons. Often applied to tankers.

[821] UCS1/5/81, Report, 21 July 1953

[822] Ship 688/689, 2 x 32,000 dwt. tankers for Alvion Steamship Corp. Ship 690, a 26,000 dwt. tanker for A Ravano & Sons and Ship 695, a 19,000 dwt tanker for SLA Ltd. A cancellation fee of £25,000 was negotiated for Ship 695 and £65,000 for Ship 690. See UCS 1/5/72, reports for 29 May 1953 and 7 February 1954. The amount of compensation received for the other two is unknown

[823] Friedman, op. cit., page 328

[824] UCS 1/5/81, Report, 27 March 1953

[825] After much procrastination, a large dock was built at Inchgreen, Port Glasgow, operated by the Firth of Clyde Drydock Co. The Board of this company included a John Brown director. It was not until 1966 that John Brown's made use of the facility when the *Queen Elizabeth* was docked for a partial refit.

[826] UCS 1/5/81, Report, 12 February, 1953

[827] UCS 1/5/82, Report, 14 January 1954

[828] Ibid.

[829] UCS 1/5/84, Report, 23 March 1956

[830] UCS 1/5/83, Report, 24 May 1955

[831] Dawson, Philip S, *British Superliners of the Sixties*, Conway Maritime Press, London, 1990, page 25

[832] UCS 1/5/91, Draft letter from John Brown, Managing Director, to Sir John Brocklebank. n.d. but probably October 1961

[833] UCS 1/5/84, Report, 15 June 1956

[834] UCS 1/5/84, Report, 20 September 1956

[835] UCS 1/22/31, Papers relating to sale of Dalmuir ordnance factory to Babcock & Wilcox. The factory was not taken over by Babcock's until January 1959When it became clear that they would not employ many boilermakers, James McNeill established a good neighbour policy with them.

[836] UCS1/22/17, West yard reconstruction. Memo, 16 January 1957

[837] UCS1/5/84, Report, 27 January and 1 February 1956

[838] Ibid.

[839] UCS 1/22/17, West yard reconstruction, letter dated 28 August 1956

[840] UCS 1/22/17, West yard reconstruction, undated memo: 'After reconstruction, it has been arranged that the West Yard berths will build the undernoted ships already on order and under option over the next 7.5 years and will earn profits as follows.

No 709 Cadet Ship NZ Shipping Co Ltd £150,600, No 709 Tanker for Chartered Shipping Co Ltd £305,500, No 705 Tanker for BP Tanker Co £180,000, No 708 Tanker for Federal SN Co £304,500, No 714 Tanker for BP Tanker Co £300,000, No 715 Tanker for BP Tanker Co £300,000, No 716 Tanker for BP Tanker Co £350,000, Option a) Tanker for BP Tanker Co £300,000, Option b) Tanker for BP Tanker Co £350,000

    Changes say £100,000

    Total £2,639,600

    Deduct taxation etc. £1,300,000

    Balance of profit available £1,339,600

Expenditure of £1,028,000 on the West Yard berths will therefore be recovered in 6 years from profits actually earned by those berths.

[841] Interview with Fred Reid, 12 December 1996. Fred Reid later became Lloyds Assistant Chief Ship Surveyor

[842] The Glasgow Herald, 16 July 1957

[843] Lloyd's Register of Shipping.

[844] The Journal of Commerce and Shipping Telegraph, 25 September 1959

[845] UCS 1/5/88, Report, 16 June 1960

[846] UCS 1/5/82, Report, February 1954 and UCS 1/5/87, Report, 16 June 1960

[847] Figures courtesy of Graeme Smith CA

[848] The Daily Express, 9 April 1959, for example

[849] Conversation with Willie McLaughlin, 23 September 1996

[850] Unpublished and incomplete memoirs of Graham Strachan held at Glasgow University Archives

[851] Cunard's specification for Q3 stated an overall length of 1,037 feet. Letter from Roy Turner, who was Naval Architect at Vickers Armstrong shipyard at Barrow, 5 December 1996

[852] Strachan, op. cit

[853] Letter from Roy Turner, formerly Vickers Armstrong's naval architect, 5 December 1996

[854] The Glasgow Herald, 11 August 1961

[855] UCS 1/5/90, A four page report headed 'Investigation of Clydebank's Q3 Tender' dated 13 November 1961, which looks in detail at the price difference between the John Brown and Swan/Vickers tenders. The report was based on information obtained confidentially from Cunard technical staff

[856] Telephone conversation with Roy Turner, 5 November 1996

[857] Ibid.

[858] UCS 1/5/90. op. cit.

[859] Letter from Tom Kameen, formerly Cunard's Chief Superintendent Engineer, 5 December 1996

[860] Gardiner, Robert, editor, *Conway's History of the Ship*, 12 Volumes, Conway Maritime Press, London, 1994, *The Golden Age of Shipping*, p151, Chapter by Ian Buxton

[861] Telephone conversation with Norman Gilchrist, 3 November 1996. Gilchrist was chief draughtsman at Swan Hunter & Wigham Richardson and, in 1961, in charge of the tender drawings for Q3,

[862] UCS 1/5/91, Letters written by Lord Aberconway and Mr John Brown, Managing Director at Clydebank, to Sir John Brocklebank. Submitted with Report, September 1961

[863] UCS 1/5/90, Report, 17 November 1961

[864] UCS 1/5/90, Report, 21 September 1961

[865] UCS 1/5/92, Report, 27 April 1962. John Brown received a cancellation fee of £270,000

[866] UCS 1/5/97, Forecast of annual profit & loss for year 1963/64. Submitted with Report, September 1963

[867] Cash flow also continued to be positive and, within the profits declared, the interest from surplus monies grew from an average of around £25,000 per annum in the early 1950s to an average exceeding £170,000 per annum in the first four years of the 1960s. Figures courtesy of Graeme Smith CA.

[868] UCS 1/5/92, Clydebank and the Patton Report, a memorandum submitted to the monthly Board meeting on 18 June 1962

[869] UCS 1/5/90, Report, 14 November 1961

[870] UCS 1/5/91, Report, 23 March 1962 and UCS 1/5/92 report for 27 April 1962

[871] *Sagafjord* was built by Forges et Chantiers de la Mediterranée at La Seyne

[872] UCS 1/5/92, Report, 18 June 1962

[873] UCS 1/5/92, Report, 18 June 1962

[874] Alexander Stephen took this order with overheads reduced to 75% and no profit. Interview with John Innes, 1 December 1997, Stephen's estimator in 1962.

[875] According to notes accompanying the chart, Alexander Stephen had accepted a loss to obtain *Avalon*; *Sagafjord* finally went to a French builder with a £900,000 subsidy; *Orissa* and *Ottawa* were taken at substantial losses to sustain existing owner's options. UCS 1/5/94, December 1962

[876] UCS 1/5/94, Report, 'Clydebank Competitiveness and Notes on Tendering Experience' December 1962 and march 1963

[877] *News from Clydebank*. Issue 1, Autumn 1963John Brown in-house journal

[878] UCS 1/5/96, Report, 21 June 1963

[879] UCS 1/5/98, Report, 20 December 1963

[880] Friedman, op. cit., pages 343/4

[881] Interview with Sir John Brown, 2 April 1997

[882] *Shipbuilding Enquiry Committee 1965-1966 Report*, HM Stationery Office, London, reprinted 1970, p185

[883] Ibid.

[884] UCS 1/107/405, *Kungsholm* tender document, 31 May 1963

[885] University of Liverpool Archives, John Brocklebank's message to staff, March 1962. Document in QE2 folder

[886] Letter from Lord Aberconway to author, 23 September 1998

[887] Interview with John F Starks, September 1996 and telephone conversation with Tom Kameen, 19 November 1996

[888] Telephone conversation with Tom Kameen, 19 November 1996

[889] John Brown & Co. Ltd, Report and Accounts 1966, Lord Aberconway's statement, page 16

[890] UCS 1/107/405, Draft letter by Robin Williamson dated 31 January 1966

[891] UCS 1/107/405, Table of losses

[892] John Brown & Co. Ltd, Report and Accounts 1966, page 16

[893] UCS 1/5/101, Report, 25 February 1966

[894] John Brown & Co. Ltd, Report and Accounts 1966, page 16

[895] This was an 'on-deck' unit developing 12,000 shp which, in turn, drove two 5,000 shp propulsion motors. Shipbuilding and Shipping Record 24 November 1972, page 8.

[896] Based on conversations with Bill Connell and Jim Turner, respectively John Brown Engineering Sales Manager and Technical Director.

[897] *Japanese Shipyards*, Board of Trade 1965 A report on the visit of the Minister of State (Shipping) in January 1965

[898] UCS 1/22/34 to 39. Numerous papers concerned with the Newshot Isle Project

[899] The consultants were commissioned to undertake a detailed feasibility study of the proposal, for which a sum of £25,000 had been reserved by the John Brown Board

[900] Ardrossan and Greenock were, at that time, alternative sites then under consideration

[901] Including Sir William Arrol's for dock gates, cranes and fabrication shops; Drysdales for dock pumping equipment etc.

[902] Moss & Hume, op. cit., page 425

[903] UCS 1/8/88 and UCS 1/8/89 / / /

[904] Figures courtesy of Graeme Smith CA

[905] The Warship Group consisted of 12 shipyards. Geddes expressed the view that naval orders spread thinly over these yards had a negative effect on competitiveness. See the Shipbuilding Inquiry Committee 1965 - 1966 Report (Geddes Report) page 136.

[906] *Shipbuilding Enquiry Committee 1965-1966 Report*, HM Stationery Office, London, reprinted 1970, page 92

[907] Paulden, & Hawkins, *Whatever Happened at Fairfields?*, Gower Press, London, 1969, page 152

[908] Paulden, & Hawkins, op. cit., pages 150/152

[909] Hepper was also Managing Director of Pretty Polly, the stockings manufacturer

[910] McGill, Jack, *Crisis on the Clyde*, Davis-Poynter Ltd, London, 1973, page 16

[911] UCS 1/5/102, Report, 31 March 1967

[912] Paulden, & Hawkins, op. cit., pages 160/162 for a fuller account of Iain Stewart's recognition of this yard's potential

[913] UCS 1/5/102, Minutes of John Brown & Company (Shipbuilders) Ltd, 20 December 1967

[914] UCS 5/1/5, Executive Committee meeting, 10 June 1968

[915] UCS 5/1/5, Executive Committee minutes, 22 April and 27 May 1968

[916] UCS 5/1/5, Executive Committee minutes, July 1968

[917] UCS 5/1/5, Executive Committee minutes, 2 September 1968

[918] UCS 5/1/2 Minutes, 11 September 1968. It was also agreed that if labour troubles arose in docking the ship at Greenock, she would be taken to Belfast and docked there.

[919] *Upper Clyde News*, Journal of Upper Clyde Shipbuilders, Volume 1 No. 4, December 1968, page 2

[920] Numerically controlled flame cutting was cited as an example of established European practice absent at UCS. At the same time, the Board considered concentrating the building of hulls at Govan and fitting them out at Clydebank. However, referring to his old yard, Sir Charles Connell, a UCS director, pointed out that this profitable yard should not be sacrificed for the sake of the other yards which were making losses. Connell asked for £325,000 to be spent at his old Scotstoun yard where, he estimated, this would result in the building of another ship of a saleable type each year. See UCS 5/1/2 Minutes, 9 December 1968.

[921] UCS 5/1/2, Minutes, 11 September 1968

[922] University of Liverpool Archives, D42/B10/3, Minutes of Cunard Board, 22 October and 27 November 1968

[923] UCS 5/1/5, Executive Committee minutes, 2 December 1968

[924] UCS 5/1/5 Executive Committee minutes, 17 December 1968

[925] Graham Strachan described the damage: 'Each high pressure turbine consisting of 13 rows of blading through which the steam expanded giving up its energy to driving the turbine, had suffered considerable damage. The 9th stage was completely stripped in the starboard turbine and partially stripped in the port with partial stripping of the 10th and cracking observed in the 8th and 10th stages of the port rotor. Further cracking was later discovered in some other rows when the rotors were closely inspected' Unpublished and incomplete memoirs of Graham Strachan held by Glasgow University Archives.

[926] Of over 200 steam turbines designed by Pametrada, QE2's were the only ones to fail due to this cause. See *40 Years of Progress, A History of the Wallsend Research Station 1945 -85*, RF Darling, 1985

[927] The Scottish Sunday Express, 9 February 1969

[928] Strachan, op. cit.

[929] Letter to the author from Tom Kameen, 5 December 1996

[930] Strachan, op. cit.

[931] UCS 5/1/2, Minutes, 13 November 1968

[932] UCS 5/1/2, Minutes, 13 February 1969

[933] Ibid.

[934] UCS 5/1/5, Executive Committee minutes, 17 February 1969

[935] UCS 5/1/5, Executive Committee minutes, 3 March 1969

[936] UCS 5/1/2, Minutes, 18 March 1969

[937] UCS 5/1/2 Minutes,13 February 1969

[938] UCS 5/1/2, minutes, 18 March 1969

[939] UCS 5/1/2, Minutes, 10 March 1969

940 UCS 5/1/2, Minutes, 13 March 1969

941 The UCS Board had formed the opinion that he was unable to override the SIB; see UCS 5/1/2 Minutes, 13 March 1969

942 UCS 5/1/2, Minutes, 13 February 1969

943 UCS 5/1/2, Minutes, 18 March and the issue of the letters from UCS which the SIB had demanded they withdraw

944 UCS 5/1/2, Minutes, 19 March 1969

945 UCS 5/2/12, Report of Working Party on contraction to a two yard operation, May 1969

946 Letter from Lord Aberconway to the author of 23 September 1998.

947 McGill, op cit., page 43

948 UCS 5/1/2, Minutes, 7 May 1969

949 Ibid.

950 UCS 5/2/12, Report of Working Party on contraction of business to a two yard operation, May 1969. The ensuing report concluded that the Govan yard should close on the basis that Clydebank was best suited to the development of a rational steelwork layout and that Clydebank could build anything the Govan yard could and more

951 UCS 5/1/2, Minutes, 13 August 1969

952 UCS 5/1/2, Minutes, 12 November 1969

953 McGill, op. cit., page 60

954 UCS 5/1/2, Minutes, 12 January 1970

955 UCS 5/1/2, Minutes, 3 February 1970

956 UCS 5/1/2, Minutes, 22 March 1970

957 UCS 5/1/2, Minutes, 16 April 1970

958 UCS 5/1/2, Minutes, 16 December 1970

959 Ibid.

960 McGill, op. cit., page 80

961 UCS 5/1/2, Minutes, 5 February 1970

962 UCS 5/1/2, Minutes, 10 June 1970

963 From papers supplied by Sir Robert Courtney Smith, Official Liquidator of UCS, employment at Clydebank on 15 June 1971 was 489 staff, 2,468 hourly paid and 123 apprentices. Numbers employed in the other divisions were: Linthouse headquarters 336, Govan 3,064, Linthouse 422, Scotstoun 1,192, Training Centre 355. Total for UCS 8,449.

964 UCS 5/1/2, Minutes, 12 June 1970

965 Of the Glasgow Chartered Accountants Arthur Young McClelland Moores. Smith had been appointed liquidator at the winding-up of Denny's Dumbarton shipyard. He became Official Liquidater of UCS on the granting of a winding-up order on 30 July 1971.

966 UCS was far from being the only British shipbuilding group in serious financial difficulties. Harland & Wolff, Cammell Laird and Swan Hunter were losing money. During the four years of its existence, UCS attracted £12 million from the SIB and another £9.5 million from the Government. In liquidation, a further £11 million had been consumed by the summer of 1972. See Management Today, June 1972, The Shipbuilding Shambles, page 77

967 UCS 5/2/15, Report by P A Management Consultants Ltd. on Possible Industrial Uses for Clydebank Shipyard. No date.

968 From papers supplied by Sir Robert Courtney Smith, Official Liquidator of UCS, employment at Clydebank on 14 June 1972 was 376 staff, 2,036 hourly paid and 108 apprentices. Numbers employed in the other divisions were: Linthouse headquarters 197, Govan 2,738, Linthouse 329, Scotstoun 823, Training Centre 275. Total for UCS 6,882.

969 UCS 5/1/2, Minutes, 12 June 1970

970 UCS Limited (in Liquidation) Report of the Official Liquidator,. page 6.

971 The Motor Ship, September 1972, page 269

APPENDICES

MANAGEMENT BIOGRAPHIES
A FEW FROM THE MANY

Sir Thomas Bell

Sir Donald McLean Skiffington

SIR THOMAS BELL

Thomas Bell was born in India in 1865, the son of Imrie Bell, a Scottish engineer and brother of Arthur Bell the whisky distiller. In 1880, he entered the Royal Naval Engineering College at Keyham, Devonport graduating after six years as an engineering officer. Poor eyesight prevented him pursuing a service career and he joined the engineering staff at J&G Thomson's Clydebank engine works. Bell's ability was soon recognised and he rose through the company becoming Engine Works Manager in 1902. In the following year he became a member of the influential Turbine Committee appointed to investigate the use of turbine machinery in the new Cunard express steamers *Lusitania* and *Mauretania*. In 1908, Bell secured agreement with Charles Curtis to develop his turbine at Clydebank. This resulted in the Brown-Curtis turbine subsequently fitted in many British warships. In the following year, Thomas Bell was appointed Managing Director of the Clydebank Works and a Director on the main John Brown Board. In May 1917, at Admiralty request, he served as Deputy Controller of Dockyards and War Shipbuilding returning to Clydebank in January 1919. He was knighted in 1918. Despite the depressed years of the 1920s, Bell was able to retain a healthy order book and introduce marine diesel engine manufacture to Clydebank. The excellent business relationship established with Cunard leading to the contracts for both Queens was largely of his making. He took great interest in the welfare of employees and when unemployment reached its peak during the suspension of Ship Number 534, *Queen Mary*, he was instrumental in making allotments available to keep men busy. He retired in 1935 although remained as a director until 1946. Sir Thomas Bell was a disciplinarian with a quiet sense of humour. His comment after listening patiently to a lengthy, enthusiastically delivered description of a new submarine by a young niece was 'is that so'. He died in 1952 at his home in Helensburgh.

SIR DONALD MacLEAN SKIFFINGTON

Donald Skiffington was the son of a carpenter employed at J&G Thomson's shipyard. He served his apprenticeship as an ironworker and was rapidly promoted becoming foreman, head foreman, assistant manager and finally, in 1921, Shipyard Manager, a position he would retain until 1949. He was held in awe by those underneath him. He had a commanding physical presence and was a rigid disciplinarian. On his frequent tours of inspection around the yard, he gained notoriety by prodding workers thought to be working less than wholeheartedly with the point of the tightly rolled umbrella which he invariably carried. During weekly meetings, foremen had to accompany him up staging and onto hulls under construction and account for progress or the lack of it. Skiffington was particularly skilled at walking swiftly across widely spaced deck beams obliging his entourage of often elderly foremen to follow in this precarious high wire activity. This ritual became known as the 'Glee Party'. Of Skiffington Lord Aberconway recalls 'I remember once standing with him near the offices just before the 5 o'clock hooter went: he had his back to the yard, and I could see behind him, peeping around the corners, various men wanting to run out of the yard but not daring to while he was there. He was of course aware of the position behind his back and about fifteen seconds before the hooter went he looked at his very accurate watch, and moved away with me; the hooter immediately went and the men rushed out. Donald Skiffington was awarded the MBE in 1918, the CBE in 1939 and was knighted in 1949. He retired from Clydebank in 1949 remaining on the John Brown Board until 1953. Sir Donald Skiffington died in Glasgow in 1963.

SIR STEPHEN JOSEPH PIGOTT

Stephen Pigott was born in Cornwall, New York State in 1880 of Irish parents. After graduating with a degree in Mechanical and Marine Engineering from Columbia University in 1903, Pigott met Charles Curtis, inventor of the impulse steam turbine which bore his name. Curtis asked Pigott to become his assistant in further developing the turbine at General Electric's Schenectady Works, New York. In 1907, Curtis turbines were selected to propel the battleship *North Dakota*, the first instance of turbines being installed in US Navy ships. In the same year, Thomas Bell, John Brown's Engineering Manager, was sent by the Admiralty to look at the Curtis turbine and assess its suitability for service in HM ships as an alternative to the Parsons reaction type. Bell was impressed with both the turbine and the young Stephen Pigott and, in 1908, was successful in negotiating a contract to build an experimental Curtis turbine under license at Clydebank. As part of the deal struck with Curtis, Pigott was sent to Clydebank to oversee construction of this turbine and further experimental work. This resulted in the development of the very successful Brown-Curtis turbine which was later fitted in many British warships including the battlecruiser *Hood*. In 1920, Pigott became manager of the Engine Works during which time he was responsible for the manufacture of the first marine diesels and the turbine machinery for *Queen Mary*. He succeeded Sir Thomas Bell in 1935 as Managing Director of the Clydebank Works. In 1938, he was knighted in recognition of his work in connection with the Queens. One of the greatest achievements at Clydebank during the early war years was the sailing of *Queen Elizabeth* at high speed to New York. On this voyage, the liner's machinery performed effortlessly without having had any previous trials. Sir Stephen Pigott retired in 1949 taking up full time residence in his home at Closeburn Castle Dumfries. He died there in March 1955.

SIR JAMES MCFADYEN MCNEILL

James McNeill was born in 1892 on the Island of Islay. Following the death of his mother days after he was born, much of his childhood was spent on Arran in the care of an Aunt. In 1908, James became an apprenticeship draughtsman in John Brown's shipyard where his father had been a foreman. James complemented his day work in the yard by attending evening classes at the Royal Technical College in Glasgow. In 1912 he became a student at Glasgow University with a Lloyd's Scholarship in Shipbuilding, graduating with a BSc in naval architecture in 1915. In 1916 he was enlisted in the Lowland Brigade of the Royal Field Artillery. McNeill rose swiftly to the rank of Major and, standing in for a wounded battery commander, won the Military Cross in the German offensive of early 1918. On his return to the shipyard after the war, he

was made assistant naval architect in charge of the design section. In 1928, after the departure of John Black, he was appointed naval architect. His first major task in this position was the design of Canadian Pacific's *Empress of Britain*, the largest ship built in the UK since the *Aquitania* This experience was invaluable when the order for the much larger *Queen Mary* was awarded to Clydebank in 1930. McNeill, with a few other senior colleagues at Clydebank, was responsible for the smooth progress of this unprecedentedly large ship from inception to completion. In 1948, he succeeded Sir Stephen Pigott as Managing Director of the Clydebank Works, the first naval architect to do so. In 1959, he relinquished control of Clydebank to become Deputy Chairman of John Brown & Co. He retired in 1962 and died in Glasgow in 1964. In recognition of his ability, he was given a number of honours including that of LLD from Glasgow University in 1939, Fellow of the Royal Society in 1948, a CBE in 1950 and a knighthood in 1954.

Sir Stephen Joseph Pigott

SIR JOHN BROWN

John Brown, the son of a Glasgow lath splitter and plasterer, was born in 1901. Coincidentally, he had the same name as the company he would later work for. He left Hutcheson's Grammar School, Glasgow in 1918 with a leaving certificate and distinction in modern languages. However, it was to naval architecture and Glasgow University that John applied for and was accepted. After one year of study he applied for employment in various Clyde shipyards. At Clydebank they agreed to take him on as an apprentice draughtsman and he started work in June 1919. As a young apprentice in 1919 he recalled slipping out of the drawing office one lunch time to see the battlecruiser *Hood*, in the fitting-out dock. Within minutes, and strictly against the rules, he had climbed to the top of *Hood's* foremast for a look around. During the slump of the early 20s, he was permitted to resume his studies at University and graduated with a BSc in 1923. He completed his apprenticeship in the following year and was moved into the design office under James McNeil, the Assistant Naval Architect. In 1926, in secret, he began preliminary work on the ship that would become *Queen Mary*. In the following year, he was sent to Spain to work as a designer/estimator with the Sociedad at Bilbao. On McNeill's promotion to Naval Architect, Brown was promoted to Assistant Naval Architect on his return from Spain in 1929. During this time he again became closely involved with

Sir James McFadyen McNeill

Sir John Brown

design work on the *Queen Mary*. In 1948, John Brown again followed in James McNeill's path becoming Naval Architect (Technical Director) on the latter's appointment as Managing Director. He was heavily involved in the tendering process which resulted in the contract for *QE2*, last of the great Cunarders to be built at Clydebank. Brown retired in December 1963 although he continued as Deputy Chairman of John Brown until 1967. He was awarded an LLD by the University of Glasgow in June 1965 and a knighthood in 2000.

DR JOHN RANNIE CBE

Dr John Rannie

John Rannie was a native of Clydebank who started his apprenticeship as a shipwright in John Brown's in 1919 where his grandfather was under-foreman in the joiner's shop. Rannie's diligence was noticed by the shipyard manager, Donald Skiffington, who urged him to attend evening classes in preparation for applying to a course in naval architecture at the University of Glasgow. After four years of study between the University and the shipyard, Rannie qualified with a first class degree in naval architecture. In 1929, John Rannie went to work for the Sociedad in Bilbao, Spain as chief designer and estimator for a period of two years. On his return, he was made manager of the West Yard at Clydebank under Skiffington. Rannie was known for his sense of humour one of his quips being that he was the only man at Clydebank who did not build the *Queen Mary* because he was in charge of all the other ships in the yard. In 1936, he left Clydebank to become a ship surveyor with Lloyds. In this capacity, Rannie moved around shipbuilding districts at home and abroad ending up in North America during the Second World War. He was at the Henry Kaiser shipyard in California, at Mobile in Alabama and later at a yards in Victoria, British Columbia and Montreal. It was from United Shipyards in Montreal that he was asked by Sir Donald Skiffington to return to Clydebank in 1944 as Shipyard Director. As a Clydebank man, John Rannie could talk the local language and he established a good working rapport with the men under his control. Largely as a result of this the shipyard enjoyed relatively trouble free industrial relations for a long period. In January 1964, John Rannie became Managing Director of the works following Dr John Brown's retiral. When Clydebank became part of Upper Clyde Shipbuilders in 1968, Rannie was given the post of Special Director in charge of *QE2*, a job which he relished. He retired in December 1968. In 1971, he returned to Canada to

John Starks

manage the small yard at Marystown, Newfoundland. In recognition of this work he received a doctorate of engineering from Memorial University, St John's Newfoundland. He returned to Glasgow in 1974 and died there in 1989 He was made an Honorary Freemen of Clydebank in 1966 and a CBE in 1969.

JOHN STARKS

John Starks entered HM Dockyard, Devonport in 1932. After four years' apprenticeship he was awarded a cadetship in Naval Construction and subsequently spent three years at the RN College, Greenwich obtaining a First Class Certificate in Naval Architecture prior to joining the Royal Corps of Naval Constructors. He was appointed, in 1939, to the Submarine Design Section at the Admiralty, Bath and spent the early years of the war on the design, construction and trials of new construction submarines before joining the staff of Flag Officer Submarines as a Constructor Commander until late 1948.

He then began his association with the Clyde as Principal Ship Overseer covering the construction and refitting of daring Class destroyers, the cruiser *Tiger* and submarines at John Browns, Yarrows and Scotts. In 1951 he was appointed Constructor Commander on the British Joint Services Mission in Washington DC for liaison with the United States Navy until 1955 when he returned to the Admiralty as Chief Constructor of the Submarine Design Section which included *Dreadnought*, Britain's first nuclear submarine. In the late 1950s, he received an invitation to join John Browns as Technical Director - an invitation he felt he could not refuse - and took up the appointment in November 1959 following the launch of *Dreadnought*. He was later appointed Assistant Managing Director of John Browns. Following the formation of Upper Clyde Shipbuilders in February 1968, John was appointed Technical Director of UCS a post he held until January 1972. He then accepted an appointment from Vosper Thornycroft to be their representative in Brazil advising the Brazilian Navy on the construction of frigates. He retired in 1977 and died in 1998.

CLYDEBANK MANAGEMENT 1847 - 1972

MANAGING DIRECTOR

James Thomson 1847 - 1863
George Thomson 1863 - 1866
James Roger Thomson 1870 – 1899
John Gibb Dunlop 1899 – 1909
Thomas Bell 1909 – 1935
(Luke and Wood 1917 – 1920)
Stephen Joseph Pigott 1935 – 1949
James McNeill 1949 - 1959
John Brown 1959 – 1964
John Rannie 1964 – 1968

ENGINE WORKS MANAGER/DIRECTOR

James Pattison 1855 - 1870
John Parker 1870 – 1888
John Gibb Dunlop 1888 – 1899
Thomas Bell 1899 – 1909
Commander W H Wood 1909 – 1920
Steven Joseph Pigott 1920 – 1935
Tom A Crowe 1935 - 1951
George Strachan 1951 - 1962
Graham Strachan 1962 -

SHIPYARD MANAGER/DIRECTOR

Andrew Burns 1851 – 1877
George Paul Thomson 1871 - 1899
Samuel Crawford 1877 – 1892
David McGhee 1892 – 1908
William J Luke 1908 – 1921
Donald M Skiffington 1921 – 1949
John Rannie 1949 – 1964
George H Parker 1963 - 1970

NAVAL ARCHITECT /TECHNICAL DIRECTOR

John H Biles 1880 – 1891
William D Archer 1891 – 1898
William J Luke 1898 – 1908
John Paterson 1908 – 1921
John Black 1921 – 1928
James McNeill 1928 – 1949
John Brown 1949 – 1959
John F Starks 1959 – 1972

GENERAL MANAGER

John P Wilson 1883 – 1887

CHAIRMAN

William Donaldson 1897 - 1899
John Devonshire Ellis 1899 - 1907
Sir Charles McLaren MP 1907 - 1934
(Lord Aberconway from 1913)
Lord Aberconway II 1934 - 1953
Lord Aberconway III 1953 - 1967

SECRETARY

John Grant 1847 - 1897
Archibald McMillan - 1902
Robert Carswell 18 - 1887
Donald Bremner 1887 - 1901
John Henderson 1902 - 1934
Bridge 1934 -
John W Beck - 1958
A N Benson - 1958 - 1964
Robin Williamson 1964 - 1968

UPPER CLYDE SHIPBUILDERS LTD

Role of John Brown managers on formation of UCS in 1968.

FINANCIAL DIRECTOR

Robin Williamson 1968 - 1972

TECHNICAL DIRECTOR

John F Starks 1968 - 1972

DEPUTY CHAIRMAN

Tom Burleigh

Part based on private salaries books UCS 1/48/3 to 11

JOHN BROWN & CO LTD
GROUP STRUCTURE AND MANAGEMENT AT CLYDEBANK SHIPYARD 1924

John Brown & Co Ltd
Group Structure and
Management at Clydebank

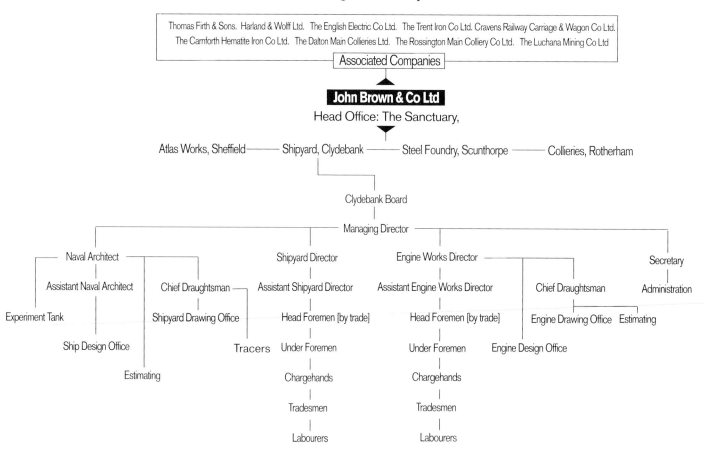

DEVELOPMENT OF THE COMPANY 1847-2000

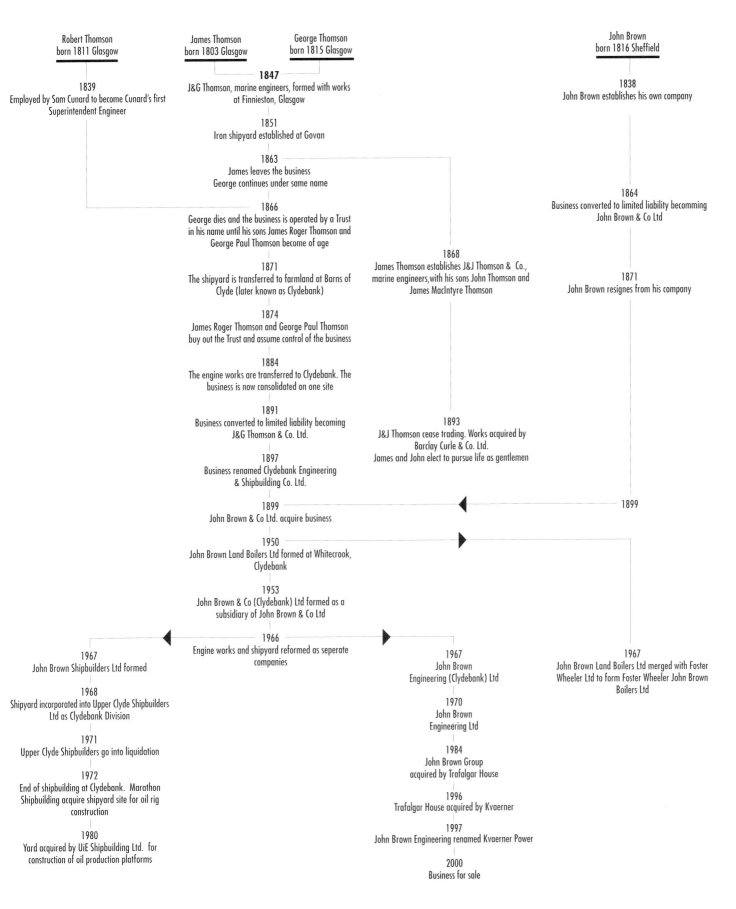

Robert Thomson
born 1811 Glasgow

James Thomson
born 1803 Glasgow

George Thomson
born 1815 Glasgow

John Brown
born 1816 Sheffield

1847
J&G Thomson, marine engineers, formed with works at Finnieston, Glasgow

1839
Employed by Sam Cunard to become Cunard's first Superintendent Engineer

1838
John Brown establishes his own company

1851
Iron shipyard established at Govan

1863
James leaves the business
George continues under same name

1864
Business converted to limited liability becomming
John Brown & Co Ltd

1866
George dies and the business is operated by a Trust in his name until his sons James Roger Thomson and George Paul Thomson become of age

1868
James Thomson establishes J&J Thomson & Co., marine engineers, with his sons John Thomson and James MacIntyre Thomson

1871
The shipyard is transferred to farmland at Barns of Clyde (later known as Clydebank)

1871
John Brown resignes from his company

1874
James Roger Thomson and George Paul Thomson buy out the Trust and assume control of the business

1884
The engine works are transferred to Clydebank. The business is now consolidated on one site

1891
Business converted to limited liability becoming
J&G Thomson & Co. Ltd.

1893
J&J Thomson cease trading. Works acquired by Barclay Curle & Co. Ltd.
James and John elect to pursue life as gentlemen

1897
Business renamed Clydebank Engineering & Shipbuilding Co. Ltd.

1899
John Brown & Co Ltd. acquire business

1899

1950
John Brown Land Boilers Ltd formed at Whitecrook, Clydebank

1953
John Brown & Co (Clydebank) Ltd formed as a subsidiary of John Brown & Co Ltd

1966
Engine works and shipyard reformed as seperate companies

1967
John Brown Shipbuilders Ltd formed

1967
John Brown
Engineering (Clydebank) Ltd

1967
John Brown Land Boilers Ltd merged with Foster Wheeler Ltd to form Foster Wheeler John Brown Boilers Ltd

1968
Shipyard incorporated into Upper Clyde Shipbuilders Ltd as Clydebank Division

1970
John Brown
Engineering Ltd

1971
Upper Clyde Shipbuilders go into liquidation

1984
John Brown Group
acquired by Trafalgar House

1972
End of shipbuilding at Clydebank. Marathon Shipbuilding acquire shipyard site for oil rig construction

1996
Trafalgar House acquired by Kvaerner

1980
Yard acquired by UiE Shipbuilding Ltd. for construction of oil production platforms

1997
John Brown Engineering renamed Kvaerner Power

2000
Business for sale

PROFIT AND LOSS

J&G Thomson (also showing drawings of original partners until 1864)

Year	Profit (Loss)	James	George
16 months to 31/7/1848	1450	318	140
1849	2809	222	339
18 months to 31/1/1850	1970	732	750
7 months to 31/7/1851	1969	263	287
12 months to 31/7/1852	1359	568	590
1853	1922	862	829
1854	775	894	890
1855	2891	1080	1101
11 months to 30/6/1856	13954	1052	906
12 months to 30/6/1857	8349	1737	2363
1858	15730	1660	2999
1859	(3956)	590	1012
1860	6397	1288	1688
1861	5105	1693	1967
1862	10979	1948	2410
1863	3853	5127	5238
1864	13774	2111	4289

Original partnership ceased trading on 30 June 1864. On 1 July 1864 business recommenced with George Thomson as sole partner

1865	90273
1866	40711

On George Thomson's death in June 1866, the business was carried on under the control of the George Thomson Trust

1867	17103
1868	(5105)
1869	1989
1870	19550
1871	14239
1872	(22079)
1873	(13736)
1874	(15095)

Co-partnery of young James and George established from 30 June 1874

1875	(2102)
1876	(10537)
1877	(14241)
1878	(7597)
1879	(12684)
1880	2556
1881	15840
6 months to 31/12/1881	(31701)
12 months to 31/12/1882	(58017)
6 months to 30/6/1883	(5307)
1884	20749
1885	(13572)
1886	22363(before depreciation)
1887	14508 (before depreciation)
1888	15305 (before depreciation)
1889	11648 (before depreciation)
nine months to 31/3/1890	(23780)

J&G Thomson & Co Ltd from 9 April 1890

nine months to 31/3/1891	38313
1892	58874
1893	24283
1894	(31882)
1895	18463
1896	70080

Clydebank Engineering & Shipbuilding Co Ltd from 1 February 1897

1897	103748
1898	118709
1899	102876

Notes for years 1866 to 1890: the profits/(losses) are the trading results before interest payable to the family Trust in the years to 1890, and exclude the effect of the asset revaluation in 1866 (which was a paper gain of £24,210) For the years 1886 to 1889, the depreciation figures are not available, and most likely the firm made a small loss during these years or managed to break-even.

John Brown & Co Ltd from September 1899

Note: Results for years 1900 to 1919 are not archived.

1920	319273
1921	188196
1922	92664
1923	81590
1924	70170
1925	68766
1926	29444
1927	20014
1928	52570
1929	18192
1930	32353
1931	10907
1932	21320
1933	14096
1934	(51405)
1935	23545
1936	179245
1937	318830
1938	161891
1939	233537
1940	587121
1941	996727
1942	507599
1943	421006
1944	412202
1945	284683
1946	356661
1947	404350
1948	402528
1949	(299129)
1950	630200
1951	477256
1952	426686
1953	547725

John Brown & Co (Clydebank) Ltd from 27 March 1953

1954	281567
1955	349386
1956	322984
1957	717722
1958	706951
1959	1064019
1960	935461
1961	1384748
1962	824834
1963	832500
1964	(1399413)
1965	(444399
1966	(2299611)
1967	(932175)

Note: results are stated after charging depreciation but before taxation

Sources: UCS 1/34/1 and 2: UCS 1/6 and 1/7

SHIP LIST

Ships built by J & G Thomson, Clydebank Engineering & Shipbuilding Co. Ltd, John Brown & Co Ltd and Upper Clyde Shipbuilders Ltd (Clydebank Division) at Clydebank shipyard, Govan and Clydebank.

This ship and engine contracts list has been based on details recorded by Clydebank shipyard staff supplemented by Ian Buxton's extensive shipbuilding notes and references, supported by the British Shipbuilding (Raper) Database. Not all ship contract numbers are in chronological order, e.g. numbers 596 to 599. There are several gaps in the sequence e.g. 200 to 219 which were never allocated. Some numbers refer to machinery contracts although the engine and boiler shops manufactured many more engines, engine components, boilers and other engineering products than shown on this list.

Number: numbers allocated to ship and machinery contracts by the Company

Name: the original ship name is given followed by subsequent names in italics where known.

Owner: the owner for whom the ship or machinery was built.

Dates: where known are given as; keel laying / launch /completion, trials (t) or commissioning (c).

Dimensions: length overall x beam x moulded depth.

Tonnage: gt. = gross tons (merchant ships); dwt = deadweight tons (tankers and bulk carriers); disp. = displacement tons (warships)

Machinery: paddle, screw, triple expansion, turbine, diesel, etc. (BC) indicates Brown Curtis turbines fitted.

Horsepower: nhp = nominal horse power; ihp = indicated horse power (generally for compound, triple and quadruple expansion machinery); shp = shaft horse power (for turbine machinery); bhp = brake horse power (diesel machinery).

Speed: in some cases service speed is given, in others that recorded at trials (t).

Armament: simple details of weapon fit is given for warships.

Fate: is mainly used to indicate loss or disposal of vessel but may include other details. Where a day/month/year is given for scrapping, this invariably refers to the date of sale for scrapping.

(SV) after a ship's name indcates a sailing ship.
Imperial units have been used throughout.

No.	Name	Owner	Dates	Details	Fate
1	Jackal	Charles McIver	22/12/51 - 18/3/52 - 14/4/52	125'4" x 19'5" x 9'8" x 180gt. Oscillating paddle, 86nhp	
2	Venus	Largs Steamboat Co.	? - 1/5/52 - 17/6/52	160' x 17'6" x 9'5" x 178gt. Oscillating paddle, 95nhp	
3	Mountaineer	David Hutcheson & Co.	? - 29/5/52 - 15/7/52	174' x 17'6" x 8'2" x 190gt. Oscillating paddle, 95nhp	Wrecked 1889
4	Corriere Sciciliano	Samuel Howes & Co.	22/3/52 - 14/8/52 - 21/9/52	170' x 24' x 16' x 190gt. Oscillating paddle, 180nhp	
5	Calpe	John Bibby & Co.	3/4/52 - 16/10/52 - 26/11/52	200' x 28'6" x 21' x 799gt. Direct acting screw, 180nhp	Missing 1868
6	Mona's Queen	Isle of Man S.P.Co.	3/6/52 - 27/11/52 - 21/2/53	165' x 25' x 15' x 451gt. 2 leverpaddle, 262nhp 13.02k	Scrapped 1880
7	Chevalier	David Hutcheson & Co.	2/11/52 - 24/3/53 - 11/5/53	176'9" x 22' x 13' x 329gt. Oscillating paddle, 180nhp	Wrecked Iron Rocks, Sound of Jura 24/11/1854
8	Telegraph	Belfast S.S. Co.	4/6/52 - 26/2/53 - 17/6/53	241' x 27'6" x 15'2" x 820gt. Lever paddle, 450nhp 14.26k	
9	Rhone	John Bibby & Co.	1/2/53 - 1/10/53 - 21/11/53	212' x 28'6" x 23' x 837gt. Direct acting screw, 238nhp	
10	Danube	John Bibby & Co.	1/2/53 - 20/8/53 - 11/10/53	212' x 28'6" x 23' x 837gt. Direct acting screw, 238nhp	
	Neptune	Charles McIver	1853	69' x 9'6" x 5'9"	
11	Jura	G&J Burns	17/2/53 - 27/6/54 - 27/7/54	313'8" x 35'8" x 28'5" x 2,240gt. Beam screw, 440nhp	Wrecked River Mersey 3/11/1864
12	Sicilia	L&S de Pace, Palermo	15/3/53 - 16/1/54 - 30/3/54	220'5" x 28'1" x 23' x 828gt. Direct acting screw, 249nhp	Sunk Tyrrhenian Sea 9/1854
13	Wonga Wonga	Australasian S. N. Co.	? - 15/5/54 - 15/8/54	212' x 27' x 19'5" x 662gt. Direct acting screw, 249nhp	Scrapped Sydney 1880
14	Telegraph	Australasian S. N. Co.	? - 1/4/54 - 17/8/54	193'9" x 23' x 13'7" x 468gt. Oscillating paddle, 180nhp	Sunk, Cape Perpendicular 10/1867
15	(iron yacht)	John Hamilton	shipped 15/5/54 (for Canada)	175' x 27' x 11' x 600gt.	
16	Lebanon (launched as Aerolith)	Burns & McIver	? - 22/11/54 - 19/1/55	243'6" x 31'6" x 25'6" x 1,383gt. Direct acting screw, 220nhp	
17	Arcadia	Papayanni & Mussabini	? - 21/12/54 - 3/3/55	230' x 31' x 20' x 1,166gt. Direct acting screw, 200nhp	Scrapped T W Ward, Preston 1898
18		Cancelled			
19	Iona	David Hutcheson & Co.	? - 22/3/55 - 26/5/55	220' x 21' x 12' x 325gt. Oscillating paddle, 180nhp	Sunk in collision, Gourock Bay 2/10/1862
		Purchased by Confederate agent Henry Lafone 19/9/1862 for use as blockade runner but lost at start of voyage across the Atlantic			
20	Thessalia	Papayanni & Mussabini	? - 30/6/55 - 27/8/55	257' x 30'8" x 26' x 1,169gt. Direct acting screw, 220nhp	
21	Forth	Carron Co.	? - 28/4/55 - 23/6/55	177'3" x 22'8" x 16'5" x 406gt. Direct acting screw, 100nhp	Sold, General S.N. 1863
22	Clansman	David Hutcheson & Co.	? - 16/6/55 - 17/8/55	185' x 23' x 15' x 414gt. Oscillating paddle, 180nhp	Wrecked, Sanda Island 1869
23	Ossian	Belfast Screw S.S. Co.	? - 27/9/55 - 2/11/55	213' x 23' x 20'5" x 714gt. Direct acting screw, 120nhp	Sunk in collision with Clansman, Kattegat 24/11/1869
24	Express	London & Edinburgh S.S. Co.	? - 8/1/56 - 23/1/56	199'7" x 24'9" x 19'5" x 499gt. Direct acting screw, 100nhp	Scrapped Barcelona 1913
	Caprera, Aurora, Diana				
25	James Brown	T S Begbie	? - 25/3/56 - 10/5/56	190' x 28'6" x 23' x 724gt. Direct acting screw, 100nhp	
26	Stirling	T S Begbie	? - 6/5/56 - 14/6/56	190' x 28'6" x 23' x 728gt. Direct acting screw, 100nhp	
27	Laconia	Papayanni & Mussabini	? - 6/3/56 - 16/4/56	314'3" x 31'9" x 20'1" x 1,151gt. Direct acting screw, 200nhp	Scrapped Genoa 1902
28	Brisbane	Australasian S. N. Co.	? - 25/6/56 - 7/7/56	136'6" x 18'6" x 8' x 103gt. Paddle, 40nhp (Replaced original Brisbane lost on delivery voyage 1855) Scrapped 1891	
29	Grange	Carron Co.	? - 2/8/56 - 18/9/56	178'5" x 25'1" x 18' x 408gt. Direct acting screw, 90nhp	
30	Governor Higginson	G A Odier, Mauritius	? - 17/7/56 - 11/9/56	208' x 27'1" x 20'5" x 599gt. Screw, 150nhp,	Wrecked, Japan 1870
31	Elizabeth Jane	William Marr	? - 11/12/56 - 19/1/57	211'5" x 30'6" x 22' x 858gt. Screw, 120nhp	
32	Etna	Florio	? - 20/12/56 - 26/3/57	160' x 22' x 14'5" x 339gt. Paddle, 110nhp,	
33	Australasian Calabria	European & Australian R. M.	1/11/56 - 10/6/57 - 21/8/57	331'7" x 42'1" x 34' x 2,761gt. Screw, 700nhp	Scrapped 1898
34	(screw lighter)	Carron Co.	? - ? - 1857	64' x 16' x 8' x 50gt. 20nhp	
35	(screw lighter)	Carron Co.	? - ? - 1857	64' x 16' x 8' x 50gt. 20nhp	
36	Agia Sofia	Papayanni & Mussabini	? - 19/9/57 - 19/11/57	250' x 34'6" x 26' x 1,437gt. Screw, 288nhp	Scrapped Livorno 1903
37	Prince Consort	Aberdeen, Leith & Clyde	? - 2/1/58 - 4/3/58	210' x 25' x 18'5" x 623gt. Paddle, 300nhp	

No.	Name	Owner	Dates	Details	Fate
38	**Havelock**	Dublin & Glasgow S. N. Co.	? - 13/5/58 - 29/6/58	223'2" x 26'2" x 14'3" x 629gt. Side lever paddle, 280nhp	
	General Beauregard	11/1862 purchased by Confederate agents and renamed General Beauregard for operation as blockade runner.			
39	**Kaptepia**	Papayanni & Mussabini	? - ? - 25/8/58	185' x 25' x 18' x 469gt. Screw, 120nhp	
40	**Heather Bell**	Christall, Gray & Bateson	? - 21/8/58 - 18/9/58	135'5" x 18'1" x 10'5" x 152gt. 2 Oscillating paddle, 60nhp	Scrapped 1877
41	**Salto**	Apolinario & Co.	? - 20/11/58 - 15/12/58	159'3" x 20'1" x 10' x 215gt. Paddle 90nhp	
42	(Barge)	Charles Thorburn & Co.		105' x 23' x 9'	
43	**Adela**	Ardrossan Sg. Co.	? - ? - 30/8/59	210' x 23' x 12' x 398gt. Paddle 194nhp	Operated as blockade runner
44	**Rangatira**	Australasian S.N. Co.	? - ? - 9/11/59	207' x 25'2" x 18 x 592gt. 130nhp	Wrecked near Noumea, 31/5/1875
45	**Olympus**	Charles McIver	? - 10/1/60 - 18/2/60	276'8" x 36'2" x 26' x 1,794gt. Screw, 270nhp	
46	**Atlas**	Charles McIver	? - 8/3/60 - ?	276'8" x 36'2" x 26' x 1,794gt. Screw, 270nhp	Scrapped in 1896
47	**Giraffe**	G & J Burns	? - 16/5/60 - ?	250' x 25' x 16'5" x 677gt. Paddle, 290nhp	Operated as blockade runner
	Robert E. Lee, Fort Donelson, Isabella.	10/1862 purchased by Confederate agents and renamed Robert E. Lee for operation as blockade runner			
48	(lighter)	Carron Co.		76' x 16' x 8'5" x 35gt.	
49	(lighter)	Carron Co.		76' x 16' x 8'5" x 35gt.	
50	**Squirrel** (barge)	British & Foreign SN		101'5" x 21'1" x 8'5" x 140gt. Dumb	
51	**Amalia**	Papayanni Brothers	? - 13/12/60 - 2/5/61	277'7" x 37'4" x 25'6" x 1,825gt. Screw, 250nhp	Foundered Bay of Biscay 1866
52	**Prince Alfred**	North Lancs. S.N.Co.	? - 26/2/61 - 16/5/61	227'2" x 28'2" x 19' x 745gt. Paddle, 330nhp	
53	**Fingal**	David Hutcheson & Co.	? - 9/5/61 - 18/6/61	185'5" x 25'4" x 18' x 462gt. Direct acting inverted cylinder, 120nhp	Lost, December 1869 en route to Haiti
	Atlanta	Purchased by Confederate Agents 9/61 for operation as blockade runner. Converted to a casemated ironclad 1862/3 and renamed Atlanta			
54	**Fairy**	David Hutcheson & Co.	? - 3/6/61 - 23/7/61	149'4" x 21' x 11' x 151gt. Paddle, 75nhp	Operated as blockade runner
55	**Express**	Lyall, Still & Co.	? - 21/9/61 - 6/11/61	229'5" x 30'1" x 11' x 490gt. Paddle, 180nhp	
56	**Villa Del Salto**	Nueva Compania Saltona	? - 9/7/61 - 10/10/61	165' x 23' x 12' x 314gt. Oscillating paddle, 110nhp	
57	**Cortes**	Spanish Co.	? - 17/12/61 - 25/2/62	280' x 39' x 26' x 2,045gt. Direct acting cylinder, 420 nhp	
58	**Emerald Isle**	Dundalk & Newry S.P.Co.	? - 26/3/62 - 14/5/62	234' x 28' x 15'6" x 718gt. Oscillating paddle engine, 325 nhp	Scrapped 1899
59	**Clydesdale**	David Hutcheson & Co.	? - 23/4/62 - 28/5/62	180'2" x 24'1" x 13'2" x 403gt. Inverted 2 cylinder, 120 nhp	
60	**City of Melbourne**	Australasian S. N. Co.	? - 13/8/62 - 22/10/62	250'4" x 28'2" x 16'6" x 838gt. Geared 4 piston radial, 200 nhp	Scrapped Sydney 1898
61	**Danmark**	Danish Government	1862 - 23/2/64 - 26/8/64	270' x 50' x 36' x 2,517gt. 440 nhp 8.5k	Scrapped 1907
		Broadside ironclad		20 - 60pdr, 8 - 18pdr. Later 12 - 8" muzzle loader, 12 - 26pdr.	
		Originally built for Confederate Government under cover name *Santa Maria*. Contract terminated and ship sold to Danish Government 12/1863			
62	**Corsica**	Burns & McIver	17/7/62 - 22/1/63 - 12/3/63	215' x 32' x 26' x 1,134gt. Oscillating geared, 200 nhp	Wrecked Portugal 1881
63	**Tripoli**	British & Foreign S.N. Co.	17/9/62 - 15/8/63 - 19/9/63	280' x 38' x 32'5" x 2,061gt. 280 nhp	Wrecked, Tuskar Rock 17/5/1872
64	**Canton**	Captain Sinclair	1862 - 29/10/63 - 12/1863	230' x 32' x 23' x 963gt. Direct acting horizontal, 350 nhp 13k	
	Texas, Tornado	Blockade runner for Confederate Government built under cover name of *Pampero*. Confederate name *Texas*			
65	**Iona**	David Hutcheson & Co.	? - 12/5/63 - 19/6/63	245' x 25' x 11'5" x 368gt. 2 cyl. oscillating paddle, 180 nhp	Wrecked, Lundy Island 2/2/1864 en route for Nassau
		Purchased by Confederate agents 11/63 for operation as blockade runner.			
66	**Southern Cross**	Tasmanian S.N.Co.	? - 11/11/63 - 25/1/64	205' x 26'6" x 17'8" x 640gt. Oscillating screw, 170 nhp	Wrecked, 1890
67	**City of Adelaide**	Australasian S.N.Co.	? - 23/12/63 - 17/3/64	251'6" x 28'3" x 24'4" x 839gt. 170 nhp	Scuttled off Townsville 1915
68	**Staffa**	David Hutcheson & Co.	? - 29/10/63 - ?	149' x 23' x 11'2" x 272gt. 2 cyl. simple, 100 nhp	Wrecked Gigha, August 1885
69	(lighter)	Lyall Still & Co.	? - ? - /63	145' x 26' 14' x 232gt.	
70	(lighter)	Lyall Still & Co.	? - ? - /63	145' x 26' 14' x 232gt.	
71	(lighter)	Lyall Still & Co.	? - ? - /63	145' x 26' 14' x 232gt.	
72	**Lilian**	Henry Lafone	? - 24/3/64 - 26/4/64	225' x 26' x 11' x 438gt. Oscillating paddle, 180 nhp 14k	Lost off Mariel, November 1870
	Victoria de las Tunas	Blockade runner for Confederate Government			
73	**Little Hattie**	Henry Lafone	? - 8/4/64 - 17/5/64	225' x 26' x 11' x 439gt. Oscillating paddle, 180 nhp	
		Blockade runner for Confederate Government			
74	**Wild Rover**	Henry Lafone	? - 7/6/64 - 27/7/64	225' x 26' x 11' x 438gt. Oscillating paddle, 180 nhp	
		Blockade runner for Confederate Government			
75	**Rio De La Plata**	Uruguay River Inspection	? - 24/5/64 - 11/8/64	210' x 25' x 12' x 483gt. Oscillating paddle, 150 nhp	
76	**Swan** (barge)	Burns & McIver	? - 3/5/64 - 7/5/64	106' x 23' x 9'	
77	**Iona**	David Hutcheson & Co.	? - 10/5/64 - 18/6/64	255'5" x 25'6" x 9' x 393gt. 2 cyl. Oscillating screw, 180 nhp	Scrapped Dalmuir 1936
78	**Aleppo**	Burns & McIver.	? - 1/11/64 - 28/12/64	292'5" x 38'2" x 26'2" x 2,057gt. Oscillating screw, 280 nhp	Scrapped Preston 1909
79	**Tarifa**	Burns & McIver.	? - 12/1/65 - 7/3/65	292'5" x 38'2" x 26'2" x 2,058gt. Oscillating screw, 280 nhp	Scrapped, Italy 1899
80	**Java**	British & North American	? - 24/6/65 - 29/9/65	327' x 42' x 29' x 2,696gt. Direct acting screw, 600 nhp	Lost 1895
	Zeeland, Electrique, Lord Spencer				
81	**Emma Henry**	Henry Lafone	? - 1/9/64 - 13/10/64	210' x 25' x 10' x 377gt. Oscillating paddle, 135 nhp	Captured 1864
		Blockade runner for Confederate Government			
82	**Corcovado** (launched as Black Adder)	Henry Lafone	? - ? - /65	240' x 28' x 20' x 705gt. Oscillating paddle, 240 nhp	
83	**Guyane**	La Comp. Transatlantique	? - 12/4/65 - 8/10/65	240' x 28' x 20' x 705gt. Oscillating paddle, 240 nhp	
84	**Malta**	J Burns	? - 19/10/65 - 30/11/65	290' x 39' x 25' x 2,132gt. 280 nhp	Wrecked, Land's End 15/10/1889
85	**Iona** *Iosto*	London & Edin. S.Co.	? - 18/1/66 - 5/3/66	238'6" x 30' x 18'6" x 909gt. Direct acting surface cond. 220 nhp	
86	**Villa Del Salto**	Nueva Compania Saltona	? - 15/2/66 - 3/5/66	190' x 24'6" x 13' x 474gt. Oscillating paddle 150 nhp	
87	**Gondolier**	David Hutcheson & Co.	? - 3/5/66 - ?	152' x 20'2" x 8' x 169gt. 2 cyl. oscillating paddle 80 nhp	Blockship at Scapa 21/3/1940
88	**Chevalier**	David Hutcheson & Co.	? - 12/4/66 - ?	210' x 22' x 9'6" x 292gt. 2 cyl. oscillating paddle 150 nhp	Scrapped, Troon 1927 after stranding
89	**Weasel** *Scotia*	G&J Burns	? - 1/3/66 - 23/4/66	195' x 26' x 14' x 489gt. 2 cyl. simple 150 nhp	
90	**Malvina**	London & Edin. S.Co.	? - 14/9/66 - 30/10/66	238'4" x 30'3" x 17'6" x 898gt. Direct acting 220 nhp	Torpedoed, Flamborough Head 2/8/1918
91	**Snipe**	G & J Burns	? - 26/5/66 - 14/8/66	200' x 28' 19'5" x 638gt. 2x2 cyl. simple 150 nhp	
92	**Linnet**	David Hutcheson & Co.	? - 1/6/66 - ?	86' x 16'2" x 2'8" x 34gt. 4 cyl. simple 15 nhp	Wrecked, Gareloch 1/1932
93	**Russia** *Waesland*	British North American.	? - 20/3/67 - 26/5/67	346' x 42'6" x 29'6" x 2,960gt. Inverted 2 cylinder 600 nhp	Sunk in collision 7/3/1902 off Anglesey
94	**Salto**	Compania Uruguaya	? - 26/10/66 - 24/12/66	160' x 25' x 10'3" x 310gt. 2 Direct acting 70 nhp	
95	**Siberia** *Sumatra*	G&J Burns	? - 2/7/67 - 7/9/67	320' x 39'2" x 26'3" x 2,498gt. Inverted 2 cylinder 300 nhp 13.28k	Wrecked 19/1/1881

No.	Name	Owner	Dates	Details	Fate
96	**Jupiter**	Nueva Compania Saltona	shipped 12/66	85'6" x 16' x 3'6"	
97	**Monte Video**	Nueva Compania Saltona	shipped 12/66	85'6" x 16' x 3'6"	
98	**Hart**	Admiralty Beacon Class Gunvessel	? - 20/8/68 - 5/9/68	155' x 24'2" x 15' x 584disp. Horizontal direct acting screw 690 ihp 10.5k 1 - 7", 1 - 64pdr, 2 - 20pdr.	Scrapped 12/1888
99	**Stamboul**	Turkish Government	? - 27/4/69 - 4/8/69	250' x 32' 23' x 1,401gt. Direct acting 200 nhp	Originally built to own account
100	**Samaria**	G&J Burns	? - 4/7/68 - 18/9/68	320'6" x 39'5" x 28'3" x 2,605gt. Direct acting surface cond. 280 nhp Scrapped 1902	
101	**Clanranald** (SV) *Loch Rannoch*	Kidston & Co.	? - 4/6/68 - ?	210' x 35' x 23' x 1,243gt. Sailing ship	
102	(barge)	C Thorburn & Co.		50' x 14'6" x 5"	
103	(barge)	C Thorburn & Co.		44' x 10'6" x 3'6"	
104	(barge)	C Thorburn & Co.		44' x 10'6" x 3'6"	
105	**Racoon**	G&J Burns	? - 5/8/68 - 18/11/68	250' x 27'6" x 14'9" x 831gt. 2 cyl. oscillating paddle 300 nhp 14.64k	Scrapped 1907
106	**Raven** *Karystos Toyta, Pintos*	G&J Burns	? - 29/10/68 - 11/1/69	220' x 28'2" x 15'9" x 778gt. 2 cyl. simple 150 nhp	
107	**Ada Beatrice** (yacht) *L'Espiegle, Columba, Aetos*	Samuel T Cooper	? - /69 - 17/4/69	138' x 21' x 12' x 173gt. Direct acting 60 nhp	
108	**Hebe** (yacht)	Charles McIver	? - /69 - 12/5/69	145'6" x 21'7" x 12'6" x 180gt. Direct act. surface cond. 60 nhp 11.3k	
109	**Orissa** (SV)	John Kerr & Co.	? - 7/10/69 - 2/1/70	218' x 35' x 22'9" x 1,256gt. Sailing ship	Originally built to own account
110	**Abyssinia**	G&J Burns	? - 3/3/70 - 19/3/70	360' x 42' x 35'6" x 3,253gt. Surface cond., 409 nhp 14.5k	Lost 18/12/1891 after fire
111	**Algeria** *Pennland*	G&J Burns	? - 12/7/70 - 15/9/70	360' x 42' x 35'6" x 3,298gt. Surface cond., 409 nhp 14.5k	Scrapped, Italy 1903
112	**Clansman**	David Hutcheson & Co.	? - 28/4/70 - 21/6/70	205' x 27' x 14'3" x 600gt. 2 cyl. simple, 150 nhp 13.22k	Sold W Reed of Tynemouth 1910
113	**Bear** *Calypso*	G&J Burns	? - 12/9/70 - 26/10/70	220' x 28' x 14'9" x 632gt. 2 cyl. Compound, 150 nhp 12k	Wrecked, Paros 31/1/1914
114	**Westmoreland**	J Currie & Co.	? - 8/11/70 - ?	240' x 31'6" x 17'9" x 933gt. Compound, 150 nhp 10.75	
115	**Gothland** *Trude Bremer*	J Currie & Co.	? - 10/1/71 - 28/2/71	250' x 31'6" x 17'9" x 1,469gt. Compound, 150 nhp 10.25k	Scrapped Germany 1924
116	**Iceland**	J Currie & Co.	? - 22/2/71 - ?	250' x 31'6" x 17'9" x 1,474gt. Compound, 150 nhp 11.5k	
117	**Marmion** *Claire*	London & Edin. S.Co.	? - 23/1/71 - 11/4/71	248'6" x 30'3" x 18' x 1,045gt. Compound, 300 nhp 12.75k	(Hull subcontracted to J G Lawrie)
118	**Bison** *Belize*	G&J Burns	? - 20/4/71 - 24/6/71	231'1" x 28'2" x 22'7" x 1,015gt. 2 cyl. Compound, 160 nhp 12.5k	
119	**Gordon Castle**	Thomas Skinner & Co.	? - 7/8/71 - 18/11/71	306' x 34' x 26' x 1,988gt. Compound, 200 nhp 11.5k	Sunk, collision Stormarn 10/9/1900 Cardigan Bay
120	**Drummond Castle**	Thomas Skinner & Co.	? - 28/12/71 - 18/3/72	306' x 34' x 26' x 1,985gt.. Compound, 200 nhp 11.5k	
121	**Trinidad**	G&J Burns	? - 9/4/72 - 2/7/72	306' x 34'6" x 25'6" x 1,899gt.. Compound, 300 nhp	lost, 1898 China Sea
122	**Demerara**	G&J Burns	? - 6/9/72 - 23/11/72	306' x 34'6" x 25'6" x 1,904gt. Compound, 300 nhp	Lost, 1887
123	**Maggie**	J&G Thomson	? - ? - ?	63'6" x 13'5" x 7'4" x 28gt. Compound, 20 nhp	
124	**Ferret** *India*	G&J Burns	? - 24/11/71 - 26/12/71	170' x 23' x 13' 344gt. 2 cyl. Compound, 70 nhp	'Stolen' 1880. Wrecked, Yorke Peninsula 11/1920
127	**Ben-Tan**	J Guthrie & Co.	? - 13/5/72 - 26/6/72	170' x 23' x 18'6" x 530gt. Compound, 100 nhp	

J&G THOMSON & CO. at Clydebank from May 1871. First keel laid was Bothnia but first launch was Braemar Castle

No.	Name	Owner	Dates	Details	Fate
125	**Braemar Castle**	Thomas Skinner & Co.	14/4/72 - 14/2/73 - 17/5/73	325' x 35' x 27'6" x 2,182gt. Compound, 300 nhp	
126	**Cawdor Castle**	Thomas Skinner & Co.	9/2/72 - 13/5/73 - 15/7/73	325' x 35' x 27'6" x 2,173gt. Compound, 300 nhp	
128	**Bothnia**	Burns & McIver	31/12/71 - 4/3/74 - 23/6/74	420' x 42'6" x 36' x 4,535gt. Compound, 3,332ihp 13.75k	Scrapped Marseilles 1899
129	**Scythia**	Burns & McIver	3/73 - 28/10/74 - 23/2/75	420' x 42' 6" x 36' x 4,557gt. Compound, 3,332ihp	Scrapped Italy 1899
130	**Saragossa**	Burns & McIver	24/12/72 - 5/5/74 - 18/6/74	315' x 35' x 26' x 2,263gt. Compound, 1,570ihp	Scrapped TW Ward Preston 1910
131	**Klopstock** *Saint Germain*	Adler Line	21/3/73 - 30/6/74 - 23/10/74	375' x 40' x 34'6"' x 3,659gt. Compound, 550nhp 14k	Scrapped Boness 10/07
132	**Fleurs Castle**	T Skinner & Co.	8/6/73 - 27/8/74 - 28/10/74	325' x 35'4" x 28'6" x 2,472gt. Compound, 1,275ihp 11.5k	Wrecked Ras Asir Cape Guardafui, Aden 9/7/82
133	**Cherbourg**	Burns & McIver	24/6/73 - 12/11/74 - 4/2/75	251'2" x 32'4" x 27'3" x 1,614gt. Compound, 794ihp 11.25k	Scrapped 1909
134	(Barge)	Guthrie	-	-	
135	**Dunnottar Castle** (SV)	T Skinner & Co.	15/5/74 - 24/12/74 - 27/1/75	258'2" x 38'6" x 24'10" x 1,750gt	Wrecked Cure Island 15/6/86
136	**Espirito Santo**	Brazilian S.N.Co.	11/7/74 - 22/4/75 - 4/5/75	250' x 38' x 21' x 1,737gt. Compound, 1,953ihp 13k tr	
137	**Blairgowrie** (SV) *Contessa, Hilda*	Thomson & Gray	14/7/74 - 26/3/75 - 16/4/75	245' x 38'3" x 23'8" x 1,646gt	
138	**Pernambuco**	Brazilian S.N.Co.	1/10/74 - 7/7/75 - 14/7/75	252' x 38' x 20'1" x 1,736gt. Compound, 2,104ihp 12.9k tr	
139	**Loch Vennachar** (SV)	Glasgow Shipping Co.	21/1/75 - 4/8/75 - 2/9/75	240' x 38' x 23'10" x 1,557gt	Wrecked on Young Rocks Kangaroo 9/05
140	**Loch Garry** (SV)	Glasgow Shipping Co.	3/3/75 - 1/10/75 - 14/10/75	240' x 38' x 23'10" x 1,565gt	
141	**Bellver**	Charles Henderson	15/4/75 - 22/12/79 - 22/1/80	240' x 30'6" x 23'1" x 1,260gt. Compound, 160nhp	
142	**Tuscany** *Madeirense, Margarita, Capo Zafferano*	David MacIver & Co.	6/5/75 - 26/1/76 - 28/2/76	275' x 32' x 25'3" x 1,642gt. Compound, 1,12 ihp 11k	
143	**Sir Walter Raleigh** (SV)	Donaldson, Rose & Co.	25/6/75 - 24/2/76 - 24/4/76	235' x 38'6" x 22'3" x 1,579gt	Wrecked near Boulogne 1888
144	**Sea Snake**	James Galbraith	27/12/75 - 12/5/76 - 18/5/76	100' x 15' x 9' x 78gt. Compound, 17 nhp 11k	
145	**Pioneer**	Henry Koch	27/12/75 - 28/4/76 - 4/5/76	100' x 15' x 9' x 78gt Compound, 17 nhp 11.5k	
146	**Loudoun Castle** *Marco, Minghetti*	Thomas Skinner & Co.	19/2/76 - 19/10/76 - 13/1/77	340' x 36'6" x 27' x 2,472gt. Compound, 2,790ihp 13.5k	
147	**Cape of Good Hope** (SV) Refered to as *Emerald* in Thomson records. Later named *Amy*	Abram Lyle & Sons	10/1/76 - 13/7/76 - 31/7/76	238'8" x 37'7" x 22'5" x 1,493gt	Wrecked 8/7/94
148	**Loch Long** (SV)	General Shipping Co.	8/2/76 - 20/11/76 - 9/12/76	228'5" x 22'8" x 21'3" x 1,261gt	Wrecked on the Chatham Islands 1903
149	**Loch Fyne** (SV)	General Shipping Co.	17/2/76 - 5/10/76 - 22/11/76	228'5" x 22' x 21'3" x 1,270gt	
150	**Loch Ryan** (SV) *Murray, John Murray*	General Shipping Co.	14/3/76 - 31/1/77 - 3/3/77	228'5" x 22'8" x 21'3" x 1,264gt	
151	**Loch Linnhe** (SV)	J&R Wilson	11/4/76 - 5/12/76 - 5/1/77	234'7" x 37'2" x 23'9" x 1,468gt	
152	**Firebrand** *Hoi Tin*	Admiralty Forester Class Gunboat	21/6/76 - 30/4/77 - 23/12/77	125' x 23'6" x 12' x 455gt. Compound, 360ihp 10.17k 2 - 64pdr, 2 - 20pdr	
153	**Firefly** *Egmont*	Admiralty Forester Class Gunboat	3/6/76 - 28/6/77 - 23/12/77	125' x 23'6" x 12' x 455gt. Compound, 360ihp 9.99k 2 - 64pdr, 2 - 20pdr	Sold Malta 5/1931

No.	Name	Owner	Dates	Details	Fate
154	**Cape Breton** (SV)	Abram Lyle & Sons	24/12/76. 6/12/77 - 21/1/78	239'3" x 37'8" x 23'8" x 1,504t	Wrecked Chile 25/7/1894
155	**Cape St Vincent** (SV)	Abram Lyle & Sons	3/2/76 - 7/12/77 - 21/1/78	239'1" x 37'8" x 23'8" x 1,504gt	Missing South Atlantic 2/1910
	Lady Lina, Angelo, Repetto				
156	**Salamanca** (SV)	J Hardie	3/11/76 - 11/4/77 - 11/5/77	227'7"x35'8" x 22'8" x 1,262gt	
157	**Orthes** *Mataura* (SV)	J Hardie	21/11/76 - 9/11/77 - 7/12/77	228' x 35'8" x 22'8" x 1,270gt	
158	**Elspeth** (yacht)	Col. Campbell of Possil.	26/12/76 - 30/5/77 - 25/6/77	125' x 17' x 10'3" x 131gt. Compound, 36nhp	
	Surirella. Elspeth, Amalinda				
159	**Summerlee**	Summerlee & Co.	28/2/77 - 12/7/77 - 27/8/77	251' x 34'8' x 18' x 1,102gt. Compound, 80nhp 11k	
160	**Walrus** *Kanaris*	Burns & McIver	22/8/77 - 6/3/78 - 29/4/78	240' x 30' x 15'3" x 870gt. 2 cyl. Compound, 220nhp 13.85k	
161	**Mastiff** *Gibel Dersa*	Burns & McIver	10/8/77 - 3/4/78 - ?	230'4" x 30'3" x 18'3" x 871gt. 2 cyl. Compound 220nhp 13.6k	Scrapped Genoa 1/24
162	**Columba**	David Hutcheson	10/10/77 - 9/4/78 - 30/6/78	295' x 27' x 9'6" x 543gt. 2 cyl. Oscillating paddle, 220nhp 15.8k	Scrapped Dalmuir 20/2/1936
163	**Gallia**	Cunard S.S.Co. Ltd	10/10/77 - 12/11/78 - 27/3/79	430' x 44' x 36' x 4,809gt. 3 cyl. Compound, 5,300ihp 15.7k	Scrapped Cherbourg 1900
164	**Rook** *Palmerston*	Burns & McIver	7/2/78 - 4/6/78 - 12/7/78	175'3" x 25' x 13'7" x 463gt. 2 cyl. Compound, 70nhp	
	Originally named Moorcock				
165	**Sir Walter**	London & Edin. S. Co.	25/2/78 - 19/6/78 - 25/6/78	175'4" x 25'1" x 13'7" x 424gt. Compound 70nhp	
	Launched as Mustang				
166	**Dunmore**	Clyde Shipping Co.	12/3/78 - 28/9/78 - 26/12/78	230' x 32'6" x 16' x 1,080gt Compound, 220nhp	Wrecked Ballyquinton Point 17/12/1882
167	**Bay of Cadiz** (SV)	J&G Bulloch & Co.	10/4/78 - 13/12/78 - 8/3/79	250' x 40' x 24'6" x 1,700gt	Missing South Pacific 4/1889
168	**Arab**	Union Steamship Co.	20/6/78 - 23/1/79 - 28/4/79	350' x 40'2" x 32'6" x 3,192gt. Compound, 2,830ihp 14k	Scrapped Germany 1900
169	**Mercutio**	Gledhill & Dishart, Leith	15/8/78 - 11/3/79 - 28/5/79	200'1" x 29'1" x 16' x 872gt. Compound, 95nhp 9.38k	
170	**Malvina**	London & Edinburgh S Co.	2/10/78 - 29/3/79 - 4/6/79	254'4" x 31'2" x 19'3" x 1,182gt Compound, 250nhp 13.92k	Torpedoed and sunk, Flamborough Head 2/8/1918
171	(steam launch)	Rangoon	25/9/78 - 22/11/78 -30/11/78	39'5" x 7' x 4'. 8k	
172	(steam launch)	Rangoon	25/9/78 - 24/12/78 - 30/1/79	39'5" x 7' x 4'. 8k	
173	**Lake Winnipeg**	Canada Shipping Co.	15/11/78 - 26/5/79 - 4/8/79	355' x 40' x 31'6" x 3,311gt. Compound, 400hp 12.7k	Torpedoed and sunk by Italian warship 1912?
	Garbi Garb				
174	**Matador**	John Burns,Castle Wemyss	30/1/79 - 3/6/79 - 5/7/79	125' x 19'10" x 11'10" x 157gt. Compound, 42nhp 10.76k	
175	**Belair** *Sophie Annet*	D Caw & Co., Glasgow	27/6/79 - 16/10/79 - 10/11/79	244' x 32'6" x 19'1" x 1,419gt. Compound, 150nhp 10.57k	Collision off Farne Island 25/9/1903
176	**Cipero**	D Caw & Co., Glasgow	30/6/79 - 5/11/79 - 5/12/79	244' x 32'6" x 19'1" x 1,419gt. Compound, 150nhp 9.8k	
	Massalia, Diadochos, Constantinos, Galatz, Diadochus, Constantinos, Emanual, Repoulis				
177	**Trojan** *Islam, Tosca Maru*	Union S.S.Co.	13/8/79 - 27/2/80 - 22/4/80	365' x 42' x 32'6" x 3,554gt. 3 cyl. Compound, 3,530ihp 14.85k	
178	**Lake Manitoba**	Canada Shipping Co..	17/12/79 - 26/4/80 - 1/6/80	355' x 40' x 31'6" x 3,311gt. Compound, 2,450ihp 13.95k	Wrecked on Miquelon Island 14/6/1885
179	**Servia**	Cunard S.S.Co. Ltd	7/2/80 - 1/3/81 - 16/11/81	515' x 52 x 41'3" x 7,392gt. 3 cyl. Compound, 10,300ihp 16.77k	Scrapped TW Ward Preston 1902
180	**Catalonia**	Cunard S.S.Co. Ltd	29/4/80 - 14/5/81 - 29/7/81	430' x 43' x 35'1" x 4,841gt. Compound, 3,765ihp 14.02k	Scrapped Italy 1901
181	**Duchess of Edinburgh**	South Eastern Rly. Co.	1/3/80 - 23/6/80 - 4/10/80	250' x 29'6" x 812gt 2 cyl. compound oscillating paddle (returned on 24/2/81 for alterations - trials 8/5/81)	Scrapped, Garston 1907
	Manx Queen				
182	**Spartan** *Fiume*	Union S.S. Co.	19/6/80 - 12/7/81 - 4/11/81	365' x 43' x 32'6" x 3,491gt. 3 cyl. Compound, 3,610ihp 14.6k	Scrapped 1902
183	**Thames**	P&O S.N. Co.	6/10/80 - 20/9/81 - 5to7/3/82	390' x 42' x 34'1.5" x 4,100gt. Compound, 5,648ihp 15.3k	
184	**Moor** *La Plata, Viking*	Union S.S. Co.	6/12/81 - 23/12/81 - 6/5/82	365' x 45'6" x 32'6" x 3,687gt 3 cyl. Compound, 4,129ihp 15.22k	Scrapped 1913
185	**Claymore**	D MacBrayne & Co.	10/12/80 - 14/7/81 - 11/10/81	220' x 29'6" x 22'9" x 726gt 2 cyl. compound, 1,460ihp 14.06k	Scrapped Boness 1931
186	**Pavonia**	Cunard S.S.Co. Ltd.	10/12/80 - 3/6/82 - 31/8/82	430' x 46' x 36'6" x 5,588gt Compound, 4,390ihp 14.33	Scrapped 1900
187	**Aurania**	Cunard S.S. Co. Ltd.	27/12/80 - 26/12/82 - 5/3/83	470' x 57' x 38'6" x 7,268gt 3 cyl. Compound, 8,500ihp 17.26k	Scrapped Genoa 1905
188	**Hammonia** *Versailles*	Hamburg Amerika Line	21/5/81 - 3/9/82 - 27/1/83	375' x 45' x 34'8" x 4,247gt 3 cyl. Compound, 4,350ihp 15.24k	Scrapped Genoa 1914
189	**Hansa** *Krautsand*	Hamburg Amerika Line	21/5/81 - 22/12/81 - 31/12/81	156'2.5" x 32' x 16'6" x 549gt Compound, 600ihp 10.5k	
190	**Chiapas**	D Caw & Co.	16/3/82 - 27/10/82 - 27/12/82	275' x 33' x 22'9" x 1,582gt Compound 1,336ihp 11.5k	Foundered Queenstown 30/12/1882
191	**Moruca**	D Caw & Co.	27/3/82 - 23/1/83 - 10/3/83	275' x 33' x 22'9" x 1,585gt Compound, 1,480ihp 12.12k	
	Brunswick, Hans Wagner, Kiangching, Nikko Maru				
192	**Iona** *Jorge Juan*	London & Edin. Ship.Co.	30/5/82 - 23/2/83 - 28/4/83	260'7" x 32'1" x 19'3" x 1,180gt Compound, 2,400ihp 14.75k	
193	**Sargasso**	Scrutton Sons & Co.	24/11/82 - 7/5/83 - 21/6/83	275' x 33'1" x 20'6" x 1,441gt Compound, 120nhp 11.49k	Sank in collision with *Mary Ada* R. Tyne 18/4/1912
194	**Burnley**	D Caw & Co.	1/2/83 - 25/6/83 - 3/9/83	275' x 33'2" x 22'9" x 1,556gt Compound, 176nhp 12.29k	Wrecked 15/11/1895
195	**America** *Eritrea, Trinacria*	National S.S.Co. Ltd.	? - 29/12/83 - 29/4/84	480' x 51.25" x 37'6" x 5,528gt Compound, 8,660ihp 16.79k	Scrapped Italy 1925
196	**Barracouta** *Granco*	Leaycroft & Co.	? - 18/9/83 - 24/10/83	275' x 35'1" x 21'6" x 2,152gt Compound, 176nhp 11.21k	
197	**Manaos**	Brazilian S. N. Co.	? - 5/11/83 - 5/2/84	266'3" x 36'1" x 21' x 1,719gt Compound, 2,000ihp 13.16k	
198	**Arecuna** *Ville de Sousse*	D Caw & Co., Glasgow	? - 13/6/84 - 16/8/84	275'5" x 36'1" x 23' x 1,735gt Compound, 209nhp 11.92k	Scrapped 1913
199	**Atlantis** *Fortuna, Atlantis*	Scrutton Sons & Co.	? - 26/6/84 - 5/9/84	280' x 33' x 20'6" x 1,528gt Compound, 1,060ihp 12.6k	
200 - 219	not allocated				
220	**Buzzard** *Sfactirea*	J Burns, Glasgow	? - 15/3/84 - 28/5/84	210'5" x 32'6" x 15'9" x 831gt Double compound, 2,400ihp 15.14k	
221	**Skirmisher**	Cunard S.S. Co. Ltd	? - 14/5/84 - 28/6/84	165' x 32'2" x 15'6" x 607gt Twin screw compound, 1,100ihp 12.26k	Scrapped Hale, Mersey 1946
222	**Lake Superior**	Canada Shipping Co. Ltd	? - 4/12/84 - 6/4/85	400' x 44'2" x 32' x 4,562t Compound 3,600ihp 12.5k	Wrecked near St Johns New Brunswick 31/3/1902
223	**Scout**	Admiralty	8/1/84 - 30/7/85 - 20/8/86	220'pp x 34' x 14'6" x 1,580disp. Horiz. Direct Act. Compound 3,200ihp 17.23k	Scrapped, Thames 1904
		Scout Class Cruiser (3rd class)		4 - 5", 8 - 3pdr, 2 - mgs, 1 - TT, 2 - TC	
224	**Grenadier**	D MacBrayne, Glasgow	? - 19/3/85 - 11/5/85	220' x 23' x 9'6" x 372gt 2 cyl. compound oscillating 150nhp 14.7k	Scrapped Ardrossan 8/1928
225	**Albuera** *Cis* (SV)	John Hardie, Glasgow	? - 19/5/85 - ?	236'6" x 39'2" x 24'4" x 1,554gt	Sunk 9/4/1917
226	**Archer**	Admiralty	2/3/85 - 23/12/85 - 20/4/86	240' x 36' x 19'2" x 1,770t Compound 3,500 ihp 17.53k	Sold for scrap by Forrester, Swansea 4/4/1905
		Archer Class Torpedo Cruiser (3rd class)		6 - 6", 8 - 3pdr, 2 - mgs, 3 - 14"TT	
227	**Mohawk**	Admiralty	2/3/85 - 6/2/86 - 30/4/86	240' x 36' x 19'2" x 1,770disp Compound 3,200 ihp 17k	Sold by auction at Chatham 4/4/1905
		Archer Class Torpedo Cruiser (3rd Class)		6 - 6", 8 - 3pdr, 2 - mgs, 3 - 14"TT	
228	**Brisk**	Admiralty	2/3/85 - 8/4/86 - 7/6/86	240' x 36' x 19'2" x 1,770disp. Compound 3,200 ihp 17k	Scrapped by Ward at Preston 15/5/1906
		Archer Class Torpedo Cruiser (3rd Class)		6 - 6", 8 - 3pdr, 2 - mgs, 3 - 14"TT	

No.	Name	Owner	Dates	Details	Fate
229	Porpoise	Admiralty Archer Class Torpedo Cruiser (3rd Class)	2/3/85 - 7/5/86 - 13/6/86	240' x 36' x 19'2" x 1,770disp. Compound 3,200 ihp 17k 6 - 6", 8 - 3pdr, 2 - mgs, 3 - 14"TT	Sold at Bombay for scrapping 1905
230	Cossack	Admiralty Archer Class Torpedo Cruiser (3rd Class)	2/3/85 - 3/6/86 - 27/10/86	240' x 36' x 19'2" x 1,770disp. Compound 3,200 ihp 17k 6 - 6", 8 - 3pdr, 2 - mgs, 3 - 14"TT	Scrapped, Thames 1905
231	Tartar	Admiralty Archer Class Torpedo Cruiser (3rd Class)	2/3/85 - 28/10/86 - ?	240' x 36' x 19'2" x 1,770disp. Compound , 3,200ihp 17k 6 - 6", 8 - 3pdr, 2 - mgs, 3 - 14"TT	Sold, Forrester, Swansea 1906
232	Itamaraty	Megaw & Norton, Rio de Janeiro -	15/10/85 - 2/12/85	220'5" x 30'4" x 7'6" x 401gt 2 cyl. paddle,160nhp 14.66k	
233	Wiborg	Russian Government Torpedo boat	? - 6/7/86 - ?	142'6.5" x 17' x 9'6" x 126disp. Compound, 1,400ihp 21.62k 2 x 1pdr, 3 x 15"TT	
234	El Destructor	Spanish Navy torpedo gunboat	? - 29/7/86 - 16/12/86	192'6" x 25' x 12' x 386disp. Compound, 3,800ihp 21.22k 1 x 3.5", 4 x 6pdr, 5 x 15"TT	
235	Aurora	Admiralty	Engines only for cruiser building at Pembroke DYd. Triple expansion 8,500ihp		
236	Reina Regente	Spanish Navy Protected cruiser	19/6/86 - 24/2/87 - 1/12/87	317'pp x 50' x 32'6" x 4,725t Triple expansion, 11,500ihp 20.5k 4 x 7.9", 6 x 4.7", 6 x 6pdr, 6 mg's, 5 x 15"TT	Foundered March 1895
237	Meteor	London & Edin. Ship. Co.	23/9/86 - 7/4/87 - 6/6/87	260' x 32'1" x 16'9" x 1,179gt Triple expansion, 290 hp 15.15k	
238		Machinery for **Primero de Algeciras** building in Spain			
239	Maranhao	Brazilian S. N. Co.	28/2/87 - 9/6/87 - 1/9/87	276' x 38'1" x 21'6" x 1,916gt Triple expansion, 250hp 13.44k	
240	City of New York *New York*	Inman & Intl. S.S. Co.	7/6/87 - 15/3/88 - 18/6/88	560' x 63'2" x 42' x 10,499gt Triple expansion, 2,000nhp 19.84k	Scrapped Genoa 1923
241	City of Paris *Paris, Yale, Philadelphia, Harrisburg*	Inman Int. S.S. Co.	14/9/87 - 23/10/88 - 19/3/89	560' x 63'2" x 42' x 10,669gt Triple expansion, 2,000nhp 21.75k	Scrapped Genoa 1923
242	Friesland *La Plata*	Soc. Anon Belge Americ.	24/10/88 - 15/8/89 - 23/11/89	437' x 51'2" x 38' x 7,116gt Triple expansion, 800nhp 13.69k	Scrapped 1912
243	Tauranga (launched as Phoenix)	Royal Australian Navy Pearl Class Cruiser (3rd Class)	1/12/88 - 28/10/89 - 15/12/90	278' x 41' x 21'3" x 2,575disp. Triple expansion, 5,450ihp 17.71k 8 - 4.7", 8 - 3pdr, 4 - mgs, 2 - 14"TT, 2 - TC	Scrapped Ward, Preston 10/7/1906
244	Ringarooma (launched as Psyche)	Royal Australian Navy Pearl Class Cruiser (3rd Class)	6/12/88 - 10/12/89 - 14/12/90	278' x 41' x 21'3" x 2,575disp. Triple expansion, 5,450ihp 17k 8 - 4.7", 8 - 3pdr, 4 - mgs, 2 - 14"TT, 2 - TC	Scrapped Forth Shipbreaking Co 1/5/1906
245	Chiyoda	Japanese Navy Cruiser	1/5/89 - 3/6/90 - 18/12/90	310'wl x 42' x 23'8" x 2,540disp. Triple expansion, 5,600ihp 19k 10 - 4.7", 14 - 3pdr., 3mg, 3 - 14"TT	Scrapped 1927
246	Brazil	Brazilian S.N. Co.	12/8/89 - 12/3/90 - 24/5/90	282' x 38'1" x 22' x 2,003gt Triple expansion, 250nhp 13.43k	
247	Terpsichore	Admiralty Apollo Class Cruiser (2nd Class)	19/9/89 - 30/10/90 - 2/7/91	314' x 43' x 22'11" x 3,400disp. Triple expansion, 7,000ihp 19.81k 2 - 6", 6 - 4.7", 8 - 6pdr, 1 - 3pdr., 4mg, 4 - 14"TT	Scrapped 1914
248	Thetis	Admiralty Apollo Class Cruiser (2nd Class)	24/10/89 - 13/12/90 - 19/8/92	314' x 43' x 22'11" x 3,400disp. Triple expansion, 7,000ihp 20k 2 - 6", 6 - 4.7", 8 - 6pdr, 1 - 3pdr., 4mg, 4 - 14"TT	Sunk as blockship at Zeebrugge 23/4/1918
249	Tribune	Admiralty Apollo Class Cruiser (2nd Class)	28/12/89 - 24/2/91 - 19/9/91	314' x 43' x 22'11" x 3,400disp. Triple expansion, 7,000 ihp 20k 2 - 6", 6 - 4.7", 8 - 6pdr, 1 - 3pdr., 4mg, 4 - 14"TT	Scrapped Cashmore Newport 9/5/1911
250	Frederica *Nilufer*	London & S.W. Rly. Co.	27/1/90 - 5/6/90 - 12/7/90	253' x 35'1" x 15'8" x 1,059gt Triple expansion, 5,700ihp 19.46k	Mined Bosphorus 22/11/1914
251	Lydia *Ierac, Ierax*	London & S.W. Rly. Co.	9/2/90 - 16/7/90 - 11/9/90	253' x 35'1" x 15'8" x 1,133gt Triple expansion, 5,700ihp 19.52k	Scrapped 1937
252	Stella	London & S.W. Rly. Co.	9/2/90 - 15/9/90 - 22/10/90	253' x 35'1" x 15'8" x 1,059gt Triple expansion, 5,700ihp	Wrecked Casquet Roads 30/3/1899
253	Ramillies	Admiralty Royal Sovereign Class Battleship	13/8/90 - 1/3/92 - 1/4/93	410'6" x 75' x 44'5" x 14,100disp. Triple expansion, 13,000ihp 17.25k 4 - 13.5", 10 - 6", 16 - 6pdr., 12 - 3pdr., 7 - 18"TT	Scrapped 1913
254	San Salvador *Sao Salvador*	Comp. de Nav. a Vapor- de Bahia, Brazil	26/12/90 - 9/6/91 - 11/9/91	282' x 38'1" x 20'7" x 2,020gt Triple expansion, 318nhp 13.44k	
255	Olinda *Joao Alfredo*	"	29/1/91 - 7/8/91 - 22/10/91	282' x 38'1" x 22' x 2,020gt Triple expansion, 318nhp 13.58k	
256	Itasca	Companhia Nac. de Nav. Costeira, Rio de Janiero	10/9/91 - 18/1/92 - 16/2/92	280' x 36' x 18' x 1,300gt Triple expansion, 15.1k	
257	Itaipu *Carlos Gomes*	Compania Nac. de Nav. Costeira, Rio de Janiero	24/9/91 - 12/3/92 - 29/3/92	280' x 36' x 18' x 1,306gt Triple expansion 315nhp 15.14k	
258	Glen Sannox	Glasgow & S.W. Rly. Co.	19/12/91 - 26/3/92 - 23/5/92	260'5" x 30'1" x 10'6" x 610gt 2 cyl. compound diagonal paddle, 353nhp 19.23k t	Scrapped Smith, Port Glasgow 1925
259	Borneo	Netherlands Navy Gunboat	20/6/92 - 24/11/92 - 31/3/93	177'2" x 33'1" x 14'9" x 787disp. 1,040ihp 13.2k 6 - 4.1", 4 - 1pdr.	
260		Admiralty Machinery for cruiser Hermione building at Devonport DYd. Triple exp. 7,500 ihp. Machinery loaded out at Clydebank on SS Portland 3/8/93 and Cumbrian 28/10/93			
261	Nile	Royal Mail S.P. Co.	2/8/92 - 21/3/93 - 12/9/93	420' x 52' x 35'5" x 5,946gt Triple expansion 934nhp 17.04k	Scrapped Oakland USA 1927
262	Danube *Mediterranean Star*	Royal Mail S.P. Co.	12/8/92 - 16/5/93 - 12/4/93	420' x 52' x 35'5" x 5,946gt Triple expansion 934nhp 17.17k	Scrapped 1922
263	Kensington	International Nav. Co.	14/1/93 - 26/10/93 - 19/6/94	480' x 57'2" x 37' x 8,669gt Quad Expansion 1,237nhp 15.6k	Scrapped Italy 1910
264	Minerva	Glasgow & S. W. Rly. Co.	22/2/93 - 6/5/93 - 1/6/93	200' x 25' x 9' x 306gt 2 cyl. compound diagonal paddle, 185nhp 17.03k	Scrapped 1927
265	Glen Rosa	Glasgow & S. W. Rly. Co.	24/3/93 - 31/5/93 - 27/6/93	200' x 25' x 9' x 306gt 2 cyl. compound diagonal paddle, 185nhp 17.46k	Scrapped Dalmuir 1939
266	Slieve Donard *Albion*	Belfast & Co. Down Rly.	10/3/93 - 20/5/93 - 16/6/93	200' x 25' x 9' x 341gt 2 cyl. compound diagonal paddle, 185nhp 17.6k	Scrapped 1920
267		Admiralty Machinery for battleship Sultan reconstructed at Portsmouth DYd. T. exp. 6,531ihp. Machinery loaded out at Clydebank on SS Avalon 9/8/94. Second load 23/8/94			
268	Slieve Bearnagh	Belfast & Co. Down Rly.	? - 21/11/93 - 27/4/94	225'6" x 26'1" x 9' x 383gt 2 cyl. compound diagonal 178nhp 17.66k	Scrapped, Ward Inverkeithing 1922
269	Rocket	Admiralty Destroyer	14/3/94 - 14/8/94 - 10/5/95	205'6" x 19'5" x 12'6" x 280disp. Triple expansion, 4,200ihp 27.4k 1 - 12pdr, 5 - 6pdr, 2 - 18"TT	Scrapped 1912
270	Shark	Admiralty Destroyer	16/3/94 - 22/9/94 - 16/5/95	205'6" x 19'5" x 12'6" x 280disp. Triple expansion, 4,250ihp 27.6k 1 - 12pdr, 5 - 6pdr, 2 - 18"TT	Scrapped Ward, Preston 11/6/1911
271	Surly	Admiralty Destroyer	19/3/94 - 10/11/94 - 16/5/95	205'6" x 19'5" x 12'6" x 280disp. Triple expansion, 4,400ihp 28.05k 1 - 12pdr, 5 - 6pdr, 2 - 18"TT	Scrapped Ward, Milford Haven 23/3/1920
272	Terrible *Fisgard III*	Admiralty Powerful Class Protected Cruiser (1st Class)	31/3/94 - 27/5/95 - 23/6/96	538' x 71' x 43'4" x 14,200disp. Triple expansion, 25,000ihp 21.1k 2 - 9.2", 12 - 6", 16 - 12pdr, 12 - 3pdr, 4 - 18"TT	Scrapped Cashmore Newport 8/1931
273	Jupiter	Admiralty Majestic Class Battleship	22/6/94 - 18/11/95 - 11/2/97	421' x 75' x 45'2" x 14,900disp. Triple expansion 10,000ihp 16.25k 4 - 12", 12 -6", 16 - 12pdr., 12 - 2pdr., 5 - 18"TT	Scrapped Hughes Bolckow Tyne 1920
274	Columbia *Sitges*	London & S.W. Rly. Co.	14/5/94 - 4/9/94 - 17/10/94	270'7" x 34' x 14'6" x 1,145gt Triple expansion 217 nhp 19.3k	

No. Name	Owner	Dates	Details	Fate
275 **Alma** *Shokiku Maru No23*	London & S.W. Rly. Co.	26/6/94 - 4/10/94 - 8/12/94	270'7" x 34' x 14'6" x 1,145t Triple expansion 217 nhp 19.205k	Deleted from Lloyds after 1923
276 **Duchess of Rothesay**	Caledonian S. P. Co.	30/1/95 - 20/4/95 - 17/5/95	225'6" x 26'1" x 8'6" x 385gt 2 cyl. comp. diagonal paddle 206 nhp 18.1k	Scrapped Nieuw Lekkerland, Holland 1946
277 **Greyhound** *Buyuk Ada*	North Pier S.S.Co.	18/2/95 - 16/5/95 - 11/6/95	230' x 27'1" x 9'7" x 542gt 2 cyl. compound diagonal paddle, 234 nhp 18.07k	Scrapped 1936
278 **Urania**	Exmo Don Francisco Recur	6/3/95 - 7/6/95 - 3/7/95	205' x 26'1" x 16'5" x 640gt 11.68k	Scrapped 1935
279 **Kiev**	Russian Volunteer Fleet	1/7/95 - 18/2/96 - 6/5/96	433' x 49'9" x 32' x 5,465gt Triple expansion, 519 nhp 13.93k	
280 **Hernan Cortes**	Spanish Navy Gunboat	30/7/95 - 24/8/95 - 4/9/95	155' x 21'6" x 11' x 300disp. Triple expansion, 13.41k	
281 **Pizarro**	Spanish Navy Gunboat	1/8/95 - 5/9/95 - 12/9/95	155' x 21'6" x 11' x 300disp. 12.74k	
282 **Vasco Nunez de Balboa**	Spanish Navy Gunboat	1/8/95 - 12/9/95 - 19/9/95	155' x 21'6" x 11' x 300disp. 13.44k	
283 **Diego Velazquez**	Spanish navy Gunboat	24/7/95 - 7/9/95 - 16/9/95	135' x 19' x 10'6" x 200disp. 13.14k	
284 **Ponce de Leon**	Spanish Navy Gunboat	24/7/95 - 13/9/95 - 21/9/95	135' x 19' x 10'6" x 200disp. 11.88k	
285 **Alvarado**	Spanish Navy	24/7/95 - 19/9/95 - 26/9/95	110' x 156'6" x 8'9" x 106disp. Triple expansion, 10.69k	
286 **Sandoval**	Spanish Navy	24/7/95 - 20/9/95 - 28/9/95	110' x 156'6" x 8'9" x 106disp. Triple expansion, 10.79k	
287	Admiralty		Machinery for cruiser Pelorus building at Sheerness DYd. Triple expansion 7,000hp 20.5k. Machinery loaded out at Clydebank on SS Marsden and sailed on 4/5/1896	
288 **Brazen**	Admiralty Destroyer	18/10/95 - 3/7/96 - 3/5/99	218' x 20' x 12'9" x 335disp. 5,700 hp 30k 1 - 12pdr, 5 - 6pdr, 2 - 18"TT	Scrapped J H Lee, 4 November 1919
289 **Electra**	Admiralty Destroyer	18/10/95 - 14/7/96 - 17/5/99	218' x 20' x 12'9" x 335disp Triple expansion, 5,760ihp 30k 1 - 12pdr, 5 - 6pdr, 2 - 18"TT	Scrapped by Barking Ship Breaking Co 29/4/1920
290 **Recruit**	Admiralty Destroyer	18/10/95 - 22/8/96 - 10/00	218' x 20' x 12'9" x 335disp Triple expansion, 5,700ihp 30k 1 - 12pdr, 5 - 6pdr, 2 - 18"TT	Sunk by Submarine off Galloper Light Vessel 1/5/1915
291 **Vulture**	Admiralty Destroyer	20/12/95 - 22/3/98 - 10/3/99	218' x 20' x 12'9" x 335disp Triple expansion, 5,700ihp 30.17k 1 - 12pdr, 5 - 6pdr, 2 - 18"TT	Scrapped by Hayes, Porthcawl 25/7/1919
292 **Jupiter**	Glasgow & SW Rly.Co.	16/12/95 - 21/3/96 - 16/5/96	230' x 28' x 9'6" x 394gt 2 cyl. compound diagonal paddle, 18.49k	Scrapped by TW Ward, Barrow 25/12/1935
293 **Europa**	Admiralty Diadem Class Cruiser (1st Class)	10/1/96 - 20/3/97 - 13/4/98	462'6" x 69' x 39'8" x 11,000disp. Triple expansion, 16,500 ihp 19.45k 16 - 6", 14 - 12pdr, 3 - 3pdr, 3 - 18"TT	Scrapped Genoa 1920
294 **Terror**	Spanish Navy Torpedo boat	19/2/96 - 28/8/96 - 20/11/96	220' x 22' x 13' x 450disp Triple expansion 26.04k 2 - 14pdr, 2 - 6pdr, 2 - 1pdr, 2 - 14"TT	Wrecked off San Juan, Puerto Rico 22/6/1898
295 **Furor**	Spanish Navy Torpedo boat	21/2/96 - 7/8/96 - 21/11/96	220' x 22' x 13' x 450disp Triple expansion 28.35k 2 - 14pdr, 2 - 6pdr, 2 - 1pdr, 2 - 14"TT	Sunk in battle of Santiago 3/7/1898
296 **Mayflower** *Butte Mala*	Ogden Goelet, New York	25/3/96 - 17/11/96 - 3/5/97	294'1" x 36'7" x 21' x 1,779gt 4 cyl. triple expansion 594nhp 16.36k	
297 **Victoria**	London & SW Rly Co.	26/3/96 - 15/6/96 - 15/7/96	220'5" x 28'1" x 16'3" x 709gt Triple expansion 107nhp 16.48k	Scrapped 1938
298 **Kestrel**	Admiralty Destroyer	18/9/96 - 25/3/98 - 17/3/99	222'6" x 20'6" x 12' 9" x 350disp. Triple expansion, 5,800ihp 30k 1 - 12pdr, 5 - 6pdr, 2 - 18"TT	Scrapped TW Ward, Rainham 17/3/1921
299 **Arab**	Admiralty Destroyer	15/3/00 - 9/2/01 - 9/10/02	232' x 22'3" x 13'10" x 470disp. Triple expansion, 8,600ihp 31.78k 1 - 12pdr, 5 - 6pdr, 2 - 18"TT	Scrapped by Fryer, Sunderland 23/7/1919
300 **Nahma** *Istar*	Robert Goelet, New York	7/8/96 - 19/2/97 - 14/7/97	288'8" x 36'7" x 21' x 969gt Triple expansion, 594nhp 16.78k	
301 **Audaz**	Spanish Navy Torpedo boat	24/8/96 - 6/2/97 - 9/3/98	225' x 22'6" x 13'6" x 430disp. Triple expansion, 7,500ihp 29.2k 2 - 14pdr, 2 - 6pdr, 2 - 1pdr, 2 - 14"TT	
302 **Osado**	Spanish Navy Torpedo boat	5/9/96 - 16/3/97 - 25/11/97	225' x 22'6" x 13'6" x 430disp. Triple expansion, 7,500ihp 29.39k 2 - 14pdr, 2 - 6pdr, 2 - 1pdr, 2 - 14"TT	

CLYDEBANK ENGINEERING & SHIPBUILDING COMPANY LIMITED from 1 February 1897

No. Name	Owner	Dates	Details	Fate
303 **Ariadne**	Admiralty Diadem Class Cruiser (1st Class)	24/2/97 - 22/4/98 - 6/2/99	462'6" x 69' x 39'8" x 11,000disp Triple expansion 18,000 ihp 21.5k 16 - 6", 14 - 12pdr, 3 - 3pdr, 3 - 18"TT	Sunk by UC65 26/7/1917 English Channel
304 **Pluton**	Spanish Navy Torpedo boat	12/2/97 - 13/7/97 - 4/11/97	225' x 22'6" x 13'6" x 460disp Triple expansion, 7,200ihp 30k 2 - 14pdr, 2 - 6pdr, 2 - 1pdr, 2 - 14"TT	Sunk Battle of Santiago de Cuba 3/7/1898
305 **Prosperina**	Spanish Navy Torpedo boat	2/3/97 - 25/10/97 - 9/2/98	229' x 22'6" x 13'6" x 467disp Triple expansion 7,200ihp 30k 2 - 14pdr, 2 - 6pdr, 2 - 1pdr, 2 - 14"TT	
306 **Brighton Queen**	Brighton, Worthing & South Coast S.P. Co.	8/3/97 - 20/5/97 - 14/6/97	240'5" x 28'1" x 10' x 603gt 2 cyl. compound diagonal paddle, 273nhp 18.44k	Mined 6/10/1915
307 **Moskva**	Russian Volunteer Fleet	17/9/97 - 23/5/98 - 5/10/98	487' x 58'2" x 37' x 7,267gt Triple expansion, 2,310nhp 20.2k	
308 to 327(Barges)	Chinese Eastern Rly. Co.	1898	180' x 35' x 7'	
328 **Asahi**	Japanese Government Battleship	23/11/97 - 13/3/99 - 23/3/00	400'6"' x 75'3" x 43'7" x 15,200disp Triple expansion 15,000ihp 18k 4 - 12", 14 - 6", 20 - 12pdr, 6 - 3pdr, 6 - 2.5pdr, 4 - 18"TT	Torpedoed and sunk Indo China 25/5/1942
329 **Sheelah** (yacht) *Ariane*	WA Donaldson	9/2/98 - 6/6/98 - 21/6/98	194' x 26'6" x 14'6" x 211gt 63nhp 13.10k	
330 **Vera**	London & SW Rly. Co.	11/3/98 - 4/7/98 - 19/9/98	276' x 35'1" x 15'3" x 1,136gt Triple expansion, 254nhp 19.51k	Scrapped Ward, Pembroke 10/1933
331 **Juno**	Glasgow & SW Rly. Co.	30/3/98 - 17/6/98 - 5/7/98	245' x 29'1" x 10'3" x 592gt 2 cyl. compound diagonal paddle, 325nhp 19.2k	Scrapped Alloa 1932
332 **Fifeshire**	Elderslie SS Co. Ltd	30/4/98 - 15/10/98 - 17/12/98	420' x 54'7" x 32' x 5,672gt Triple expansion, 493nhp	Wrecked 20miles south of Cape Guarda 9/8/1911
333 **Nairnshire** *Broadholme, Gothic Star*	Elderslie SS Co. Ltd	2/5/98 - 16/12/98 - 21/2/99	420'5" x 54'7" x 32' x 5,673gt Triple expansion, 493nhp 12.76k	
334 **Thorn**	Admiralty Destroyer	21/6/99 - 17/3/00 - 6/12/00	222' x 20'6" x 13' x 425disp. Triple expansion, 6,400 ihp 30.27k 1 - 12pdr, 5 - 6pdr, 2 - 18"TT	Scrapped Portsmouth 1919
335 **Tiger**	Admiralty Destroyer	27/7/99 - 19/5/00 - 22/8/00	222' x 20'6" x 13' x 425disp. Triple expansion, 6,400ihp 30.27k 1 - 12pdr, 5 - 6pdr, 2 - 18"TT	Sunk in collision with Berwick Isle of Wight 2/4/1908
336 **Vigilant**	Admiralty Destroyer	15/8/99 - 16/8/00 - 16/1/01	222' x 20'6" x 13' x 380disp. Triple expansion, 6,000ihp 30.29k 1 - 12pdr, 5 - 6pdr, 2 - 18"TT	Scrapped South Alloa SB Co. 10/2/1920

No.	Name	Owner	Dates	Details	Fate
337	Sutlej	Admiralty	13/10/98 - 18/11/99 - 5/2/01	472' x 69'6" x 39'2" x 12,000disp. Triple expansion, 21,000ihp 21.7k	Scrapped Ward, Preston, 1924
		Cressy Class Cruiser (1st Class)		2 - 9.2", 12 - 6", 12 - 12pdr, 3 - 3pdr, 2 - 18"TT	
338	Bacchante	Admiralty	8/3/99 - 21/2/01 - 7/12/01	472' x 69'6" x 39'2" x 12,000disp. Triple expansion, 21,000ihp 21.7k	Scrapped by Castle, Plymouth 1/7/1920
		Cressy Class Cruiser (1st Class)		2 - 9.2", 12 - 6", 12 - 12pdr, 3 - 3pdr, 2 - 18"TT	
339	Saxonia	Cunard SS Co. Ltd.	22/11/98 - 16/12/99 - 21/4/00	580' x 64'2" x 41'7" x 14,221gt Quadruple expansion, 10,000ihp 16.59k	Scrapped Holland 1925
340	Duchess of Fife	London, & SW Rly. Co.	22/3/99 - 28/4/99 - 18/5/99	215' x 26' x 9'6" x 443gt 2 cyl. compound diagonal paddle, 185nhp 16.74k	Scrapped Holland 1929
341	Vaderland Southland	American Line	19/4/99 - 12/7/00 - 28/11/00	560'8" x 60' x 42' x 12,018gt Quadruple expansion, 10,000ihp 16.82k	Torpedoed off northern Ireland 1917
342	Zeeland Northland, Minnesota	American Line	22/5/99 - 24/11/00 - 5/4/01	561'6" x 60' x 42' x 11,667gt Quadruple expansion, 10,000ihp	Scrapped Ward Inverkeithing 20/10/1929
343	Leviathan	Admiralty	22/1/00 - 3/7/01 - 11/3/02	533'6" x 71' x 40' x 14,100disp Triple expansion, 30,000ihp 22.86k	Scrapped Hughes Bolckow Blyth 3/3/1920
		Drake Class Cruiser (1st Class)		2 - 9.2", 16 - 6", 14 - 12pdr, 3 - 3pdr, 2 - 18"TT	
344	Haverford	American Line	1/8/99 - 4/5/01 - 26/8/01	531 x 59'2" x 39' x 11,635gt Triple expansion, 5000ihp 14.71k	Scrapped Italy 1925
345	Merion	American Line	8/5/00 - 26/11/01 - 26/2/02	530'5" x 59'2" x 39' x 11,621gt Triple expansion, 5000ihp 13.07k	Torpedoed in Aegean Sea as dummy HMS Tiger 30/5/1915

JOHN BROWN & COMPANY LIMITED from 22 September 1899

No.	Name	Owner	Dates	Details	Fate
346	Alberta Mykali	London, & S W Rly. Co.	4/10/99 - 3/4/00 - 22/5/00	270' x 35'6" x 22'7" x 1,236gt 4 cylinder Triple expansion, 5000ihp 19.85k	Sunk by German aircraft, Salamis 23/4/41
347		Admiralty		Machinery for armoured cruiser Essex building at Pembroke DYd. Triple expansion, 22,00 ihp 23k	
348	Pannonia	Cunard S. S. Co.Ltd.	22/10/01 - 5/9/02 - 13/2/04	486'5" x 59'3" x 36' x 9,851gt Triple expansion, 811nhp 14.93k	Scrapped 1922
349	Suffolk	Birt, Trinder, Bethell	12/9/01 - 23/5/02 - 15/7/02	460' x 58'2" x 34'3" x 7,573gt Triple expansion, 918nhp 13.57k	Scrapped Boness 1927
350	Energetic	Admiralty	22/10/01 - 22/5/02 - ?	144' x 27'3" x 15'9" x 700disp Triple expansion, 1,250ihp 10k	Scrapped by Shaw at Rainham 1953
		Paddle tug			
351	Mars Marsa	Glasgow & S W Rly. Co.	8/11/01 - 14/3/02 - 4/4/02	200'4" x 26'1" x 9' x 317gt 2 cyl. Comp. diagonal, 172nhp 17.27k	Run down by destroyer off Harwich 18/11/1918.
352	Duchess of Montrose	Caledonian S P Co.	19/12/01 - 8/5/02 - 4/6/02	210'2" x 25'1" x 9' x 322gt 4 cyl. Triple exp. diagonal, 206nhp 16.1k	Mined and sunk off Gravelines 18/3/1917
353	Duke of Connaught	Lancs & Yorks and Lond & N W Rly. Co.	4/2/02 - 20/8/02 - 15/10/02	315' x 38'2" x 25' 6" x 1,680gt Triple expansion, 340nhp 17.58k	Scrapped Holland 1934
354	Essex Van	Federal S. N. Co.	5/5/02 - 1/11/02 - 24/12/02	460' x 58' x 34'3" x 7,016gt Triple expansion, 918nhp 14.09k	Scrapped Boness 1933
355	Sheelah (yacht)	W A Donaldson	8/2/02 - 22/5/02 - 19/8/02	202' x 27' x 14'6" x 466gt Triple expansion, 100nhp 13.68k	
356	Antrim	Admiralty	27/8/02 - 8/10/03 - 19/5/05	473'6" x 68'6" x 38' 5" x 10,850disp Triple expansion, 21,000ihp 22.25k	Scrapped Hughes Bolckow Tyne 19/12/1922
		Devonshire Class Cruiser (1st Class)		4 - 7.5", 6 - 6", 2 - 12pdr, 18 - 3pdr, 2 - 18"TT	
357	Dorset	Birt, Trinder, Bethell	15/8/02 - 14/2/03 - 20/4/03	460' x 58' x 34'3" x 6,990gt Triple expansion, 918nhp 14.36k	Scrapped Boness 1927
358	Somerset	Federal S. N. Co.	17/9/02 - 25/4/03 - 23/6/03	460'5" x 58'2" x 34' 3" x 7,150gt Triple expansion, 918nhp 14.91k	Torpedoed off Ushant 26/7/1917
359	Hindustan	Admiralty	25/10/02 - 19/12/03 - 22/8/05	453'9" x 78' x 42'5" x 17,500disp Triple expansion, 18,000ihp 18.9k	Scrapped Ward Preston 14/10/1923
		King Edward VII Class Battleship		4 - 12", 4 - 9.2", 10 - 6", 14 - 12pdr, 14 - 3pdr, 4 - 18"TT	
360	Kaikoura Giano, Ferrania	New Zealand S. Co.	10/12/02 - 27/6/03 - 10/9/03	460' x 58'2" x 34'3" x 6,998gt Triple expansion, 918nhp 14.27k	Scrapped Savona 1929
361	Kaipara	New Zealand S. Co	13/3/03 - 8/9/03 - 10/11/03	460' x 58' x 34'3" x 7,392gt Triple expansion, 918nhp 14.37k	Sunk by Kaiser Wilhelm der Grosse 16/8/1914
362	Caronia Taiseiyo Maru	Cunard S. S. Co. Ltd.	29/9/03 - 13/7/04 - 4/2/05	650' x 72' x 52' x 19,594gt Triple expansion, 22,000ihp 19.52k	Scrapped Japan 1933
363	Antrim Ramsey Town	Midland Rly. Co.	1/10/03 - 22/3/04 - 19/5/04	330'9" x 42'2" x 25'6" x 2,083gt Triple expansion, 386nhp 21.86k	Scrapped Ward Preston 5/11/1936
364		Admiralty		Machinery for battleship Africa building at Chatham DYd. Triple expansion, 18,000ihp 18.9k	
365	Atalanta	Glasgow & S.W. Rly. Co.	24/11/05 - 23/4/06 - 12/5/06	210'4" x 30'1" x 10'6" x 486gt Turbines (experimental) 1700shp 17.31k	Scrapped Ghent 1945
366	Carmania	Cunard S. S. Co. Ltd	19/5/04 - 21/2/05 - 14/11/05	650' x 72'2" x 44' x 19,524gt Turbines,19,000shp 19.43k	Scrapped Hughes Bolckow Blyth 22/11/1932
367	Lusitania	Cunard S.S.Co.Ltd.	17/8/04 - 7/6/06 - 30/7/07	787' x 87'6" x 60'4.5" x 32,500gt Turbines, 76,000shp 26.7k(t)	Torpedoed off Old Head of Kinsale Ireland 7/5/1915
368	Gwalia Lady Moyra, Brighton Queen	Barry & Bristol C. S.S.Co.	5/10/04 - 24/2/05 - 23/3/05	245' x 29' x 10'3" x 562gt 2 cyl. compound diagonal, 325nhp 19.81k	Sunk Dunkirk June 1940
369	Devonia	Barry & Bristol C. S.S.Co.	8/10/04 - 22/3/05 - 27/3/05	245' x 29' x 10'3" x 563gt 2 cyl. compound diagonal, 325nhp 19.74k	Sunk 28/10/1940
370	St David Rosslare	Fishguard& Rosslare Harbour Rly.Co.	19/4/05 - 25/1/06 - 15/6/06	350' x 41' x 25'11" x 2,387gt Turbines, 11,000shp 22.6k	Scrapped Newport Monmouth 1933
371	St Patrick	Fishguard & Rosslare Harbour Rly.Co.	16/5/05 - 24/2/06 - 3/7/06	350' x 41' x 25'11" x 2,380gt Turbines, 11,000 shp 22.64k	Scrapped Ward, Preston 10/1929 after fire at Fishguard
372	Woodcock Woodnut, Woodcock, Lairdswood, Lochnagar, Rena, Blue Star	G&J Burns Ltd	5/10/05 - 10/4/06 - ?	270'3" x 36' x 25' 1" x 1,523gt Triple expansion, 460nhp 15.53k	Scrapped La Spezia 1952
373	Partridge Partridge II, Partridge, Lairdsloch	G&J Burns Ltd	24/10/05 - 23/5/06 - 5/7/06	270'4" x 36'1" x 25'1" x 1,523gt Triple expansion, 460nhp	Scrapped Dalmuir 1936
374	Inflexible	Admiralty	5/2/06 - 26/6/07 - 2/10/08	567' x 78'5" x 40' 4" x 17,250disp Turbines, 46,947shp 26.48k (trials)	Scrapped Germany 1922
		Invincible Class Battlecruiser		8 - 12", 16 - 4", 7 - Maxim mg, 5 - 18"TT	
375	Northbrook	Indian Government Troopship	28/11/05 - 6/7/06 - 25/9/06	360' x 52'3" x 39' x 5,100gt Triple expansion, 7,200ihp 17.07k	
376	Duke of Albany	Lancs. & Yorks and Lond & N.W.Rly.Co.	26/2/07 - 13/6/07 - 17/9/07	330'5" x 41'1" x 26' x 2,184gt Triple expansion, 7,600ihp 20.53k	Sunk by Submarine 24/8/1916
377	Kenuta Vassilios, Pandelis	Pacific S.N.Co.	22/2/07 - 7/9/07 - 23/10/07	401'3" x 52'2" x 28'6" x 5,005gt. Triple expansion, 2,300ihp 13.17k	
378	Lima	Pacific S.N.Co.	10/4/07 - 6/11/07 - 17/12/07	401' x 52' x 28'6" x 4,946gt Triple expansion, 2,300ihp 13.2k	Wrecked Huamblin Island 5/2/1910
379	Barry Waverley, Snaefell	Barry Rly. Co.	23/2/07 - 4/5/07 - 31/5/07	225'6" x 26'6" x 9' x 497gt 2 cyl. compound diagonal, 1,400ihp 17.31k	Sunk by aircraft 5/7/1941
380	Copenhagen	Great Eastern Rly. Co.	27/5/07 - 22/10/07 - 27/12/07	343' x 43' x 26'5" x 2,600gt Turbines, 7,600shp 20.22k	Torpedoed by sub. off Hinder lightship 5/3/1917
381		Admiralty		Engines only for cruiser Boadicea building at Pembroke DYd. Turbines, 18,000shp 25k	
382	St Andrew Fishguard	Fishguard & Rosslare Co.	12/8/07 - 19/12/07 - 13/4/08	350' x 41' x 25'11" x 2,520gt Turbines, 11,000shp 22.95k	Scrapped by Cashmore, Newport 8/1933
*Harland & Wolff No. 1		Turbine for White Star liner SS Laurentic building at Belfast			
383	Orsova	Orient S.N.Co.	28/5/08 - 7/11/08 - 11/5/09	552' x 61'3" x 46' 12,000gt Triple expansion 11,000ihp 18.05k	Scrapped MacLellan Boness 21/10/1936
384	Munich St Denis	Great Eastern Rly. Co.	7/4/08 - 26/8/08 - 29/10/08	343' x 43' x 26'6" x 2,570gt Turbines 8,000shp 21.03k	Scrapped, Sunderland 1950
385	Rambler	Admiralty	1/9/08 - 21/12/08 - 11/5/09	145' x 27'11.25" x 15' x 690gt 1,250ihp 12.29k	Scrapped Charlestown 1953
386	Golden Eagle	General S. N. Co.	23/2/09 - 17/4/09 - 3/6/09	290' x 32' x 10'9" x 793gt Triple expansion, 455nhp 18.61k	Scrapped by Ward, at Gray's Essex, 18/9/1951

No. Name	Owner	Dates	Details	Fate
387 **Beagle**	Admiralty	27/7/09 - 16/10/09 - 29/4/10	269' x 27' x 16'5" x 860disp Turbines, 14,300shp 27.04k	Scrapped by Fryer, Sunderland 1/11/1921
	Beagle Class Destroyer		1 - 4", 3 - 12pdr, 2 - 21"TT	
388 **Bulldog**	Admiralty	10/8/09 - 13/11/09 - 7/7/10	269' x 27' x 16'5" x 860disp Turbines, 14,300shp 27.08k	Scrapped by Ward, Rainham 21/11/1920
	Beagle Class Destroyer		1 - 4", 3 - 12pdr, 2 - 21"TT	
389 **Foxhound**	Admiralty	20/8/09 - 11/12/09 - 28/5/10	269' x 27' x 16'5" x 860disp Turbines, 14,300shp 27.07k	Sold to Fryer, Sunderland 1/11/1921
	Beagle Class Destroyer		1 - 4", 3 - 12pdr, 2 - 21"TT	
390 **Bristol**	Admiralty	23/3/09 - 23/2/10 - 16/12/10	453' x 47' x 26'9" x 4,800disp Turbines (BC) 22,000shp 26.84k	Sold to Ward, Hayle 9/5/1921
	Bristol Class Cruiser		2 - 6", 10 - 4", 4 - 3pdr, 2 - 18"TT	
391	Admiralty		Engines for battlecruiser **Indefatigable** building at Devonport DYd. 1909/11. Turbines, 43,000shp 25k	
*Harland & Wolff No. 2			Turbines for battleship **Neptune** building at Portsmouth DYd. 1909/10. Turbines 25,000 shp 21k.	
392 **Zealandia**	Huddart Parker & Co.	24/8/09 - 28/12/09 - 3/5/10	410'3" x 54'7" x 23'4" x 6,660gt Quadruple expansion 1,157nhp 15.51k	Lost 19/2/1942
*Harland & Wolff No. 3			Turbine for White Star liner SS **Olympic** building at Belfast	
*Harland & Wolff No. 4			Turbine for White Star liner SS **Titanic** building at Belfast	
393 **Acorn**	Admiralty	1/2/10 - 1/7/10 - 1/11/10	246' x 25'6" x 15' 6" x 800disp Turbines, 13,500shp 26.66k	Scrapped Marple & Gillett, Saltash, 29/11/1921
	Acorn Class Destroyer		2 - 4", 2 - 12pdr, 2 - 21"TT	
394 **Alarm**	Admiralty	22/2/10 - 29/8/10 - 28/3/11	246' x 25'6" x 15' 6" x 800disp Turbines, 13,500shp 27.74k	Scrapped by Ward, Hayle, 1921
	Acorn Class Destroyer		2 - 4", 2 - 12pdr, 2 - 21"TT	
395 **Brisk**	Admiralty	17/5/10 - 20/9/10 - 29/5/11	246' x 25'6" x 15' 6" x 800disp Turbines (BC) 13,500shp 27.91k	Scrapped by Distin, Devonport,15/11/1921
	Acorn Class Destroyer		2 - 4", 2 - 12pdr, 2 - 21"TT	
396 **Doris** (yacht)	SB Joel	8/1/10 - 9/4/10 - 7/7/10	270' x 31' x 19' x 963gt 4 cylinder triple expansion, 2,500ihp 14.94k	
Eileen, Girundia II, Poupela, Al Salimi				
397 **St Petersburg** *Archangel*	Great Eastern Rly. Co.	14/1/10 - 25/4/10 - 27/6/10	331' x 43'2" x 26'6" x 2,450gt Turbines, 9,000shp 21.22k	Lost 16/5/1941
398	Admiralty		Machinery for cruiser **Yarmouth** building at London & Glasgow Sb. Co. Turbines (BC) 22,000shp 25k	
*Harland & Wolff No. 5			Turbine for **Demosthenes** building at Belfast	
399 **Argyllshire** *Clan Urquhart*	Scottish Shire Line	13/5/10 - 27/2/11 - 30/6/11	526' x 61' x 33'3" x 10,392gt Quadruple expansion, 6,500ihp 14.89k	Scrapped by Ward, Briton Ferry, 10/1936
400 **Shropshire** *Roturua*	Federal S. N. Co.	9/6/10 - 27/4/11 - 20/9/11	526'4" x 61'4" x 38'3" x 12,184gt Quadruple expansion, 6,500ihp 14.95k	Torpedoed off St Kilda 11/12/1940
401 **Wiltshire**	Federal S. N. Co.	7/2/11 - 19/12/11 - 15/2/12	526'4" x 61'4" x 38'3" x 12,160gt Quadruple expansion, 6,500ihp 15.25k	Wrecked 31/5/22 Great Barrier Island
402 **Australia**	Admiralty	23/6/10 - 25/10/11 - 18/6/13	590' x 80' x 42' 2.5" 19,200disp Turbines, 44,000shp 26.89k	Scuttled off Sydney 12/4/1924
	Indefatigable Class Battlecruiser		8 - 12", 16 - 4", 4 - 3pdr, 3 - 18"TT	
403 **Orama**	Orient S. N. Co.	8/2/11 - 27/6/11 - 2/11/11	550' x 64' x 42' x 12,927gt Triple expansion/turbines 11,250hp 18.22k	Torpedoed south of Ireland 19/10/1917
404 **Hind**	Admiralty	13/2/11 - 28/7/11 - 21/11/11	246' x 25'9" x 15' 6" x 750disp Turbines, 13,500shp 28.21k	Scrapped Ward, Preston 6/6/1924
	Acheron Class Destroyer		2 - 4", 2 - 12pdr, 2 - 21"TT	
405 **Hornet**	Admiralty	24/1/11 - 20/12/11 - 21/3/12	246' x 25'9" x 15' 6" x 750disp Turbines, 13,500shp 28.77k	Sold Ward, Rainham 9/5/1921
	Acheron Class Destroyer		2 - 4", 2 - 12pdr, 2 - 21"TT	
406 **Hydra**	Admiralty	23/2/11 - 19/2/12 - 19/4/12	246' x 25'9" x 15' 6" x 750disp Turbines, 13,500shp 28.47k	Sold Ward, Portishead 9/5/1921
	Acheron Class Destroyer		2 - 4", 2 - 12pdr, 2 - 21"TT	
407 **Southampton**	Admiralty	14/9/11 - 16/5/12 - 23/11/12	458' x 49'5" x 25' 10" x 5,400disp Turbines (BC) 22,000shp 25.52k	Scrapped Ward Pembroke 7/1926
	Chatham Class Cruiser		8 - 6", 4 - 3pdr, 2 - 21"TT	
408 **Jeanette** (yacht)	Mr H Livesey	7/2/11 - 29/3/11 - 25/5/11	267' x 31' x 18'9" x 931gt Triple expansion, 2,300ihp 15.41k	
Komninos, Eilath				
409 **Aquitania**	Cunard S.S. Co. Ltd.	5/6/11 - 21/4/13 - 10/5/14	901' x 97' x 49'7" x 45,647gt Turbines 62,000shp 23.35k	Scrapped, Metal Industries, Faslane 21/2/1950
410	Admiralty		Machinery for battlecruiser **Queen Mary** building at Palmers Shipbuilding Co. Turbines 78,700shp 28k	
411 **Sapphire**	Duke of Bedford	20/12/11 - 7/3/12 - 18/6/12	242' x 35' x 20'3.5" x 1,707gt Triple expansion, 329nhp 15.18k	Sunk in collision Campbeltown Loch 18/2/1944
Sapphire II, Sapphire, Breda				
412 **Acasta**	Admiralty	16/11/11 - 10/9/12 - 30/11/12	267'6" x 27' x 16'6" x 810disp Turbines (BC) 24,500shp 29.15k	Scrapped by Ward, Hayle, 9/5/1921
	Acasta Class Destroyer		3 - 4", 2 - 21"TT	
413 **Achates**	Admiralty	5/3/12 - 14/11/12 - 27/3/13	267'6" x 27' x 16'6" x 810disp Turbines (BC) 24,500shp 32.88k	Scrapped by Ward, Rainham, 9/5/1921
	Acasta Class Destroyer		3 - 4", 2 - 21"TT	
414 **Ambuscade**	Admiralty	26/3/12 - 25/1/13 - 27/6/13	267'6" x 27' x 16'6" x 810disp. Turbines (BC) 24,500shp 30.63k	Scrapped by Petersen & Albeck, 6/9/1921
	Acasta Class Destroyer		3 - 4", 2 - 21"TT	
415 **Niagara**	Union S.S. New Zealand	2/12/11 - 17/8/12 - 1/3/13	524'7" x 66'3" x 37'6" x 13,415gt Triple exp./Turbine 15,000shp 17.88k	Mined and sunk off Hauraki Gulf N.Z. 18/6/40
416	Chilean Government		Engines only for battleship **Almirante Latorre** (originally called Valparaiso) building at Armstrong Whitworth. Turbines (BC) 37,000shp 23k later *Canada*	
*417 **Preussen**	Hamburg Amerika PAG	14/4/10 - 25/8/10 - 13/12/10	470' x 58'2" x 32'4" x 7,997gt Quadruple expansion, 3,700ihp	Scrapped Japan 1934
Trevithick, Papanui				
418 **Tiger**	Admiralty	20/6/12 - 15/12/13 - 3/10/14	704' x 90'5" x 44'3" x 35,000disp. Turbines (BC) 108,000shp 29k	Scrapped by Ward, Inverkeithing 1932
	Battlecruiser		8 - 13.5", 12 - 6", 2 - 3", 4 - 3pdr, 5mgs, 10 lewis, 4 - 21"TT	
419 **Emperor Peter the Great**	Russian S.N. Co.	25/9/12 - 11/6/13 - 20/10/13	380' x 51'5" x 30'6" x 5,750gt Triple expansion 788nhp 15.03k	Scrapped South Korea 1987
Morskaja II, Jakutia				
420 **Emperor Nicholas I**	Russian S.N.Co.	1/10/12 - 20/9/13 - 10/12/13	380' x 51'6" x 30'6" x 5,146gt Triple expansion 788nhp 15.1k	Lost 2/9/1943
Pierre Loti				
421	Russian Government		Machinery for Russian battleship **Imperatritsa Mariya** building at Russud Yard, Nikolaev. Turbines (BC) 26,500shp 21k	
422	Russian Govt.		Machinery for Russian battleship **Imperator Alexander III** building at Russud Yard, Nikolaev. Turbines (BC) 26,500shp 21k later *Volya*	
423	Chilean Government		Machinery for battleship **Almirante Cochrane** (originally called Santiago) building by Armstrong Whitworth. Geared turbines (BC) 50,000 shp 24k	
424 **Barham**	Admiralty	24/2/13 - 31/12/14 - 10/15	634'6" x 90'6" x 44'9" x 31,100disp. Turbines (BC) 76,575 shp (tr) 24k	Torpedoed Eastern Med. by U331 25/11/1941
	Queen Elizabeth Class Battleship		8 - 15", 14 - 6", 2 - 3", 4 - 3pdr, 4 - 21"TT	
425 **Ormonde**	Orient S.N.Co.	21/10/13 - 10/2/17 - 27/10/17	580'5" x 66'7" x 40'5" x 14,853gt Turbines 17,000 shp	Scrapped Arnott Young, Dalmuir 4/12/1952
426 **Milne**	Admiralty	17/2/14 - 5/10/14 - 7/12/14	273'4" x 26'7" x 16'3" x 860disp. Turbines (BC) 25,000 shp 34k	Scrapped Germany 1921
	M Class Destroyer		3 - 4", 2 - 1pdr, 4 - 21"TT	
427 **Moorsom**	Admiralty	27/2/14 - 20/12/14 - ?	273'4" x 26'7" x 16'3" x 860disp. Turbines (BC) 25,000 shp 34k	Scrapped Germany 1921
	M Class Destroyer		3 - 4", 2 - 1pdr, 4 - 21"TT	

No. Name	Owner	Dates	Details	Fate
428 **Morris**	Admiralty M Class Destroyer	26/3/14 - 19/11/14 - 31/12/14	273'4" x 26'7" x 16'3" x 860disp. Turbines (BC) 25,000 shp 34k 3 - 4", 2 - 1pdr, 4 - 21"TT	Scrapped Germany 1921
429 **Medea** (EX Kriti)	Admiralty Medea Class Destroyer	6/4/14 - 30/1/15 - 22/6/15	273'4" x 26'7" x 16'3" x 860disp. Turbines (BC) 25,000 shp 32k 3 - 4", 4 - 21"TT	Scrapped by Ward, Milford, 9/5/1921
430 **Medusa** (EX Lesvos)	Admiralty Medea Class Destroyer	6/4/14 - 27/3/15 - 1/7/15	273'4" x 26'7" x 16'3" x 860disp. Turbines (BC) 25,000 shp 32k 3 - 4", 4 - 21"TT	Sunk in collision with Laverick North Sea 25/3/16
431 **Pegasus** ex Stockholm	Admiralty Seaplane Carrier	21/5/14 - 9/6/17 - 17/8/17	332' x 43' x 26'6" x 3,070disp. Turbines (BC) 9,500 shp 2 - 3", 2 - 12pdr, 9 aircraft	Scrapped Morecambe 8/1931
432 **Platypus** Penguin, Platypus	Admiralty (RAN) Submarine depot ship	6/4/15 - 28/10/16 - 30/3/17	325' x 44' x 15'8" x 3,455disp. Triple expansion 3,500 ihp 15.5k	Scrapped Australia 1960
433 **Mons**	Admiralty Repeat M Class Destroyer	30/9/14 - 1/5/15 - 14/7/15	273'8" x 26'9" x 16'3" x 860disp. Turbines (BC) 25,000 shp 34k 3 - 4", 1 - 2pdr, 4 - 21"TT	Scrapped Germany 1921
434 **Marne**	Admiralty Repeat M Class Destroyer	30/9/14 - 29/5/15 - 14/7/15	273'8" x 26'9" x 16'3" x 860disp. Turbines (BC) 25,000 shp 34k 3 - 4", 1 - 2pdr, 4 - 21"TT	Scrapped Germany 1921
435 **Canterbury**	Admiralty Cambrian Class Cruiser	14/10/14 - 21/12/15 - 9/5/16	446' x 41'6" x 16'3" x 3,750disp. Turbines 40,000 shp 29k 2 - 6", 8 - 4", 4 - 3pdr, 1 - 13pdr, 2 - 21"TT	Scrapped Metal Industries Rosyth 5/10/1934
436 **E35**	Admiralty E Class Submarine	7/12/14 - 20/5/16 - 14/7/16	182'6" x 22'7" x 15' x 807disp. Diesels/elec.1,600 hp/840 hp 15k/9k 5 - 18"TT, 1 - 12pdr.	Scrapped Ellis & Co. Newcastle 6/9/1922
437 **E36**	Admiralty Submarine	7/1/15 - 16/9/16 - 16/11/16	182'6" x 22'7" x 15' x 807disp. Diesels/elec.1,600 hp/840 hp 15k/9k 5 - 18"TT, 1 - 12pdr.	Lost North Sea 19/1/1917
438 **E50**	Admiralty Submarine	29/6/15 - 13/11/16 - 23/1/17	182'6" x 22'7" x 15' x 807disp. Diesels/elec.1,600hp/840hp 15k/9k 5 - 18"TT, 1 - 12pdr.	Lost North Sea 31/1/1918
439 **Mameluke**	Admiralty Repeat M Class Destroyer	23/12/14 - 14/8/15 - 30/10/15	273'8" x 26'9" x 16'3" x 860disp. Turbines (BC) 25,000shp 34k 3 - 4", 1 - 2pdr, 4 - 21"TT	Sold Cohen. Scrapped Germany 22/9/1921
440 **Ossory**	Admiralty Repeat M Class Destroyer	23/12/14 - 9/10/15 - 4/12/15	273'8" x 26'9" x 16'3" x 860disp. Turbines (BC) 25,000shp 34k 3 - 4", 1 - 2pdr, 4 - 21"TT	Scrapped Germany 1921
441	Admiralty	Engines for destroyer **Noble** building by Alexander Stephen. Turbines (BC) 25,000shp 34k		
442	Admiralty	Engines for destroyer **Nomad** building by Alexander Stephen. Turbines (BC) 25,000shp 34k		
443 **Repulse**	Admiralty Renown Class Battlecruiser	25/1/15 - 8/1/16 - 14/8/16	794' x 90' x 40' 10" x 30,835disp. Turbines (BC) 119,025shp 31.72k (t) 6 - 15", 17 - 4", 2 - 3", 4 - 3pdr, 2 - 21"TT	Sunk off Malaya 10/12/1941
444 **Napier**	Admiralty Repeat M Class Destroyer	6/7/15 - 27/11/15 - 22/1/16	273'8" x 26'9" x 16'3" x 860disp. Turbines (BC) 25,000shp 34k 3 - 4", 1 - 2pdr, 4 - 21"TT	Sold Slough TC. Scrapped Germany 8/11/1921
445 **Narborough**	Admiralty Repeat M Class Destroyer	13/7/15 - 2/3/16 - 29/4/16	273'8" x 26'9" x 16'3" x 860disp. Turbines (BC) 25,000shp 34k 3 - 4", 1 - 2pdr, 4 - 21"TT	Wrecked off Orkney Islands 12/1/1918
446	Admiralty	Half set of turbine machinery for battlecruiser **Furious** building by Armstrong Whitworth to order of the Wallsend Slipway & Engineering Co. Ltd. (BC) 90,000 shp. 31.5k		Scrapped Arnott Young, Dalmuir 15/3/1948
447 **Penn**	Admiralty Repeat M Class Destroyer	9/6/15 - 8/4/16 - 31/5/16	273'8" x 26'9" x 16'3" x 860disp. Turbines (BC) 25,000shp 34k 3 - 4", 1 - 2pdr, 4 - 21"TT	Scrapped W Burden 1921
448 **Peregrine**	Admiralty Repeat M Class Destroyer	9/6/15 - 29/5/16 - 10/7/16	273'8" x 26'9" x 16'3" x 860disp. Turbines (BC) 25,000shp 34k 3 - 4", 1 - 2pdr, 4 - 21"TT	Scrapped Cashmore, Newport, 5/11/1921
449 **Romola**	Admiralty R Class Destroyer	25/8/15 - 14/5/16 - 17/8/16	275' x 26'9" x 16'3" x 975disp. Turbines (BC) 27,000shp 36k 3 - 4", 1 - 2pdr, 4 - 21"TT	Scrapped Troon 1930
450 **Rowena**	Admiralty R Class Destroyer	25/8/15 - 1/7/16 - 29/9/16	275' x 26'9" x 16'3" x 975disp. Turbines (BC) 27,000shp 36k 3 - 4", 1 - 2pdr, 4 - 21"TT	Scrapped Ward, Milford Haven, 1937
451 **Restless**	Admiralty R Class Destroyer	22/9/15 - 12/8/16 - 21/10/16	275' x 26'9" x 16'3" x 975disp. Turbines(BC) 27,000shp 36k 3 - 4", 1 - 2pdr, 4 - 21"TT	Scrapped Ward, Briton Ferry 11/1936
452 **Rigorous**	Admiralty R Class Destroyer	22/9/15 - 30/9/16 - 27/11/16	275' x 26'9" x 16'3" x 975disp. Turbines (BC) 27,000shp 36k 3 - 4", 1 - 2pdr, 4 - 21"TT	Scrapped Cashmore, Newport 5/11/1926
453	Admiralty	Geared turbines (BC) for K Class **K1** submarine building at Portsmouth Dyd. 10,500shp		
454	Admiralty	Geared turbines (BC) for K Class **K2** submarine building at Portsmouth Dyd. 10,500shp		
455 **Simoom**	Admiralty R Class Destroyer	23/5/16 - 30/10/16 - 22/12/16	275' x 26'9" x 16'3" x 975disp. Turbines (BC) 27,000shp 36k 3 - 4", 1 - 2pdr, 4 - 21"TT	Sunk North Sea 23/1/1917
*456 **Windsor Castle**	Union Castle Mail S.S. Co.	4/6/19 - 9/3/21 - 10/3/22	630' x 72'3" x 41'5" x 19,600gt Geared turbines 14,500shp 18k	Lost 23/3/1943
457 **Tarpon**	Admiralty R Class Destroyer	12/4/16 - 10/3/17 - 26/4/17	276' x 26'9" x 16'3" x 900disp. Turbines (BC) 27,000shp 3 - 4", 1 - 2pdr, 4 - 21"TT	Scrapped Cashmore, Newport, 8/1927
458 **Telemachus**	Admiralty R Class Destroyer	12/4/16 - 21/4/17 - 16/6/17	276' x 26'9" x 16'3" x 900disp. Turbines 27,000shp 3 - 4", 1 - 2pdr, 4 - 21"TT	Scrapped Hughes Bolckow, Blyth 8/1927
459 **Ceres**	Admiralty Cruiser Class cruiser	26/4/16 - 24/3/17 - 15/6/17	450' x 43'6" x 24' 9" x 4,190disp. Turbines 39,425shp 29.1k 5 - 6", 2 - 3", 4 - 3pdr, 8 - 21"TT	Scrapped Hughes Bolckow, Blyth 12/7/1946
460 **Hood**	Admiralty Battlecruiser	1/9/16 - 22/8/18 - 15/5/20 c	860' 7" x 104' 2" x 40' 10" 46,680disp. Geared turbines (BC) 151,280shp 32.07k(t) 8 x 15", 12 x 5.5", 4 x 4", 6 x 21"TT	Sunk 24/5/1941 Denmark Straits
461 **Skate**	Admiralty R Class Destroyer	12/1/16 - 11/1/17 - 19/2/17	275' x 26'9" x 16'3" x 975disp. Turbines (BC) 27,000shp 36k 3 - 4", 1 - 2pdr, 4 - 21"TT	Scrapped Newport 1947
462 **Vanoc**	Admiralty V Class Destroyer	20/9/16 - 14/6/17 - 15/8/17	312' x 29'6" x 18' 3" x 1,490disp. Geared turbines (BC) 27,000shp 34k 4 - 4", 1 - 3", 4 - 21"TT	Lost 1946 en route to shipbreakers
463 **Vanquisher**	Admiralty V Class Destroyer	29/9/16 - 18/8/17 - 2/10/17	312' x 29'6" x 18' 3" x 1,490disp. Geared turbines (BC) 27,000shp 34k 4 - 4", 1 - 3", 4 - 21"TT	Scrapped Charlestown 1948
464 **Montcalm** Wolfe	Canadian Pacific Rly.	10/1/19 - 3/7/20 - 15/12/21	575' x 70'2" x 43'3" x 16,418gt Geared turbines 14,000 shp 17.5k	Scrapped, Dalmuir 1952
465 **Montclare**	Canadian Pacific Rly.	17/9/19 - 17/12/21 - 2/8/22	575" x 70'6" x 43'3" x 16,314gt Geared turbines 14,000 shp 17k	Scrapped Inverkeithing 1958

No.	Name	Owner	Dates	Details	Fate
466	**Wakeful**	Admiralty W Class Destroyer	17/1/17 - 6/10/17 - 16/11/17	312' x 29'6" x 18' 3" x 1,490disp. Geared turbines (BC) 27,000shp 34k	Sunk off Dunkirk 30/5/1940
467	**Watchman**	Admiralty W Class Destroyer	17/1/17 - 1/12/17 - 26/1/18	312' x 29'6" x 18' 3" x 1,490disp. Geared turbines (BC) 27,000shp 34k	Scrapped 1945
468	**War Thistle** *Emilie D*	Ship Controller	2/3/17 - 1/9/17 - 9/10/17	412' x 52'2" x 31' x 5,152gt Triple expansion 2,500ihp	Wrecked near Finisterre 8/10/1927
469	**War Hermit** *Anatina, Mindanao*	Anglo Saxon Petroleum	12/3/17 - 28/3/18 - 29/3/18	412' x 52'3" x 31' x 5,256gt Triple expansion 2,500ihp (engine constructed by Fullerton Hodgart & Barclay, Paisley)	Sunk Japanese aircraft Mindoro Island 10/2/1942
470	**War Rider** *Fort de Troyon, Eridano, Al Kuwait, Spetsai Sailor*	Chargeurs Reunis	7/9/17 - 6/9/18 - ?/1/19	412' x 52'4" x 31' x 5,269t Triple expansion 2,500ihp	Sunk off Aden 11/10/58 after springing leak
471	**War Crane** *Bodnant*	African S.S. Co.	8/4/18 - 3/6/19 - 2/7/19	412' x 52'3" x 31' x 5,258t Triple expansion 2,500ihp	Sunk after collision south of Iceland 30/12/40
472	**Simoom**	Admiralty S Class Destroyer	2/7/17 - 26/1/18 - 12/3/18	276' x 26'9" x 16' 3" x 1,075disp. Geared turbines (BC) 27,000shp 36k 3 - 4", 1 - 2pdr, 4 - 21"TT	Scrapped Metal Industries, Charlestown 2/31
473	**Scimitar**	Admiralty S Class Destroyer	30/5/17 - 27/2/18 - 29/4/18	276' x 26'9" x 16' 3" x 1,075disp. Geared turbines (BC) 27,000shp 36k 3 - 4", 1 - 2pdr, 4 - 21"TT	Scrapped Ward, Briton Ferry 1947
474	**Scotsman**	Admiralty S Class Destroyer	10/12/17 - 30/3/18 - 21/5/18	276' x 26'9" x 16' 3" x 1,075disp. Geared turbines (BC) 27,000shp 36k 3 - 4", 1 - 2pdr, 4 - 21"TT	Scrapped Ward, Briton Ferry 1937
475	**Scout**	Admiralty S Class Destroyer	25/10/17 - 27/4/18 - 15/6/18	276' x 26'9" x 16' 3" x 1,075disp. Geared turbines (BC) 27,000shp 36k 3 - 4", 1 - 2pdr, 4 - 21"TT	Scrapped Ward, Briton Ferry 1946
476	**Scythe**	Admiralty S Class Destroyer	4/1/18 - 25/5/18 - 8/7/18	276' x 26'9" x 16' 3" x 1,075disp. Geared turbines (BC) 27,000shp 36k 3 - 4", 1 - 2pdr, 4 - 21"TT	Scrapped Newport 1931
477	**Seabear**	Admiralty S Class Destroyer	13/12/17 - 6/7/18 - 7/9/18	276' x 26'9" x 16' 3" x 1,075disp. Geared turbines (BC) 27,000shp 36k 3 - 4", 1 - 2pdr, 4 - 21"TT	Scrapped, Ward (Grays) 2/31
478	**Seafire**	Admiralty S Class Destroyer	27/2/18 - 10/8/18 - 24/10/18	276' x 26'9" x 16' 3" x 1,075disp. Geared turbines (BC) 27,000shp 36k 3 - 4", 1 - 2pdr, 4 - 21"TT	Scrapped, Ward, Inverkeithing 7/36
479	**Searcher**	Admiralty S Class Destroyer	30/3/18 - 11/9/18 - 25/11/18	276' x 26'9" x 16' 3" x 1,075disp. Geared turbines (BC) 27,000shp 36k 3 - 4", 1 - 2pdr, 4 - 21"TT	Scrapped, Ward, Barrow 3/38
480	**Seawolf**	Admiralty S Class Destroyer	30/4/18 - 2/11/18 - 28/1/19	276' x 26'9" x 16' 3" x 1,075disp. Geared turbines (BC) 27,000shp 36k 3 - 4", 1 - 2pdr, 4 - 21"TT	Scrapped, Newport following collision 1930
481		Admiralty		Machinery for destroyer **Sesame** building at Wm. Denny. Geared turbines (BC) 27,000shp 36k	
482	**Venomous** (ex Venom)	Admiralty Modified W Class Destroyer	31/5/18 - 21/12/18 - 6/19	312' x 29'6" x 18' 3" x 1,508disp. Geared turbines (BC) 27,000shp 34k 4 - 4.7", 1 - 3" or 2 - 2pdr, 6 - 21"TT	Scrapped, Charlestown 1946
483	**Verity**	Admiralty Modified W Class Destroyer	17/5/18 - 19/3/19 - 17/9/19	312' x 29'6" x 18' 3" x 1,508disp. Geared turbines (BC) 27,000shp 34k 4 - 4.7", 1 - 3" or 2 - 2pdr, 6 - 21"TT	Scrapped, Newport 1945
484	**Enterprise**	Admiralty Emerald Class Cruiser	28/6/18 - 23/12/19 - 9/4/20	570' x 54'6" x 16'6" x 7,558disp. Geared turbines (BC) 80,000shp 33k 7 - 6", 5 - 4", 4 - 3pdr, 3 -2pdr, 12 - 21"TT	Scrapped, Newport 1946
485	**Veteran**	Admiralty Modified W Class Destroyer	30/8/18 - 26/4/19 - 12/11/19	312' x 29'6" x 18' 3" x 1,508disp. Turbines 27,000shp 34k 4 - 4.7", 1 - 3" or 2 - 2pdr, 6 - 21"TT	Sunk, 30/10/42
486	**Vigo**	Admiralty Modified W Class Destroyer	CANCELLED	312' x 29'6" x 18' 3" x 1,508disp. Turbines 27,000shp 34k 4 - 4.7", 1 - 3" or 2 - 2pdr, 6 - 21"TT	
487	**Wistful** (ex Vigorous)	Admiralty Modified W Class Destroyer	CANCELLED	312' x 29'6" x 18' 3" x 1,500disp. Turbines 27,000shp 34k 4 - 4.7", 1 - 3" or 2 - 2pdr, 6 - 21"TT	
488	**Virulent**	Admiralty Modified W Class Destroyer	CANCELLED	312' x 29'6" x 18' 3" x 1,500disp. Turbines 27,000shp 34k 4 - 4.7", 1 - 3" or 2 - 2pdr, 6 - 21"TT	
489	**Volage**	Admiralty Modified W Class Destroyer	CANCELLED	312' x 29'6" x 18' 3" x 1,500disp. Turbines 27,000shp 34k 4 - 4.7", 1 - 3" or 2 - 2pdr, 6 - 21"TT	
490	**Volcano**	Admiralty Modified W Class Destroyer	CANCELLED	312' x 29'6" x 18' 3" x 1,500disp. Turbines 27,000shp 34k 4 - 4.7", 1 - 3" or 2 - 2pdr, 6 - 21"TT	
491	**Bata** *Tower Abbey, Willandra, Utide Maru*	Elder Dempster Lines	19/12/18 - 10/9/19 - 14/10/19	412' x 52'3" x 31' x 5,100gt Triple expansion 2,500ihp (by H&W)	Sunk by submarine USS Sargo 29/2/1944
492	**Franconia**	Cunard S.S. Co. Ltd.	12/8/19 - 21/10/22 - 28/5/23	624' x 73'8" x 45' x 20,341gt DR Geared Turbines (BC) 13,500 shp 16k	Scrapped Inverkeithing 1956
493	**Antwerp**	Great Eastern Rly. Co.	14/3/19 - 25/10/19 - 19/5/20	321'6" x 43'1" x 26'6" x 2,957gt Turbines 10,000 shp	Scrapped Milford Haven, 1951
494	**Bruges**	Great Eastern Rly. Co.	30/4/19 - 20/3/20 - 25/9/20	321'6" x 43'1" x 26'6" x 2,949gt Turbines 10,000 shp	Sunk off Le Havre 11/6/1940
495	**Alaunia**	Cunard S.S.Co.Ltd.	8/4/20 - 7/2/25 - 3/7/25	538' x 65'2" x 43' x 14,030t Geared Turbines 8,500 shp 15k	Scrapped Blyth 1957
496				Turbines 2,700 shp for **British Monarch** building by Napier & Miller at Old Kilpatrick.	
497	**Restless** (yacht) *Sans Peur, King Faisal I*	Alex. S Cochran	7/7/22 - 17/2/23 - 7/4/23	200' x 29'6" x 15'5" x 742gt Triple expansion 1,000 ihp	
498	**Mirror**	Eastern Telegraph Co.	2/11/22 - 12/5/23 - 12/7/23	271'3" x 37'2" x 18'1" x 1,869t Triple expansion 1,500 ihp	Scrapped Belgium 25/11/1964
499	**Norseman**	Western Telegraph Co.	22/11/22 - 26/9/23 - 29/11/23	271'3" x 37'2" x 18' x 1,892gt Triple expansion	Scrapped Belgium 3/1965
500	**Oronsay**	Orient Steam Nav. Co.	1/3/23 - 14/8/24 - 14/1/25	659' x 75'2" x 33' x 20,000gt SR Geared Turbines (BC) 20,000 shp 20k	Sunk by torpedo 9/10/1942
501				Sulzer diesel 2 x 3,000 bhp for **Limerick** building by W. Hamilton at Port Glasgow	
502				Fullagar Diesel 2,500 bhp each for two ships, **Florida Maru** and **Cuba Maru,** building by Kawasaki Dockyard Co. at Kobe	
503	**Thalassa** (yacht) *Suilven*	Eugene Higgins, New York	22/10/23 - 23/4/24 - 17/6/24	182'1" x 29'2" x 16'3" x 876gt Triple expansion 1,000 ihp	
504	**Princess Kathleen**	Canadian Pacific Rly.	12/3/24 - 27/9/24 - 22/12/24	350'1" x 60'1" x 20' x 5,875gt Turbines 13,500 shp 22k	Wrecked Lena Point, Alaska 7/9/1952
505	**Princess Marguerite**	Canadian Pacific Rly.	12/3/24 - 29/11/24 - 25/3/25	350'1" x 60'1" x 20' x 5,875gt Turbines 13,500 shp 22k	Sunk 17/8/1942
506	**Lumen** *Empire Light*	H E Moss & Co.	11/7/24 - 23/4/25 - 9/9/25	420'1" x 54'4" x 32'8" x 6,483gt Sulzer diesel 2,500 bhp	Torpedoed, N Atlantic, 7/3/1943
507	**British Diplomat** *Empire Diplomat*	British Tanker Co.	29/4/25 - 2/4/26 - 30/6/26	420'2" x 54'4" x 32'8" x 6,484gt Sulzer diesel 2,500 bhp	Scrapped Gateshead 1946
508	**LochKatrine**	Royal Mail S.P.Co.	16/2/20 - 5/8/21 -1/22	485'4" x 62'3" x 38'6" x 9,409gt Diesel (by H&W) 4,600 bhp	Sunk 3/8/1942
509	**St Julien**	Great Western Rly.	3/7/24 - 23/2/25 - 2/5/25	291'6" x 40'1" x 24'8" x 1,943gt Turbines 4,500 shp	Scrapped Belgium 14/3/1961
510	**St Helier**	Great Western Rly.	4/7/24 - 26/3/25 - 4/6/25	291'6" x 40'1" x 24'8" x 1,943gt Turbines 4,500 shp	Scrapped Ghent 29/12/1960

No. Name	Owner	Dates	Details	Fate
511	Quadruple expansion machinery for **Imperial Monarch** building by Napier & Miller at Old Kilpatrick			
512 **Australia**	Royal Australian Navy Kent Class Cruiser	9/5/25 - 17/3/27 - 24/4/28	630' x 68'4" x 43'6" x 13,630disp. Geared turbines (BC) 80,000shp 31.5k 8 - 8", 4 - 4", 4 - 3pdr, 4 - 2pdr, 8 - 21"TT	Scrapped Barrow 1955
513 **Canberra**	Royal Australian Navy Kent Class Cruiser	23/6/25 - 31/5/27 - 10/7/28	630' x 68'4" x 43'6" x 13,630disp. Geared turbines (BC) 80,000shp 31.5k 8 - 8", 4 - 4", 4 - 3pdr, 4 - 2pdr, 8 - 21"TT	Sunk 8/8/1942 off Solomon Islands
514 **Avila** *Avila Star*	Blue Star Line (1920) Ltd	14/9/25 - 22/9/26 - 10/3/27	550'4" x 68'2" x 42'6" x 12,872gt SR Geared turbines 8,400shp 17k(t)	Sunk by U201 in Atlantic 5/7/1942
515 **Avelona** *Avelona Star*	Blue Star Line (1920) Ltd	21/10/25 - 6/12/26 - 5/5/27	550'4" x 68'2" x 42'6" x 12,858gt SR Geared turbines 8,400shp 17k(t)	Sunk by U43 in North Atlantic 31/6/1940
516 **Rangitiki**	New Zealand Ship. Co.	27/4/27 - 29/8/28 - 26/1/29	553' x 70'2" x 43' 3" x 16,755gt Sulzer diesels 2 x 5,000 bhp 16k	Scrapped Spain 7/1962
517 **Rangitata** *Rang*	New Zealand Ship. Co.	25/5/27 - 26/3/29 - 15/10/29	553' x 70'2" x 43' 3" x 16,737gt Sulzer diesele 2 x 5,000 bhp 16k	Scrapped Yugoslavia 3/1962
518 **Duchess of Bedford** *Empress of France*	Canadian Pacific Rly.	6/1/27 - 24/1/28 - 25/5/28	601' x 75' x 53' x 20,123gt SR Geared turbines 21,000 shp 19k	Scrapped Newport 12/1960
*519 **Ekari** *Stanleyville*	African Steamship Co.	31/3/19 - 12/1/20 - 13/4/20	405'2" x 54'2" x 35'3" x 6,741gt DR Geared turbines 2,500 shp	Scrapped Japan 1933
520 **Princess Elaine**	Canadian Pacific Rly.	8/4/27 - 26/10/27 - 22/2/28	291' x 48'1" x 27' 6" x 2,125gt SR Geared turbines (BC) 934nhp 19.5k	Sold for use as floating restaurant 8/1963
521	Quadruple expansion machinery for **Caledonian Monarch** building by Napier & Miller at Old Kilpatrick 370nhp			
522 **Rangitane**	New Zealand S. Co.	11/2/28 - 27/5/29 - 8/10/29	553' x 70'2" x 43' 3" x 16,733gt Sulzer Diesels 2 x 5,000 bhp 16k	Sunk 26/11/1940
523 **Duchess of Richmond** *Empress of Canada*	Canadian Pacific Rly.	15/6/27 - 18/6/28 - 20/12/28	600' x 75' x 53' x 20,022gt Geared turbines 21,000 shp 19k	Destroyed by fire at Gladstone dock 25/1/1953 Scrapped in Italy 1954
524 **Duchess of York**	Canadian Pacific Rly.	10/8/27 - 28/9/28 - 2/3/29	601' x 75' x 53' x 20,500gt Geared turbines 21,000 shp 19k	Sunk by bombers off Spanish coast 11/7/1943
525 **Acasta**	Admiralty A Class Destroyer	13/8/28 - 8/8/29 - 6/2/30	323' x 32'3" x 19' x 1,330disp. Geared turbines (BC) 34,000shp 35k 4 - 4.7", 2 - 2pdr, 8 - 21"TT	Sunk by Scharnhorst & Gneisenau 8/6/1940
526 **Achates**	Admiralty A Class Destroyer	11/9/28 - 4/10/29 - 27/3/30	323' x 32'3" x 19' x 1,330disp. Geared turbines (BC) 34,000shp 35k 4 - 4.7", 2 - 2pdr, 8 - 21"TT	Sunk 31/12/1942
527 **Vienna**	L. N. E. Rly.	20/6/28 - 10/4/29 - 27/6/29	365' x 50' x 27' x 4,218gt Geared turbines 1,520nhp	Scrapped Ghent 5/9/1960
528 **Prague**	L. N. E. Rly.	2/3/29 - 18/11/29 - 14/2/30	350'8" x 50'1" x 27' x 4,220gt Geared turbines 1,520nhp	Scrapped Barrow 14/3/1948 after fire at Clydebank
529 **Amsterdam**	L. N. E. Rly.	12/4/29 - 30/1/30 - 11/4/30	365' x 50' x 27' x 4,100gt Geared turbines 1,520nhp	Sunk 7/8/1944
530 **Empress of Britain**	Canadian Pacific Rly.	28/11/28 - 11/6/30 - 5/4/31	760' x 97'6" x 60'9" x 42,500gt Geared turbines 66,500 shp 25.5k	Sunk off Ireland 28/10/1940 after being bombed and torpedoed
531 **Basilisk**	Admiralty B Class Destroyer	19/8/29 - 6/8/30 - 19/2/31	323' x 32'3" x 19' 1,330disp. Geared turbines (BC) 34,000shp 35k 4 - 4.7", 2 - 2pdr, 8 - 21"TT	Sunk off Denmark 1/6/1940
532 **Beagle**	Admiralty B Class Destroyer	11/10/29 - 26/9/30 - 9/3/31	323' x 32'3" x 19' 1,330disp. Geared turbines (BC) 34,000shp 35k 4 - 4.7", 2 - 2pdr, 8 - 21"TT	Scrapped Rosyth 1946
533 **Nahlin** (yacht) *Luceafarul, Libertatea*	Lady Yule	23/9/29 - 28/4/30 - 7/7/30	296' x 36'3" x 21' x 2,050gt Geared turbines (BC) 4,000shp 17.5k	
534 **Queen Mary**	Cunard S.S.Co.	1/12/30 - 26/9/34 - 24/3/36	1,019'6" x 118'7" x 92' x 81,237gt Geared turbines 160,000shp 32k(t)	Museum/Hotel ship, Long Beach California
535	Number originaly set aside for Queen Elizabeth but assigned to sloop engines and valve gearing			
536 **Halcyon**	Admiralty Halcyon Class Minesweeper	24/3/33 - 20/12/33 - 18/4/34	245'6" x 33'6" x 16' x 815disp. Compound 1,770ihp 16.5k 2 - 4"	Scrapped Ward, Milford Haven 19/4/1950
537 **Skipjack**	Admiralty Halcyon Class Minesweeper	24/3/33 - 18/1/34 - 3/5/34	245'6" x 33'6" x 16' x 815disp. Compound 1,770ihp 16.5k 2 - 4"	Sunk at Dunkirk 1/6/1940
538 **Fortune** *Saskatchewan*	Admiralty F Class Destroyer	25/7/33 - 29/8/34 - 27/4/35	329' x 33'3" x 19' 6" x 1,350disp. Turbines 36,000shp 36k 4 - 4.7", 8 - 21"TT	Scrapped 1946, Sydney
539 **Foxhound** *Qu'Appelle*	Admiralty F Class Destroyer	21/8/33 - 12/10/34 - 21/6/35	329' x 33'3" x 19' 6" x 1,350disp. Turbines 36,000shp 36k 4 - 4.7", 8 - 21"TT	Scrapped 1947, Sydney
540 **Enchantress** *Lady Enchantress*	Admiralty Bittern Class Sloop	9/3/34 - 21/12/34 - 4/4/35	282' x 37' x 17'6" x 1,085disp. Geared turbines (BC) 3,300shp 18.75k 2 - 4.7", 4 - 3pdr	Scrapped Clayton & Davie, Dunston 16/2/1952
541 **Port Wyndham**	Port Line Ltd.	10/2/34 - 23/10/34 - 23/1/35	511' x 65'2" x 43'10" x 8,702gt Doxford diesel 9,400 bhp	Scrapped Far East 11/1966
542 **Southampton** (ex *Polyphemus*)	Admiralty Southampton Class Cruiser	21/11/34 - 10/3/36 - 6/3/37	591'6" x 61'8" x 33'3" x 11,350disp. Geared turbines 75,000shp 32k 12 - 6", 8 - 4", 4 - 3pdr, 8 - 2pdr, 6 - 21"TT, 3 aircraft	Bombed and Sunk 10/1/1941 east of Malta
543	Admiralty		Machinery for cruiser **Birmingham** building at Devonport DYd. Geared turbines 75,000shp	
544 **Comanchee** *Esso Plymouth*	Anglo American Oil Co.	29/7/35 - 9/1/36 - 5/3/36	469'3" x 61'3" x 32'2" x 6,837gt Doxford diesel 3,350 bhp	Scrapped Norway 8/1962
545 **Essex** *Paringa, Norfolk*	P&O S.N. Co.	14/12/35 - 17/9/36 - 17/12/36	537'3" x 70'5" x 47'6" x 11,080gt Doxford diesels 13,250 bhp	Scrapped Yokosuka Japan 7/62
546 **Sussex** *Palana, Cambridge*	P&O S.N. Co.	7/1/36 - 17/11/36 - 10/2/37	537'3" x 70'5" x 47'6" x 11,073gt Doxford Diesels 13,250 bhp	Scrapped Sakai Japan 8/62
547 **Icarus**	Admiralty I Class Destroyer	9/3/36 - 26/11/36 - 3/5/37	312' x 33' x 19'3" x 1,370disp. Geared turbines 34,000 shp 36k 4 - 4.7", 10 - 21"TT	Scrapped Troon 1946
548 **Ilex**	Admiralty I Class Destroyer	16/3/36 - 28/1/37 - 7/7/37	312' x 33' x 19'3" x 1,370disp. Geared turbines 34,000 shp 36k 4 - 4.7", 10 - 21"TT	Scrapped Italy 1948
549 **Maidstone**	Admiralty Maidstone Class Submarine Depot Ship	17/8/36 - 21/10/37 - 5/5/38	531' x 73' x 44' x 11,815disp. Geared turbines 7,000 shp 17k 8 - 4.5", 8 - 2pdr	Scrapped by Ward at Inverkeithing 1978
550 **San Juan**	Argentine Navy Buenos Aires Class Destroyer	7/10/36 - 24/6/37 - 18/8/38	323' x 33' x 19'3" x 1,375disp. Geared turbines 34,000 shp 35k 4 - 4.7", 8 - 2pdr, 8 - 21"TT	Scrapped 1973
551 **San Luis**	Argentine Navy Buenos Aires Class Destroyer	17/10/36 - 24/8/37 - 18/8/38	323' x 33' x 19'3" x 1,375disp. Geared turbines 34,000 shp 35k 4 - 4.7", 8 - 2pdr, 8 - 21"TT	Scrapped 1971
552 **Queen Elizabeth** *Seawise University*	Cunard White Star Ltd.	4/12/36 - 27/9/38 - 2/40	1,031' 118'7" x 92'6" x 83,673gt Geared turbines 160,000 shp 30k	Sunk Hong Kong after fire 1/72
553	Doxford diesel engines for **Kaikoura** building at Alexander Stephen, Linthouse.			
554 **Duke of York**	Admiralty King George V Class Battleship	5/5/37 - 28/2/40 - 4/11/41	745' x 103' x 50'8" x 42,970f.l.disp. Geared turbines 111,200 shp 28.6k(t) 10 - 14", 16 - 5.25", 48 - 2pdr, 6 - 20mm, 2 aircraft	Scrapped Faslane 18/2/58
555 **Forth**	Admiralty Maidstone Class Submarine Depot Ship	30/6/37 - 11/8/38 - 14/5/39	574' x 73' x 47' 6" x 11,815disp. Geared turbines (BC) 7,000 shp 17k 8 - 4.5", 8 - 2pdr	Scrapped Medway 1985

No. Name	Owner	Dates	Details	Fate
556 **Jackal**	Admiralty J Class Destroyer	24/9/37 - 25/10/38 - 13/4/39	348' x 35' x 20' 6" x 1,690disp. Geared turbines 40,000 shp 35.32k 6 - 4.7", 4 - 2pdr, 10 - 21"TT	Sunk, eastern Mediterranean 11/5/42
557 **Javelin**	Admiralty J Class Destroyer	11/10/37 - 21/12/38 - 8/6/39	348' x 35' x 20' 6" x 1,690disp. Geared turbines 40,000 shp 36k 6 - 4.7", 4 - 2pdr, 10 - 21"TT	Scrapped Troon 1949
558 **Fiji**	Admiralty Fiji Class Cruiser	30/3/38 - 31/5/39 - 17/5/40	555' x 62' x 32' x 8,000disp. Geared turbines 72,500 shp 32k 12 - 6", 8 - 4", 8 - 2pdr, 6 - 21"TT, 2 aircraft	Sunk, Crete 22/5/41
559 **Suffolk**	Federal S.N.Co.	19/8/38 - 3/5/39 - 11/9/39	551'4" x 70'5" x 47'6" x 11,145gt Doxford diesel 13,250 bhp 17k	Scrapped Kaohsiung 9/68
560 **Hecla**	Admiralty Tyne Class Destroyer Depot Ship	25/1/39 - 14/3/40 - 6/1/41	621'2" x 66' x 43' x 11,000 disp. Geared turbines 7,500 shp 17k 8 - 4.5", 8 - 2pdr	Sunk, Algeria 10/11/42
561 **Fernie**	Admiralty Hunt Class Escort Destroyer	8/6/39 - 9/1/40 - 29/5/40	280' x 29' x 17' 2" x 1,490 disp. Geared turbines 19,000shp 25k 4 - 4", 4 - 2pdr	Scrapped Port Glasgow 1956
562 **Garth**	Admiralty Hunt Class Escort Destroyer	8/6/39 - 14/2/40 - 1/7/40	280' x 29' x 17' 2" x 1,490 disp. Geared turbines 19,000shp 25k 4 - 4", 4 - 2pdr	Scrapped Barrow 1958
563 **Piorun** (ex Nerissa) *Noble*	Admiralty N Class Destroyer	26/7/39 - 7/5/40 - 4/11/40	356'6" x 35'8" x 20' 6" x 2,540 disp. Geared turbines 40,000shp 32k 6 - 4.7", 4 - 2pdr, 10 - 21"TT	Scrapped Dunston 1955
564 **Nizam**	Admiralty N Class Destroyer	27/7/39 - 4/7/40 - 8/1/41	356'6" x 35'8" x 20' 6" x 2,540 disp. Geared turbines 40,000shp 32k 6 - 4.7", 4 - 2pdr, 10 - 21"TT	Scrapped Grays 1955
565 **Indefatigable**	Admiralty (J1565) Implacable Class Aircraft Carrier	3/11/39 - 8/12/42 - 3/5/44	766' 6" x 95'9" x 70'3" x 32,101disp. Geared turbines 148,000shp 32k 16 - 4.5", 44 - 2pdr, 60 aircraft	Scrapped Dalmuir 1956
566 **Hororata**	New Zealand S.Co.	26/10/39 - 9/10/41 - 4/42	551'4" x 70'5" x 47'6" x 14,246t Geared turbines 12,300 shp 17k	Scrapped, Kaoshiung 1967
567 **Vanguard**	Admiralty Battleship	2/10/41 - 30/11/44 - 12/7/46	814'4" x 108'6" x 52' 6" x 51,420 disp. Geared turbines 132,950shp 30.3k 8 - 15", 16 - 5.25", 73 - 40mm, 4 - 3pdr	Scrapped Faslane 9/8/60
568 **Bermuda**	Admiralty Fiji Class Cruiser	30/11/39 - 11/9/41 - 5/8/42	555'6" x 62' x 32' x 11,270f.l.disp. Geared turbines 72,500 shp 31.5k 12 - 6", 8 - 4", 8 - 2pdr, 6 - 21"TT, 2 aircraft	Scrapped Briton Ferry, 8/65
569 **Avon Vale**	Admiralty Hunt Class Escort Destroyer (Type 2)	12/2/40 - 23/10/40 - 17/2/41	280' x 31'6" x 17' 2" x 1,610 disp. Geared turbines 19,000shp 25k 6 - 4", 4 - 2pdr	Scrapped Sunderland 1958
570 **Blankney**	Admiralty Hunt Class Escort Destroyer (Type 2)	17/5/40 - 19/12/40 - 11/4/41	280' x 31'6" x 17' 2" x 1,610 disp. Geared turbines 19,000shp 25k 6 - 4", 4 - 2pdr	Scrapped Blyth, 1959
571 **Onslow** *Tippu Sultan*	Admiralty O Class Destroyer	1/7/40 - 31/3/41 - 8/10/41	345' x 35' x 20' 4" x 1,540 disp. Geared turbines 40,000shp 34k	Scrapped 1958
572 **Paladin**	Admiralty P Class Destroyer	22/7/40 - 11/6/41 - 12/12/41	345' x 35' x 20'4" x 1,540 disp. Geared turbines 40,000shp 34k 6 - 4", 4 - 2pdr, 8 - 21"TT	Scrapped Dunston, 11/62
573 **Roberts**	Admiralty Monitor	30/4/40 - 1/2/41 - 27/10/41	373'4" x 89'9" x 27' 3" x 9,380 disp. Geared turbines 4,800shp 12k 2 - 15", 8 - 4", 16 - 2pdr	Scrapped Inverkeithing 1965
574 **LC8** (salvage lifting craft)	Admiralty Lifting craft	22/3/40 - 30/9/40 - 31/10/40	181' x 39' x 17'6" x 940 gt non propelled 1200 ton lift	
575 **Rotherham** *Rajput*	Admiralty R Class Destroyer	10/4/41 - 21/3/42 - 16/11/42	358'3" x 35'8" x 20'6" x 2,510 disp. Geared turbines 40,000shp 32k 4 - 4.7", 4 - 2pdr, 8 - 21"TT	To India 29/7/1949. Scrapped 1976
576 **Racehorse**	Admiralty R Class Destroyer	25/6/41 - 1/6/42 - 30/10/42	358'9" x 35'9" x 20'6" x 1,705 disp. Geared turbines 40,000shp 32k 4 - 4.7", 4 - 2pdr, 8 - 21"TT	Scrapped Troon 1949
577 **Nairana** *Karel Doorman, Port Victor*	Admiralty Vindex Class Escort Carrier converted from Port Line refrigerated cargo ship	2/11/41 - 20/5/43 - 12/12/43	529' x 68'5" x 72' 3" x 11,290 disp. Diesel 11,000 bhp 2 - 4", 16 - 2pdr, 16 - 20mm, 18 aircraft	Scrapped Shipbreaking Industries, Faslane 7/71
578 **Airedale**	Admiralty Hunt Class Escort Destroyer (Type 3)	20/11/40 - 12/8/41 - 8/1/42	264' x 31'6" x 17'2" x 1,620disp. Geared turbines 19,000shp 25k 4 - 4", 4 - 2pdr, 2 - 21"TT	Sunk Mediterranean 3/7/42
579 **Albrighton** *Raule*	Admiralty Hunt Class Escort Destroyer	30/12/40 - 11/10/41 - 22/2/42	280' x 31'6" x 17'2" x 1,620disp. Geared turbines 19,000shp 25k 4 - 4", 4 - 2pdr, 2 - 21"TT	Scrapped 1969
580 **LCM 103 - 110**	Admiralty	6/12/40 (date of trials)	40' x 13'6" x 4' motor landing craft	
581 **LCT13**	Admiralty Landing Craft, Tank Mk 1	24/9/40 - 9/12/40 - 18/12/40	152' x 29' x 8'9.5" x 372disp. 2 petrol engines 500bhp 10k 2 - 2pdr, 3 - 40 ton tanks or 6 - 20 ton tanks.	
582 **LCT14**	Admiralty Landing Craft, Tank Mk 1	7/10/40 - 10/12/40 - 18/12/40	152' x 29' x 8'9.5" x 372disp. 2 petrol engines 500bhp 10k 2 - 2pdr, 3 - 40 ton tanks or 6 - 20 ton tanks.	
583 **LCT27**	Admiralty Landing Craft, Tank Mk 1	20/12/40 - 22/3/41 - 3/41	152' x 29' x 8'9.5" x 372disp. 2 petrol engines 500bhp 10k 2 - 2pdr, 3 - 40 ton tanks or 6 - 20 ton tanks.	
584 **LCT28**	Admiralty Landing Craft, Tank Mk 1	21/12/40 - 22/3/41 - 4/4/41	152' x 29' x 8'9.5" x 372disp. 2 petrol engines 500bhp 10k 2 - 2pdr, 3 - 40 ton tanks or 6 - 20 ton tanks.	
585	Admiralty		Diesel engines (2 x 1,250 bhp) for T Class submarine **Talent** building at Vickers Armstrong Completed 6/12/1943	
586	Admiralty		Diesel engines (2 x 1,250 bhp) for T Class submarine **Tally Ho** building at Vickers Armstrong. Completed 12/4/1943	
587	Admiralty		Diesel engines (2 x 1,250 bhp) for T Class submarine **Tantivy** building at Vickers Armstrong. Completed 25/719/43	
588	Admiralty		Diesel engines (2 x 1,250 bhp) for T Class submarine **Truculent** building at Vickers Armstrong. Completed 31/12/1942	
589 **Redoubt** *Ranjit*	Admiralty R Class Destroyer	19/6/41 - 2/5/42 - 1/10/42	358'3" x 35'8" x 20' 6" x 2,425disp. Geared turbines 40,000shp 32k 4 - 4.7", 4 - 2pdr, 8 - 21"TT	To India 4/7/1949. Scrapped 1979
590 **Relentless**	Admiralty R Class Destroyer	21/6/41 - 15/7/42 - 30/11/42	358'3" x 35'8" x 20' 6" x 2,425disp. Geared turbines 40,000shp 32k 4 - 4.7", 4 - 2pdr, 8 - 21"TT	Scrapped T W Ward Inverkeithing 6/1971
591 **Troubridge**	Admiralty (J1591) T Class Destroyer	10/11/41 - 23/9/42 - 8/3/43	362'9" x 35'8" x 20' 6" x 2,530disp. Geared turbines 40,000shp 32k 4 - 4.7", 2 - 40mm, 8 - 21"	Scrapped Newport 1970
592 **Tumult**	Admiralty (J1592) T Class Destroyer	16/11/41 - 9/11/42 - 2/4/43	362'9" x 35'8" x 20' 6" x 2,510disp. Geared turbines 40,000shp 32k 4 - 4.7", 2 - 40mm, 8 - 21"	Scrapped Arnott Young Dalmuir 10/1965
593 **Tiger** (ex Bellerophon)	Admiralty Tiger Class Cruiser	1/10/41 - 25/10/45 - 19/1/59	555'6" x 64' x 32' x 11,700disp. Geared turbines 80,000shp 31.5k 4 - 6", 6 - 3"	Scrapped Spain 1986

No.	Name	Owner	Dates	Details	Fate
594	Snipe	Admiralty Black Swan Class Frigate	Order transferred to Wm. Denny		
595	Sparrow	Admiralty Black Swan Class Frigate	Order transferred to Wm. Denny		
*596	Calgary	Elder Dempster Line	3/10/19 - 27/8/20 - 3/2/21	454' 10" x 59'2" x 33'9" x 7,275gt Geared turbines	Scrapped, Grays, 1958
*597	Cochrane	Elder Dempster Line	24/3/20 - 28/12/20 - 8/3/23	454' 10" x 59'2" x 33'9" x 7,276gt Geared turbines	Scrapped, Hendrik ido Ambacht, 1958
*598	Calumet	Elder Dempster Line	4/9/20 - 1/7/22 - 15/3/23	454' 10" x 59'2" x 33'9" x 7,346gt Geared turbines	Scrapped Osaka 1960
*599	Caribo	Elder Dempster line	30/12/20 - 22/3/24 - 3/7/24	440' x 59' x 33'9" x 7,268gt Geared turbines	Sunk Keis Kamma, East London 24/11/1928
600	Hardy	Admiralty V Class Destroyer	14/5/42 - 18/3/43 - 14/8/43	362'9" x 35'8" x 20'6" x 2,700disp. Geared turbines 40,000shp 32k 4 - 4.7", 2 - 40mm, 8 - 21"	Torpedoed off Bear Island 30/1/1944
601	Valentine *Valentine, Algonquin*	Admiralty V Class Destroyer	8/10/42 - 2/9/43 - 28/2/44	362'9" x 35'8" x 20'6" x 2,525disp. Geared turbines 40,000shp 32k 4 - 4.7", 2 - 40mm, 8 - 21"	To RCN 1944. Scrapped Taiwan 1971
602	Kempenfelt *Kempenfelt, Kotor*	Admiralty (J1602) W Class Destroyer	24/6/42 - 8/5/43 - 25/10/43	362'9" x 35'9" x 20'6" x 2,530disp. Geared turbines 40,000shp 32k 4 - 4.7", 2 - 40mm, 8 - 21"	To Yugoslavia 1958
603	Wager *Pula*	Admiralty (J1603) W Class Destroyer	20/11/42 - 1/11/43 - 14/4/44	362'9" x 35'8" x 20'6" x 2,505disp. Geared turbines 40,000shp 32k 4 - 4.7", 2 - 40mm, 8 - 21"	To Yugoslavia 1958
604	Norfolk *Hauraki*	Federal Steam Nav. Co.	14/5/45 - 13/6/46 - 7/3/47	560'8" x 70'2" x 32'6.75" x 14,350gt Doxford diesels 12,800 bhp 17.7k	Scrapped Kaosiung 1973
605	Caesar (ex Ranger)	Admiralty (J1605) Destroyer, Ca Class	3/4/43 - 14/2/44 - 5/10/44	362'9" x 35'9" x 20'6" x 2,530disp. Geared turbines 40,000shp 4 - 4.7", 2 - 40mm, 8 - 21"	Scrapped Blyth 1/67
606	Cavendish (ex Sybil)	Admiralty (J1606) Destroyer, Ca Class	19/5/43 - 12/4/44 - 13/12/44	362'9" x 35'8" x 20'6" x 2,530disp. Geared turbines 40,000shp 32k 4 - 4.7", 2 - 40mm, 8 - 21"	Scrapped Hughes Bolckow, Blyth 29/8/67
607	Crescent	Admiralty (RCN) (J1607) Destroyer, Cr Class	16/8/43 - 20/7/44 - 21/8/45	362'9" x 35'8" x 20'6" x 2,566disp. Geared turbines 40,000shp 32k 4 - 4.7", 2 - 40mm, 8 - 21"	Scrapped Taiwan 1971
608	Crusader	Admiralty (RCN) (J1608) Destroyer, Cr Class	15/11/43 - 5/10/44 - 26/11/45	362'9" x 35'8" x 20'6" x 2,560disp. Geared turbines 40,000shp 32k 4 - 4.7", 2 - 40mm, 8 - 21"	Scrapped Canada 1963
1113	Milne	Admiralty	Transferred after launch from Scotts S & E Co. Ltd. 1942		
1121	Roebuck	Admiralty	Transferred after launch from Scotts S & E Co. Ltd. January 1943		
609		Admiralty	Diesel engines (2 x 1,250 bhp) for T Class submarine **Tapir** building at Vickers Armstrong. Completed 30/12/44		
610		Admiralty	Diesel engines (2 x 1,250 bhp) for T Class submarine **Teredo** building at Vickers Armstrong. Completed 5/4/46		
611		Admiralty	Diesel engines (2 x 1,250 bhp) for T Class submarine **Tiptoe** building at Vickers Armstrong. Completed 13/6/44		
612		Admiralty	Diesel engines (2 x 1,250 bhp) for T Class submarine **Tabard** building at Vickers Armstrong.		
613		Admiralty	Machinery (40,000 shp) for destroyer **Cambrian** building at Scotts Sb & E Co Ltd. Completed 17/7/44		
614	Loch Fada	Admiralty (J1614) Loch Class Frigate	8/6/43 - 14/12/43 - 10/4/44	307' x 38.5' x 17'9" x 2,260disp. Triple expansion 5,500ihp 19.5k 1 - 4", 4 - 2pdr., 2 squid, 15 depth charges, 150 Squid bombs	Scrapped Faslane 1970
615	Barrosa	Admiralty (J1615) Battle Class Destroyer	28/12/43 - 17/1/45 - 14/2/47	379' x 40.5 x 22' x 3,375disp. Geared turbines 50,000shp 32k 5 - 4.5", 8 - 40mm, 10 - 21"TT	Scrapped Blyth 1978
616	Matapan	Admiralty (J1616) Battle Class Destroyer	11/3/44 - 30/4/45 - 5/9/47	379' x 40.5 x 22' x 3,375disp. Geared turbines 50,000shp 32k 5 - 4.5", 8 - 40mm, 10 - 21"TT	Scrapped Blyth 1979
617	Talavera	Admiralty (J1617) Battle Class Destroyer	4/9/44 - 27/8/45	379' x 41 x 22' x 3,375disp. Geared turbines 50,000shp 32k 5 - 4.5", 8 - 40mm, 10 - 21"TT	Launched, not completed, broken up Troon 1946
618	Trincomalee	Admiralty (J1618) Battle Class Destroyer	5/2/45 - 8/1/46	355' x 41 x 22' x 3,375disp. Geared turbines 50,000shp 32k 5 - 4.5", 8 - 40mm, 10 - 21"TT	Launched, not completed, broken up Troon 1946
619		Admiralty	Machinery for Weapons Class destroyer **Carronade** building at Scotts Sb & E Co Ltd.		Cancelled 18/9/1945
620		Admiralty	Machinery for Weapons Class destroyer **Grenade** building at Scotts Sb & E Co Ltd.		Cancelled 18/9/1945
621		Admiralty	Diesel engines (2 x 2,150 bhp) for A Class submarine building at Devonport Dockyard		Cancelled 1945
622		Admiralty	Diesel engines (2 x 2,150 bhp) for A Class submarine building at Devonport Dockyard		Cancelled 1945
623		Admiralty	Diesel engines (2 x 2,150 bhp) for A Class submarine building at Devonport Dockyard		Cancelled 1945
624	Malta	Admiralty Malta Class Fleet Aircraft Carrier	Ordered 1943. Cancelled 1/46	916'6" x 136' x 34'6" draft x 56,800disp. Geared turbines 200,000 shp 33.5k 16 - 4.5", 64 - 2pdr., 81 aircraft	Berth realigned and prepared but ship not laid down
625		Admiralty	Spare turbines and gearing for cruiser or light fleet carrier		Cancelled 3/10/1945
626		Admiralty	Engines for A Class submarines building at Vickers Armstrong		Cancelled 19/9/1944
627		Admiralty	Engines for A Class submarines building at Vickers Armstrong		Cancelled 19/9/1944
628	Port Wellington	Port Line Ltd.	11/2/44 - 4/2/46 - 23/9/46	528'10" x 68'5" x 42' x 11,100gt Doxford diesels 10,700 bhp 17.4k	Scrapped Castellon, Spain 7/1971
629	Media *Flavia, Flavian, Lavia*	Cunard White Star Ltd.	12/11/45 - 12/12/46 - 8/8/47	531'5" x 70'4" x 46' x 13,345t Turbines 13,600 shp 19.23k	Destroyed by fire 7/1/1989, Hong Kong
630	Target vessel	Admiralty	6/2/45 - 19/12/45 - 10/1/46	64' x 30'6" x 48'9"	Section of Malta Class aircraft carrier hull
631	Target vessel	Admiralty	6/2/45 - 19/12/45 - 10/1/46	64' x 30'6" x 48'9"	Section of Malta Class aircraft carrier hull
632	Diamond	Admiralty (J1632) Daring Class destroyer	15/3/49 - 14/6/50 - 29/10/51	391' x 43' x 22'6" x 3,700disp. Geared turbines 54,000shp 34.75k 6 - 4.5", 6 - 40mm, 10 - 21"TT	Scrapped Rainham, Kent 1981
633	Desperate	Daring Class destroyer	Cancelled	as above	
634	Haparangi	New Zealand Ship. Co.	21/1/46 - 20/2/47 - 30/8/47	560'8" x 70'2" x 47'6" x 14,410gt Doxford diesels 12,800 bhp 18.07k	Scrapped Kaohsiung 1973
635	Caronia *Columbia, Caribia*	Cunard White Star Ltd.	13/2/46 - 30/10/47 - 17/12/48	715' x 91'5" x 53'3" x 34,183gt Geared turbines 35,000 shp 23k t	Broke-up 14/8/1974 outside Apra harbour, Guam
636	Arnhem	LNER	30/11/45 - 7/11/46 - 8/5/47	377'1" x 52'1" x 27' x 5,005t Geared turbines 12,000 shp 22.5k	Scrapped T Ward, Inverkeithing 1968
637			Machinery for Pacific Fortune building at Blythswood Sb. Co. Sea trials completed 27 February 1947		
638	Suffolk Ferry	LNER	1/5/46 - 7/5/47 - 19/8/47	404'6" x 58'10" x 19' x 3,138gt Sulzer diesels 3,200 bhp 14.6k	Sold for scrapping to Boelwerf, Burcht Belgium 1980
639		New Zealand Ship. Co.	Reconditioning of **Rangitiki**. Started 9/10/47, completed 26/8/48 Doxford diesels 14,000 bhp		
640		New Zealand Ship. Co.	Reconditioning of **Rangitata**. Started 8/12/48, completed 1/9/49 Doxford diesels 14,000 bhp		
641	Patria	Co.Colonial. Nav. Lisbon	19/6/46 - 30/6/47 - 22/12/47	531'7" x 68'4" x 44' x 13,916gt G. turbines 13,200 shp 18.54k t	Scrap'd Chi Shun Hwa Co, Kaohsiung, arr. 1/8/1973
642	Imperio	Co.Colonial. Nav. Lisbon	30/5/46 - 27/12/47 - 8/6/48	531'7" x 68'5" x 44' x 13,186gt G. turbines 13,200 shp 19.89k t	Scrap'd Chi Shun Hwa Co, Kaohsiung, arr. 29/3/1974

No. Name	Owner	Dates	Details	Fate
643 **Sussex**	Federal S. N. Co.	4/8/47 - 7/10/48 - 22/4/49	560'8" x 70'2" x 47'6" x 11,280gt Doxford diesels 12,800 bhp 18.03k	Scrapped Hong Kong 1976
*644 **Invergordon** Mount Helmos	British Mexican Pet. Co.	4/8/20 - 20/1/23 - 5/4/23	412'9" x 55'6" x 39' x 6,921gt Triple expansion 540nhp	Sunk 24/1/1942
645 **City of Oxford** Union Arabia	Ellerman lines Ltd.	20/6/47 - 24/6/48 - 21/12/48	481'4" x 61'6" x 41'9" x 7,340gt Geared turbine 7,200 shp 16.98k	Scrapped Kaohsiung 1978
646 **City of Birmingham**	Ellerman lines Ltd.	20/6/47 - 18/11/48 - 3/5/49	481'4" x 61'6" x 41'9" x 7,3404gt Geared turbine 7,200 shp 16.38k	Scrapped Castellon 1971
647 **Hinakura**	New Zealand Ship. Co.	4/8/47 - 21/1/49 - 27/6/49	560'8" x 70'2" x 47'6" x 11,280gt Doxford diesels 12,800 bhp 17.75k	Scrapped Kaohsiung 1974
648 **Rangitane**	New Zealand Ship. Co.	18/12/47 - 30/6/49 - 15/12/49	609'3" x 78' x 53' x 21,867gt Doxford diesels 15,500 bhp 17.9k	Scrap'd Kaohsiung by I Shing Steel & Ironworks 1976
Oriental Esmeralda				
649	North of Scotland HEB	Closed cycle gas turbine 12,500kW		
650	Coventry Power Station	Closed cycle gas turbine		
651 **Vikland**	Tanker Corp. of Panama	14/5/48 - 26/7/49 - 28/12/49	571'4" x 72'4" x 41' x 12,803gt Doxford diesel 6,500 bhp 15.26k	Scrapped Japan 2/1967
Monte, Real, Minoan				
652 **Vikfoss**	Tanker Corp. of Panama	6/10/48 - 24/11/49 - 31/3/50	571'4" x 72'4" x 31'9" x 12,803gt Doxford diesel 6,500 bhp 15.08k	
San Mateo, Silver Star				
653 **Nottingham**	Federal S.N. Co.	6/1/49 - 22/12/49 - 9/6/50	480'9" x 61'7" x 34'5" x 6,689gt x 6 cyl. Doxford 6,200bhp 16.00k	Scrapped Kaohsiung 7/1971
654 **Ottawa**	Maritime Trading Ltd.	3/8/49 - 17/5/50 - 18/8/50	547'4" x 72'3" x 41' x 19,308dwt Doxford diesel 6,500 bhp 14.9k	Scrapped Spain 16/2/1965
Monterray, Manzanillo				
655 **Franconia**	Cunard White Star Ltd.	refit		
656 **Kipawa**	Maritime Trading Co.	21/12/49 - 2/5/51 - 31/7/51	571'4" x 72'4" x 41' x 19,284dwt Doxford diesel 6,500 bhp 15.08k	
Hoegh Lance, Marlaura, Endeavour, Dona Alexandra				
657 **Adelaide Star**	Blue Star Line	31/1/49 - 2/8/50 - 7/12/50	573'10" x 72'10" x 49' 9" x 12,037gt Doxford diesels 15,000 bhp 20.36k	Scrapped by Hankook Steel Co. S. Korea 1975
658 **Ruahine** Oriental Rio	New Zealand Ship. Co.	24/10/49 - 11/12/50 - 3/5/51	563'5" x 75'2" x 49'6" x 17,851dwt Doxford diesel 14,200 bhp 19.8k	Scrapped Kaohsiung. Arrived 31/12/1973
659 **Amsterdam** Fiorita	British Transport Com.	1/3/49 - 19/1/50 - 23/3/50	360'7" x 52'2" x 27' x 5,092gt Geared turbines 12,000 shp 22.67k	Sank off Fethiye, Turkey in storm 27/1/1987
660 **Singapore**	P&O S. N. Co. Ltd.	21/1/50 - 1/12/50 - 11/4/51	522' 11" x 69'3" x 45' x 9,236gt Geared turbines 13,000 shp 20.29k	Scrapped Bilbao 1972
Comorin, Pando Cove				
661 **Norfolk Ferry** BB3	British Transport Com.	31/3/50 - 8/3/51 - 25/6/51	399'10" x 63'1" x 34' 9" x 3,151gt Sulzer diesels 3,200 bhp 14.34k	
662 **Scythia**	Cunard S.S. Co. Ltd	refit		
663 **Clydewater** Charitas	Tidewater Commercial Co.	27/7/50 - 7/6/51 - 19/10/51	571'4" x 72'4" x 41' x 19,310dwt Doxford diesel 7,500 bhp 15.44k	
664 **Almak** World Hope	Alva Steam Ship Co.	18/12/50 - 18/10/51 - 24/1/52	559' x 72'4" x 40' x 19,050dwt Doxford diesel 6,800 bhp 15.28k	Scrapped Kaohsiung 1974
665 **Clan MacIntosh**	Clan Line Steamers	16/10/50 - 19/7/51 - 22/11/51	471' x 60'8" x 37'9" x 6,558gt Doxford diesel 6,000 bhp	Scrapped Bombay 1980
666 **Clan MacIntyre** Eastern Express	Clan Line Strs.	20/3/51 - 31/10/51 - 27/2/52	471' x 60'8" x 26'1.5" x 6,560gt Doxford diesel 6,000 bhp	Wrecked near La Spezia 22/11/1971
667	Diesels (6,000 bhp) for **Clan MacInnes** building at Greenock Dockyard Co. Ship in service July 1952			
668 **Samaria**	Cunard S.S. Co. Ltd.	refit		
669 **Algol**	Alva Steam Ship Co.	10/5/51 - 13/3/52 - 21/5/52	559' x 72'4" x 40' x 19,070dwt Doxford diesel 6,800 bhp 15.3k	Scrapped 4/1969 Hamburg
670 **Wellington Star**	Blue Star Line	26/12/50 - 7/5/52 - 29/8/52	573'10" x 72'8" x 48'9" x 11,994gt Doxford diesels 14,000 bhp 20.56k	Scrapped Kaohsiung 1979
671 **Otaki** Mahmoud, Natalia	New Zealand Ship. Co.	26/10/51 - 24/10/52 - 1/5/53	525'10" x 70'2" x 36' x 10.934gt Sulzer diesels 11,500 bhp 17.73k	Scrapped Aliaga, Turkey 1984
672 **Sunda** Pando Strait	P&O S.N.Co Ltd	4/5/51 - 11/6/52 - 2/10/52	522'11" x 69'2" x 45' x 10,571dwt Geared turbines (by Parsons MST Co.) 20.51k	
673 **Media**	Cunard White Star Ltd	Fitting stabilisers (delivered early 1952)		
674 **Essex** Golden Gulf	Federal S.N.Co.	22/10/52 - 21/12/53 - 30/4/54	525'10" x 70'2" x 36' x 10,936gt Sulzer diesels 11,500 bhp	Scrapped Gadani Beach 1977
675 **Arcadia**	P&O S.N.Co Ltd	28/6/51 - 14/5/53 - 27/1/54	721'4" x 90'8" x 49'9" x 29,734gt Geared turbines 42,500 shp 24.65k	
676 **Northumberland**	Federal S.N.Co.	31/3/54 - 7/2/55 - 11/5/55	499'4" x 64'9" x 42' x 10,335gt Sulzer diesel 9,000 bhp 17.83k	Scrapped Hong Kong 1978
Kavo Astrapi, Golden City				
677 **British Sailor**	British Tanker Co. Ltd.	30/10/51 - 18/12/52 - 9/4/53	664'10" x 86'8" x 46'8" x 31,825dwt 2 Geared turbines 12,500 shp 16.k	Scrapped Kaohsiung 1980
678 **British Soldier**	British Tanker Co. Ltd.	8/4/52 - 30/6/54 - 26/10/54	664'10" x 86'8" x 46'8" x 31,611dwt Geared turbines 12,500 shp 16.k	Scrapped Kaohsiung 1976
679 **Lynx** Abu Bakr	Admiralty	13/8/53 - 12/1/55 - 14/3/57	340' x 40' x 26'6" x 2,323disp. 8 Admiralty diesels (Vickers) 14,400bhp 23.82k	Sold to Bangladesh 1982
	Leopard Class frigate		4 - 4.5", 2 - 40mmSTAAG, 1 - Squid	
680 **Brahmaputra**	Indian Navy	20/10/55 - 15/3/57 - 2/58	340' x 40' x 26'6" x 2,325disp. 8 Admiralty diesels (Vickers) 14,400bhp 23.82k	
(originally Panther)	Leopard Class frigate		4 - 4.5", 2 - 40mmSTAAG, 1 - Squid	
681 **Stanvac Australia**	Standard Vacuum	1/5/54 - 24/5/55 - 22,23/9/55	628' x 82'10" x 42'6" x 17,297t Geared turbines 13,750 shp 17.38k	
Esso Australia	Trans. Co.			
682 **East River**	International Nav. Corp.	5/12/52 - 22/4/54 - 30/9/54	571'4" x 72'4" x 41' x 19,524dwt Geared turbines 7,500 shp 15.79k	Scrapped Kaohsiung 1974
683 **Alvega**	Alvion Steamship Corp.	2/3/55 - 21/9/55 - 1,6/2/56	662'9" x 86'10" x 46'3" x 32,000dwt Geared turbines 13,750 shp 16.33k	Scrapped Busan, Korea 1977
684 **Whangaroa**	New Zealand Ship. Co.	16/8/54 - 21/6/55 - 15/10/55	471'9" x 63' x 39'6" x 8,701gt Doxford diesel 7,200 bhp 17.78k	Scrapped Kaohsiung 1974
Wainui, Warina, Garonfalia, Dromeus				
685 **Wharanui** Waipara	New Zealand Ship. Co.	26/1/55 - 11/5/56 - 27/9/56	471'9" x 63' x 39'6" x 8,706gt Doxford diesel 7,200 bhp 17.53k	Scrapped Kaohsiung 1979
Golden Lion				
686 **Salsette** Aradina, Tairea	P&O S.N.Co Ltd	17/2/55 - 1/2/56 - 25/6/56	499' x 64'6" x 42' x 8,202gt Doxford diesel 8,000 bhp 17.36k	Scrapped Kaohsiung 1979
Strathlomond, United Viscount				
687 **Salmara** Arakawa	P&O S.N.Co Ltd	9/6/55 - 25/6/56 - 13/11/56	499' x 64'6" x 42' x 8,202gt Doxford diesel 8,000 bhp 17.36k	Scrapped Pakistan 1978
Teesta, Strathloyal				
688 Cancelled	Alvion Steamship Corporation of Panama 32,000 dwt turbine tanker for completion in November 1955			
689 Cancelled	Alvion Steamship Corporation of Panama 32,000 dwt turbine tanker for completion in November 1956			
690 Cancelled	A Ravano & Sons (Compania Atlantica Pacifica) 26,000 dwt turbine tanker, ordered January 1952 for delivery October 1956			
691 **Britannia**	Admiralty	16/6/52 - 16/4/53 - 3/11/54	413' x 55' x 32'6" x 5,769gt. Geared turbines 12,000shp 21k	
692 **Saxonia**	Cunard S.S. Co. Ltd.	8/1/53 - 17/2/54 - 18/8/54	608'4" x 80'4" x 46'3" x 21,637gt. Geared turbines 24,500 shp 22.09k	
Carmania, Leonid Sobinov				
693 **Ivernia**	Cunard S.S. Co. Ltd.	19/10/53 - 14/12/54 - 13/6/55	608'4" x 80'4" x 46'3" x 21,717gt. Geared turbines 24,500 shp 22.19k	
Franconia, Fedor Shalyapin				
694 **Essex Ferry**	British Trans. Commis.	8/2/56 - 24/10/56 - 9/1/57	380' x 58' x 35'6" x 3,242t 2 Sulzer diesels 3,200 bhp 14.21k	Scrapped Rainham, Kent 1/83. Hull towed to Norway and converted into two pontoons
695 Cancelled	Tanker Corporation of Panama 19,000 dwt turbine tanker for completion in November 1957			

No.	Name	Owner	Dates	Details	Fate
696		Cunard S.S. Co. Ltd.	Refit and fitting stabilisers to **Parthia**		
697	**British Industry** *Stephanie Conway*	BP Tanker Co.	25/8/54 - 10/10/56 - 7/2/57	664'9" x 85'10" x 46'8" x 32,000dwt Geared turbines 15,500 shp 16.96k	Scrapped Castellon 1975
698	**British Trader** *Pelopidas*	BP Tanker Co.	2/2/56 - 26/6/57 - 31/10/57	664'9" x 85'10" x 46'8" x 32,000dwt Geared turbines 15,500 shp 17.32k	Scrapped Kaohsiung 1976
699	**Carinthia** *Fairland, Fairsea*	Cunard S.S.Co. Ltd.	23/12/54 - 14/12/55 - 14/6/56	608'3" x 80'4" x 46'3" x 21,947gt. Geared turbines 24,500 shp 21.47k	
700	**Sylvania** *Fairwind*	Cunard S.S.Co. Ltd.	9/11/55 - 22/11/56 - 27/5/57	608'3" x 80'4" x 46'3" x 21,989gt. Geared turbines 24,500 shp 22.29k	
701	**Scottish Ptarmigan** *Markab, Eleni V*	Thomson S.S.Co. Ltd.	29/10/56 - 24/10/57 - 25/1/58	559' x 72' x 39' x 18,300dwt Doxford diesel 6,800 bhp 13.33k	
702	**Edgewater**	International Nav. Corp.	26/7/56 - 9/8/57 - 25/11/57	571' x 72'4" x 41' x 19,500dwt Geared turbines 8,000 shp 15.59k	
703	**British Duchess** *Petrola 25*	BP Tanker Co.	18/12/56 - 2/6/58 - 1/10/58	710' x 95'4" x 51' x 42,000dwt Geared turbines 17,600 shp 17.06k	Scrapped Barcelona 1978
704	**British Queen**	BP Tanker Co.	29/10/57 - 16/9/59 - 19/12/59c	725' x 97' x 54' x 49,309dwt Geared turbines 17,600 shp 15.5k	Scrapped Kaohsiung 1975
705	**British Judge**	BP Tanker Co.	7/8/57 - 11/12/58 - 30/4/59c	710' x 95'4" x 51' x 42,000dwt Geared turbines 17,600 shp17.09k	Scrapped Valencia 1975
706	**Derby** *Okeanis*	Federal S.N.Co.	17/6/58 - 14/1/60 - 11/5/60	759' x 97'2" x 52' x 48,884dwt Geared turbines 18,000 shp 16.25k	Scrapped Kaohsiung 1976
707	**Lincoln** *Amphion* *Phillips New Jersey*	Federal S.N.Co.	6/9/57 - 11/9/58 - 28/12/58c	559' x 72'4" x 39' x 18,500dwt Geared turbines 7,750 shp 15.3k	Scrapped Brownsville 1978
708	**Kent** *Leslie Conway*	Federal S.N.Co.	18/12/58 - 20/9/60 - 15/12/60c	759' x 97'2" x 52' x 48,873dwt Geared turbines 18,000 shp 16.25k	Scrapped Kaohsiung 1976
709	**Otaio** *Eastern Academy*	New Zealand S. Co.	12/11/56 - 29/12/57 - 10/4/58	526'2" x 73'3" x 43' x 13,314gt. 2 Doxford diesels 12,400 bhp 18.33k	Scrapped Gadani Beach 1982
710	**Yarmouth** Rothesay Class Frigate	Admiralty	29/11/57 - 23/3/59 - 18/4/60	370' x 40'11" x 28'3" x 2,560disp. 2 Geared turbines 30,000 shp 30.3k 2 - 4.5", 2 - 40mmSTAAG, 12 - 21"TT, 2 - Limbo	
711	**Hampshire** County Class Destroyer	Admiralty	26/3/59 - 16/3/61 - 17/3/63	521' 6" x 54' x 40'6" x 6,200disp. 2 shaft COSAG Geared turbines 60,000shp 32.5k 4 - 4.5", 1 - Seaslug, 2 - Seacat GWS, 2 - 20mm, 1 helicopter.	Scrapped Briton Ferry 1979
712	**Clan MacIndoe** *Gulf Heron*	Neptune Ship. Co. Bermuda	30/9/58 - 20/8/59 - 20/11/59	492' x 61'6" x 38'8" x 7,395gt. Doxford diesel 5,400 bhp 16.32k	Sank Basrah 11/9/80 after being shelled
713	**Clan MacNair** *Lichiang*	Thompson Ship. Co.	14/9/60 - 26/10/61 - 9/2/62	506' x 61'6" x 38' x 9,338gt. Doxford diesels 6,400 bhp 15.5k	Scrapped Kaohsiung 1987
714	**British Hussar**	BP Tanker Co.	15/1/60 - 23/1/62 - 30/5/62c	760' x 97' x 54' x 50,771dwt Geared turbines 16,000 shp 15.5k	Scrapped Kaohsiung 1975
715	**British Mariner**	BP Tanker Co.	28/2/61 - 23/4/63 - 16/10/63	815' x 112'6" x 58' x 71,018dwt Geared turbines 20,000 shp 16.25k	Scrapped Kaohsiung 1975
716	**British Confidence**	BP Tanker Co.	10/9/63 - 17/2/65 - 30/7/65	815' x 108' x 55' 9" x 71,018dwt Geared turbines 20,000 shp 16.25k	Scrapped Kaohsiung 1976
717	**Somerset** *Aegean Sky*	Federal S.N.Co.	7/11/61 - 30/7/62 - 17/11/63	488' x 66' x 41' x 10,027gt Sulzer diesel 10,400 bhp	Scrapped Chittagong 1984
718	allocated to Q3	Cunard Steamship Co. Ltd.			
719	Cancelled	A Ravano & Sons	(53,000dwt turbine tanker cancelled February 1962)		
720	**Transvaal Castle** *S A Vaal , Festivale*	Union Castle S.S. Co. Ltd	19/1/59 - 17/1/61 - 16/12/61	760' x 90'2" x 50' x 32,697gt Geared turbines 44,000 shp 23.5k	
721	**Aurora** Leander Class frigate	Admiralty	1/6/61 - 28/11/62 - 10/4/64	372' x 41' x 28'3" x 2,860disp. Geared turbines 30,000shp 28.5k 2 - 4.5", 2 - 40mm, 1 - Limbo, 1 - helicopter	Scrapped Barrow 1990
722	**Centaur** *Hai Da*	Ocean S.S. Co Ltd	4/4/62 - 20/6/63 - 31/12/63	435' x 66' x 38'9" x 8,261gt. B&W diesels 21.5k	
723	**Intrepid** Assault Ship	Admiralty	16/1/63 - 25/6/64 - 14/3/67	520' x 80' x 51' x 12,120disp. Geared turbines 22,000shp 20k 2 - 40mm, 4 Seacat, 4 LCM	
724		Cunard S.S. Co Ltd	Conversion of **Carmania** (ex Saxonia) to cruising. Trials completed 30/3/63		
725		Cunard S.S. Co Ltd	Conversion of **Franconia** (ex Ivernia) to cruising. Trials completed 25/5/63		
726		Cunard S.S. Co Ltd	Diesels (7,600 bhp) for **Parthia** building at Caledon Shipbuilding Co.		
727		Cunard S.S. Co Ltd	Diesels (7,600 bhp) for **Ivernia** building at Caledon Shipbuilding Co.		
728	**Kungsholm** *Sea Princess*	Swedish America Line	3/1/64 - 14/4/65 - 17/3/66	660' x 86'3" x 58'10.5" x 26,677gt. 2 Gotaverken diesels 27,700bhp 23k	
729			Sulzer diesel (9,467 bhp) for **Tenbury** building at Burntisland Shipbuilding Co.		
730	**Vennachar** *Ocean Mariner, Lu Hai*	Aiden Ship. Co. Ltd.	3/2/64 - 21/10/64 - 12/1/65	610' x 82.5' x 47.25' x 28,469dwt Sulzer diesel 13,600 bhp 15.25k	
731	**Glenfinlas**	Glen Line	22/12/64 - 3/8/66 - 29/12/66	564' x 77.5' x 44' x 13,297gt. B&W diesel	
732	**Sylvania**	Cunard S.S. Co Ltd	Refit. Completed 5/2/65		
733	**North Star** (Jackup rig)	International Drilling Co.	2/11/64 - 14/6/65 - 21/9/65	170' x 130' x 17' x 3,500gt	
734	**Constellation** (Jackup rig)	International Drill Co.	22/12/64 - 9/11/65 - 28/1/66	179' x 150' x 17' x 3,600gt	
735	**Cape St. Vincent** *Cornish Wasa, Casparia, Jezara*	William Dennison Ltd.	30/4/65 - 5/5/66 - 14/6/66	495' x 72' x 41.5' x 20,022dwt. Sulzer diesel 9,700 bhp 15.5k	Scrapped Santander 1984
736	**Queen Elizabeth 2**	Cunard S.S. Co. Ltd.	2/7/65 - 20/9/67 - 18/4/69	963' x 105' x 82' 3" 65,863gt 2 Geared turbines 110,000 shp 28.5k	
737	**Orion** (Jackup rig)	Gas Council Amoco	12/11/65 - 9/5/66 - 28/6/66	179' x 150' x 17' x 3,723gt	
738	**Queen Elizabeth**	Cunard S.S. Co Ltd	Refit. Completed 3/66		
739	**Gulftide** (Jackup rig)	Husky Oil Alberta Ltd.	6/1/67 - 26/7/67 - 14/10/67	179' x 150' x 20' x 3,618gt.	
740	**Volnay** *Argaman Sea*	Aiden Shipping Co.	19/9/67 - 25/9/68 - 18/3/69	633' x 90' x 50' x 37,849dwt Sulzer diesel 13,800 bhp 15.75k	

UPPER CLYDE SHIPBUILDERS (Clydebank Division) from 7 February 1968

No.	Name	Owner	Dates	Details	Fate
741	**Vancouver Forest** *Beaufort Island*	Charles Connell & Co Ltd	18/4/68 - 4/2/69 - 23/5/69	575' x 87' x 45' x 26,700dwt Barclay Curle Sulzer diesel 10,500 bhp 15.25k	
742	**Kyoto Forest** *Caleta Leones*	Scotscraig Shipping Co. Ltd	25/10/68 - 7/1/69 - 10/2/69	575' x 87' x 45' x 26,591dwt Barclay Curle Sulzer diesel 10,500 bhp 15.25k	
743	**Offshore Mercury** (Jackup rig)	International Drill Co.	25/7/68 - 6/5/69 - 3/12/69	276' x 130' x 22' x 5,519gt. 7k	
744	**Blenheim** *Scandinavian Sea, Venus Venturer, Discovery 1*	Fred Olsen Lines	28/11/68 - 10/1/70 - 1/9/70	490' x 65'7" x 28'10" x 10,420gt. Crossley Pielstick 18,000 bhp 22.5k	
843	**Victoria City**	Sir W Reardon Smith	12/11/69 - 18/5/70 - 8/12/70	570' x 83' 8" x 46' x 25,874dwt B&W diesel by J&G Kincaid, 11,600 bhp	Transferred from Govan Division

Upper Clyde Shipbuilders operated a new sequence of ship numbers starting at 100. Clydebank contracts were given the suffix 'c'

No.	Name	Owner	Dates	Details	Fate
102c	**Temple Hall**	Lambert Brothers (Shipping) Ltd	4/4/70 - 10/12/70 - 10/6/71	527' x 75' x 42.9' x 22,175dwt. Ruston Paxman diesels 12,000 bhp 16k	Transferred from Govan Division

No. Name	Owner	Dates	Details	Fate
107c **Ocean Tide**	Rimrock (UK) Ltd Self propelled jack-up drilling vessel	22/8/69 - 16/1/71 - 9/9/71	276' x 130' x 22' x 5,567gt.	
111c **Arahanga**	New Zealand Railways	2/12/70 - 3/2/72 - 14/10/72	418' 4" x 61' 6" x 16' x 3,893gt. 2 Crossley Pielstick diesels, 12,000 bhp 17k	
112c **Samjohn Pioneer**	John Samonas & Sons Ltd.	26/6/70 - 25/3/71 - 19/1/72	482' x 75' x 45' x 11,506gt. Sulzer diesel by G. Clark and NEM, 9,000 bhp 17k	
117c **Samjohn Governor**	John Samonas & Sons Ltd.	16/12/70 - 24/6/71 - 25/4/72	482' x 75' x 45' x 11,506gt. Sulzer diesel by G. Clark and NEM, 9,000 bhp 17k	
118c **Varda** *Gold Varda*	Haverton Shipping Ltd.	25/1/71 - 22/12/71 - 8/3/73	482' x 75' x 45' x 11,895gt. Sulzer diesel by G. Clark and NEM, 9,000 bhp 16k	
119c **Orli** *Gold Orli*	Haverton Shipping Ltd.	7/4/71 - 30/5/72 - 11/7/73	482' x 75' x 45' x 11,897gt. Sulzer diesel by Barclay Curle, 9,000 bhp	
120c **Alisa** *Gold Alisa*	Haverton Shipping Ltd.	25/6/71 - 5/10/72 - 27/12/73	482' x 75' x 45' x 12,000gt. Sulzer diesel by G. Clark and NEM, 9,000 bhp	

Intended for Clydebank at the time of Upper Clyde Shipbuilder's collapse:

No. Name	Owner	Details	Fate
121c	Haverton Shipping Ltd.	482' x 75' x 45' x 12,000gt. Sulzer diesel by G. Clark, 9,000 bhp	Order switched to Scotstoun Division
124c	Cardigan Shipping Co. Ltd.		Cancelled
125c	Cardigan Shipping Co. Ltd.		Cancelled
128c **Harfleet**	Gowland Steamship Co. Ltd.	535' x 83' x 46' x 25,874dwt.	Order switched to Scotstoun Division
129c **Harfleur**	J&C Harrison & Co. Ltd.	535' x 83' x 46' x 25,874dwt.	Order switched to Scotstoun Division
130	Reardon Smith & Sons Ltd.	535' x 83' x 46' x 25,874dwt.	Order switched to Govan Division 6/1/71
131	Irish Shipping Co. Ltd.	535' x 83' x 46' x 25,874dwt.	Order switched to Govan Division 6/1/71
132	Irish Shipping Co. Ltd.	535' x 83' x 46' x 25,874dwt.	Order switched to Govan Division 6/1/71
133	Lyle Shipping Co. Ltd.	27,000dwt.	Cancelled 12/71
134	Lyle Shipping Co. Ltd.	27,000dwt.	Cancelled 12/71
135	H Hogarth & Sons Ltd.	27,000dwt.	Order switched to Govan Division
136	H Hogarth & Sons Ltd.	27,000dwt.	Order switched to Govan Division

The following numbers were originally allocated to contracts which were cancelled and then reallocated to other contracts.

No.	Owner	
497	Admiralty	Battlecruiser (G3) Number transferred to steam yacht *Restless*
567	Admiralty	Lion Class battleship *Conqueror*. Number transferred to battleship *Vanguard*
535		Originally intended for *Queen Elizabeth* to follow *Queen Mary's* 534 but realocated to engines for sloops and valve gearing
571	Admiralty	Machinery for Fiji Class cruiser. Number transferred to destroyer *Onslow*

DRILLING RIGS, MODULES, DECKS ETC.
Constructed by Marathon Manufacturing Co. from 30 September 1972

Name	Owner	Dates	Details
Penrod 64	Penrod Drilling Co.	1973	Complete jack-up drilling rig, 7,100te
Key Victoria	Keydrill	1974	Complete jack-up drilling rig, 5,850te
Penrod 65	Penrod Drilling Co.	1975	Complete jack-up drilling rig, 7,100te
Douglas Carver	Reading & Bates	1975	Drill ship conversion, 6,870te
Al Ittihad	KCA Drilling Co.	1975	Complete jack-up drilling rig, 4,430te
Penrod 67	Penrod Drilling Co.	1976	Complete jack-up drilling rig, 7,100te
Key Gibraltar	Keydrill	1976	Complete jack-up drilling rig, 7,100te
Al Ghallan	National Drilling Co.	1976	Complete jack-up drilling rig, 4,050te
Penrod 80	Penrod Drilling Co.	1978	Complete jack-up drilling rig, 7,060te
Penrod 81	Penrod Drilling Co.	1979	Complete jack-up drilling rig, 7,550te
Black Dog	Saipem AG Milan	1980	Complete jack-up drilling rig, 7,580te

Constructed by UiE Shipbuilding Ltd. from 29 April 1980

Name	Owner	Dates	Details
Uxmal	Permargo	8/1980 - 8/1981	Complete jack-up drilling rig, 7,600te
Chicken Itza	Permargo	11/1980 - 3/1982	Complete jack-up drilling rig, 7,600te
Morecambe Flame	Hydrocarbons GB	4/1981 - 6/1982	Complete jack-up drilling rig, 7,200te
Bay Driller	Houlder Marine Drilling	1/1982 - 5/1983	Complete jack-up drilling rig, 7,200te
(Rough Storage Project)	British Gas Corporation	1982 - 5/1983	Derrick module 17m x 17m x 15m; Power Module 31.5m x 11m x 11m; Storage Module 31.5m x 11m x 11m; Mud Module 31.5m x 11m x 11m. Total all four 3,065te
(Morecambe Bay Project)	Hydrocarbons GB	1984 - 11/1985	Control Module 43m x 12m x 10m x 1,329te. Five other wellhead and production modules built elsewhere totalling 9,290te were transported to Clydebank by barge for completion as part of this contract.
Mr Mac	Transworld	4/1985 - 8/1986	Gorilla Class jack-up drilling rig, 297' x 292' x 30' x 17,500te
Alwyn North	Total	1985 - 11/1986	Treatment Modules (2) 36m x 14m x 15m x 1,751te; 36m x 14m x 13,5m x 2,090te
Vulcan 1	Conoco UK Ltd	1986 - 1987	Integrated Deck 23.75m x 22.5m x 16m x 910te
Vulcan 2	Conoco UK Ltd	1986 - 1987	Integrated Deck 23.75m x 22.5m x 16m x 873te
Vanguard	Conoco UK Ltd	1986 - 1987	Integrated Deck 23.75m x 22.5m x 16m x 817te
South Valiant	Conoco UK Ltd	1986 - 1987	Integrated Deck 23.75m x 22.5m x 16m x 831te
Amethyst 1	BP	9/1989 - 7/1989	Integrated Decks (2) each 20m x 30m x 18m although x 1,029te and 1,044te. Jacket 1, 1,047te; Jacket 2, 957te; Piles, 1,862te
(Various)	Shell	7/1990 - 10/1990	Six Sub Sea Units constructed for following fields- Sean P-P 330te; Leman AP 330te; Leman BT 330te; Brent A 230te; Cormorant A 230te; Cormorant North 230te
Anglia	Ranger Oil Uk Ltd	1990 - 6/1991	Process Deck 750te; Jacket, 500te. Piles 720te
Amethyst 2	BP	5/1991	Integrated Decks (2) 22m x 36m x 18m x 760te; 22m x 35m x 18m x 805te. Jacket, 1,195te; Jacket, 960te Piles 1,001te
Lomond	Amoco	1991 - 11/1992	Integrated Process Deck 9,750te. Flare Boom 350te
Hyde	BP	1992 - 3/1993	Process Deck 21m x 30m x 18m x 700te Jacket, 1,057te.
Dunbar	Total Oil Marine	1992 - 4/1994	Process/Drilling/Accommodation Deck 11,000te
Captain	Texaco	1/1995 - 7/1996	Process/Drilling/Accommodation Deck 7,000te. Jacket, 5,000te. Piles (8) 2,800te; Drilling Template 170te
Baldur	Esso Norge	1997 - 1999	FPU (Floating Production Unit) conversion
Talisman Ross	Bluewater	1997 - 1999	FPSO (Floating Production Storage Offloading Vessel)

GAS TURBINES
John Brown Engineering 1967 to 1997 and Kvaerner Energy to 1999

Model	Number Constructed	Total Rating MW
For Power Generation		
MS3002	4	39
MS5001	265	5,728
MS5002	1	25
MS6001	90	3,353
MS7001	4	299
MS9001	49	5,868
LM2500	28	61
LM2500+	1	26
LM6000	3	121
For Marine Propulsion & Mechanical Drives		
MS3002	90	911
MS5001	2	27
MS5002	45	1,157
LM500	6	25
LM1600	15	194
LM2500	23	479
Total	**626**	**18,313**

EMERGENCY REPAIRS AND CONVERSIONS 1939-1945

Repair and conversion work carried out during World War 2 by John Brown & Co. Ltd at their Clydebank and Dalmuir yards in addition to shipbuilding and marine engineering work. The Admiralty attached the highest priority, even over the construction of new vessels, to the repair and quick return to service of battle damaged ships. Work undertaken at Dalmuir or Clydebank is indicated by a (D) or (C) after date of arrival. Based on monthly reports.

Ship Name and Contract Number	Arrived	Left/handed over	Details (where known)
Cilicia	9 October 1939 (D)	–	conversion to AMC
Worcestershire	21 November 1939 (D)	–	conversion to AMC
Wolfe (ex Montcalm)	25 October (D)	6 January 1940	conversion to AMC
Corfield	(C) 1997	December 1939.(D)	conversion to magnetic mine sweeper
Bushwood J1343	15 January 1940 (D)	–	reinforcing of hull forward
Southern Prince	25 Dec. 1939 (D)	27 June 1940	converted into a mine layer
Glengyle J1355	27 June 1940 (D)	7 September	conversion to troopship
Breconshire J1356	12 July 1940 (D)	30 August	conversion to fuel and ammunition transport
HMS Illustrious J 3986	24 July 1940 (C)	5 August 1940	repairs to arrester gear and fitting degaussing gear
HMS Fiji	27 July 1940	2 August 1940	
HMS Athene	26 January 1941	27 Oct. 1941	conversion to aircraft transport
HMS Fiji	9 Sept. 1940 (Govan)	21 Feb. 1941	repair torpedo damage
HMS Crispin ER 1214	mid Nov. 1940 (C)	17 Dec. 1940	special alterations
Glenroy J1361	3 Dec. 1940 (D)	29 Dec. 1940	repairs
HMS Argus ER 1245	15 Jan 1941 (C)	30 Jan 1941	
HMCS St Laurent ER 1232	25 Dec. 1940 (D)	14 Jan 1941	Canadian destroyer
Glenearn	13 Jan 1941 (D)	15 Jan 1941	erecting RDF hut
HMS Castleton ER129	2 April 1941 (C)	–	erecting RDF hut
HMS Snowdrop ER1297	5 April 1941 (C)	–	alignment of main engine.
HMS Mistral J1392	11 March. 1941 (D)	18 Oct. 1941	ex French destroyer
AMC Ascania	arrived Dalmuir 22 October but left 25th without repairs.		
AMC Alaunia ER1394	26 Oct. 1941 (D)	15 Dec. 1941	
La Cordeliere ER1397	31 Oct. 1941 (D)	–	French torpedo boat
ORP Piorun ER1410	14 Nov. 1941 (D)	–	

Note; **HMS Roberts** returned to Clydebank and left 13 November 1941

Ship Name and Contract Number	Arrived	Left/handed over	Details (where known)
HMS Keren ER1426	23 Dec. 1941 (D)	15 Jan. 1942	
HMS Cardiff ER1434	(D)	28 Feb. 1942.	
HMS Hecla ER1442	1 March 1942 (D)	13 April 1942	
HMS Javelin ER1450	13 March 1942 (C)	22 March 1942	
La Flore (R1460	30 March 1942 (C)	22 April 1942	French torpedo boat
HMS Partridge ER1467	7 April 1942 (C)	13 April 1942	
HMS Charleston ER1471	25 April 1942 at Elderslie Dock		ex US destroyer
HMS Warwick ER1474	24 April 1942	30 April 1942	
HMS Chesterfield ER1476	27 April 1942 (C)	23 June 1942	ex US destroyer
HMS Orion ER1479	6 May 1942 (D)	22 June 1942	
HMS Mistral	13 June 1942	15 June 1942	
HMS Charleston	30 May 1942	31 May 1942	
HMS Bulldog	1 June 1942	–	
HMS Hawkins ER1500	30 June 1942 (D)	15 July 1942	
HMS Newark ER1496	4 July 1942 (D)	19 July	
HMS Boadicea	1 August 1942 (D)	1 Sept.	
HMS Keren ER1526	Sept.? (D)	10 Oct. 1942	
HMS Karanja ER1527	Sept.? (D)	5 Oct. 1942	
Misoa ER1533	2 October 1942 (D)	19 Oct. 1942	

Queen Mary arrived Firth of Clyde 3 Oct. 1942 for emergency repairs to bow after collision with cruiser Curacoa on 2 October 1942. Work completed on 8 Oct. 1942. Sailed to Boston for dry docking and permanent repairs.

Ship Name and Contract Number	Arrived	Left/handed over	Details (where known)
HMS Enterprise ER1576	24 Dec. 1942 (D)	15 Oct. 1943	
HMS Princess Iris ER1554	13 Nov. 1942 (D)	–	
HMS Daffodil ER1555	13 Nov. 1942 (D)	–	
HMS Redoubt ER1559	14 Nov. 1942	26 Nov. 1942	
Rosslyn (Dredger)	13 Nov. 1942 (D)	–	

Repairs to hull and machinery of 13 landing craft completed by 27 Nov. 1942 with work continuing on a further 12.

Ship Name and Contract Number	Arrived	Left/handed over	Details (where known)
HMS Glasgow	(D)	18 Dec. 1942	for arcticisation
Z5	Feb. 1943 (C)	–	Netherlands destroyer
HMS Sheffield ER1611	9 March 1943	6 June 1943	
HMS Glengyle ER1600	8 Feb. 1943 (D)	–	
HMS Newcastle ER1527	April 1943 (D)	–	
OPR Garland (Polish) ER1630	29 April 1943	–	
HMS Vanquisher ER1646	15 May 1943 (D)	2 June 1943	
HMS Euryalus ER1703	16 Oct. 1943 (D)	–	
Port Quebec J1851	5 Dec. 1943 (D)	conversion to aircraft repair ship	

LST 13, **216** and **217** ER1735, 1737, 1738 resp. American LST's arrived Clydebank Jan 1944 conversion to headquarters ships (Fighter Direction Tenders) with highest priority. Last departed 12 Feb. 1944

Ship Name and Contract Number	Arrived	Left/handed over	Details (where known)
Prince David & **Prince Henry** ER1757 & 1758 22 Feb. 1944 (C) Prince David departed 13 April 1944			
ORP Piorun ER1725	30 November 1943 (D)	1 Feb. 1944	
HMS Frobisher ER1782	11 April 1944 (D)	28 April 1944	
Arbutus J1529 will complete at Dalmuir early June 1944			
HMS Loch Alvie J1813	8 May 1944 (D)	21 August 1944	from Barclay Curle
HMS Ambuscade ER1803	20 June 1944 (D)	31 July 1944	
HMS Bermuda J1805	5 July 1944 (D)	left Clydebank 5 March 1945	
HMS Loch Gorm J3397	8 July 1944(C)	from H&W Belfast	for completion
HMS Loch Craggie J3373	8 July 1944(C)	from H&W Belfast	for completion
LST 413 ER1823	20 Sept. 1944(D)	25 Nov. 1944	
HMS Indefatigable ER1826	Sept. 1944 C)	–	preparations for tropical conditions.
LST 406 ER1822	Sept. 1944. (D)	22 Nov. 1944	
TF21[*] J1858 Transport ferry	23 Nov. 1944 (D)	–	from Lithgows
LST's ER1836 & ER 1837 conversion for Far East left Dalmuir 17 Feb. 1945			
TF 31 J1864 Transport ferry	30 Jan 1945 (D)	11 July 1945	from Charles Connell
TF 32 J1865 Transport ferry	19 May 1945 (D)	from Connell (not completed, towed to Falmouth)	
TF41 J1866 Transport ferry	(D)	28 May 1945	from H&W
TF 22 J1859 Transport ferry	(D)	5 Oct. 1945	from Lithgow
TF 42 J1867 Transport ferry	(D)	31 Oct. 1945	from H&W Govan
Pintade (tug)	8 May 1945 (D)	25 June 1945	
TF 23 J1860 Transport ferry	31 July 1945 (D)	from Lithgow (not completed, towed to Falmouth)	
TF 39 J11725 Transport ferry	(D)	from Fairfield (not completed, towed to Falmouth)	
Empire Halladale ex German Antonio Delfino converted to troop carrier 12 November (D) 1945			
HMS Patroller		12 Nov. 1945	conversion to troop transport

Fitting-out at Dalmuir - **Allington Castle** (Fleming & Ferguson), Charlock (Ferguson), **Humberstone** (A&J Inglis), Barnard Castle completed as **Empire Shotton** (George Brown), York Castle completed as **Empire Comfort** (Ferguson), **Loch Coulside** later Padstow Bay (Robb), **Arbutus**, (George Brown), **Longbranch** (from A & J Inglis), **Loch Fada** (from John Brown), **Loch Alvie** (from Barclay Curle), **Loch Tarbert** (from Ailsa Sb.)

[*]The pendant numbers allocated to transport ferrys were later increased by 3000.

335

A WARTIME REFIT 1943-1944

ORP Piorun (ex HMS Nerissa)

The work carried out below on just one ship, the destroyer Piorun, gives an indication of the demands made on John Brown & Co. to repair and refit fighting ships in addition to maintaining its construction programme for new ships. To provide additional space, some of this work was carried out at Dalmuir basin which was adjacent to John Brown's Clydebank works. This work, emergency repair number ER1725, was carried out at Dalmuir. (Based on Report UCS1/22/26)

Piorun arrived at John Browns on 30 November 1943 and was taken in hand immediately. She was dry-docked at Govan on 19 January and undocked on 27 January 1944. Work was completed on 1 February 1944 at which time the ship sailed to resume active service.

The following units of machinery were overhauled, defects made good and tested on completion —

* Steering Gear, feed and sea water pumps, turbo-generators, capstan engine, diesel generator, paravane winches and refrigerating machinery.
* Galley ranges rebricked and soup pots retinned.
* New diesel engine fitted in motor cutter. Trial run completed.
* New diesel generator fitted in gearing room and subjected to a test of 3 hours duration.
* Wear and waste test on one boiler.
* Boilers cleaned and rebricked.
* Auxilliaries and valves refitted. Joints remade.
* Wear down on all turbine and gear case bearings taken.
* Sea valves refitted.
* A bracket bushes remettaled.
* Shaft glands repacked and wear down of stern tubes taken.
* Canvas covers, black-out covers and mess deck covers repaired and renewed as necessary.
* Rigging surveyed and blackened down and new rigging fitted to main mast, fore mast ladders, boat spans, guys and ladders.
* New tonnage wire, D/C and P/V securing and torpedo tube guard wires supplied.
* 57 sidelights rerubbered.
* All davits tested.
* Loose rivets in fore peak, Nos. 3 and 4 oil fuel tanks, 4.7" magazine and lower naval store drilled out and re-riveted.
* Reserve feed tanks water tested and painted.
* Numbers 3 and 4 oil fuel tanks water tested and cleaned also CL bulkhead.
* Lower Naval Store. Crack in starboard shell plate re-welded and riveted. Plate approximately 4' x 2'6" x 12.5 lbs fitted over same.
* Shell hose tested and compartment air tested.
* Chernikeeff log plus echo sounding examined and defects made good.
* Numbers 5 and 6 oil fuel tanks air tested.
* Feed water tanks in boiler room and under naval store forward coated with Rosbonite where necessary.
* Insulation to feed water tanks and reserve feed tanks repaired.
* Fo'c'sle deck shell racks reversed, splinter protection fitted and breakwater repaired.
* Asdic dome and raft found to be defective and were landed. New units were fitted.
* Erosion on shaft brackets considerable, particularly at the fillet of the arms to barrel. This was all made good by welding.
* Sea cocks and valves examined and zincs renewed.
* Single oerlikon mountings removed and twin oerlikon power mountings (4 off) fitted in lieu of same.
* Additional ready use lockers fitted.
* Range finder, director tower and pelorous defects made good.
* Pom-pom mounting removed and new power operated mountings fitted.
* All new mountings tested and found satisfactory.
* 44" searchlight and sights removed and returned to Rosyth.
* 5 tons pig iron ballast placed in numbers 1 and 2 boiler rooms. (total 2 tons port and 3 tons starboard)
* Miscellaneous defects to furniture, deck coverings, piping and Arctic insulation all made good.
* Type 271 and 291 RDF fitted and tested.
* Type 242 dismantled and refitted.
* Duplicate supplies for type 285 fitted.
* HF/DF aerial rewired.
* Torpedo tubes lifted for examination. Rewired for new heating arrangements but new heaters not fitted owing to late delivery of same.
* All 4.7" mountings examined.
* Wiring for ABU units completed but unit not available.
* RDF communications installed to suit the above sets.

CONSTRUCTION OF THE CUNARD EXPRESS STEAMER LUSITANIA SHIP NO 367

Date	Progress of Lusitania	Other yard events
18 May 1904	Preparing berth. (No 4 berth East Yard)	*Antrim* and *Hindustan* fitting-out. TSS *Antrim* preparing for trials. *Carmania* laid down 19 May.
22 June 1904	Berth being prepared. Keel blocks being laid. Keel plates commenced.	
13 July 1904	Berth prepared. Ground logs and keel logs laid. Keel plates being bored in West Shed.	*Caronia* launched.
17 August 1904	Keel blocks laid complete. Commenced laying keel. Framing commenced	Only two berths in yard occupied. *Antrim*, *Hindustan* and *Caronia* now fitting-out.
21 September 1904	Keel being riveted; double bottom frames being laid out in berth ready for erecting.	
25 October 1904	Keel complete from aft knuckle to stem. Riveted from engine space to stem. Garboards in place and riveted from engine space to three fourths length forward. Commenced to set side frames. Commenced to erect double bottom frames.	Orders received for *Gwalia* and *Devonia*
16 November 1904	Bottom frames erected from engine room to Peak Bulkhead. Riveting of shell on bottom plates commenced	
20 December 1904	Bottom shell plating and hydraulic riveting forward of engine space being carried out. Patterns being made for stern castings.	
18 January 1905	Shell plating and riveting of bottom forward of engine space making slow progress.	
21 February 1905	Outer and inner bottom plating forward of machinery space and hydraulic riveting proceeding slowly. Bulkheads being wrought in West Yard.	*Carmania* launched. Gwalia launched on 24 February.
28 March 1905	Working at framing in machinery space. Erecting uprights for side framing.	Orders received for *St David* and *St Patrick*. Devonia launched on 22 March.
2 May 1905	Turbine seating being erected. Bow frames erected from frame 245 to frame 285. Margin plate being erected in position. Bulkheads and decks being taken off boards.	St David laid down on April. St Patrick laid down on 16 May.
17 May 1905	Side frames erected from frame 210 to stem. After keel and heel piece riveted. Framing of turbine seating being erected and riveted. Frames aft of machinery space being erected.	
22 June 1905	Turbine seats erected and riveted. Side frames from frame 163 to stem; commencing to erect from frame 163 right aft. Decks and shell plating from frame 163 to stem making good progress. Commencing to erect fore and aft bulkheads.	
13 July 1905	Framed and beamed to shelter deck from frame 108 to stem. Fore and Aft and thwartships bunkers being erected. Shell plating fully one third completed. Heel piece in position and keel finished to this point. Stern frame and brackets cast. About six weeks required to complete framing.	
18 August 1905	Framed from frame 73 to stem. Stern frames being completed. Stern castings being machined. Decks, shell plating and internal steel work making good progress.	
15 September 1905	Preparing to erect stern frame. Frames all off boards except forecastle. Shell making good progress. Preparing to start topside plating to permit hydraulic riveting of topsides.	Orders received for *Woodcock* and *Partridge*
18 October 1905	Frames erected as far as wants of stern frame permits. Topside plating making good progress and preparing to commence hydraulic riveting. Deck plating and inside work making good progress. All progress in carpenter and joinery work and other trades being delayed waiting approval of plans. All stern bracket castings in position except forward brackets. Erection of frames being completed	*Woodcock* laid down 5 October. *Partridge* laid down 24 October.
24 November 1905	aft. Topside riveting and plating making good progress but delay being caused by non-delivery of steel material.	*Atalanta* laid down. *Northbrook* laid down 28 November
21 December 1905	Shell about three quarters completed. Stern framing being erected. Topside riveting making steady progress. Laying of decks (wood) commenced. Joiners preparing to start on board.	
30 January 1906	90% of shell plated. Commencing hydraulic riveting of shelter deck stringers. Stern making good progress. Bosses being prepared for boring-out. Laying decks. Top part of rudder cast.	*St David* launched from West Yard 25 January.
14 February 1906	Shell plating approaching completion. Preparing to bore out bosses. Upper part of rudder left Darlington (Forge). Hydraulic riveting making good progress. Decks being laid.	*Inflexible* laid down 5 February *St Patrick* launched from West Yard 24 February.
21 March 1906	Hydraulic riveting of topsides about complete up to shelter deck. Promenade deck frames and beams being erected. Rudder being machined. Commenced boring out forward bosses. After bosses bored out.	

Date	Progress of Lusitania	Other yard events
30 April 1906	Preparing for launch. Stern tubes and shafts being shipped. Rudder ready for shipping. Hawsepipes fitted into position.	*Woodcock* launched from West Yard 10 April.
23 May 1906	Sliding ways in position. Preparing for launch. Propellers being fitted. Rudder completed. Water testing approaching completion.	*Partridge* launched from West Yard.
7 June 1906	Ship launched.	
26 June 1906	Preparing to ship boilers.	
6 July 1906	Laying decks (wood). Inside work making fair progress. Shifted from sheers until machinery is shipped in *Northbrook*.	*Northbrook* launched
22 August 1906	In position for shipping boilers. Opening up for turbine generators.	
17 October 1906	Boilers all shipped. Boiler hatches being closed in. Smoke boxes fitted ready for funnels. Auxiliary machinery being shipped. Decks being laid.	
21 November 1906	Funnels all shipped. Preparing to ship condensers. Steering gear being shipped. Decks up to Promenade Deck in general laid and caulked; boat deck half laid.	
21 December 1906	Condensers shipped and structure over well closed in. Opening up for high pressure turbines. Steel work of upper work, joinery and carpentry work, making good progress. Cunard Company still delaying settlement regarding special cabins, 1st class passenger lifts, upholstery work and other items. This delay on their part may delay delivery date.	
16 January 1907	Port and starboard bedplates for high pressure turbines in position. Preparing to ship starboard rotor. Joinery work making good progress.	Berth 6 being prepared for *Duke of Albany*.
20 February 1907	Port and starboard turbines shipped. Port custom bottom casing shipped. Main mast shipped. Other work making good progress.	*Kenuta* laid down 22 February. *Barry* laid down 23 February. *Duke of Albany* laid down 26 February.
20 March 1907	Last of heavy turbine lifts on board. Closing in of decks and turbines commenced. Good progress being made towards completion.	
17 April 1907	Finishing closing in turbines. Joiner work and general outfitting work all over, making good progress.	*Lima* laid down 10 April
15 May 1907	Ready to test steam gear. Testing deck machinery; sanitary piping etc, upholstery work being fitted. Joiner work in 1st class smoke room commenced.	*Copenhagen* laid down 27 April *Duke of Albany* launched 13 June.
26 June 1907	Ready to proceed to Tail of the Bank on 27th inst.	*Inflexible* launched.

EMPLOYMENT NUMBERS IN SHIPYARD DURING CONSTRUCTION OF LUSITANIA
MAY 1904 - JUNE 1907

		Ironworkers	Carpenters	Joiners	Engineers & Patternmkrs	Blacksmiths	SheetIronwkrs	Plumbers	Painters	Riggers	Electricians	Sawmillmen	Labourers	TOTAL
1904	18 May	1782	469	514	487	233	128	64	172	128	76	155	137	4345
	22 June	1733	480	791	526	257	167	66	210	109	87	170	147	4743
	13 July	1445	447	807	533	258	174	74	187	112	103	147	143	4430
	17 August	1406	463	713	510	265	182	81	151	119	107	121	140	4258
	21 September	1779	388	757	542	262	195	83	221	124	119	119	146	4735
	25 October	1902	397	756	542	282	193	89	242	120	128	118	134	4903
	16 November	1846	461	705	451	285	200	93	250	117	129	121	132	4790
	20 December	1518	456	721	416	260	205	95	255	117	122	111	128	4398
1905	18 January	1269	443	771	456	252	203	94	203	116	121	113	128	4169
	21 February	1020	395	827	480	200	203	76	254	112	113	120	125	3925
	28 March	873	324	852	476	198	204	89	281	113	111	123	143	3787
	2 May	948	319	695	339	169	193	77	244	111	115	104	136	3450
	17 May	978	330	647	341	151	191	76	241	112	116	105	157	3445
	22 June	1127	367	642	306	155	150	65	202	107	118	102	142	3483
	13 July	1068	368	557	277	168	126	54	170	105	92	102	126	3213
	18 August	1039	314	475	225	167	112	42	94	96	86	101	100	2851
	15 September	1084	297	408	218	164	81	42	149	101	88	99	110	2841
	18 October	1098	302	539	215	149	80	40	175	100	80	93	108	2979
	24 November	1395	304	427	227	160	76	46	53	100	75	102	109	3074
	21 December	1404	311	471	231	166	76	46	48	97	70	103	100	3123
1906	30 January	1500	318	511	240	188	77	45	112	101	72	103	117	3384
	14 February	1496	342	523	262	189	77	49	126	103	73	105	141	3486
	21 March	1725	374	547	298	207	87	51	129	107	74	115	143	3857
	30 April	1840	425	644	366	223	138	61	146	111	92	115	161	4322
	23 May	1825	431	666	374	224	136	62	140	107	91	114	165	4335
	26 June	1420	440	618	360	198	133	63	149	106	81	112	152	3832
	6 July	1324	436	596	360	201	146	65	173	103	81	108	145	3738
	22 August	1253	415	700	373	194	157	78	144	99	95	109	121	3738
	17 October	660	386	537	354	175	153	81	187	91	81	105	126	2936
	21 November	742	308	419	337	134	148	62	97	78	67	103	107	2602
	21 December	1581	324	842	367	185	175	76	153	80	85	110	147	4125
1907	16 January	1611	339	887	381	199	186	73	144	79	96	110	154	4259
	20 February	1642	372	946	447	218	207	78	252	98	118	111	167	4656
	20 March	1680	384	941	464	218	220	85	291	103	124	110	168	4788
	17 April	1727	372	955	477	208	225	85	260	101	124	112	153	4799
	15 May	1514	381	982	477	217	228	89	262	94	140	111	148	4643
	26 June	1331	406	819	441	234	214	87	256	101	135	109	160	4293

CLYDEBANK SHIPS IN SCALE

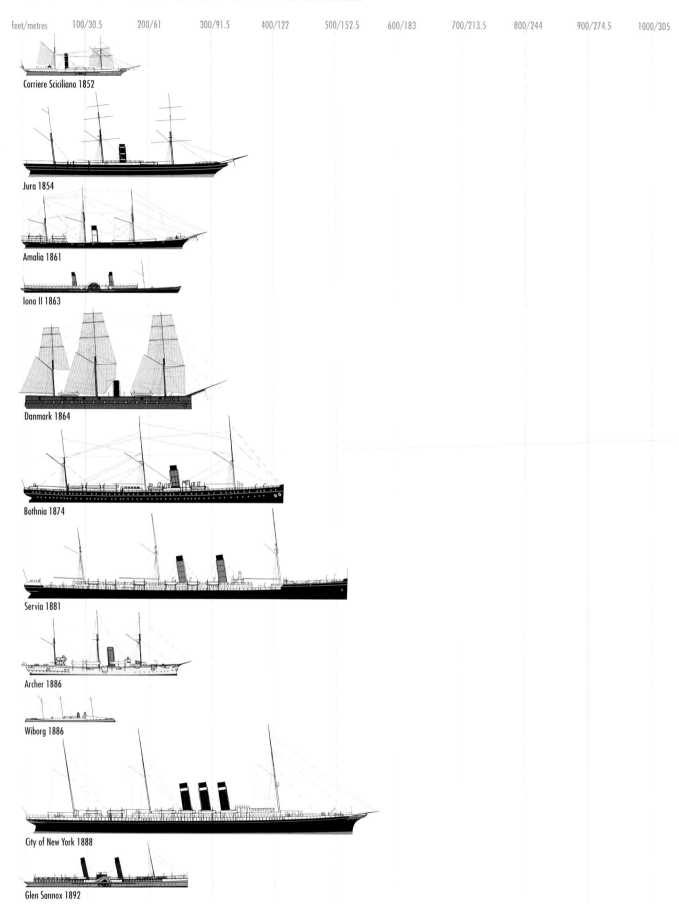

feet/metres 100/30.5 200/61 300/91.5 400/122 500/152.5 600/183 700/213.5 800/244 900/274.5 1000/305

Corriere Sciciliano 1852

Jura 1854

Amalia 1861

Iona II 1863

Danmark 1864

Bothnia 1874

Servia 1881

Archer 1886

Wiborg 1886

City of New York 1888

Glen Sannox 1892

340

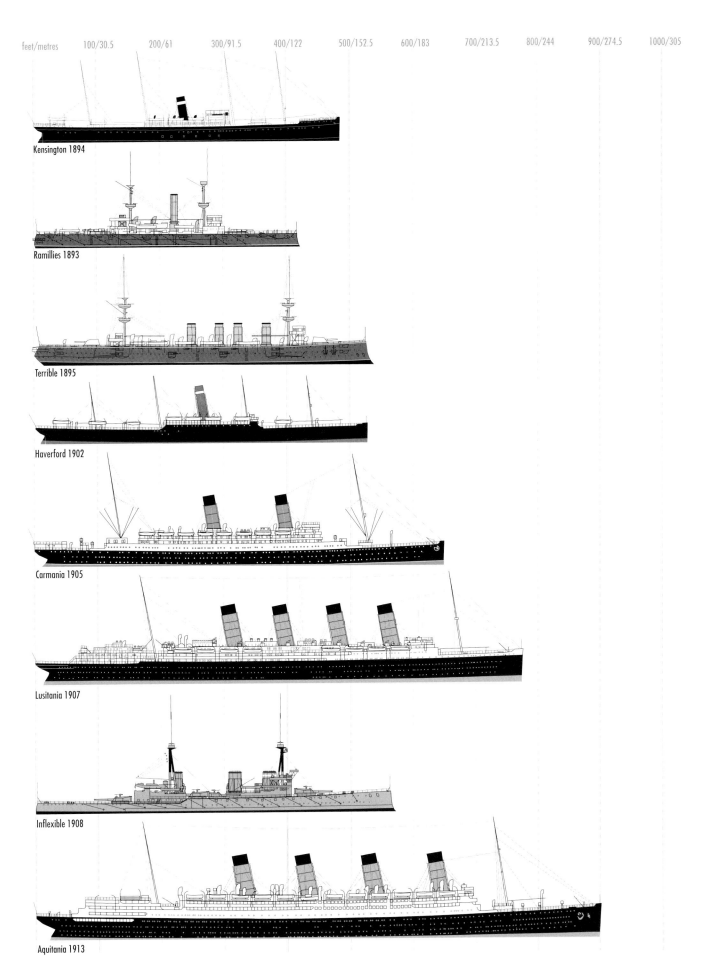

feet/metres 100/30.5 200/61 300/91.5 400/122 500/152.5 600/183 700/213.5 800/244 900/274.5 1000/305

Kensington 1894

Ramillies 1893

Terrible 1895

Haverford 1902

Carmania 1905

Lusitania 1907

Inflexible 1908

Aquitania 1913

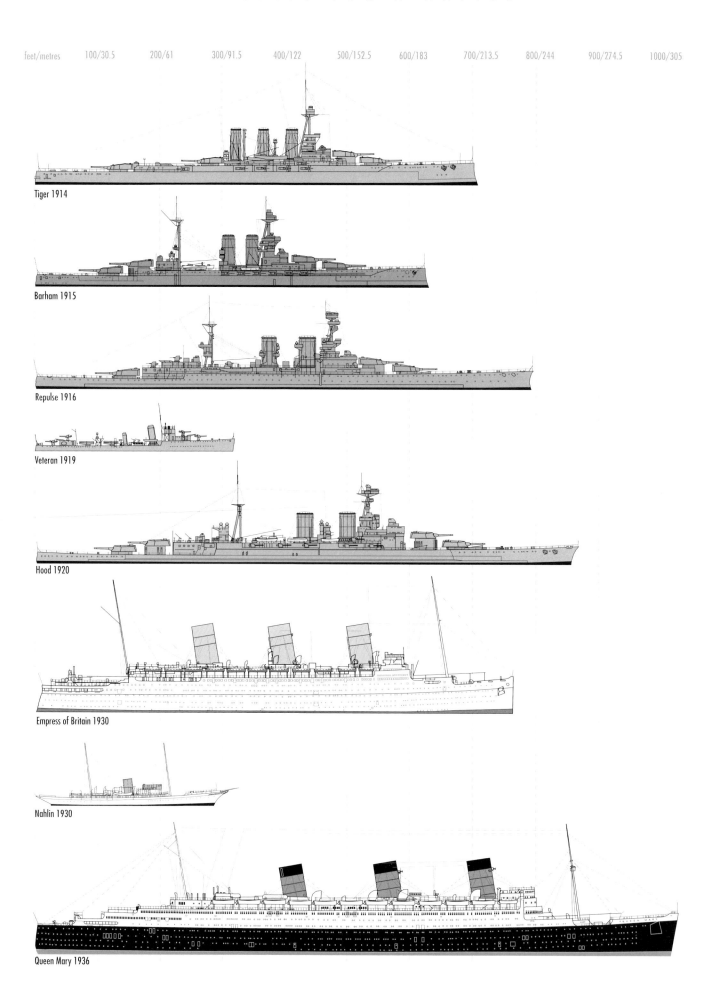

feet/metres   100/30.5   200/61   300/91.5   400/122   500/152.5   600/183   700/213.5   800/244   900/274.5   1000/305

Tiger 1914

Barham 1915

Repulse 1916

Veteran 1919

Hood 1920

Empress of Britain 1930

Nahlin 1930

Queen Mary 1936

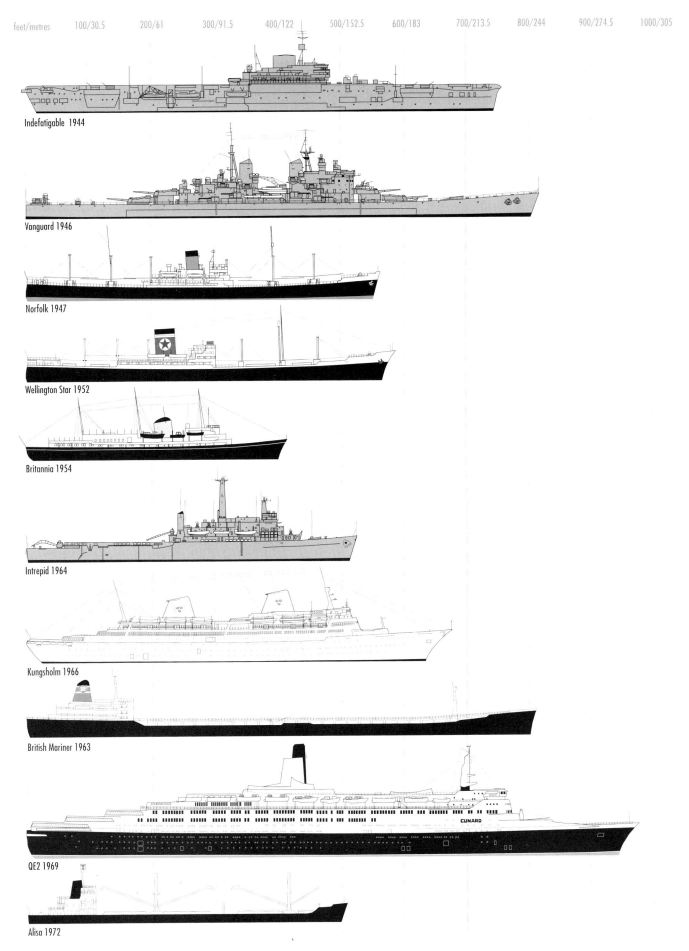

feet/metres · 100/30.5 · 200/61 · 300/91.5 · 400/122 · 500/152.5 · 600/183 · 700/213.5 · 800/244 · 900/274.5 · 1000/305

Indefatigable 1944

Vanguard 1946

Norfolk 1947

Wellington Star 1952

Britannia 1954

Intrepid 1964

Kungsholm 1966

British Mariner 1963

QE2 1969

Alisa 1972

343

Bibliography

Barry, P, *The Dockyards and Private Shipyards of The Kingdom*, London, 1863

Barry, P, *Dockyard Economy and Naval Power*, Sampson Low, london, 1863

Bellamy, Joyce M, *A Hull Shipbuilding Firm*, Business History, Volume VI, 1963

Bonsor, N R P, *North Atlantic Seaway*, T Stephenson & Sons, Prescot, 1955

Bourne, John, *A Treatise on the Screw Propeller, Screw vessels and Screw Engines as Adapted for purposes of Peace and War*, 1867

Brown, D K, *Warrior to Dreadnought*, Chatham Publishing, London, 1997

Bulloch, James D, *The Secret Service Of The Confederate States In Europe*, London 1883

Burt,R A, *British Battleships of World War One*, Arms & Armour Press, London,1986

Burton, Anthony, *The Rise and Fall of British Shipbuilding*, Constable, London, 1994

Chalmers, Rear-Admiral W S, *The Life and Letters of David Beatty Admiral of the Fleet*, Hodder and Stoughton, London 1951.

Conways all the World's Warships 1860 - 1982 (5 volumes) Conway Maritime Press, London, 1979

Crabtree, R,*The Luxury Yacht*, David & Charles 1973.

Crampsey, Bob, *The King's Grocer,* Glasgow Libraries and Museums

Credland, Artur G, *Earles of Hull*, City of Kingston upon Hull Museums and Art Galleries, 1982

Damer, Sean, *Rent Strike!*, Clydebank District Library, Clydebank 1982

Darling, RF, *40 Years of Progress, A History of the Wallsend Research Station 1945 -85*, British Maritime Technology Limited,1985

Dawson, Philip S, *British Superliners of the Sixties*, Conway Maritime Press, London, 1990

Duckworth, C L D, and Langmuir, G E, *Clyde River and other Steamers*, Brown Son & Ferguson, Glasgow, 1946

Glasgow Contemporaries, The Photo-biographical Publishing Company, Glasgow, 1901

Grant, Sir Allan, *Steel & Ships The History of John Brown's*, Michael Joseph, London, 1950

Green, Edwin and Moss, Michael, *A Business of National Importance, The Royal Mail Shipping Group 1902 -1937*, Methuen, London, 1982

Griffiths, Denis, *Power of the Great Liners*, Patrick Stephens Ltd., London, 1990

Guthrie, John, *A History of Marine Engineering*, Hutchinson Educational Ltd, London, 1971.

Foster, J and Woolfson, C, *The Politics of the UCS Work-in*, London, 1986

Paulden S and Hawkins, B, *Whatever Happened at Fairfields?*, Gower Press, London, 1969

Friedman, Norman, *British Carrier Aviation*, Conway Maritime Press, London, 1988

Gardiner, Robert, (ed.), *Conway's History of the Ship*, 12 Volumes, Conway Maritime Press, London, 1994

Half a Century of Shipbuilding, James & George Thomson Ltd, reprinted from Engineering, London, 1896

Hearn, Chester G, Gray *Raiders of the Sea*, Louisiana State University Press, 1996

Hichborn, Philip, *Report on European Dockyards*, Washington, 1889

Hood, John (Compiled) *The History of Clydebank*, Parthenon Publishing, Cranforth, 1988

Hyde, Francis E, *Cunard and the North Atlantic 1840 - 1973*, MacMillan, London, 1975

Irving, Joseph, Johnston, W & AK, *The Book of Dumbartonshire Vol 3*, Edinburgh, 1879

Jeffrey, Andrew, *This Time of Crisis*, Mainstream Publishing, Edinburgh, 1993

Johnson, Howard, *The Cunard Story*, Whittet Books 1987

Johnston, Ian, *Beardmore Built*, The Rise and Fall of a Clydeside Shipyard, Clydebank District Libraries & Museums, Clydebank, 1993.

Kludas, Arnold, *Great Passenger Ships of the World*, 5 Volumes, Patrick Stephens, Cambridge, 1975

Lyon, David, *The First Destroyers*, Chatham Publishing, London, 1996

Luraghi, Raimondo, *A History of the Confederate Navy*, Naval Institute Press, Annapolis, 1966.

McGill, Jack, *Crisis on the Clyde*, Davis-Poynter Ltd, London, 1973

McCart, Neil, *Atlantic Liners of the Cunard Line*, Patrick Stephens Ltd, London, 1990

McKinlay, Alan, *Making Ships Making Men*, Clydebank District libraries, 1991

McPhail, I M M, *The Clydebank Blitz*, Clydebank District Libraries & Museums, 1974.

McQueen, Andrew, *Clyde River Steamers of the Last Fifty Years,*

Massie, Robert K, *Dreadnought: Britain, Germany, and the Coming of the Great War*, Johnathan Cape, London, 1992

Maw, William H, *Recent Practice in Marine Engineering*, London, 1883

Maxtone-Graham, John, *Cunard, 150 Glorious Years*, David & Charles, Newton Abbot, 1989

Memoirs & Portraits of 100 Glasgow Men, published by James Maclehose, Glasgow, 1886

Mensforth, Eric, *Family Engineers*, Ward Lock, London, 1981

Moss M and Hume, J R, *Shipbuilders to the World, 125 Years of Harland & Wolff*, Blackstaff Press, Belfast, 1986.

Musk, George, *Canadian Pacific*, David & Charles, Newton Abbot, 1981

Parkes, Oscar, *British Battleships*, Seeley Service, London, 1970.

Paulden, S and Hawkins, B, *Whatever Happened at Fairfields?*, Gower Press, London, 1969

Peebles, Hugh B, *Warshipbuilding on the Clyde*, John Donald, Edinburgh, 1987.

Pollard, S and Robertson, B, *The British Shipbuilding Industry, 1870-1914*, Harvard University Press, 1979

Potter, Neil and Frost, Jack, *The Queen Mary*, Harrap, 1971

Raven, Alan and Roberts, John, *British Battleships of World War Two*, Arms & Armour Press, London, 1976

Raven, Alan and Roberts, John, *British Cruisers of World War Two*, Arms & Armour Press, London, 1980

Riddell, John F, *Clyde Navigation*, John Donald, Edinburgh, 1979

Rippon, P M, Commander, *Evolution of Engineering in the Royal Navy*, Spellmount Ltd, Tunbridge Wells, 1988

The Fairfield Shipbuilding & Engineering Works, reprinted from Engineering, London 1909.

Slaven, A and Checkland S, (editors),*Dictionary of Scottish Business Biography*, Volumes 1 and 2, Aberdeen University Press, 1986

Smout,TC, (ed.) *Scotland and the Sea*, Dept. of Scottish History, University of St Andrews, John Donald, Edinburgh1992.

Smith, Edgar, *A Short History of Naval and Marine Engineering*, Cambridge University Press, 1938

Spencer, Warren F, *The Confederate Navy in Europe*, University of Alabama Press, 1983.

Thomson, W and Hart, F, *The UCS Work-in*, London, 1972.

Vogt, Leo, *King Edward*, Clyde River Steamer Club, Glasgow 1992.

Walker, Fred M, *Song of the Clyde*, Patrick Stephens, Cambridge 1984

Westwood, J N, *Russian Naval Construction 1905-45*, University of Birmingham, Macmillan Press, 1994

PAPERS

Griffiths, D, *The British Crosshead Marine Diesel Engine Between The Wars*, Marine Management (Holdings) Ltd, 1994.

Buxton, Ian, *Mauretania And Her Builders*, Mariners World, 1996

Jung, Ingvar, *The Marine Steam Turbine. Part 3* National Maritime Museum monograph pages 121 - 125

Newman, Brian, *Materials Handling in British Shipbuilding*, The Centre for Business History in Scotland, Glasgow, 1996

Newman, Brian, *Plate and section Working Machinery in British Shipbuilding 1850 - 1945*, The Centre for Business History in Scotland, Glasgow, 1995.

Buxton, Ian, *Warship Building and Repair During the Second World War*, The Centre for Business History in Scotland, Glasgow, 1997.

Amended Report by the Committee on Marine Engines, House of Commons Papers(Parliamentary) 1859 (II) Vol.17

Slaven, Anthony, *A Shipyard in Depression*, John Brown's of Clydebank 1919-1938, Business History, Volume XIX, 1977

THESIS

Graham, Barbara, *Scottish Shipbuilding and the American Civil War*, Unpublished thesis, University of Strathclyde 1992.

Sorbie, James, *John Brown's of Clydebank*: Aspects of Accounting Practice and Financial Management Between the Wars., Unpublished Thesis, University of Glasgow, 1983

REPORTS

Shipbuilding Enquiry Committee 1965-1966 Report, HM Stationery Office, London, reprinted 1970

Report of the Advisory Group on Shipbuilding on the Upper Clyde H6544, HMSO, 29 July 1971

Shipbuilding on the Upper Clyde: Report of Hill Samuel & Co. Ltd., March 1972

UNPUBLISHED SOURCES

Stephen J Pigott, Engineer and Shipbuilder 1880 - 1955. A slim volume by his great grandson Lawrence

Jackson by courtesy of Eleanor Shipp, Sir Stephen's daughter.

Graham Strachan, Memoirs. Incomplete at the time of his death in 1995. Copy held at the Ballast Trust, Johnstone, courtesy of Dr William Lind.

Papers relating to the 1941 Apprentices Strike in the possession of Johnny Moore courtesy of his daughters, Linden Moore and Eleanor Page.

PERIODICALS
The Engineer
Engineering

RECORDS OF JOHN BROWN & CO LTD, CLYDEBANK
GLASGOW UNIVERSITY ARCHIVES (GUA)
Archives of the shipbuilding activities of John Brown & Co. and J&G Tomson & Co. catalogued under UCS1 (Upper Clyde Shipbuilders, Clydebank Division)

NATIONAL ARCHIVES OF SCOTLAND (NSA)
Collection of negatives and bound volumes made by the shipyard photographer from the 1880s until 1972.

SHEFFIELD CITY ARCHIVES
Some material relating to John Brown & Co. Ltd.

GLASGOW CITY ARCHIVES
Papers relating to the Clyde Navigation Trust

INDEX

£29.99

Photoshop® CS5 Bible